DETROIT PUBLIC LIBRARY

5674 04337143 5

J
Graphic

D0769992

FRANKLIN BRANCH LIBRARY
13651 E. MCNICHOLS RD.
DETROIT, MI 48205
(313) 852-4797

JUN - - 2006
FR

Publisher
MIKE RICHARDSON

Series Editor
DIANA SCHUTZ

Collection Editor
CHRIS WARNER

Collection Designer
CARY GRAZZINI

USAGI YOJIMBO™ (BOOK 14): DEMON MASK
Text and illustrations © 1999, 2000, 2001 Stan Sakai. Introduction © 2001 Paul Dini.
All other material, unless otherwise specified, © 2001 Dark Horse Comics, Inc. Usagi Yojimbo and
all other prominently featured characters are trademarks of Stan Sakai. All rights reserved. No portion
of this publication may be reproduced or transmitted, in any form or by any means, without the express written
permission of the copyright holders. Names, characters, places, and incidents featured in this publication
either are the product of the author's imagination or are used fictitiously. Any resemblance to actual persons
(living or dead), events, institutions, or locales, without satiric intent, is coincidental. Dark Horse Books™
is a trademark of Dark Horse Comics, Inc. Dark Horse Comics® is a trademark of Dark Horse
Comics, Inc., registered in various categories and countries. All rights reserved.

This volume collects issues 31-38 of the Dark Horse comic-book series
Usagi Yojimbo Volume Three and stories from the following publications: issue
140 of the Dark Horse comic-book series *Dark Horse Presents*; the Dark Horse comic book
Dark Horse Presents Annual 1999; issue 97 of the Gareb Shamus Enterprises, Inc. publication
Wizard: The Comics Magazine; issue 10 of the Oni Press comic-book series *Oni Double Feature*;
and issues 20-23 of the Dark Horse publication *Dark Horse Extra*.

Visit the Usagi Dojo website
www.usagiyojimbo.com

Published by
Dark Horse Books
A division of Dark Horse Comics, Inc.
10956 SE Main Street
Milwaukie, Oregon 97222

First edition: March 2001
ISBN: 1-56971-523-8

3 5 7 9 10 8 6 4
Printed in Canada

USAGI
YOJIMBO™
— DEMON MASK —

Created, Written,
and Illustrated by
STAN SAKAI

Introduction by
PAUL DINI

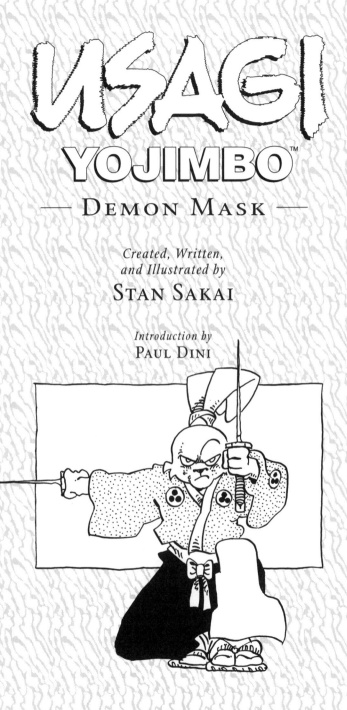

DARK HORSE BOOKS™

Usagi Yojimbo

Behind the Rabbit's Mask

FROM THE ANCIENT FABLES OF AESOP to the contemporary cartoons of Bugs Bunny, the humble rabbit has long been a symbol of cleverness and survival. Even mythology's master strategist, the fox, routinely comes off the loser when he tries to match wits with his fleet-footed adversary, as the African-American folktales of Br'er Rabbit readily attest. Whether he is called hare, cottontail, or jackrabbit, the little guy with the big ears and buck teeth is truly a timeless figure, and his legends have been told as long as there have been human beings around to tell them.

The storytelling tradition of ancient Japan holds friend rabbit in high esteem as well. As a child, one of my favorite bedtime stories was a rather ghoulish Japanese "fairy tale" telling of the murder of a farmer's kindly wife by a wicked *tanuki*, or raccoon dog. It seems the good wife fed and sheltered the little demon, who later repaid the woman for her generosity by murdering her and serving up her stewed remains to the farmer. Pretty gruesome behavior for old *tanuki*, a comical creature usually depicted wearing an oversized straw hat and toting a sake bottle. Maybe he drank too much sake and became unhinged, or maybe he was simply one seriously sociopathic raccoon dog; the story was vague on that point. What is known is that the grief-stricken farmer was horrified at the crime, as was his good friend, a rabbit who lived in the nearby woods. Playing on the *tanuki*'s greed, the rabbit lured the evil creature away on a treasure hunt, then secretly set fire to the *tanuki*'s backpack. When the nasty varmint jumped into a river to douse the flames, the rabbit clubbed him with a paddle and that was the end of that *tanuki*. In this story, as in many others told throughout the world, we witness the triumph of a small and traditionally meek character who has called upon his brains and bravery to defeat a larger, more aggressive enemy. It is a classic theme and one which writer/artist Stan Sakai weaves masterfully through his endlessly imaginative ongoing series, *Usagi Yojimbo*.

Stan often pits Usagi, a rabbit *ronin* of seventeenth-century Japan, in combat against a host of humanoid wolves, cats, bears, and other less easily defined carnivores. Far more than a funny animal conceit, it always seemed to me that Stan was making a visual comment on the true natures of heroes and villains while perhaps referencing the great print maker Tsukikoa Yoshitoshi. In his depictions of Japanese legends, Yoshitoshi often revealed the hidden, many times horrifying animalistic nature of his human subjects. A woman's shadow partially cast on a screen reveals the head of a fox. A samurai gazing into a dish of water sees not the pretty girl behind him but a reflection of her demonic inner being. In Yoshitoshi's world, the face of serenity masks the darker parts of the human id. It's only upon closer examination that we see the beast lurking within.

In the world of Usagi, the reverse is true. The animals' faces are their masks while their humanity (or lack thereof) is revealed through their personalities, or to be more accurate, through Stan's deft characterizations. Whether he is armed with swords or not, Usagi is often perceived by many to be a physically weaker character. Ignorant enemies overlook his speed and skill, to say nothing of his courageous heart, and that is their inevitable undoing. Usagi also possesses the samurai's most valuable weapon, the wisdom of knowing when to fight and when to stand down. It's a trait that some might mistakenly read as cowardice (as the boy Eizo does in the short story "A Life of Mush"), but it subtly recalls the moral put forth in director Akira Kurosawa's samurai epic *Sanjuro* that the best swords are the ones that stay in their scabbards.

With the stories collected in this volume, Stan Sakai shows off every facet of Usagi's engaging and complex personality. We see him as Usagi the warrior certainly, but in "The Inn on Moon Shadow Hill" we also meet Usagi the trickster. After discovering the truth about a colony of *obakemono* (goblins) infesting the woods near a lonely inn, Usagi adds his own fantastic spin on the tale, preserving the legend of the creatures while slyly arranging a tidy profit for his efforts.

A much more serious encounter with demons is recounted in "Kumo." Here Usagi joins forces with the mysterious demon-hunter Sasuke to destroy a terrifying spider-creature that has laid siege to a mountain village. The fox-like Sasuke is a terrific addition to Usagi's extended cast of allies and enemies, and unlike the reluctant Usagi, I can't wait for the mystic to make a return appearance.

The collection's longest tale, "The Mystery of the Demon Mask," places Usagi in a situation that calls on him to be as much detective as he is samurai. While searching for the masked fiend that has been killing masterless samurai, the rabbit *ronin* fights to stay alive in a tightening web of tragedy, betrayal, and madness. As with all good mysteries, the outcome is both surprising and satisfying, but Sakai goes a step further to add a final bitter yet not inappropriate twist to the epic. It's the sort of human touch that has placed *Usagi Yojimbo* far in front of every other "funny animal" book published since Carl Barks bid adieu to Duckburg thirty-five years ago.

It's the mark of a great storyteller. It's the stuff of legends.

PAUL DINI

CONTENTS

THIS ONE IS FOR
STAN AND FRANCISCA HIRTLE

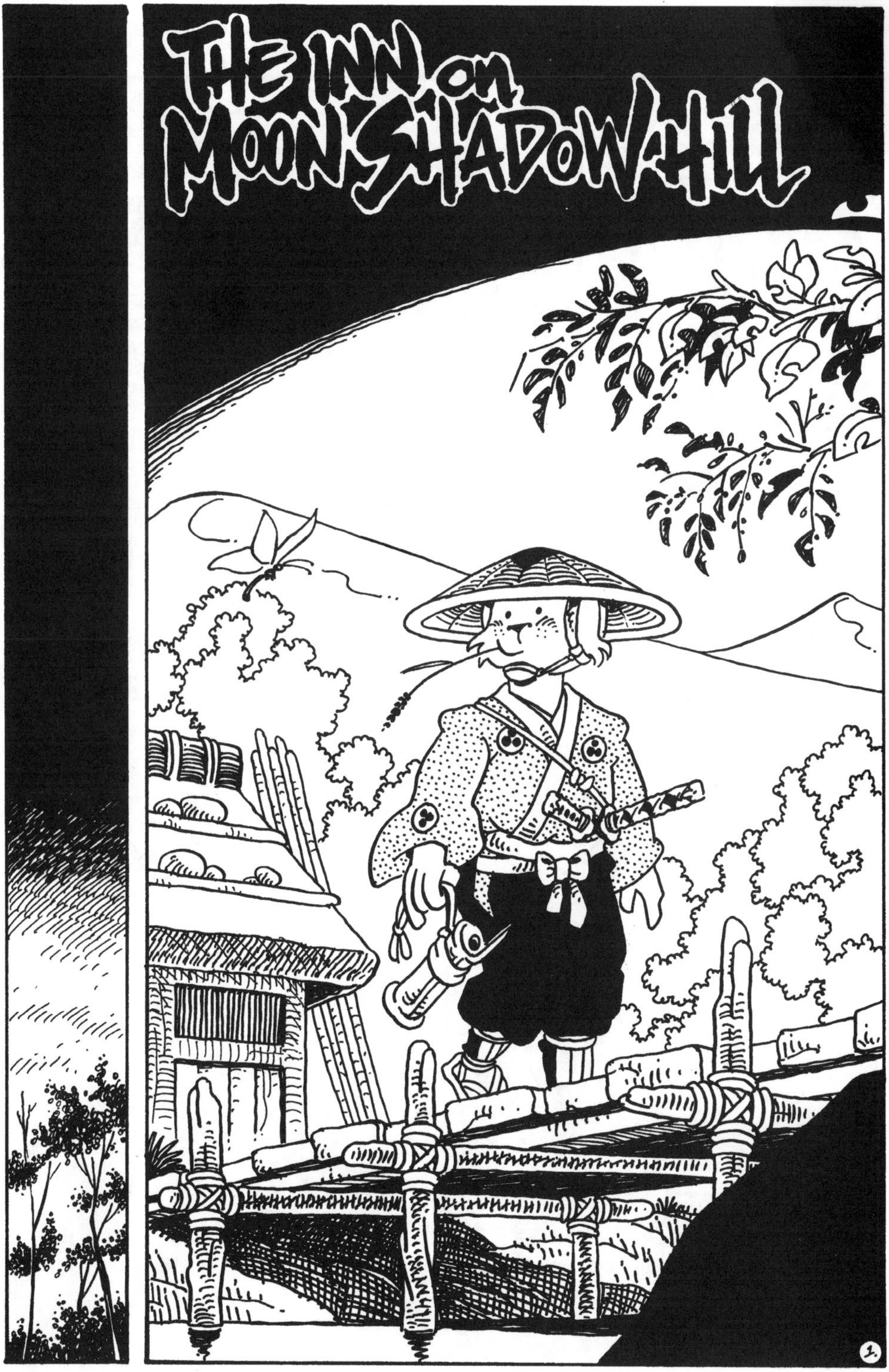
THE INN ON MOON SHADOW HILL
1.

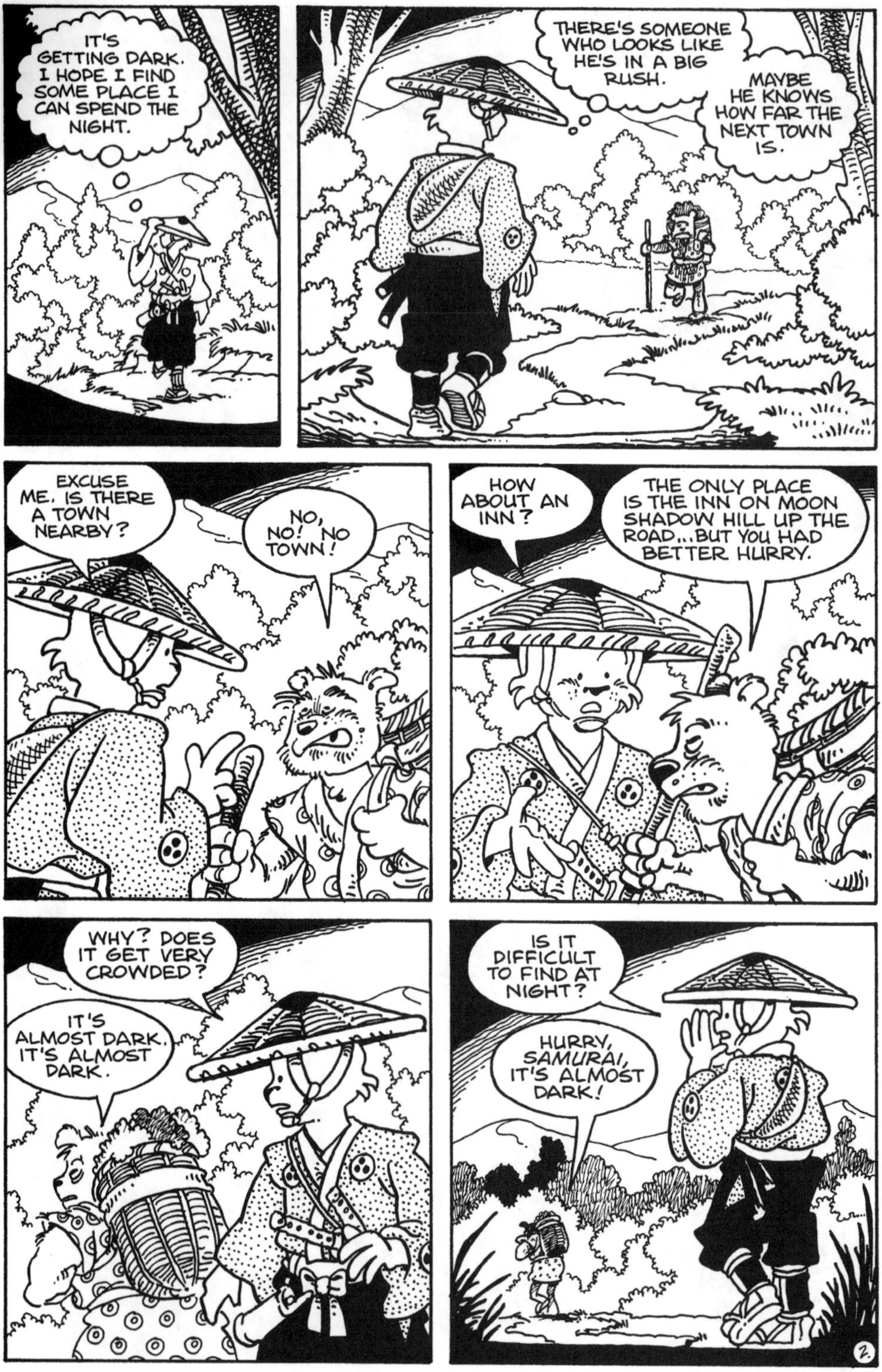
IT'S GETTING DARK. I HOPE I FIND SOME PLACE I CAN SPEND THE NIGHT.
THERE'S SOMEONE WHO LOOKS LIKE HE'S IN A BIG RUSH.
MAYBE HE KNOWS HOW FAR THE NEXT TOWN IS.
EXCUSE ME. IS THERE A TOWN NEARBY?
NO, NO! NO TOWN!
HOW ABOUT AN INN?
THE ONLY PLACE IS THE INN ON MOON SHADOW HILL UP THE ROAD...BUT YOU HAD BETTER HURRY.
WHY? DOES IT GET VERY CROWDED?
IT'S ALMOST DARK. IT'S ALMOST DARK.
IS IT DIFFICULT TO FIND AT NIGHT?
HURRY, SAMURAI, IT'S ALMOST DARK!
2.

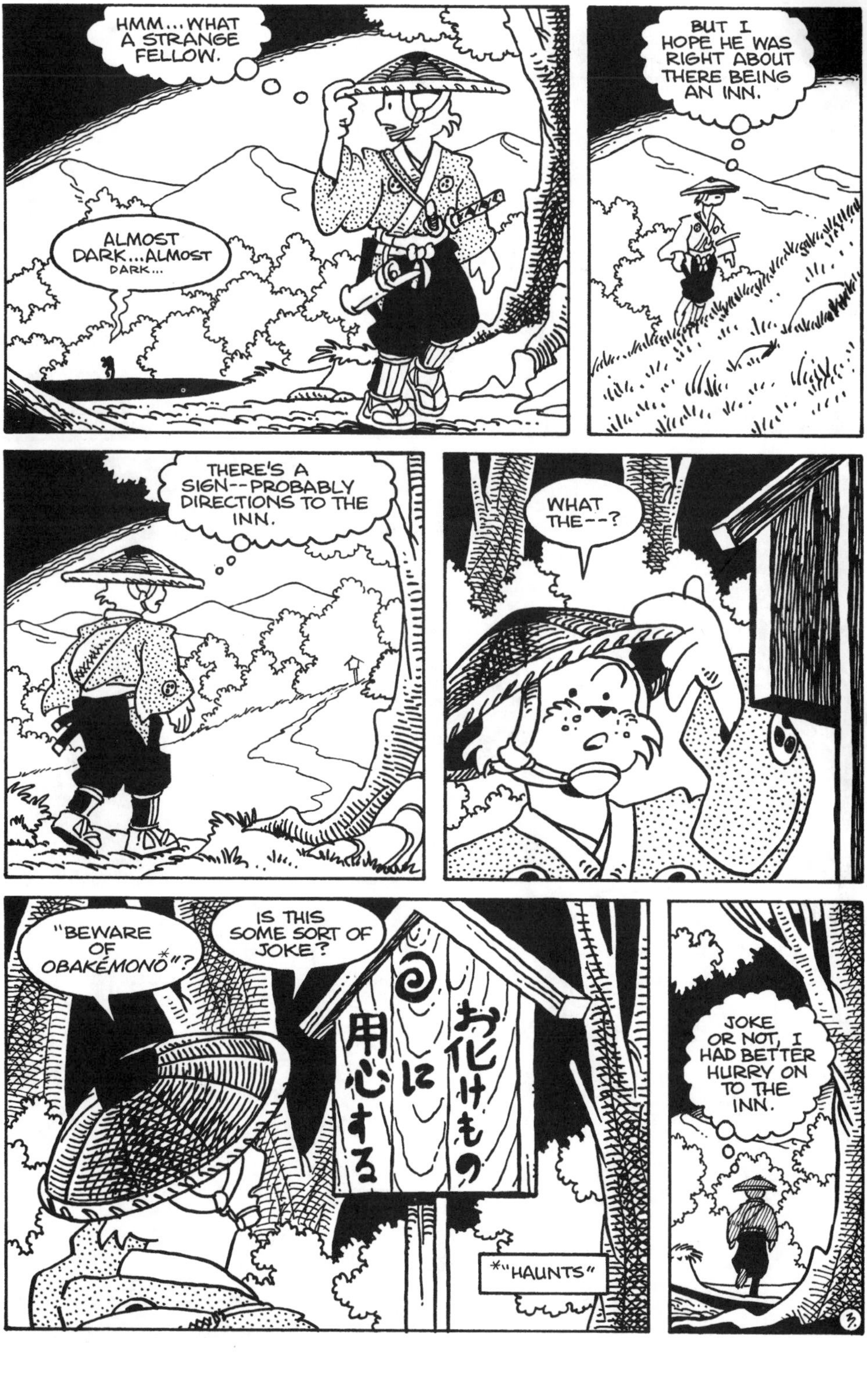
HMM...WHAT A STRANGE FELLOW.
ALMOST DARK...ALMOST DARK...
BUT I HOPE HE WAS RIGHT ABOUT THERE BEING AN INN.
THERE'S A SIGN--PROBABLY DIRECTIONS TO THE INN.
WHAT THE--?
"BEWARE OF OBAKÉMONO*"?
IS THIS SOME SORT OF JOKE?
お化けものに用心する
*"HAUNTS"
JOKE OR NOT, I HAD BETTER HURRY ON TO THE INN.
3.

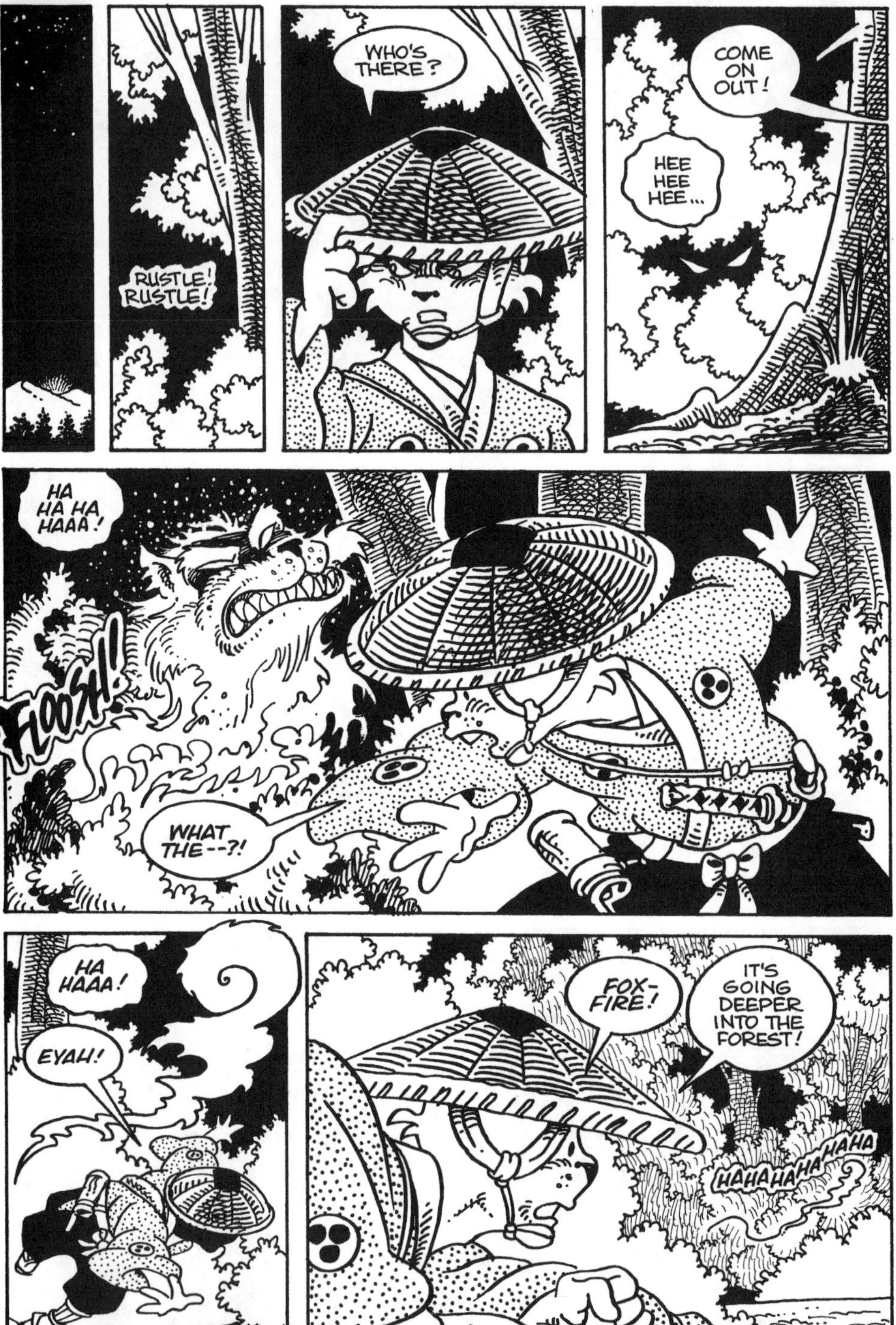
RUSTLE! RUSTLE!
WHO'S THERE?
COME ON OUT!
HEE HEE HEE...
HA HA HA HAAA!
FLOOSH!
WHAT THE--?!
HA HAAA!
EYAH!
FOX-FIRE!
IT'S GOING DEEPER INTO THE FOREST!
HAHAHAHAHAHAHA
4.

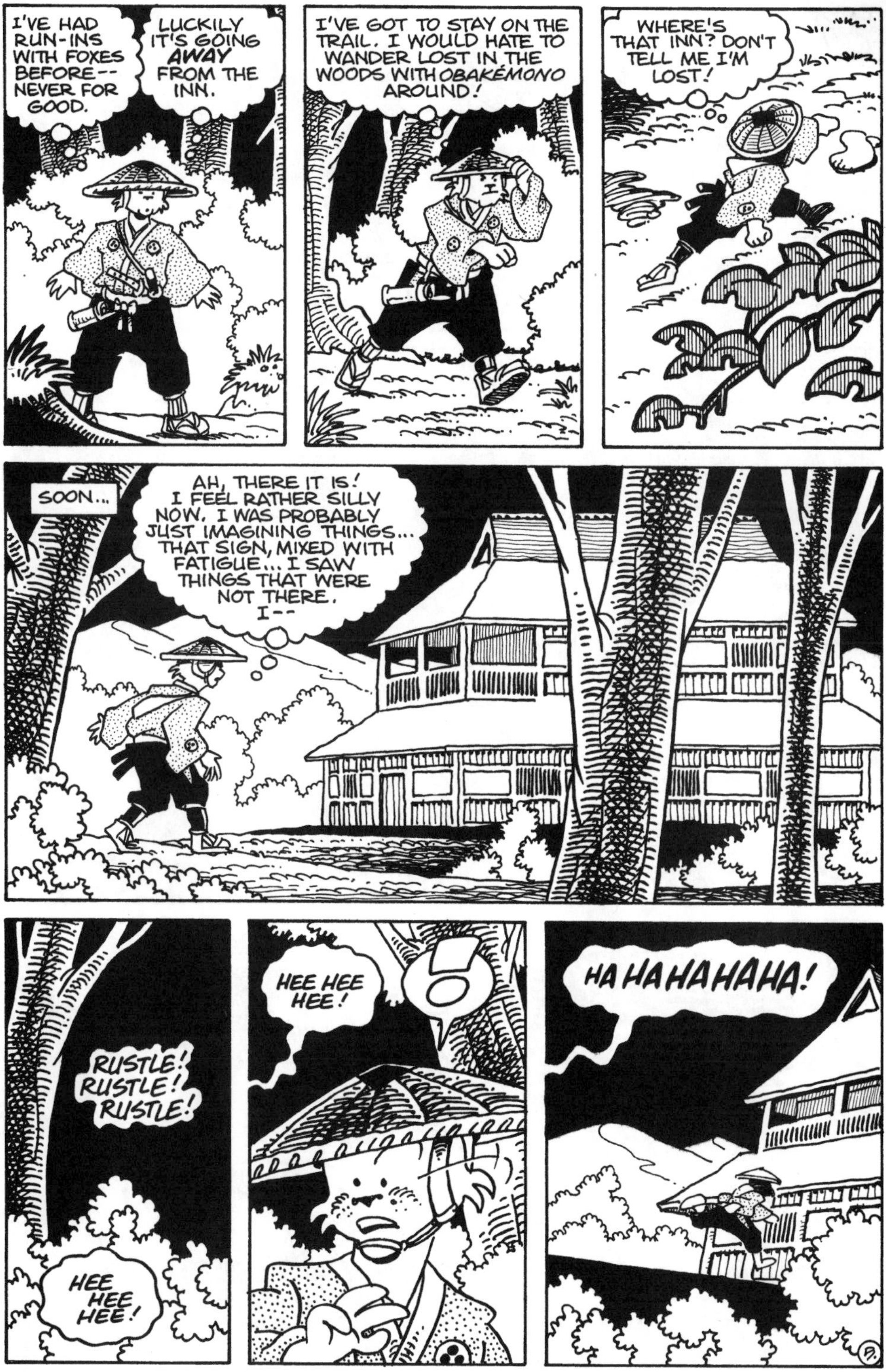
I'VE HAD RUN-INS WITH FOXES BEFORE-- NEVER FOR GOOD.
LUCKILY IT'S GOING AWAY FROM THE INN.
I'VE GOT TO STAY ON THE TRAIL. I WOULD HATE TO WANDER LOST IN THE WOODS WITH OBAKÉMONO AROUND!
WHERE'S THAT INN? DON'T TELL ME I'M LOST!
SOON...
AH, THERE IT IS! I FEEL RATHER SILLY NOW. I WAS PROBABLY JUST IMAGINING THINGS... THAT SIGN, MIXED WITH FATIGUE... I SAW THINGS THAT WERE NOT THERE. I--
RUSTLE! RUSTLE! RUSTLE!
HEE HEE HEE!
HEE HEE HEE!
!
HA HA HA HA HA HA!

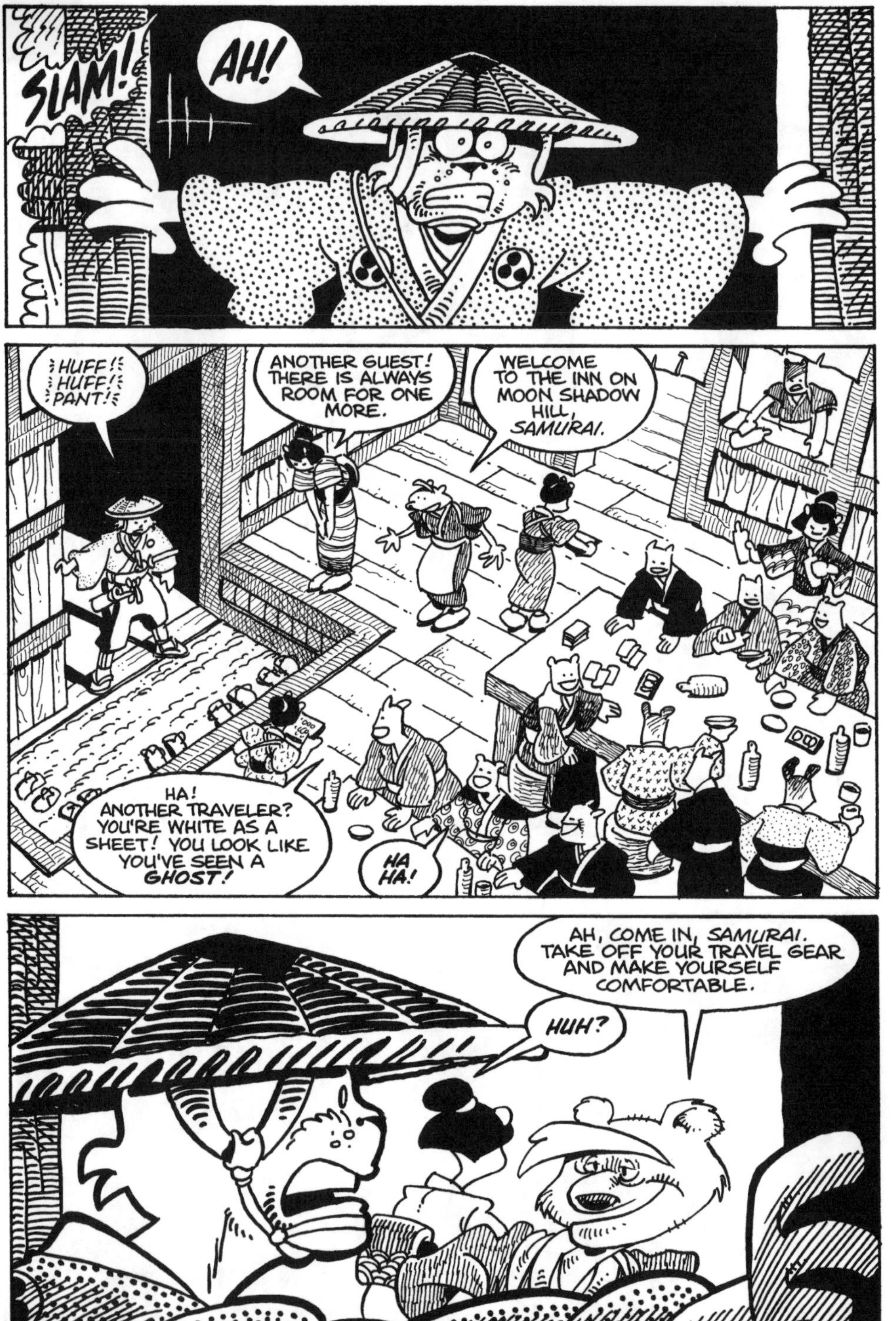
SLAM!
AH!
HUFF! HUFF! PANT!
ANOTHER GUEST! THERE IS ALWAYS ROOM FOR ONE MORE.
WELCOME TO THE INN ON MOON SHADOW HILL, SAMURAI.
HA! ANOTHER TRAVELER? YOU'RE WHITE AS A SHEET! YOU LOOK LIKE YOU'VE SEEN A GHOST!
HA HA!
AH, COME IN, SAMURAI. TAKE OFF YOUR TRAVEL GEAR AND MAKE YOURSELF COMFORTABLE.
HUH?
6.

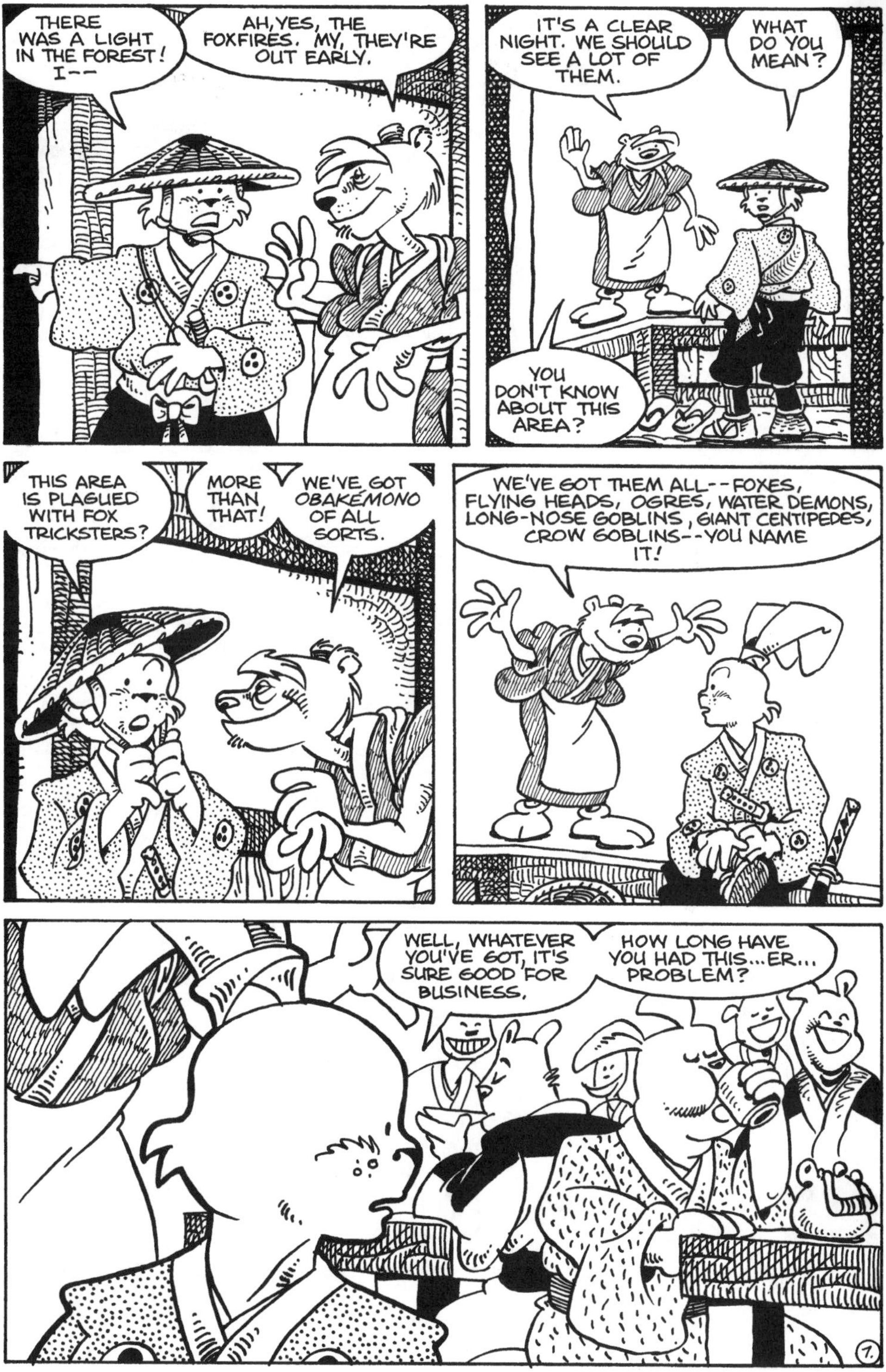
THERE WAS A LIGHT IN THE FOREST! I--
AH, YES, THE FOXFIRES. MY, THEY'RE OUT EARLY.
IT'S A CLEAR NIGHT. WE SHOULD SEE A LOT OF THEM.
WHAT DO YOU MEAN?
YOU DON'T KNOW ABOUT THIS AREA?
THIS AREA IS PLAGUED WITH FOX TRICKSTERS?
MORE THAN THAT!
WE'VE GOT *OBAKÉMONO* OF ALL SORTS.
WE'VE GOT THEM ALL--FOXES, FLYING HEADS, OGRES, WATER DEMONS, LONG-NOSE GOBLINS, GIANT CENTIPEDES, CROW GOBLINS--YOU NAME IT!
WELL, WHATEVER YOU'VE GOT, IT'S SURE GOOD FOR BUSINESS.
HOW LONG HAVE YOU HAD THIS...ER... PROBLEM?
7.

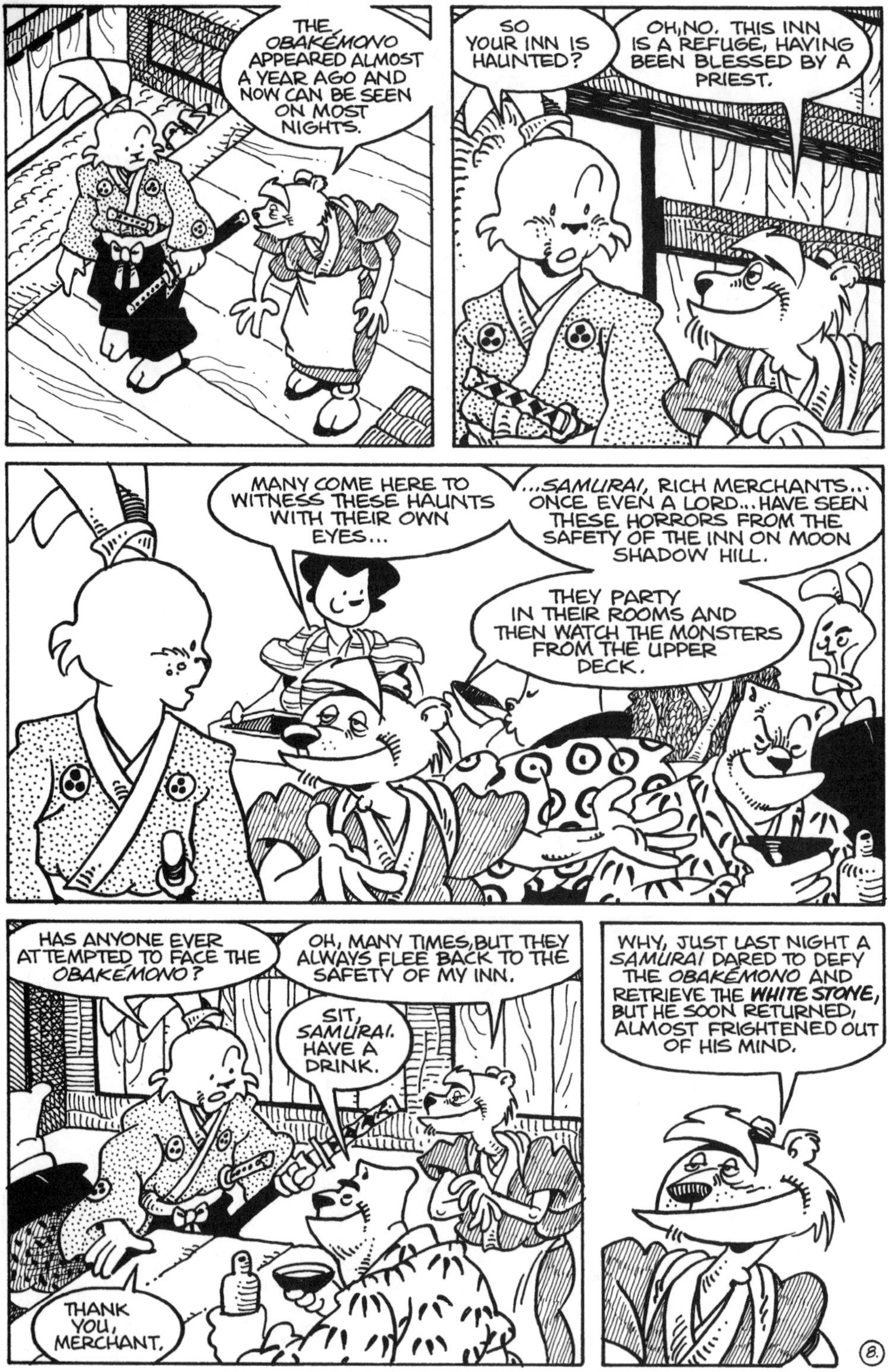
THE OBAKÉMONO APPEARED ALMOST A YEAR AGO AND NOW CAN BE SEEN ON MOST NIGHTS.
SO YOUR INN IS HAUNTED?
OH, NO. THIS INN IS A REFUGE, HAVING BEEN BLESSED BY A PRIEST.
MANY COME HERE TO WITNESS THESE HAUNTS WITH THEIR OWN EYES...
...SAMURAI, RICH MERCHANTS... ONCE EVEN A LORD... HAVE SEEN THESE HORRORS FROM THE SAFETY OF THE INN ON MOON SHADOW HILL.
THEY PARTY IN THEIR ROOMS AND THEN WATCH THE MONSTERS FROM THE UPPER DECK.
HAS ANYONE EVER ATTEMPTED TO FACE THE OBAKÉMONO?
OH, MANY TIMES, BUT THEY ALWAYS FLEE BACK TO THE SAFETY OF MY INN.
SIT, SAMURAI. HAVE A DRINK.
THANK YOU, MERCHANT.
WHY, JUST LAST NIGHT A SAMURAI DARED TO DEFY THE OBAKÉMONO AND RETRIEVE THE WHITE STONE, BUT HE SOON RETURNED, ALMOST FRIGHTENED OUT OF HIS MIND.
8.

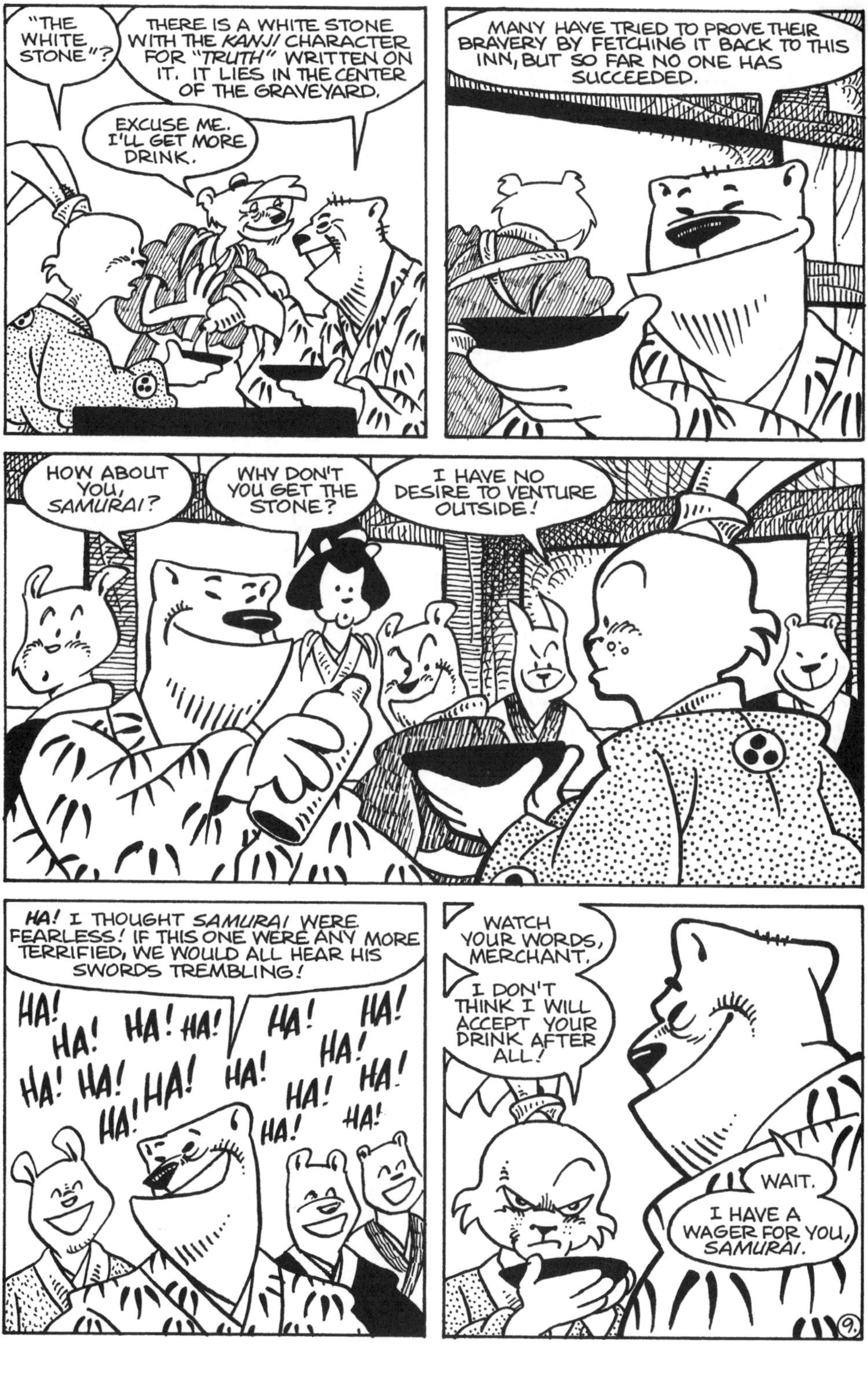
"THE WHITE STONE"?
THERE IS A WHITE STONE WITH THE KANJI CHARACTER FOR "TRUTH" WRITTEN ON IT. IT LIES IN THE CENTER OF THE GRAVEYARD.
EXCUSE ME. I'LL GET MORE DRINK.
MANY HAVE TRIED TO PROVE THEIR BRAVERY BY FETCHING IT BACK TO THIS INN, BUT SO FAR NO ONE HAS SUCCEEDED.
HOW ABOUT YOU, SAMURAI?
WHY DON'T YOU GET THE STONE?
I HAVE NO DESIRE TO VENTURE OUTSIDE!
HA! I THOUGHT SAMURAI WERE FEARLESS! IF THIS ONE WERE ANY MORE TERRIFIED, WE WOULD ALL HEAR HIS SWORDS TREMBLING!
HA! HA! HA! HA! HA! HA! HA! HA! HA! HA! HA! HA! HA! HA! HA! HA! HA!
WATCH YOUR WORDS, MERCHANT.
I DON'T THINK I WILL ACCEPT YOUR DRINK AFTER ALL!
WAIT.
I HAVE A WAGER FOR YOU, SAMURAI.
9.

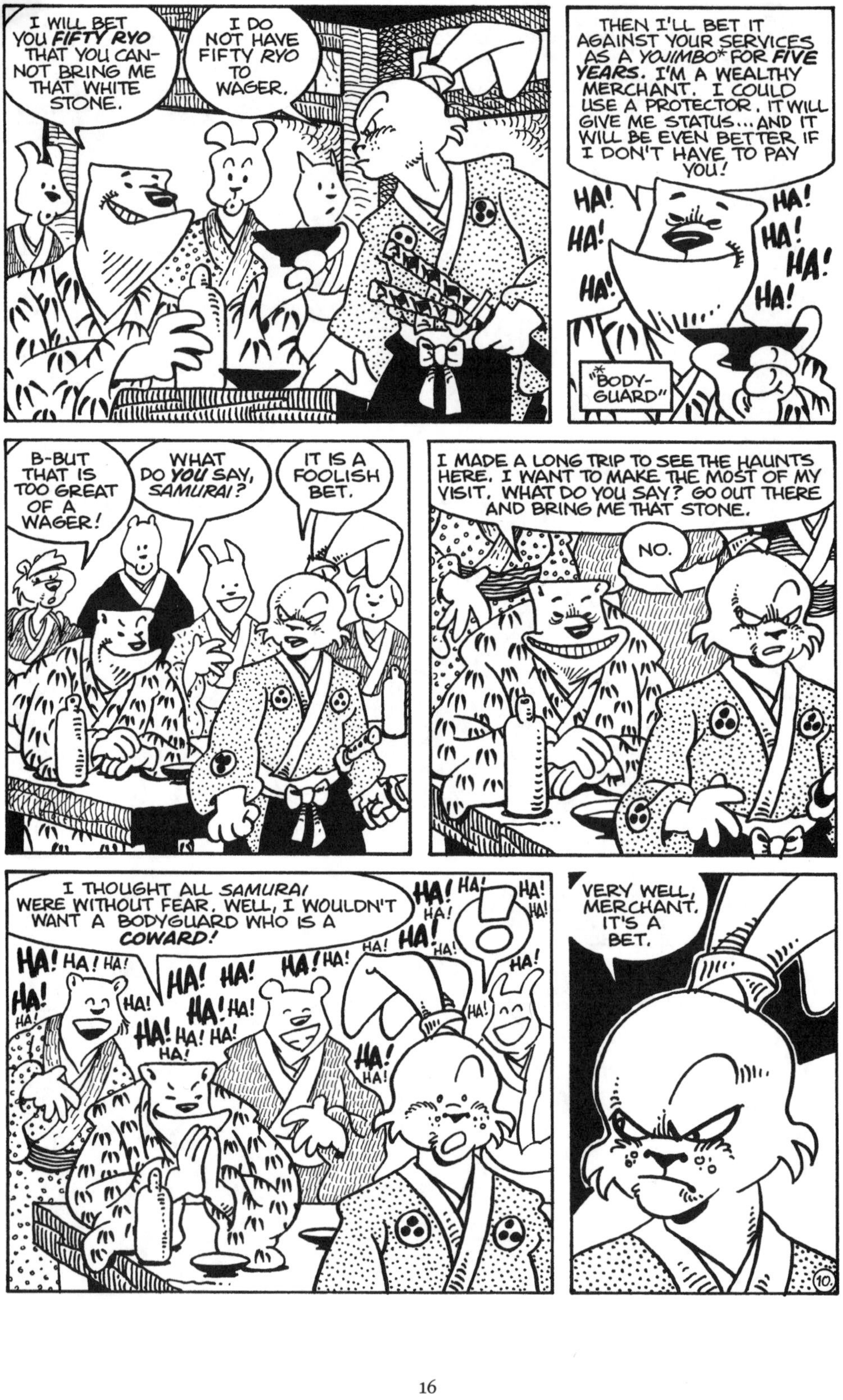

I WILL BET YOU *FIFTY RYO* THAT YOU CAN-NOT BRING ME THAT WHITE STONE.
I DO NOT HAVE FIFTY *RYO* TO WAGER.
THEN I'LL BET IT AGAINST YOUR SERVICES AS A *YOJIMBO** FOR **FIVE YEARS.** I'M A WEALTHY MERCHANT. I COULD USE A PROTECTOR. IT WILL GIVE ME STATUS... AND IT WILL BE EVEN BETTER IF I DON'T HAVE TO PAY YOU!
HA! HA! HA! HA! HA! HA! HA!
*"BODY-GUARD"
B-BUT THAT IS TOO GREAT OF A WAGER!
WHAT DO *YOU* SAY, *SAMURAI*?
IT IS A FOOLISH BET.
I MADE A LONG TRIP TO SEE THE HAUNTS HERE. I WANT TO MAKE THE MOST OF MY VISIT. WHAT DO YOU SAY? GO OUT THERE AND BRING ME THAT STONE.
NO.
I THOUGHT ALL *SAMURAI* WERE WITHOUT FEAR. WELL, I WOULDN'T WANT A BODYGUARD WHO IS A ***COWARD!***
HA! HA! HA! HA! HA! HA! HA! HA! HA! HA! HA! HA! HA! HA! HA! HA! HA! HA! HA! HA! HA! HA! HA! HA! HA! HA! HA!
!
VERY WELL, MERCHANT. IT'S A BET.
10.

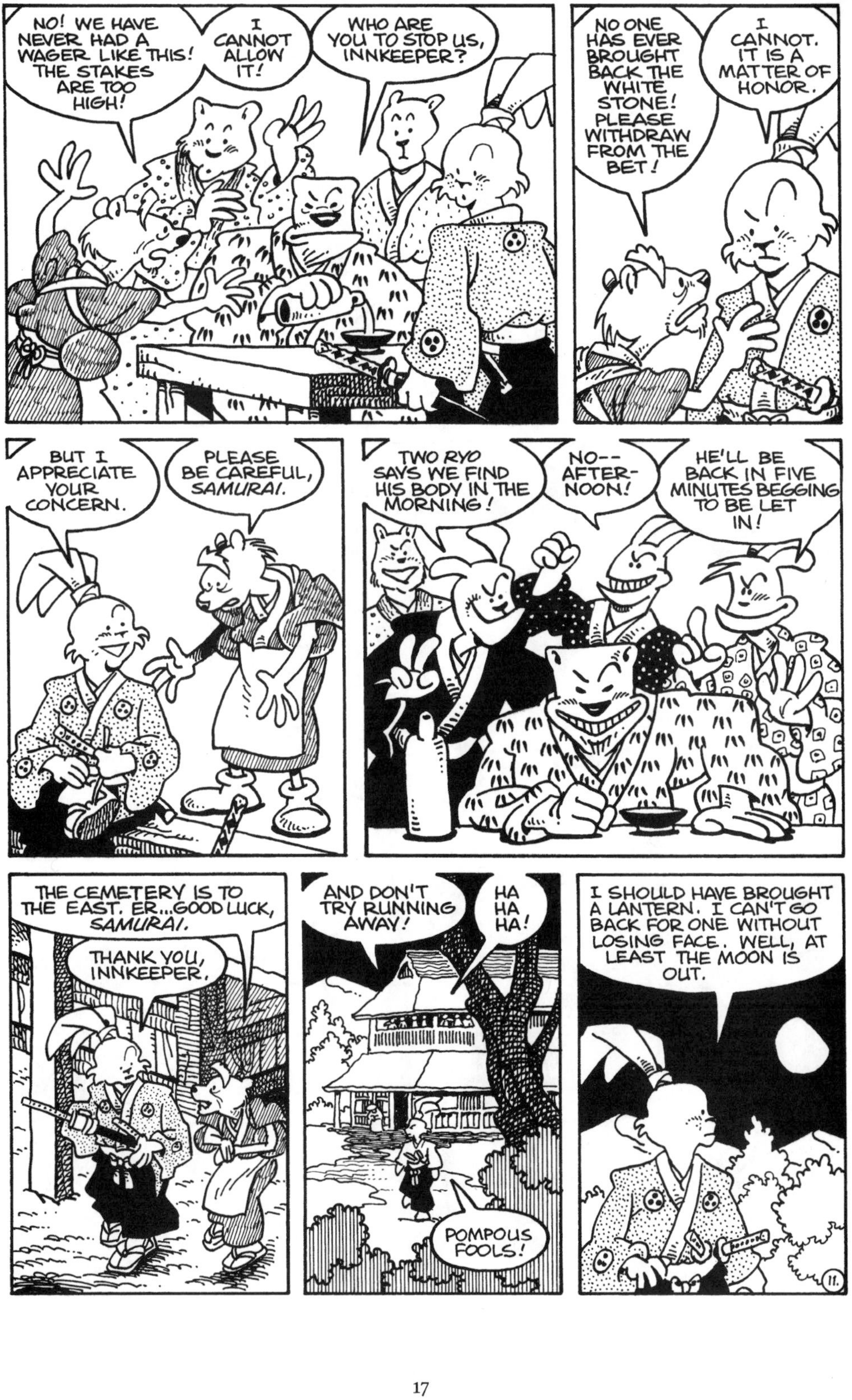
NO! WE HAVE NEVER HAD A WAGER LIKE THIS! THE STAKES ARE TOO HIGH!
I CANNOT ALLOW IT!
WHO ARE YOU TO STOP US, INNKEEPER?
NO ONE HAS EVER BROUGHT BACK THE WHITE STONE! PLEASE WITHDRAW FROM THE BET!
I CANNOT. IT IS A MATTER OF HONOR.
BUT I APPRECIATE YOUR CONCERN.
PLEASE BE CAREFUL, SAMURAI.
TWO RYO SAYS WE FIND HIS BODY IN THE MORNING!
NO-- AFTER-NOON!
HE'LL BE BACK IN FIVE MINUTES BEGGING TO BE LET IN!
THE CEMETERY IS TO THE EAST. ER...GOOD LUCK, SAMURAI.
THANK YOU, INNKEEPER.
AND DON'T TRY RUNNING AWAY!
HA HA HA!
POMPOUS FOOLS!
I SHOULD HAVE BROUGHT A LANTERN. I CAN'T GO BACK FOR ONE WITHOUT LOSING FACE. WELL, AT LEAST THE MOON IS OUT.
11.

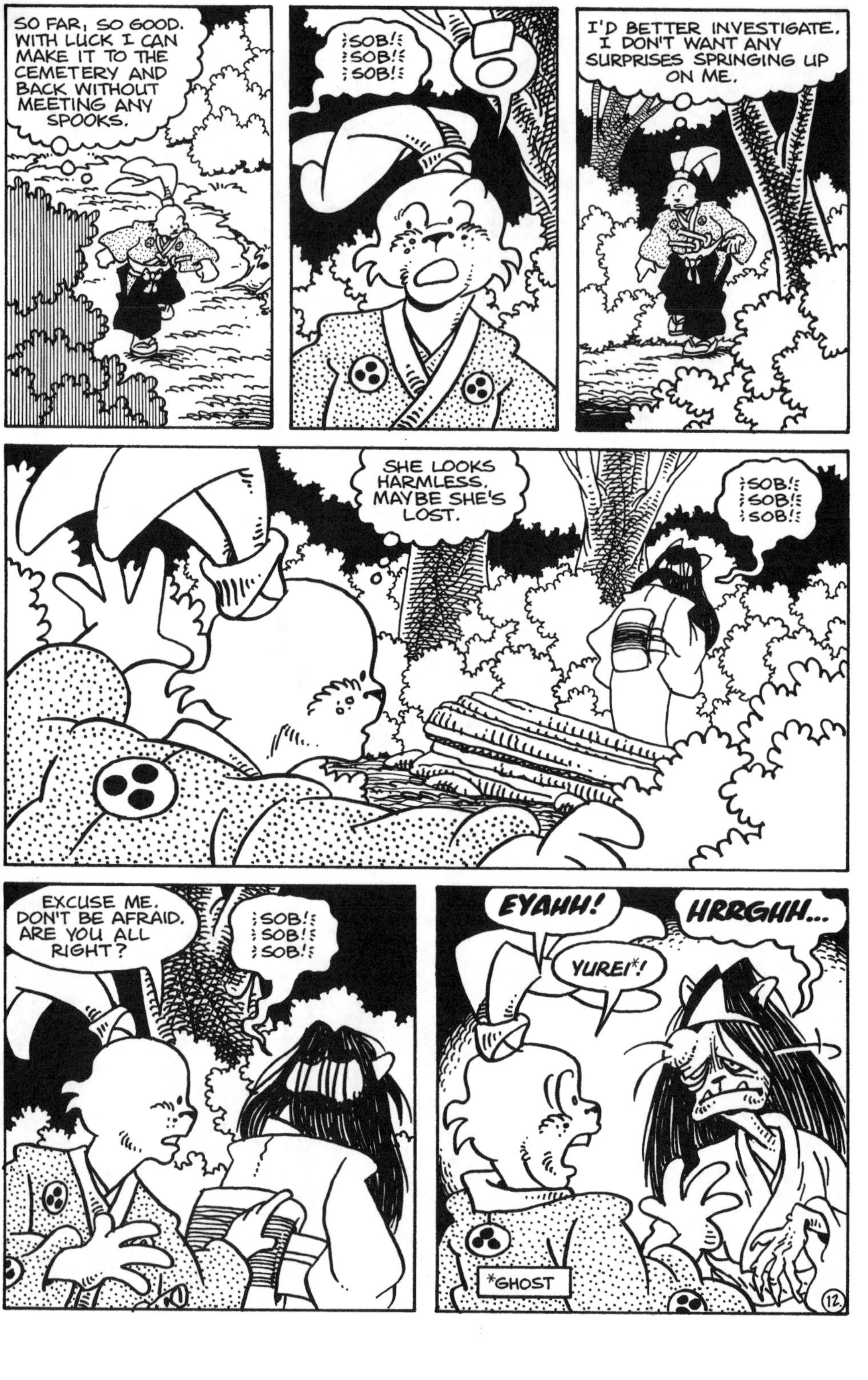
SO FAR, SO GOOD. WITH LUCK I CAN MAKE IT TO THE CEMETERY AND BACK WITHOUT MEETING ANY SPOOKS.
SOB! SOB! SOB!
I'D BETTER INVESTIGATE. I DON'T WANT ANY SURPRISES SPRINGING UP ON ME.
SHE LOOKS HARMLESS. MAYBE SHE'S LOST.
SOB! SOB! SOB!
EXCUSE ME. DON'T BE AFRAID. ARE YOU ALL RIGHT?
SOB! SOB! SOB!
EYAHH!
YUREI*!
HRRGHH...
*GHOST
12

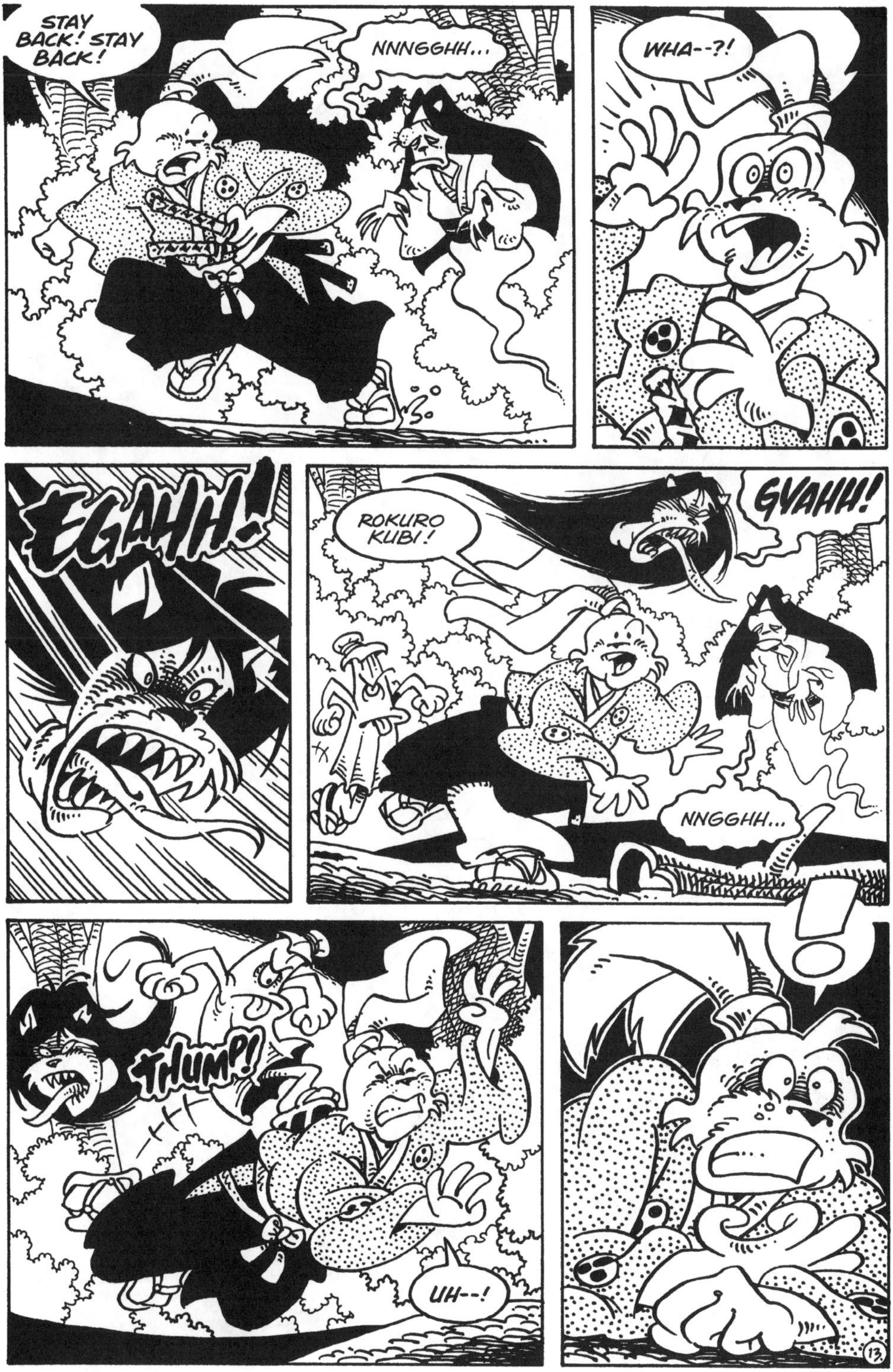
STAY BACK! STAY BACK!
NNNGGHH...
WHA--?!
EGAHH!
ROKURO KUBI!
GYAHH!
NNGGHH...
THUMP!
UH--!
!
13

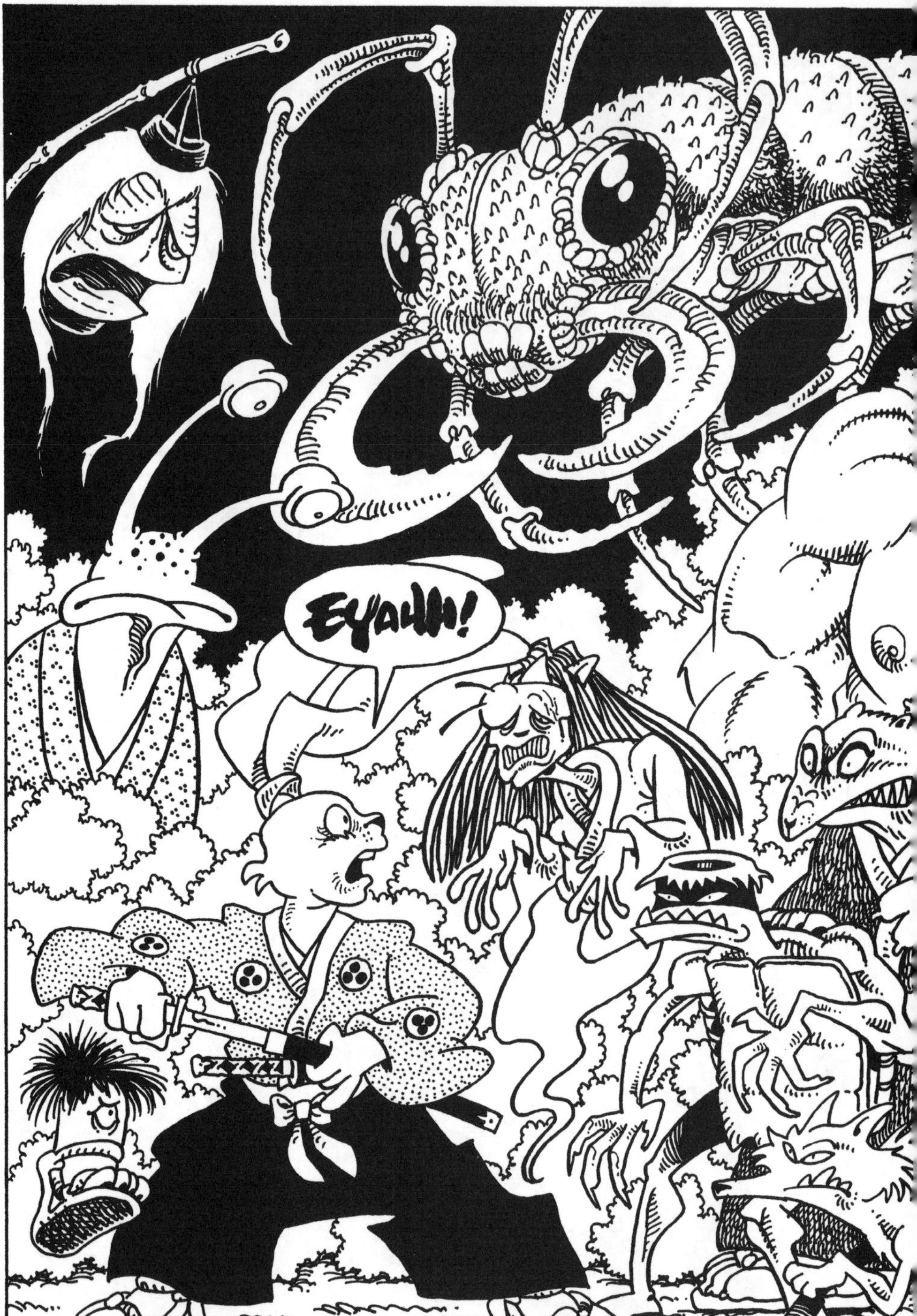
EYAHH!

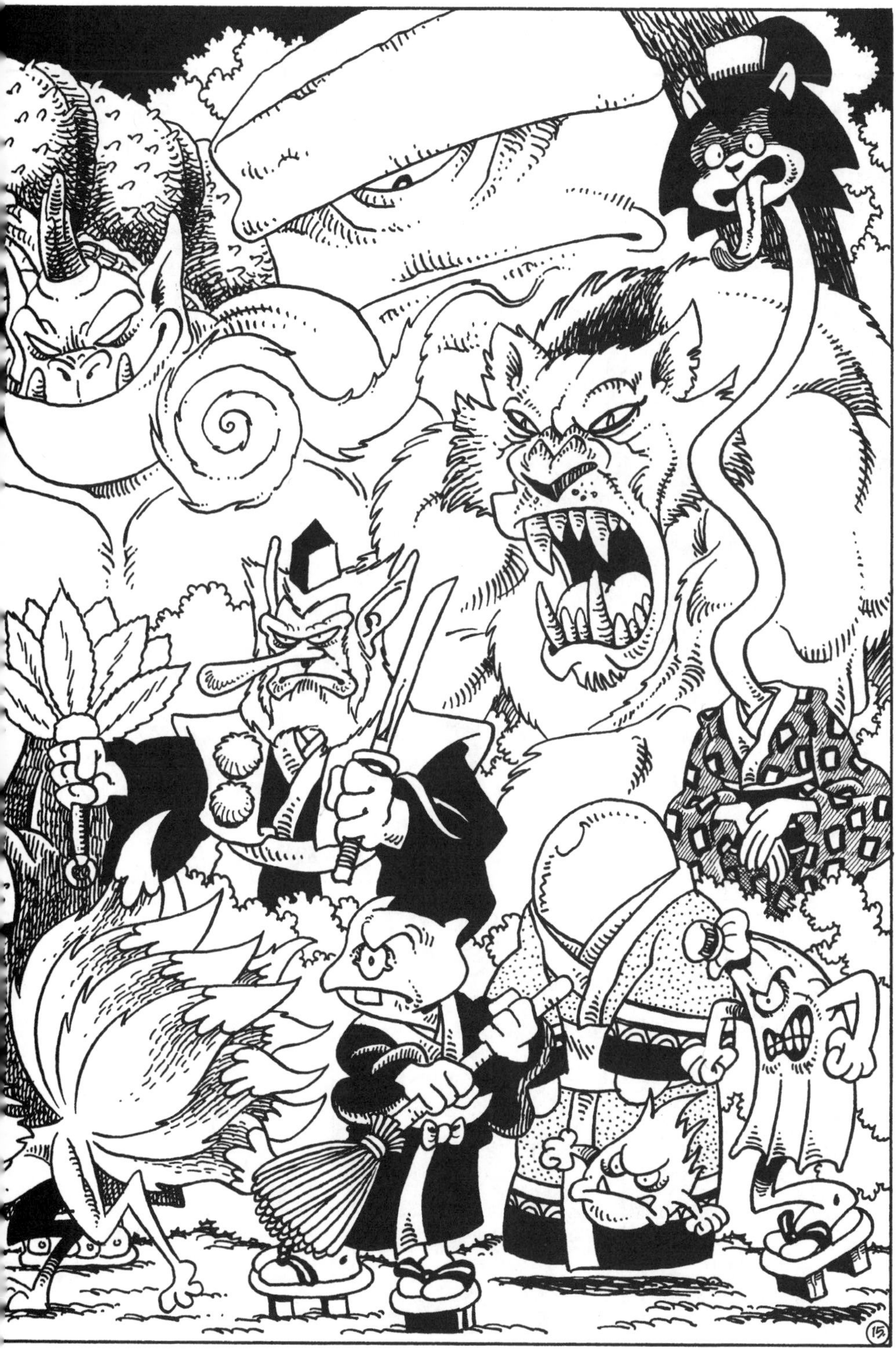

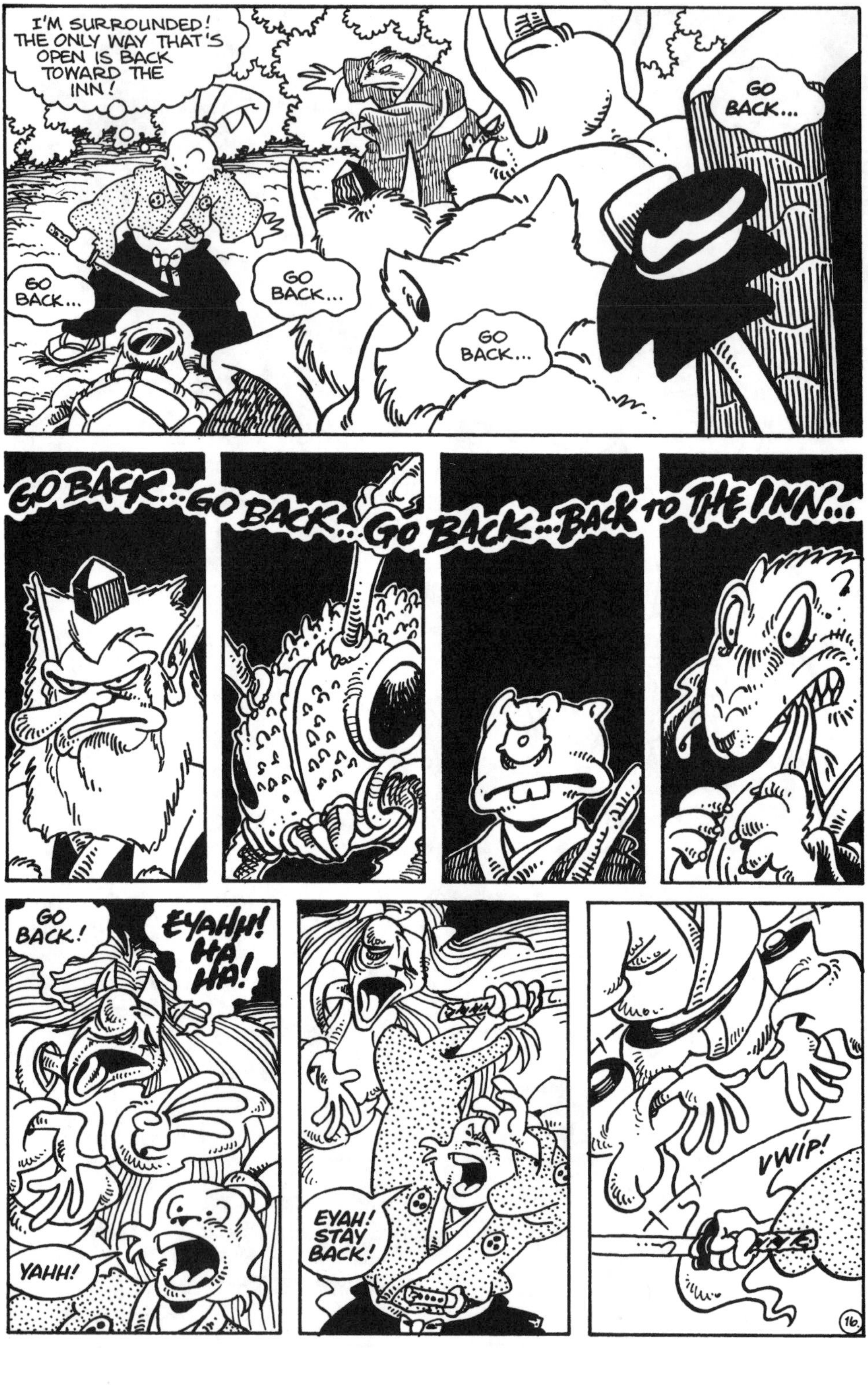
I'M SURROUNDED! THE ONLY WAY THAT'S OPEN IS BACK TOWARD THE INN!
GO BACK...
GO BACK...
GO BACK...
GO BACK...
GO BACK...GO BACK...GO BACK...BACK TO THE INN...
GO BACK!
EYAHH! HA HA!
YAHH!
EYAH! STAY BACK!
VWIP!
16.

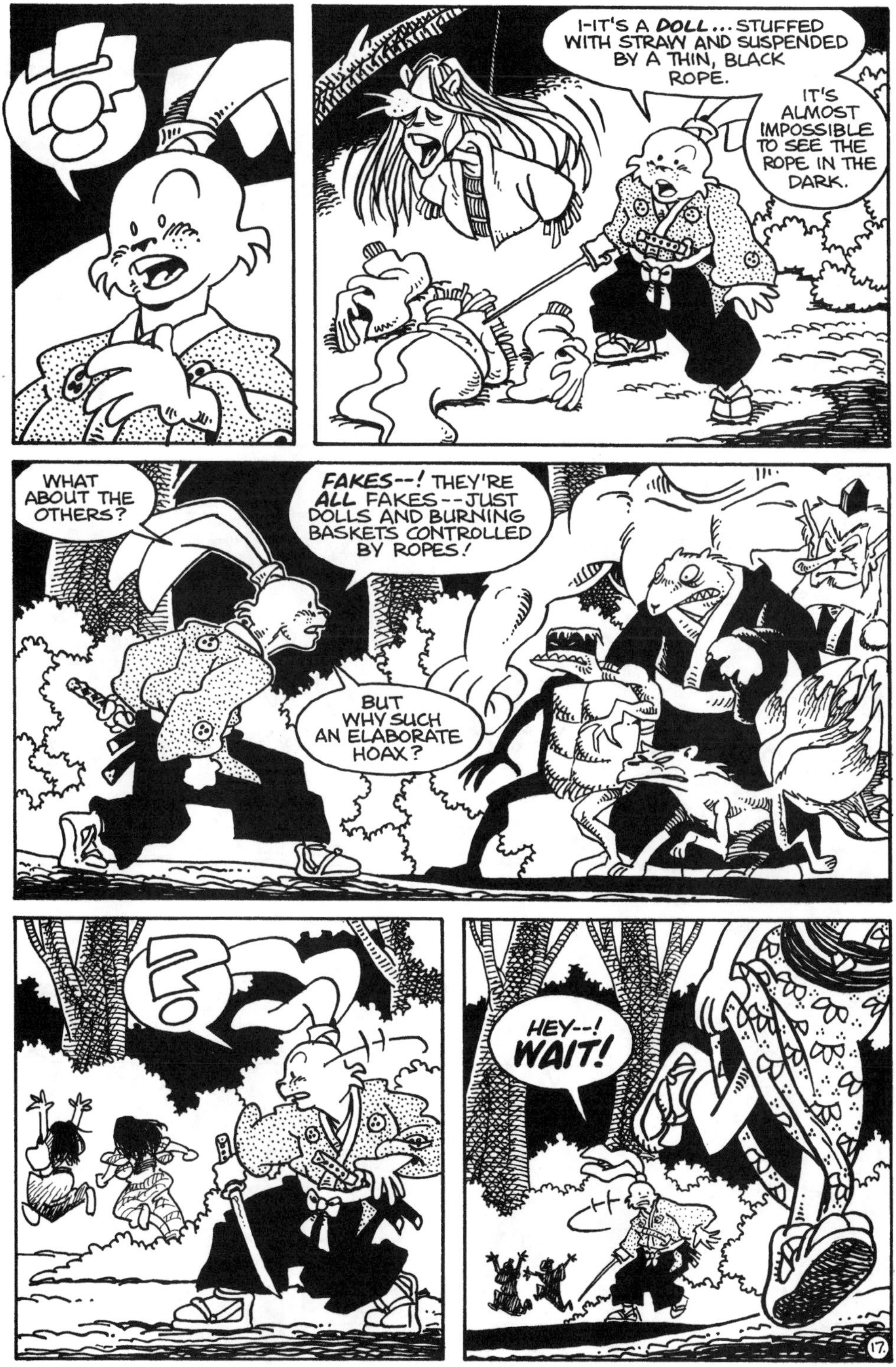
I-IT'S A DOLL... STUFFED WITH STRAW AND SUSPENDED BY A THIN, BLACK ROPE.
IT'S ALMOST IMPOSSIBLE TO SEE THE ROPE IN THE DARK.
WHAT ABOUT THE OTHERS?
FAKES--! THEY'RE ALL FAKES--JUST DOLLS AND BURNING BASKETS CONTROLLED BY ROPES!
BUT WHY SUCH AN ELABORATE HOAX?
HEY--! WAIT!
17.

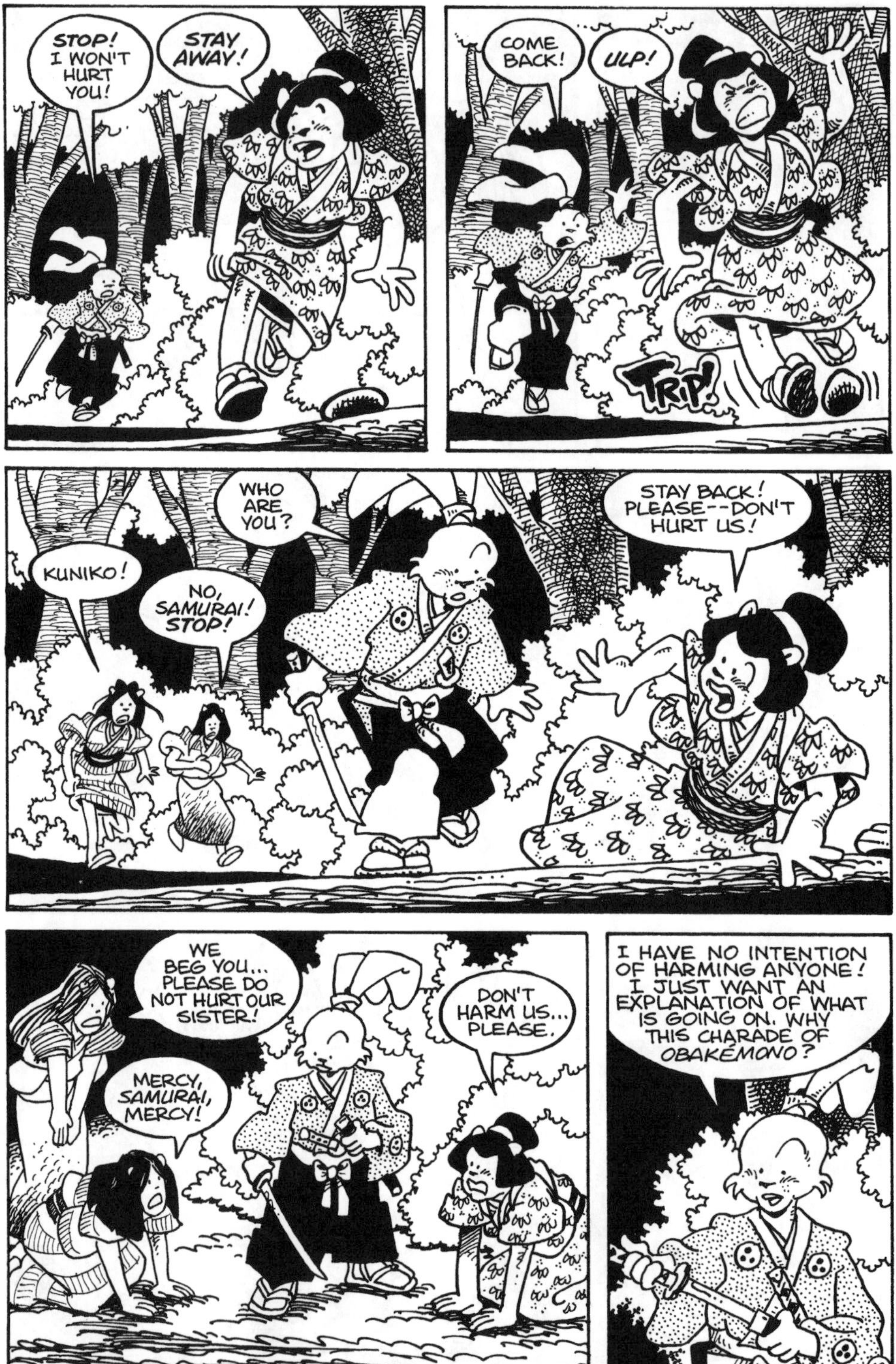
STOP! I WON'T HURT YOU!
STAY AWAY!
COME BACK!
ULP!
TRIP!
KUNIKO!
NO, SAMURAI! STOP!
WHO ARE YOU?
STAY BACK! PLEASE--DON'T HURT US!
WE BEG YOU... PLEASE DO NOT HURT OUR SISTER!
MERCY, SAMURAI, MERCY!
DON'T HARM US... PLEASE.
I HAVE NO INTENTION OF HARMING ANYONE! I JUST WANT AN EXPLANATION OF WHAT IS GOING ON. WHY THIS CHARADE OF OBAKEMONO?
18.

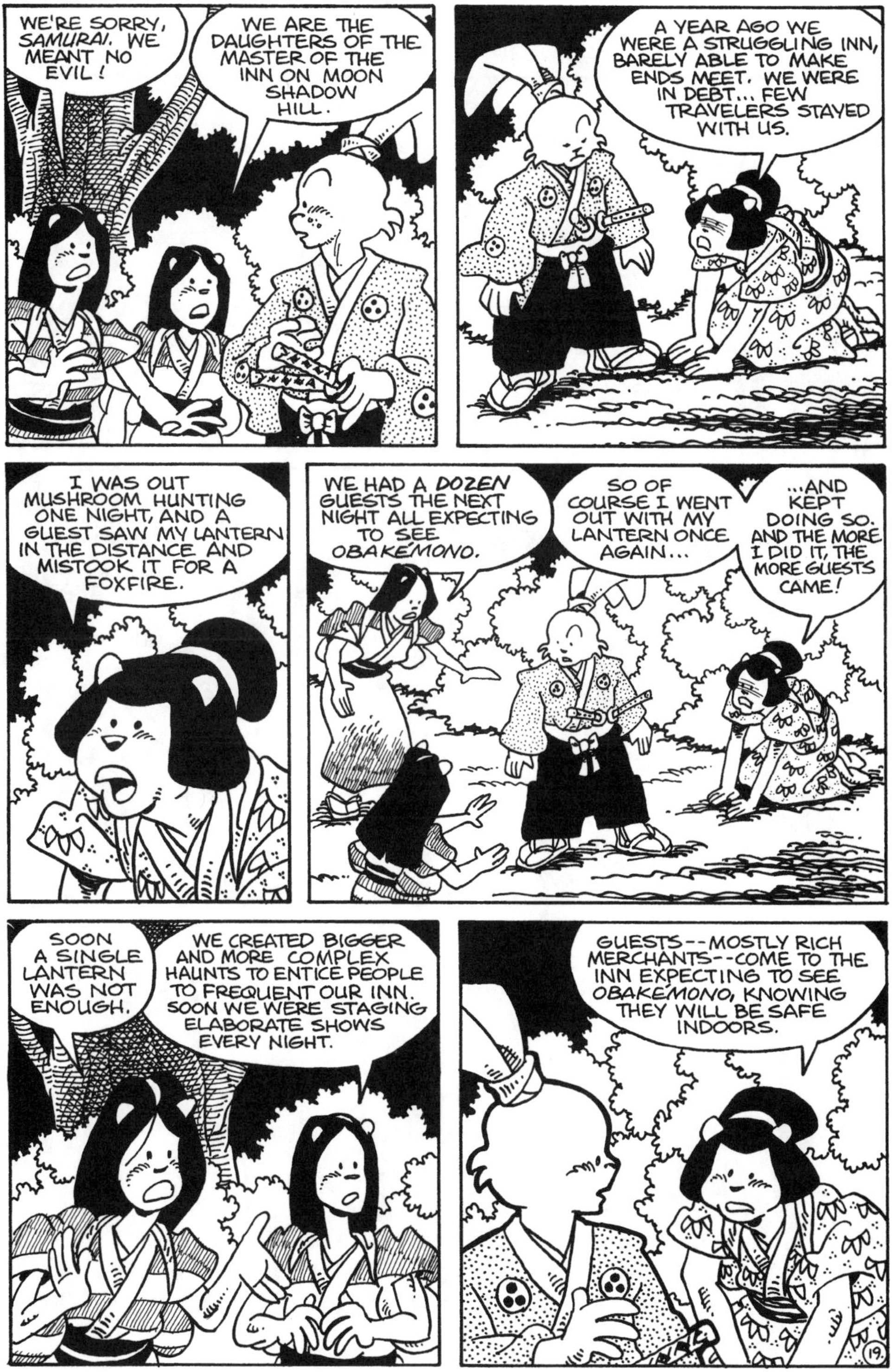
WE'RE SORRY, SAMURAI. WE MEANT NO EVIL!
WE ARE THE DAUGHTERS OF THE MASTER OF THE INN ON MOON SHADOW HILL.
A YEAR AGO WE WERE A STRUGGLING INN, BARELY ABLE TO MAKE ENDS MEET. WE WERE IN DEBT... FEW TRAVELERS STAYED WITH US.
I WAS OUT MUSHROOM HUNTING ONE NIGHT, AND A GUEST SAW MY LANTERN IN THE DISTANCE AND MISTOOK IT FOR A FOXFIRE.
WE HAD A DOZEN GUESTS THE NEXT NIGHT ALL EXPECTING TO SEE OBAKEMONO.
SO OF COURSE I WENT OUT WITH MY LANTERN ONCE AGAIN...
...AND KEPT DOING SO. AND THE MORE I DID IT, THE MORE GUESTS CAME!
SOON A SINGLE LANTERN WAS NOT ENOUGH.
WE CREATED BIGGER AND MORE COMPLEX HAUNTS TO ENTICE PEOPLE TO FREQUENT OUR INN. SOON WE WERE STAGING ELABORATE SHOWS EVERY NIGHT.
GUESTS--MOSTLY RICH MERCHANTS--COME TO THE INN EXPECTING TO SEE OBAKEMONO, KNOWING THEY WILL BE SAFE INDOORS.
19.

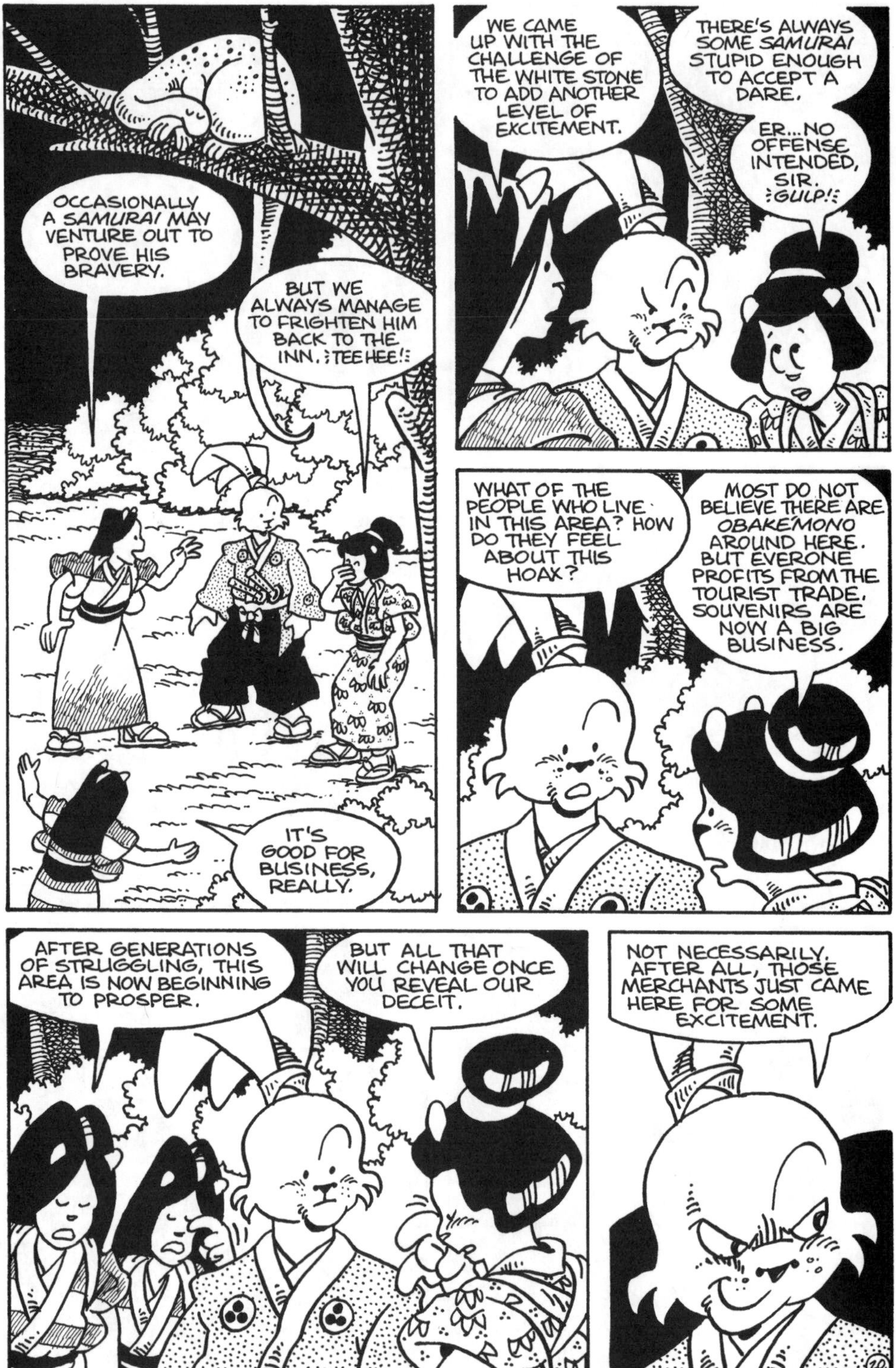
OCCASIONALLY A SAMURAI MAY VENTURE OUT TO PROVE HIS BRAVERY.
BUT WE ALWAYS MANAGE TO FRIGHTEN HIM BACK TO THE INN. TEE HEE!
IT'S GOOD FOR BUSINESS, REALLY.
WE CAME UP WITH THE CHALLENGE OF THE WHITE STONE TO ADD ANOTHER LEVEL OF EXCITEMENT.
THERE'S ALWAYS SOME SAMURAI STUPID ENOUGH TO ACCEPT A DARE.
ER...NO OFFENSE INTENDED, SIR.
GULP!
WHAT OF THE PEOPLE WHO LIVE IN THIS AREA? HOW DO THEY FEEL ABOUT THIS HOAX?
MOST DO NOT BELIEVE THERE ARE OBAKEMONO AROUND HERE. BUT EVERONE PROFITS FROM THE TOURIST TRADE. SOUVENIRS ARE NOW A BIG BUSINESS.
AFTER GENERATIONS OF STRUGGLING, THIS AREA IS NOW BEGINNING TO PROSPER.
BUT ALL THAT WILL CHANGE ONCE YOU REVEAL OUR DECEIT.
NOT NECESSARILY. AFTER ALL, THOSE MERCHANTS JUST CAME HERE FOR SOME EXCITEMENT.
20

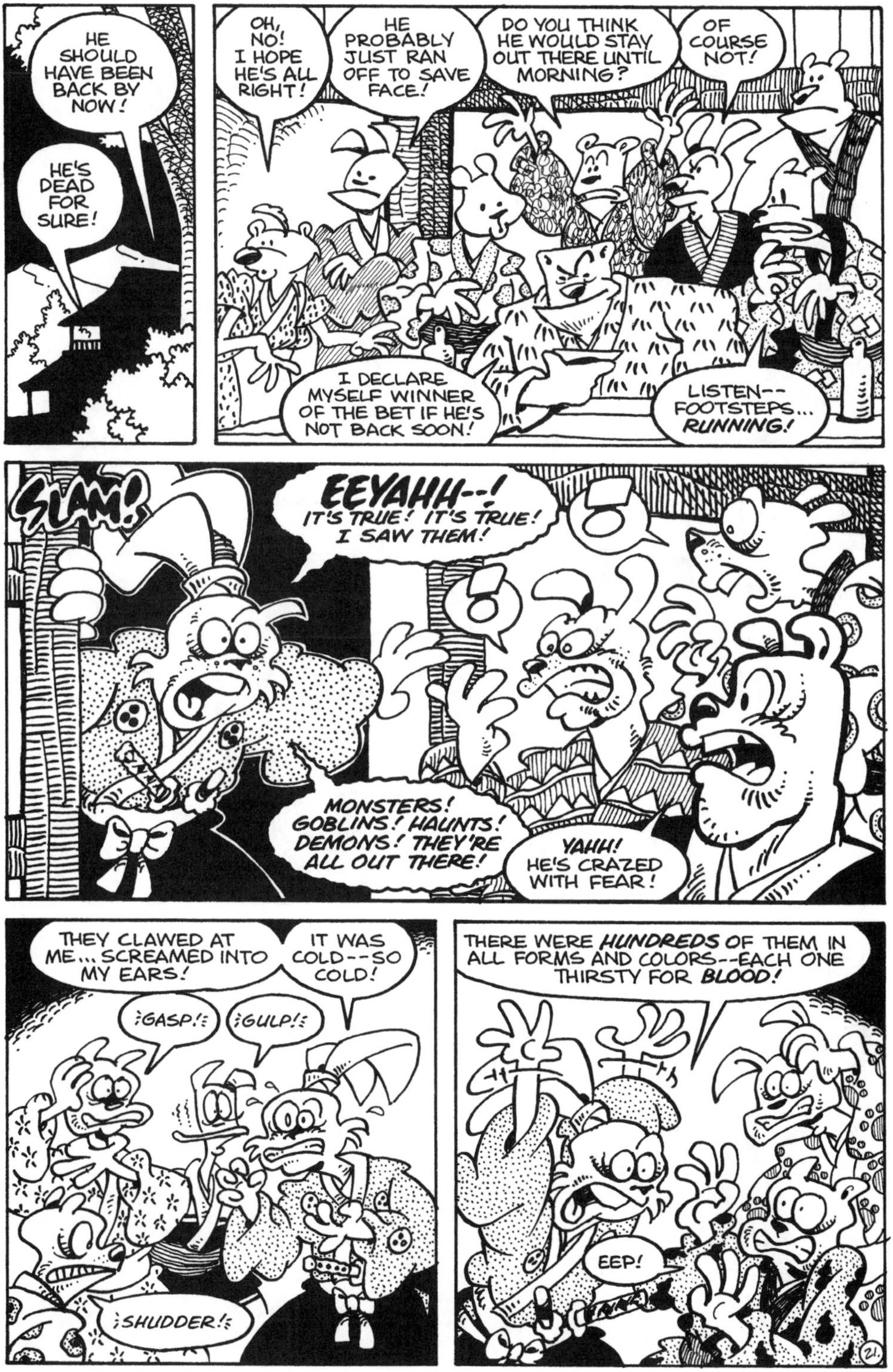

HE SHOULD HAVE BEEN BACK BY NOW!
HE'S DEAD FOR SURE!
OH, NO! I HOPE HE'S ALL RIGHT!
HE PROBABLY JUST RAN OFF TO SAVE FACE!
DO YOU THINK HE WOULD STAY OUT THERE UNTIL MORNING?
OF COURSE NOT!
I DECLARE MYSELF WINNER OF THE BET IF HE'S NOT BACK SOON!
LISTEN-- FOOTSTEPS... RUNNING!
SLAM!
EEYAHH--! IT'S TRUE! IT'S TRUE! I SAW THEM!
MONSTERS! GOBLINS! HAUNTS! DEMONS! THEY'RE ALL OUT THERE!
YAHH! HE'S CRAZED WITH FEAR!
THEY CLAWED AT ME... SCREAMED INTO MY EARS!
IT WAS COLD--SO COLD!
GASP!
GULP!
SHUDDER!
THERE WERE HUNDREDS OF THEM IN ALL FORMS AND COLORS--EACH ONE THIRSTY FOR BLOOD!
EEP!
21.

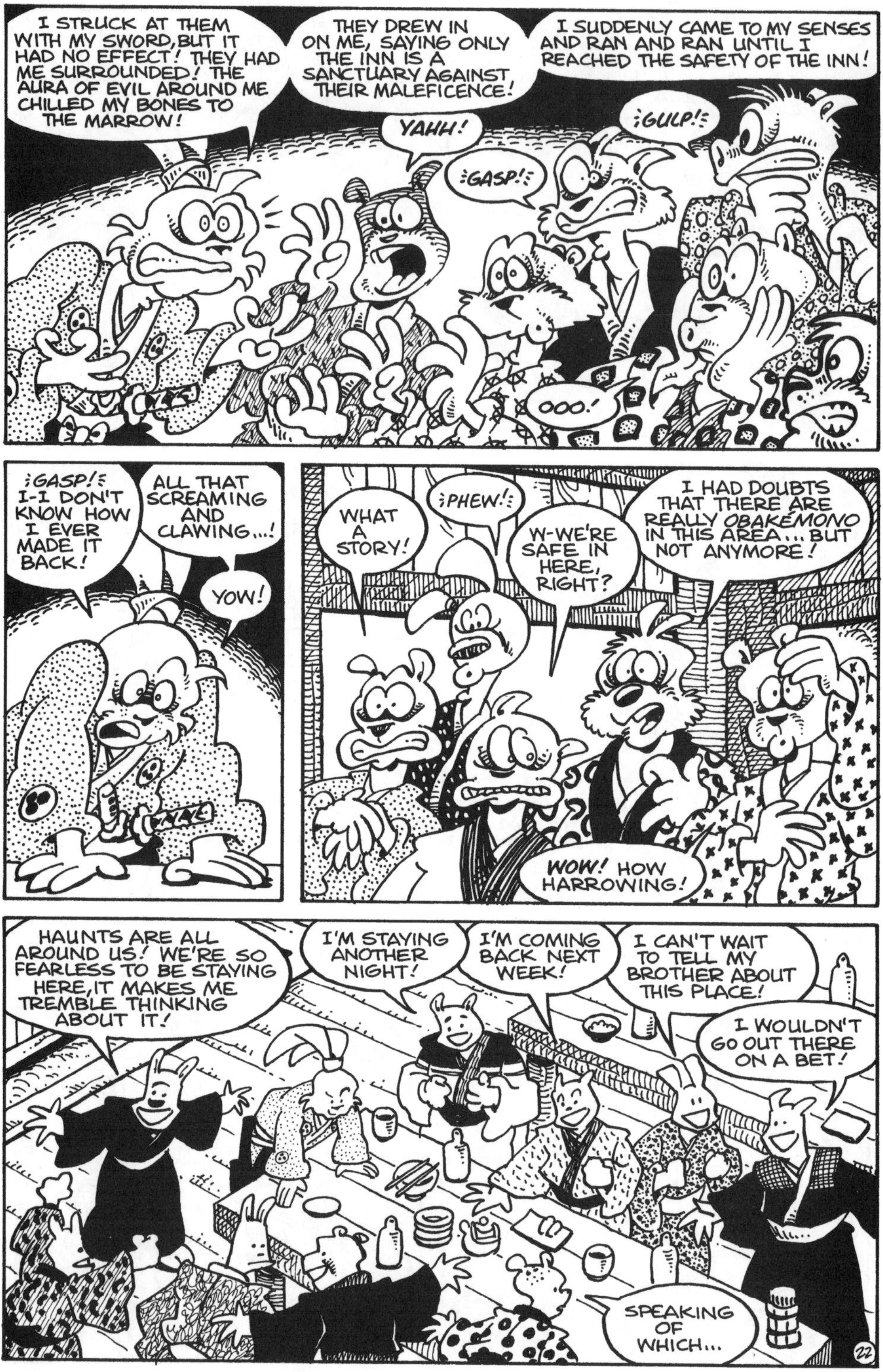
I STRUCK AT THEM WITH MY SWORD, BUT IT HAD NO EFFECT! THEY HAD ME SURROUNDED! THE AURA OF EVIL AROUND ME CHILLED MY BONES TO THE MARROW!
THEY DREW IN ON ME, SAYING ONLY THE INN IS A SANCTUARY AGAINST THEIR MALEFICENCE!
I SUDDENLY CAME TO MY SENSES AND RAN AND RAN UNTIL I REACHED THE SAFETY OF THE INN!
YAHH!
GASP!
GULP!
OOO!
GASP! I-I DON'T KNOW HOW I EVER MADE IT BACK!
ALL THAT SCREAMING AND CLAWING...!
YOW!
WHAT A STORY!
PHEW!
W-WE'RE SAFE IN HERE, RIGHT?
I HAD DOUBTS THAT THERE ARE REALLY *OBAKEMONO* IN THIS AREA... BUT NOT ANYMORE!
WOW! HOW HARROWING!
HAUNTS ARE ALL AROUND US! WE'RE SO FEARLESS TO BE STAYING HERE, IT MAKES ME TREMBLE THINKING ABOUT IT!
I'M STAYING ANOTHER NIGHT!
I'M COMING BACK NEXT WEEK!
I CAN'T WAIT TO TELL MY BROTHER ABOUT THIS PLACE!
I WOULDN'T GO OUT THERE ON A BET!
SPEAKING OF WHICH...
22

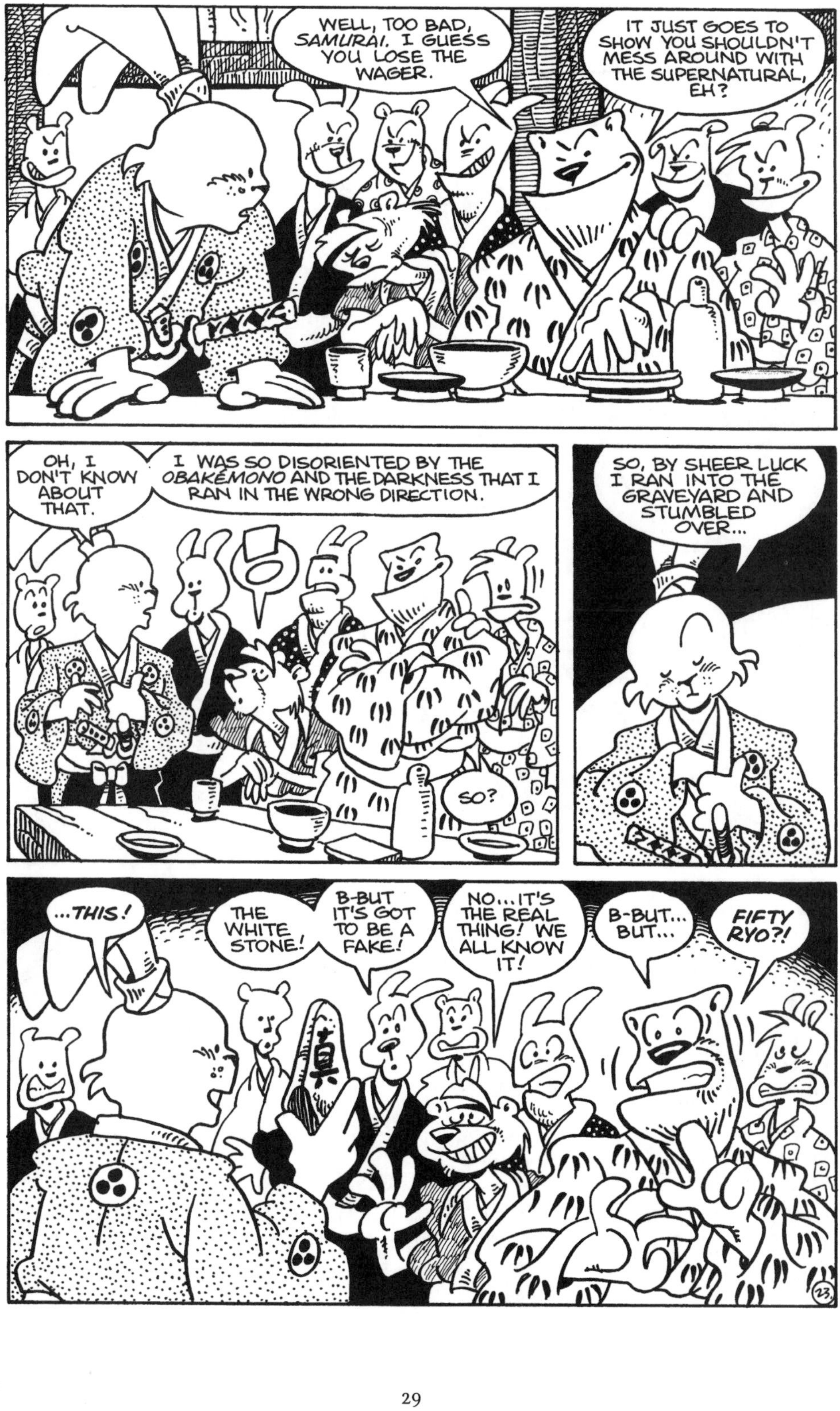

WELL, TOO BAD, SAMURAI. I GUESS YOU LOSE THE WAGER.
IT JUST GOES TO SHOW YOU SHOULDN'T MESS AROUND WITH THE SUPERNATURAL, EH?
OH, I DON'T KNOW ABOUT THAT.
I WAS SO DISORIENTED BY THE *OBAKEMONO* AND THE DARKNESS THAT I RAN IN THE WRONG DIRECTION.
SO?
SO, BY SHEER LUCK I RAN INTO THE GRAVEYARD AND STUMBLED OVER...
...THIS!
THE WHITE STONE!
B-BUT IT'S GOT TO BE A FAKE!
NO...IT'S THE REAL THING! WE ALL KNOW IT!
B-BUT... BUT...
FIFTY RYO?!
23

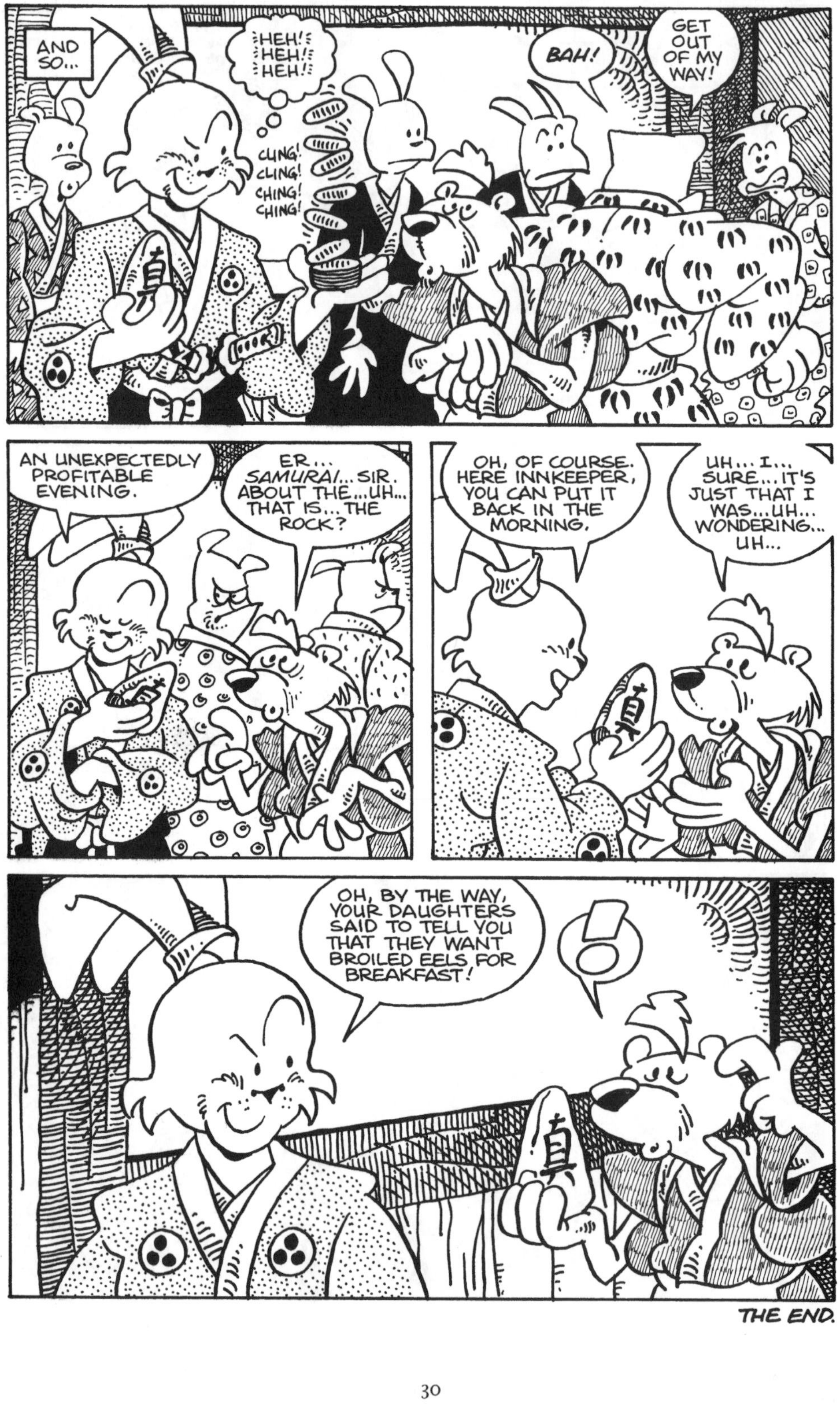
AND SO...
HEH! HEH! HEH!
CLING! CLING! CHING! CHING!
BAH!
GET OUT OF MY WAY!
AN UNEXPECTEDLY PROFITABLE EVENING.
ER... *SAMURAI*... SIR. ABOUT THE...UH... THAT IS... THE ROCK?
OH, OF COURSE. HERE INNKEEPER, YOU CAN PUT IT BACK IN THE MORNING.
UH... I... SURE... IT'S JUST THAT I WAS...UH... WONDERING... UH...
OH, BY THE WAY, YOUR DAUGHTERS SAID TO TELL YOU THAT THEY WANT BROILED EELS FOR BREAKFAST!
!

THE END.

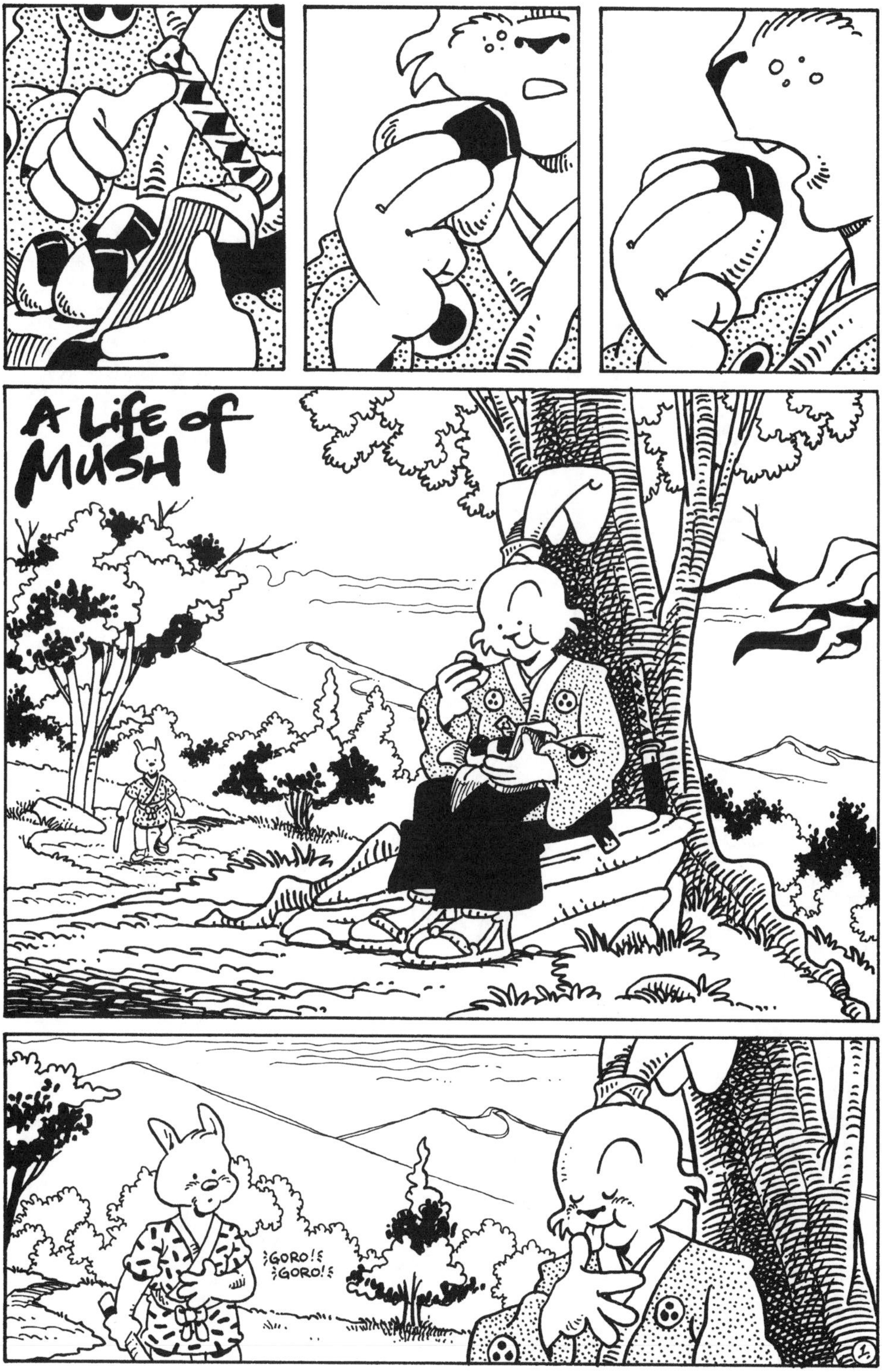
A Life of MUSH
GORO! GORO!

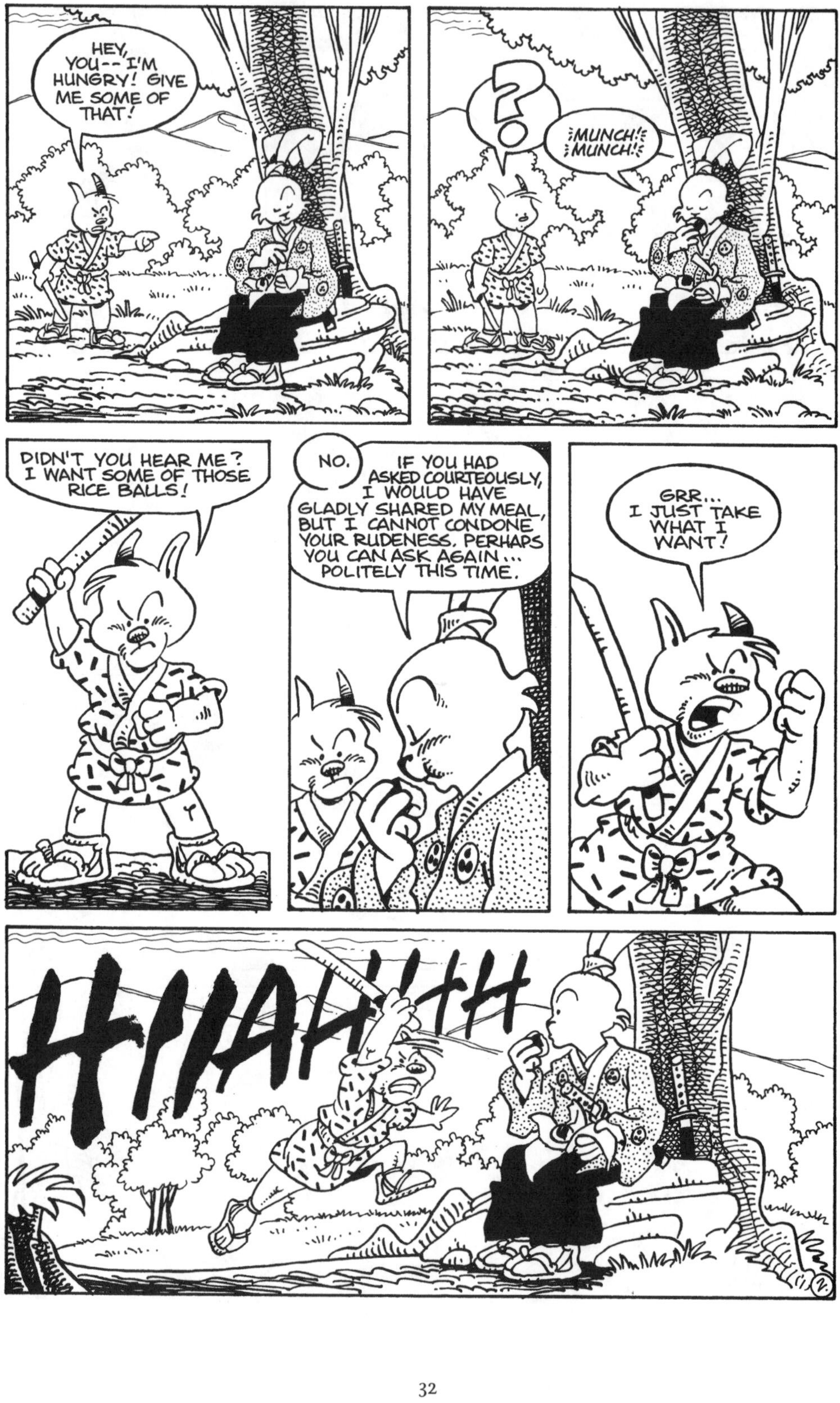
HEY, YOU-- I'M HUNGRY! GIVE ME SOME OF THAT!
?
MUNCH! MUNCH!
DIDN'T YOU HEAR ME? I WANT SOME OF THOSE RICE BALLS!
NO.
IF YOU HAD ASKED COURTEOUSLY, I WOULD HAVE GLADLY SHARED MY MEAL, BUT I CANNOT CONDONE YOUR RUDENESS. PERHAPS YOU CAN ASK AGAIN... POLITELY THIS TIME.
GRR... I JUST TAKE WHAT I WANT!
HIIAHHH
2.

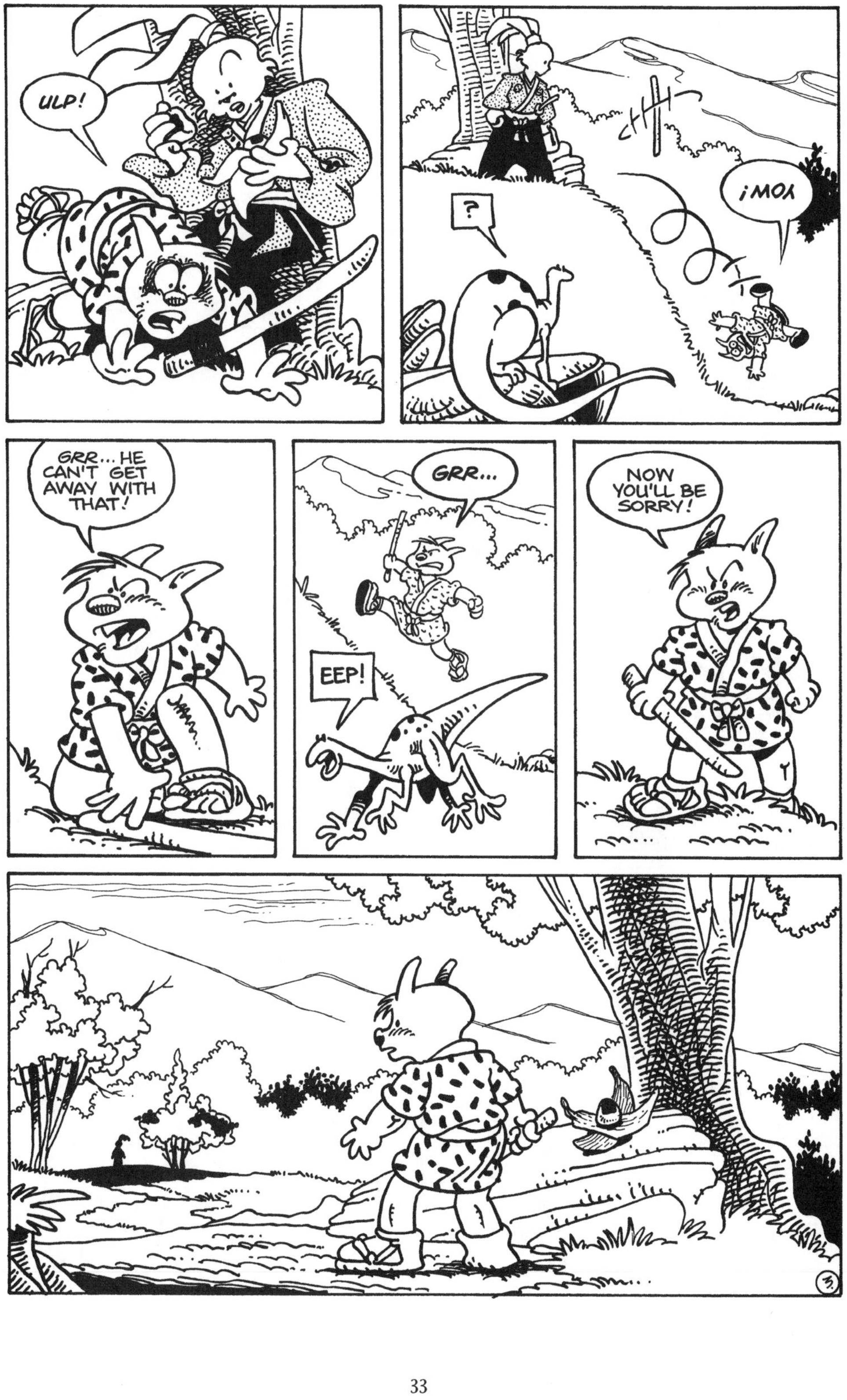
ULP!
?
YOW!
GRR... HE CAN'T GET AWAY WITH THAT!
GRR...
EEP!
NOW YOU'LL BE SORRY!

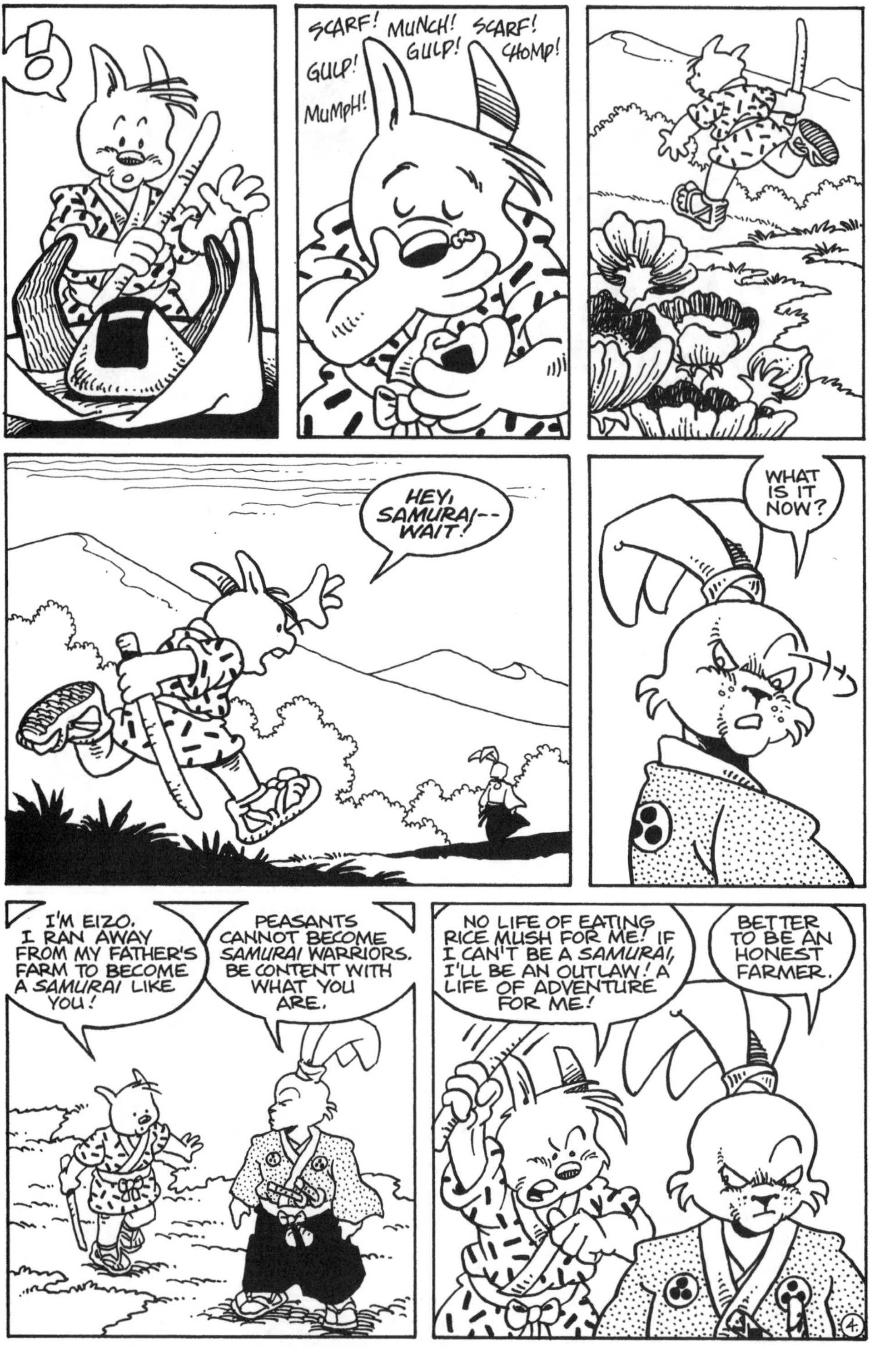
!
SCARF! MUNCH! SCARF!
GULP! GULP! CHOMP!
MUMPH!
HEY, SAMURAI-- WAIT!
WHAT IS IT NOW?
I'M EIZO. I RAN AWAY FROM MY FATHER'S FARM TO BECOME A SAMURAI LIKE YOU!
PEASANTS CANNOT BECOME SAMURAI WARRIORS. BE CONTENT WITH WHAT YOU ARE.
NO LIFE OF EATING RICE MUSH FOR ME! IF I CAN'T BE A SAMURAI, I'LL BE AN OUTLAW! A LIFE OF ADVENTURE FOR ME!
BETTER TO BE AN HONEST FARMER.
4

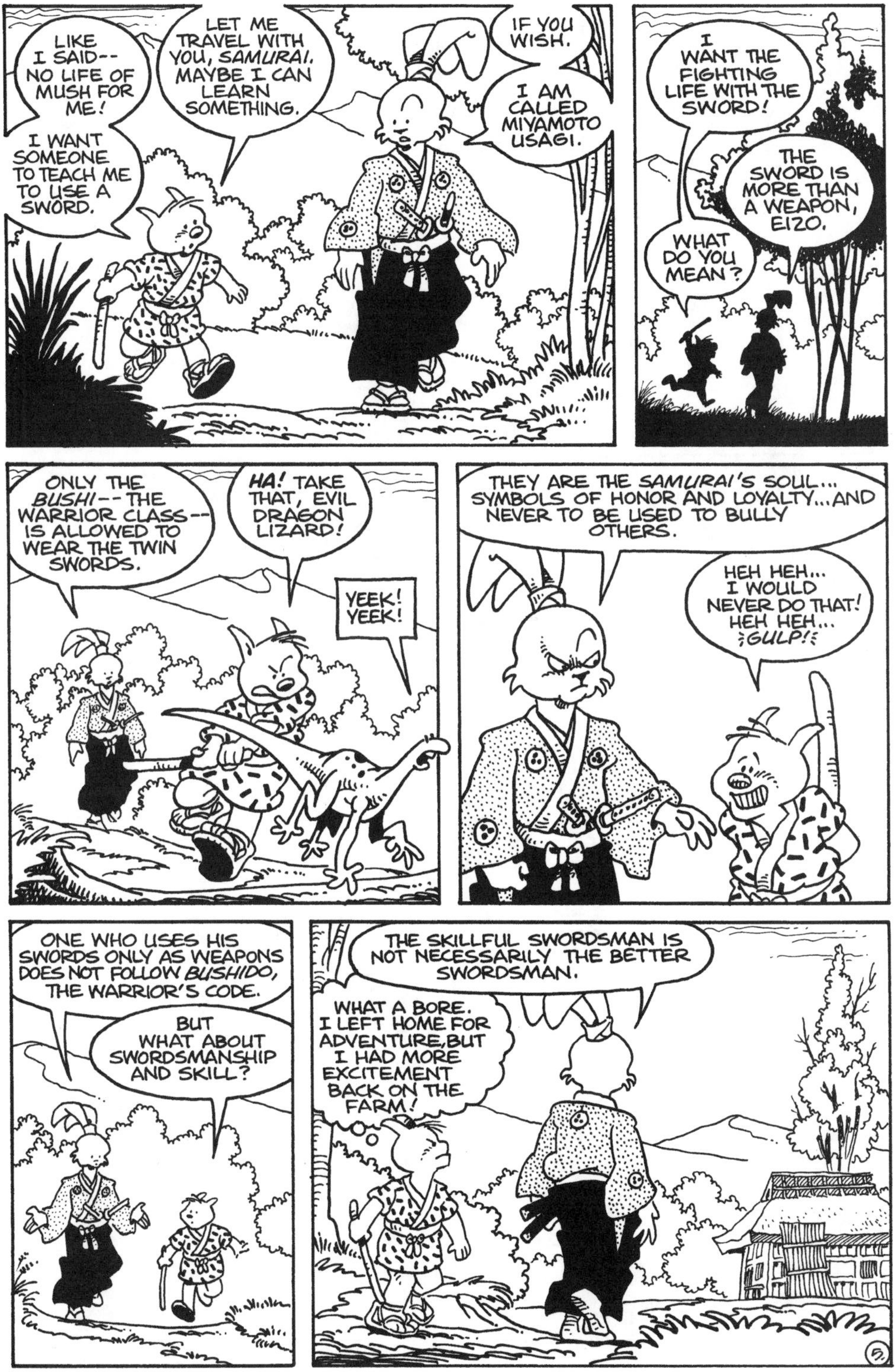
LIKE I SAID-- NO LIFE OF MUSH FOR ME!
I WANT SOMEONE TO TEACH ME TO USE A SWORD.
LET ME TRAVEL WITH YOU, SAMURAI. MAYBE I CAN LEARN SOMETHING.
IF YOU WISH.
I AM CALLED MIYAMOTO USAGI.
I WANT THE FIGHTING LIFE WITH THE SWORD!
THE SWORD IS MORE THAN A WEAPON, EIZO.
WHAT DO YOU MEAN?
ONLY THE BUSHI--THE WARRIOR CLASS--IS ALLOWED TO WEAR THE TWIN SWORDS.
HA! TAKE THAT, EVIL DRAGON LIZARD!
YEEK! YEEK!
THEY ARE THE SAMURAI'S SOUL... SYMBOLS OF HONOR AND LOYALTY... AND NEVER TO BE USED TO BULLY OTHERS.
HEH HEH... I WOULD NEVER DO THAT! HEH HEH... GULP!
ONE WHO USES HIS SWORDS ONLY AS WEAPONS DOES NOT FOLLOW BUSHIDO, THE WARRIOR'S CODE.
BUT WHAT ABOUT SWORDSMANSHIP AND SKILL?
THE SKILLFUL SWORDSMAN IS NOT NECESSARILY THE BETTER SWORDSMAN.
WHAT A BORE. I LEFT HOME FOR ADVENTURE, BUT I HAD MORE EXCITEMENT BACK ON THE FARM!
5

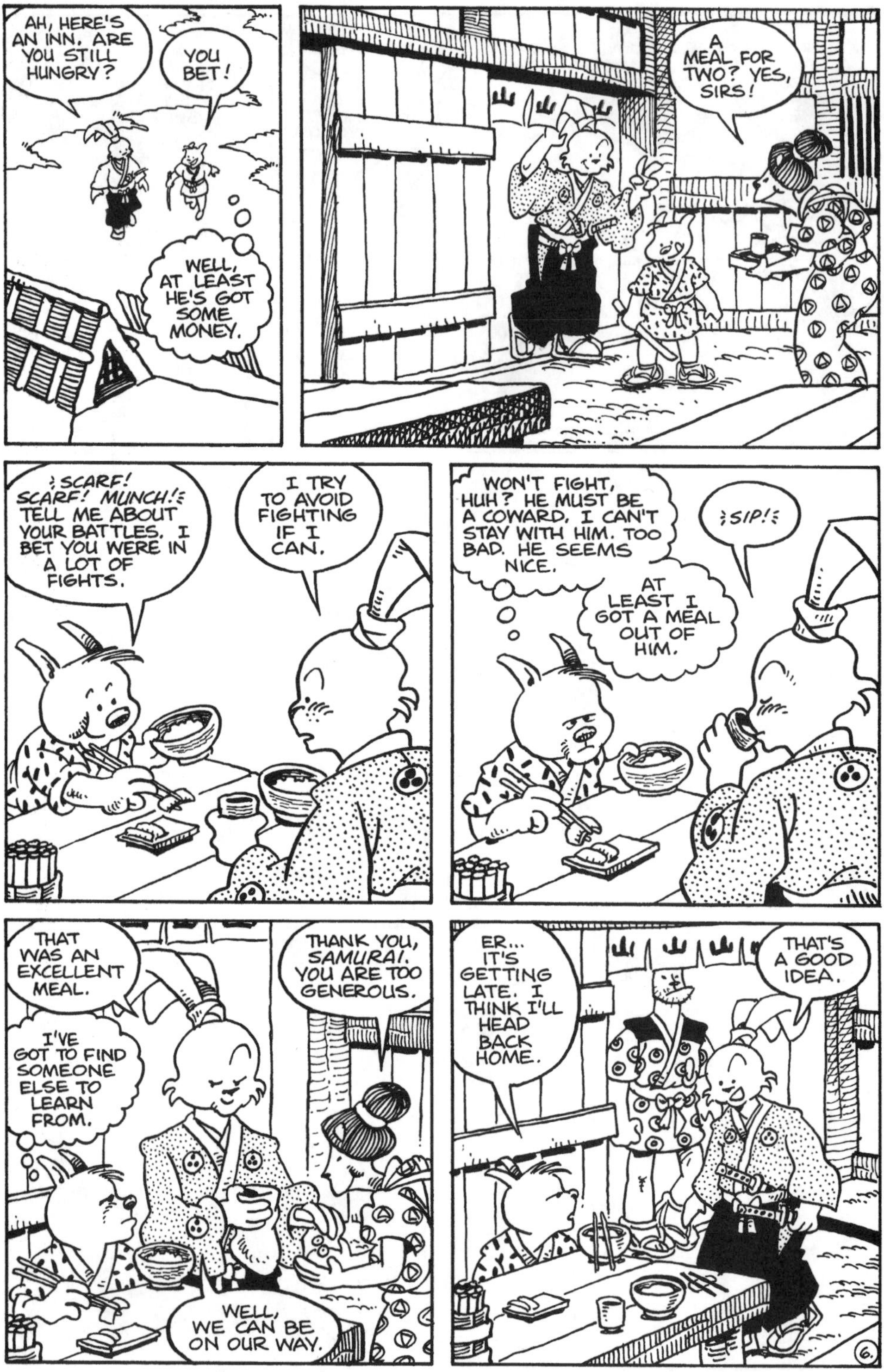
AH, HERE'S AN INN. ARE YOU STILL HUNGRY?
YOU BET!
WELL, AT LEAST HE'S GOT SOME MONEY.
A MEAL FOR TWO? YES, SIRS!
SCARF! SCARF! MUNCH! TELL ME ABOUT YOUR BATTLES. I BET YOU WERE IN A LOT OF FIGHTS.
I TRY TO AVOID FIGHTING IF I CAN.
WON'T FIGHT, HUH? HE MUST BE A COWARD. I CAN'T STAY WITH HIM. TOO BAD. HE SEEMS NICE.
AT LEAST I GOT A MEAL OUT OF HIM.
SIP!
THAT WAS AN EXCELLENT MEAL.
I'VE GOT TO FIND SOMEONE ELSE TO LEARN FROM.
THANK YOU, SAMURAI. YOU ARE TOO GENEROUS.
WELL, WE CAN BE ON OUR WAY.
ER... IT'S GETTING LATE. I THINK I'LL HEAD BACK HOME.
THAT'S A GOOD IDEA.
6.

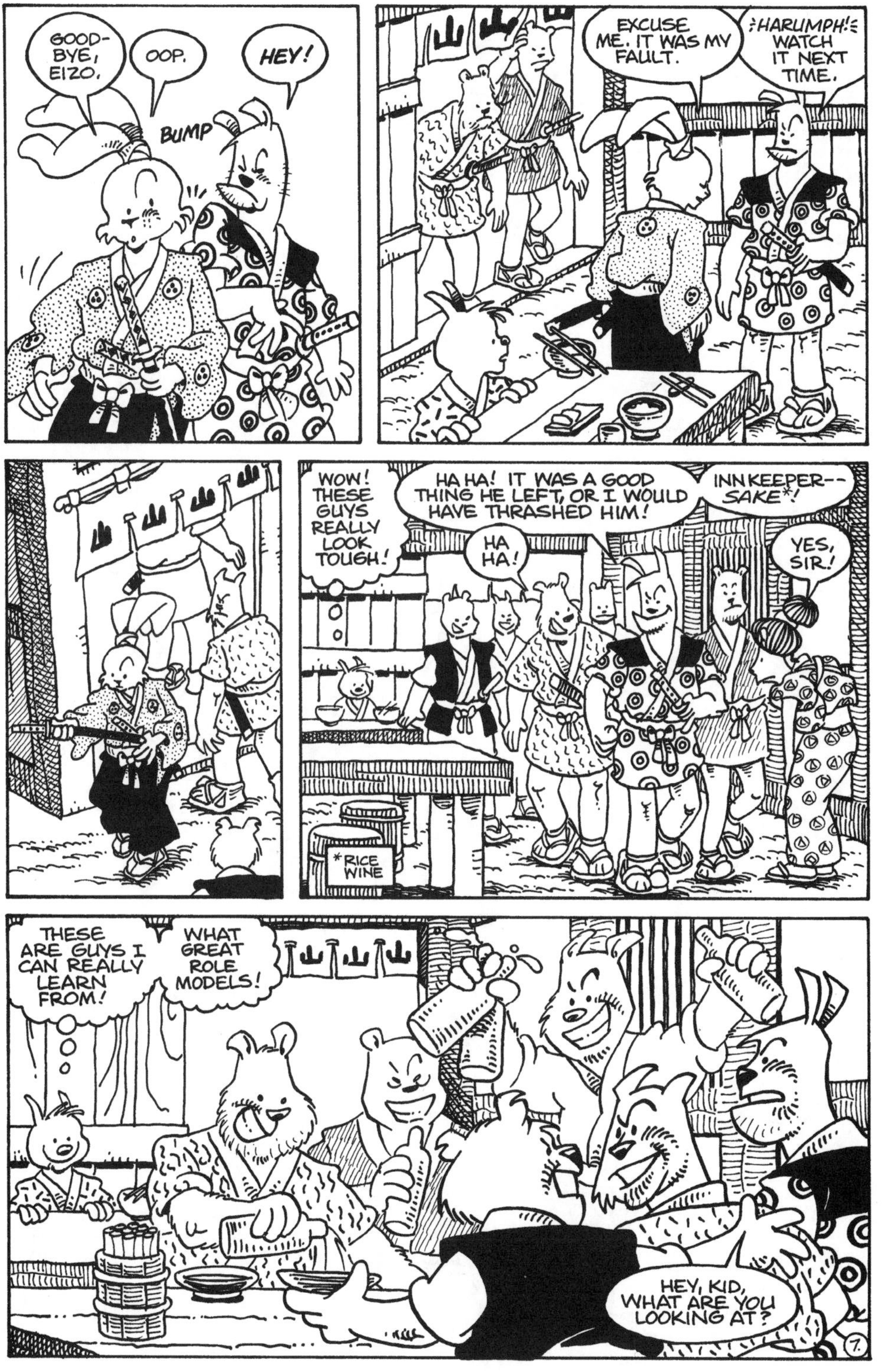
GOOD-BYE, EIZO.
OOP.
HEY!
BUMP
EXCUSE ME. IT WAS MY FAULT.
HARUMPH! WATCH IT NEXT TIME.
WOW! THESE GUYS REALLY LOOK TOUGH!
HA HA! IT WAS A GOOD THING HE LEFT, OR I WOULD HAVE THRASHED HIM!
HA HA!
INNKEEPER-- SAKE*!
YES, SIR!
*RICE WINE
THESE ARE GUYS I CAN REALLY LEARN FROM!
WHAT GREAT ROLE MODELS!
HEY, KID, WHAT ARE YOU LOOKING AT?
7.

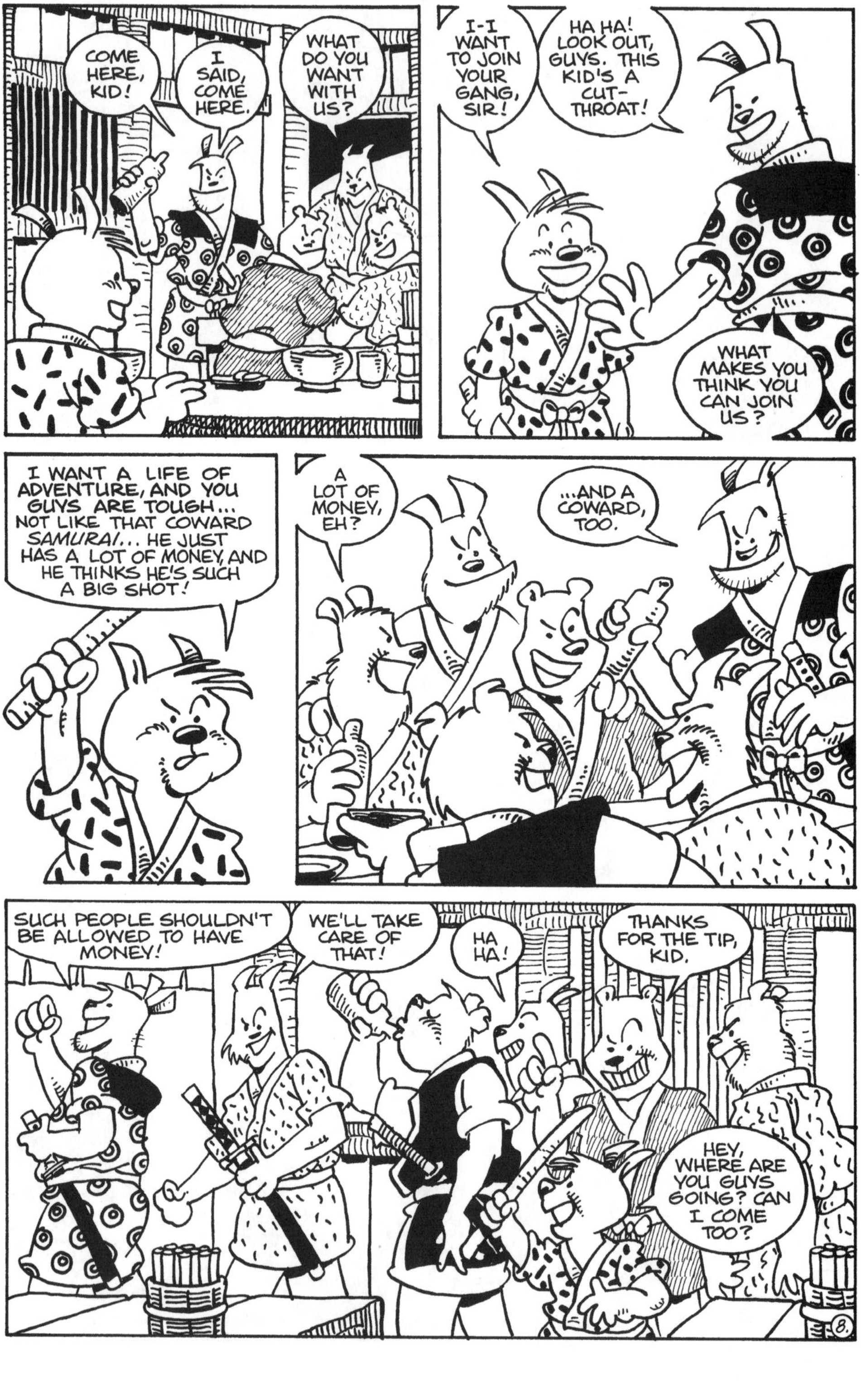
COME HERE, KID!
I SAID, COME HERE.
WHAT DO YOU WANT WITH US?
I-I WANT TO JOIN YOUR GANG, SIR!
HA HA! LOOK OUT, GUYS. THIS KID'S A CUT-THROAT!
WHAT MAKES YOU THINK YOU CAN JOIN US?
I WANT A LIFE OF ADVENTURE, AND YOU GUYS ARE TOUGH... NOT LIKE THAT COWARD *SAMURAI*... HE JUST HAS A LOT OF MONEY, AND HE THINKS HE'S SUCH A BIG SHOT!
A LOT OF MONEY, EH?
...AND A COWARD, TOO.
SUCH PEOPLE SHOULDN'T BE ALLOWED TO HAVE MONEY!
WE'LL TAKE CARE OF THAT!
HA HA!
THANKS FOR THE TIP, KID.
HEY, WHERE ARE YOU GUYS GOING? CAN I COME TOO?
8.

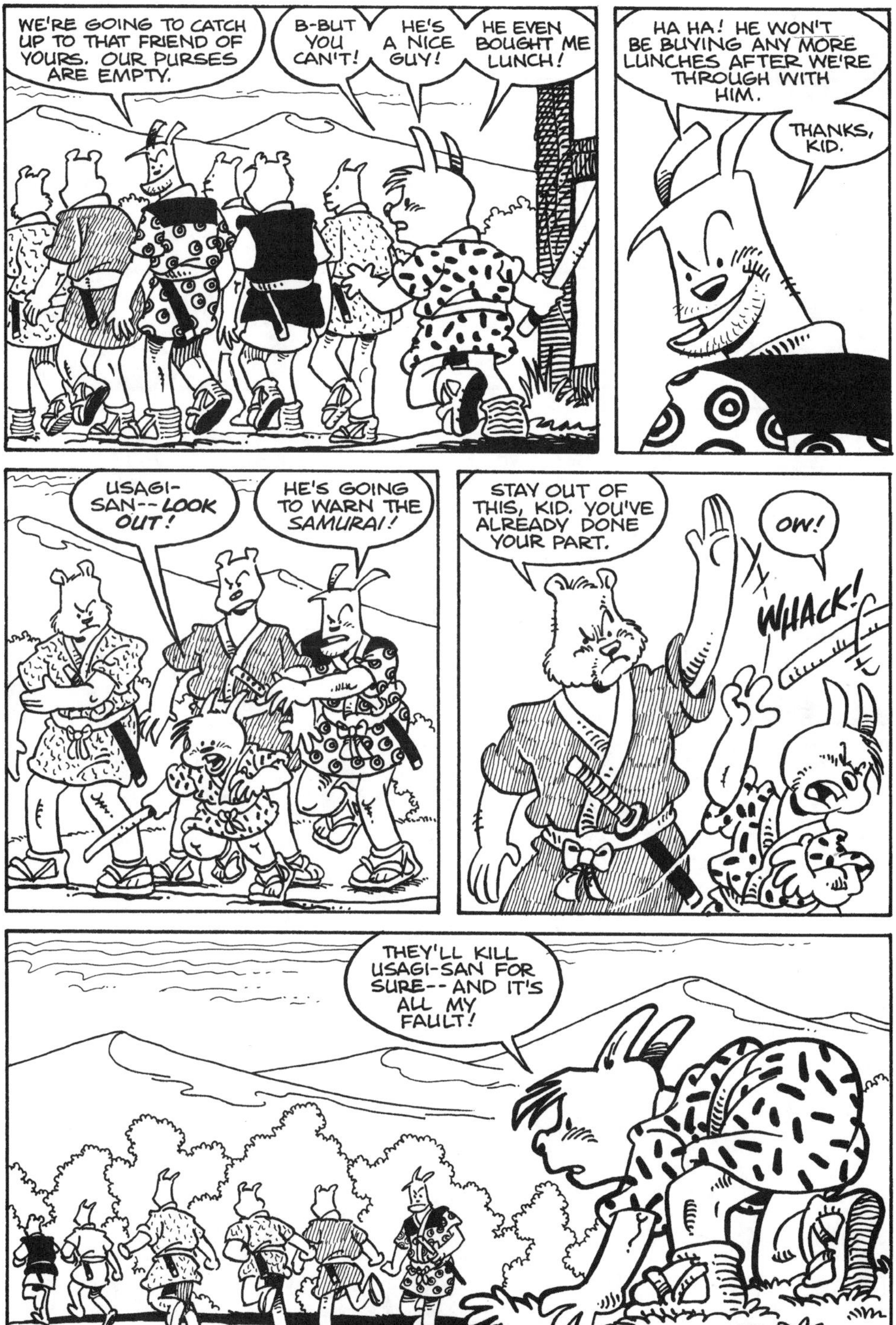
WE'RE GOING TO CATCH UP TO THAT FRIEND OF YOURS. OUR PURSES ARE EMPTY.
B-BUT YOU CAN'T!
HE'S A NICE GUY!
HE EVEN BOUGHT ME LUNCH!
HA HA! HE WON'T BE BUYING ANY MORE LUNCHES AFTER WE'RE THROUGH WITH HIM.
THANKS, KID.
USAGI-SAN--LOOK OUT!
HE'S GOING TO WARN THE SAMURAI!
STAY OUT OF THIS, KID. YOU'VE ALREADY DONE YOUR PART.
OW!
WHACK!
THEY'LL KILL USAGI-SAN FOR SURE--AND IT'S ALL MY FAULT!
9.

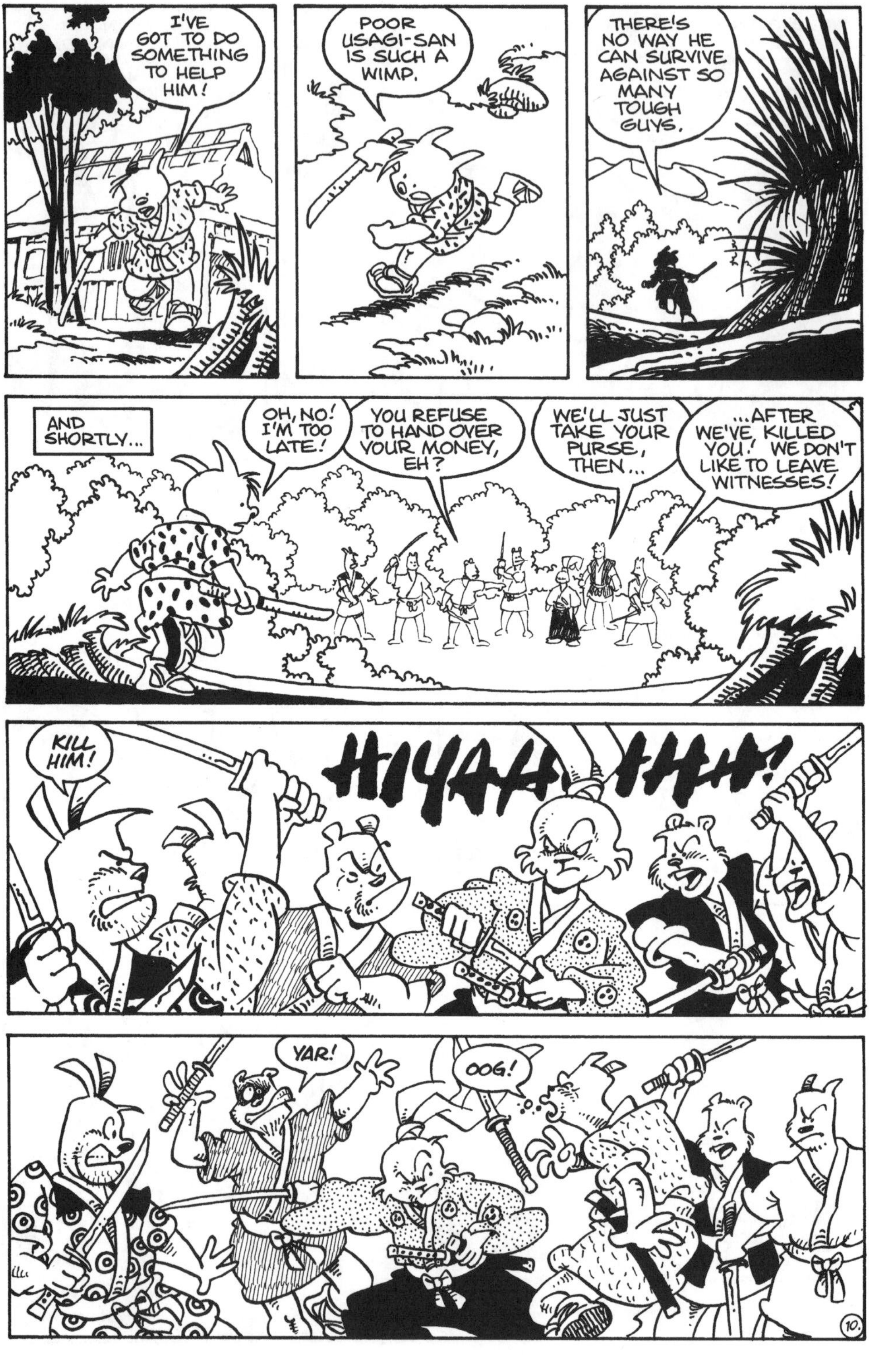
I'VE GOT TO DO SOMETHING TO HELP HIM!
POOR USAGI-SAN IS SUCH A WIMP.
THERE'S NO WAY HE CAN SURVIVE AGAINST SO MANY TOUGH GUYS.
AND SHORTLY...
OH, NO! I'M TOO LATE!
YOU REFUSE TO HAND OVER YOUR MONEY, EH?
WE'LL JUST TAKE YOUR PURSE, THEN...
...AFTER WE'VE KILLED YOU! WE DON'T LIKE TO LEAVE WITNESSES!
KILL HIM!
HIYAH HHH!
YAR!
OOG!
10.

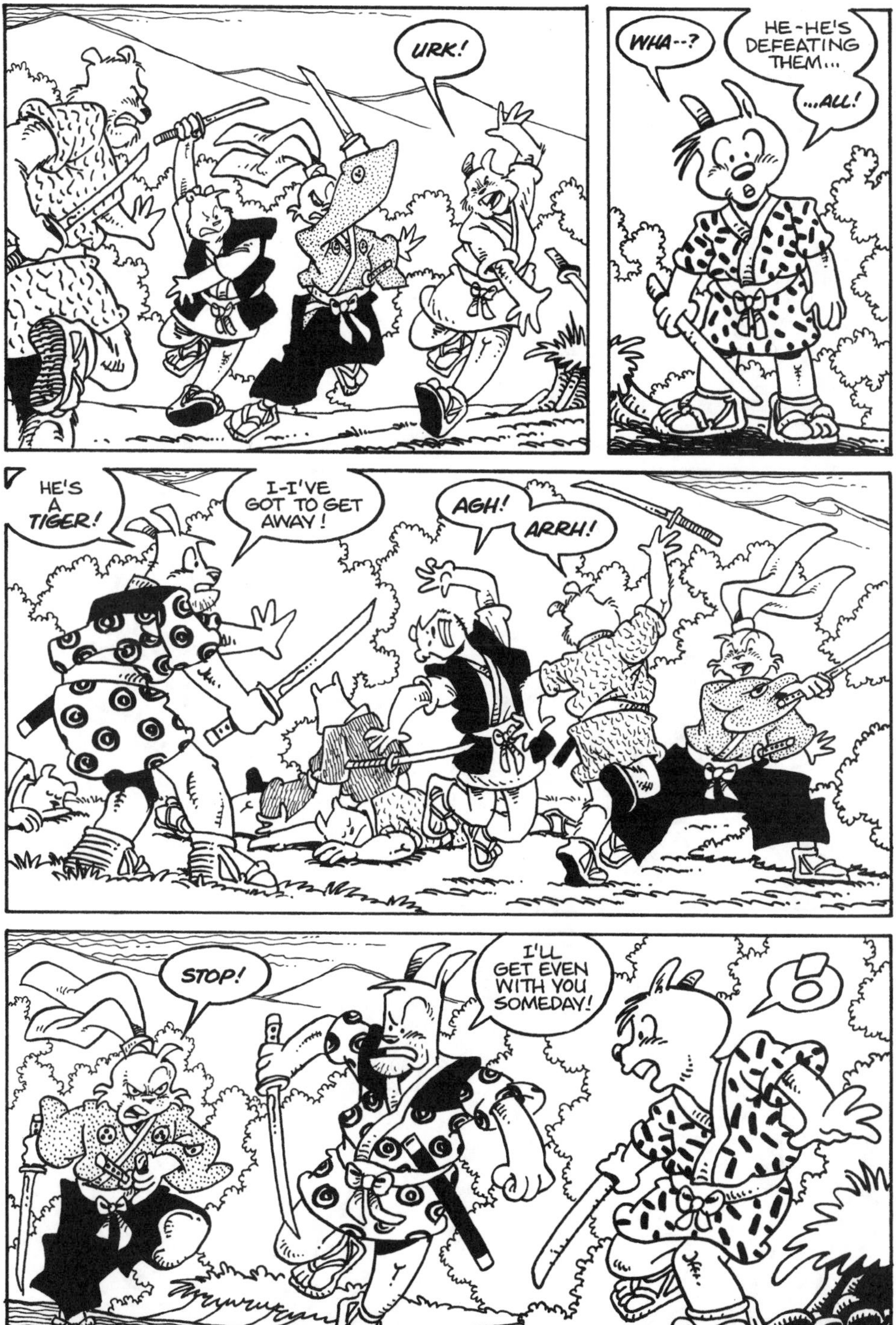
URK!
WHA--?
HE-HE'S DEFEATING THEM...
...ALL!
HE'S A TIGER!
I-I'VE GOT TO GET AWAY!
AGH!
ARRH!
STOP!
I'LL GET EVEN WITH YOU SOMEDAY!
11.

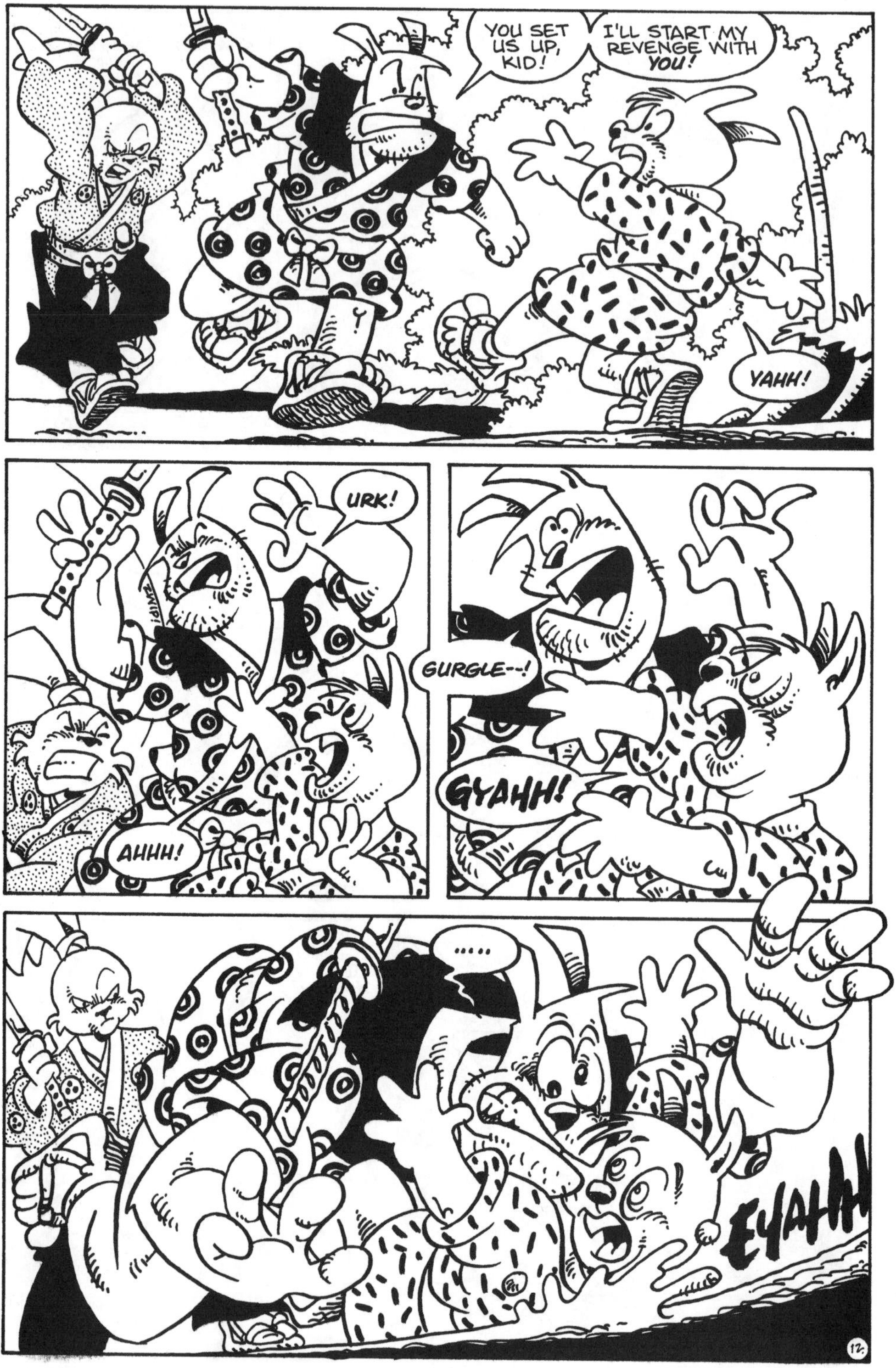
YOU SET US UP, KID!
I'LL START MY REVENGE WITH YOU!
YAHH!
URK!
GURGLE--!
AHHH!
GYAHH!
.....
EYAHH
12

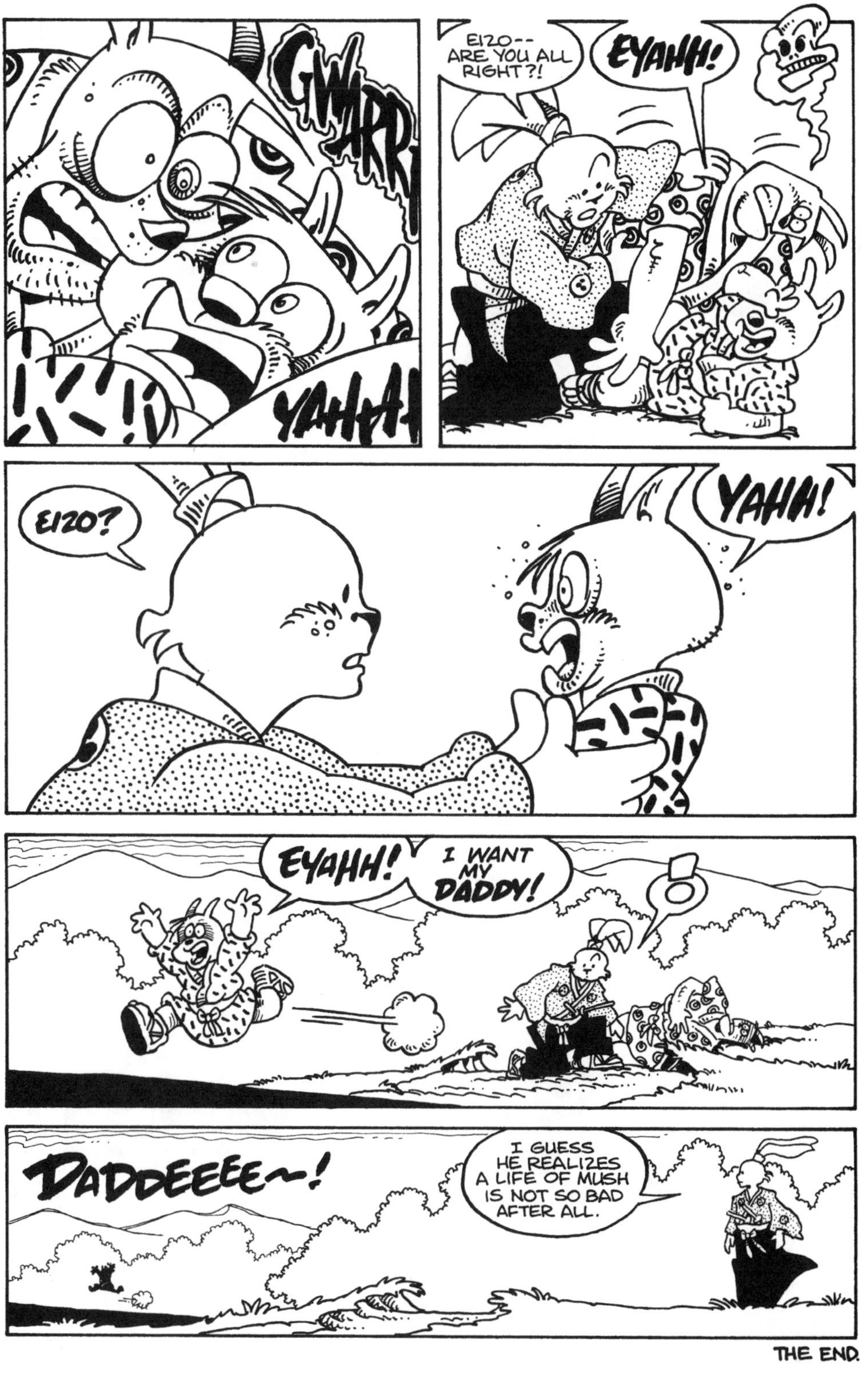
GWARR
YAHH--
EIZO-- ARE YOU ALL RIGHT?!
EYAHH!
EIZO?
YAHH!
EYAHH!
I WANT MY DADDY!
DADDEEEE~!
I GUESS HE REALIZES A LIFE OF MUSH IS NOT SO BAD AFTER ALL.
THE END.

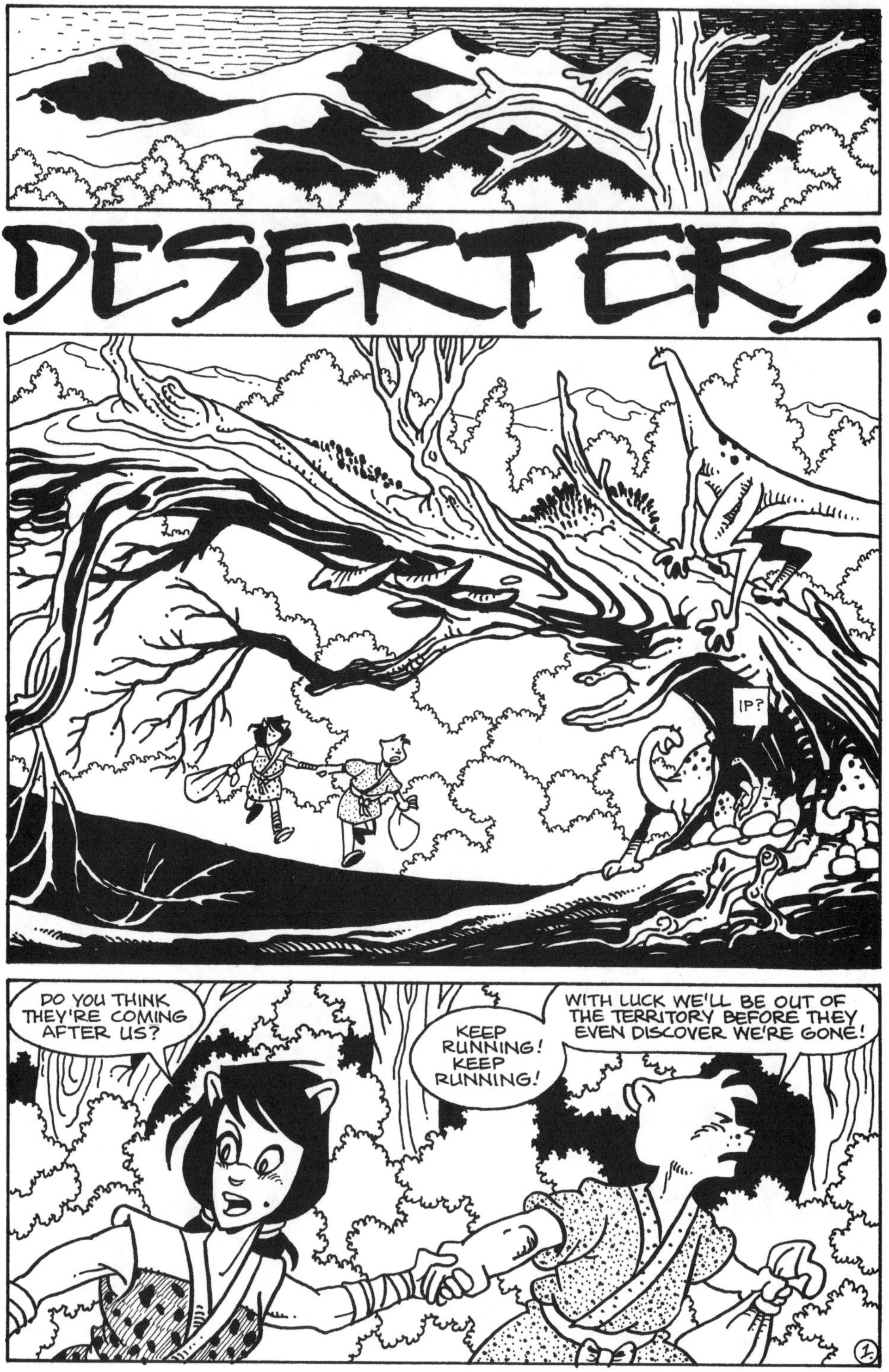
DESERTERS.
IP?
DO YOU THINK THEY'RE COMING AFTER US?
KEEP RUNNING! KEEP RUNNING!
WITH LUCK WE'LL BE OUT OF THE TERRITORY BEFORE THEY EVEN DISCOVER WE'RE GONE!
1.

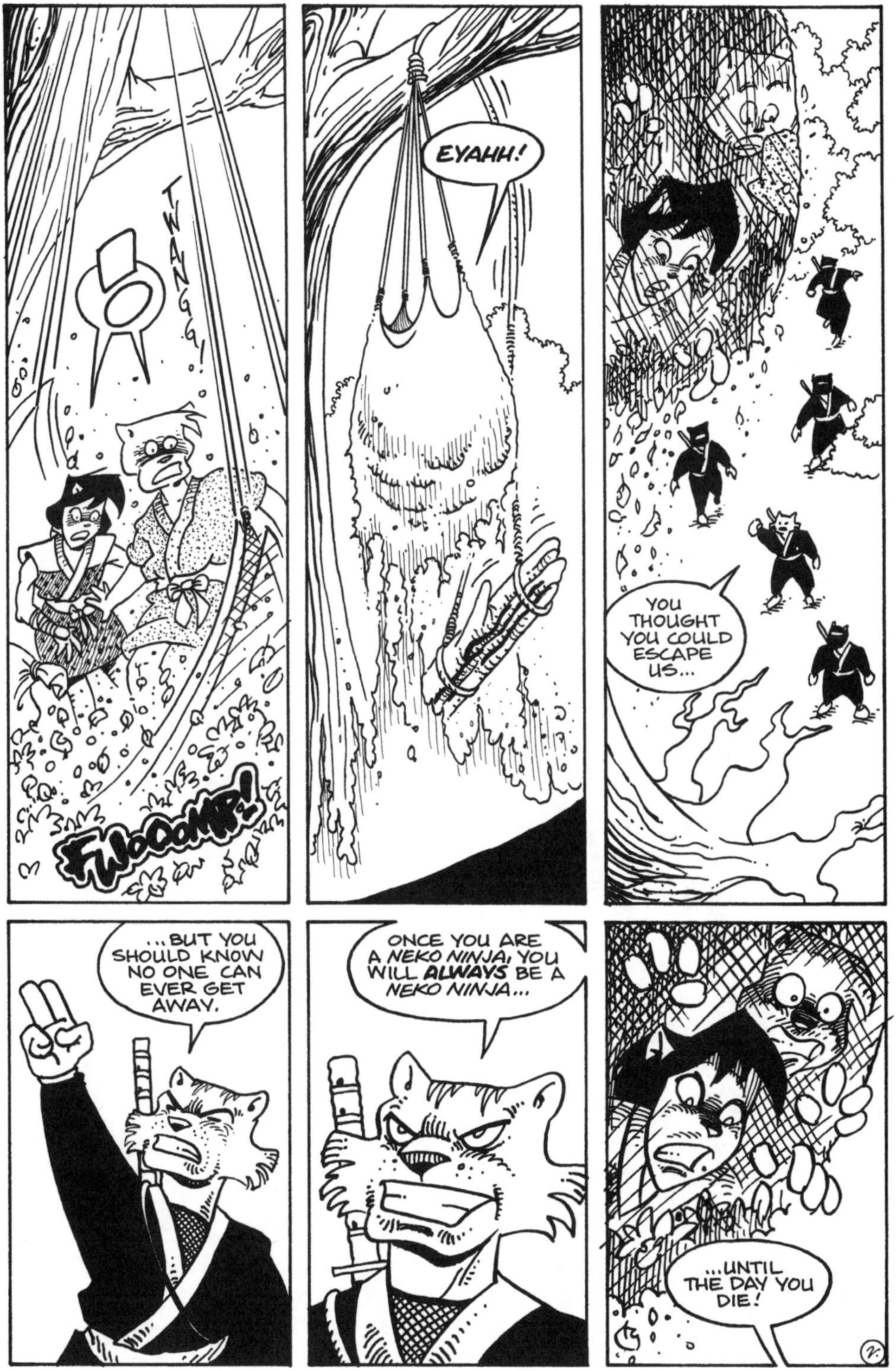
TWANGG!
FWOOOMP!
EYAHH!
YOU THOUGHT YOU COULD ESCAPE US...
...BUT YOU SHOULD KNOW NO ONE CAN EVER GET AWAY.
ONCE YOU ARE A *NEKO NINJA*, YOU WILL **ALWAYS** BE A *NEKO NINJA*...
...UNTIL THE DAY YOU DIE!
2.

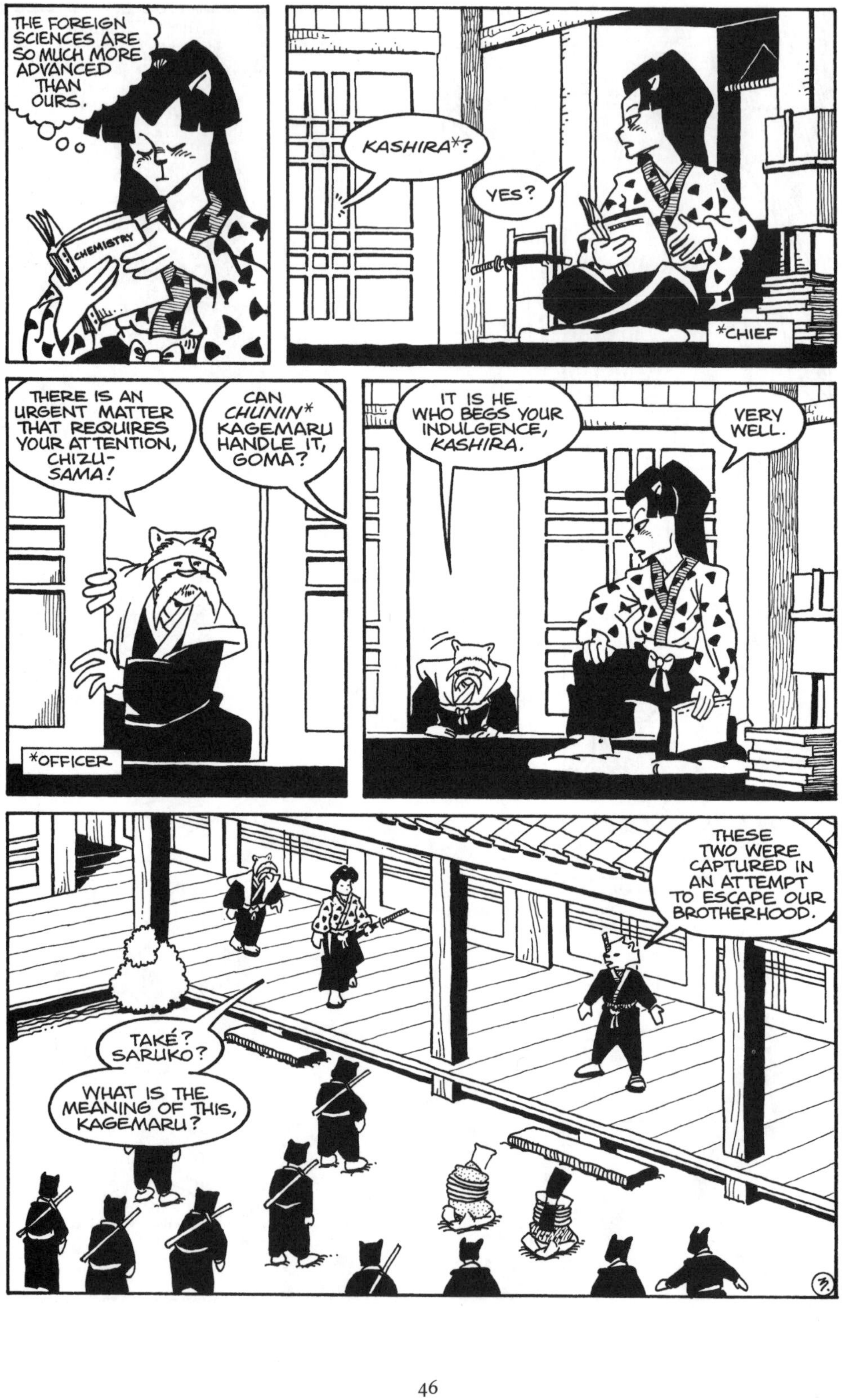
THE FOREIGN SCIENCES ARE SO MUCH MORE ADVANCED THAN OURS.
CHEMISTRY
KASHIRA*?
YES?
*CHIEF
THERE IS AN URGENT MATTER THAT REQUIRES YOUR ATTENTION, CHIZU-SAMA!
CAN CHUNIN* KAGEMARU HANDLE IT, GOMA?
*OFFICER
IT IS HE WHO BEGS YOUR INDULGENCE, KASHIRA.
VERY WELL.
TAKÉ? SARUKO?
WHAT IS THE MEANING OF THIS, KAGEMARU?
THESE TWO WERE CAPTURED IN AN ATTEMPT TO ESCAPE OUR BROTHERHOOD.
3.

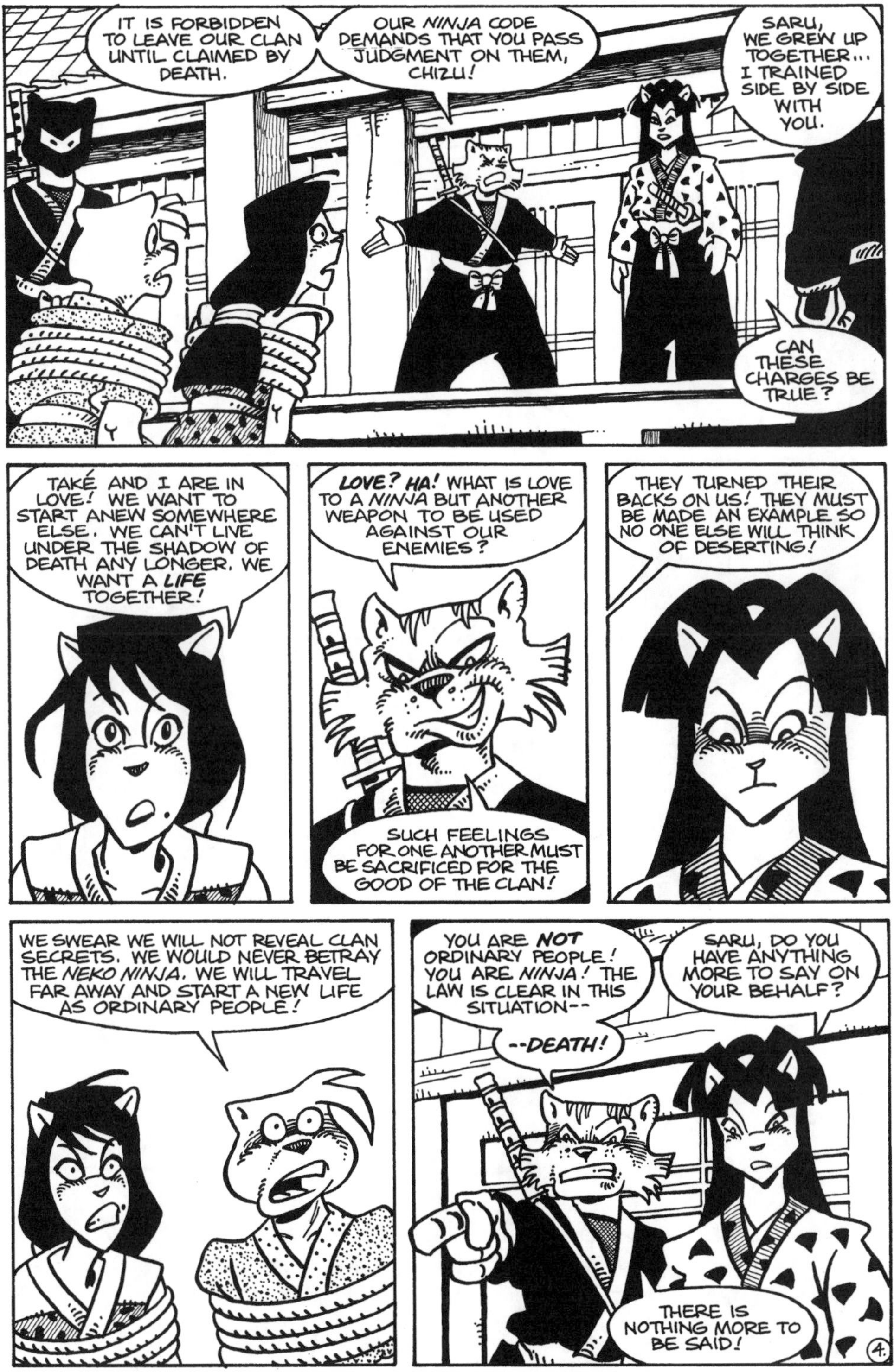

IT IS FORBIDDEN TO LEAVE OUR CLAN UNTIL CLAIMED BY DEATH.
OUR NINJA CODE DEMANDS THAT YOU PASS JUDGMENT ON THEM, CHIZU!
SARU, WE GREW UP TOGETHER... I TRAINED SIDE BY SIDE WITH YOU.
CAN THESE CHARGES BE TRUE?
TAKÉ AND I ARE IN LOVE! WE WANT TO START ANEW SOMEWHERE ELSE. WE CAN'T LIVE UNDER THE SHADOW OF DEATH ANY LONGER. WE WANT A LIFE TOGETHER!
LOVE? HA! WHAT IS LOVE TO A NINJA BUT ANOTHER WEAPON TO BE USED AGAINST OUR ENEMIES?
SUCH FEELINGS FOR ONE ANOTHER MUST BE SACRIFICED FOR THE GOOD OF THE CLAN!
THEY TURNED THEIR BACKS ON US! THEY MUST BE MADE AN EXAMPLE SO NO ONE ELSE WILL THINK OF DESERTING!
WE SWEAR WE WILL NOT REVEAL CLAN SECRETS. WE WOULD NEVER BETRAY THE NEKO NINJA. WE WILL TRAVEL FAR AWAY AND START A NEW LIFE AS ORDINARY PEOPLE!
YOU ARE NOT ORDINARY PEOPLE! YOU ARE NINJA! THE LAW IS CLEAR IN THIS SITUATION--
--DEATH!
SARU, DO YOU HAVE ANYTHING MORE TO SAY ON YOUR BEHALF?
THERE IS NOTHING MORE TO BE SAID!
4.

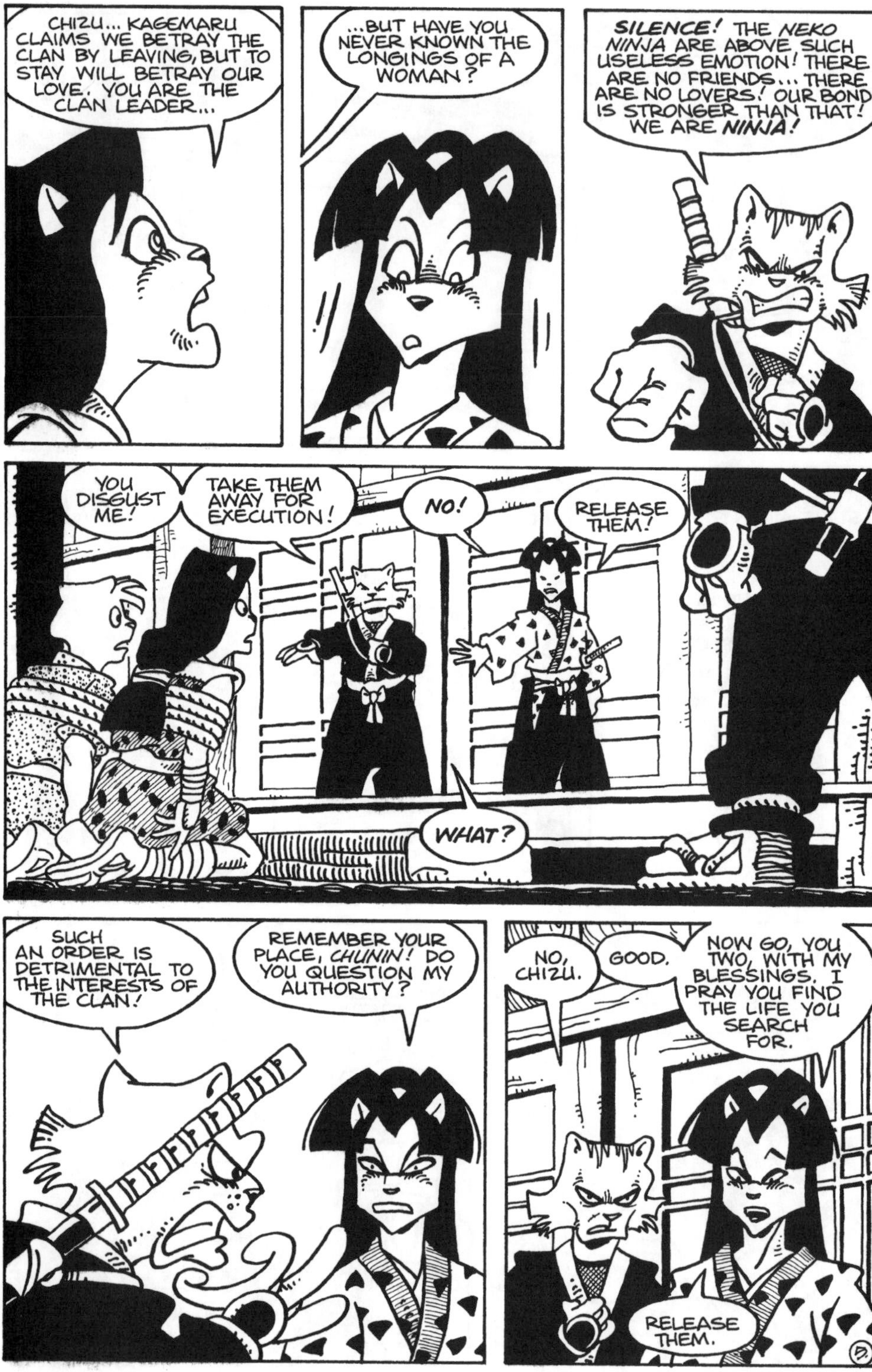
CHIZU... KAGEMARU CLAIMS WE BETRAY THE CLAN BY LEAVING, BUT TO STAY WILL BETRAY OUR LOVE. YOU ARE THE CLAN LEADER...
...BUT HAVE YOU NEVER KNOWN THE LONGINGS OF A WOMAN?
SILENCE! THE NEKO NINJA ARE ABOVE SUCH USELESS EMOTION! THERE ARE NO FRIENDS... THERE ARE NO LOVERS! OUR BOND IS STRONGER THAN THAT! WE ARE NINJA!
YOU DISGUST ME!
TAKE THEM AWAY FOR EXECUTION!
NO!
RELEASE THEM!
WHAT?
SUCH AN ORDER IS DETRIMENTAL TO THE INTERESTS OF THE CLAN!
REMEMBER YOUR PLACE, CHUNIN! DO YOU QUESTION MY AUTHORITY?
NO, CHIZU.
GOOD.
NOW GO, YOU TWO, WITH MY BLESSINGS. I PRAY YOU FIND THE LIFE YOU SEARCH FOR.
RELEASE THEM.

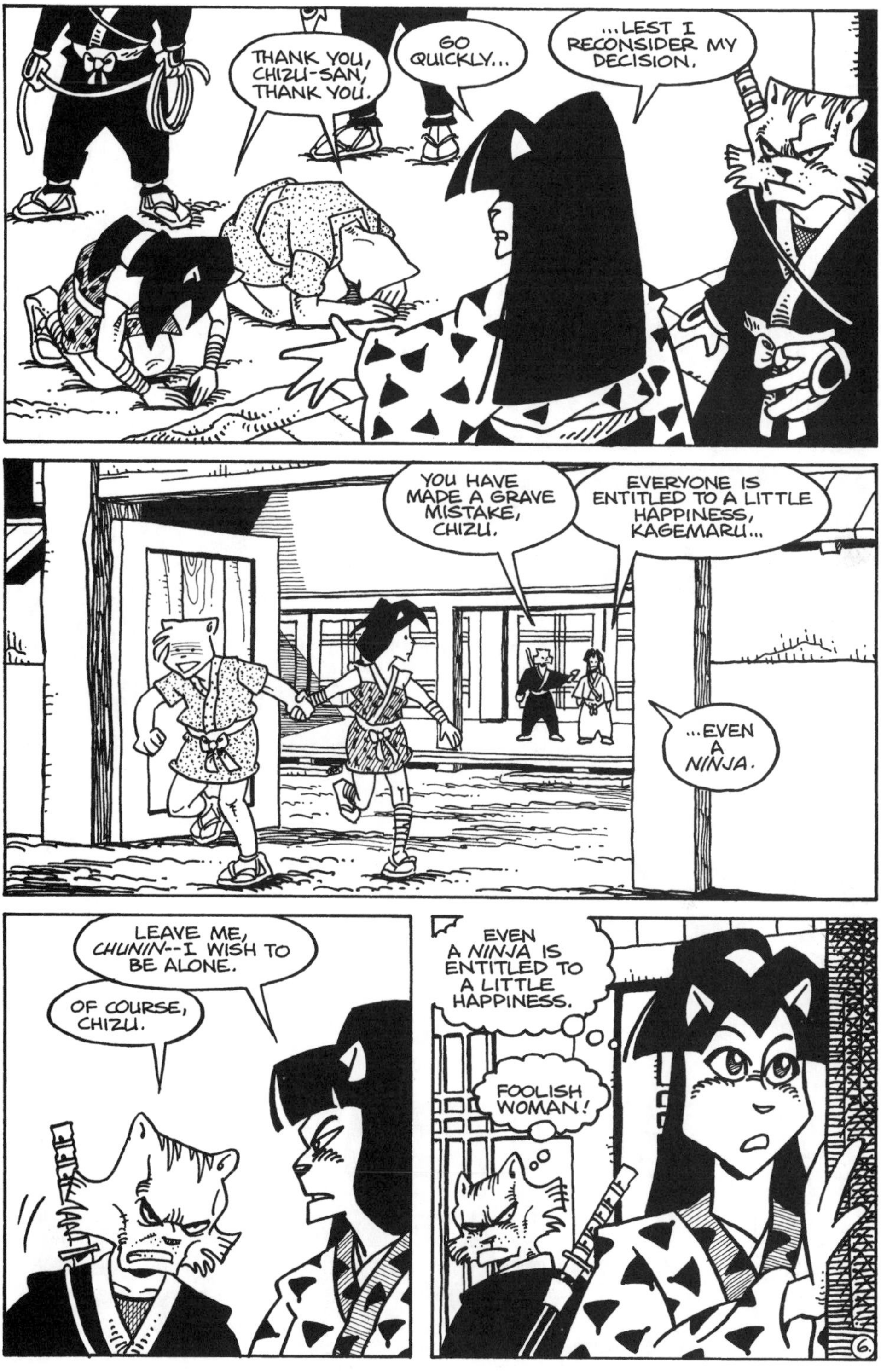
THANK YOU, CHIZU-SAN, THANK YOU.
GO QUICKLY...
...LEST I RECONSIDER MY DECISION.
YOU HAVE MADE A GRAVE MISTAKE, CHIZU.
EVERYONE IS ENTITLED TO A LITTLE HAPPINESS, KAGEMARU...
...EVEN A *NINJA*.
LEAVE ME, *CHUNIN*--I WISH TO BE ALONE.
OF COURSE, CHIZU.
EVEN A *NINJA* IS ENTITLED TO A LITTLE HAPPINESS.
FOOLISH WOMAN!
6.

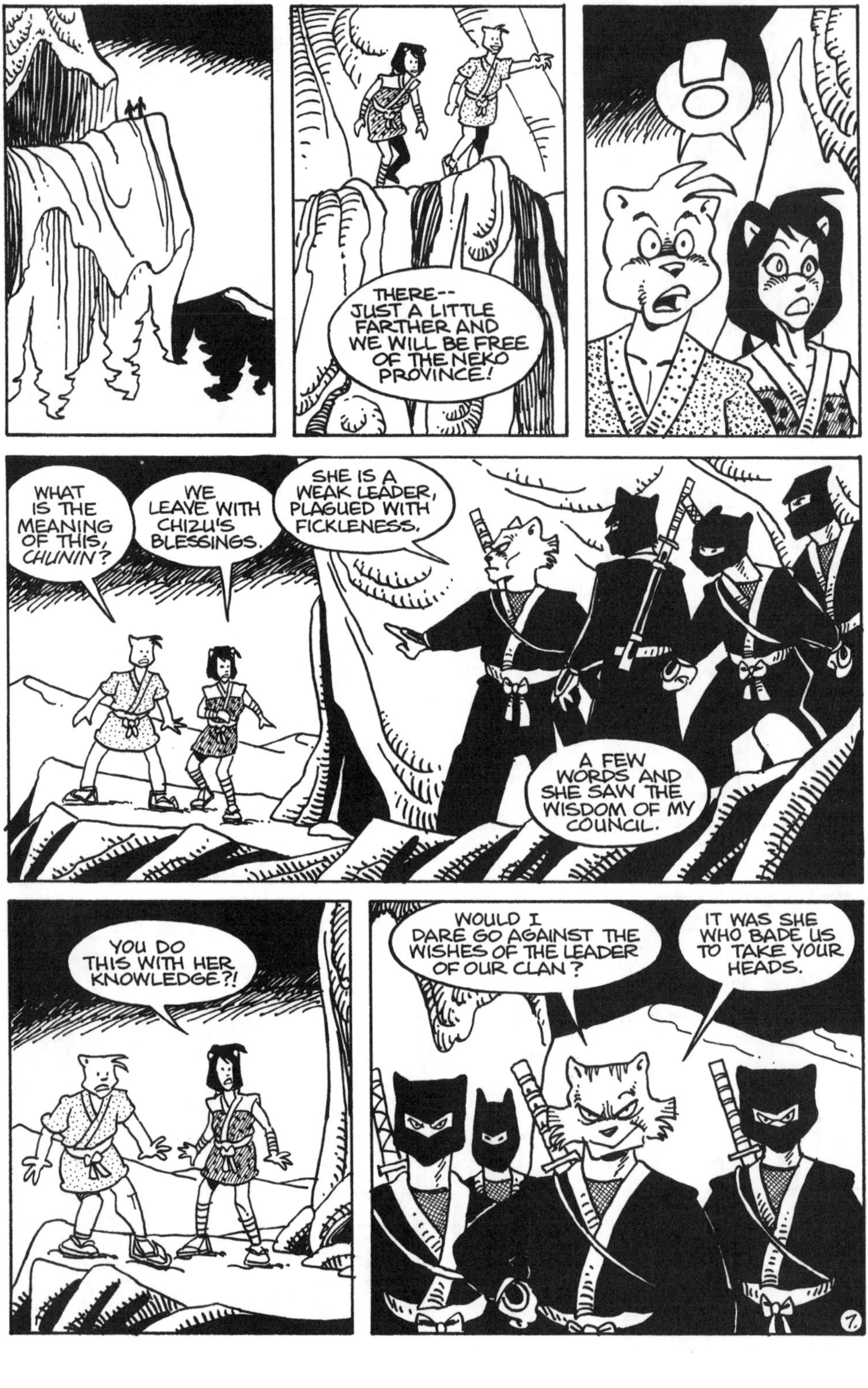

!
THERE-- JUST A LITTLE FARTHER AND WE WILL BE FREE OF THE NEKO PROVINCE!
!
WHAT IS THE MEANING OF THIS, *CHUNIN*?
WE LEAVE WITH CHIZU'S BLESSINGS.
SHE IS A WEAK LEADER, PLAGUED WITH FICKLENESS.
A FEW WORDS AND SHE SAW THE WISDOM OF MY COUNCIL.
YOU DO THIS WITH HER KNOWLEDGE?!
WOULD I DARE GO AGAINST THE WISHES OF THE LEADER OF OUR CLAN?
IT WAS SHE WHO BADE US TO TAKE YOUR HEADS.
7.

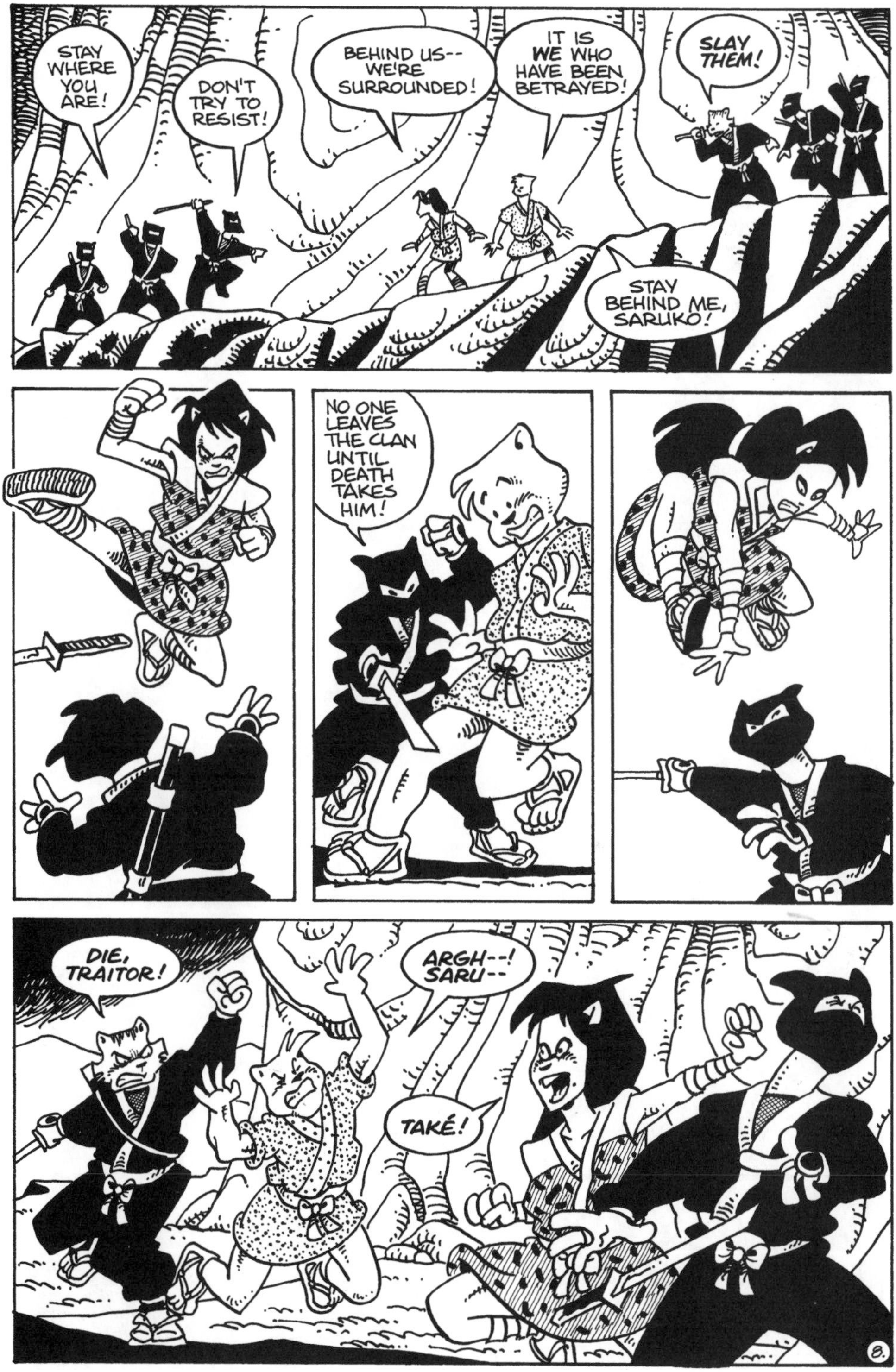
STAY WHERE YOU ARE!
DON'T TRY TO RESIST!
BEHIND US-- WE'RE SURROUNDED!
IT IS WE WHO HAVE BEEN BETRAYED!
SLAY THEM!
STAY BEHIND ME, SARUKO!
NO ONE LEAVES THE CLAN UNTIL DEATH TAKES HIM!
DIE, TRAITOR!
ARGH--! SARU--
TAKÉ!
8.

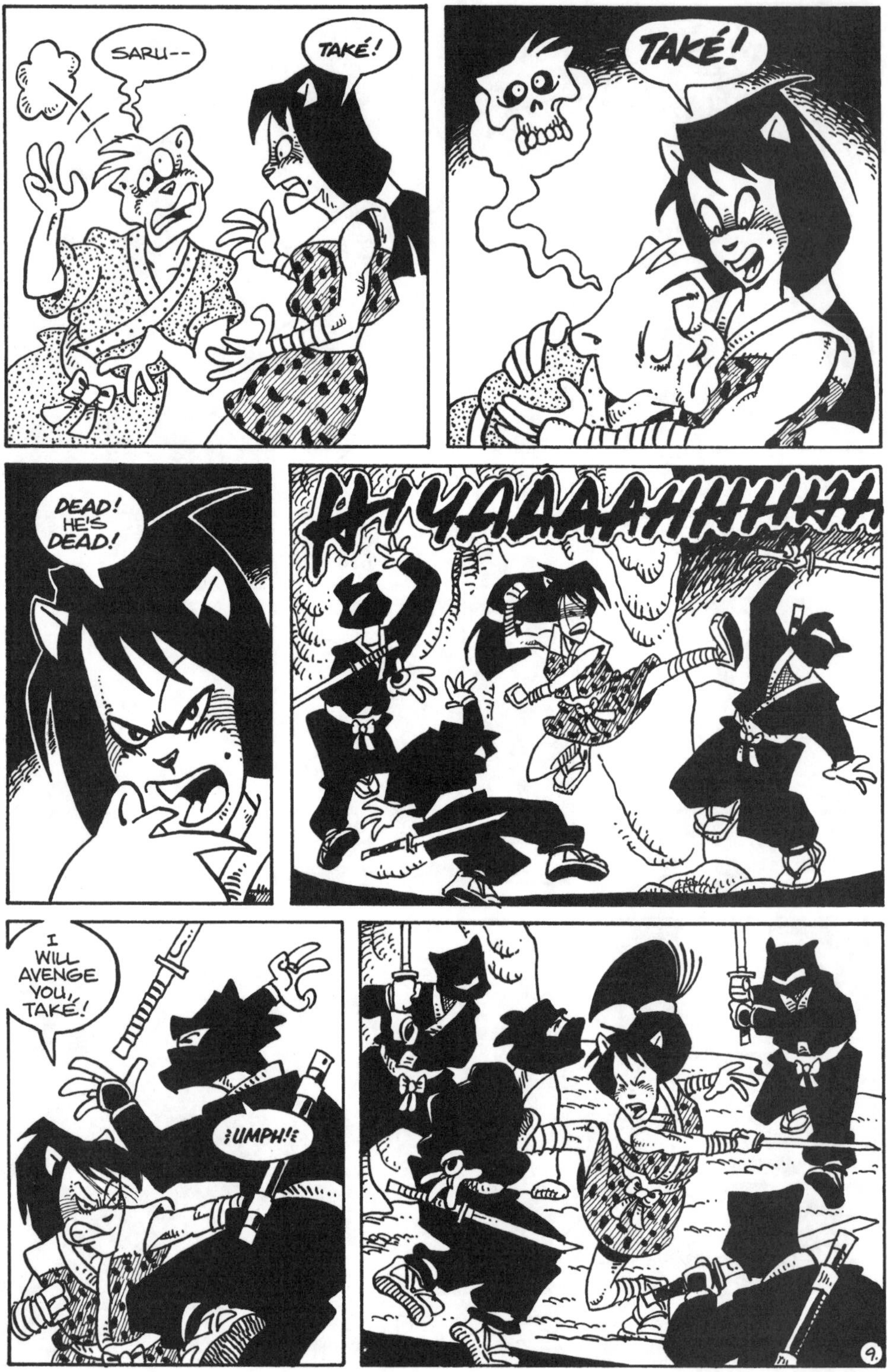
SARU--
TAKÉ!
TAKÉ!
DEAD! HE'S DEAD!
HIYAAAAAHHHHH
I WILL AVENGE YOU, TAKÉ!
UMPH!
9.

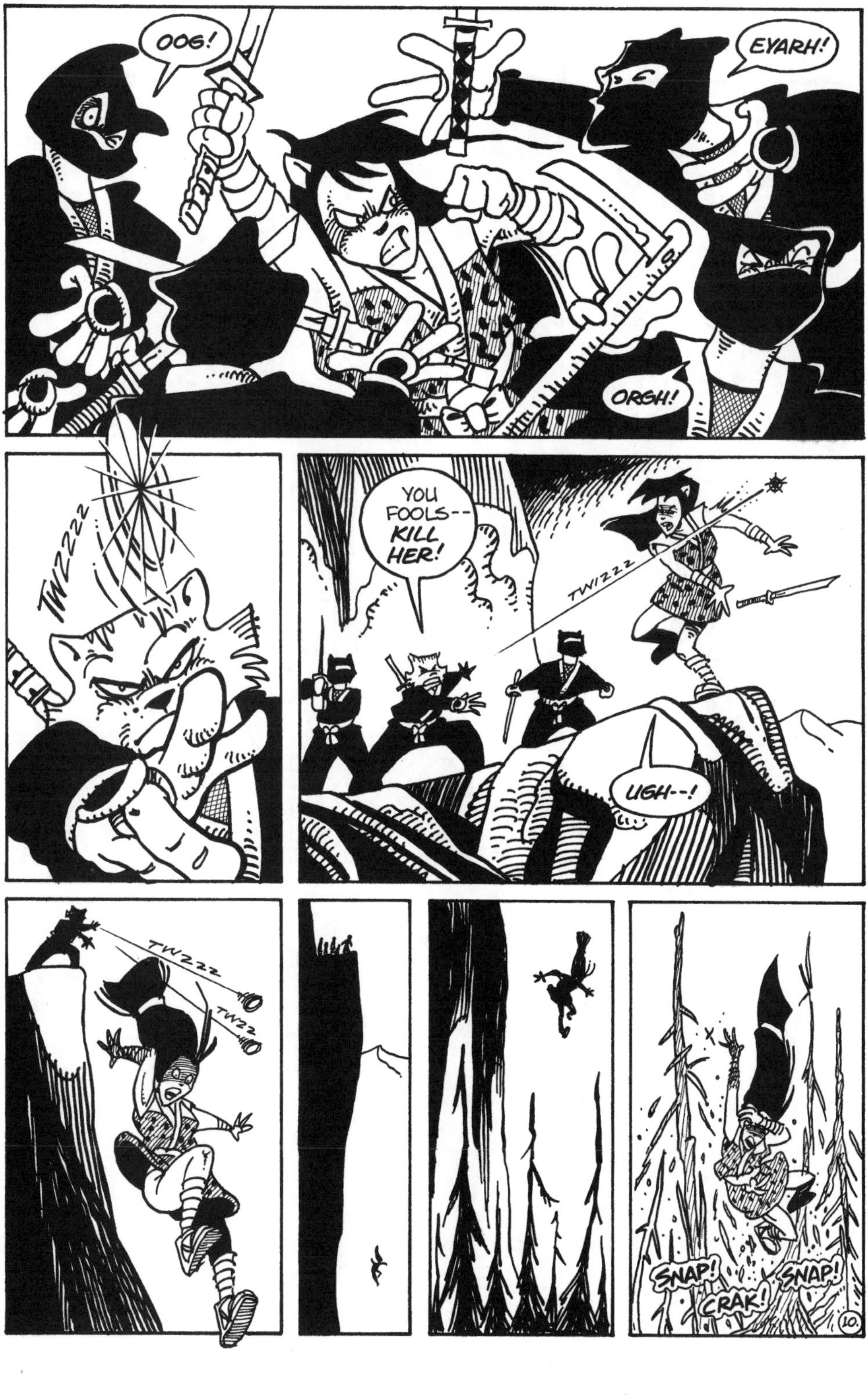

OOG!
EYARH!
ORGH!
TWZZZZ
YOU FOOLS-- KILL HER!
TWIZZZ
UGH--!
TWZZZ
TWZZ
SNAP!
CRAK!
SNAP!
10.

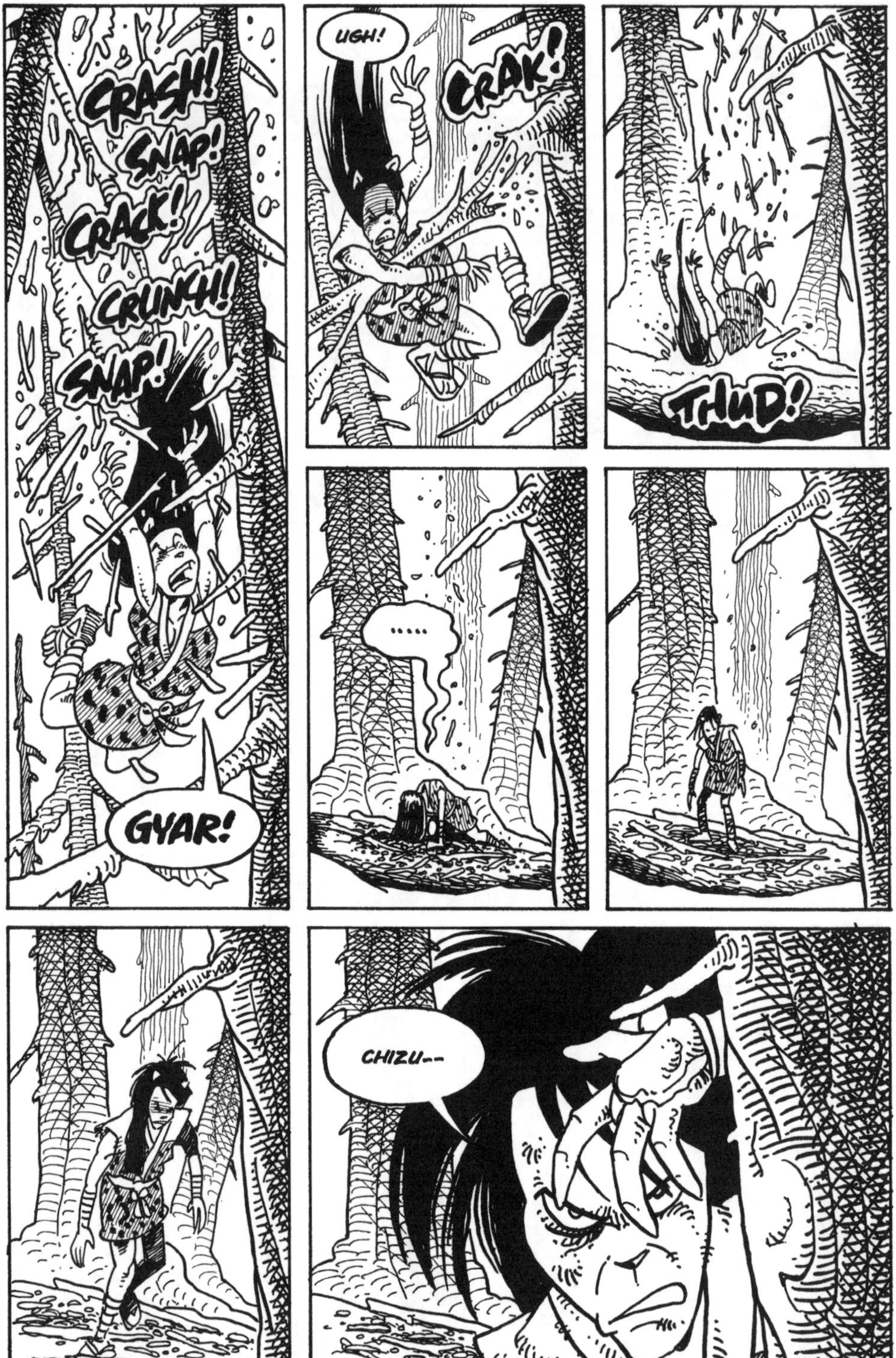
CRASH!
SNAP!
CRACK!
CRUNCH!
SNAP!
GYAR!
UGH!
CRAK!
THUD!
.....
CHIZU--

END.

A POTTER'S TALE

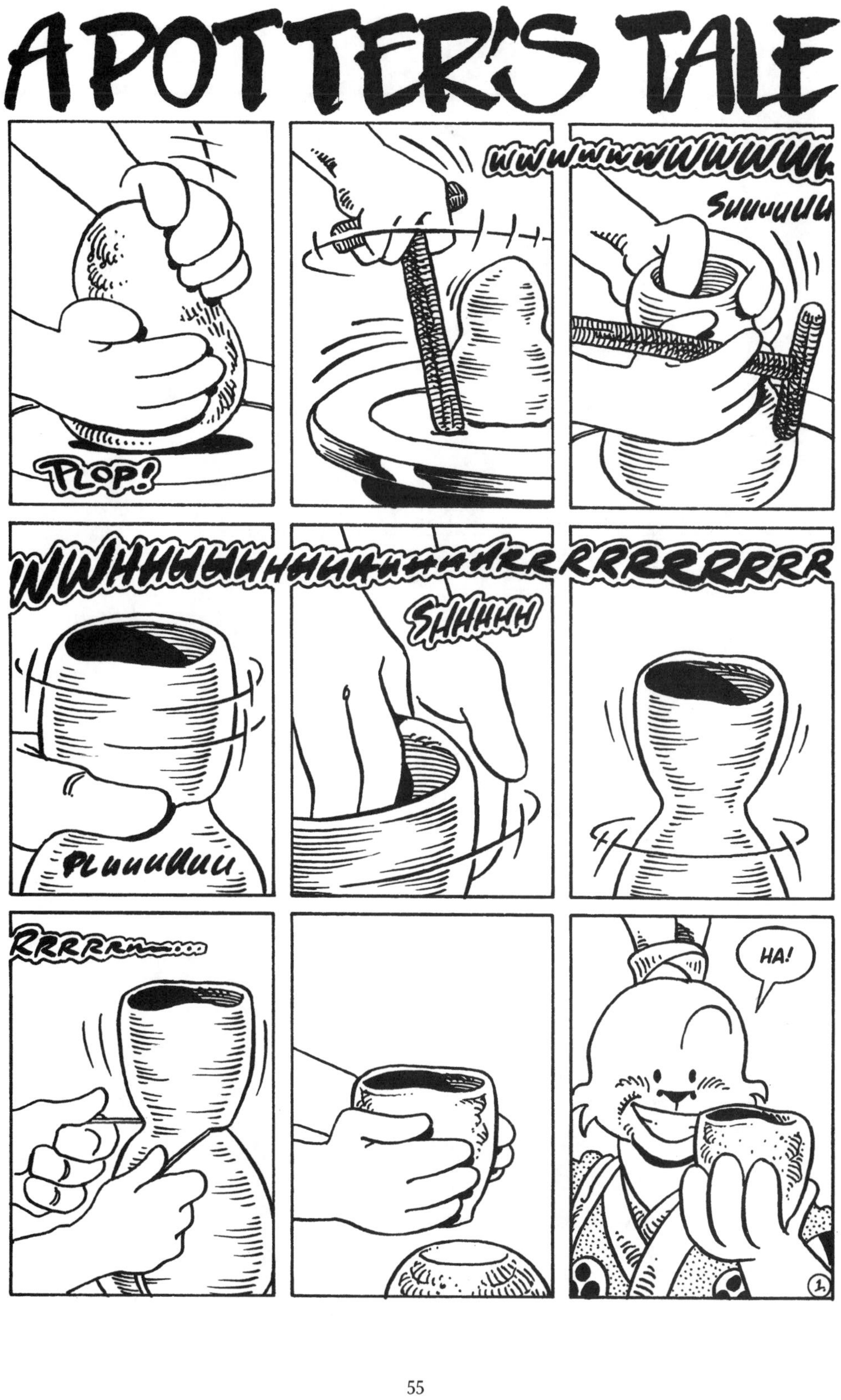
PLOP!
WWWWWWWWWWWWWWW
SUUUUUU
WHHHHHHHHHHHHHHHHHHHRRRRRRRRRRRRR
SHHHHH
PLUUUUUU
RRRRRN...
HA!
1

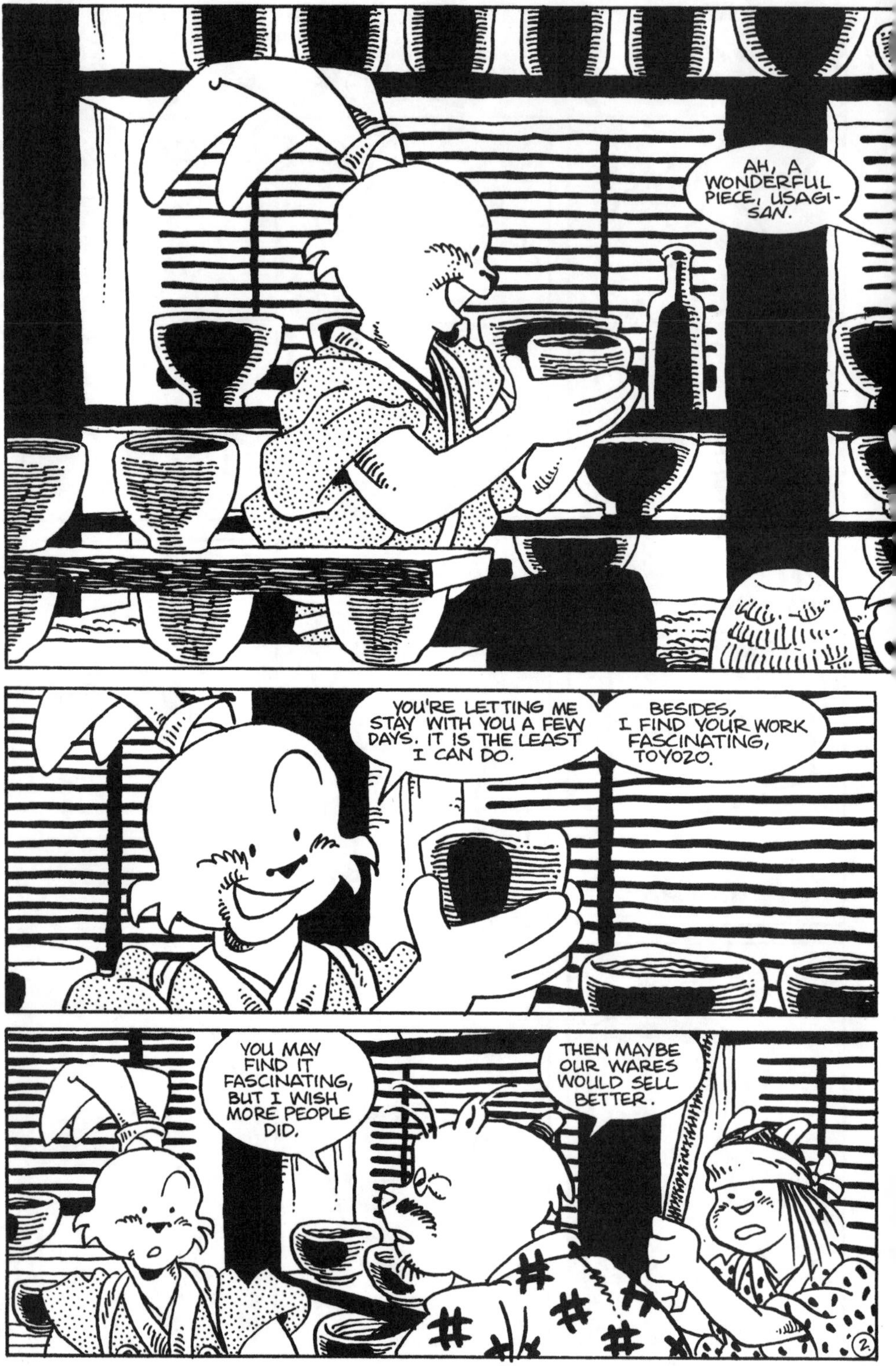
AH, A WONDERFUL PIECE, USAGI-SAN.
YOU'RE LETTING ME STAY WITH YOU A FEW DAYS. IT IS THE LEAST I CAN DO.
BESIDES, I FIND YOUR WORK FASCINATING, TOYOZO.
YOU MAY FIND IT FASCINATING, BUT I WISH MORE PEOPLE DID.
THEN MAYBE OUR WARES WOULD SELL BETTER.
2

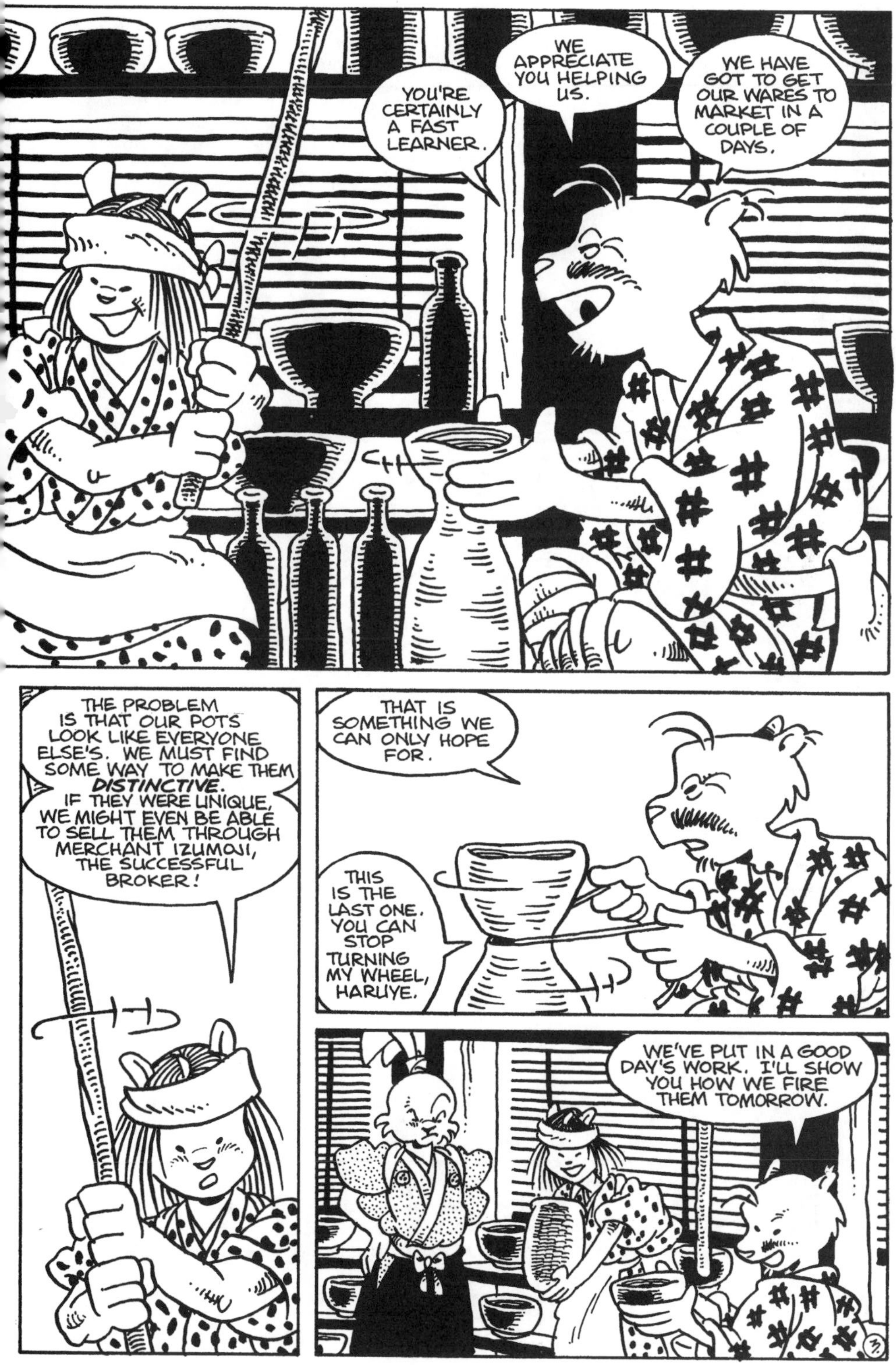
YOU'RE CERTAINLY A FAST LEARNER.
WE APPRECIATE YOU HELPING US.
WE HAVE GOT TO GET OUR WARES TO MARKET IN A COUPLE OF DAYS.
THE PROBLEM IS THAT OUR POTS LOOK LIKE EVERYONE ELSE'S. WE MUST FIND SOME WAY TO MAKE THEM DISTINCTIVE. IF THEY WERE UNIQUE, WE MIGHT EVEN BE ABLE TO SELL THEM THROUGH MERCHANT IZUMOJI, THE SUCCESSFUL BROKER!
THAT IS SOMETHING WE CAN ONLY HOPE FOR.
THIS IS THE LAST ONE. YOU CAN STOP TURNING MY WHEEL, HARUYE.
WE'VE PUT IN A GOOD DAY'S WORK. I'LL SHOW YOU HOW WE FIRE THEM TOMORROW.
3

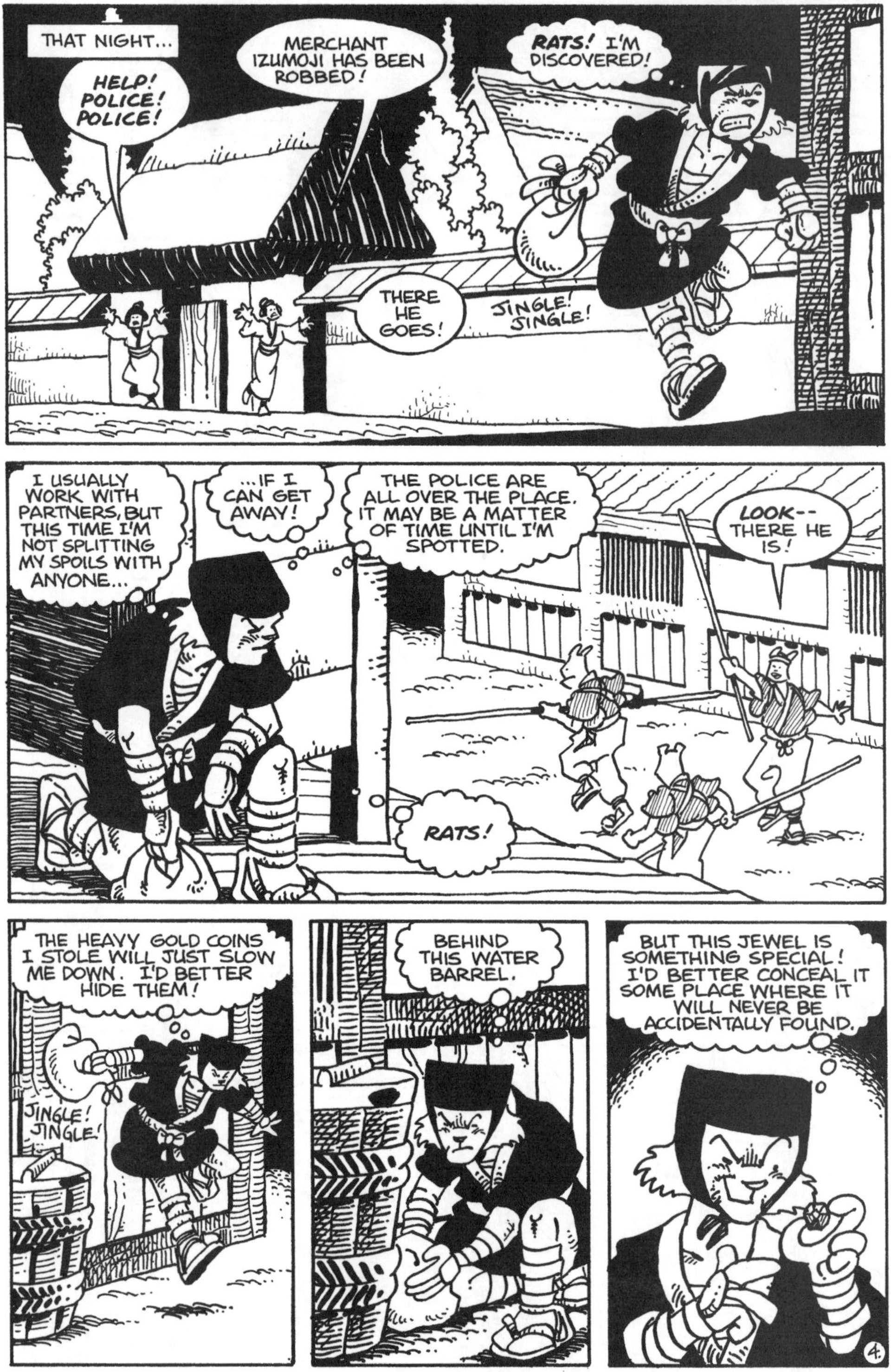
THAT NIGHT...
HELP! POLICE! POLICE!
MERCHANT IZUMOJI HAS BEEN ROBBED!
RATS! I'M DISCOVERED!
THERE HE GOES!
JINGLE! JINGLE!
I USUALLY WORK WITH PARTNERS, BUT THIS TIME I'M NOT SPLITTING MY SPOILS WITH ANYONE...
...IF I CAN GET AWAY!
THE POLICE ARE ALL OVER THE PLACE. IT MAY BE A MATTER OF TIME UNTIL I'M SPOTTED.
LOOK-- THERE HE IS!
RATS!
THE HEAVY GOLD COINS I STOLE WILL JUST SLOW ME DOWN. I'D BETTER HIDE THEM!
JINGLE! JINGLE!
BEHIND THIS WATER BARREL.
BUT THIS JEWEL IS SOMETHING SPECIAL! I'D BETTER CONCEAL IT SOME PLACE WHERE IT WILL NEVER BE ACCIDENTALLY FOUND.
4.

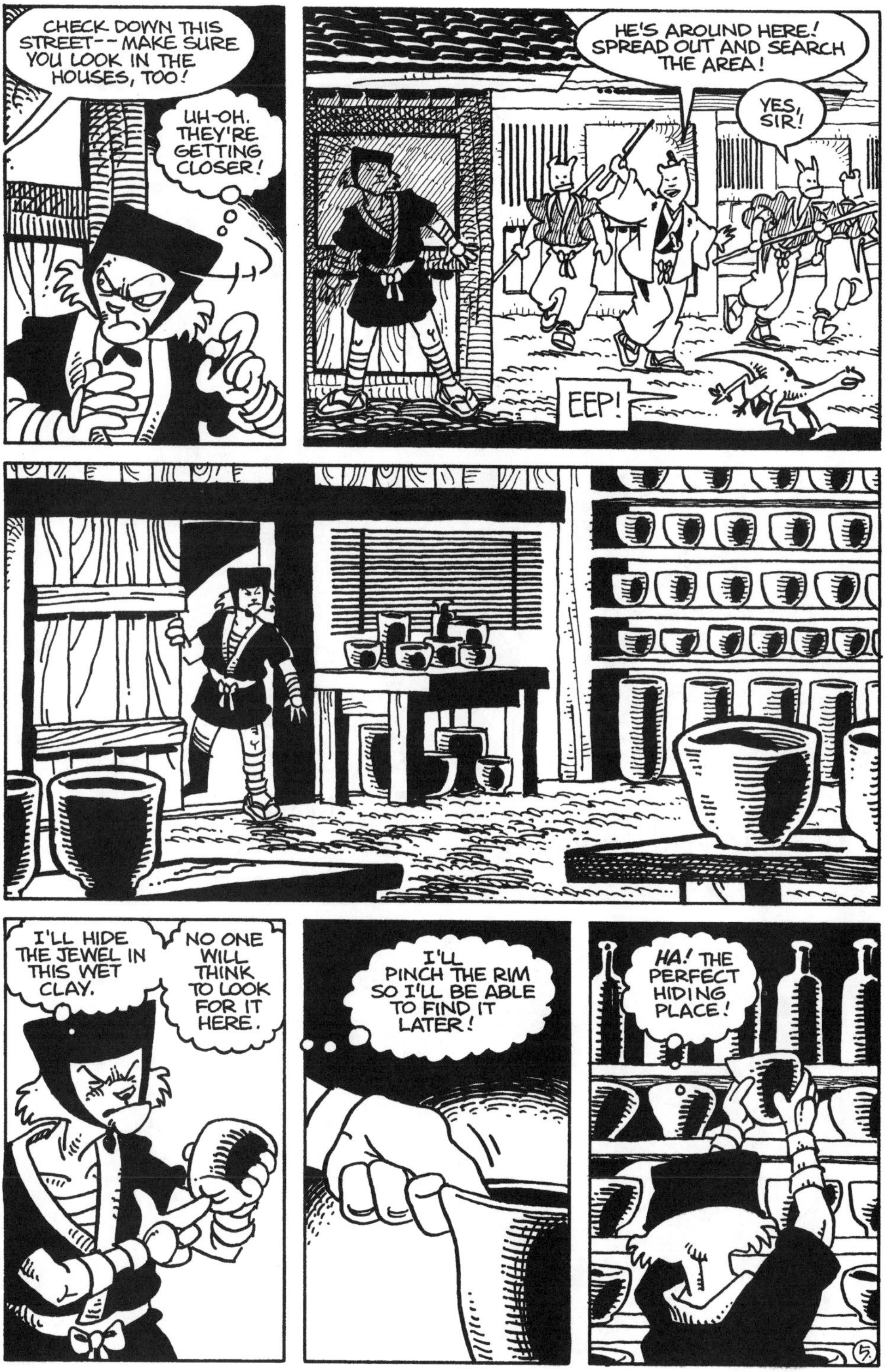
CHECK DOWN THIS STREET--MAKE SURE YOU LOOK IN THE HOUSES, TOO!
UH-OH. THEY'RE GETTING CLOSER!
HE'S AROUND HERE! SPREAD OUT AND SEARCH THE AREA!
YES, SIR!
EEP!
I'LL HIDE THE JEWEL IN THIS WET CLAY.
NO ONE WILL THINK TO LOOK FOR IT HERE.
I'LL PINCH THE RIM SO I'LL BE ABLE TO FIND IT LATER!
HA! THE PERFECT HIDING PLACE!
5

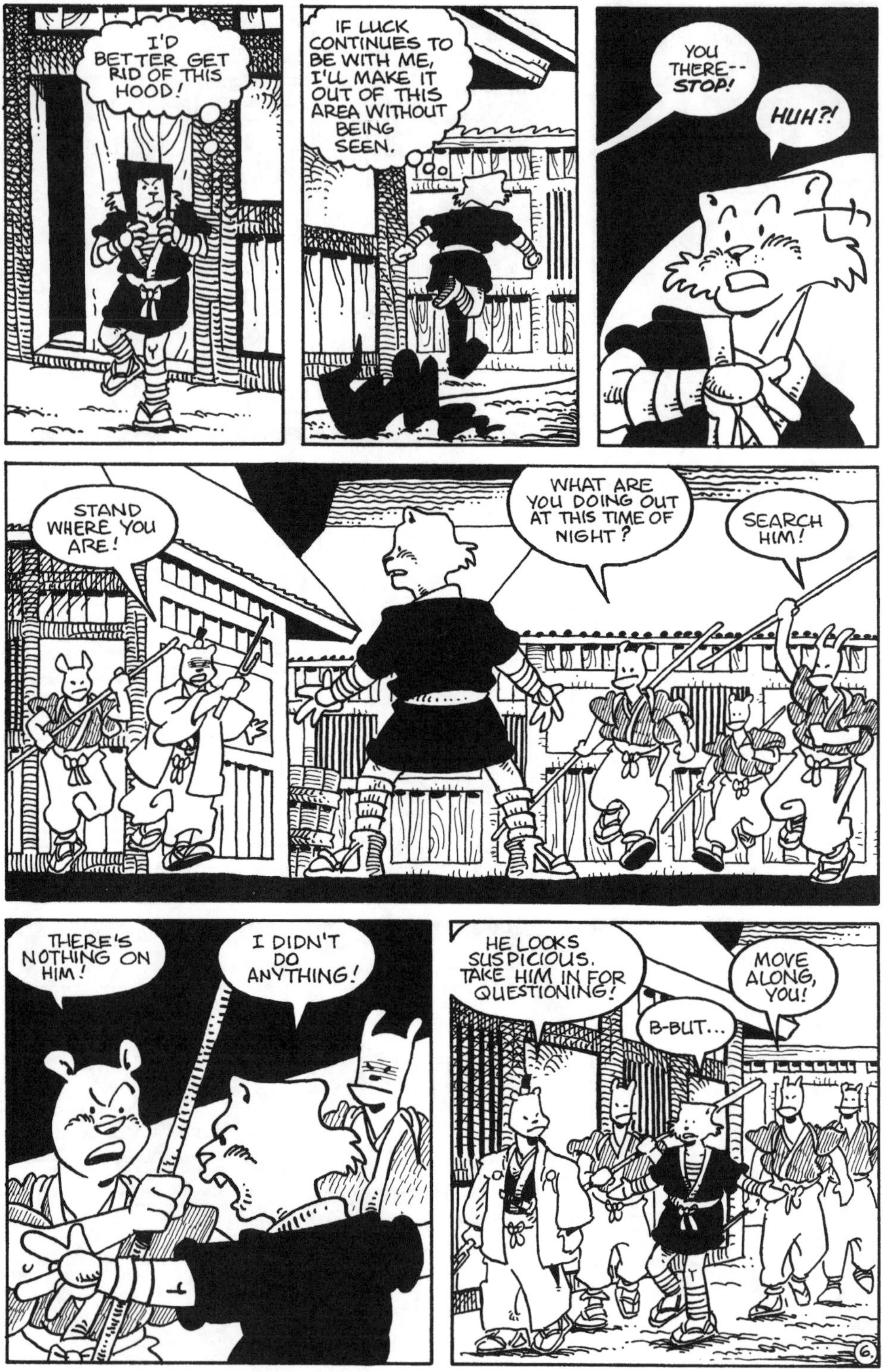
I'D BETTER GET RID OF THIS HOOD!
IF LUCK CONTINUES TO BE WITH ME, I'LL MAKE IT OUT OF THIS AREA WITHOUT BEING SEEN.
YOU THERE-- STOP!
HUH?!
STAND WHERE YOU ARE!
WHAT ARE YOU DOING OUT AT THIS TIME OF NIGHT?
SEARCH HIM!
THERE'S NOTHING ON HIM!
I DIDN'T DO ANYTHING!
HE LOOKS SUSPICIOUS. TAKE HIM IN FOR QUESTIONING!
B-BUT...
MOVE ALONG, YOU!
6.

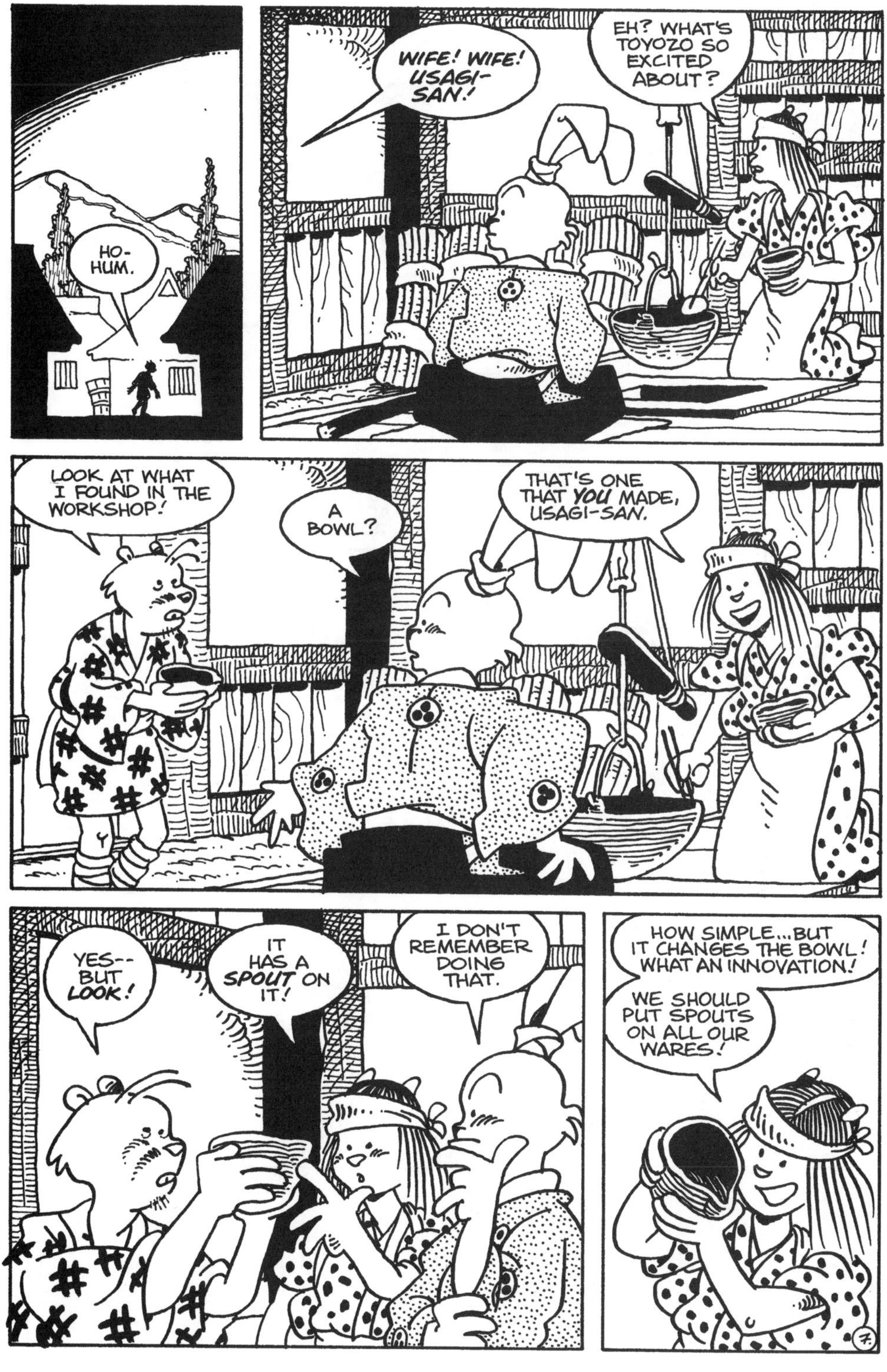
HO-HUM.
WIFE! WIFE! USAGI-SAN!
EH? WHAT'S TOYOZO SO EXCITED ABOUT?
LOOK AT WHAT I FOUND IN THE WORKSHOP!
A BOWL?
THAT'S ONE THAT YOU MADE, USAGI-SAN.
YES-- BUT LOOK!
IT HAS A SPOUT ON IT!
I DON'T REMEMBER DOING THAT.
HOW SIMPLE...BUT IT CHANGES THE BOWL! WHAT AN INNOVATION!
WE SHOULD PUT SPOUTS ON ALL OUR WARES!
7.

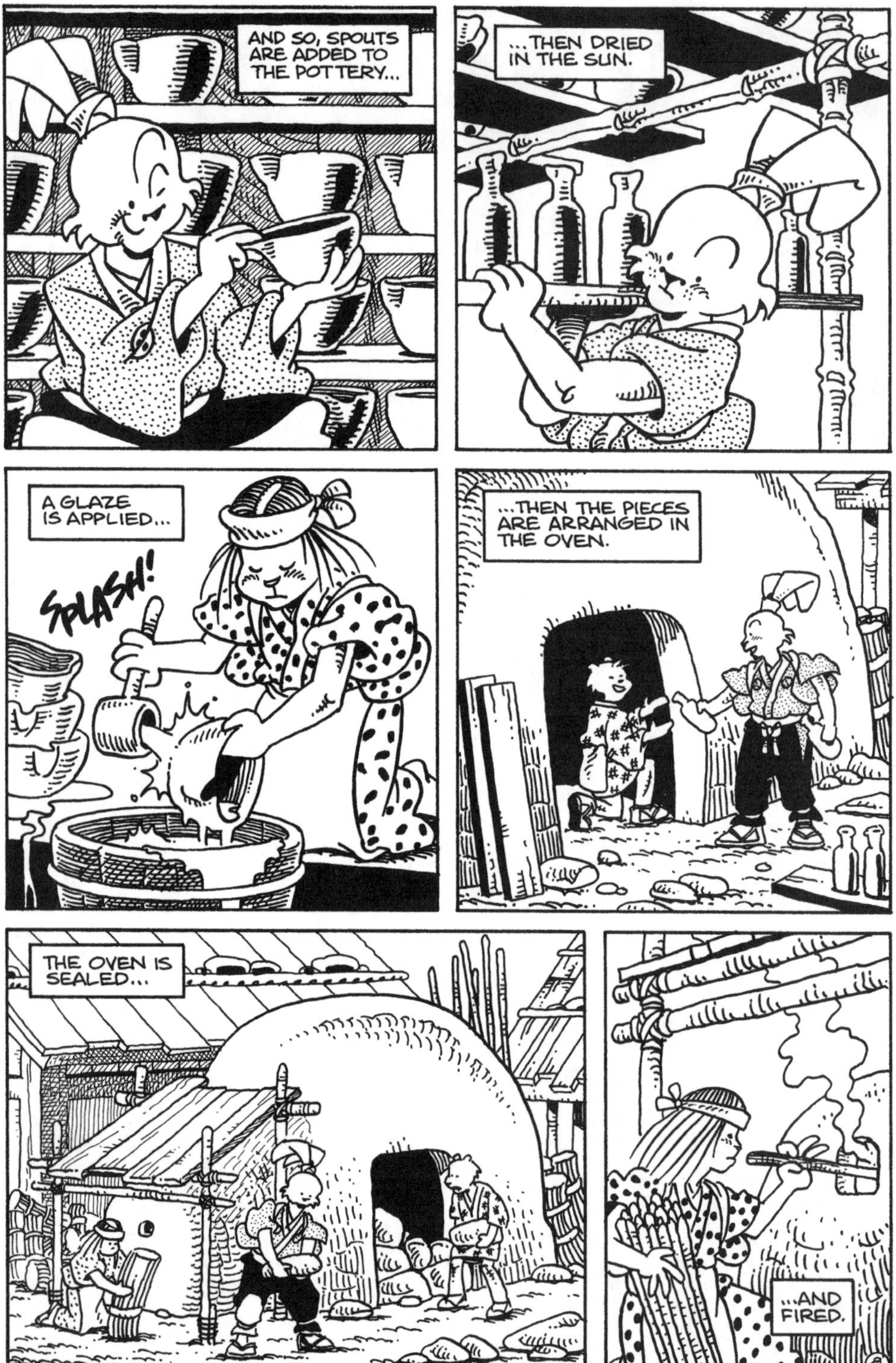
AND SO, SPOUTS ARE ADDED TO THE POTTERY...
...THEN DRIED IN THE SUN.
A GLAZE IS APPLIED...
SPLASH!
...THEN THE PIECES ARE ARRANGED IN THE OVEN.
THE OVEN IS SEALED...
...AND FIRED.
8.

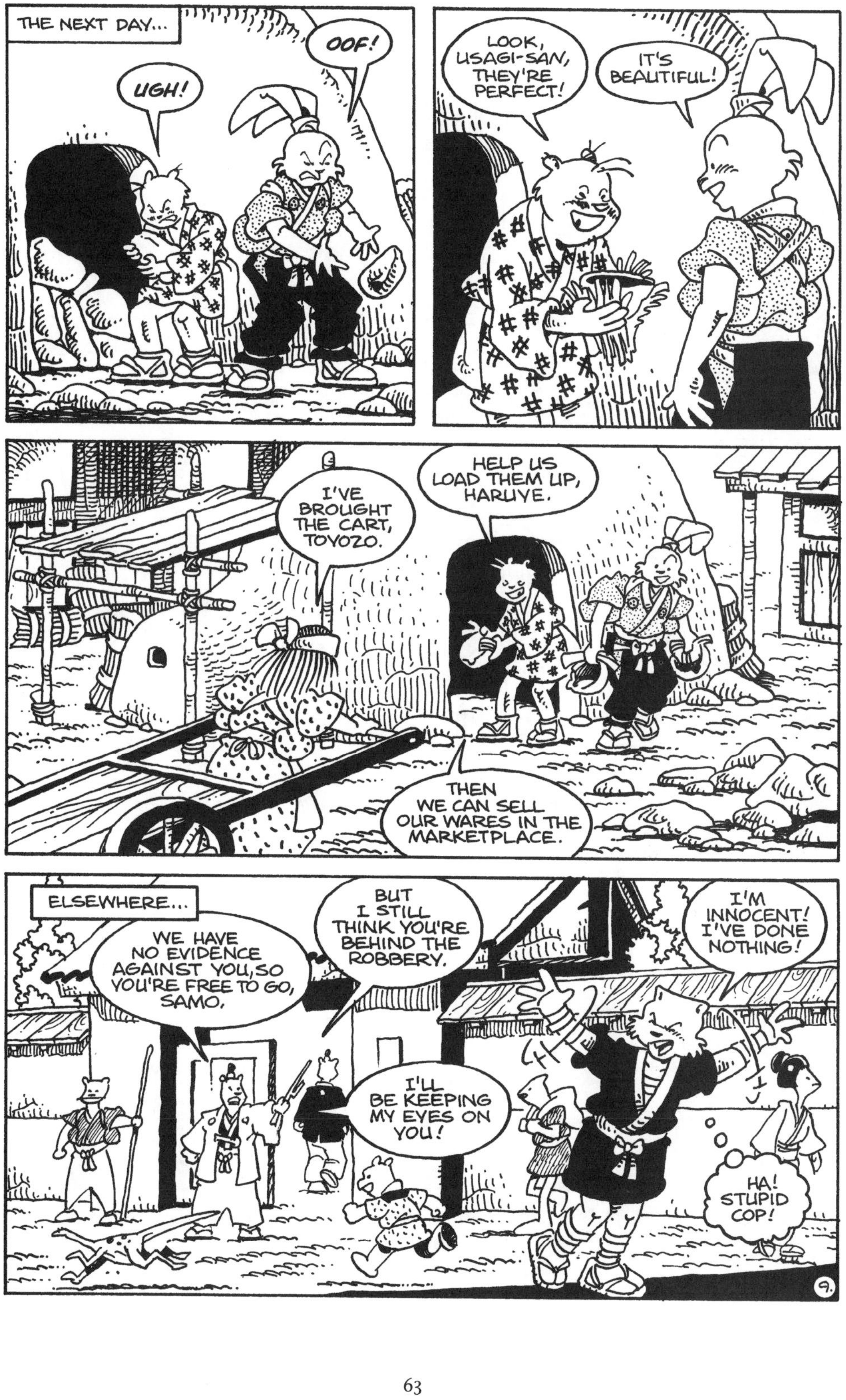
THE NEXT DAY...
UGH!
OOF!
LOOK, USAGI-SAN, THEY'RE PERFECT!
IT'S BEAUTIFUL!
I'VE BROUGHT THE CART, TOYOZO.
HELP US LOAD THEM UP, HARUYE.
THEN WE CAN SELL OUR WARES IN THE MARKETPLACE.
ELSEWHERE...
WE HAVE NO EVIDENCE AGAINST YOU, SO YOU'RE FREE TO GO, SAMO.
BUT I STILL THINK YOU'RE BEHIND THE ROBBERY.
I'LL BE KEEPING MY EYES ON YOU!
I'M INNOCENT! I'VE DONE NOTHING!
HA! STUPID COP!
9.

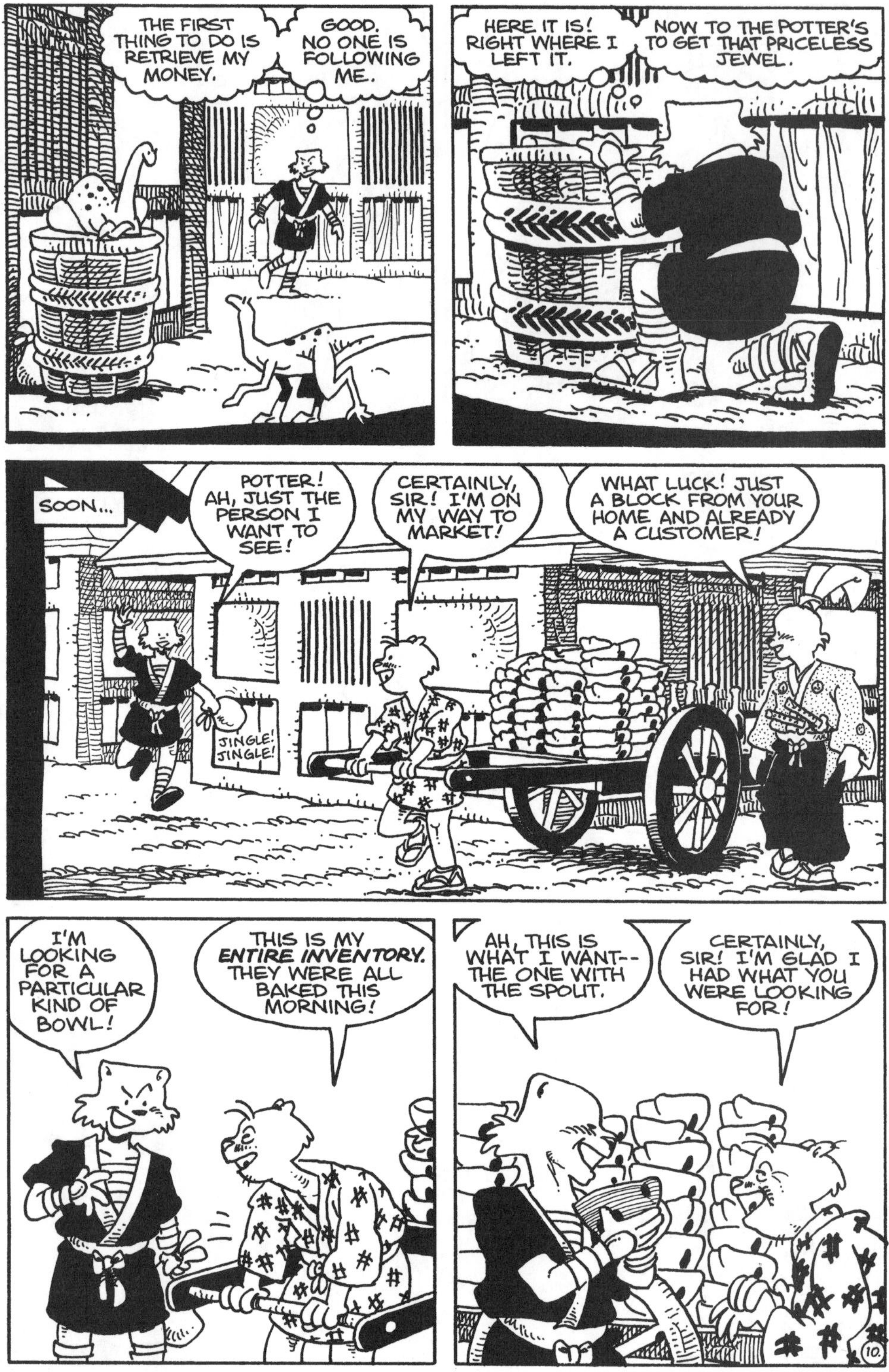
THE FIRST THING TO DO IS RETRIEVE MY MONEY.
GOOD. NO ONE IS FOLLOWING ME.
HERE IT IS! RIGHT WHERE I LEFT IT.
NOW TO THE POTTER'S TO GET THAT PRICELESS JEWEL.
SOON...
POTTER! AH, JUST THE PERSON I WANT TO SEE!
JINGLE! JINGLE!
CERTAINLY, SIR! I'M ON MY WAY TO MARKET!
WHAT LUCK! JUST A BLOCK FROM YOUR HOME AND ALREADY A CUSTOMER!
I'M LOOKING FOR A PARTICULAR KIND OF BOWL!
THIS IS MY ***ENTIRE INVENTORY.*** THEY WERE ALL BAKED THIS MORNING!
AH, THIS IS WHAT I WANT-- THE ONE WITH THE SPOUT.
CERTAINLY, SIR! I'M GLAD I HAD WHAT YOU WERE LOOKING FOR!
10.

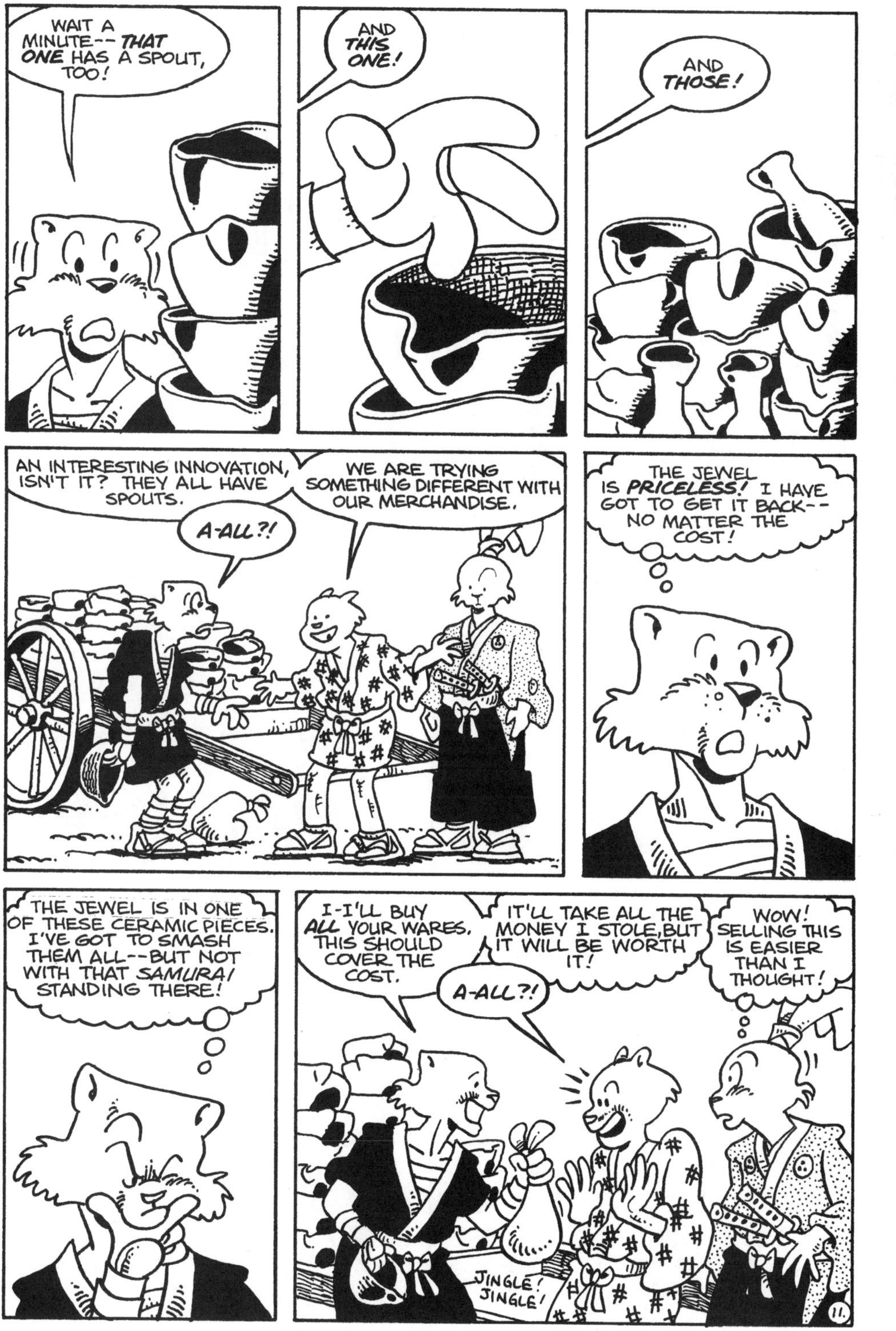
WAIT A MINUTE-- THAT ONE HAS A SPOUT, TOO!
AND THIS ONE!
AND THOSE!
AN INTERESTING INNOVATION, ISN'T IT? THEY ALL HAVE SPOUTS.
A-ALL?!
WE ARE TRYING SOMETHING DIFFERENT WITH OUR MERCHANDISE.
THE JEWEL IS PRICELESS! I HAVE GOT TO GET IT BACK-- NO MATTER THE COST!
THE JEWEL IS IN ONE OF THESE CERAMIC PIECES. I'VE GOT TO SMASH THEM ALL--BUT NOT WITH THAT SAMURAI STANDING THERE!
I-I'LL BUY ALL YOUR WARES. THIS SHOULD COVER THE COST.
A-ALL?!
IT'LL TAKE ALL THE MONEY I STOLE, BUT IT WILL BE WORTH IT!
WOW! SELLING THIS IS EASIER THAN I THOUGHT!
JINGLE! JINGLE!
11.

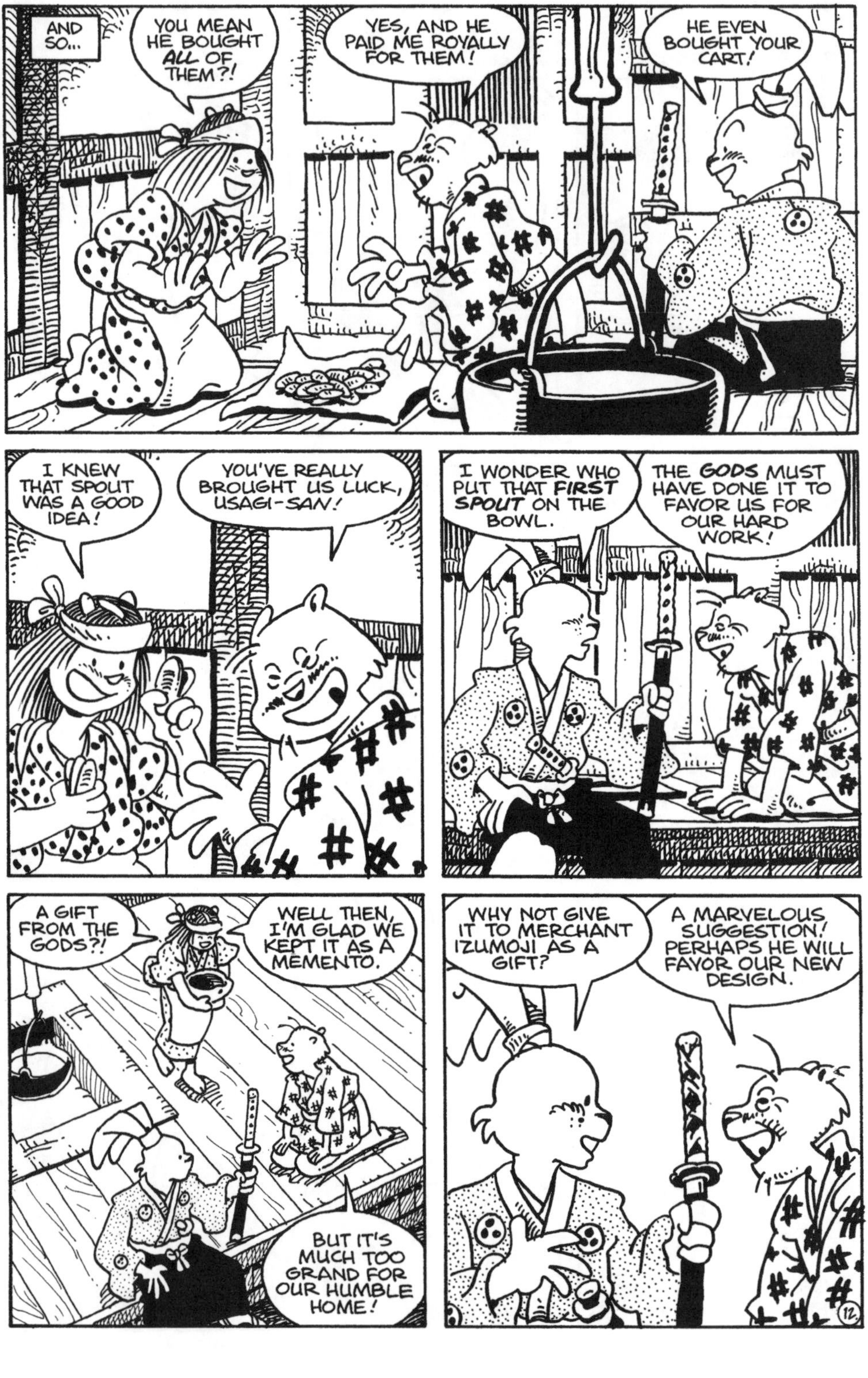
AND SO...
YOU MEAN HE BOUGHT ALL OF THEM?!
YES, AND HE PAID ME ROYALLY FOR THEM!
HE EVEN BOUGHT YOUR CART!
I KNEW THAT SPOUT WAS A GOOD IDEA!
YOU'VE REALLY BROUGHT US LUCK, USAGI-SAN!
I WONDER WHO PUT THAT FIRST SPOUT ON THE BOWL.
THE GODS MUST HAVE DONE IT TO FAVOR US FOR OUR HARD WORK!
A GIFT FROM THE GODS?!
WELL THEN, I'M GLAD WE KEPT IT AS A MEMENTO.
BUT IT'S MUCH TOO GRAND FOR OUR HUMBLE HOME!
WHY NOT GIVE IT TO MERCHANT IZUMOJI AS A GIFT?
A MARVELOUS SUGGESTION! PERHAPS HE WILL FAVOR OUR NEW DESIGN.
12.

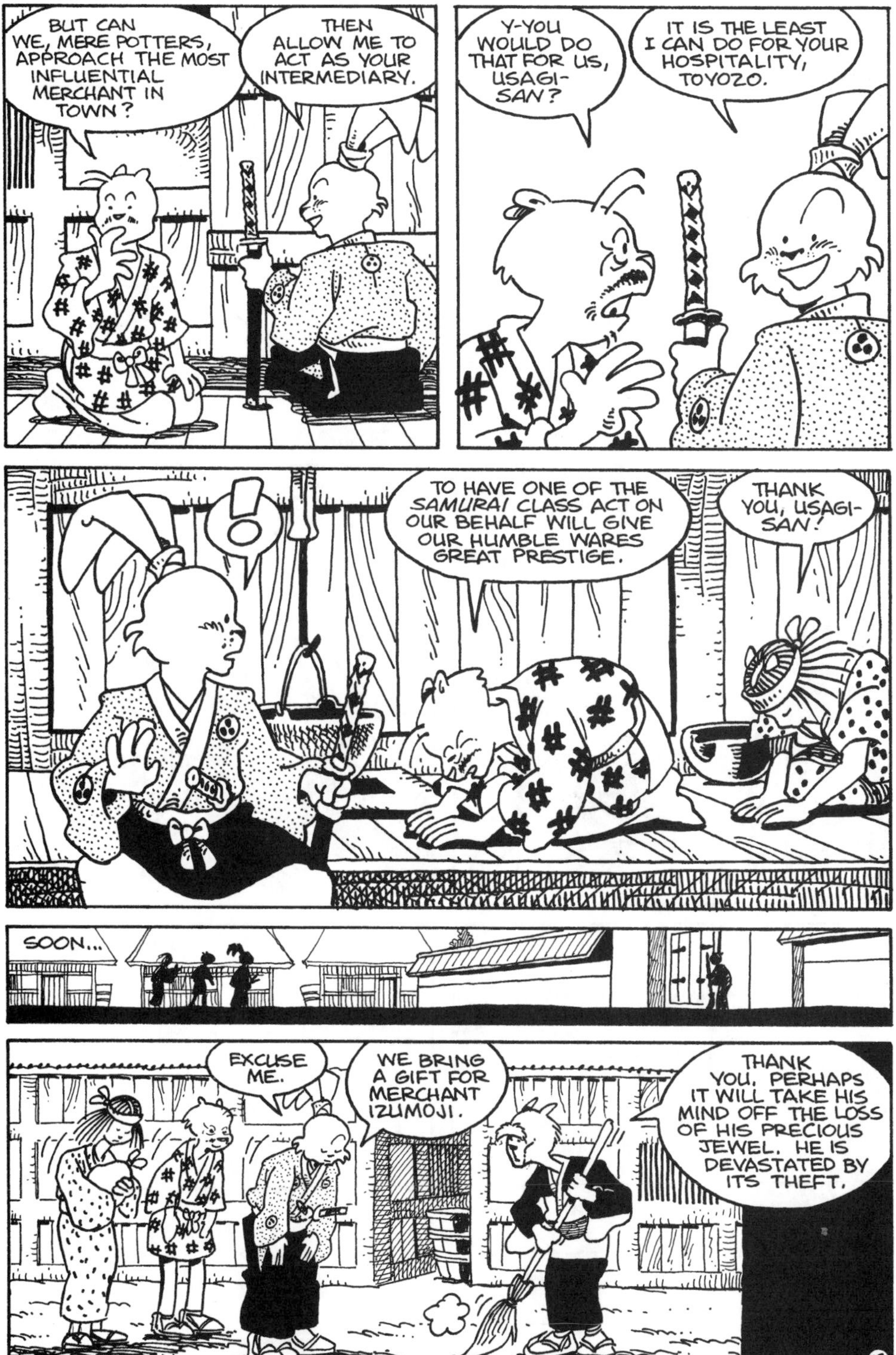
BUT CAN WE, MERE POTTERS, APPROACH THE MOST INFLUENTIAL MERCHANT IN TOWN?
THEN ALLOW ME TO ACT AS YOUR INTERMEDIARY.
Y-YOU WOULD DO THAT FOR US, USAGI-SAN?
IT IS THE LEAST I CAN DO FOR YOUR HOSPITALITY, TOYOZO.
!
TO HAVE ONE OF THE *SAMURAI* CLASS ACT ON OUR BEHALF WILL GIVE OUR HUMBLE WARES GREAT PRESTIGE.
THANK YOU, USAGI-SAN!
SOON...
EXCUSE ME.
WE BRING A GIFT FOR MERCHANT IZUMOJI.
THANK YOU. PERHAPS IT WILL TAKE HIS MIND OFF THE LOSS OF HIS PRECIOUS JEWEL. HE IS DEVASTATED BY ITS THEFT.
13

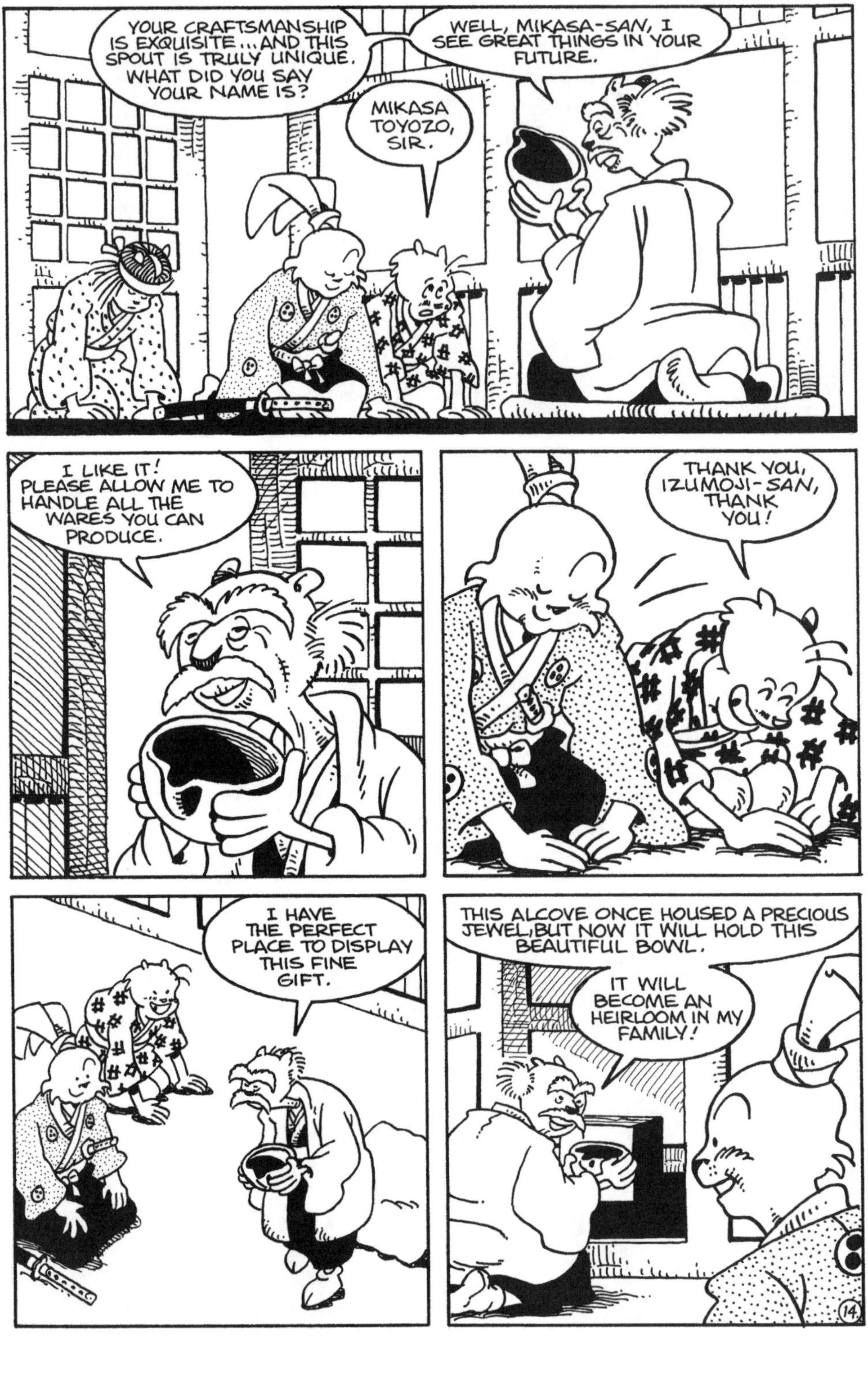
YOUR CRAFTSMANSHIP IS EXQUISITE...AND THIS SPOUT IS TRULY UNIQUE. WHAT DID YOU SAY YOUR NAME IS?
MIKASA TOYOZO, SIR.
WELL, MIKASA-SAN, I SEE GREAT THINGS IN YOUR FUTURE.
I LIKE IT! PLEASE ALLOW ME TO HANDLE ALL THE WARES YOU CAN PRODUCE.
THANK YOU, IZUMOJI-SAN, THANK YOU!
I HAVE THE PERFECT PLACE TO DISPLAY THIS FINE GIFT.
THIS ALCOVE ONCE HOUSED A PRECIOUS JEWEL, BUT NOW IT WILL HOLD THIS BEAUTIFUL BOWL.
IT WILL BECOME AN HEIRLOOM IN MY FAMILY!
14

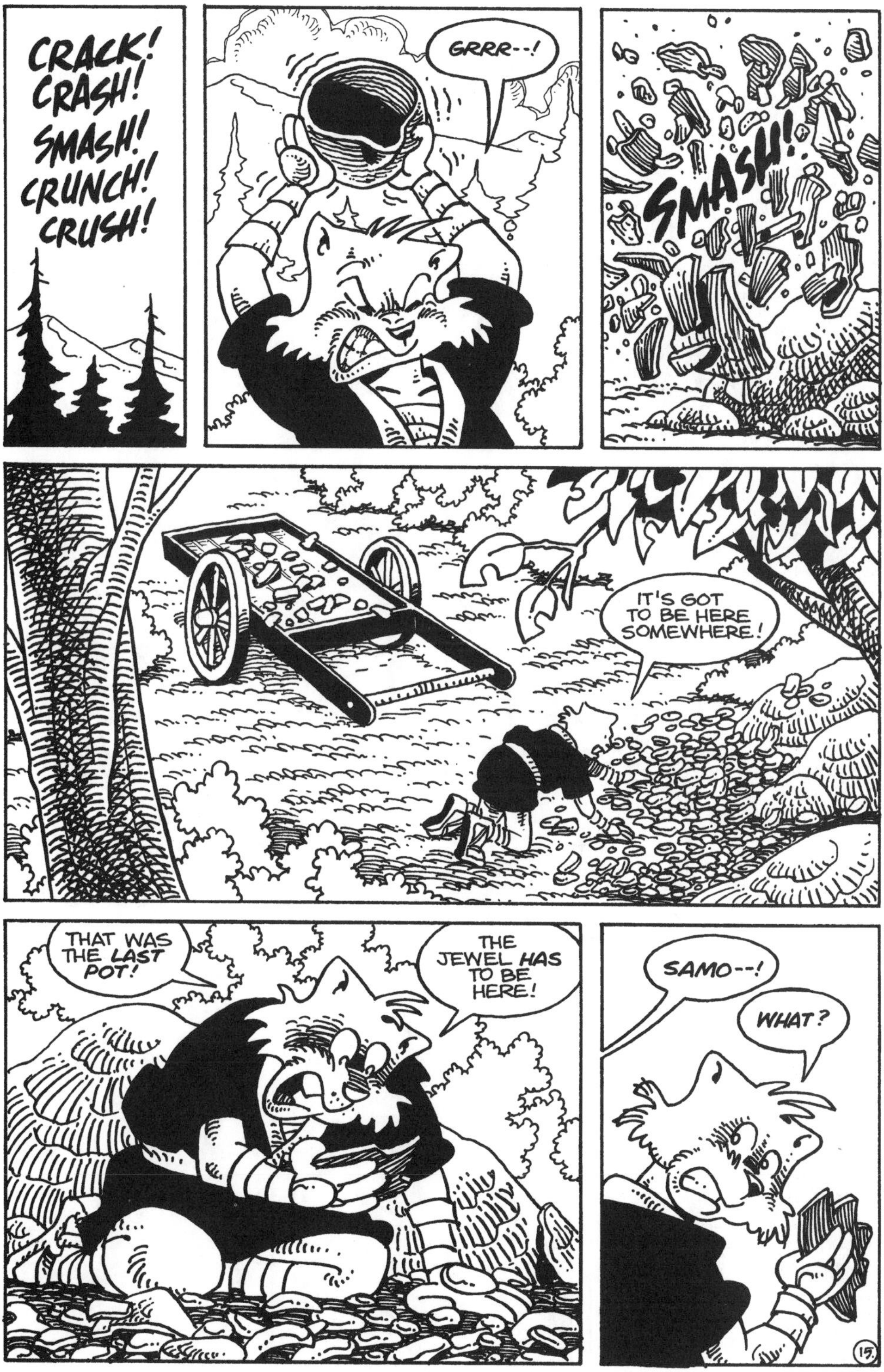
CRACK! CRASH! SMASH! CRUNCH! CRUSH!
GRRR--!
SMASH!
IT'S GOT TO BE HERE SOMEWHERE!
THAT WAS THE LAST POT!
THE JEWEL HAS TO BE HERE!
SAMO--!
WHAT?
15.

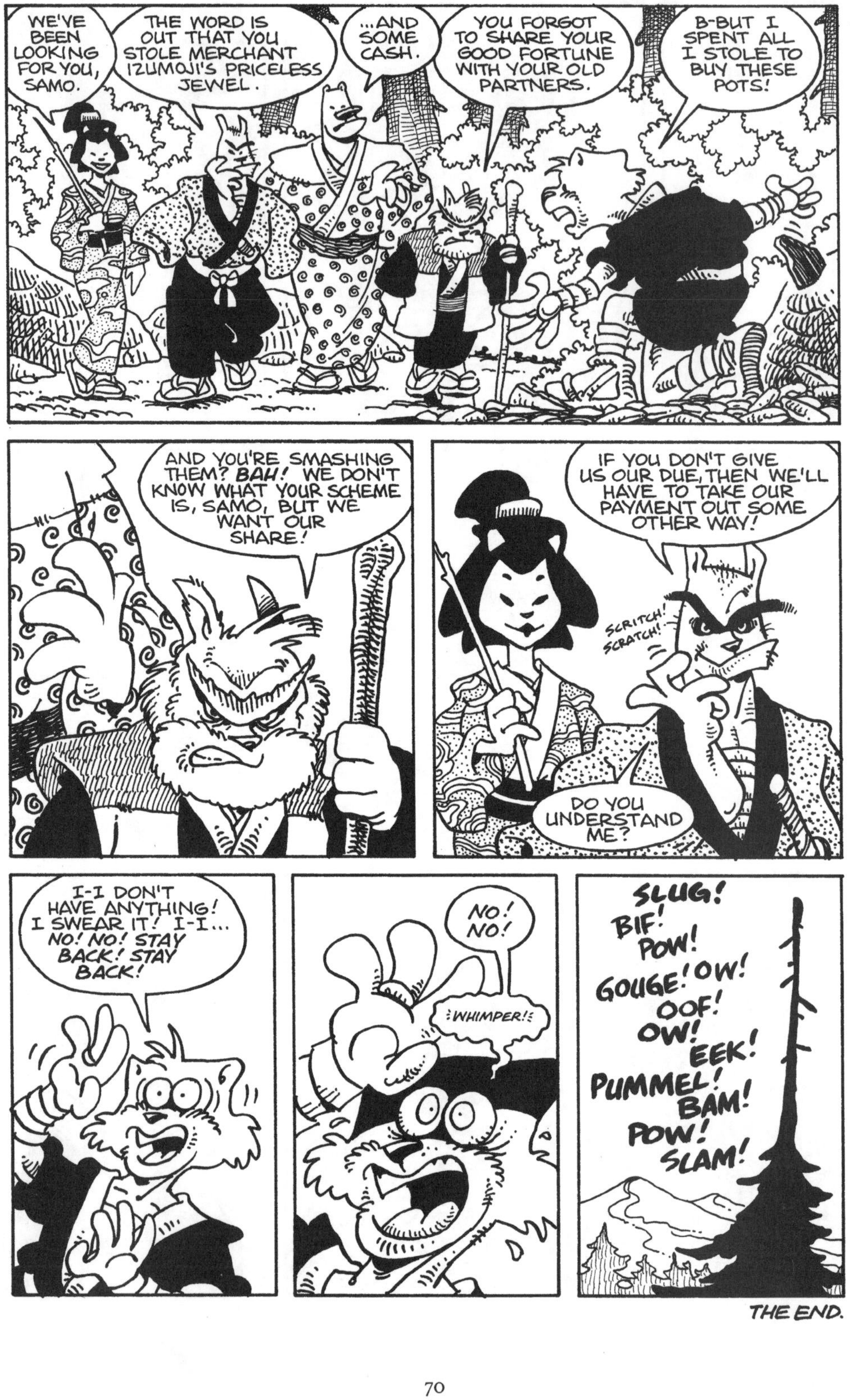
WE'VE BEEN LOOKING FOR YOU, SAMO.
THE WORD IS OUT THAT YOU STOLE MERCHANT IZUMOJI'S PRICELESS JEWEL.
...AND SOME CASH.
YOU FORGOT TO SHARE YOUR GOOD FORTUNE WITH YOUR OLD PARTNERS.
B-BUT I SPENT ALL I STOLE TO BUY THESE POTS!
AND YOU'RE SMASHING THEM? BAH! WE DON'T KNOW WHAT YOUR SCHEME IS, SAMO, BUT WE WANT OUR SHARE!
IF YOU DON'T GIVE US OUR DUE, THEN WE'LL HAVE TO TAKE OUR PAYMENT OUT SOME OTHER WAY!
SCRITCH! SCRATCH!
DO YOU UNDERSTAND ME?
I-I DON'T HAVE ANYTHING! I SWEAR IT! I-I... NO! NO! STAY BACK! STAY BACK!
NO! NO!
WHIMPER!
SLUG! BIF! POW! GOUGE! OW! OOF! OW! EEK! PUMMEL! BAM! POW! SLAM!

THE END.

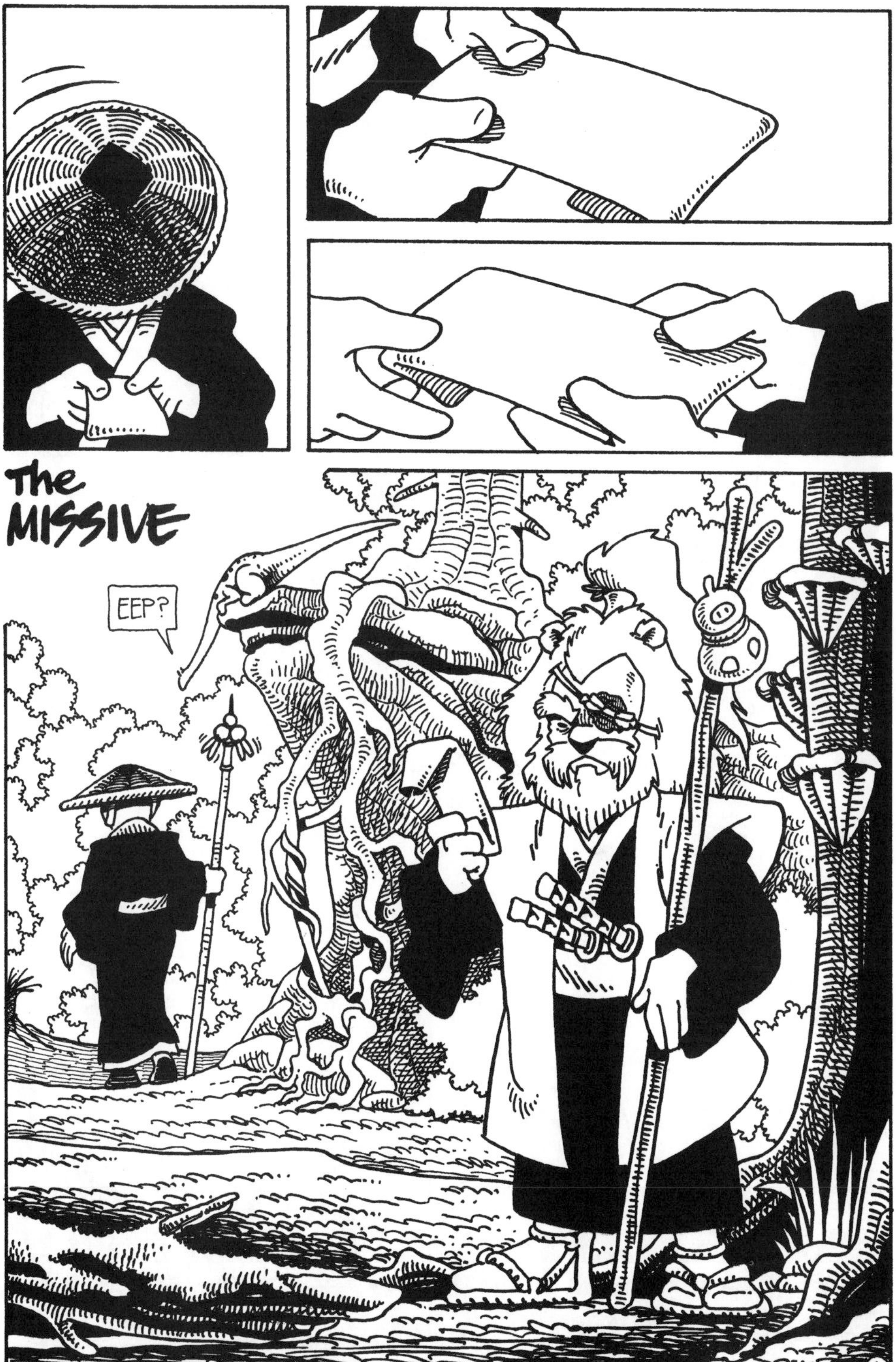
The MISSIVE
EEP?

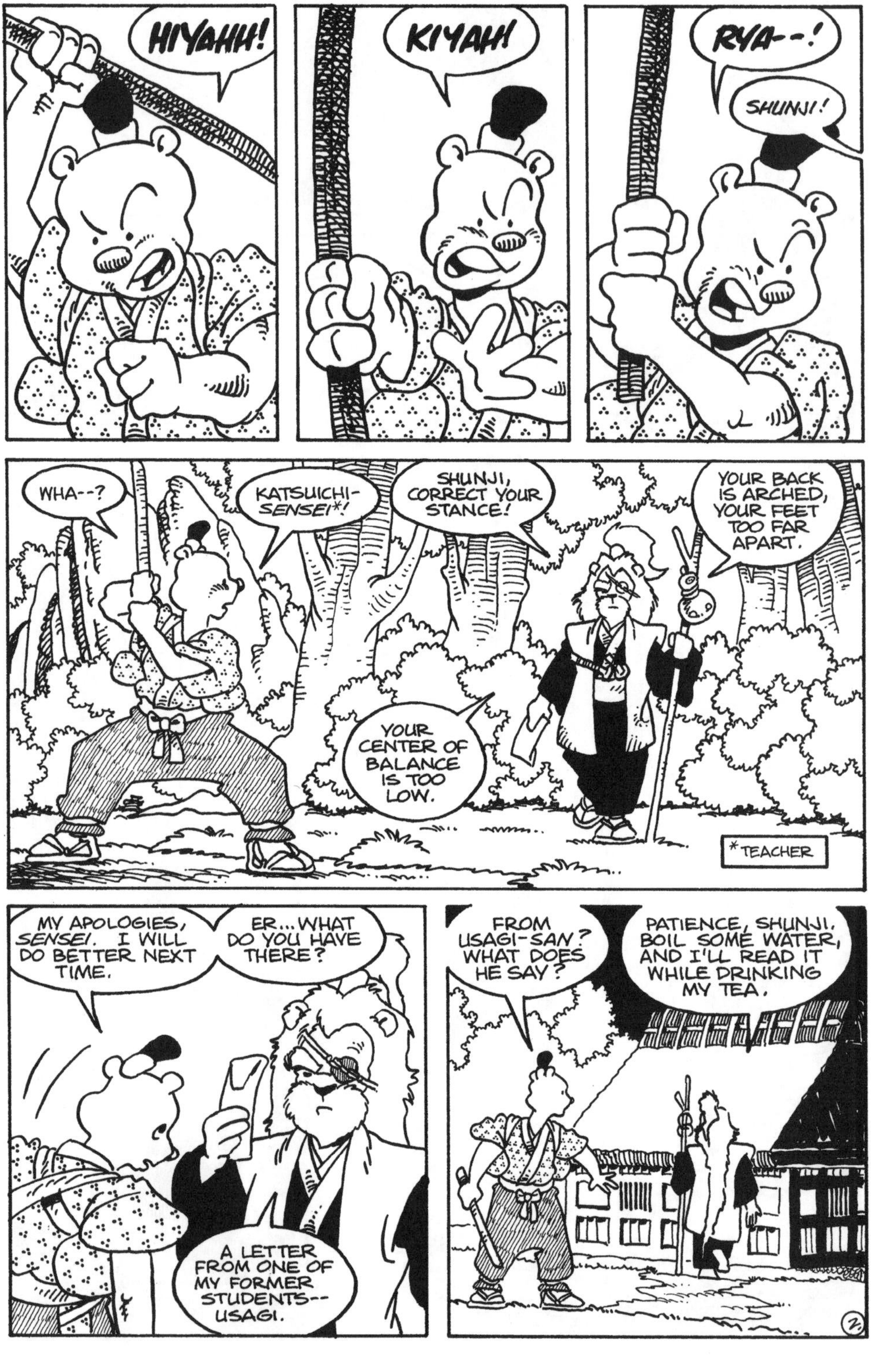
HIYAHH!
KIYAH!
RYA--!
SHUNJI!
WHA--?
KATSUICHI-SENSEI*!
SHUNJI, CORRECT YOUR STANCE!
YOUR BACK IS ARCHED, YOUR FEET TOO FAR APART.
YOUR CENTER OF BALANCE IS TOO LOW.
*TEACHER
MY APOLOGIES, SENSEI. I WILL DO BETTER NEXT TIME.
ER... WHAT DO YOU HAVE THERE?
A LETTER FROM ONE OF MY FORMER STUDENTS-- USAGI.
FROM USAGI-SAN? WHAT DOES HE SAY?
PATIENCE, SHUNJI. BOIL SOME WATER, AND I'LL READ IT WHILE DRINKING MY TEA.

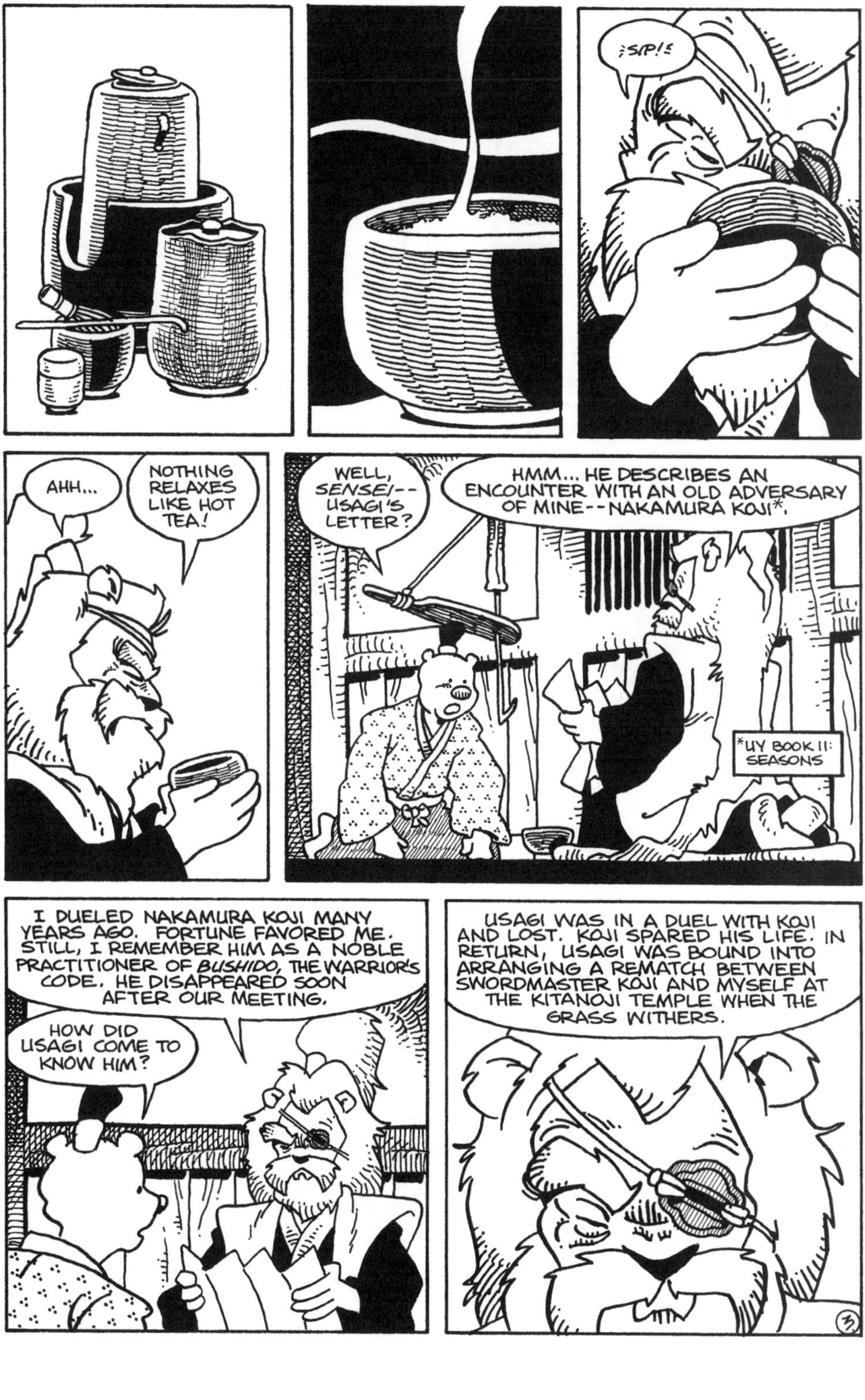
;SIP!;
AHH...
NOTHING RELAXES LIKE HOT TEA!
WELL, SENSEI-- USAGI'S LETTER?
HMM... HE DESCRIBES AN ENCOUNTER WITH AN OLD ADVERSARY OF MINE--NAKAMURA KOJI*.
*UY BOOK 11: SEASONS
I DUELED NAKAMURA KOJI MANY YEARS AGO. FORTUNE FAVORED ME. STILL, I REMEMBER HIM AS A NOBLE PRACTITIONER OF BUSHIDO, THE WARRIOR'S CODE. HE DISAPPEARED SOON AFTER OUR MEETING.
HOW DID USAGI COME TO KNOW HIM?
USAGI WAS IN A DUEL WITH KOJI AND LOST. KOJI SPARED HIS LIFE. IN RETURN, USAGI WAS BOUND INTO ARRANGING A REMATCH BETWEEN SWORDMASTER KOJI AND MYSELF AT THE KITANOJI TEMPLE WHEN THE GRASS WITHERS.
3

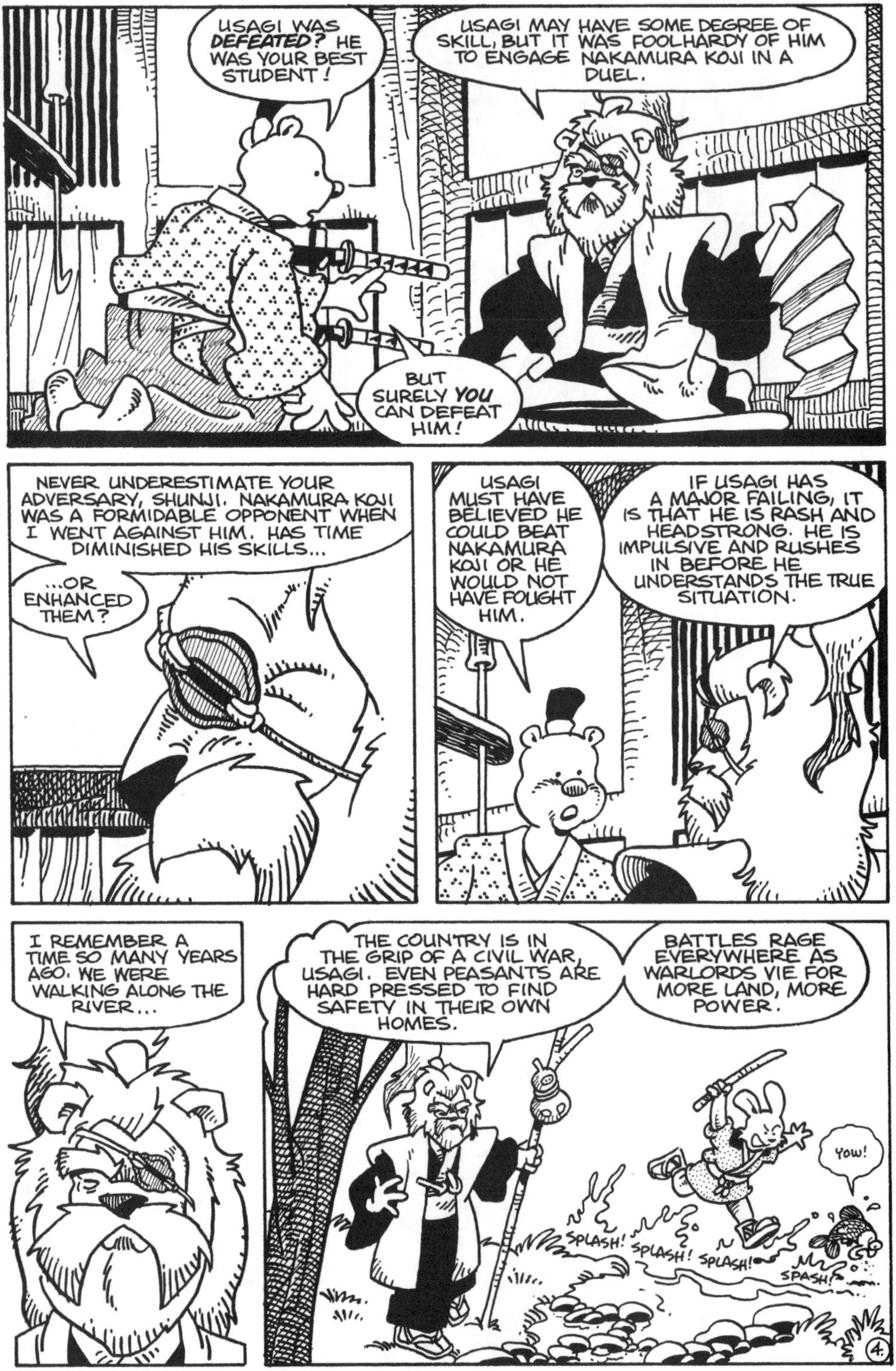
USAGI WAS DEFEATED? HE WAS YOUR BEST STUDENT!
USAGI MAY HAVE SOME DEGREE OF SKILL, BUT IT WAS FOOLHARDY OF HIM TO ENGAGE NAKAMURA KOJI IN A DUEL.
BUT SURELY YOU CAN DEFEAT HIM!
NEVER UNDERESTIMATE YOUR ADVERSARY, SHUNJI. NAKAMURA KOJI WAS A FORMIDABLE OPPONENT WHEN I WENT AGAINST HIM. HAS TIME DIMINISHED HIS SKILLS...
...OR ENHANCED THEM?
USAGI MUST HAVE BELIEVED HE COULD BEAT NAKAMURA KOJI OR HE WOULD NOT HAVE FOUGHT HIM.
IF USAGI HAS A MAJOR FAILING, IT IS THAT HE IS RASH AND HEADSTRONG. HE IS IMPULSIVE AND RUSHES IN BEFORE HE UNDERSTANDS THE TRUE SITUATION.
I REMEMBER A TIME SO MANY YEARS AGO. WE WERE WALKING ALONG THE RIVER...
THE COUNTRY IS IN THE GRIP OF A CIVIL WAR, USAGI. EVEN PEASANTS ARE HARD PRESSED TO FIND SAFETY IN THEIR OWN HOMES.
BATTLES RAGE EVERYWHERE AS WARLORDS VIE FOR MORE LAND, MORE POWER.
YOW!
SPLASH! SPLASH! SPLASH! SPASH!
4.

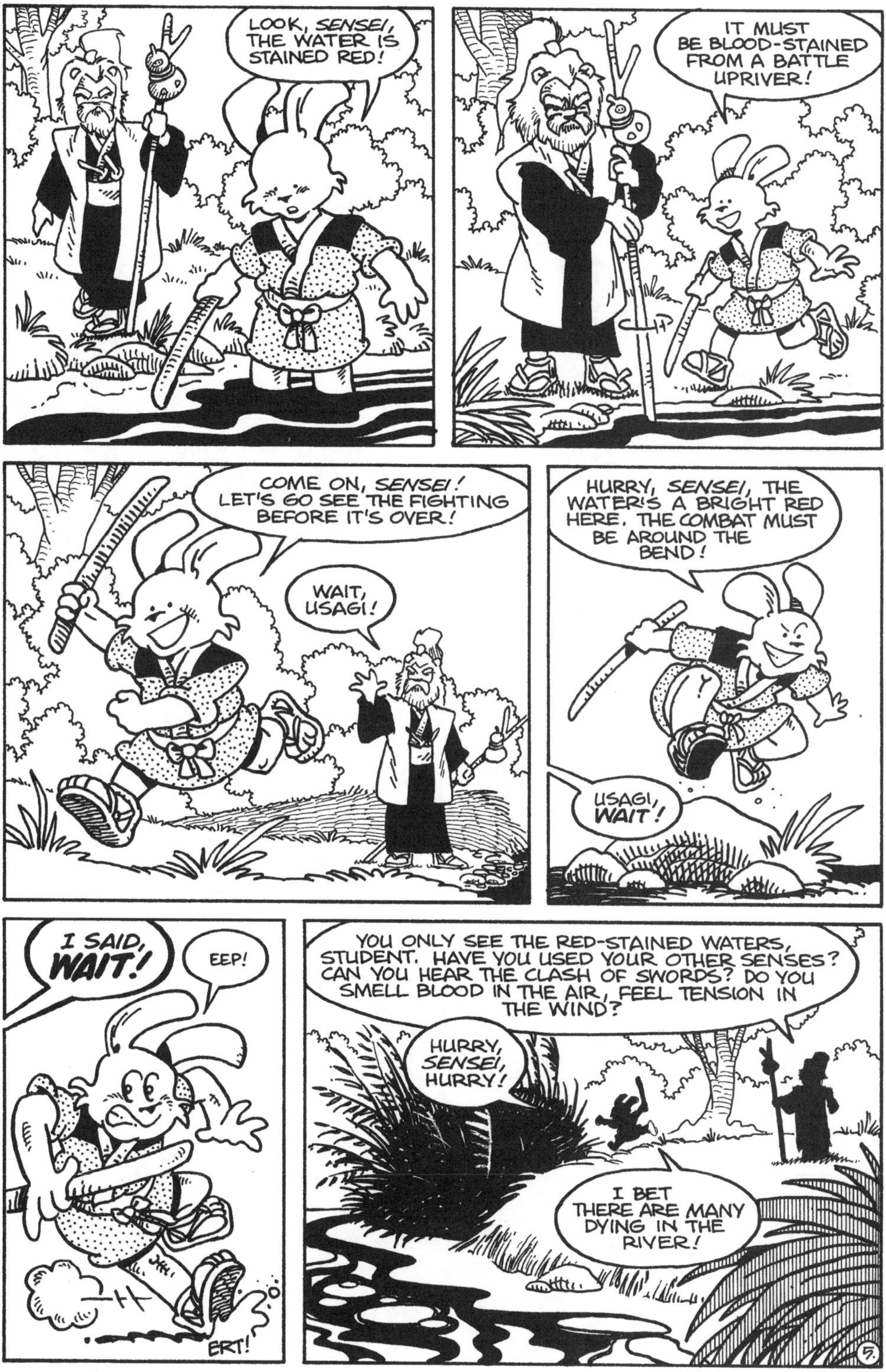
LOOK, SENSEI, THE WATER IS STAINED RED!
IT MUST BE BLOOD-STAINED FROM A BATTLE UPRIVER!
COME ON, SENSEI! LET'S GO SEE THE FIGHTING BEFORE IT'S OVER!
WAIT, USAGI!
HURRY, SENSEI, THE WATER'S A BRIGHT RED HERE. THE COMBAT MUST BE AROUND THE BEND!
USAGI, WAIT!
I SAID, WAIT!
EEP!
ERT!
YOU ONLY SEE THE RED-STAINED WATERS, STUDENT. HAVE YOU USED YOUR OTHER SENSES? CAN YOU HEAR THE CLASH OF SWORDS? DO YOU SMELL BLOOD IN THE AIR, FEEL TENSION IN THE WIND?
HURRY, SENSEI, HURRY!
I BET THERE ARE MANY DYING IN THE RIVER!
5.

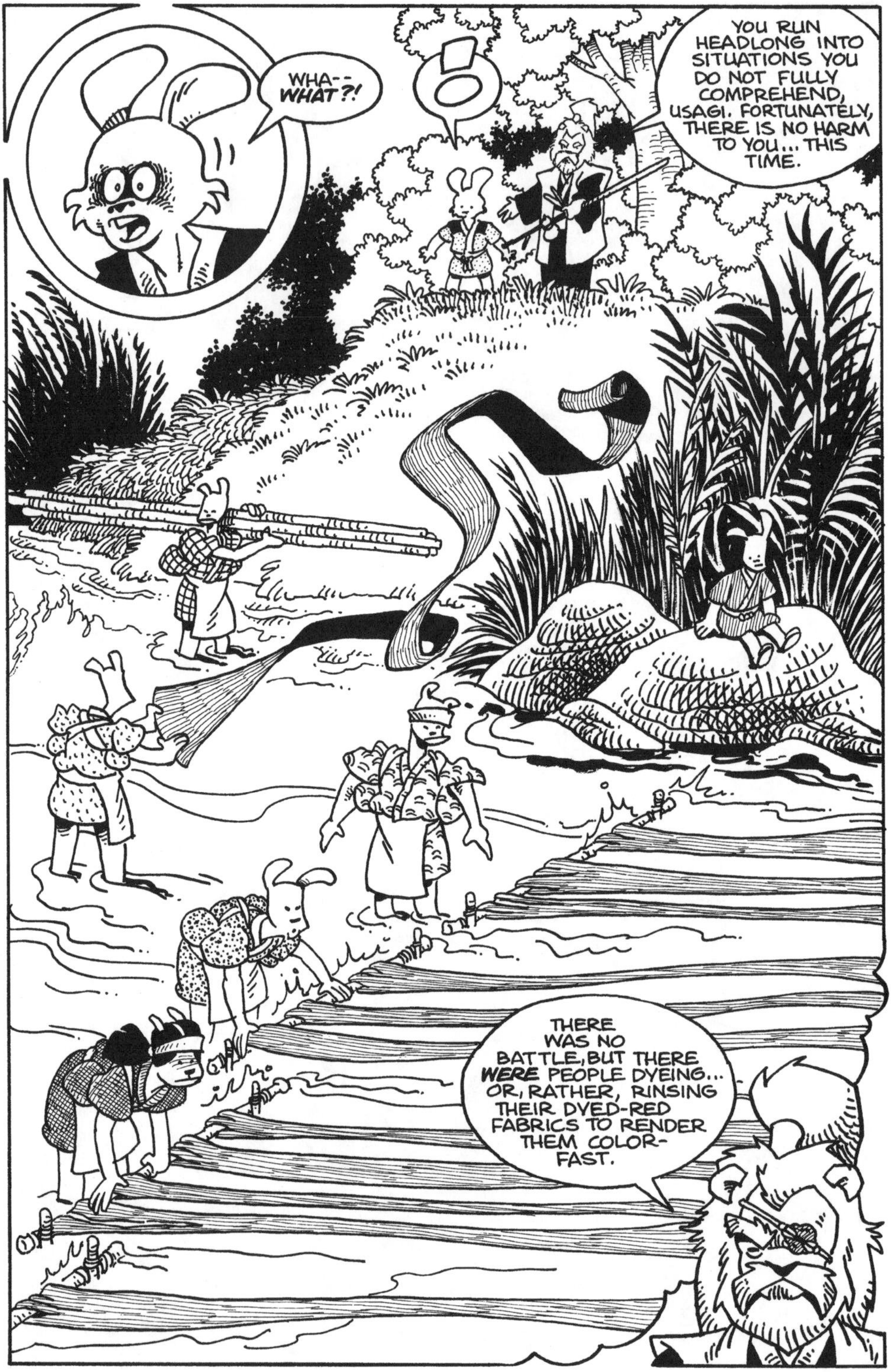
WHA-- WHAT?!
!
YOU RUN HEADLONG INTO SITUATIONS YOU DO NOT FULLY COMPREHEND, USAGI. FORTUNATELY, THERE IS NO HARM TO YOU... THIS TIME.
THERE WAS NO BATTLE, BUT THERE WERE PEOPLE DYEING... OR, RATHER, RINSING THEIR DYED-RED FABRICS TO RENDER THEM COLOR-FAST.

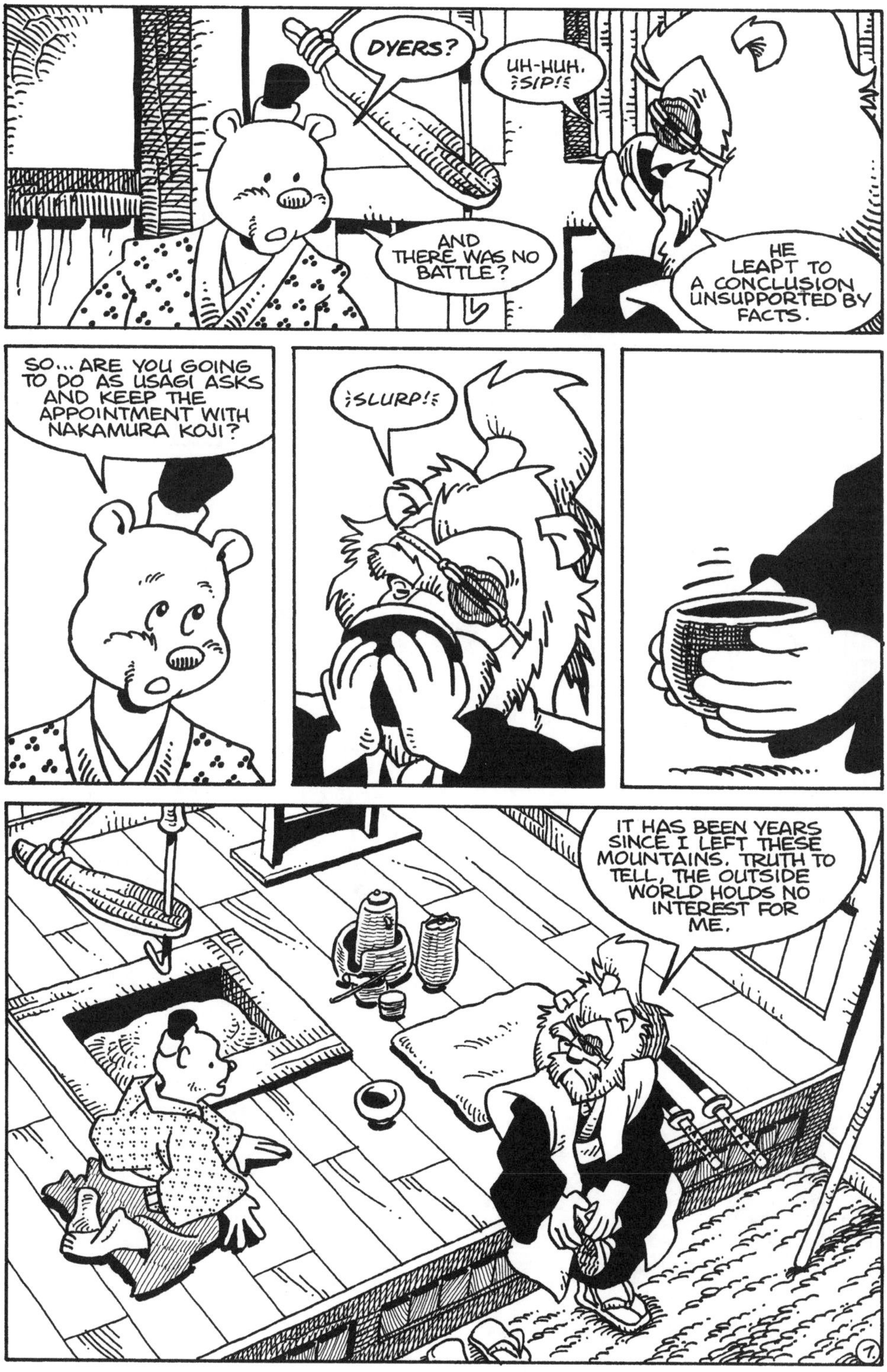
DYERS?
UH-HUH. ¡SIP!¡
AND THERE WAS NO BATTLE?
HE LEAPT TO A CONCLUSION UNSUPPORTED BY FACTS.
SO... ARE YOU GOING TO DO AS USAGI ASKS AND KEEP THE APPOINTMENT WITH NAKAMURA KOJI?
¡SLURP!¡
IT HAS BEEN YEARS SINCE I LEFT THESE MOUNTAINS. TRUTH TO TELL, THE OUTSIDE WORLD HOLDS NO INTEREST FOR ME.
7.

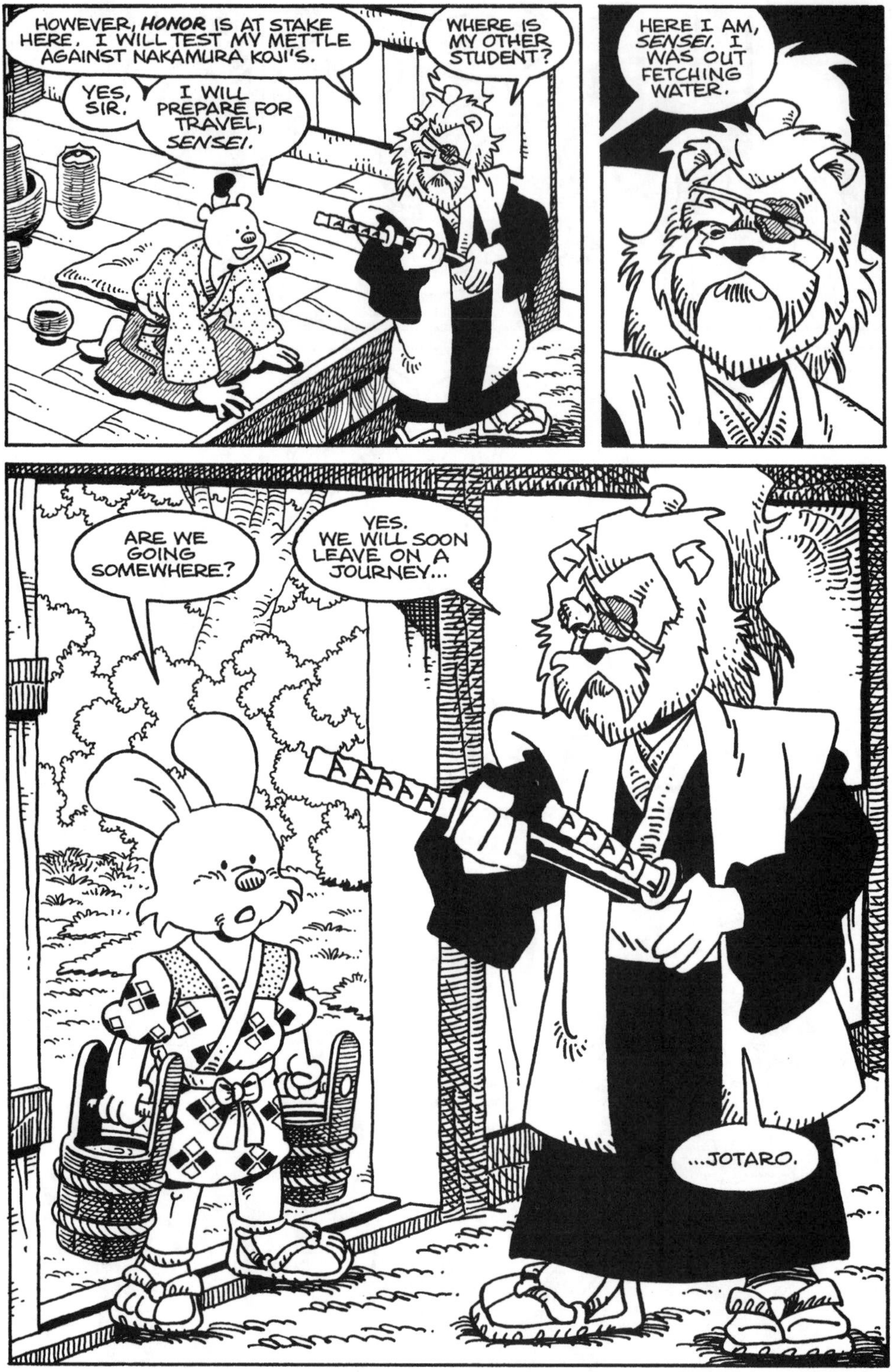
HOWEVER, **HONOR** IS AT STAKE HERE. I WILL TEST MY METTLE AGAINST NAKAMURA KOJI'S.
YES, SIR.
I WILL PREPARE FOR TRAVEL, *SENSEI.*
WHERE IS MY OTHER STUDENT?
HERE I AM, *SENSEI.* I WAS OUT FETCHING WATER.
ARE WE GOING SOMEWHERE?
YES. WE WILL SOON LEAVE ON A JOURNEY...
...JOTARO.
THE END.

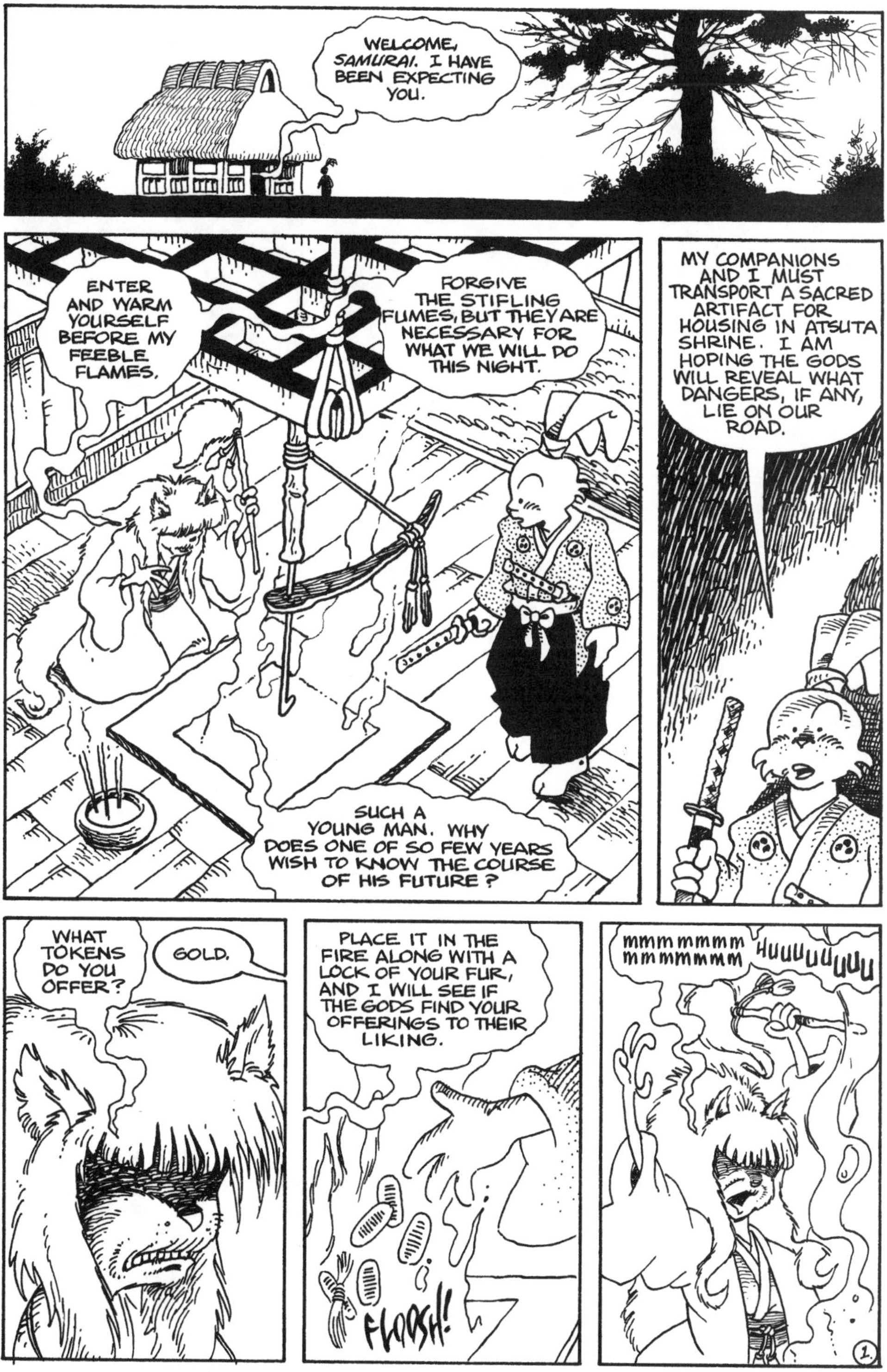

WELCOME, SAMURAI. I HAVE BEEN EXPECTING YOU.
ENTER AND WARM YOURSELF BEFORE MY FEEBLE FLAMES.
FORGIVE THE STIFLING FUMES, BUT THEY ARE NECESSARY FOR WHAT WE WILL DO THIS NIGHT.
SUCH A YOUNG MAN. WHY DOES ONE OF SO FEW YEARS WISH TO KNOW THE COURSE OF HIS FUTURE?
MY COMPANIONS AND I MUST TRANSPORT A SACRED ARTIFACT FOR HOUSING IN ATSUTA SHRINE. I AM HOPING THE GODS WILL REVEAL WHAT DANGERS, IF ANY, LIE ON OUR ROAD.
WHAT TOKENS DO YOU OFFER?
GOLD.
PLACE IT IN THE FIRE ALONG WITH A LOCK OF YOUR FUR, AND I WILL SEE IF THE GODS FIND YOUR OFFERINGS TO THEIR LIKING.
FLOOSH!
mmmmmmm mmmmmmm
HUUUUUUUU
1.

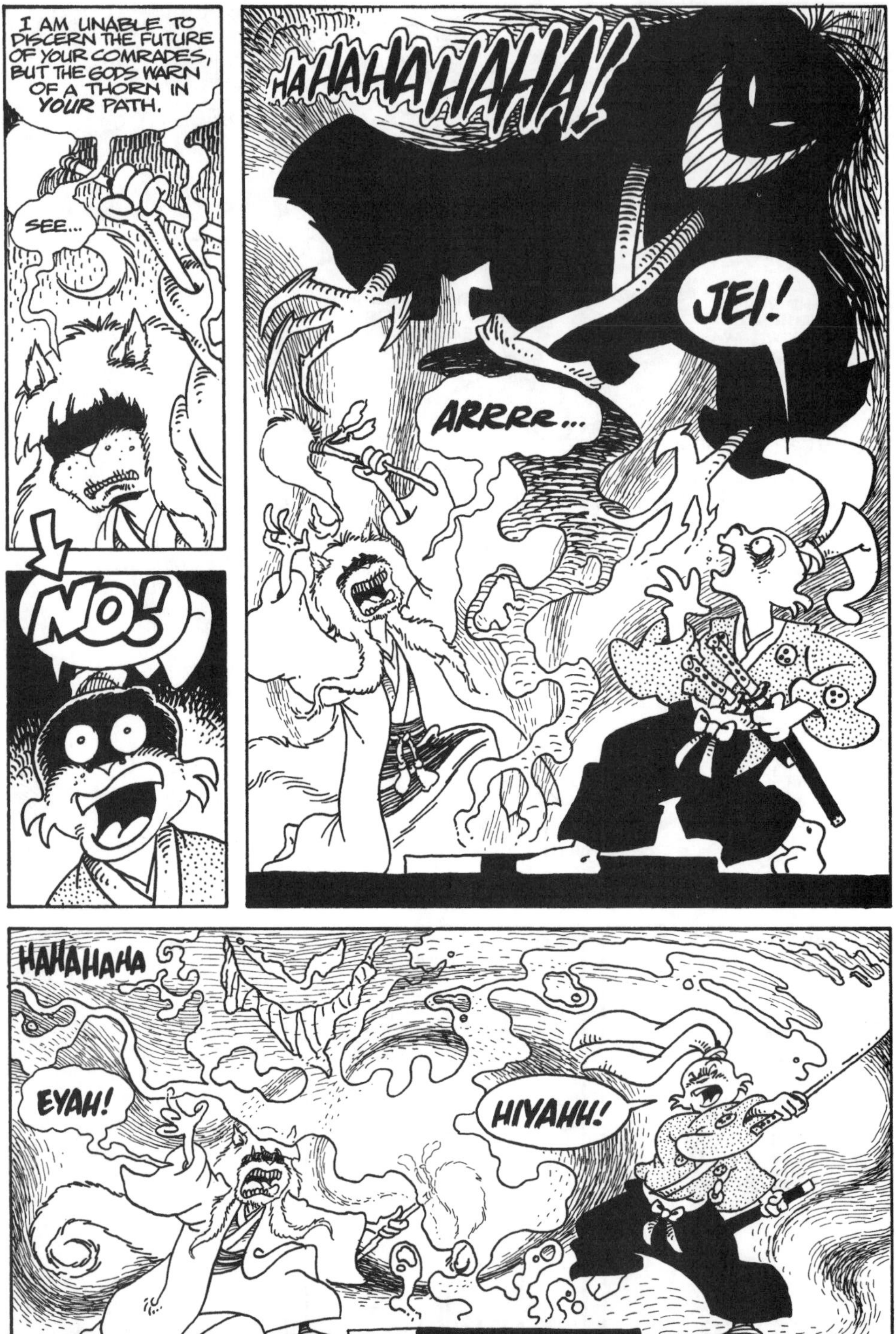
I AM UNABLE TO DISCERN THE FUTURE OF YOUR COMRADES, BUT THE GODS WARN OF A THORN IN YOUR PATH.
SEE...
NO!
HAHAHAHAHAHA!
JEI!
ARRRR...
HAHAHAHA
EYAH!
HIYAHH!

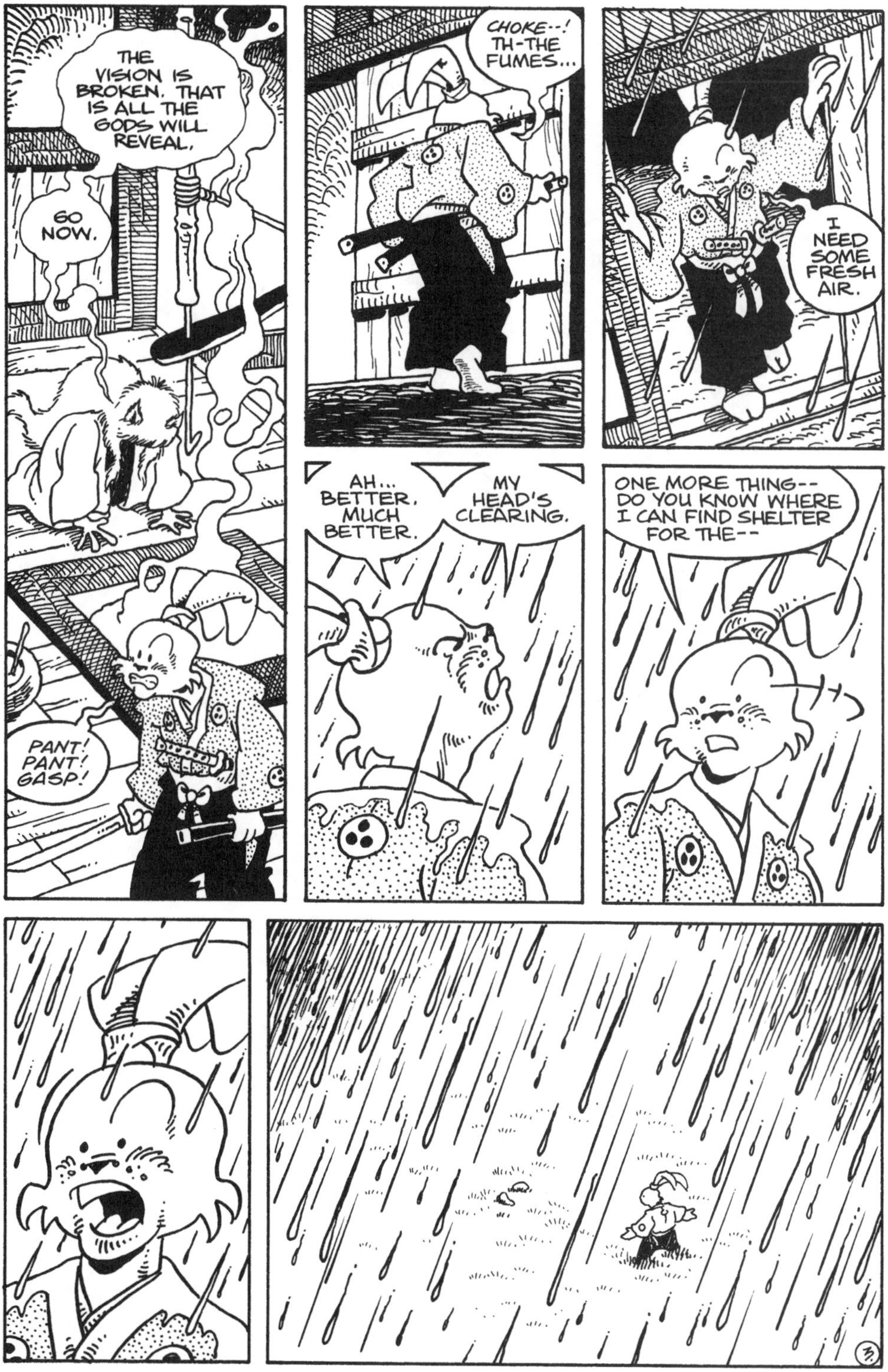
THE VISION IS BROKEN. THAT IS ALL THE GODS WILL REVEAL.
GO NOW.
PANT! PANT! GASP!
CHOKE--! TH-THE FUMES...
I NEED SOME FRESH AIR.
AH... BETTER. MUCH BETTER.
MY HEAD'S CLEARING.
ONE MORE THING-- DO YOU KNOW WHERE I CAN FIND SHELTER FOR THE--
3

THE MYSTERY OF THE DEMON MASK CHAPTER ONE

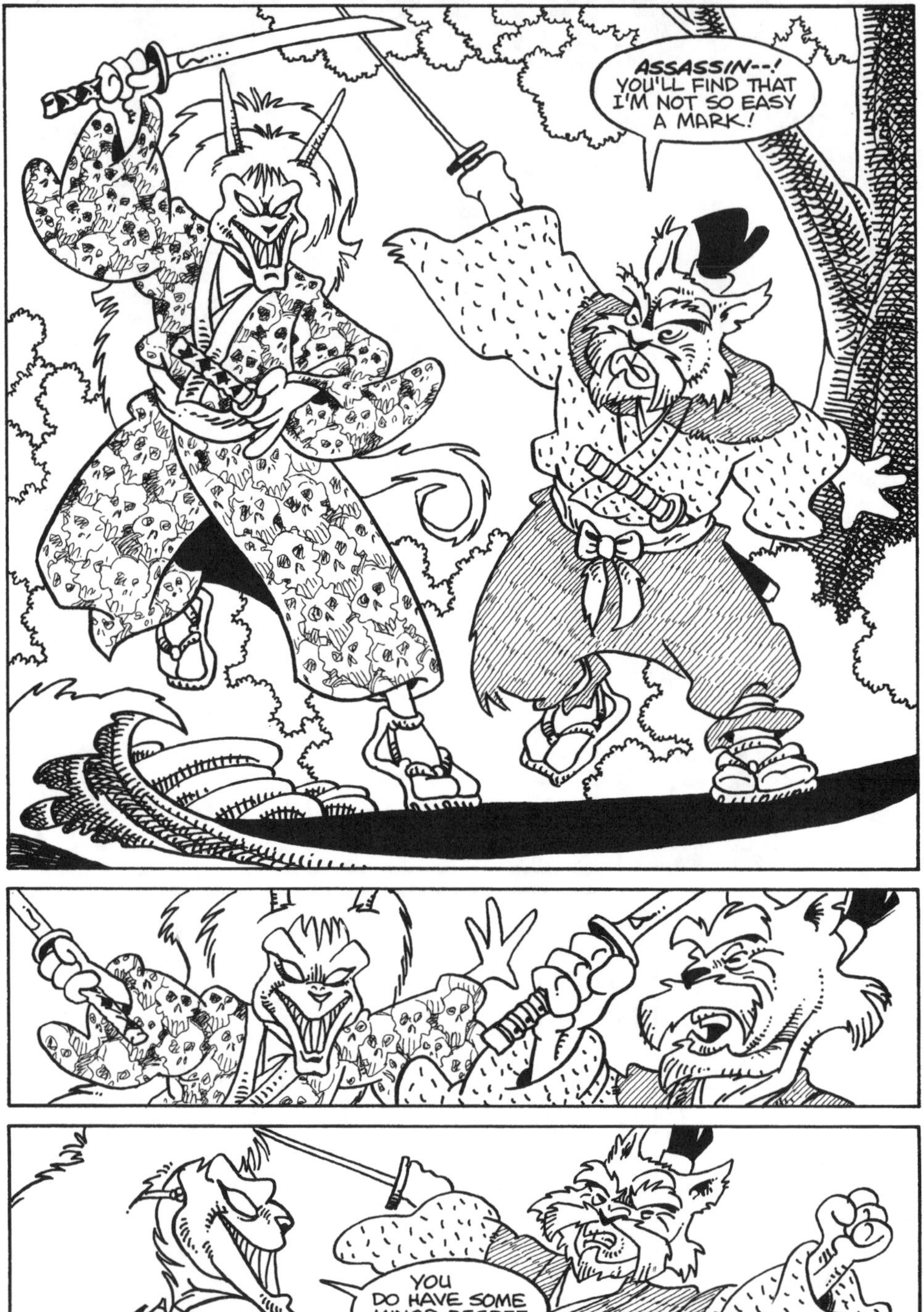
ASSASSIN--! YOU'LL FIND THAT I'M NOT SO EASY A MARK!
YOU DO HAVE SOME MINOR DEGREE OF SKILL...
4.

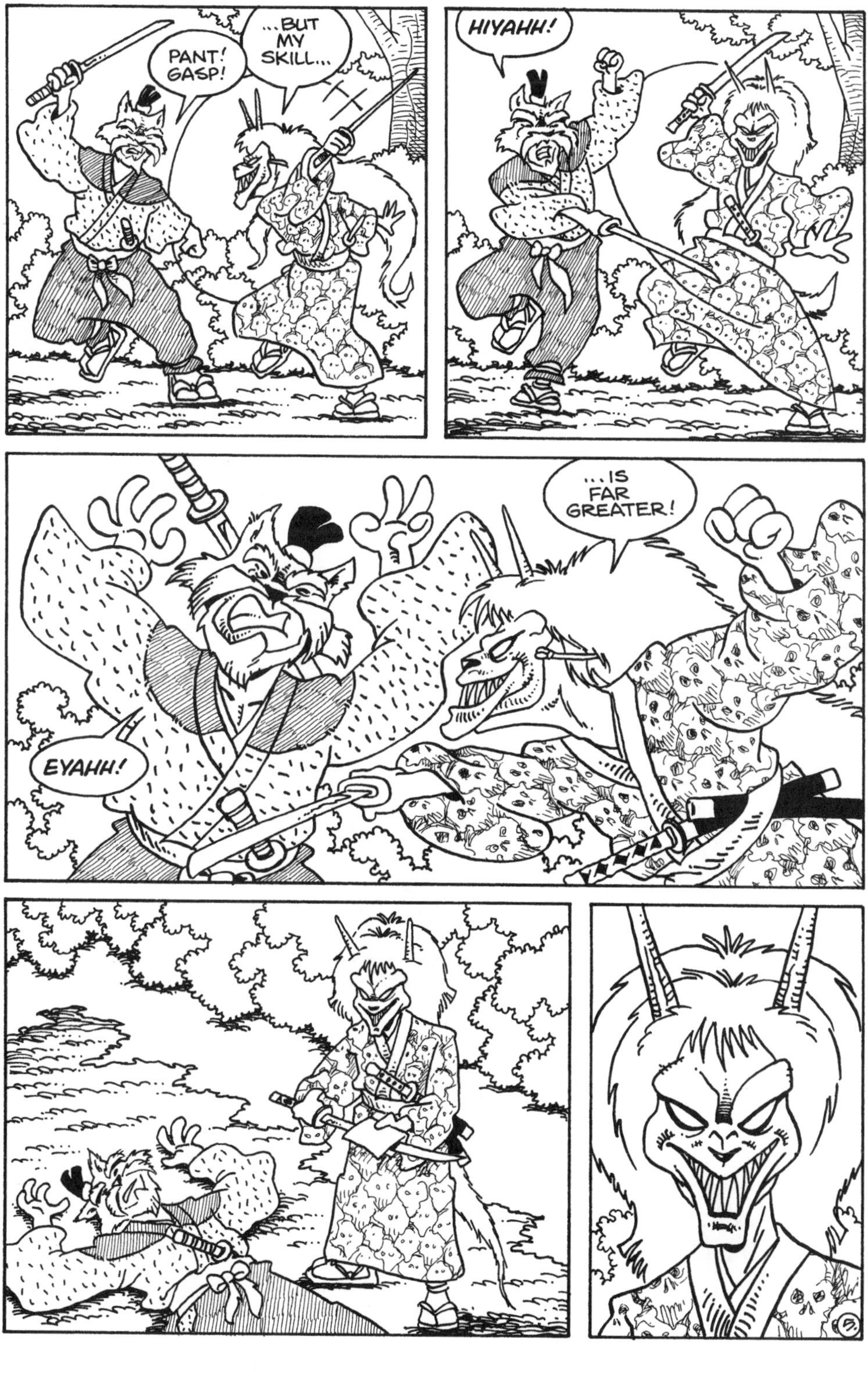
PANT! GASP!
...BUT MY SKILL...
HIYAHH!
...IS FAR GREATER!
EYAHH!

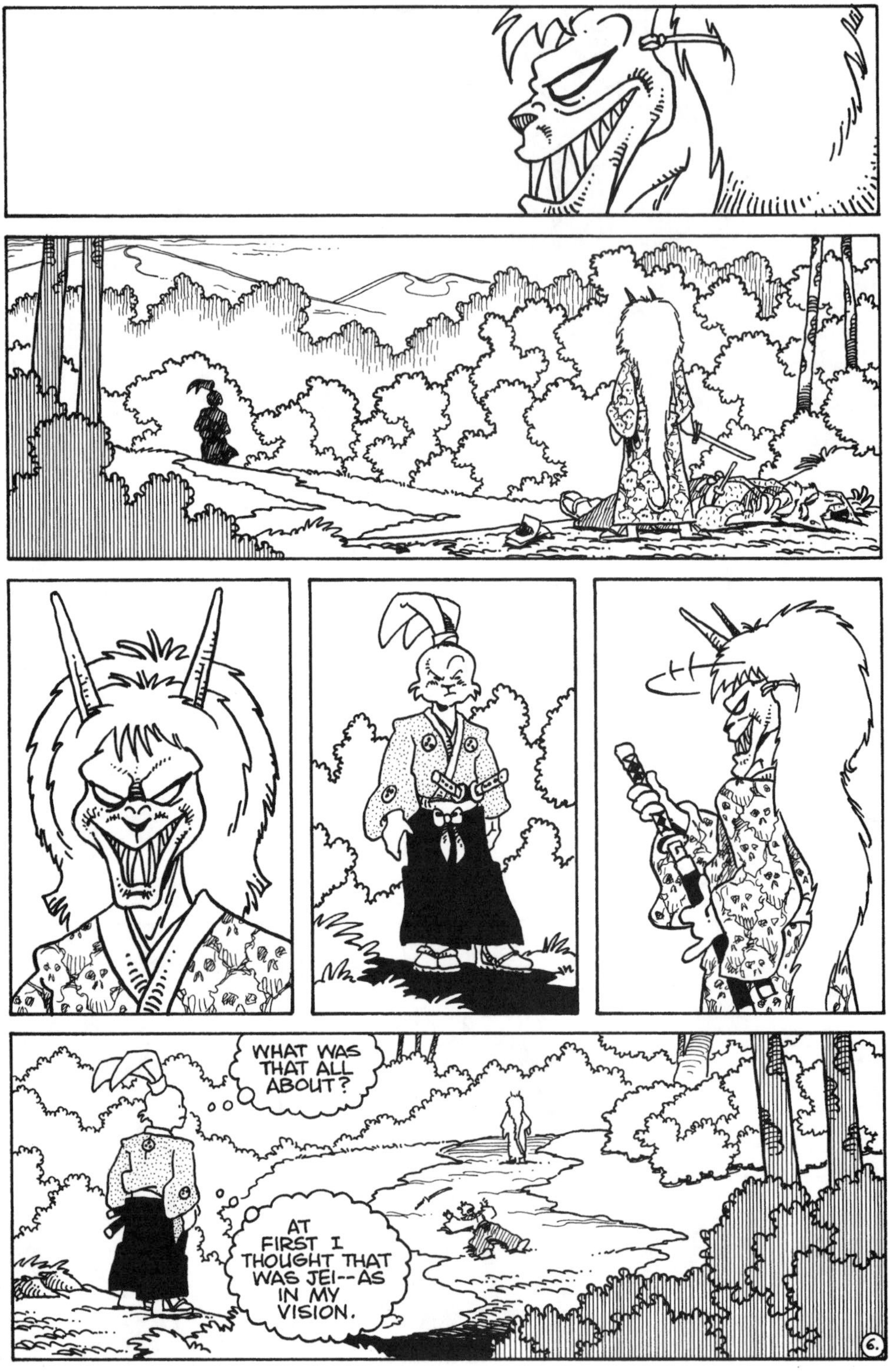
WHAT WAS THAT ALL ABOUT?
AT FIRST I THOUGHT THAT WAS JEI--AS IN MY VISION.
6.

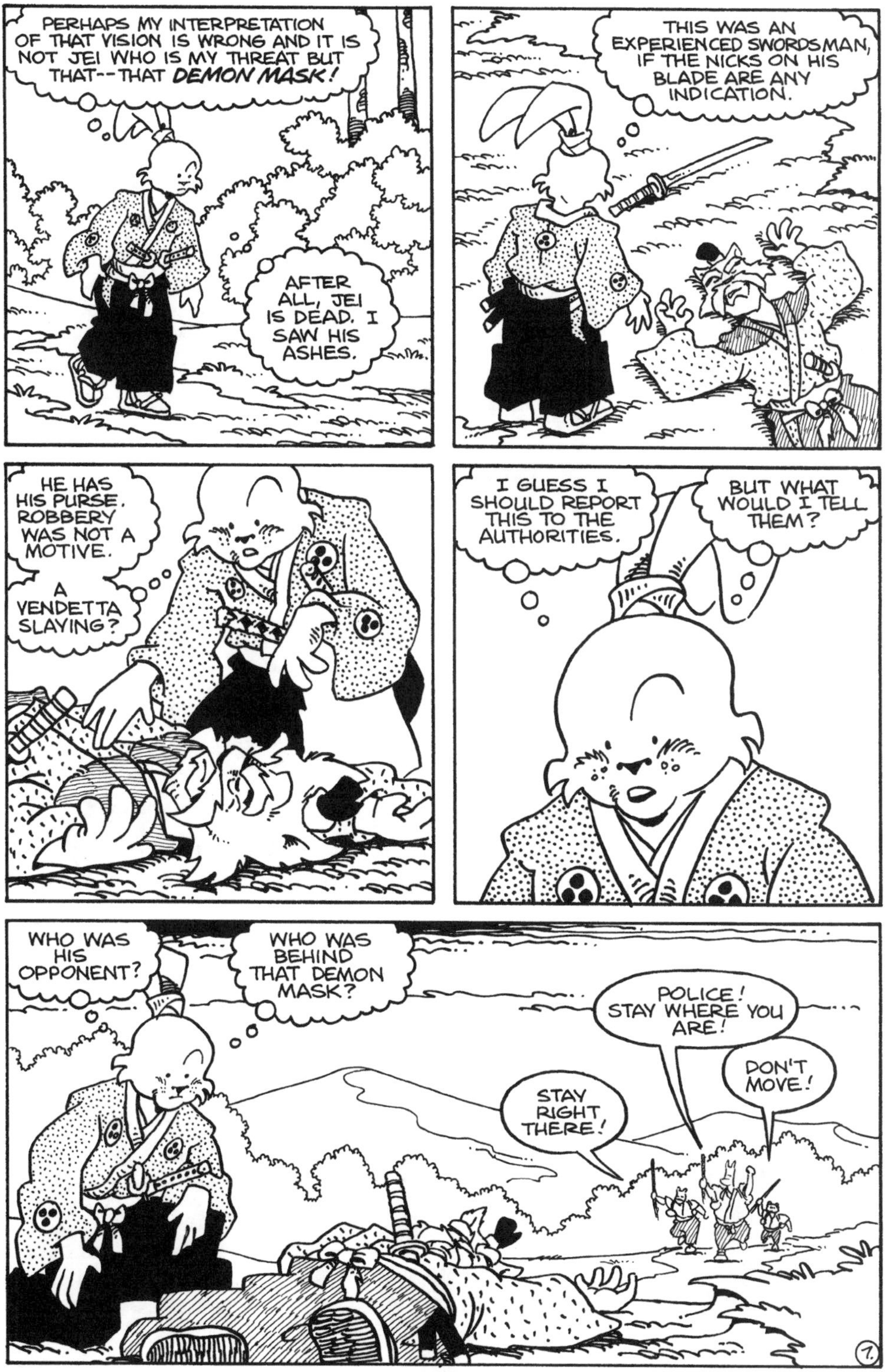
PERHAPS MY INTERPRETATION OF THAT VISION IS WRONG AND IT IS NOT JEI WHO IS MY THREAT BUT THAT--THAT *DEMON MASK!*
AFTER ALL, JEI IS DEAD. I SAW HIS ASHES.
THIS WAS AN EXPERIENCED SWORDSMAN, IF THE NICKS ON HIS BLADE ARE ANY INDICATION.
HE HAS HIS PURSE. ROBBERY WAS NOT A MOTIVE.
A VENDETTA SLAYING?
I GUESS I SHOULD REPORT THIS TO THE AUTHORITIES.
BUT WHAT WOULD I TELL THEM?
WHO WAS HIS OPPONENT?
WHO WAS BEHIND THAT DEMON MASK?
POLICE! STAY WHERE YOU ARE!
STAY RIGHT THERE!
DON'T MOVE!
7.

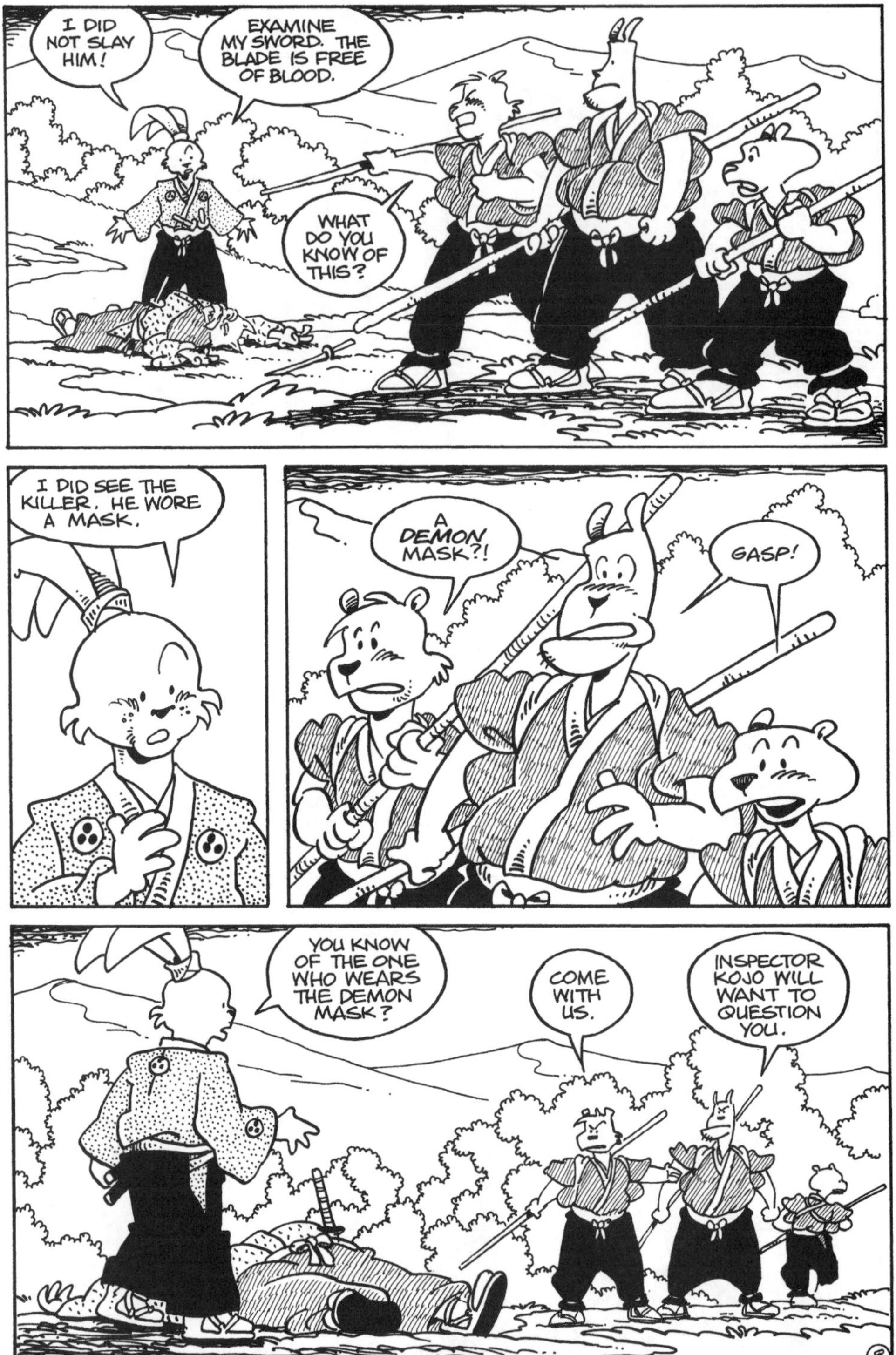
I DID NOT SLAY HIM!
EXAMINE MY SWORD. THE BLADE IS FREE OF BLOOD.
WHAT DO YOU KNOW OF THIS?
I DID SEE THE KILLER. HE WORE A MASK.
A DEMON MASK?!
GASP!
YOU KNOW OF THE ONE WHO WEARS THE DEMON MASK?
COME WITH US.
INSPECTOR KOJO WILL WANT TO QUESTION YOU.
8.

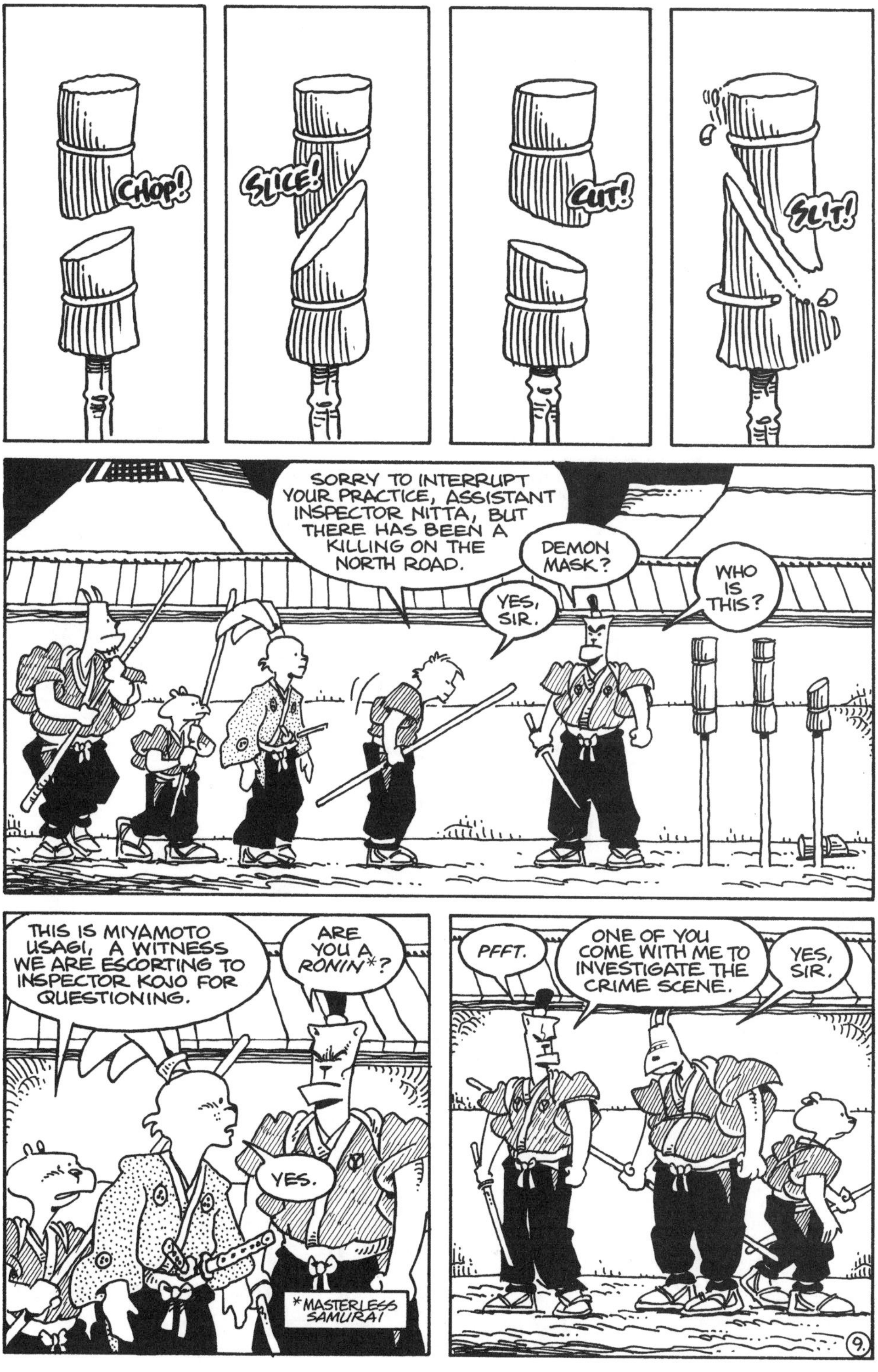
CHOP!
SLICE!
CUT!
SLIT!
SORRY TO INTERRUPT YOUR PRACTICE, ASSISTANT INSPECTOR NITTA, BUT THERE HAS BEEN A KILLING ON THE NORTH ROAD.
DEMON MASK?
YES, SIR.
WHO IS THIS?
THIS IS MIYAMOTO USAGI, A WITNESS WE ARE ESCORTING TO INSPECTOR KOJO FOR QUESTIONING.
ARE YOU A RONIN*?
YES.
*MASTERLESS SAMURAI
PFFT.
ONE OF YOU COME WITH ME TO INVESTIGATE THE CRIME SCENE.
YES, SIR.
9.

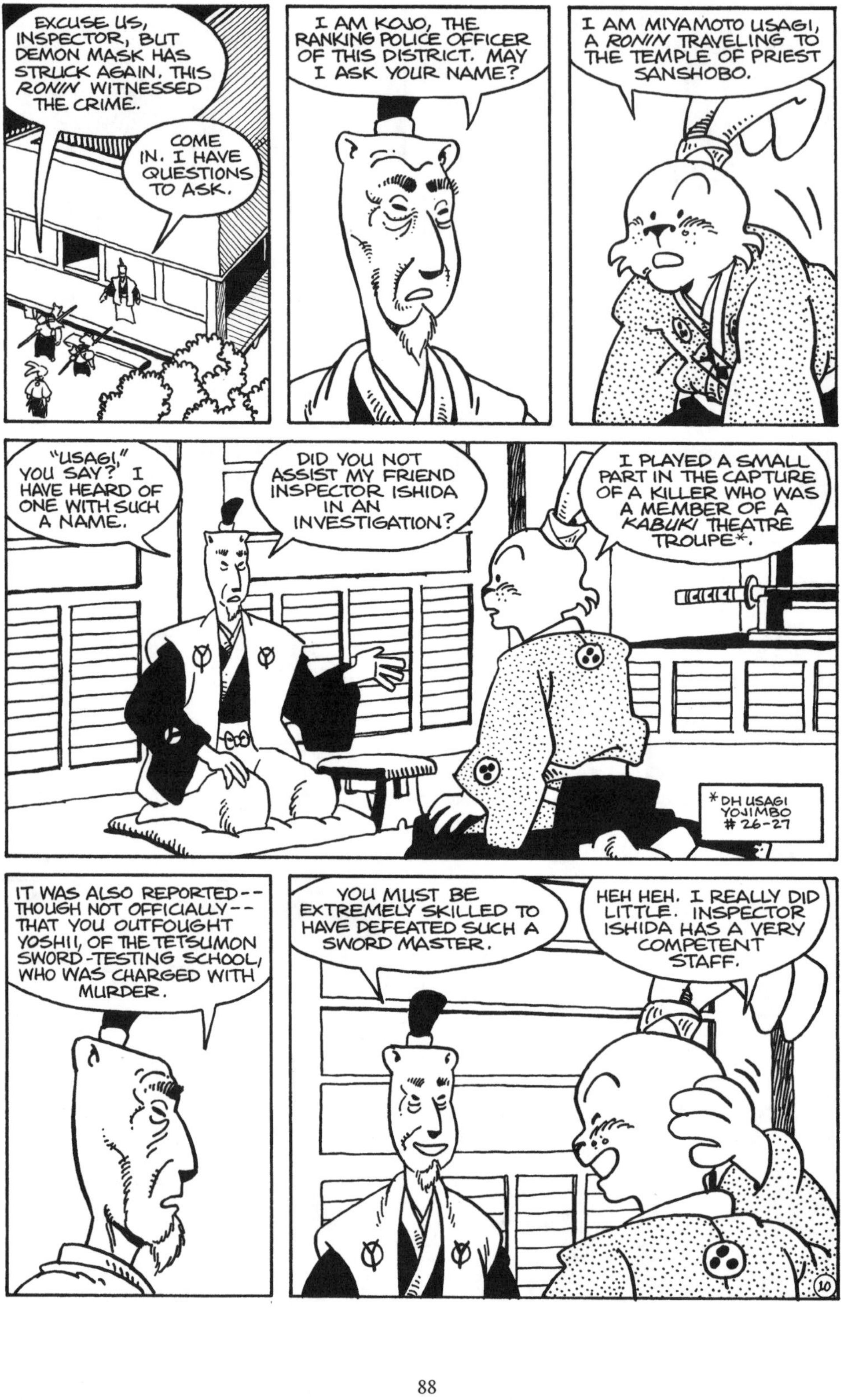
EXCUSE US, INSPECTOR, BUT DEMON MASK HAS STRUCK AGAIN. THIS *RONIN* WITNESSED THE CRIME.
COME IN. I HAVE QUESTIONS TO ASK.
I AM KOJO, THE RANKING POLICE OFFICER OF THIS DISTRICT. MAY I ASK YOUR NAME?
I AM MIYAMOTO USAGI, A *RONIN* TRAVELING TO THE TEMPLE OF PRIEST SANSHOBO.
"USAGI," YOU SAY? I HAVE HEARD OF ONE WITH SUCH A NAME.
DID YOU NOT ASSIST MY FRIEND INSPECTOR ISHIDA IN AN INVESTIGATION?
I PLAYED A SMALL PART IN THE CAPTURE OF A KILLER WHO WAS A MEMBER OF A *KABUKI* THEATRE TROUPE*.
*DH USAGI YOJIMBO #26-27
IT WAS ALSO REPORTED-- THOUGH NOT OFFICIALLY-- THAT YOU OUTFOUGHT YOSHII, OF THE TETSUMON SWORD-TESTING SCHOOL, WHO WAS CHARGED WITH MURDER.
YOU MUST BE EXTREMELY SKILLED TO HAVE DEFEATED SUCH A SWORD MASTER.
HEH HEH. I REALLY DID LITTLE. INSPECTOR ISHIDA HAS A VERY COMPETENT STAFF.
10

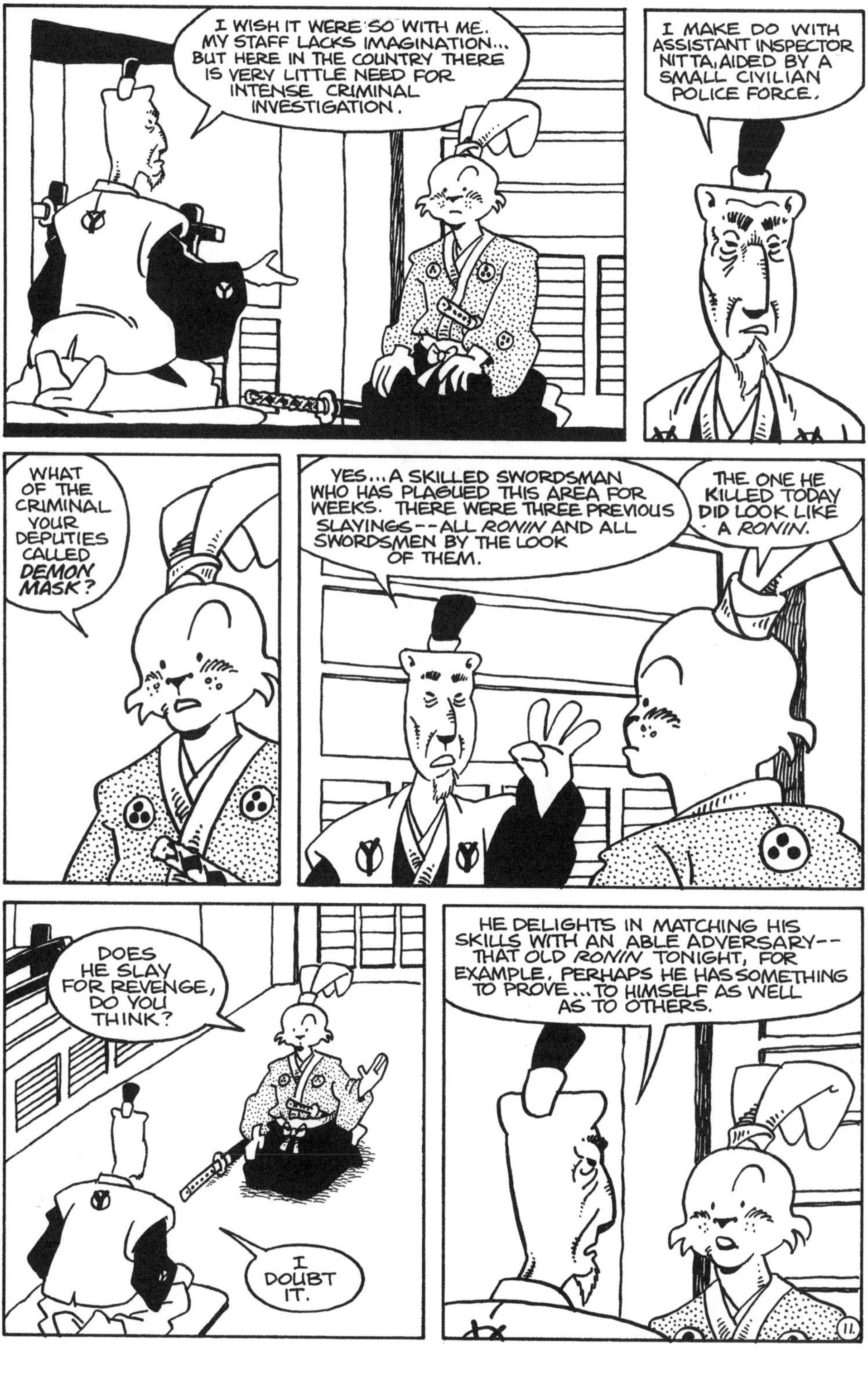
I WISH IT WERE SO WITH ME. MY STAFF LACKS IMAGINATION... BUT HERE IN THE COUNTRY THERE IS VERY LITTLE NEED FOR INTENSE CRIMINAL INVESTIGATION.
I MAKE DO WITH ASSISTANT INSPECTOR NITTA, AIDED BY A SMALL CIVILIAN POLICE FORCE.
WHAT OF THE CRIMINAL YOUR DEPUTIES CALLED *DEMON MASK*?
YES... A SKILLED SWORDSMAN WHO HAS PLAGUED THIS AREA FOR WEEKS. THERE WERE THREE PREVIOUS SLAYINGS--ALL *RONIN* AND ALL SWORDSMEN BY THE LOOK OF THEM.
THE ONE HE KILLED TODAY DID LOOK LIKE A *RONIN*.
DOES HE SLAY FOR REVENGE, DO YOU THINK?
I DOUBT IT.
HE DELIGHTS IN MATCHING HIS SKILLS WITH AN ABLE ADVERSARY-- THAT OLD *RONIN* TONIGHT, FOR EXAMPLE. PERHAPS HE HAS SOMETHING TO PROVE... TO HIMSELF AS WELL AS TO OTHERS.
11.

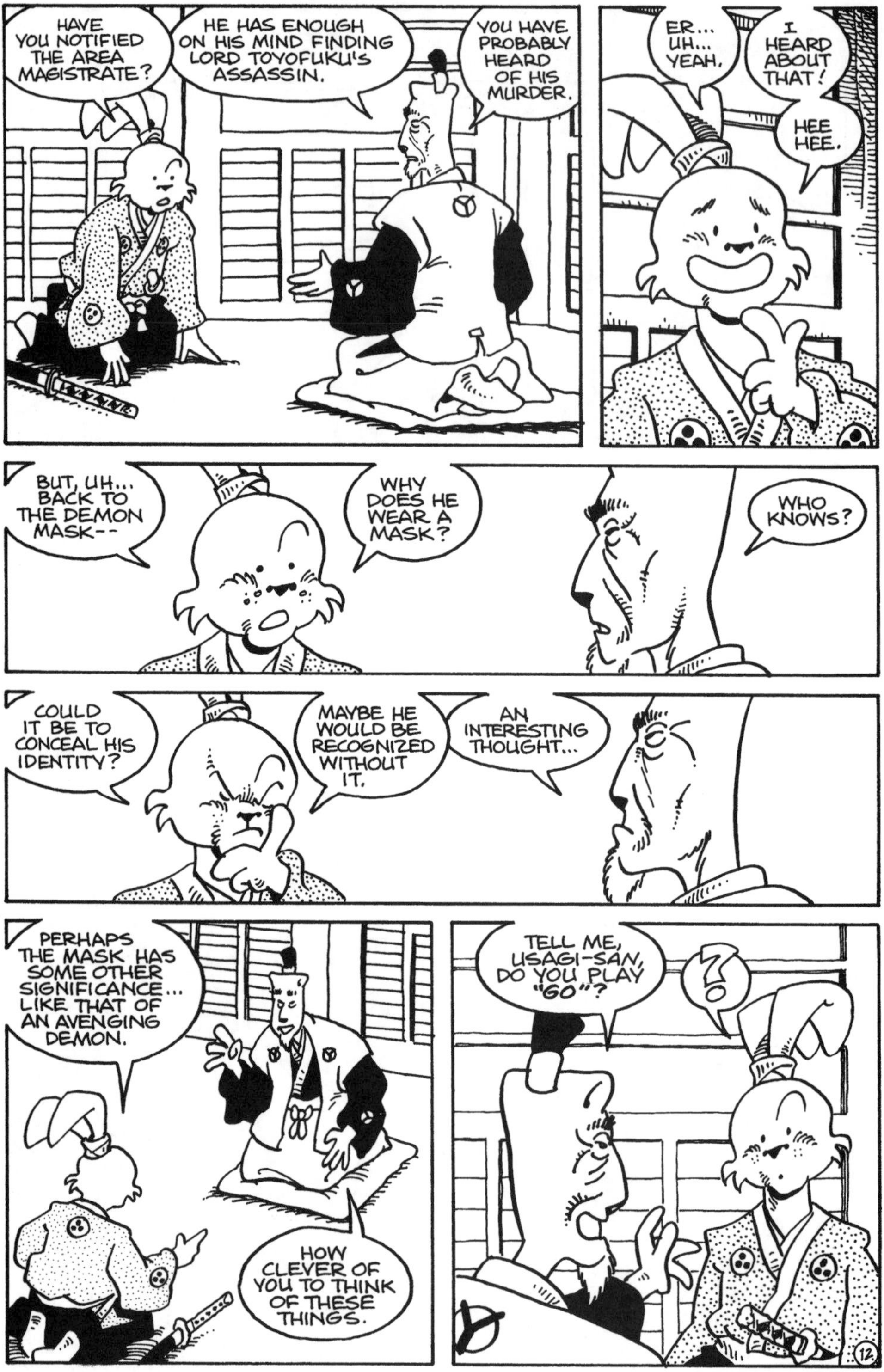
HAVE YOU NOTIFIED THE AREA MAGISTRATE?
HE HAS ENOUGH ON HIS MIND FINDING LORD TOYOFUKU'S ASSASSIN.
YOU HAVE PROBABLY HEARD OF HIS MURDER.
ER... UH... YEAH.
I HEARD ABOUT THAT!
HEE HEE.
BUT, UH... BACK TO THE DEMON MASK--
WHY DOES HE WEAR A MASK?
WHO KNOWS?
COULD IT BE TO CONCEAL HIS IDENTITY?
MAYBE HE WOULD BE RECOGNIZED WITHOUT IT.
AN INTERESTING THOUGHT...
PERHAPS THE MASK HAS SOME OTHER SIGNIFICANCE... LIKE THAT OF AN AVENGING DEMON.
HOW CLEVER OF YOU TO THINK OF THESE THINGS.
TELL ME, USAGI-SAN, DO YOU PLAY "GO"?
?
12

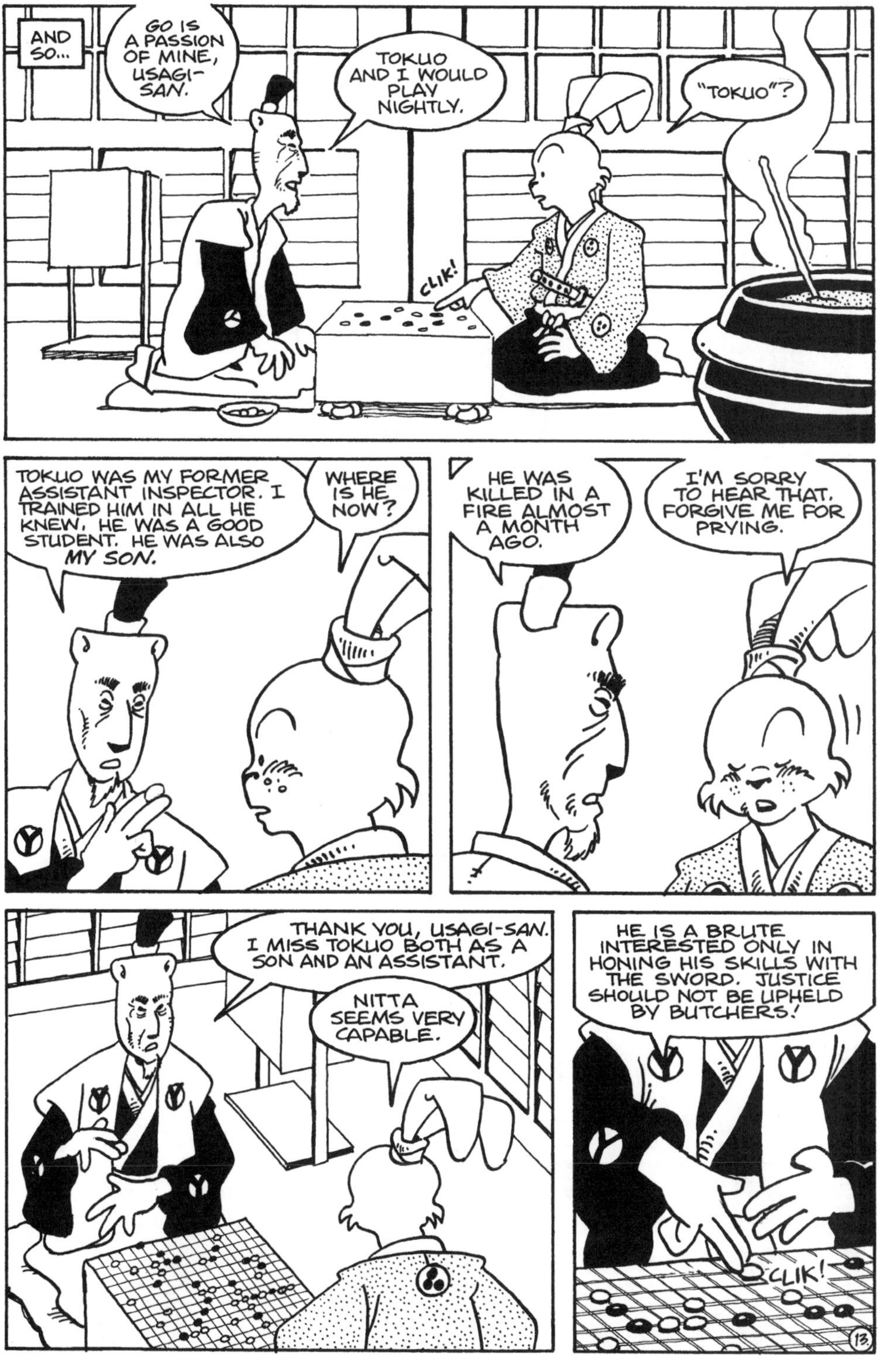
AND SO...
GO IS A PASSION OF MINE, USAGI-SAN.
TOKUO AND I WOULD PLAY NIGHTLY.
"TOKUO"?
CLIK!
TOKUO WAS MY FORMER ASSISTANT INSPECTOR. I TRAINED HIM IN ALL HE KNEW. HE WAS A GOOD STUDENT. HE WAS ALSO MY SON.
WHERE IS HE NOW?
HE WAS KILLED IN A FIRE ALMOST A MONTH AGO.
I'M SORRY TO HEAR THAT. FORGIVE ME FOR PRYING.
THANK YOU, USAGI-SAN. I MISS TOKUO BOTH AS A SON AND AN ASSISTANT.
NITTA SEEMS VERY CAPABLE.
HE IS A BRUTE INTERESTED ONLY IN HONING HIS SKILLS WITH THE SWORD. JUSTICE SHOULD NOT BE UPHELD BY BUTCHERS!
CLIK!
13.

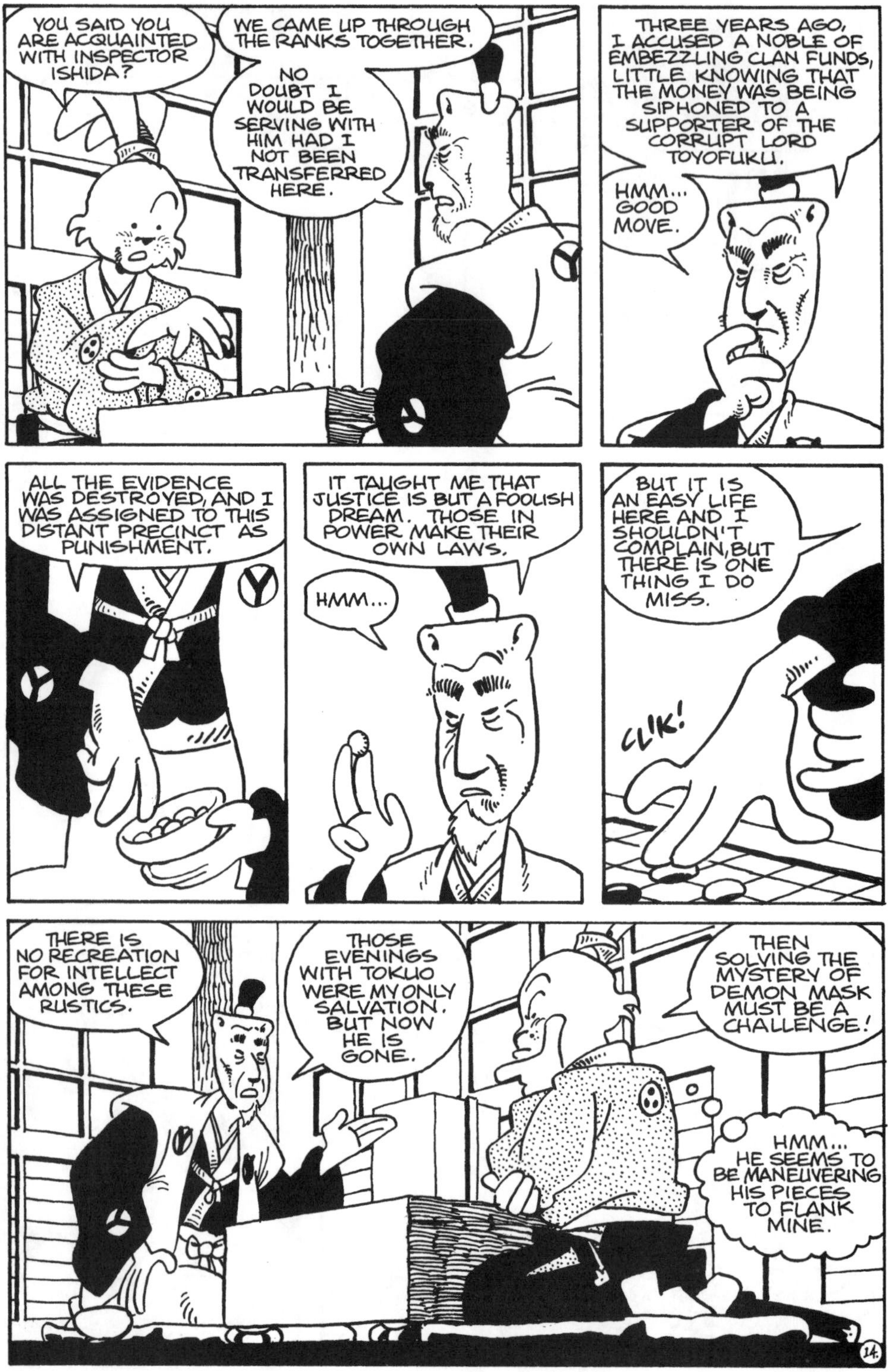
YOU SAID YOU ARE ACQUAINTED WITH INSPECTOR ISHIDA?
WE CAME UP THROUGH THE RANKS TOGETHER.
NO DOUBT I WOULD BE SERVING WITH HIM HAD I NOT BEEN TRANSFERRED HERE.
THREE YEARS AGO, I ACCUSED A NOBLE OF EMBEZZLING CLAN FUNDS, LITTLE KNOWING THAT THE MONEY WAS BEING SIPHONED TO A SUPPORTER OF THE CORRUPT LORD TOYOFUKU.
HMM... GOOD MOVE.
ALL THE EVIDENCE WAS DESTROYED, AND I WAS ASSIGNED TO THIS DISTANT PRECINCT AS PUNISHMENT.
IT TAUGHT ME THAT JUSTICE IS BUT A FOOLISH DREAM. THOSE IN POWER MAKE THEIR OWN LAWS.
HMM...
BUT IT IS AN EASY LIFE HERE AND I SHOULDN'T COMPLAIN, BUT THERE IS ONE THING I DO MISS.
CLIK!
THERE IS NO RECREATION FOR INTELLECT AMONG THESE RUSTICS.
THOSE EVENINGS WITH TOKUO WERE MY ONLY SALVATION. BUT NOW HE IS GONE.
THEN SOLVING THE MYSTERY OF DEMON MASK MUST BE A CHALLENGE!
HMM... HE SEEMS TO BE MANEUVERING HIS PIECES TO FLANK MINE.
14.

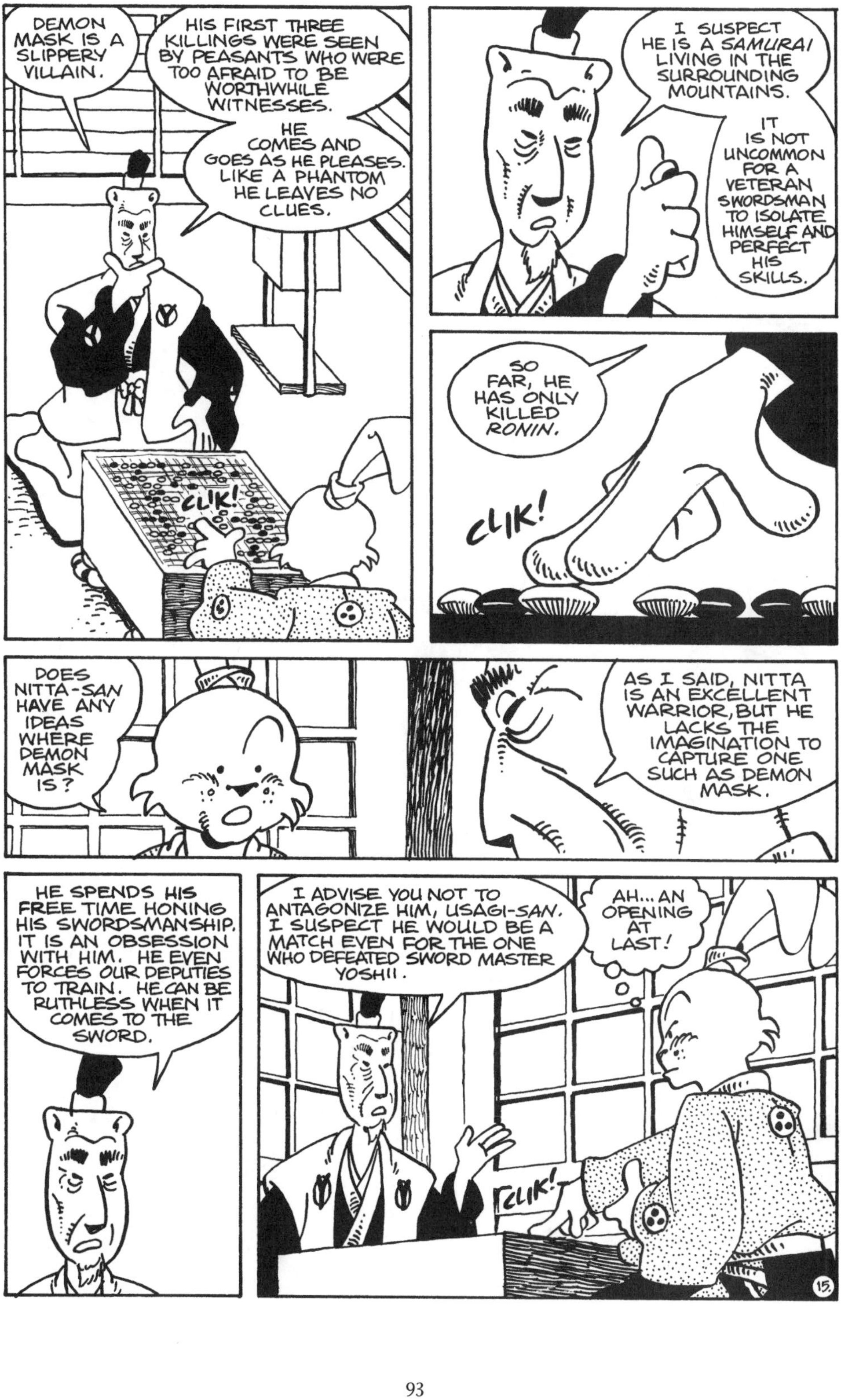
DEMON MASK IS A SLIPPERY VILLAIN.
HIS FIRST THREE KILLINGS WERE SEEN BY PEASANTS WHO WERE TOO AFRAID TO BE WORTHWHILE WITNESSES.
HE COMES AND GOES AS HE PLEASES. LIKE A PHANTOM HE LEAVES NO CLUES.
CLIK!
I SUSPECT HE IS A *SAMURAI* LIVING IN THE SURROUNDING MOUNTAINS.
IT IS NOT UNCOMMON FOR A VETERAN SWORDSMAN TO ISOLATE HIMSELF AND PERFECT HIS SKILLS.
SO FAR, HE HAS ONLY KILLED *RONIN*.
CLIK!
DOES NITTA-*SAN* HAVE ANY IDEAS WHERE DEMON MASK IS?
AS I SAID, NITTA IS AN EXCELLENT WARRIOR, BUT HE LACKS THE IMAGINATION TO CAPTURE ONE SUCH AS DEMON MASK.
HE SPENDS HIS FREE TIME HONING HIS SWORDSMANSHIP. IT IS AN OBSESSION WITH HIM. HE EVEN FORCES OUR DEPUTIES TO TRAIN. HE CAN BE RUTHLESS WHEN IT COMES TO THE SWORD.
I ADVISE YOU NOT TO ANTAGONIZE HIM, USAGI-*SAN*. I SUSPECT HE WOULD BE A MATCH EVEN FOR THE ONE WHO DEFEATED SWORD MASTER YOSHII.
AH... AN OPENING AT LAST!
CLIK!
15.

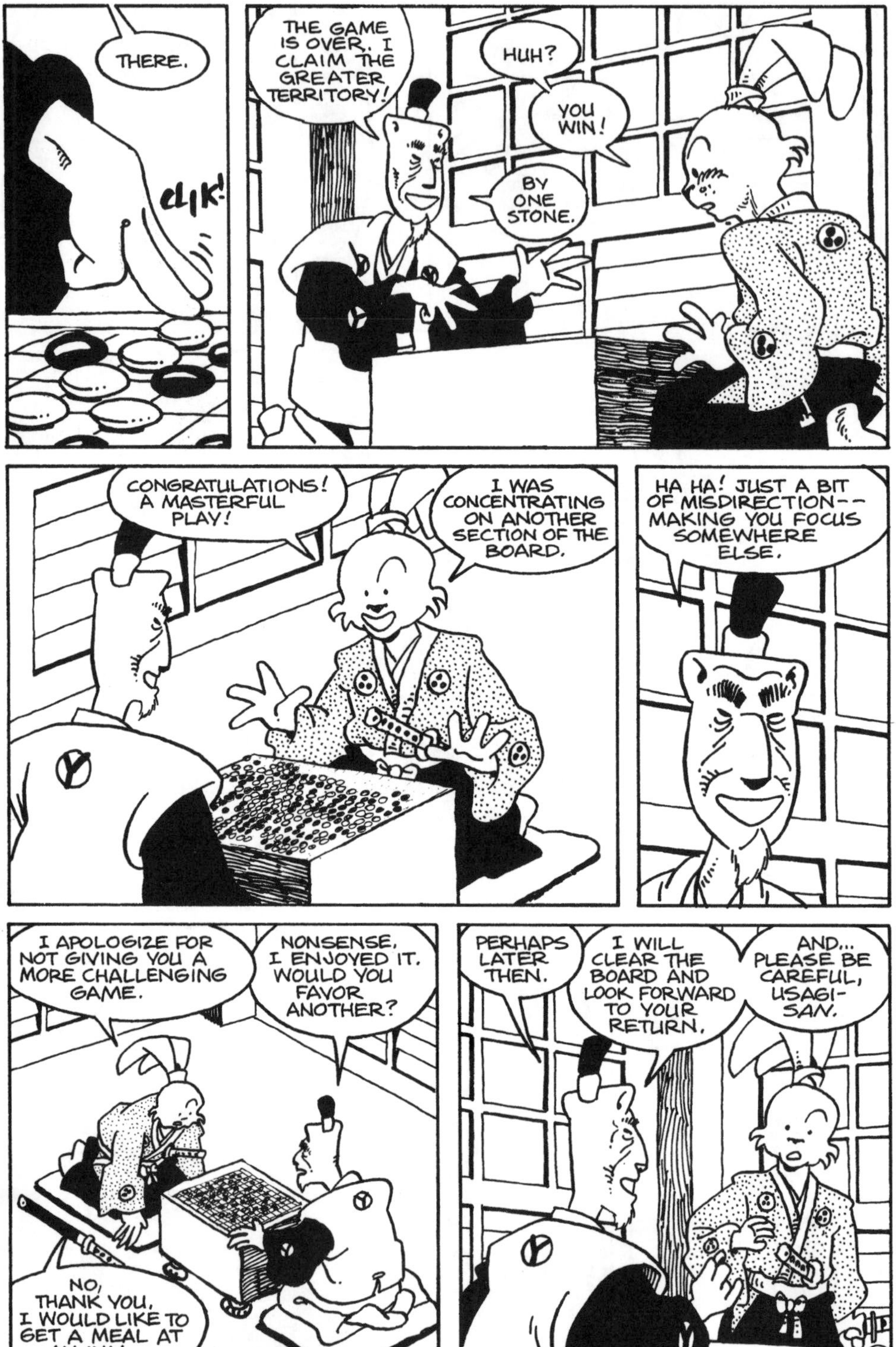
THERE.
CLIK!
THE GAME IS OVER. I CLAIM THE GREATER TERRITORY!
HUH?
YOU WIN!
BY ONE STONE.
CONGRATULATIONS! A MASTERFUL PLAY!
I WAS CONCENTRATING ON ANOTHER SECTION OF THE BOARD.
HA HA! JUST A BIT OF MISDIRECTION-- MAKING YOU FOCUS SOMEWHERE ELSE.
I APOLOGIZE FOR NOT GIVING YOU A MORE CHALLENGING GAME.
NONSENSE. I ENJOYED IT. WOULD YOU FAVOR ANOTHER?
NO, THANK YOU. I WOULD LIKE TO GET A MEAL AT AN INN.
PERHAPS LATER THEN.
I WILL CLEAR THE BOARD AND LOOK FORWARD TO YOUR RETURN.
AND... PLEASE BE CAREFUL, USAGI-SAN.
16

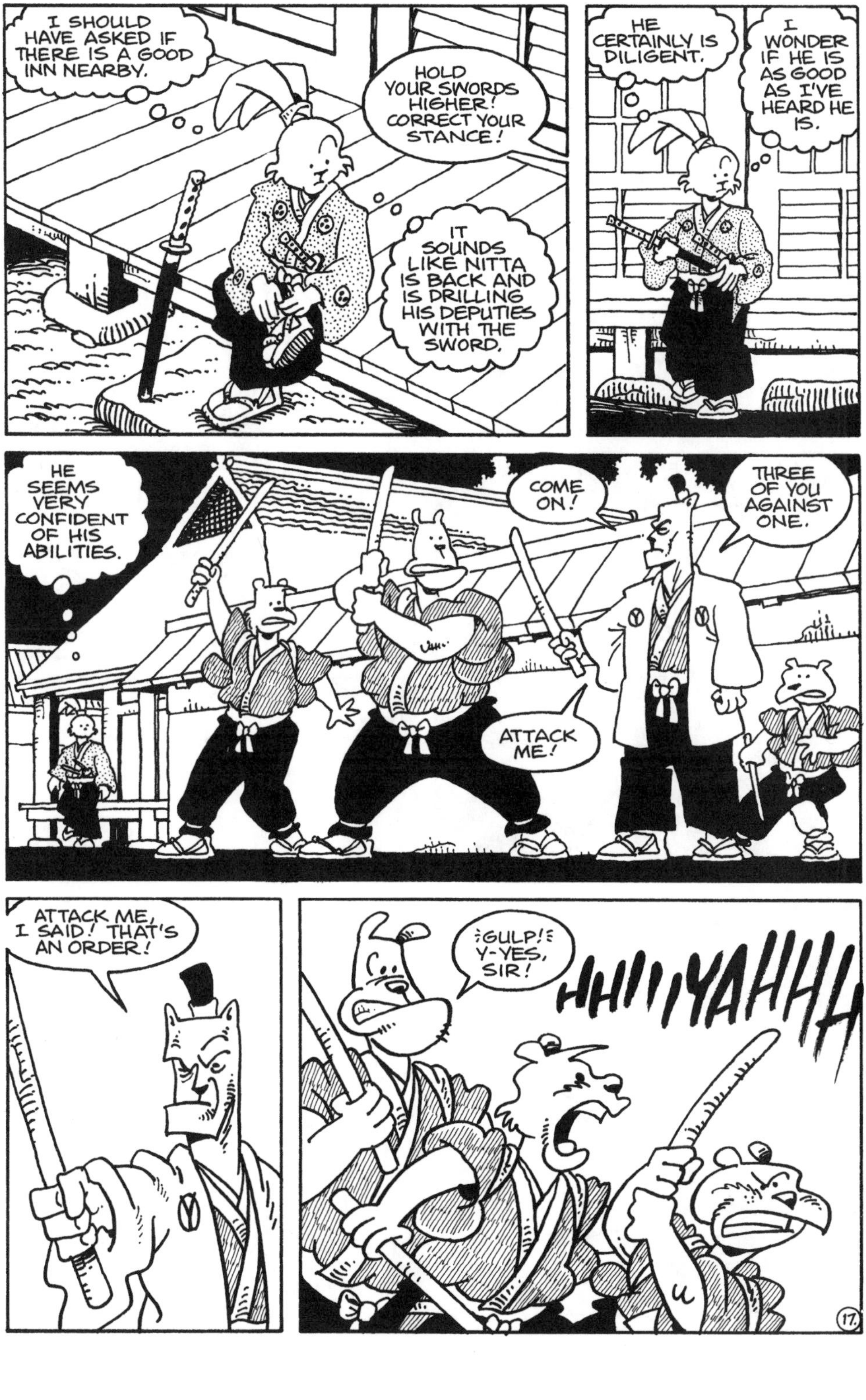
I SHOULD HAVE ASKED IF THERE IS A GOOD INN NEARBY.
HOLD YOUR SWORDS HIGHER! CORRECT YOUR STANCE!
IT SOUNDS LIKE NITTA IS BACK AND IS DRILLING HIS DEPUTIES WITH THE SWORD.
HE CERTAINLY IS DILIGENT.
I WONDER IF HE IS AS GOOD AS I'VE HEARD HE IS.
HE SEEMS VERY CONFIDENT OF HIS ABILITIES.
COME ON!
THREE OF YOU AGAINST ONE.
ATTACK ME!
ATTACK ME, I SAID! THAT'S AN ORDER!
GULP! Y-YES, SIR!
HHIIIYAHHH
17.

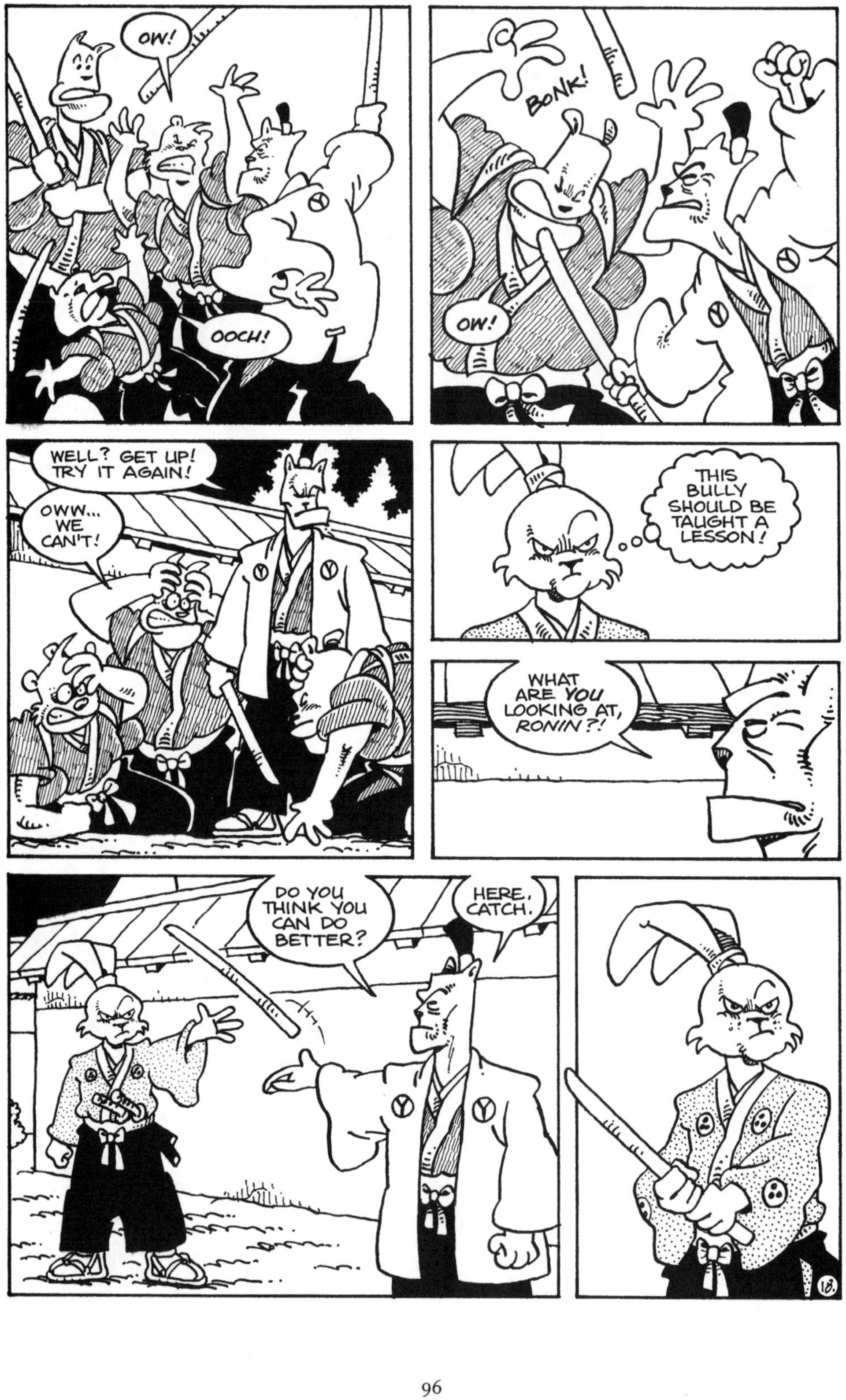
OW!
OOCH!
BONK!
OW!
WELL? GET UP! TRY IT AGAIN!
OWW... WE CAN'T!
THIS BULLY SHOULD BE TAUGHT A LESSON!
WHAT ARE *YOU* LOOKING AT, *RONIN*?!
DO YOU THINK YOU CAN DO BETTER?
HERE, CATCH.
18.

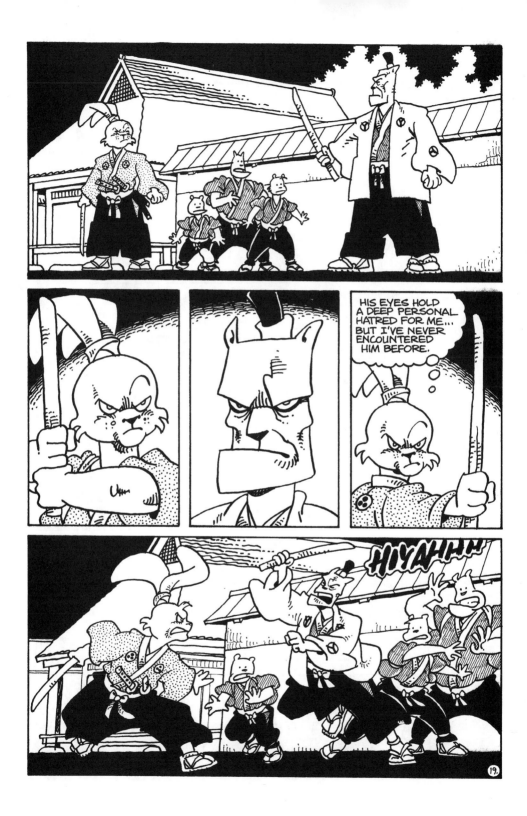

HIS EYES HOLD A DEEP PERSONAL HATRED FOR ME... BUT I'VE NEVER ENCOUNTERED HIM BEFORE.

HIYAHHH

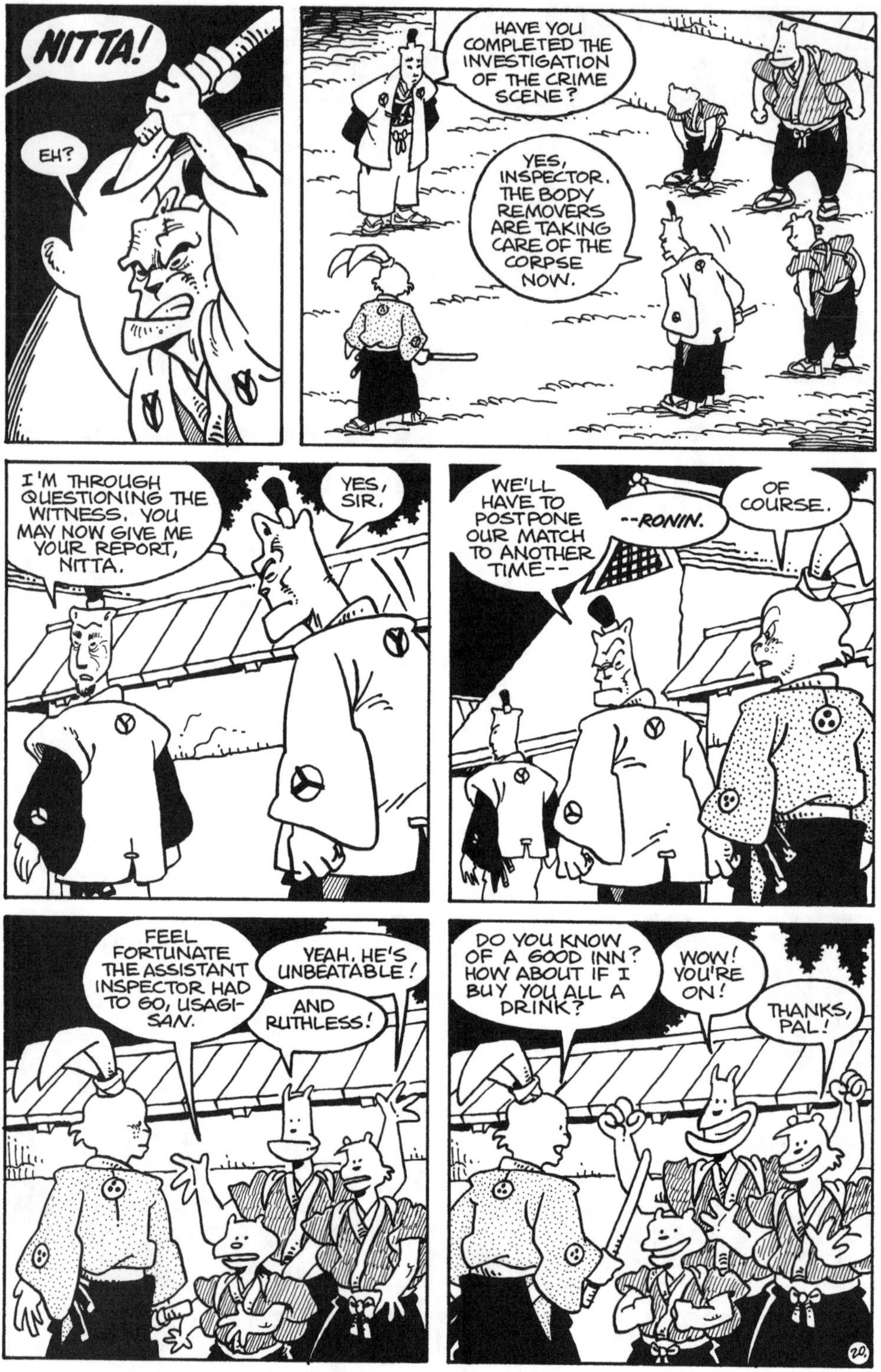
NITTA!
EH?
HAVE YOU COMPLETED THE INVESTIGATION OF THE CRIME SCENE?
YES, INSPECTOR. THE BODY REMOVERS ARE TAKING CARE OF THE CORPSE NOW.
I'M THROUGH QUESTIONING THE WITNESS. YOU MAY NOW GIVE ME YOUR REPORT, NITTA.
YES, SIR.
WE'LL HAVE TO POSTPONE OUR MATCH TO ANOTHER TIME--
--RONIN.
OF COURSE.
FEEL FORTUNATE THE ASSISTANT INSPECTOR HAD TO GO, USAGI-SAN.
YEAH, HE'S UNBEATABLE!
AND RUTHLESS!
DO YOU KNOW OF A GOOD INN? HOW ABOUT IF I BUY YOU ALL A DRINK?
WOW! YOU'RE ON!
THANKS, PAL!
20.

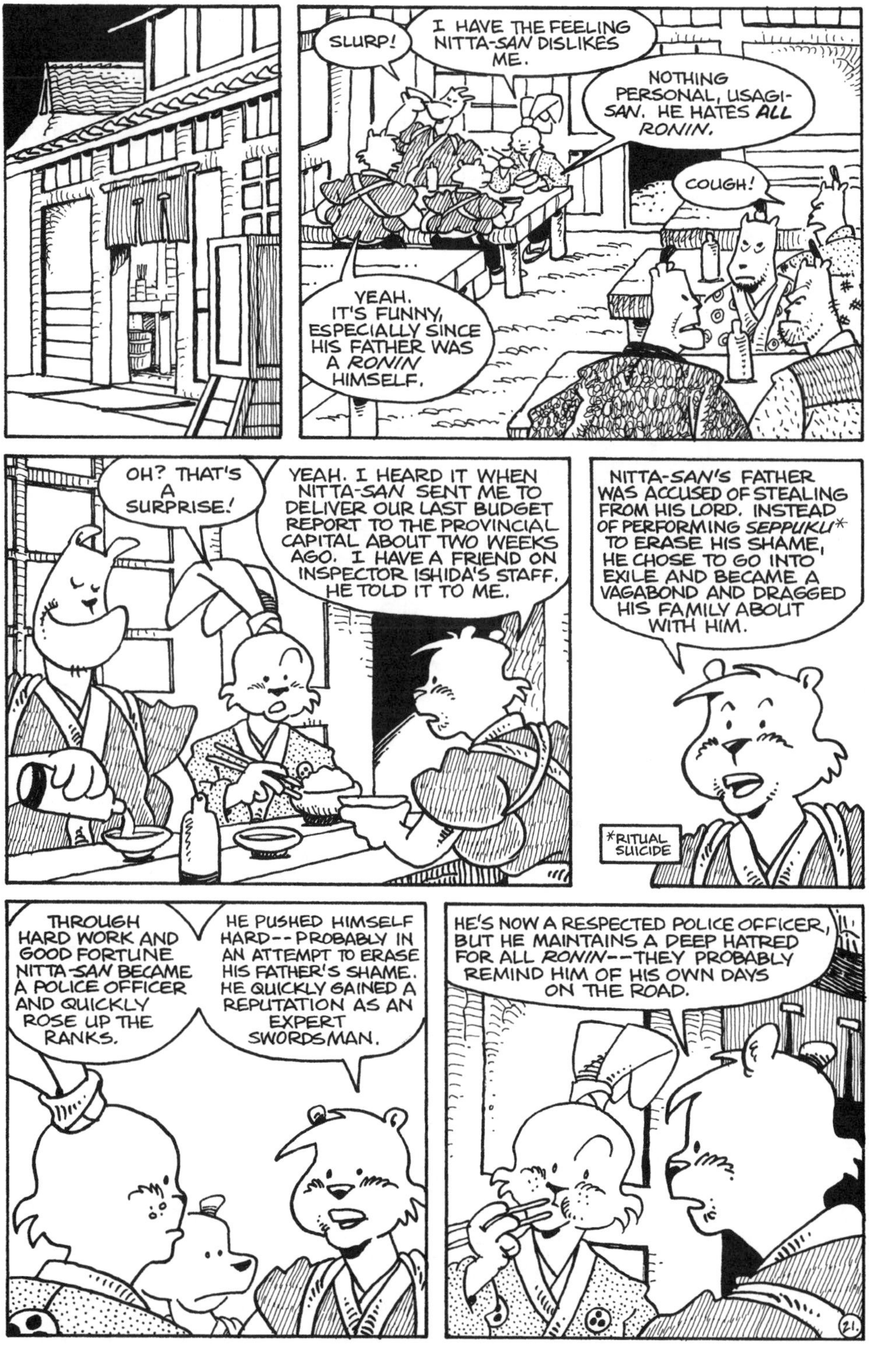
SLURP!
I HAVE THE FEELING NITTA-SAN DISLIKES ME.
NOTHING PERSONAL, USAGI-SAN. HE HATES ALL RONIN.
COUGH!
YEAH. IT'S FUNNY, ESPECIALLY SINCE HIS FATHER WAS A RONIN HIMSELF.
OH? THAT'S A SURPRISE!
YEAH. I HEARD IT WHEN NITTA-SAN SENT ME TO DELIVER OUR LAST BUDGET REPORT TO THE PROVINCIAL CAPITAL ABOUT TWO WEEKS AGO. I HAVE A FRIEND ON INSPECTOR ISHIDA'S STAFF. HE TOLD IT TO ME.
NITTA-SAN'S FATHER WAS ACCUSED OF STEALING FROM HIS LORD. INSTEAD OF PERFORMING SEPPUKU* TO ERASE HIS SHAME, HE CHOSE TO GO INTO EXILE AND BECAME A VAGABOND AND DRAGGED HIS FAMILY ABOUT WITH HIM.
*RITUAL SUICIDE
THROUGH HARD WORK AND GOOD FORTUNE NITTA-SAN BECAME A POLICE OFFICER AND QUICKLY ROSE UP THE RANKS.
HE PUSHED HIMSELF HARD--PROBABLY IN AN ATTEMPT TO ERASE HIS FATHER'S SHAME. HE QUICKLY GAINED A REPUTATION AS AN EXPERT SWORDSMAN.
HE'S NOW A RESPECTED POLICE OFFICER, BUT HE MAINTAINS A DEEP HATRED FOR ALL RONIN--THEY PROBABLY REMIND HIM OF HIS OWN DAYS ON THE ROAD.
21.

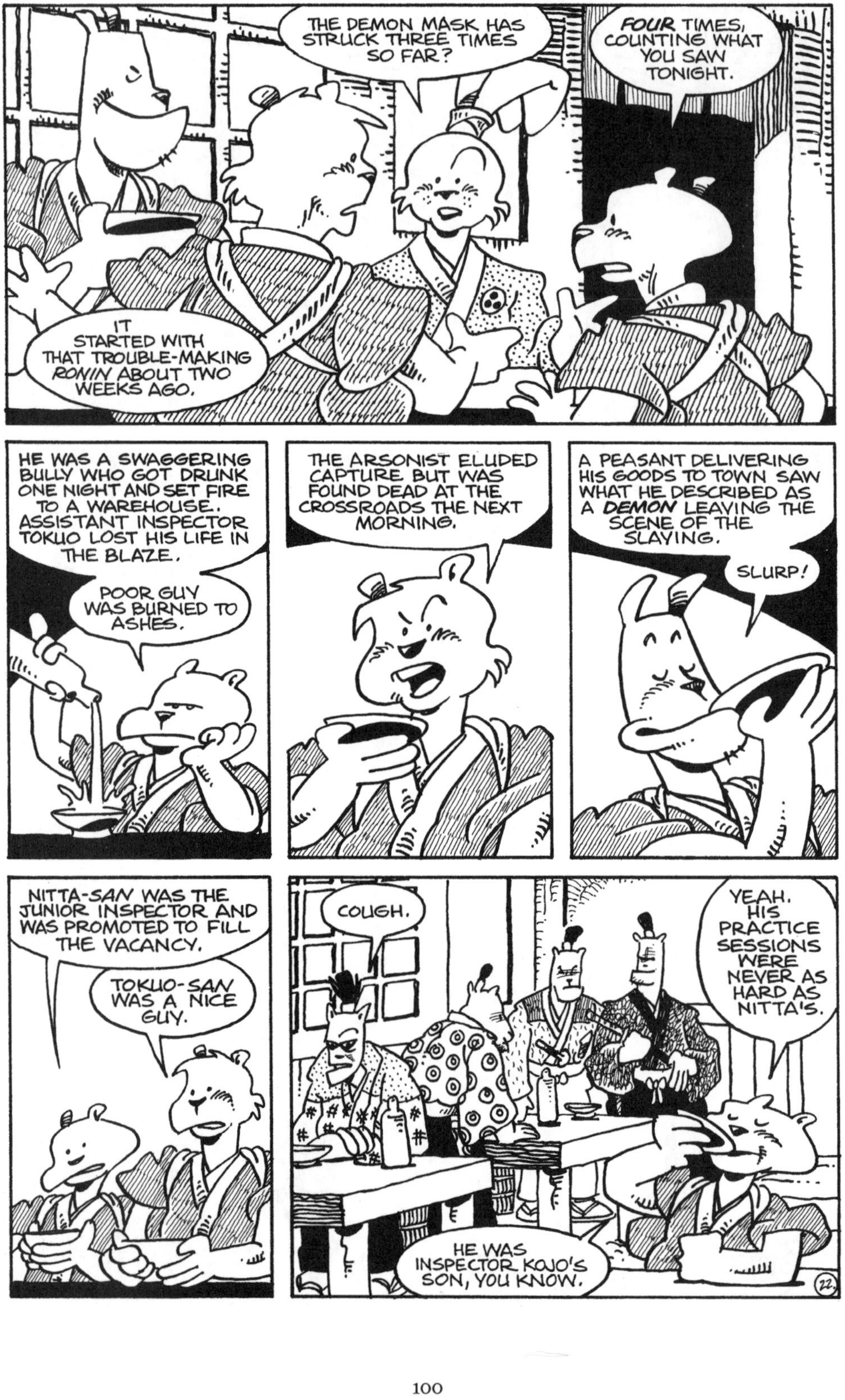
THE DEMON MASK HAS STRUCK THREE TIMES SO FAR?
FOUR TIMES, COUNTING WHAT YOU SAW TONIGHT.
IT STARTED WITH THAT TROUBLE-MAKING *RONIN* ABOUT TWO WEEKS AGO.
HE WAS A SWAGGERING BULLY WHO GOT DRUNK ONE NIGHT AND SET FIRE TO A WAREHOUSE. ASSISTANT INSPECTOR TOKUO LOST HIS LIFE IN THE BLAZE.
POOR GUY WAS BURNED TO ASHES.
THE ARSONIST ELUDED CAPTURE BUT WAS FOUND DEAD AT THE CROSSROADS THE NEXT MORNING.
A PEASANT DELIVERING HIS GOODS TO TOWN SAW WHAT HE DESCRIBED AS A *DEMON* LEAVING THE SCENE OF THE SLAYING.
SLURP!
NITTA-*SAN* WAS THE JUNIOR INSPECTOR AND WAS PROMOTED TO FILL THE VACANCY.
TOKUO-SAN WAS A NICE GUY.
COUGH.
YEAH. HIS PRACTICE SESSIONS WERE NEVER AS HARD AS NITTA'S.
HE WAS INSPECTOR KOJO'S SON, YOU KNOW.
22

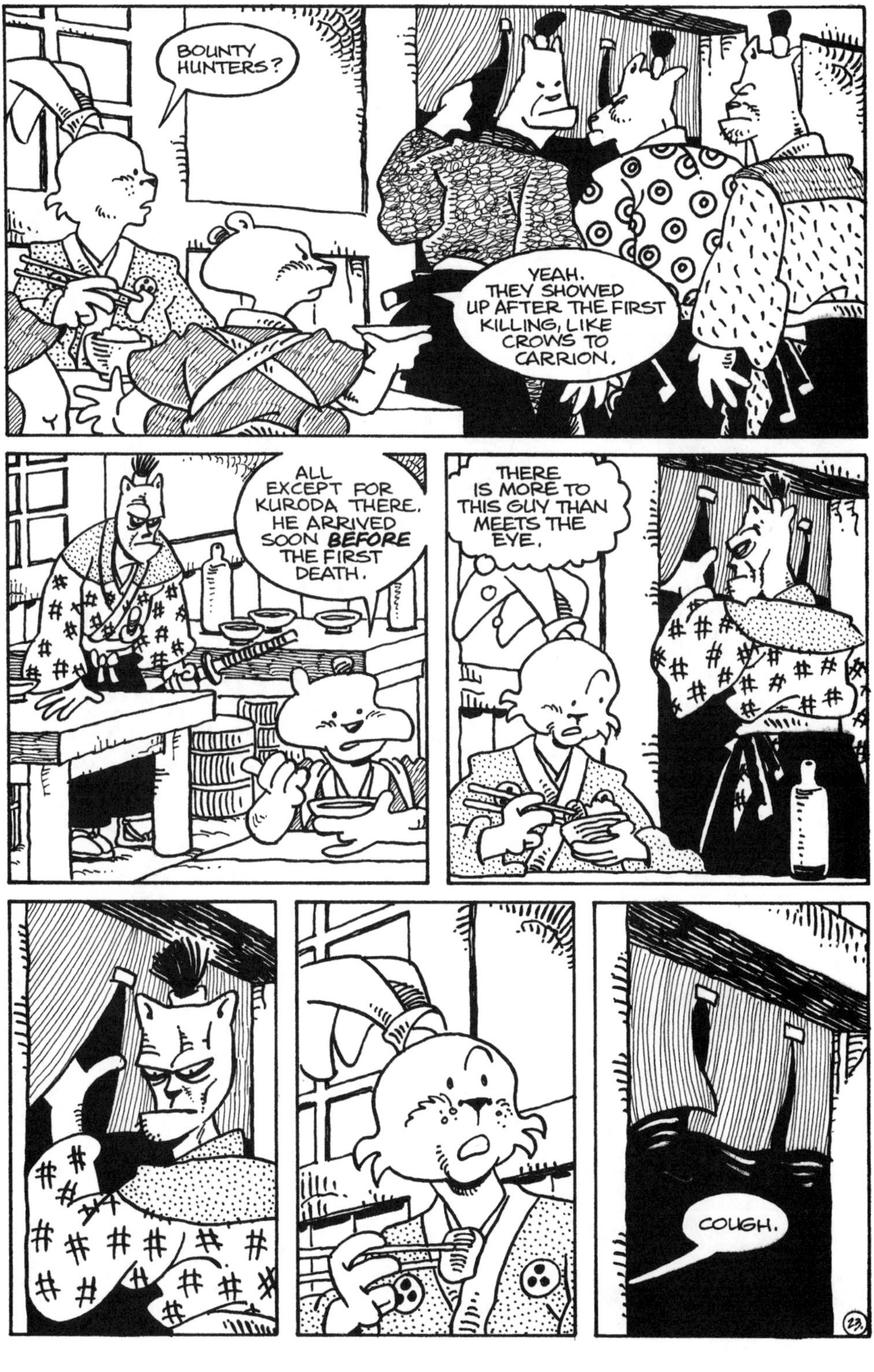
BOUNTY HUNTERS?
YEAH. THEY SHOWED UP AFTER THE FIRST KILLING, LIKE CROWS TO CARRION.
ALL EXCEPT FOR KURODA THERE. HE ARRIVED SOON **BEFORE** THE FIRST DEATH.
THERE IS MORE TO THIS GUY THAN MEETS THE EYE.
COUGH.
23.

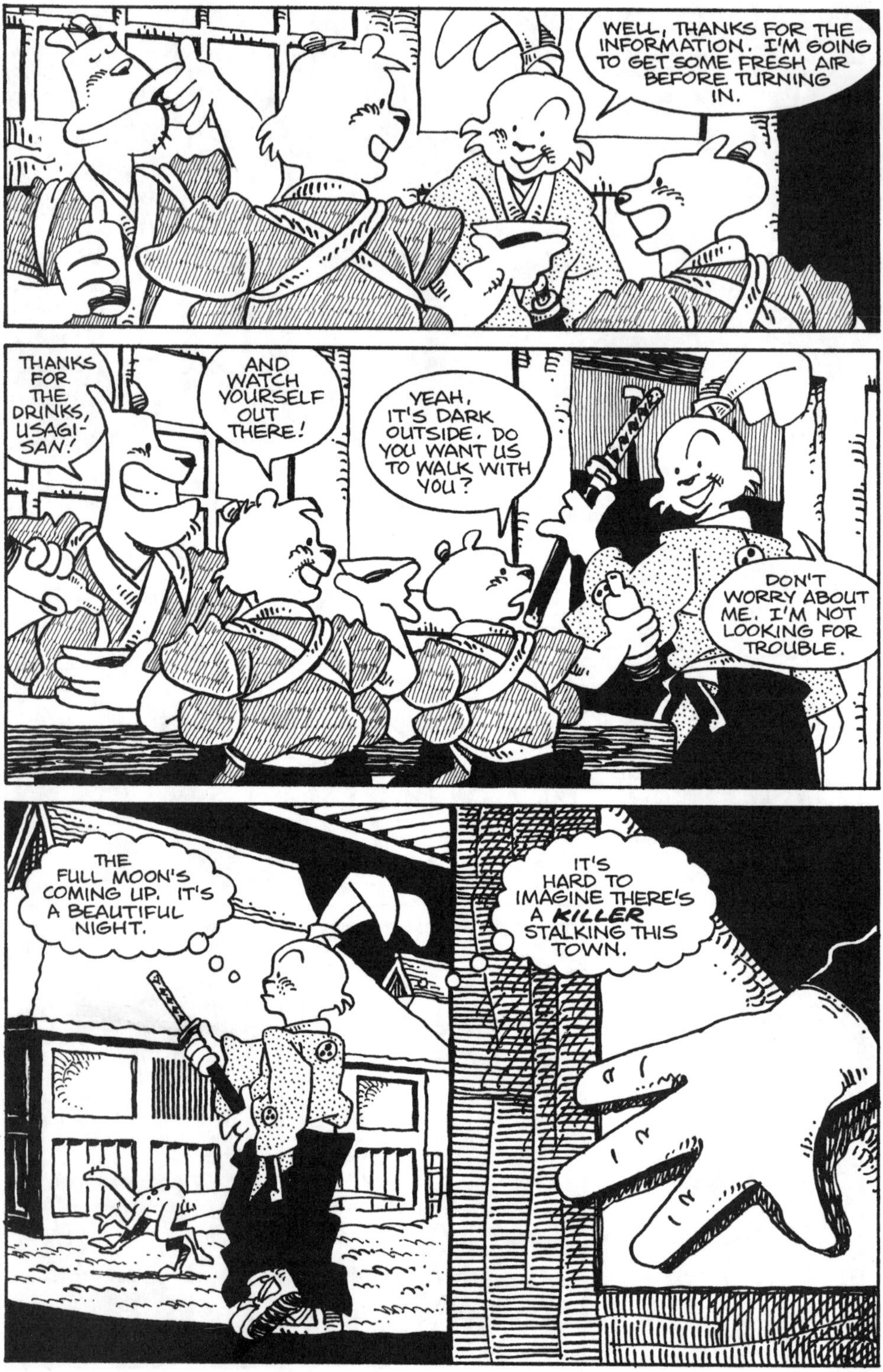
WELL, THANKS FOR THE INFORMATION. I'M GOING TO GET SOME FRESH AIR BEFORE TURNING IN.
THANKS FOR THE DRINKS, USAGI-SAN!
AND WATCH YOURSELF OUT THERE!
YEAH, IT'S DARK OUTSIDE. DO YOU WANT US TO WALK WITH YOU?
DON'T WORRY ABOUT ME. I'M NOT LOOKING FOR TROUBLE.
THE FULL MOON'S COMING UP. IT'S A BEAUTIFUL NIGHT.
IT'S HARD TO IMAGINE THERE'S A **KILLER** STALKING THIS TOWN.

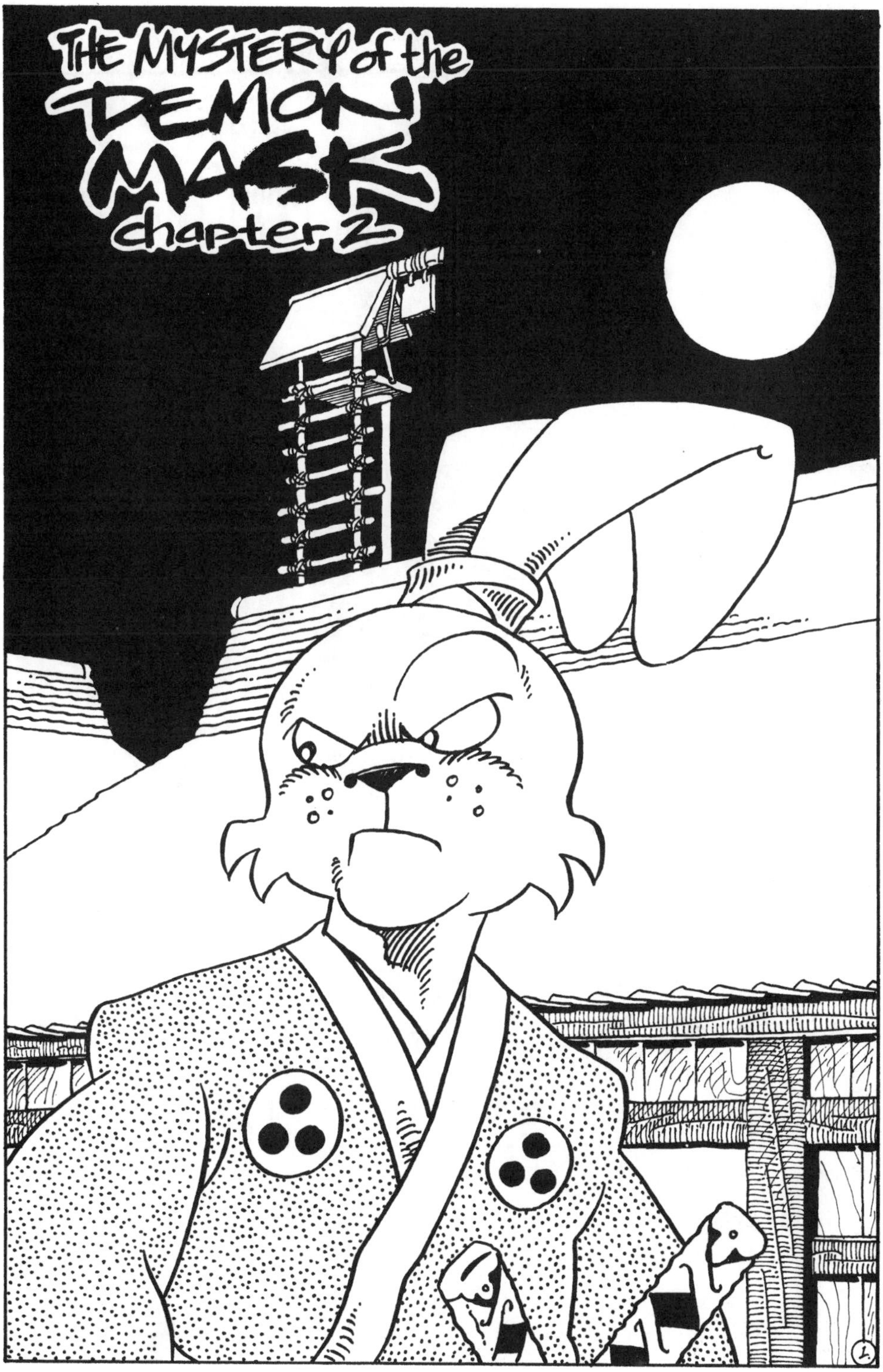
THE MYSTERY of the DEMON MASK chapter 2

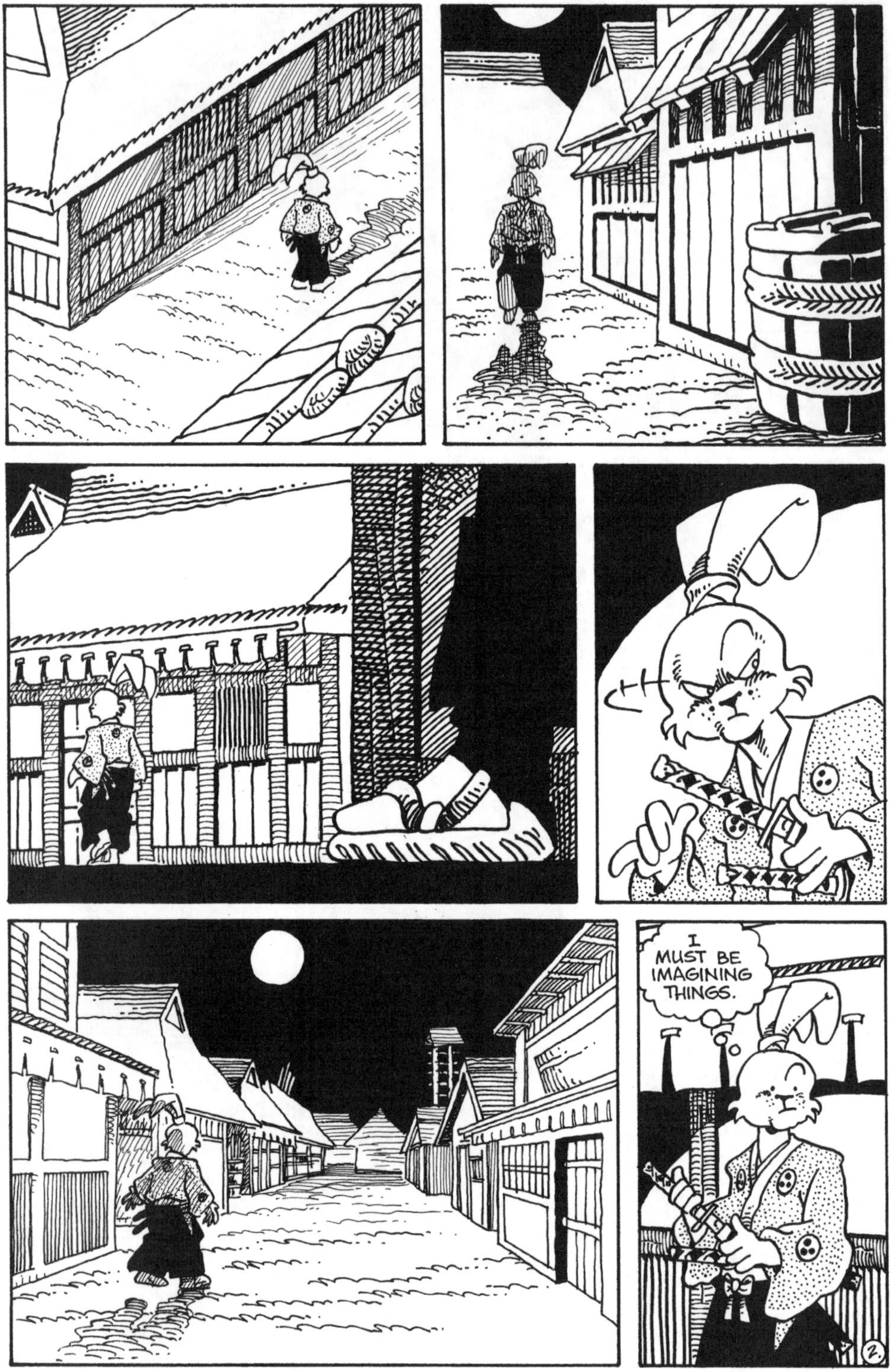
I MUST BE IMAGINING THINGS.
2.

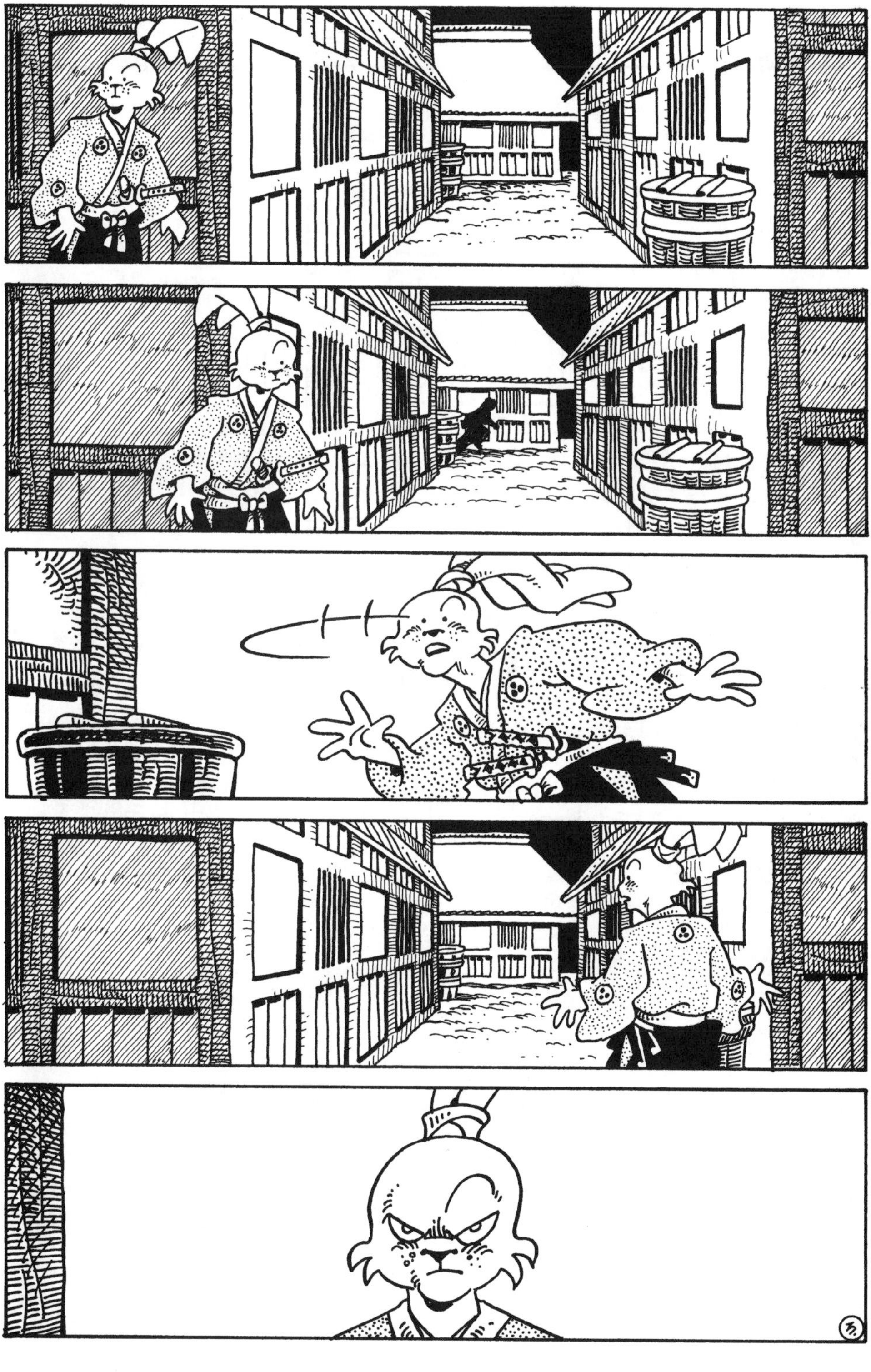

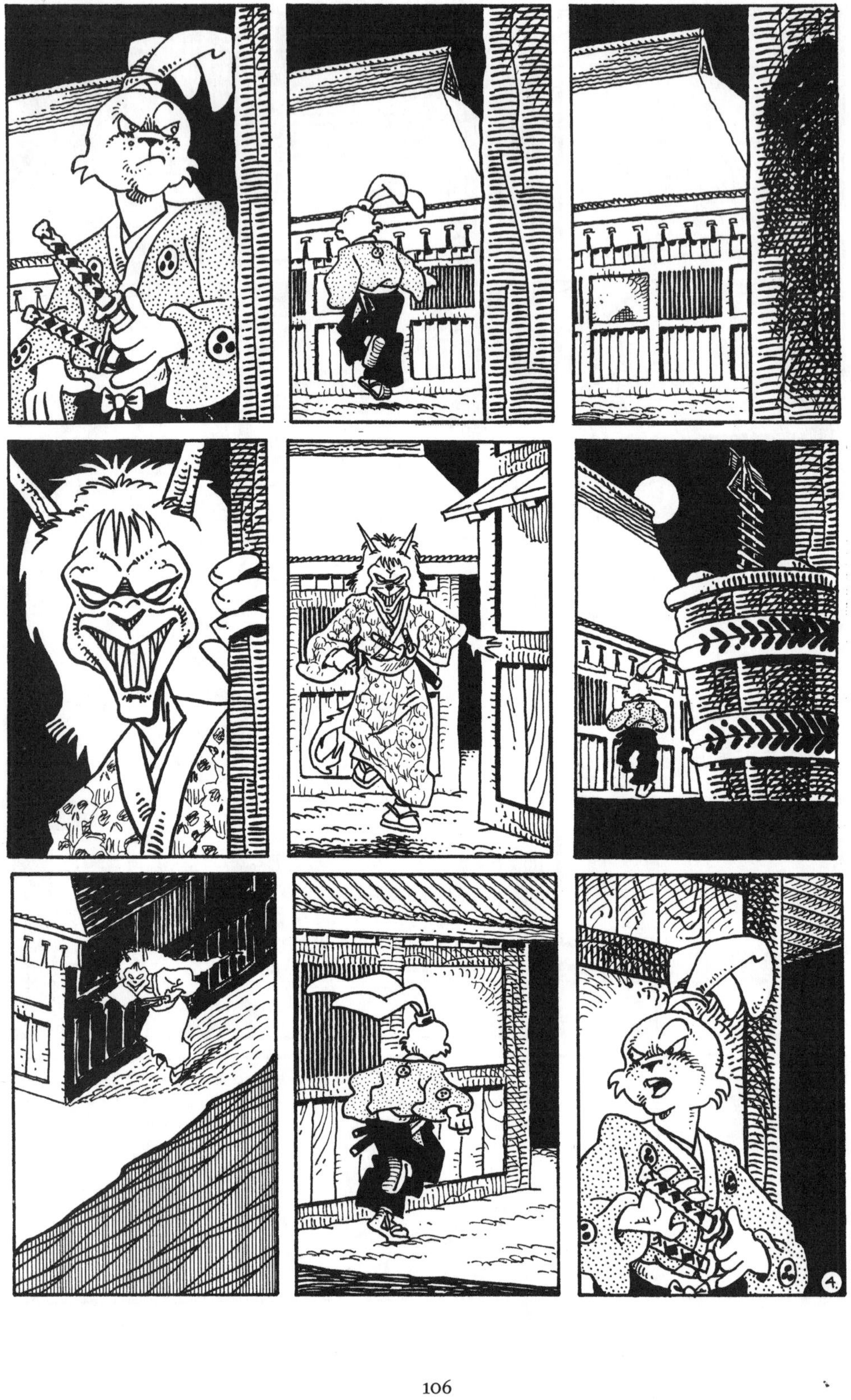
4.

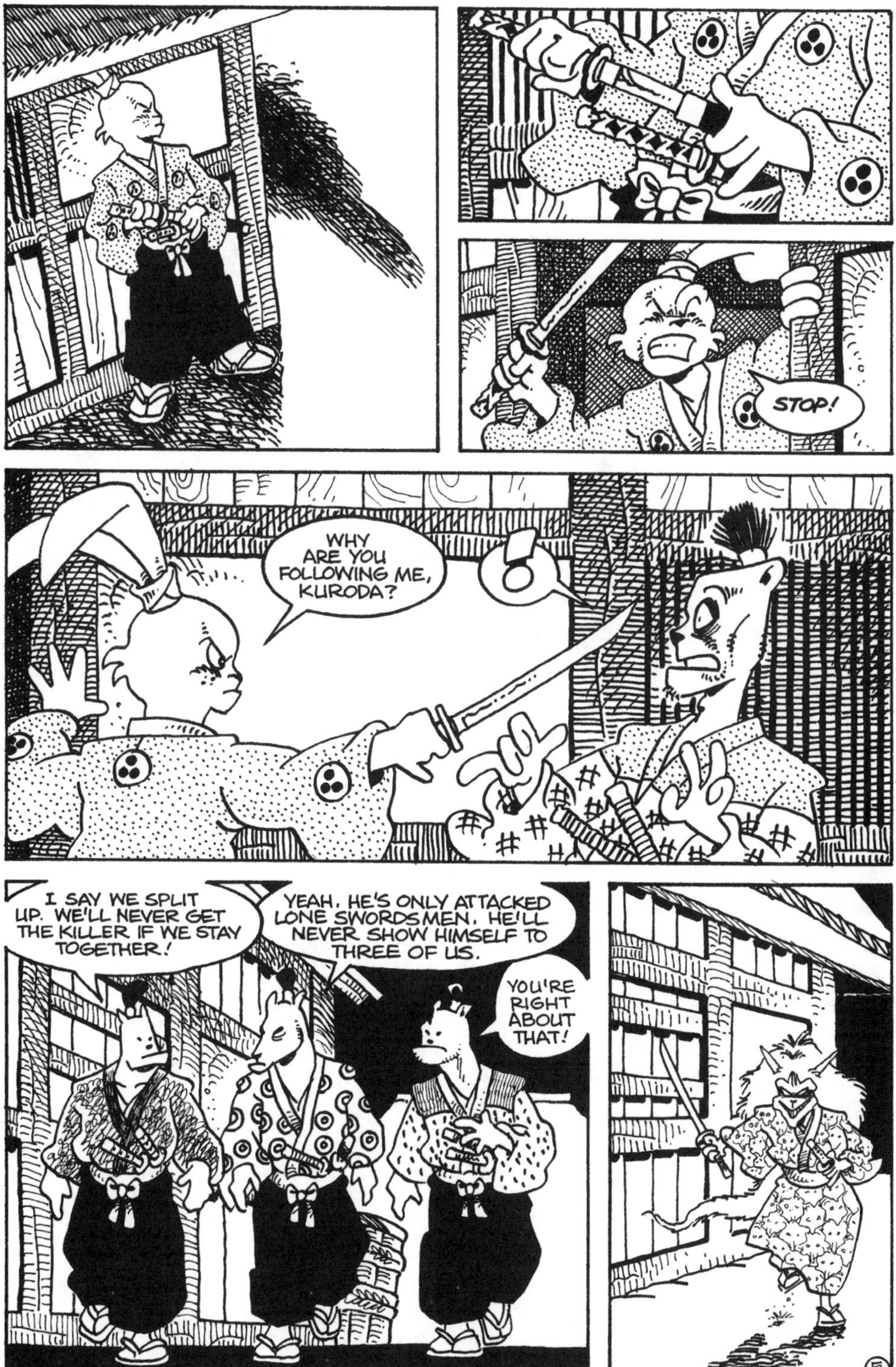
STOP!
WHY ARE YOU FOLLOWING ME, KURODA?
!
I SAY WE SPLIT UP. WE'LL NEVER GET THE KILLER IF WE STAY TOGETHER!
YEAH. HE'S ONLY ATTACKED LONE SWORDSMEN. HE'LL NEVER SHOW HIMSELF TO THREE OF US.
YOU'RE RIGHT ABOUT THAT!
5.

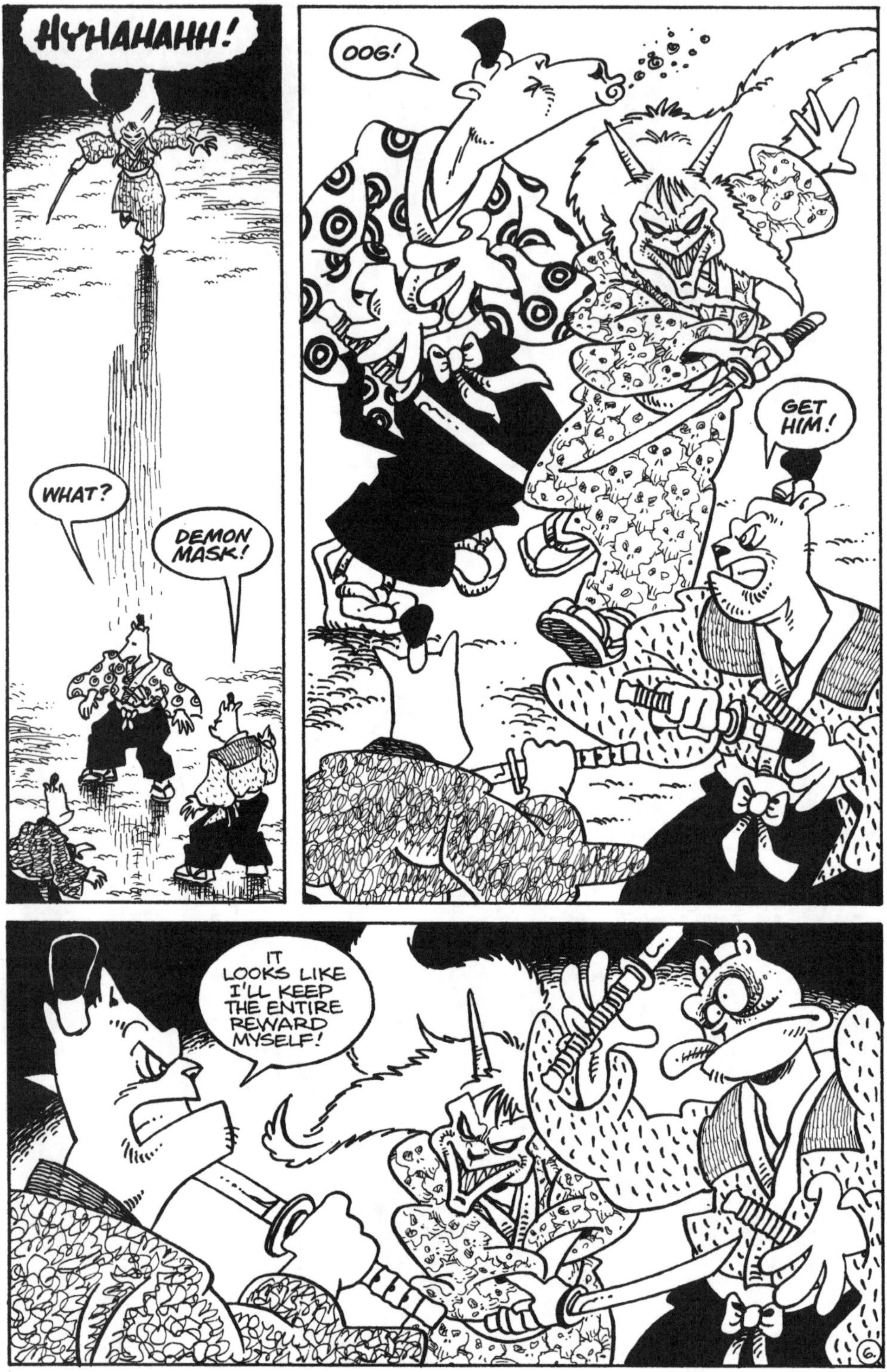
HYAHAHH!
WHAT?
DEMON MASK!
OOG!
GET HIM!
IT LOOKS LIKE I'LL KEEP THE ENTIRE REWARD MYSELF!
6.

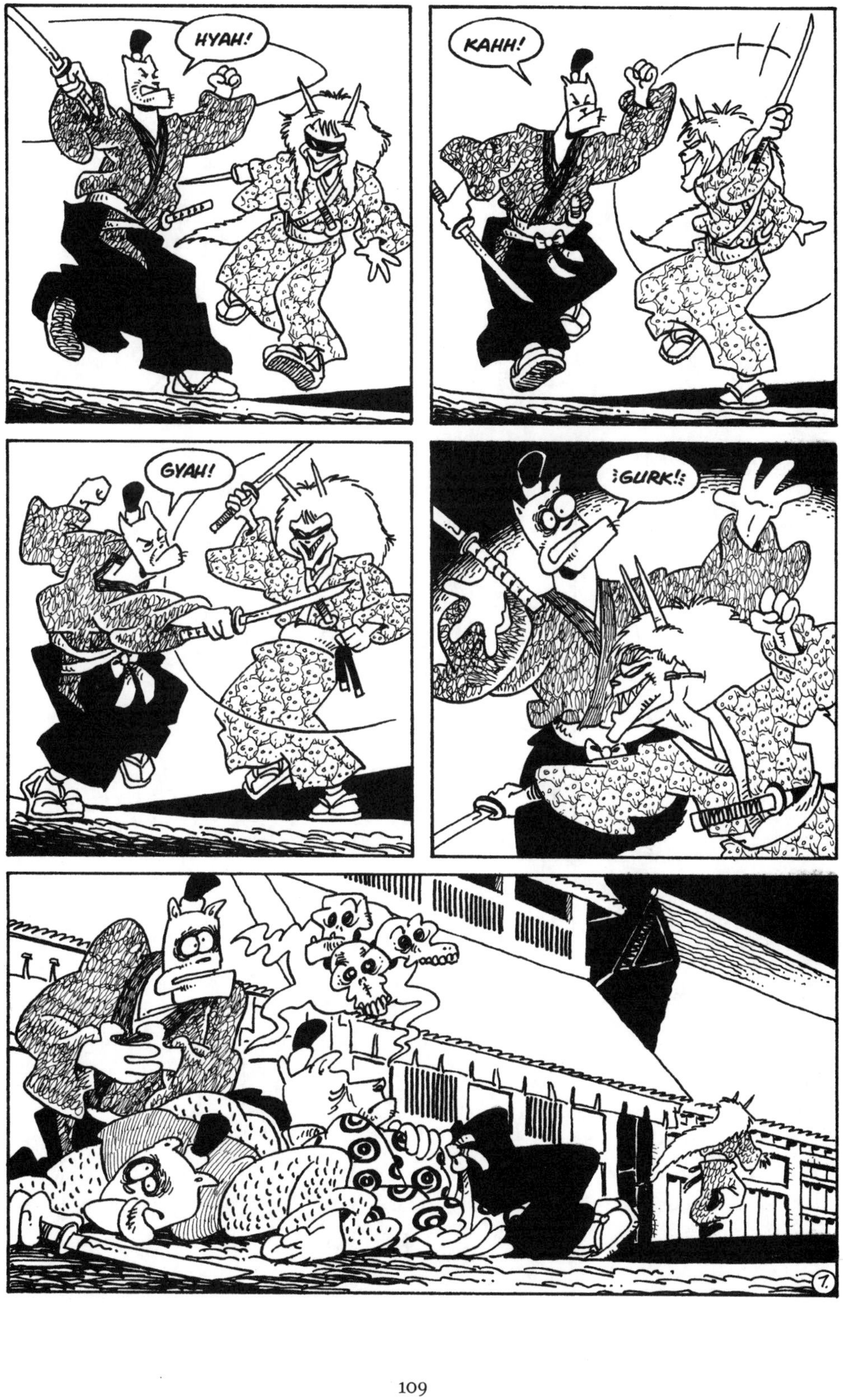
HYAH!
KAHH!
GYAH!
!GURK!
7.

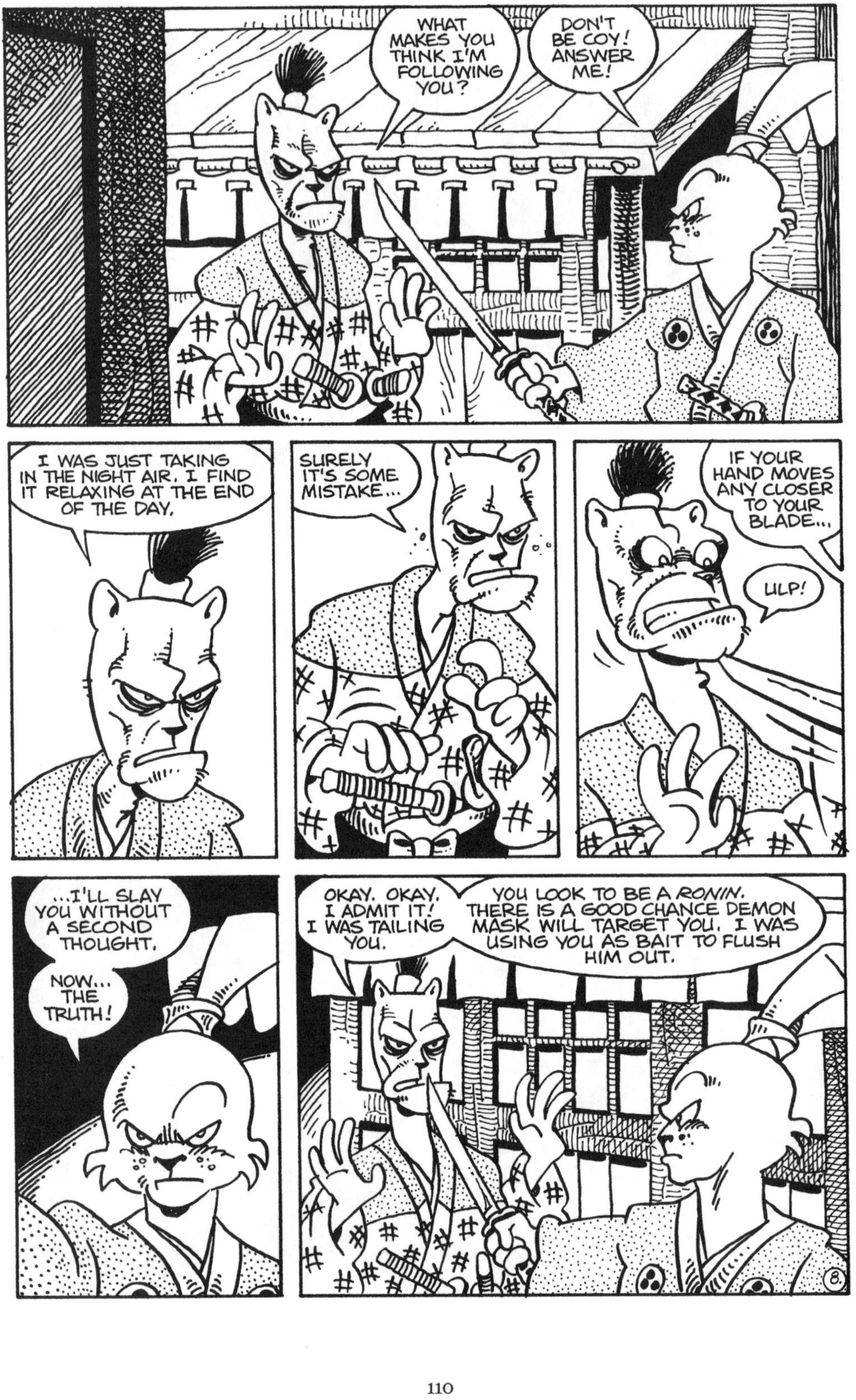
WHAT MAKES YOU THINK I'M FOLLOWING YOU?
DON'T BE COY! ANSWER ME!
I WAS JUST TAKING IN THE NIGHT AIR. I FIND IT RELAXING AT THE END OF THE DAY.
SURELY IT'S SOME MISTAKE...
IF YOUR HAND MOVES ANY CLOSER TO YOUR BLADE...
ULP!
...I'LL SLAY YOU WITHOUT A SECOND THOUGHT.
NOW... THE TRUTH!
OKAY. OKAY. I ADMIT IT! I WAS TAILING YOU.
YOU LOOK TO BE A *RONIN*. THERE IS A GOOD CHANCE DEMON MASK WILL TARGET YOU. I WAS USING YOU AS BAIT TO FLUSH HIM OUT.
8.

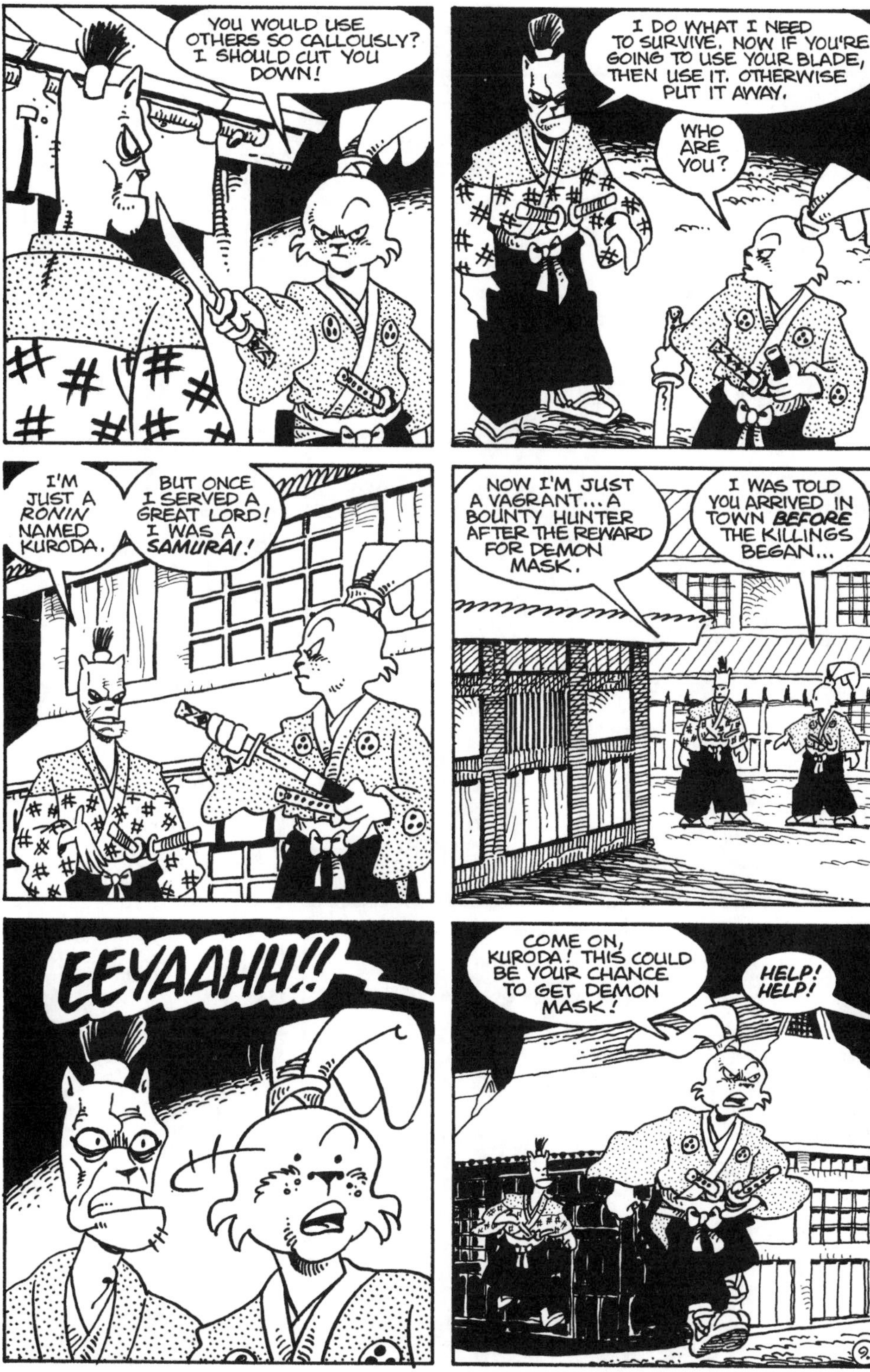
YOU WOULD USE OTHERS SO CALLOUSLY? I SHOULD CUT YOU DOWN!
I DO WHAT I NEED TO SURVIVE. NOW IF YOU'RE GOING TO USE YOUR BLADE, THEN USE IT. OTHERWISE PUT IT AWAY.
WHO ARE YOU?
I'M JUST A *RONIN* NAMED KURODA.
BUT ONCE I SERVED A GREAT LORD! I WAS A *SAMURAI*!
NOW I'M JUST A VAGRANT... A BOUNTY HUNTER AFTER THE REWARD FOR DEMON MASK.
I WAS TOLD YOU ARRIVED IN TOWN ***BEFORE*** THE KILLINGS BEGAN...
EEYAAHH!!
COME ON, KURODA! THIS COULD BE YOUR CHANCE TO GET DEMON MASK!
HELP! HELP!
9.

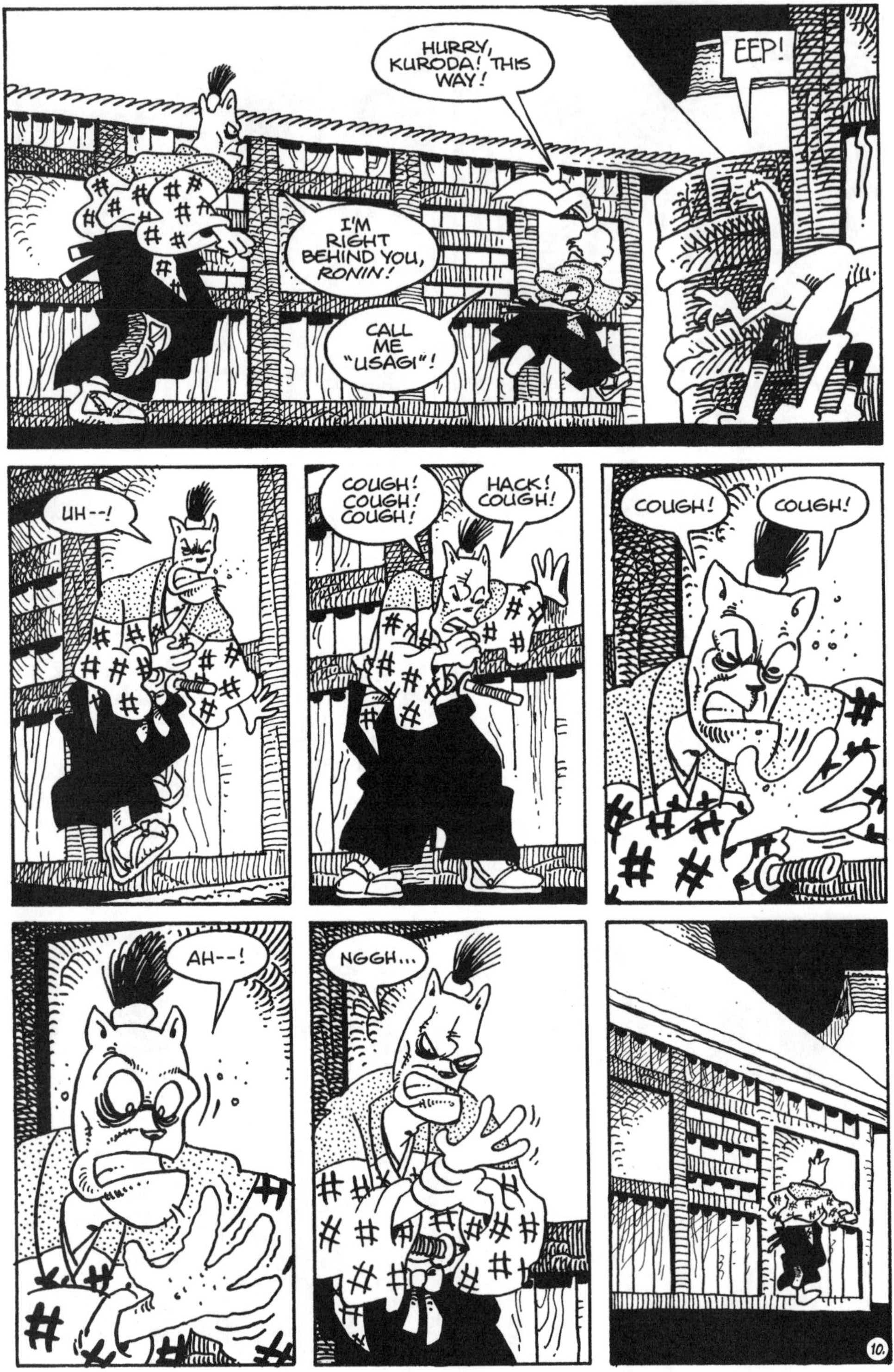
HURRY, KURODA! THIS WAY!
EEP!
I'M RIGHT BEHIND YOU, *RONIN!*
CALL ME "USAGI"!
UH--!
COUGH! COUGH! COUGH!
HACK! COUGH!
COUGH!
COUGH!
AH--!
NGGH...
10.

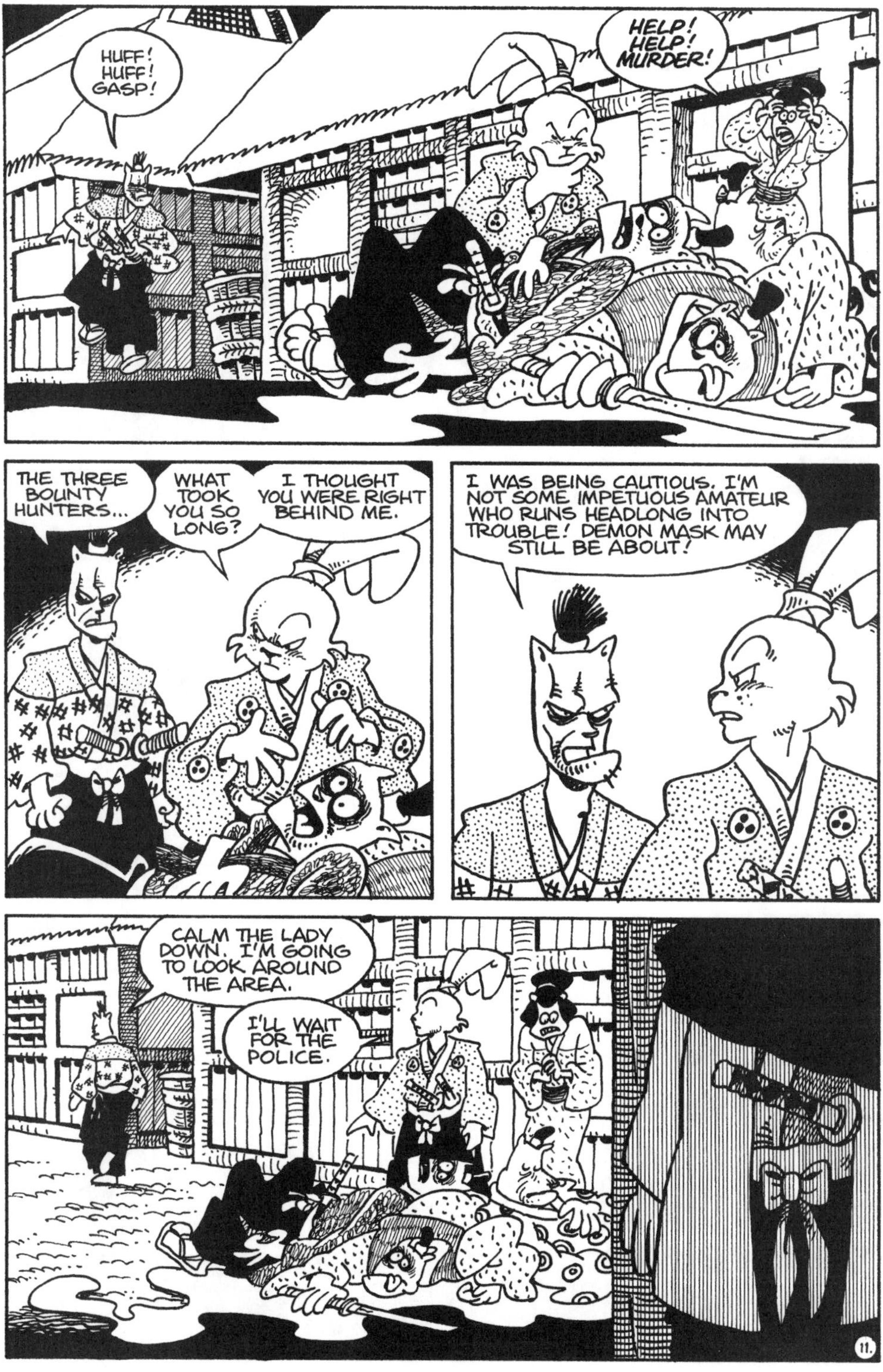
HUFF! HUFF! GASP!
HELP! HELP! MURDER!
THE THREE BOUNTY HUNTERS...
WHAT TOOK YOU SO LONG?
I THOUGHT YOU WERE RIGHT BEHIND ME.
I WAS BEING CAUTIOUS. I'M NOT SOME IMPETUOUS AMATEUR WHO RUNS HEADLONG INTO TROUBLE! DEMON MASK MAY STILL BE ABOUT!
CALM THE LADY DOWN. I'M GOING TO LOOK AROUND THE AREA.
I'LL WAIT FOR THE POLICE.
11.

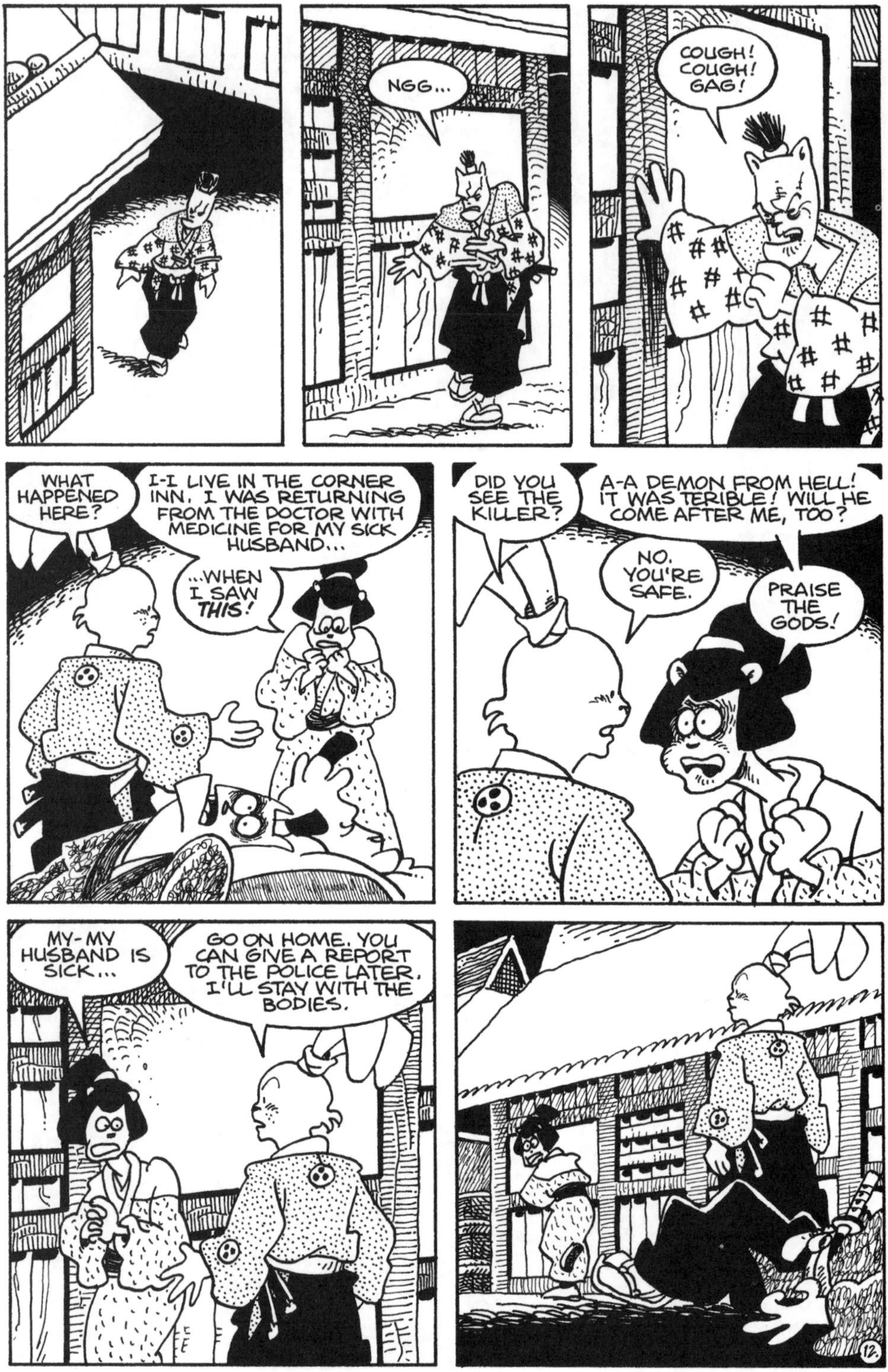
NGG...
COUGH! COUGH! GAG!
WHAT HAPPENED HERE?
I-I LIVE IN THE CORNER INN. I WAS RETURNING FROM THE DOCTOR WITH MEDICINE FOR MY SICK HUSBAND...
...WHEN I SAW *THIS*!
DID YOU SEE THE KILLER?
A-A DEMON FROM HELL! IT WAS TERIBLE! WILL HE COME AFTER ME, TOO?
NO. YOU'RE SAFE.
PRAISE THE GODS!
MY-MY HUSBAND IS SICK...
GO ON HOME. YOU CAN GIVE A REPORT TO THE POLICE LATER. I'LL STAY WITH THE BODIES.
12.

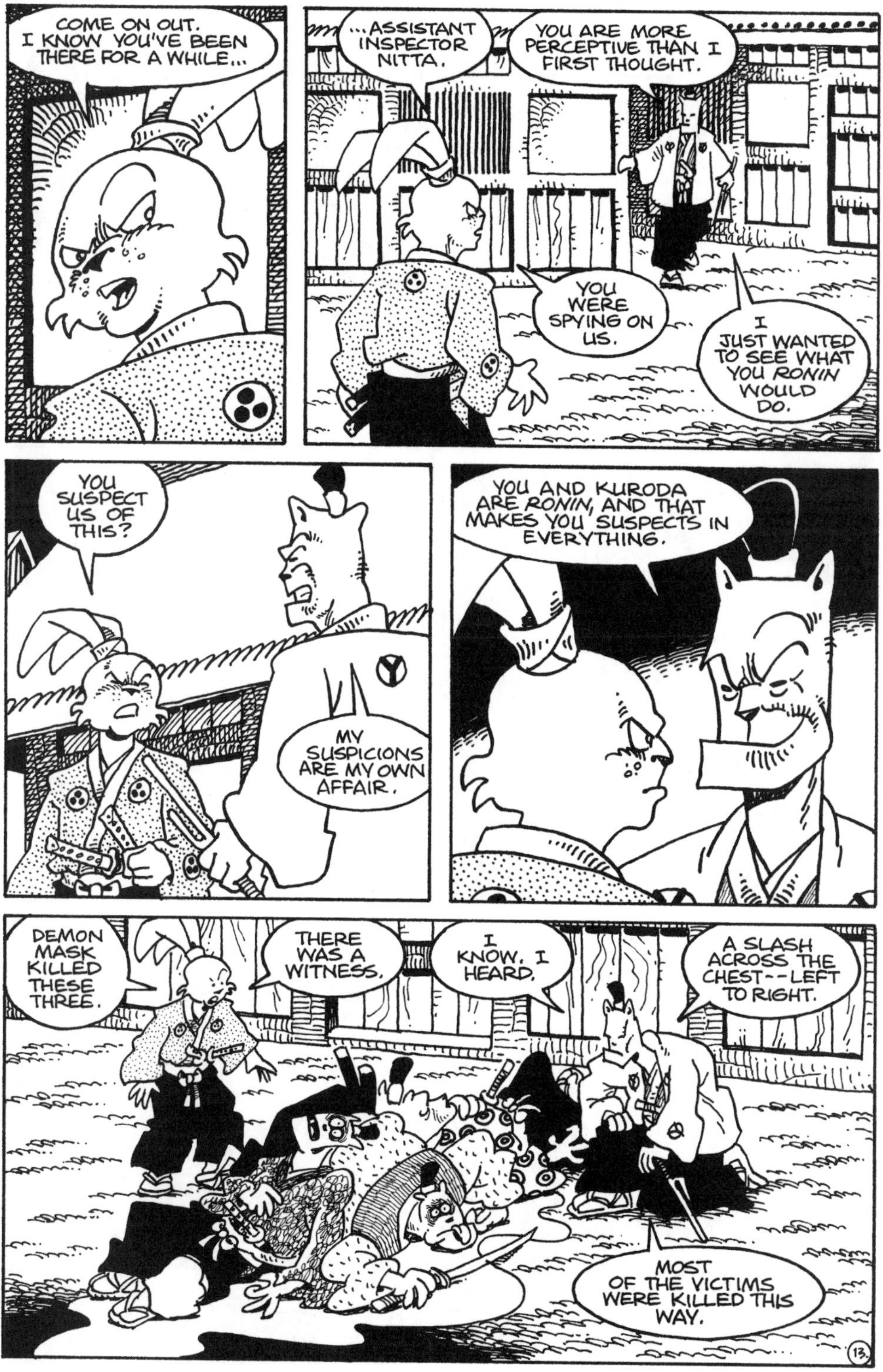
COME ON OUT. I KNOW YOU'VE BEEN THERE FOR A WHILE...
...ASSISTANT INSPECTOR NITTA.
YOU ARE MORE PERCEPTIVE THAN I FIRST THOUGHT.
YOU WERE SPYING ON US.
I JUST WANTED TO SEE WHAT YOU *RONIN* WOULD DO.
YOU SUSPECT US OF THIS?
MY SUSPICIONS ARE MY OWN AFFAIR.
YOU AND KURODA ARE *RONIN*, AND THAT MAKES YOU SUSPECTS IN EVERYTHING.
DEMON MASK KILLED THESE THREE.
THERE WAS A WITNESS.
I KNOW. I HEARD.
A SLASH ACROSS THE CHEST--LEFT TO RIGHT.
MOST OF THE VICTIMS WERE KILLED THIS WAY.
13.

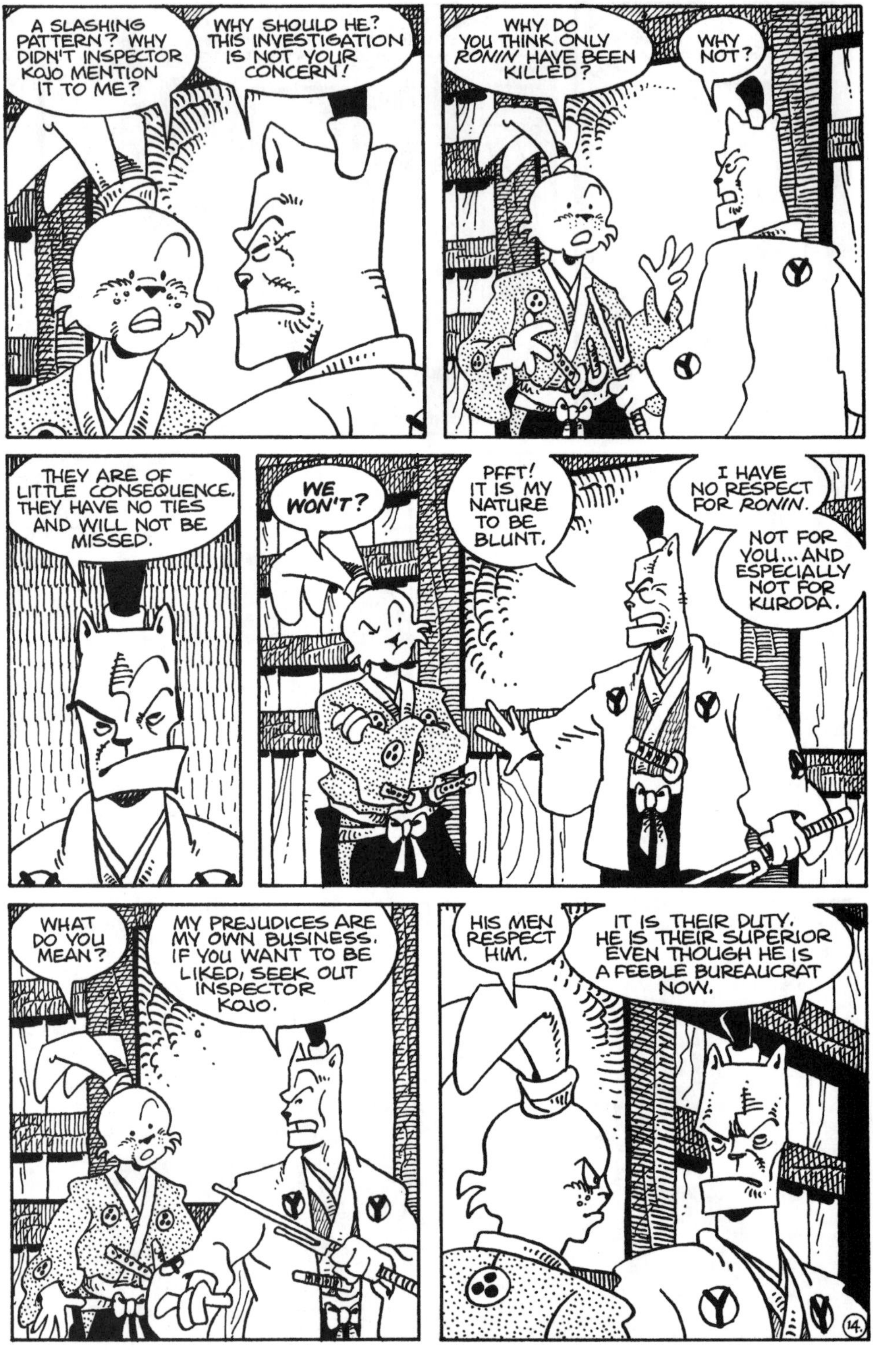
A SLASHING PATTERN? WHY DIDN'T INSPECTOR KOJO MENTION IT TO ME?
WHY SHOULD HE? THIS INVESTIGATION IS NOT YOUR CONCERN!
WHY DO YOU THINK ONLY *RONIN* HAVE BEEN KILLED?
WHY NOT?
THEY ARE OF LITTLE CONSEQUENCE. THEY HAVE NO TIES AND WILL NOT BE MISSED.
WE WON'T?
PFFT! IT IS MY NATURE TO BE BLUNT.
I HAVE NO RESPECT FOR *RONIN*.
NOT FOR YOU... AND ESPECIALLY NOT FOR KURODA.
WHAT DO YOU MEAN?
MY PREJUDICES ARE MY OWN BUSINESS. IF YOU WANT TO BE LIKED, SEEK OUT INSPECTOR KOJO.
HIS MEN RESPECT HIM.
IT IS THEIR DUTY. HE IS THEIR SUPERIOR EVEN THOUGH HE IS A FEEBLE BUREAUCRAT NOW.
14.

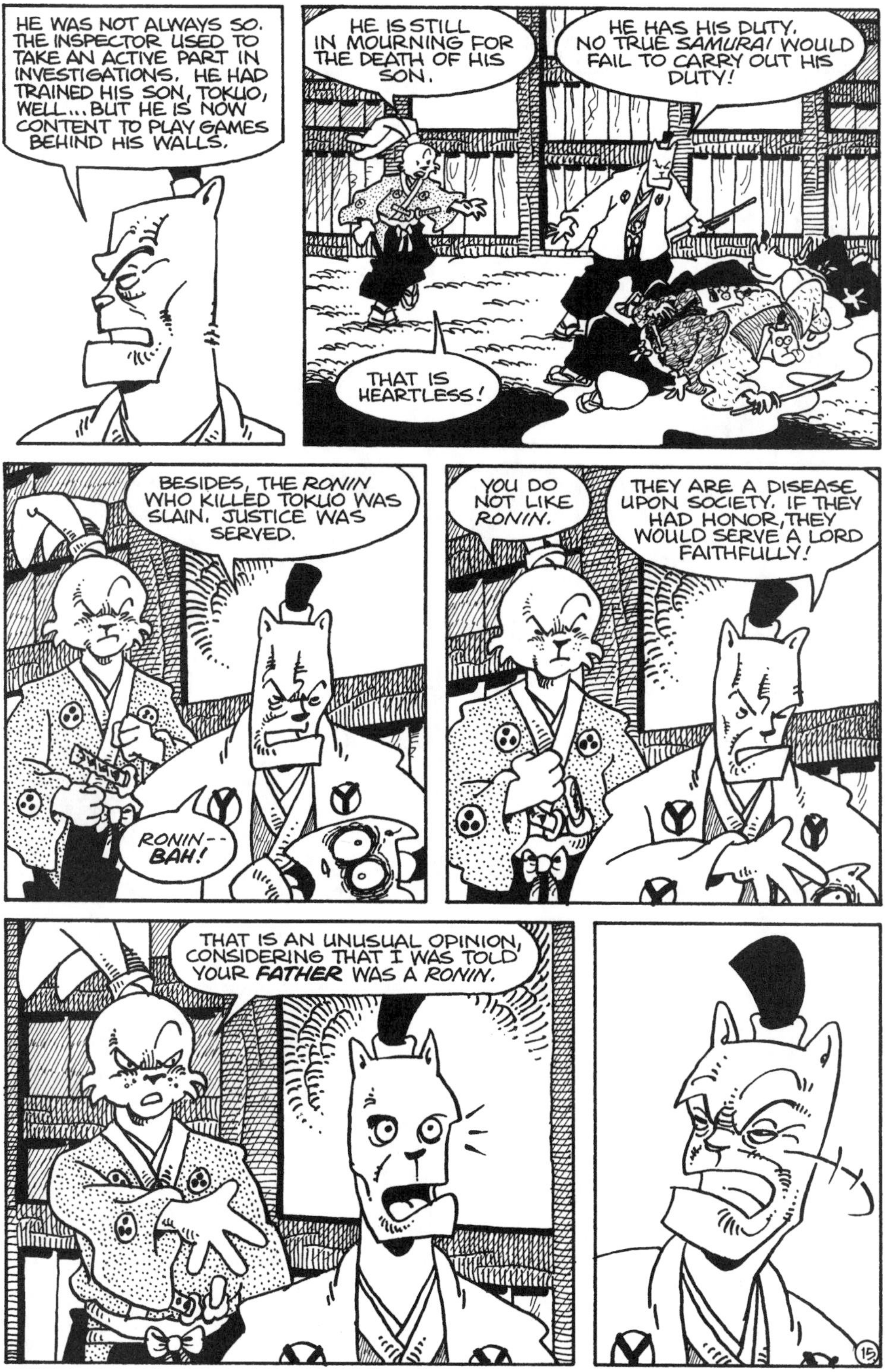
HE WAS NOT ALWAYS SO. THE INSPECTOR USED TO TAKE AN ACTIVE PART IN INVESTIGATIONS. HE HAD TRAINED HIS SON, TOKUO, WELL... BUT HE IS NOW CONTENT TO PLAY GAMES BEHIND HIS WALLS.
HE IS STILL IN MOURNING FOR THE DEATH OF HIS SON.
HE HAS HIS DUTY. NO TRUE *SAMURAI* WOULD FAIL TO CARRY OUT HIS DUTY!
THAT IS HEARTLESS!
BESIDES, THE *RONIN* WHO KILLED TOKUO WAS SLAIN. JUSTICE WAS SERVED.
RONIN-- ***BAH!***
YOU DO NOT LIKE *RONIN*.
THEY ARE A DISEASE UPON SOCIETY. IF THEY HAD HONOR, THEY WOULD SERVE A LORD FAITHFULLY!
THAT IS AN UNUSUAL OPINION, CONSIDERING THAT I WAS TOLD YOUR ***FATHER*** WAS A *RONIN*.
15

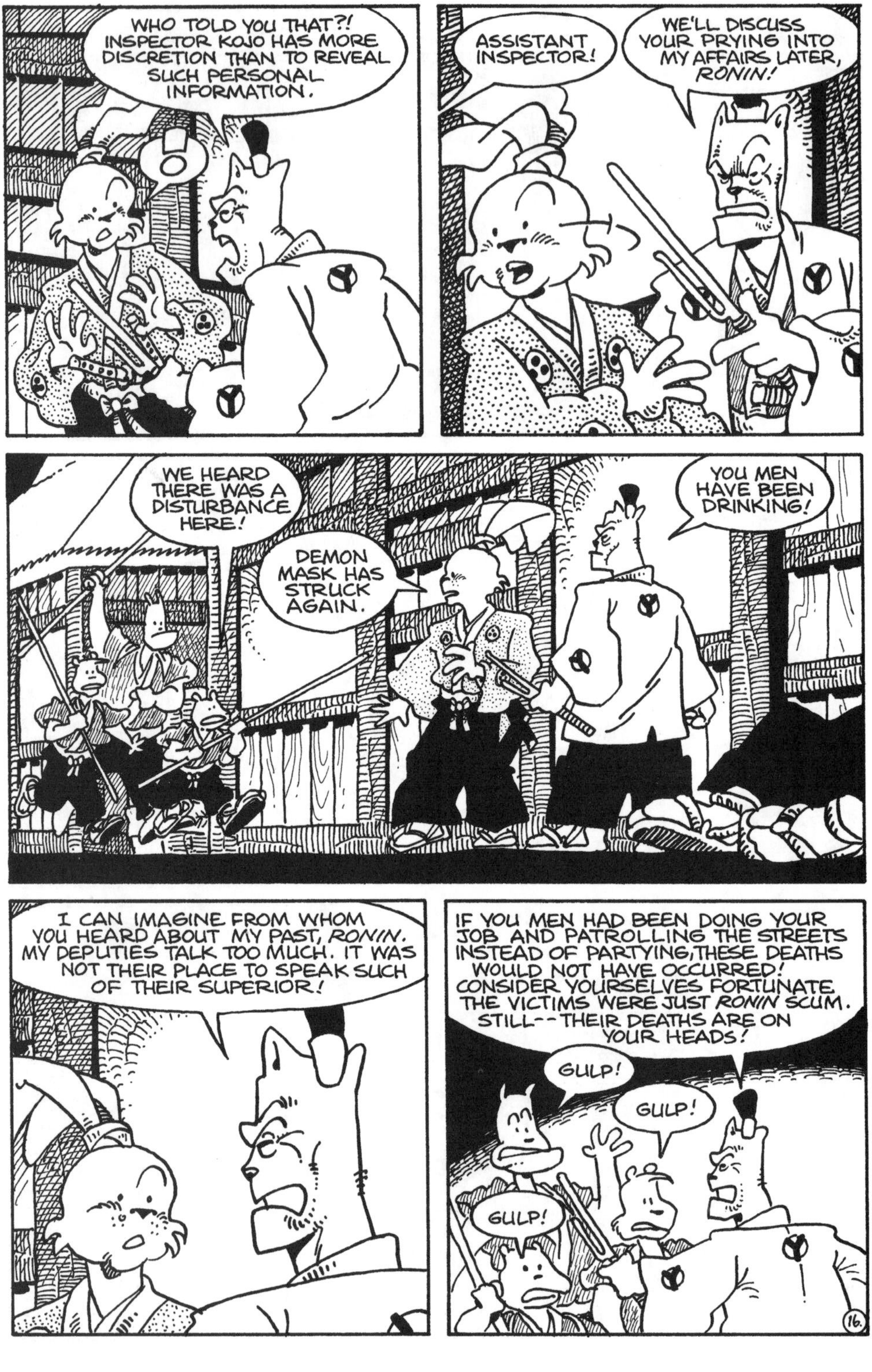
WHO TOLD YOU THAT?! INSPECTOR KOJO HAS MORE DISCRETION THAN TO REVEAL SUCH PERSONAL INFORMATION.
ASSISTANT INSPECTOR!
WE'LL DISCUSS YOUR PRYING INTO MY AFFAIRS LATER, *RONIN!*
WE HEARD THERE WAS A DISTURBANCE HERE!
DEMON MASK HAS STRUCK AGAIN.
YOU MEN HAVE BEEN DRINKING!
I CAN IMAGINE FROM WHOM YOU HEARD ABOUT MY PAST, *RONIN.* MY DEPUTIES TALK TOO MUCH. IT WAS NOT THEIR PLACE TO SPEAK SUCH OF THEIR SUPERIOR!
IF YOU MEN HAD BEEN DOING YOUR JOB AND PATROLLING THE STREETS INSTEAD OF PARTYING, THESE DEATHS WOULD NOT HAVE OCCURRED! CONSIDER YOURSELVES FORTUNATE THE VICTIMS WERE JUST *RONIN* SCUM. STILL--THEIR DEATHS ARE ON YOUR HEADS!
GULP!
GULP!
GULP!
16.

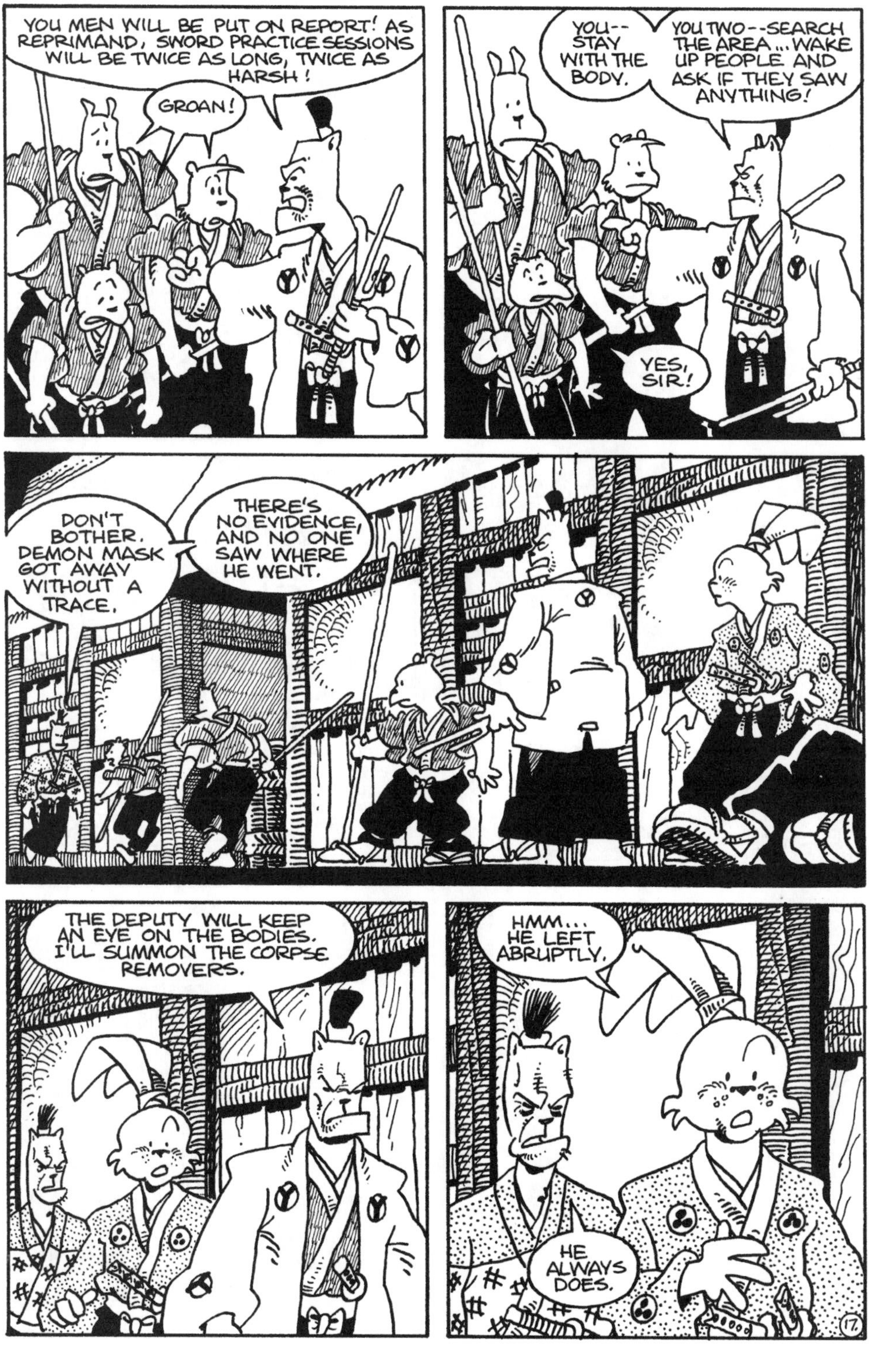
YOU MEN WILL BE PUT ON REPORT! AS REPRIMAND, SWORD PRACTICE SESSIONS WILL BE TWICE AS LONG, TWICE AS HARSH!
GROAN!
YOU-- STAY WITH THE BODY.
YOU TWO--SEARCH THE AREA... WAKE UP PEOPLE AND ASK IF THEY SAW ANYTHING!
YES, SIR!
THERE'S NO EVIDENCE, AND NO ONE SAW WHERE HE WENT.
DON'T BOTHER. DEMON MASK GOT AWAY WITHOUT A TRACE.
THE DEPUTY WILL KEEP AN EYE ON THE BODIES. I'LL SUMMON THE CORPSE REMOVERS.
HMM... HE LEFT ABRUPTLY.
HE ALWAYS DOES.
17

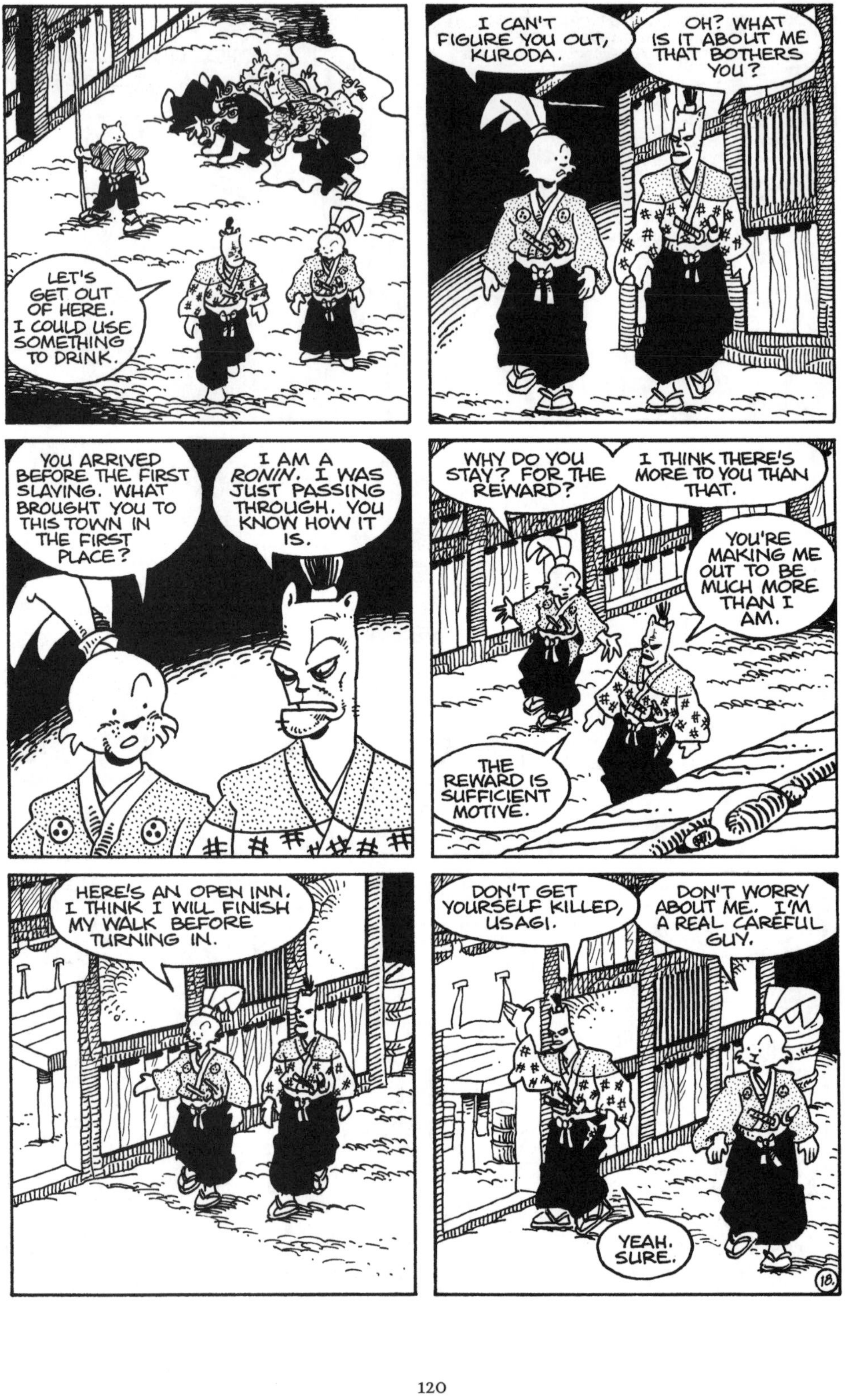
LET'S GET OUT OF HERE. I COULD USE SOMETHING TO DRINK.
I CAN'T FIGURE YOU OUT, KURODA.
OH? WHAT IS IT ABOUT ME THAT BOTHERS YOU?
YOU ARRIVED BEFORE THE FIRST SLAYING. WHAT BROUGHT YOU TO THIS TOWN IN THE FIRST PLACE?
I AM A *RONIN*. I WAS JUST PASSING THROUGH. YOU KNOW HOW IT IS.
WHY DO YOU STAY? FOR THE REWARD?
I THINK THERE'S MORE TO YOU THAN THAT.
YOU'RE MAKING ME OUT TO BE MUCH MORE THAN I AM.
THE REWARD IS SUFFICIENT MOTIVE.
HERE'S AN OPEN INN. I THINK I WILL FINISH MY WALK BEFORE TURNING IN.
DON'T GET YOURSELF KILLED, USAGI.
DON'T WORRY ABOUT ME. I'M A REAL CAREFUL GUY.
YEAH. SURE.
18.

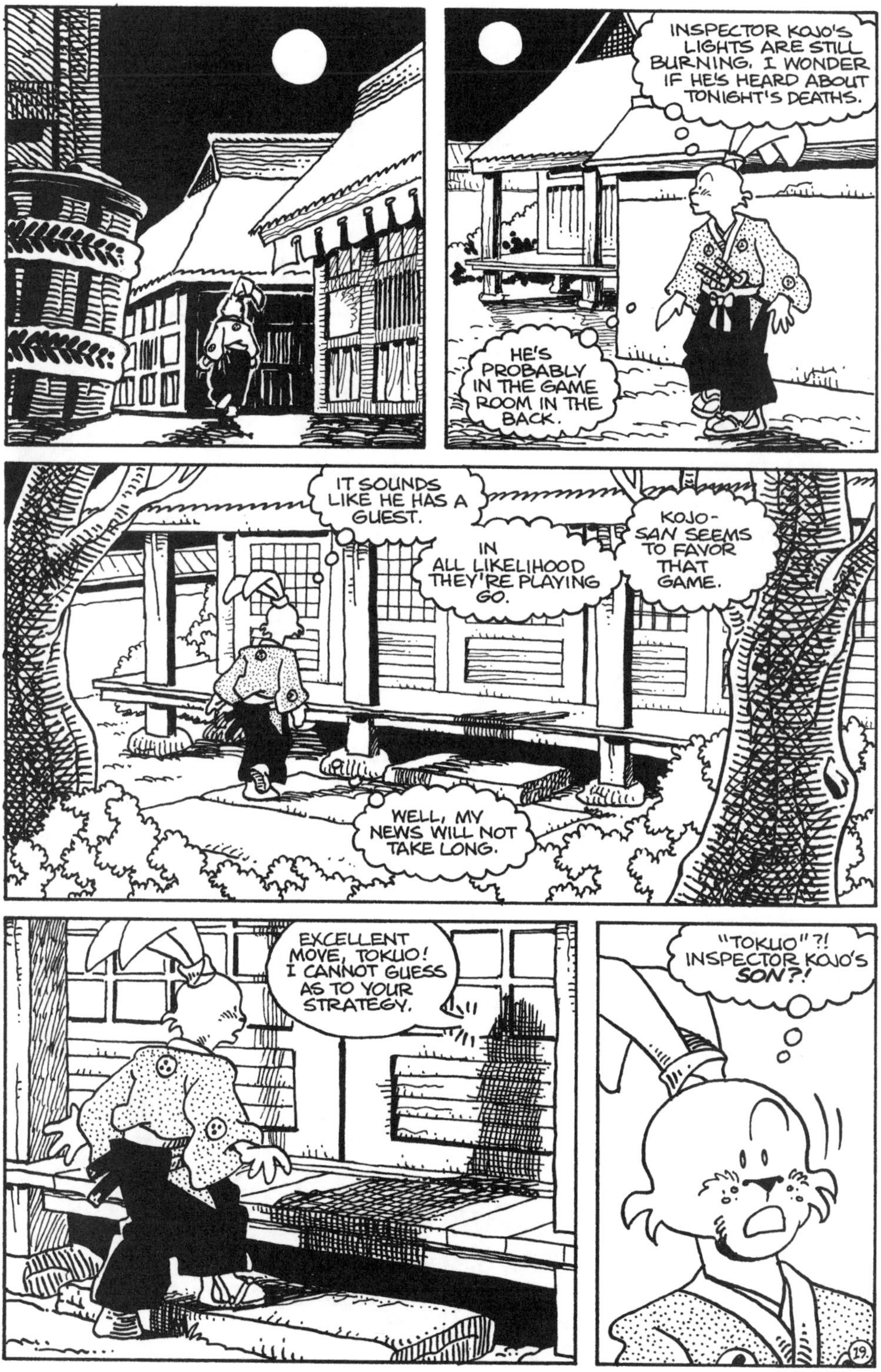
INSPECTOR KOJO'S LIGHTS ARE STILL BURNING. I WONDER IF HE'S HEARD ABOUT TONIGHT'S DEATHS.
HE'S PROBABLY IN THE GAME ROOM IN THE BACK.
IT SOUNDS LIKE HE HAS A GUEST.
IN ALL LIKELIHOOD THEY'RE PLAYING GO.
KOJO-SAN SEEMS TO FAVOR THAT GAME.
WELL, MY NEWS WILL NOT TAKE LONG.
EXCELLENT MOVE, TOKUO! I CANNOT GUESS AS TO YOUR STRATEGY.
"TOKUO"?! INSPECTOR KOJO'S SON?!
19

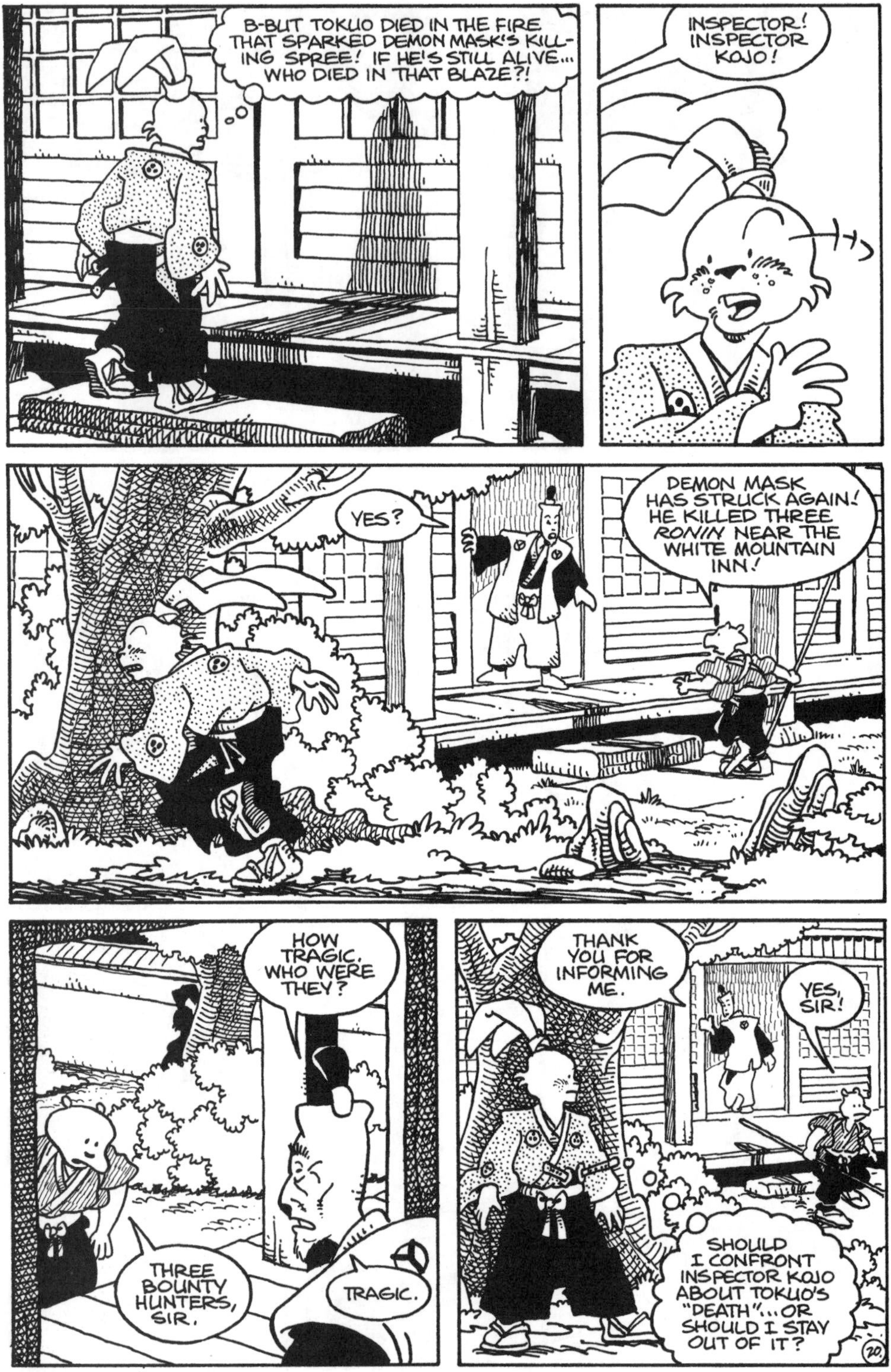
B-BUT TOKUO DIED IN THE FIRE THAT SPARKED DEMON MASK'S KILLING SPREE! IF HE'S STILL ALIVE... WHO DIED IN THAT BLAZE?!
INSPECTOR! INSPECTOR KOJO!
YES?
DEMON MASK HAS STRUCK AGAIN! HE KILLED THREE *RONIN* NEAR THE WHITE MOUNTAIN INN!
HOW TRAGIC. WHO WERE THEY?
THREE BOUNTY HUNTERS, SIR.
TRAGIC.
THANK YOU FOR INFORMING ME.
YES, SIR!
SHOULD I CONFRONT INSPECTOR KOJO ABOUT TOKUO'S "DEATH"... OR SHOULD I STAY OUT OF IT?
20.

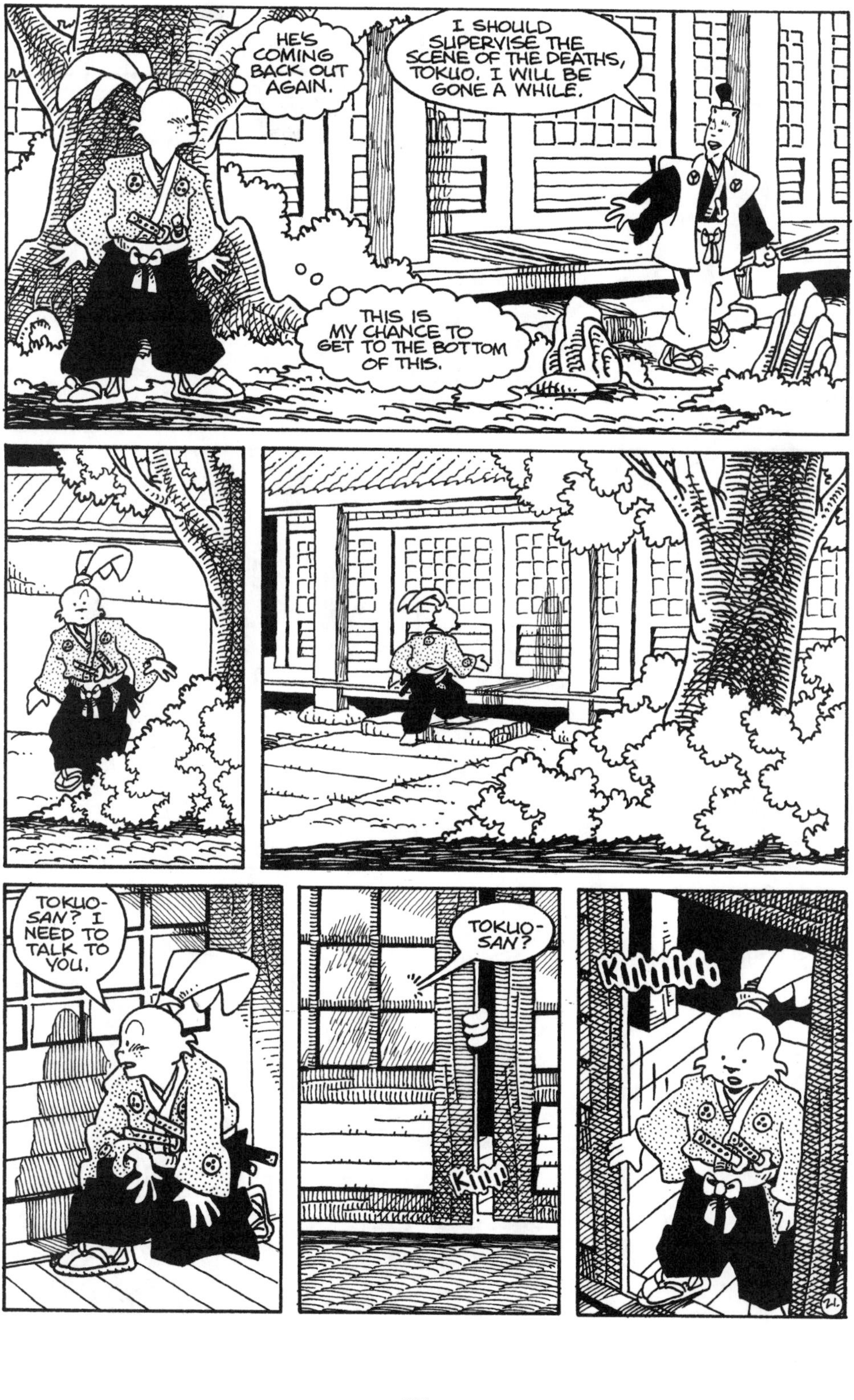
HE'S COMING BACK OUT AGAIN.
I SHOULD SUPERVISE THE SCENE OF THE DEATHS, TOKUO. I WILL BE GONE A WHILE.
THIS IS MY CHANCE TO GET TO THE BOTTOM OF THIS.
TOKUO-SAN? I NEED TO TALK TO YOU.
TOKUO-SAN?
KIIII
KIIIIIIII
21.

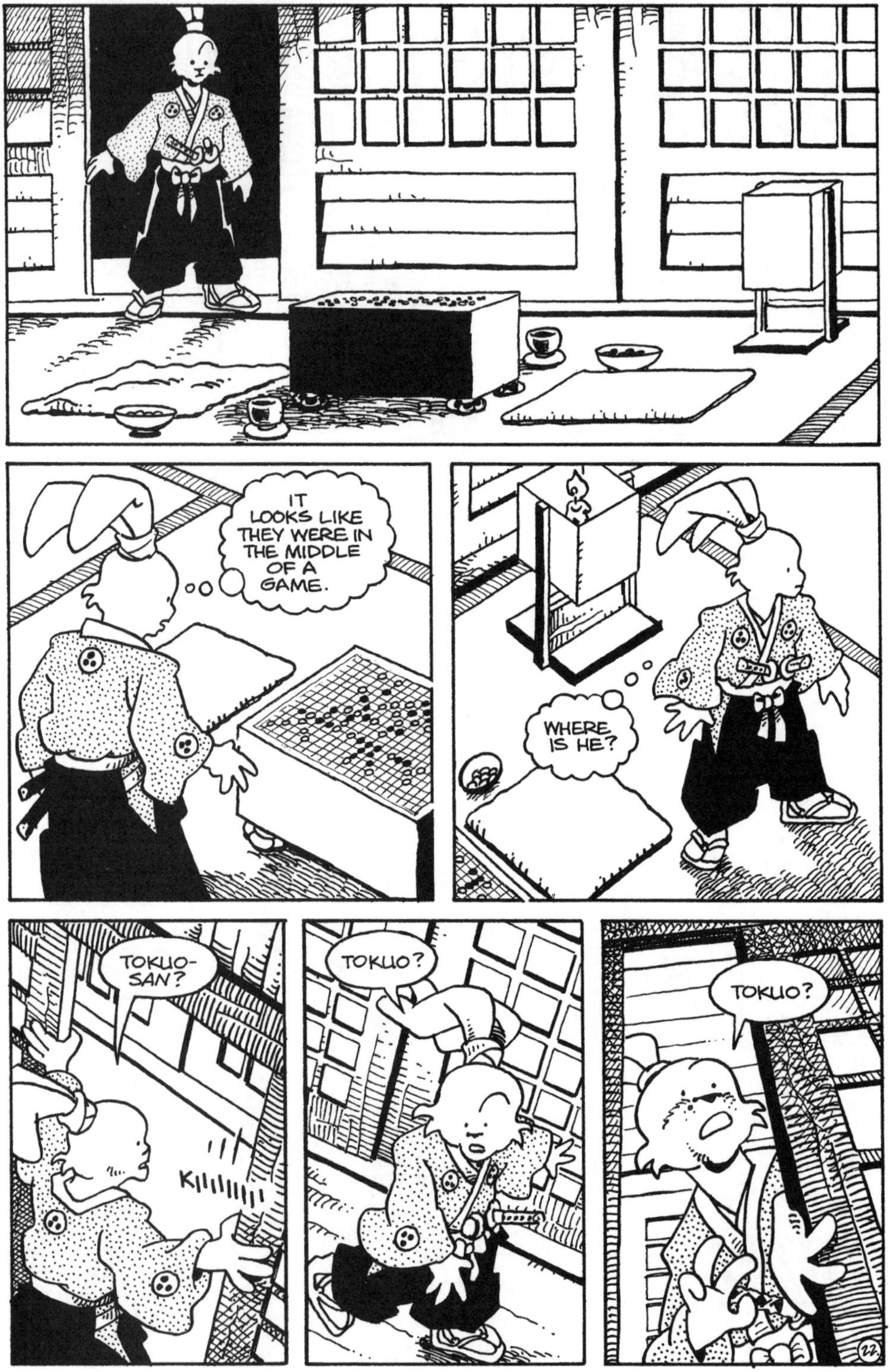
IT LOOKS LIKE THEY WERE IN THE MIDDLE OF A GAME.
WHERE IS HE?
TOKUO-SAN?
KIIIIIII
TOKUO?
TOKUO?
22.

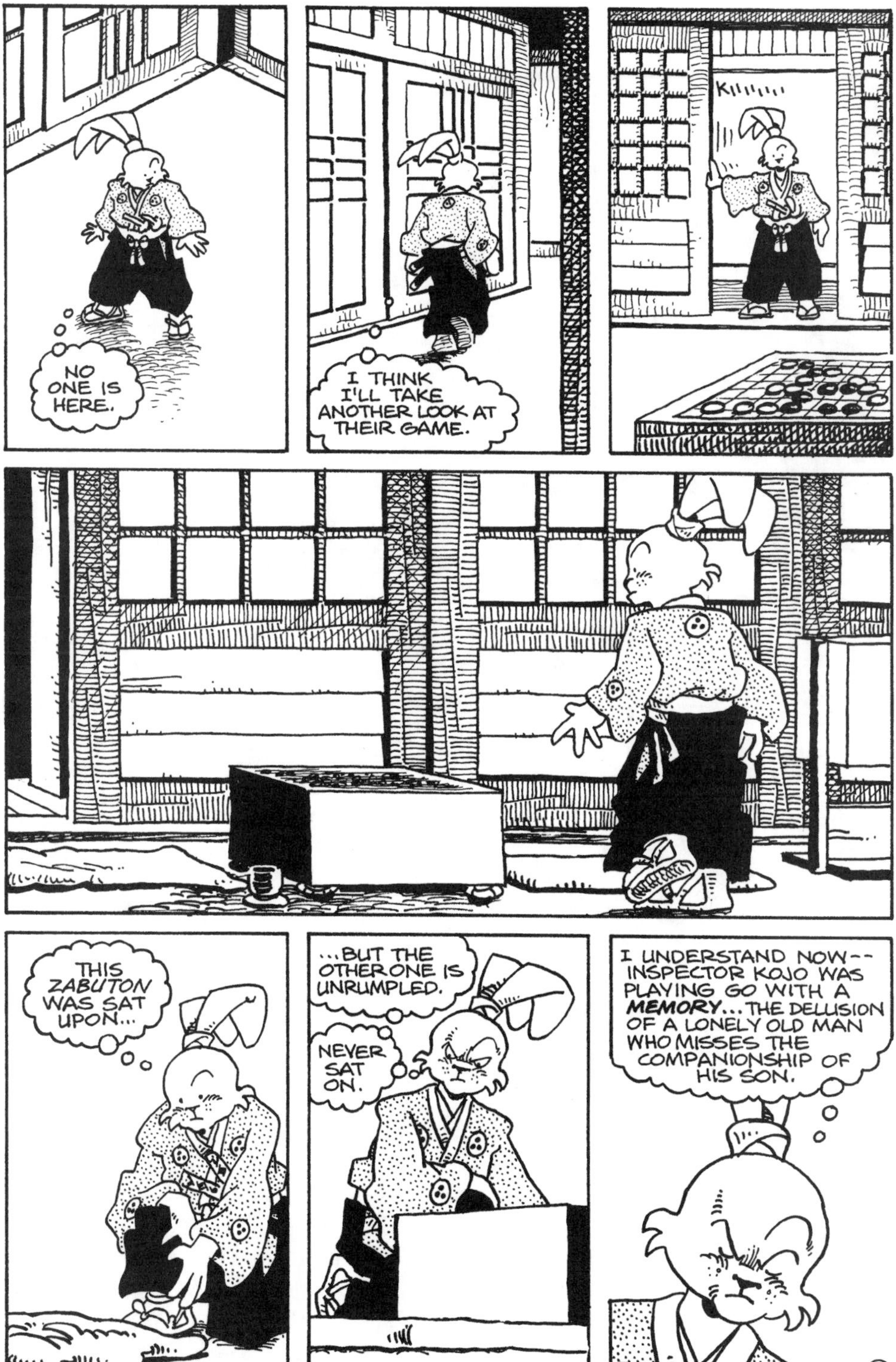
NO ONE IS HERE.
I THINK I'LL TAKE ANOTHER LOOK AT THEIR GAME.
KI...
THIS ZABUTON WAS SAT UPON...
...BUT THE OTHER ONE IS UNRUMPLED.
NEVER SAT ON.
I UNDERSTAND NOW-- INSPECTOR KOJO WAS PLAYING GO WITH A MEMORY... THE DELUSION OF A LONELY OLD MAN WHO MISSES THE COMPANIONSHIP OF HIS SON.
23

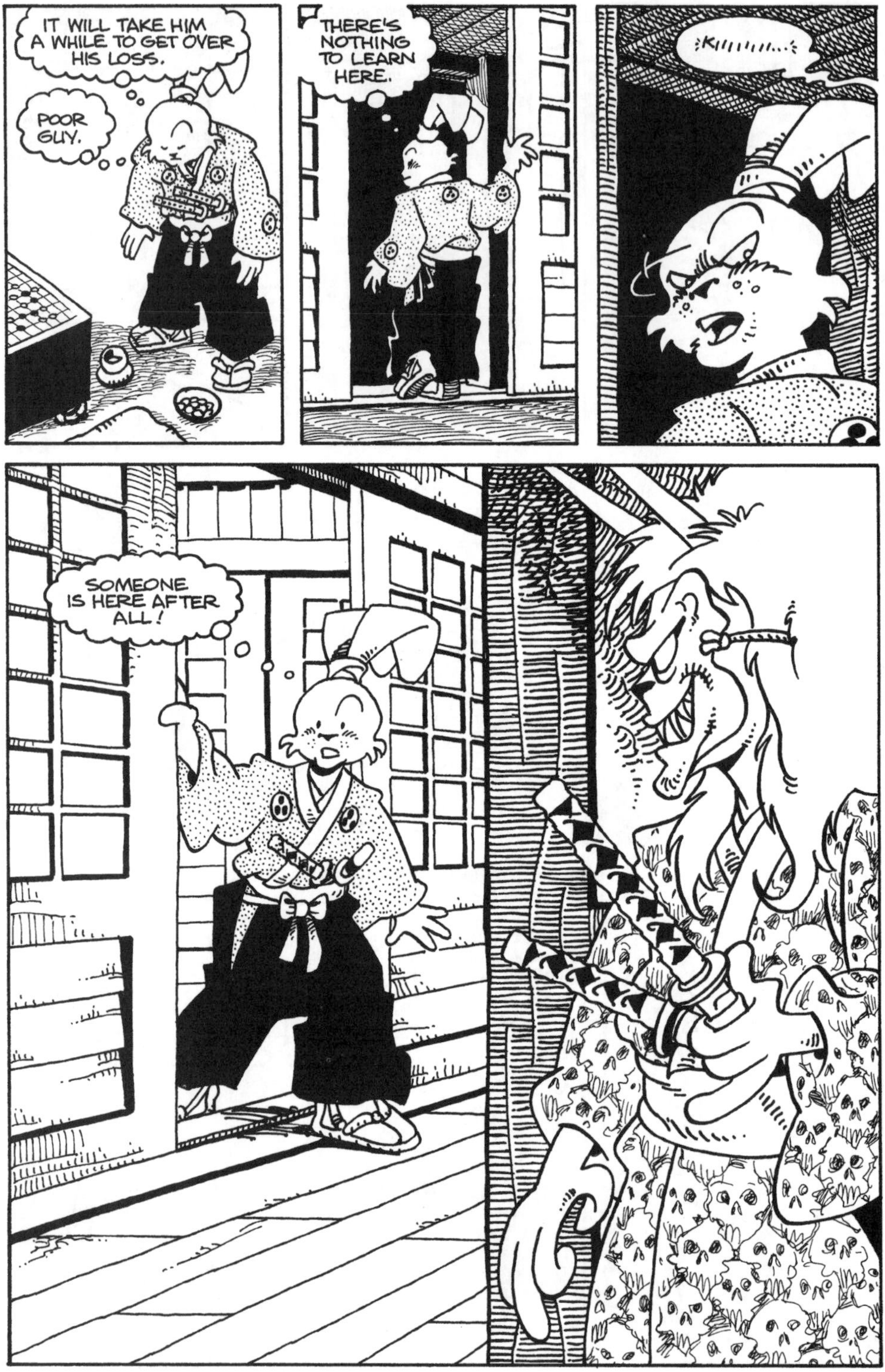

IT WILL TAKE HIM A WHILE TO GET OVER HIS LOSS.
POOR GUY.
THERE'S NOTHING TO LEARN HERE.
KIIIIIII...
SOMEONE IS HERE AFTER ALL!

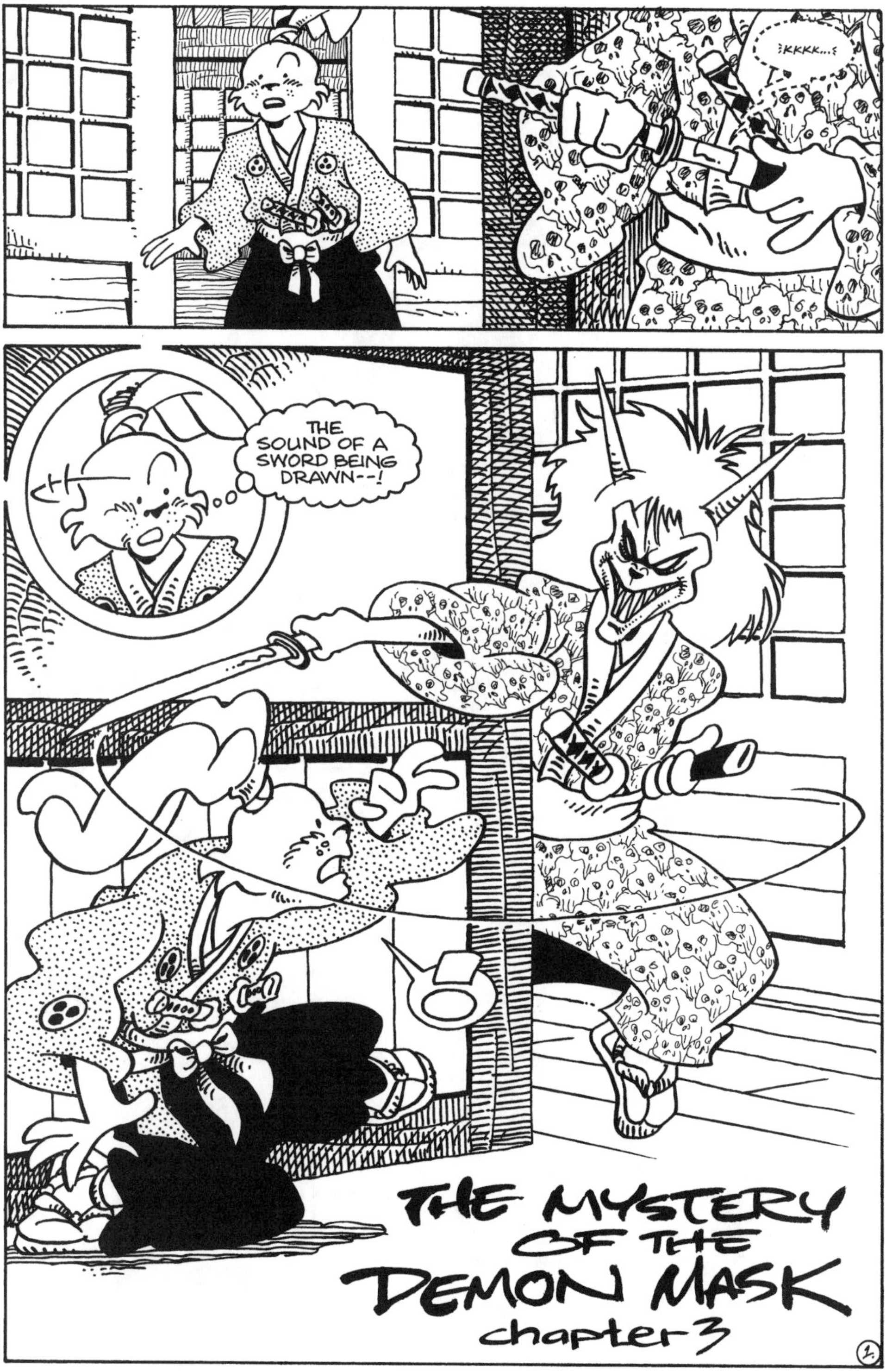
KKKK...
THE SOUND OF A SWORD BEING DRAWN--!
THE MYSTERY OF THE DEMON MASK
chapter 3
1

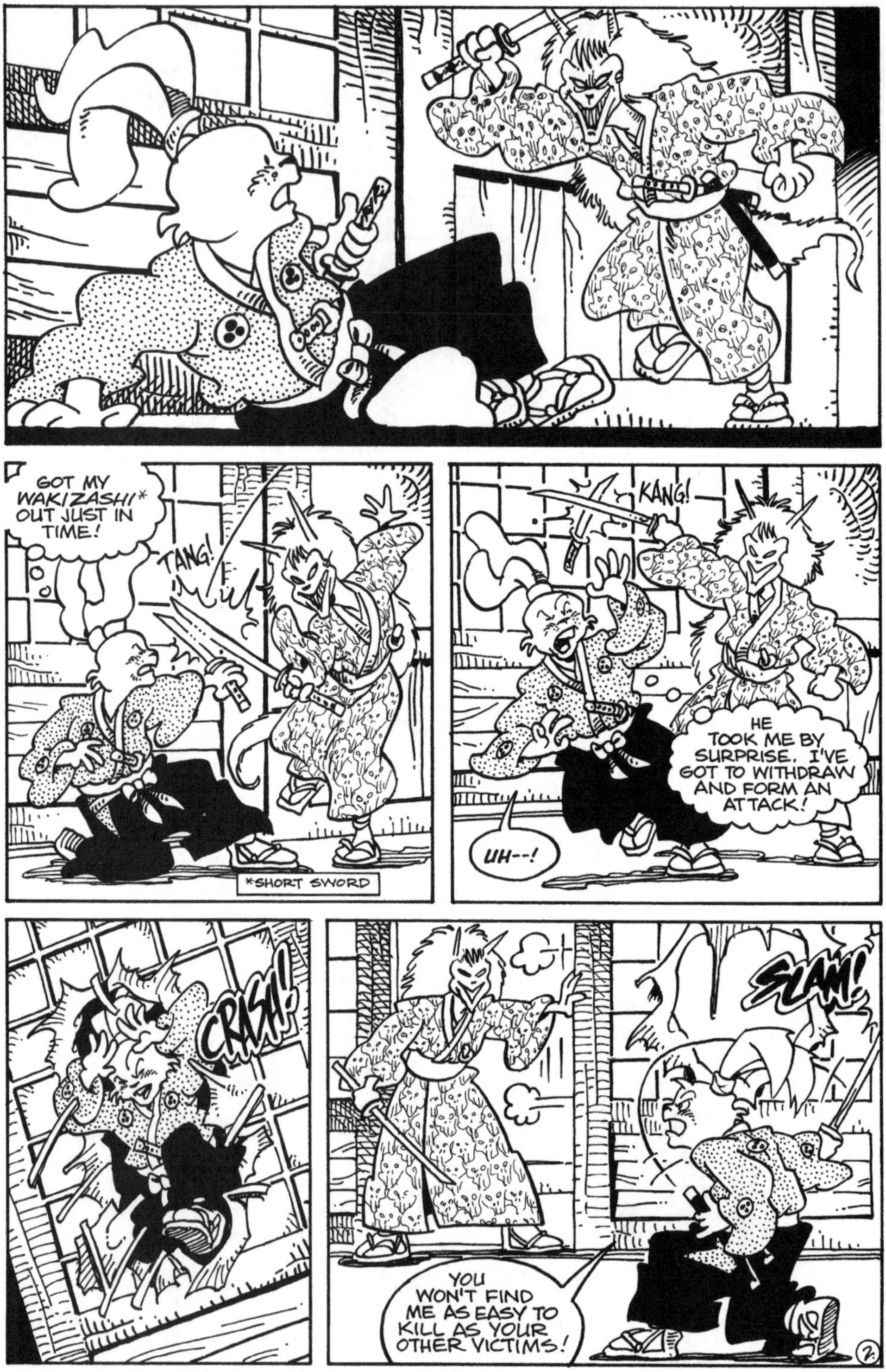
GOT MY WAKIZASHI* OUT JUST IN TIME!
TANG!
*SHORT SWORD
KANG!
UH--!
HE TOOK ME BY SURPRISE. I'VE GOT TO WITHDRAW AND FORM AN ATTACK!
CRASH!
SLAM!
YOU WON'T FIND ME AS EASY TO KILL AS YOUR OTHER VICTIMS!
2.

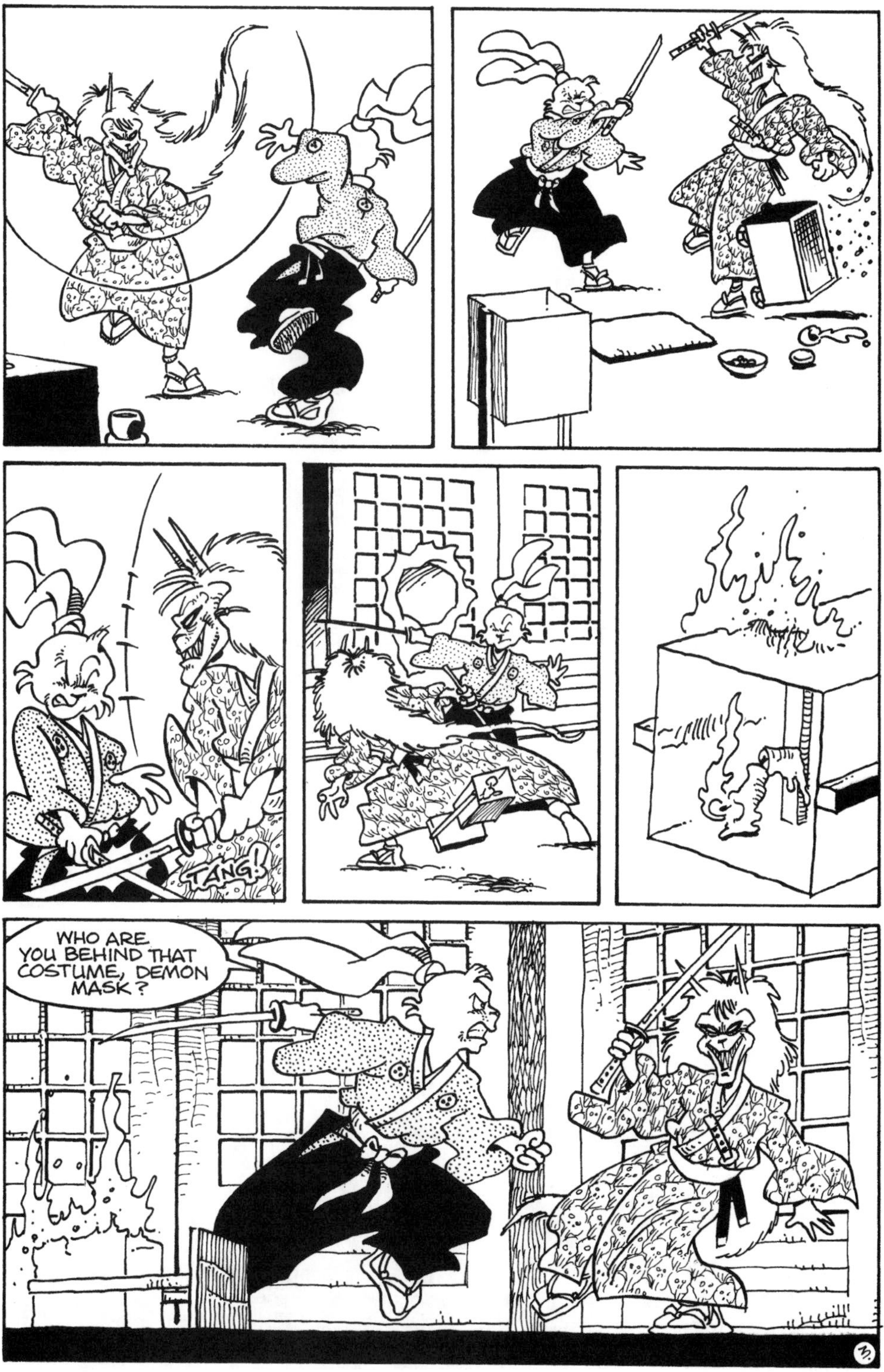
TANG!
WHO ARE YOU BEHIND THAT COSTUME, DEMON MASK?

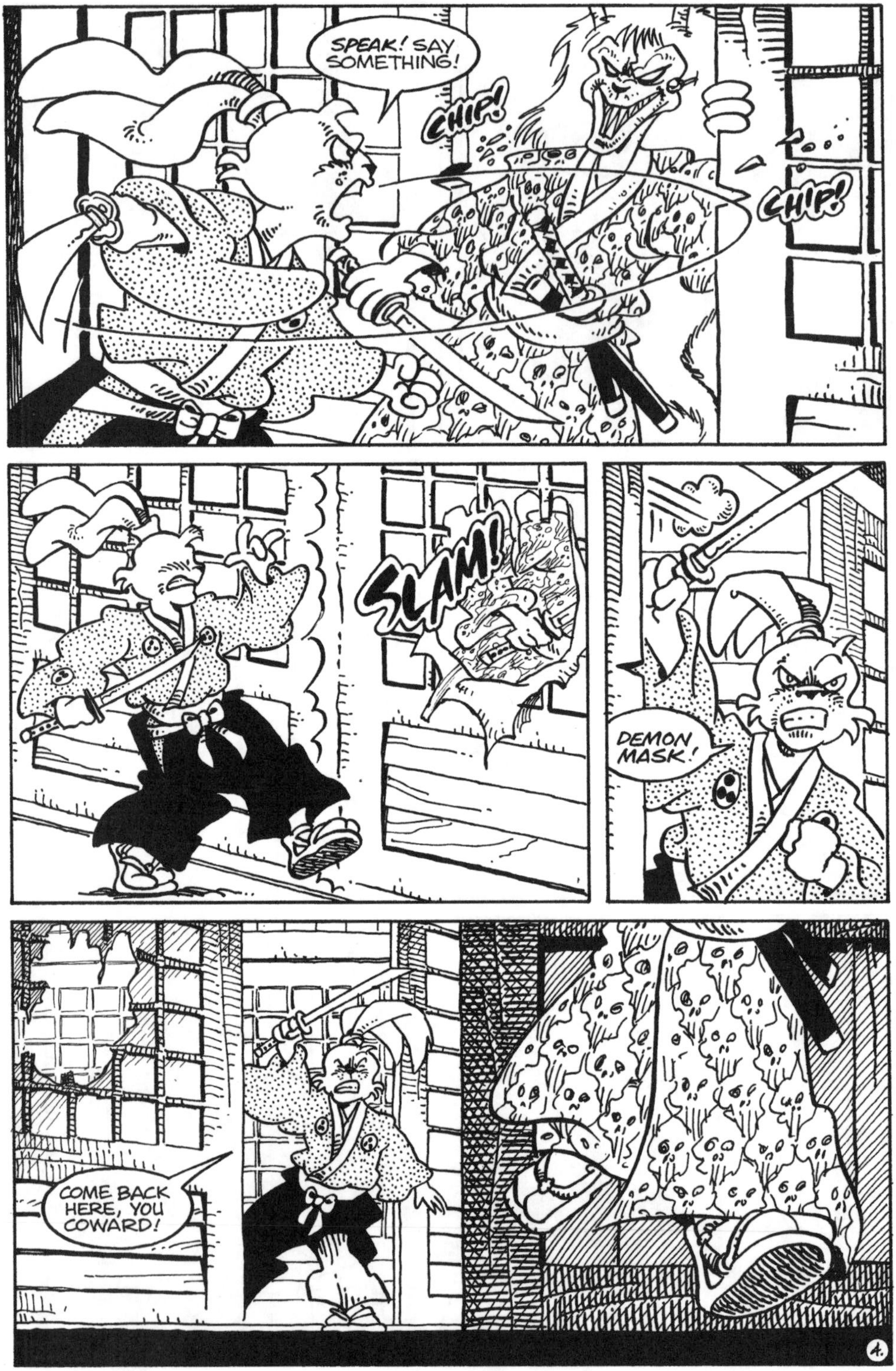
SPEAK! SAY SOMETHING!
CHIP!
CHIP!
SLAM!
DEMON MASK!
COME BACK HERE, YOU COWARD!
4.

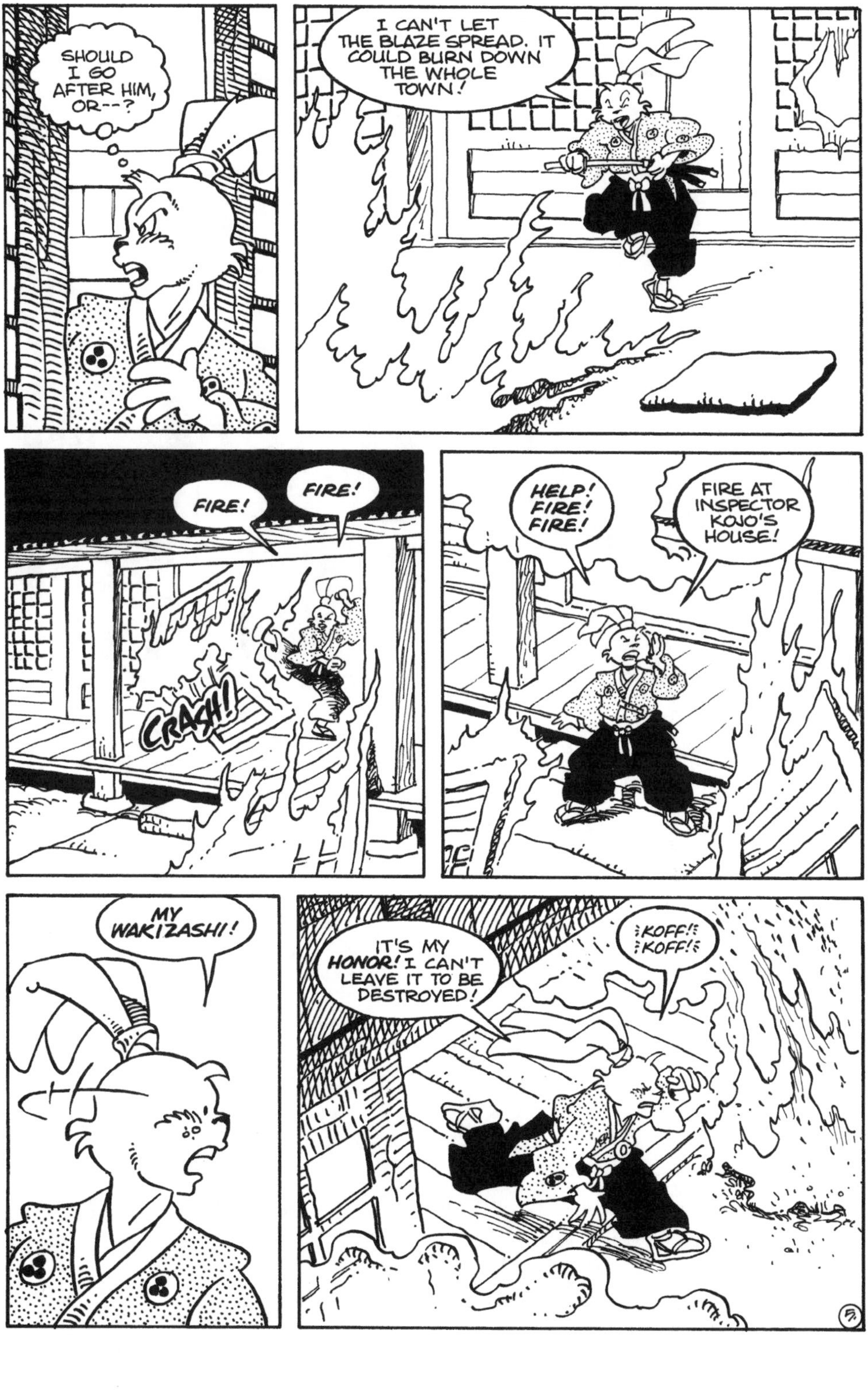
SHOULD I GO AFTER HIM, OR--?
I CAN'T LET THE BLAZE SPREAD. IT COULD BURN DOWN THE WHOLE TOWN!
FIRE!
FIRE!
CRASH!
HELP! FIRE! FIRE!
FIRE AT INSPECTOR KOJO'S HOUSE!
MY WAKIZASHI!
IT'S MY HONOR! I CAN'T LEAVE IT TO BE DESTROYED!
KOFF! KOFF!
5

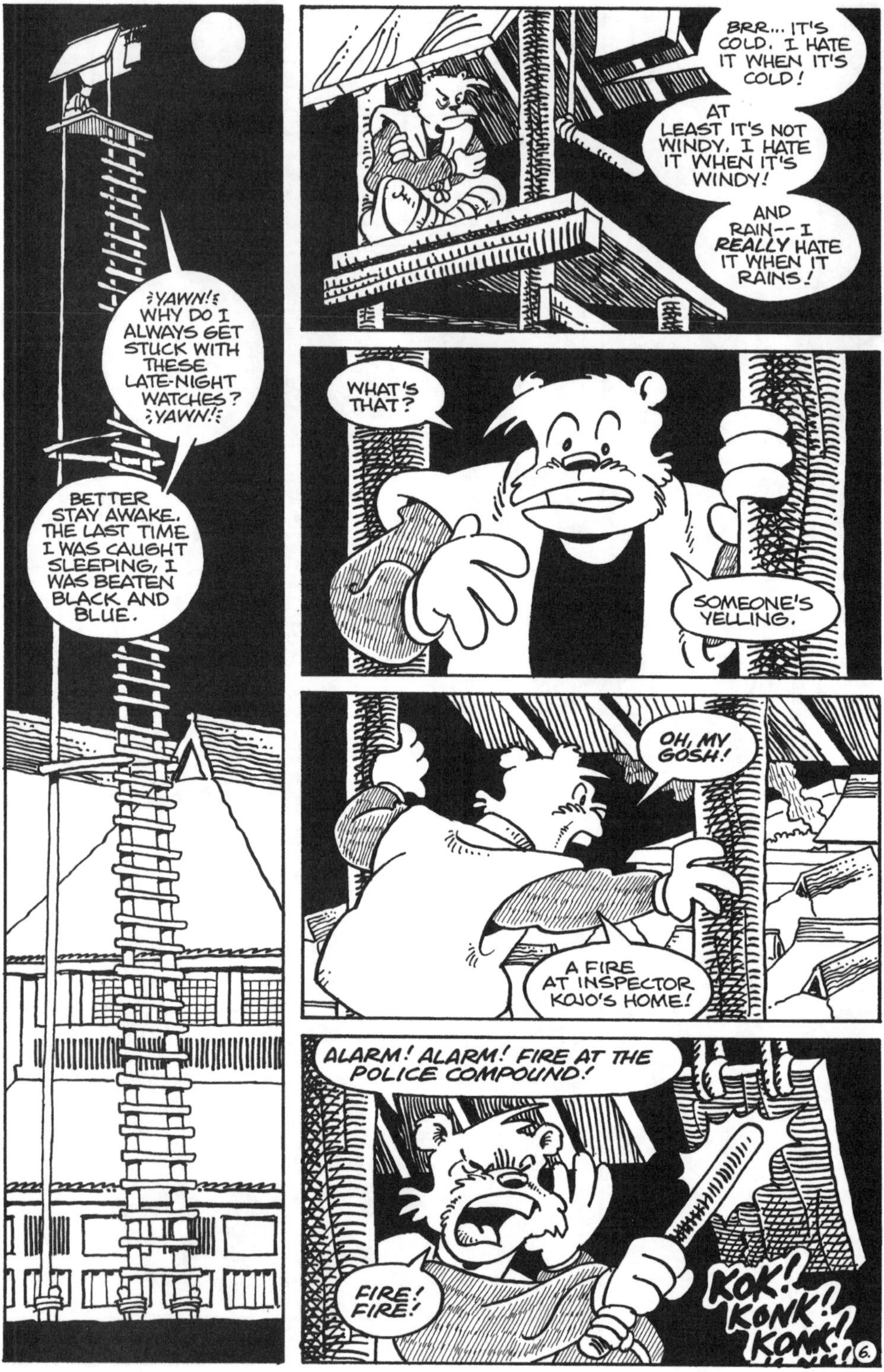

¡YAWN! WHY DO I ALWAYS GET STUCK WITH THESE LATE-NIGHT WATCHES? ¡YAWN!
BETTER STAY AWAKE. THE LAST TIME I WAS CAUGHT SLEEPING, I WAS BEATEN BLACK AND BLUE.
BRR... IT'S COLD. I HATE IT WHEN IT'S COLD!
AT LEAST IT'S NOT WINDY. I HATE IT WHEN IT'S WINDY!
AND RAIN-- I REALLY HATE IT WHEN IT RAINS!
WHAT'S THAT?
SOMEONE'S YELLING.
OH, MY GOSH!
A FIRE AT INSPECTOR KOJO'S HOME!
ALARM! ALARM! FIRE AT THE POLICE COMPOUND!
FIRE! FIRE!
KOK! KONK! KONK!
6.

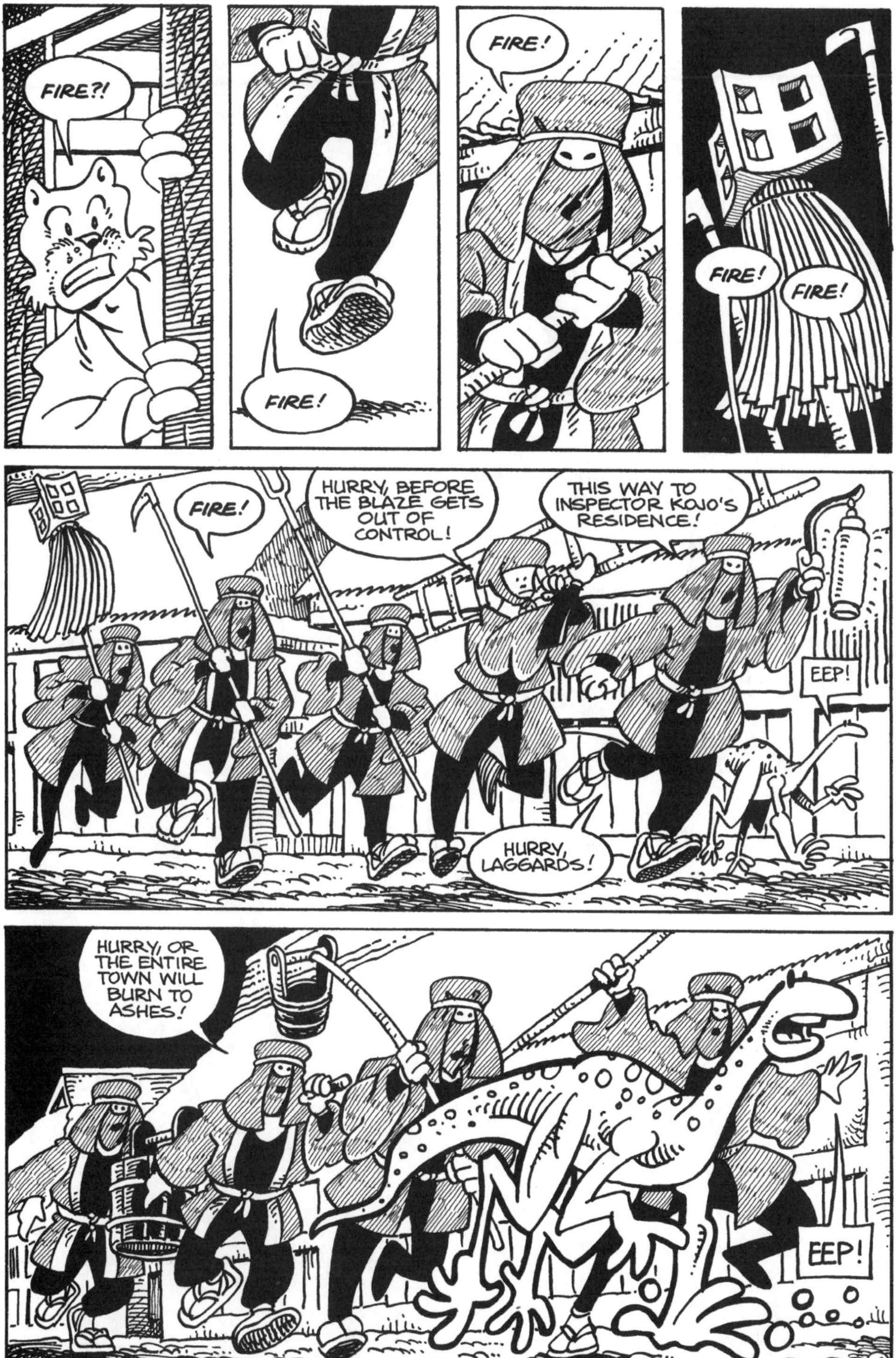
FIRE?!
FIRE!
FIRE!
FIRE!
FIRE!
FIRE!
HURRY, BEFORE THE BLAZE GETS OUT OF CONTROL!
THIS WAY TO INSPECTOR KOJO'S RESIDENCE!
EEP!
HURRY, LAGGARDS!
HURRY, OR THE ENTIRE TOWN WILL BURN TO ASHES!
EEP!
7.

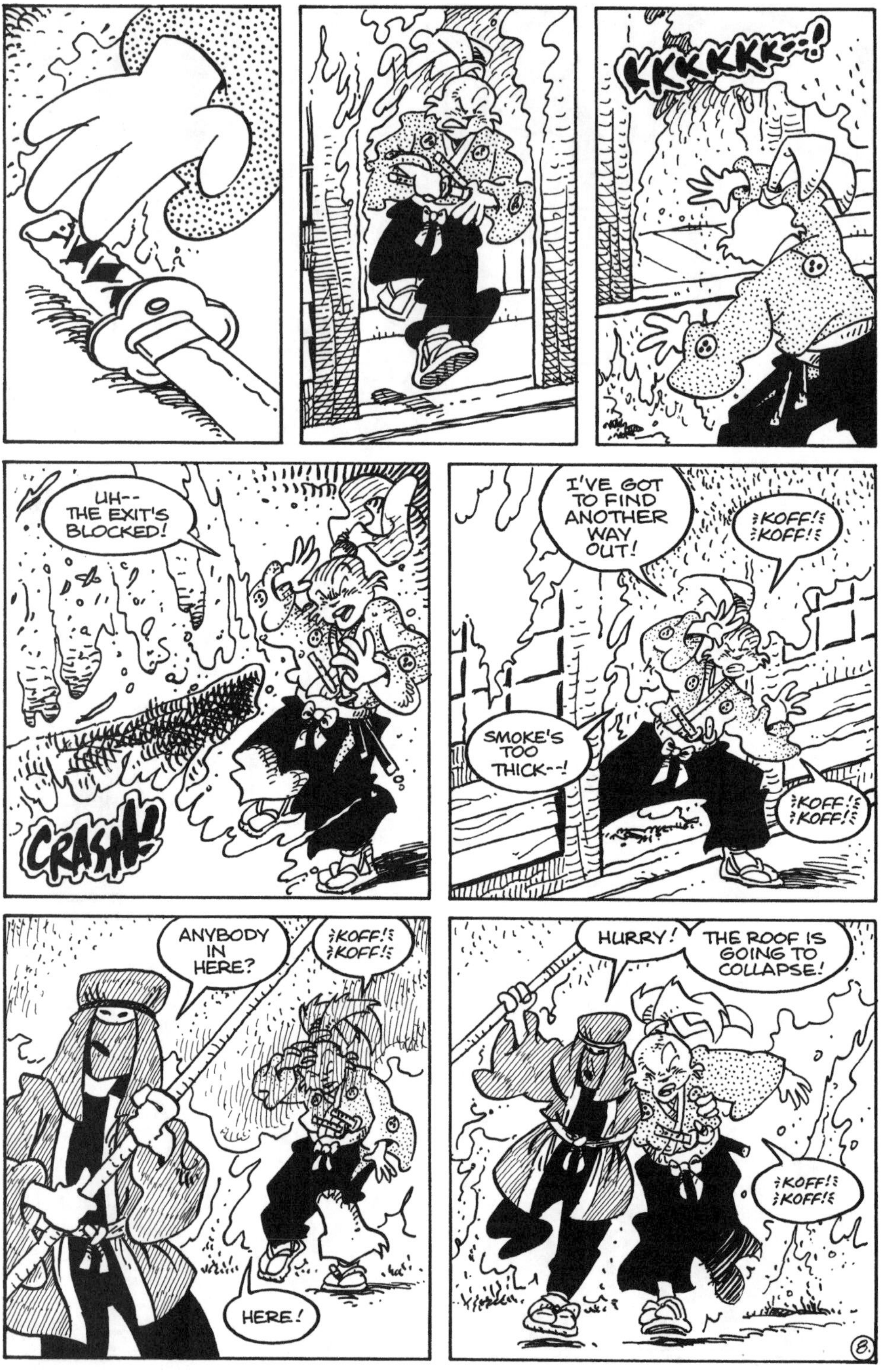
KKKKKK--!
UH-- THE EXIT'S BLOCKED!
CRASH!
I'VE GOT TO FIND ANOTHER WAY OUT!
KOFF! KOFF!
SMOKE'S TOO THICK--!
KOFF! KOFF!
ANYBODY IN HERE?
KOFF! KOFF!
HERE!
HURRY!
THE ROOF IS GOING TO COLLAPSE!
KOFF! KOFF!
8.

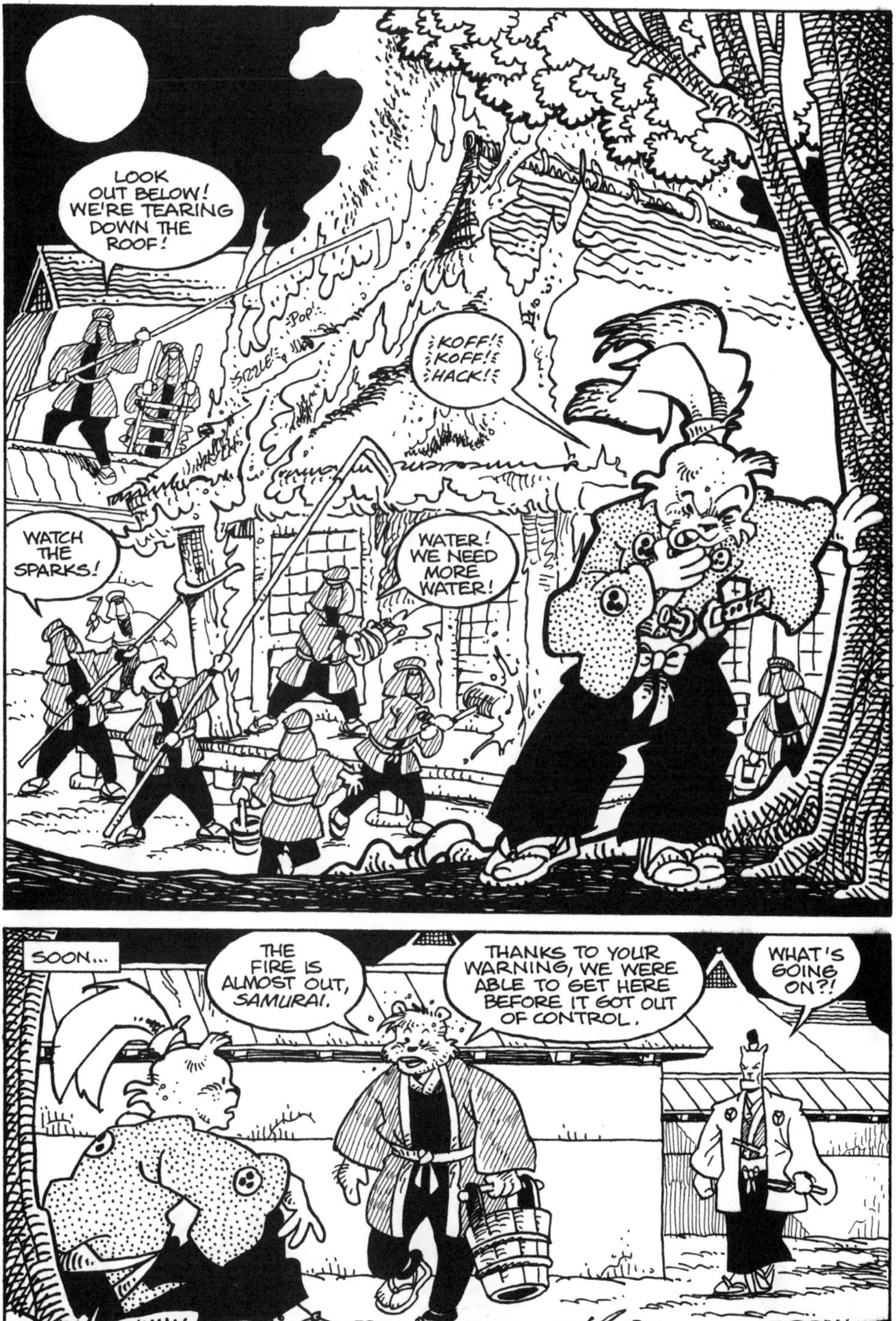
LOOK OUT BELOW! WE'RE TEARING DOWN THE ROOF!
POP
SIZZLE
KOFF! KOFF! HACK!
WATCH THE SPARKS!
WATER! WE NEED MORE WATER!
SOON...
THE FIRE IS ALMOST OUT, SAMURAI.
THANKS TO YOUR WARNING, WE WERE ABLE TO GET HERE BEFORE IT GOT OUT OF CONTROL.
WHAT'S GOING ON?!
9.

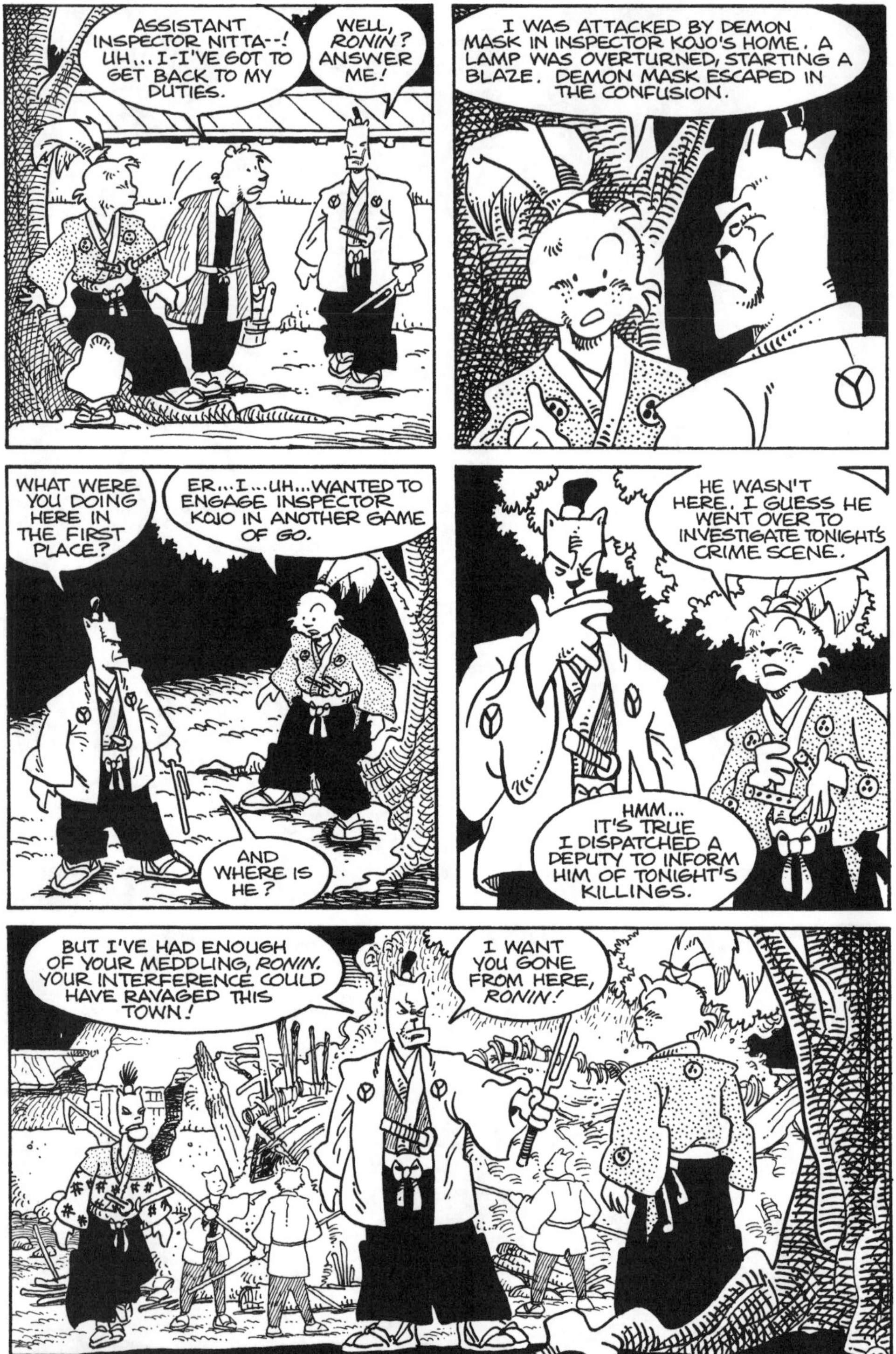
ASSISTANT INSPECTOR NITTA--! UH... I-I'VE GOT TO GET BACK TO MY DUTIES.
WELL, *RONIN*? ANSWER ME!
I WAS ATTACKED BY DEMON MASK IN INSPECTOR KOJO'S HOME. A LAMP WAS OVERTURNED, STARTING A BLAZE. DEMON MASK ESCAPED IN THE CONFUSION.
WHAT WERE YOU DOING HERE IN THE FIRST PLACE?
ER... I... UH... WANTED TO ENGAGE INSPECTOR KOJO IN ANOTHER GAME OF GO.
AND WHERE IS HE?
HE WASN'T HERE. I GUESS HE WENT OVER TO INVESTIGATE TONIGHT'S CRIME SCENE.
HMM... IT'S TRUE I DISPATCHED A DEPUTY TO INFORM HIM OF TONIGHT'S KILLINGS.
BUT I'VE HAD ENOUGH OF YOUR MEDDLING, *RONIN*. YOUR INTERFERENCE COULD HAVE RAVAGED THIS TOWN!
I WANT YOU GONE FROM HERE, *RONIN*!
10.

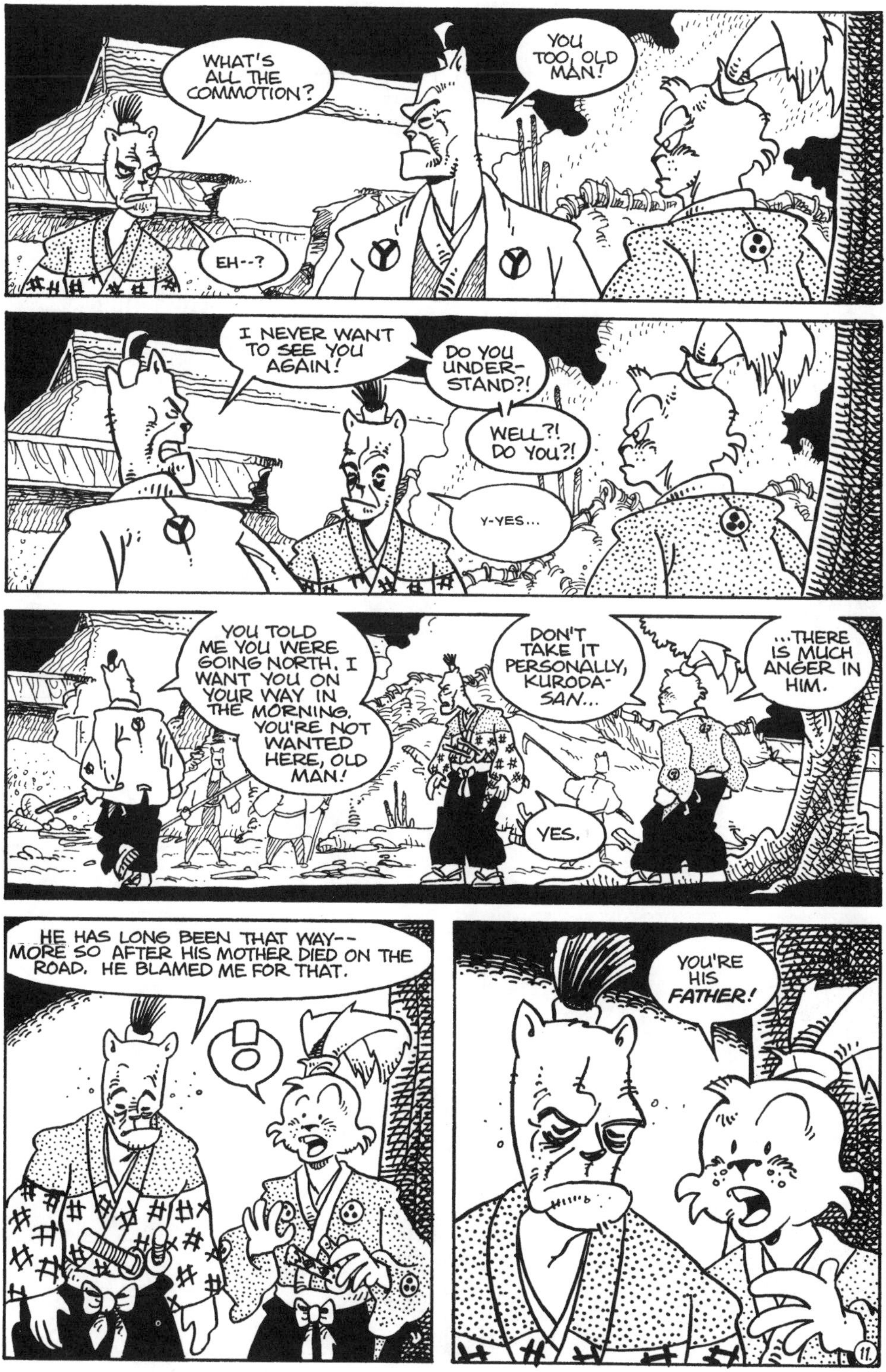
WHAT'S ALL THE COMMOTION?
EH--?
YOU TOO, OLD MAN!
I NEVER WANT TO SEE YOU AGAIN!
DO YOU UNDER-STAND?!
WELL?! DO YOU?!
Y-YES...
YOU TOLD ME YOU WERE GOING NORTH. I WANT YOU ON YOUR WAY IN THE MORNING. YOU'RE NOT WANTED HERE, OLD MAN!
DON'T TAKE IT PERSONALLY, KURODA-SAN...
YES.
...THERE IS MUCH ANGER IN HIM.
HE HAS LONG BEEN THAT WAY-- MORE SO AFTER HIS MOTHER DIED ON THE ROAD. HE BLAMED ME FOR THAT.
!
YOU'RE HIS ***FATHER!***
11.

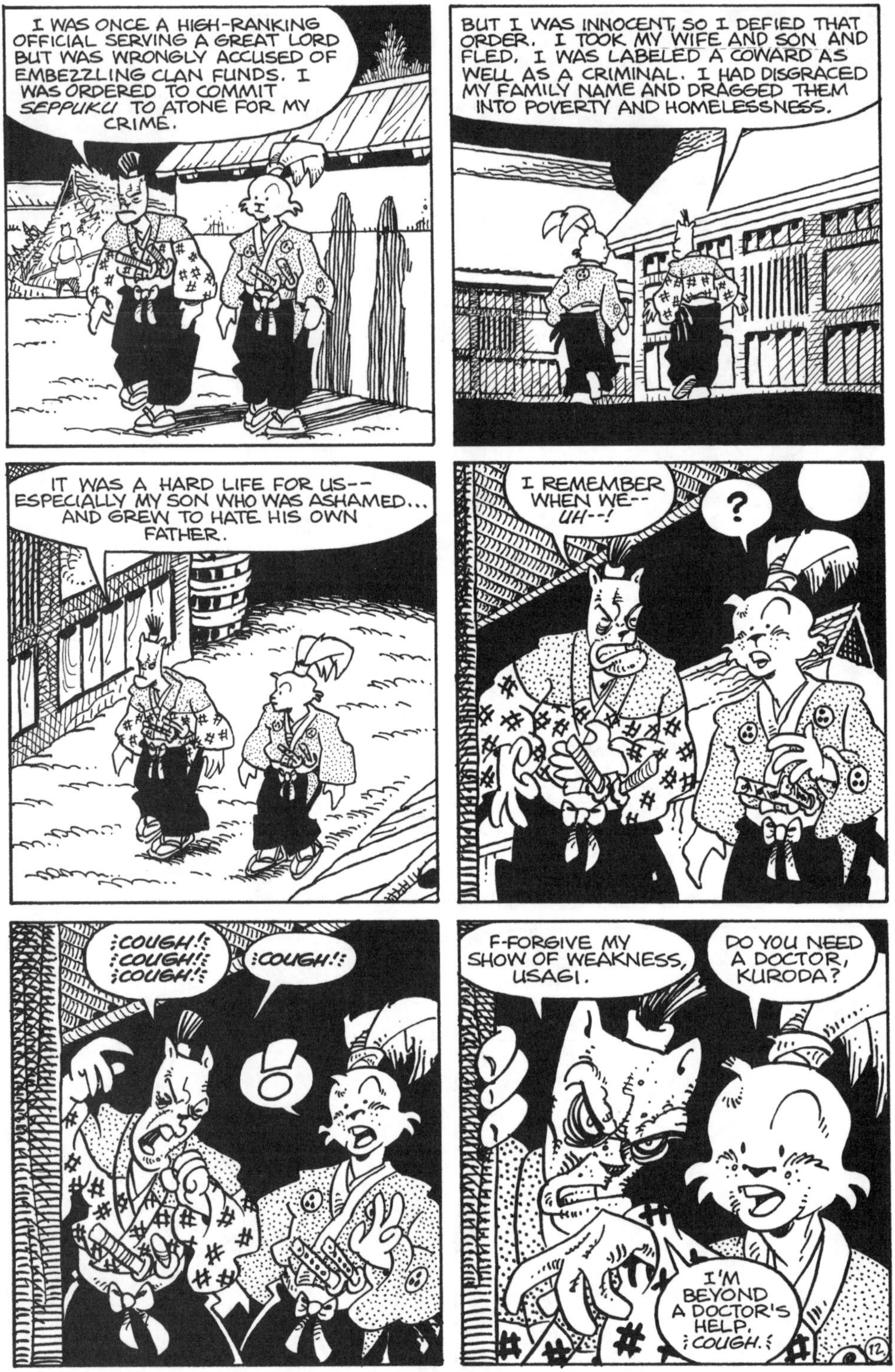
I WAS ONCE A HIGH-RANKING OFFICIAL SERVING A GREAT LORD BUT WAS WRONGLY ACCUSED OF EMBEZZLING CLAN FUNDS. I WAS ORDERED TO COMMIT *SEPPUKU* TO ATONE FOR MY CRIME.
BUT I WAS INNOCENT, SO I DEFIED THAT ORDER. I TOOK MY WIFE AND SON AND FLED. I WAS LABELED A COWARD AS WELL AS A CRIMINAL. I HAD DISGRACED MY FAMILY NAME AND DRAGGED THEM INTO POVERTY AND HOMELESSNESS.
IT WAS A HARD LIFE FOR US-- ESPECIALLY MY SON WHO WAS ASHAMED... AND GREW TO HATE HIS OWN FATHER.
I REMEMBER WHEN WE-- *UH--!*
?
;COUGH!; ;COUGH!; ;COUGH!;
;COUGH!;
F-FORGIVE MY SHOW OF WEAKNESS, USAGI.
DO YOU NEED A DOCTOR, KURODA?
I'M BEYOND A DOCTOR'S HELP. ;COUGH.;
12

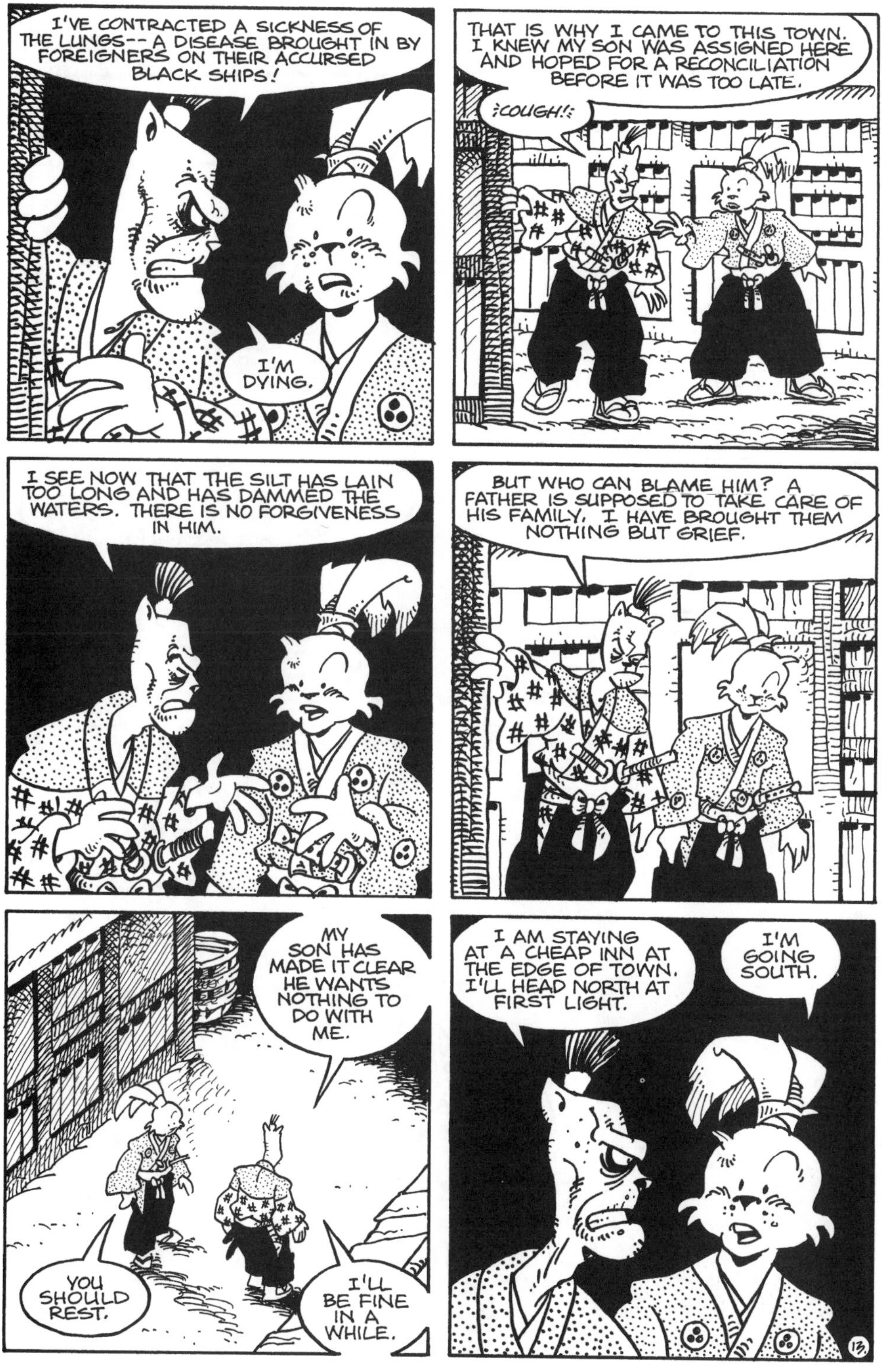
I'VE CONTRACTED A SICKNESS OF THE LUNGS-- A DISEASE BROUGHT IN BY FOREIGNERS ON THEIR ACCURSED BLACK SHIPS!
I'M DYING.
THAT IS WHY I CAME TO THIS TOWN. I KNEW MY SON WAS ASSIGNED HERE AND HOPED FOR A RECONCILIATION BEFORE IT WAS TOO LATE.
COUGH!
I SEE NOW THAT THE SILT HAS LAIN TOO LONG AND HAS DAMMED THE WATERS. THERE IS NO FORGIVENESS IN HIM.
BUT WHO CAN BLAME HIM? A FATHER IS SUPPOSED TO TAKE CARE OF HIS FAMILY. I HAVE BROUGHT THEM NOTHING BUT GRIEF.
MY SON HAS MADE IT CLEAR HE WANTS NOTHING TO DO WITH ME.
YOU SHOULD REST.
I'LL BE FINE IN A WHILE.
I AM STAYING AT A CHEAP INN AT THE EDGE OF TOWN. I'LL HEAD NORTH AT FIRST LIGHT.
I'M GOING SOUTH.
13.

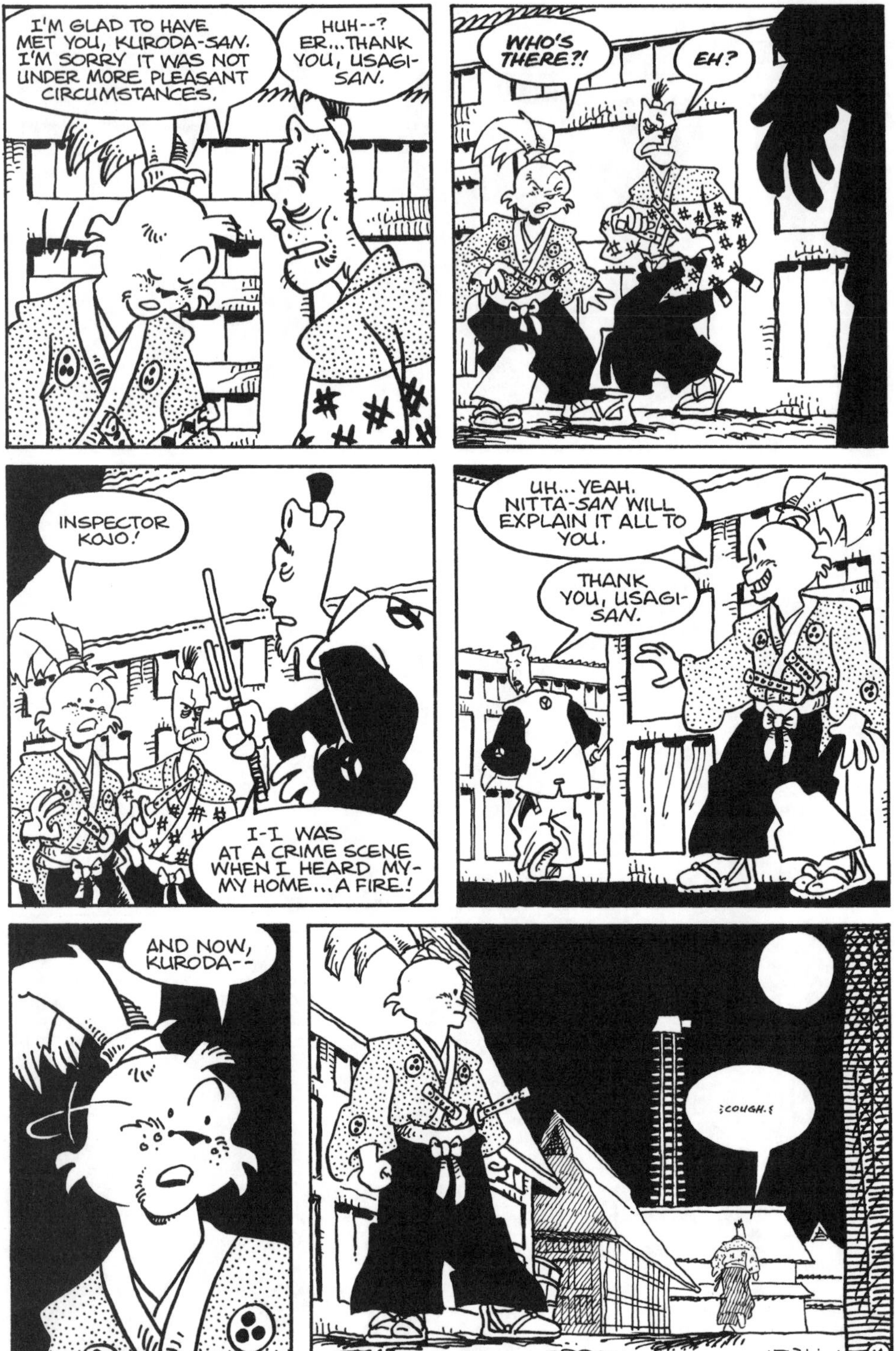
I'M GLAD TO HAVE MET YOU, KURODA-SAN. I'M SORRY IT WAS NOT UNDER MORE PLEASANT CIRCUMSTANCES.
HUH--? ER...THANK YOU, USAGI-SAN.
WHO'S THERE?!
EH?
INSPECTOR KOJO!
I-I WAS AT A CRIME SCENE WHEN I HEARD MY-MY HOME...A FIRE!
UH... YEAH. NITTA-SAN WILL EXPLAIN IT ALL TO YOU.
THANK YOU, USAGI-SAN.
AND NOW, KURODA--
COUGH.
14.

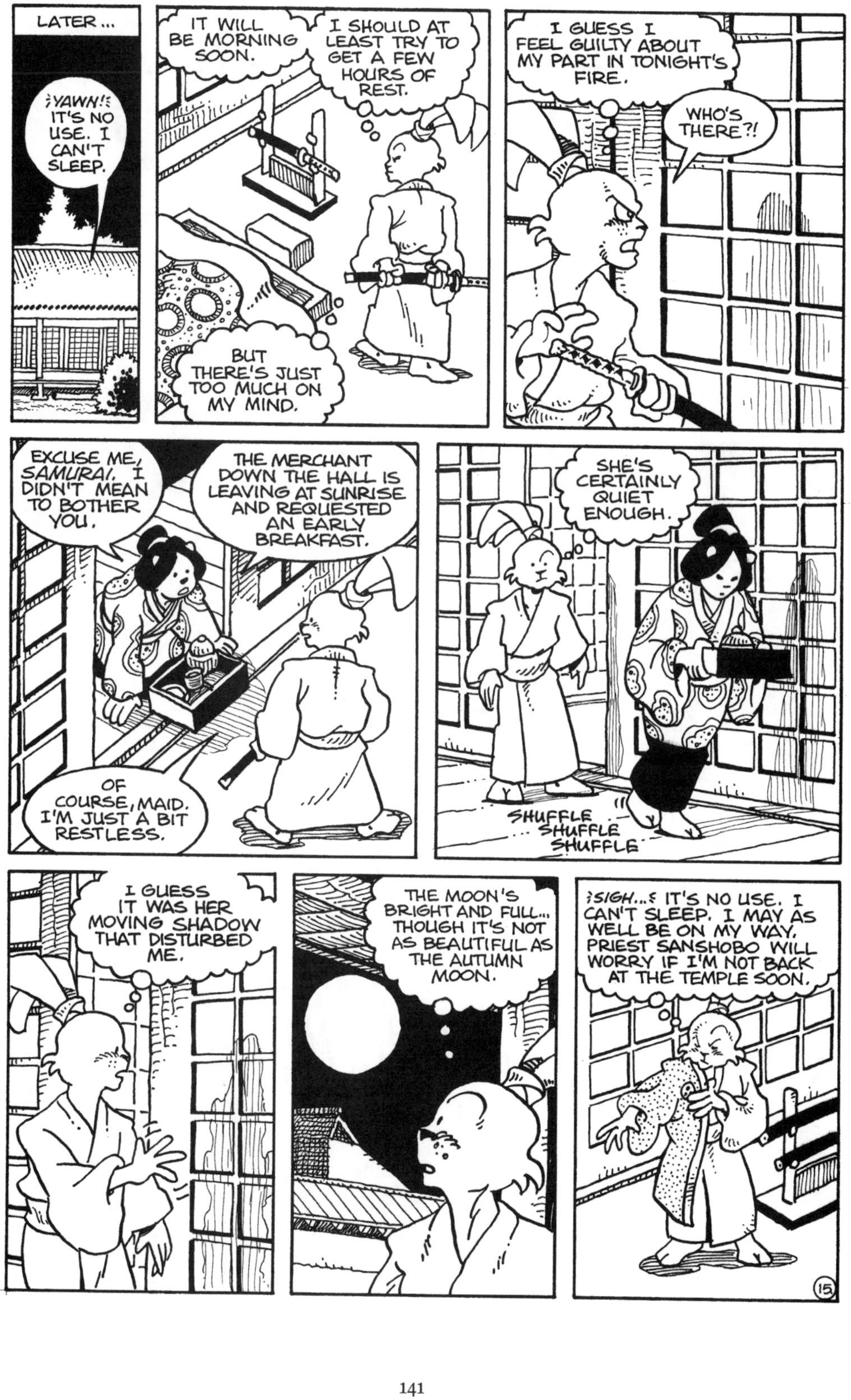
LATER...
¡YAWN!¡ IT'S NO USE. I CAN'T SLEEP.
IT WILL BE MORNING SOON.
I SHOULD AT LEAST TRY TO GET A FEW HOURS OF REST.
BUT THERE'S JUST TOO MUCH ON MY MIND.
I GUESS I FEEL GUILTY ABOUT MY PART IN TONIGHT'S FIRE.
WHO'S THERE?!
EXCUSE ME, SAMURAI. I DIDN'T MEAN TO BOTHER YOU.
THE MERCHANT DOWN THE HALL IS LEAVING AT SUNRISE AND REQUESTED AN EARLY BREAKFAST.
OF COURSE, MAID. I'M JUST A BIT RESTLESS.
SHE'S CERTAINLY QUIET ENOUGH.
SHUFFLE ... SHUFFLE SHUFFLE
I GUESS IT WAS HER MOVING SHADOW THAT DISTURBED ME.
THE MOON'S BRIGHT AND FULL... THOUGH IT'S NOT AS BEAUTIFUL AS THE AUTUMN MOON.
¡SIGH...¡ IT'S NO USE. I CAN'T SLEEP. I MAY AS WELL BE ON MY WAY. PRIEST SANSHOBO WILL WORRY IF I'M NOT BACK AT THE TEMPLE SOON.
15

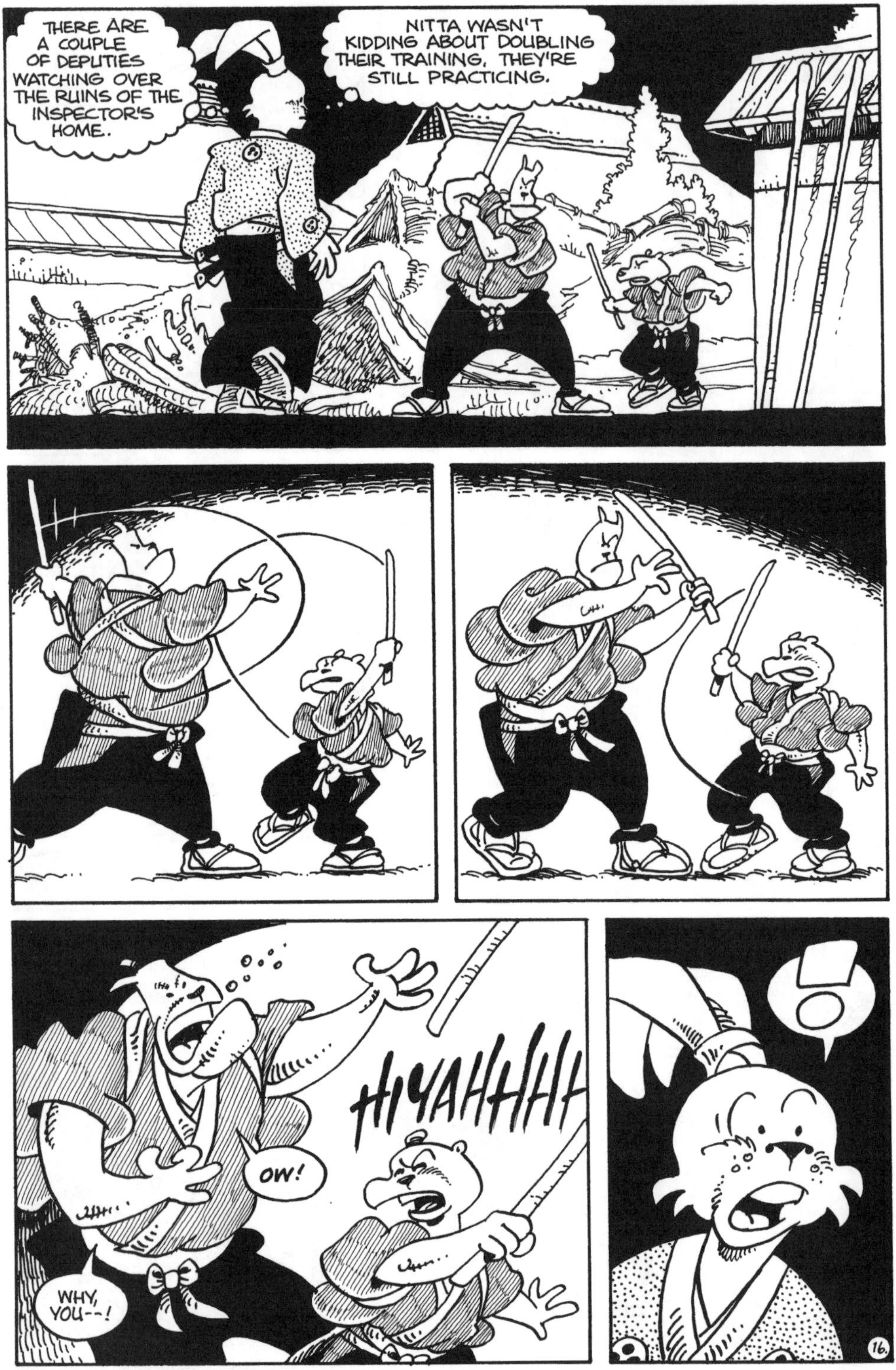
THERE ARE A COUPLE OF DEPUTIES WATCHING OVER THE RUINS OF THE INSPECTOR'S HOME.
NITTA WASN'T KIDDING ABOUT DOUBLING THEIR TRAINING. THEY'RE STILL PRACTICING.
OW!
WHY, YOU--!
HIYAHHHH
!
16.

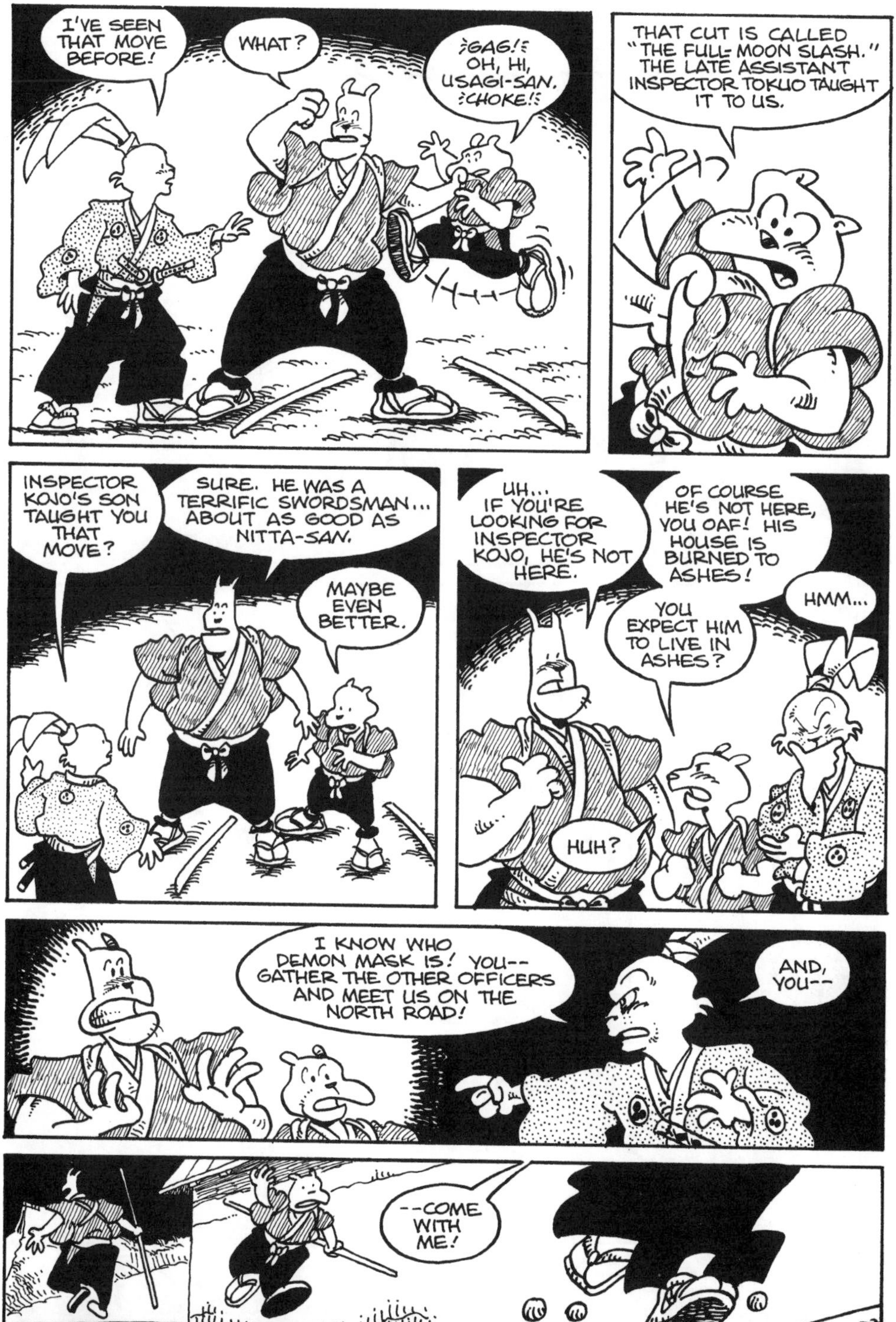
I'VE SEEN THAT MOVE BEFORE!
WHAT?
¡GAG!¡ OH, HI, USAGI-SAN. ¡CHOKE!¡
THAT CUT IS CALLED "THE FULL-MOON SLASH." THE LATE ASSISTANT INSPECTOR TOKUO TAUGHT IT TO US.
INSPECTOR KOJO'S SON TAUGHT YOU THAT MOVE?
SURE. HE WAS A TERRIFIC SWORDSMAN... ABOUT AS GOOD AS NITTA-SAN.
MAYBE EVEN BETTER.
UH... IF YOU'RE LOOKING FOR INSPECTOR KOJO, HE'S NOT HERE.
OF COURSE HE'S NOT HERE, YOU OAF! HIS HOUSE IS BURNED TO ASHES!
YOU EXPECT HIM TO LIVE IN ASHES?
HMM...
HUH?
I KNOW WHO DEMON MASK IS! YOU-- GATHER THE OTHER OFFICERS AND MEET US ON THE NORTH ROAD!
AND, YOU--
--COME WITH ME!
17.

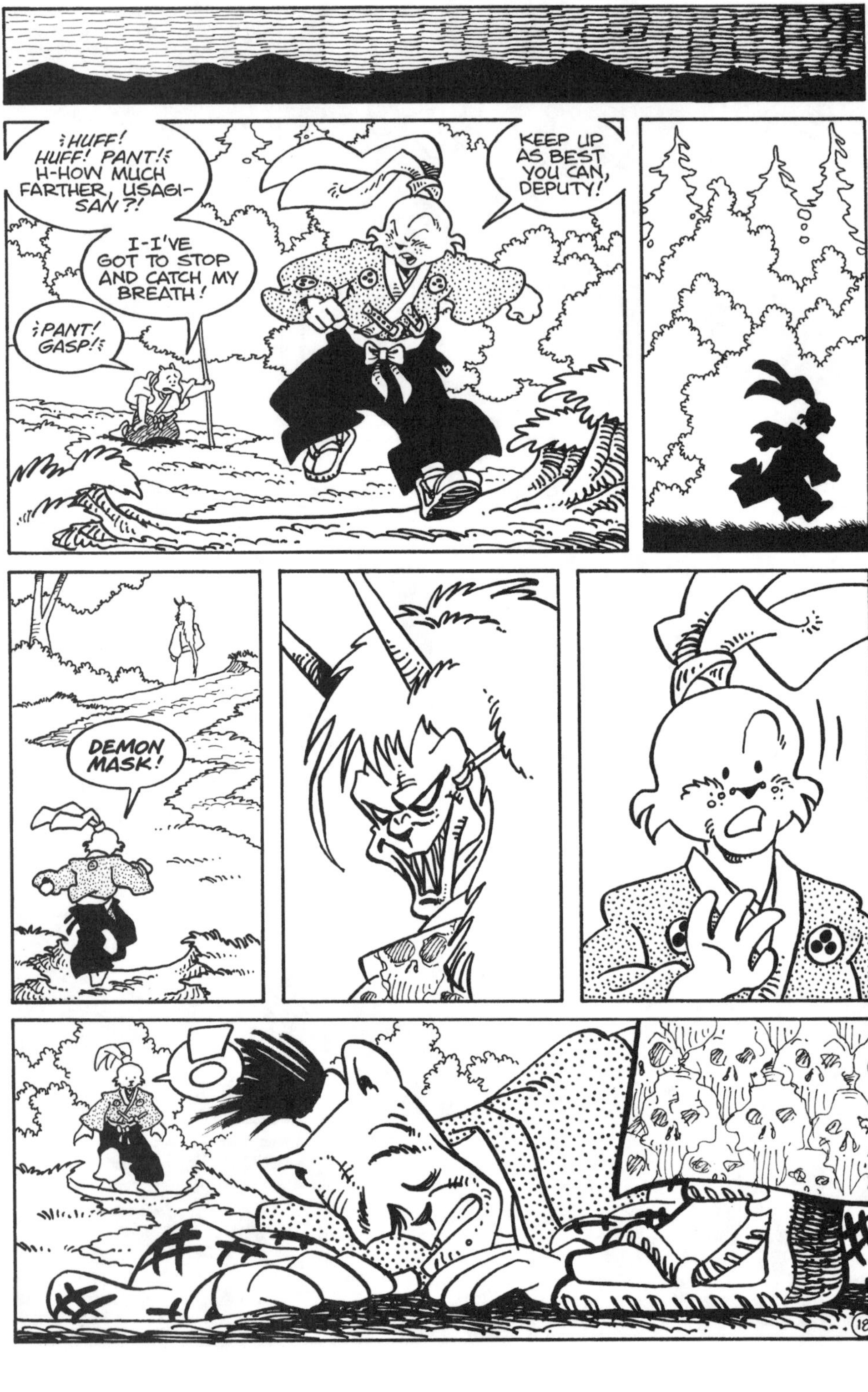

HUFF! HUFF! PANT! H-HOW MUCH FARTHER, USAGI-SAN?!
I-I'VE GOT TO STOP AND CATCH MY BREATH!
PANT! GASP!
KEEP UP AS BEST YOU CAN, DEPUTY!
DEMON MASK!
18

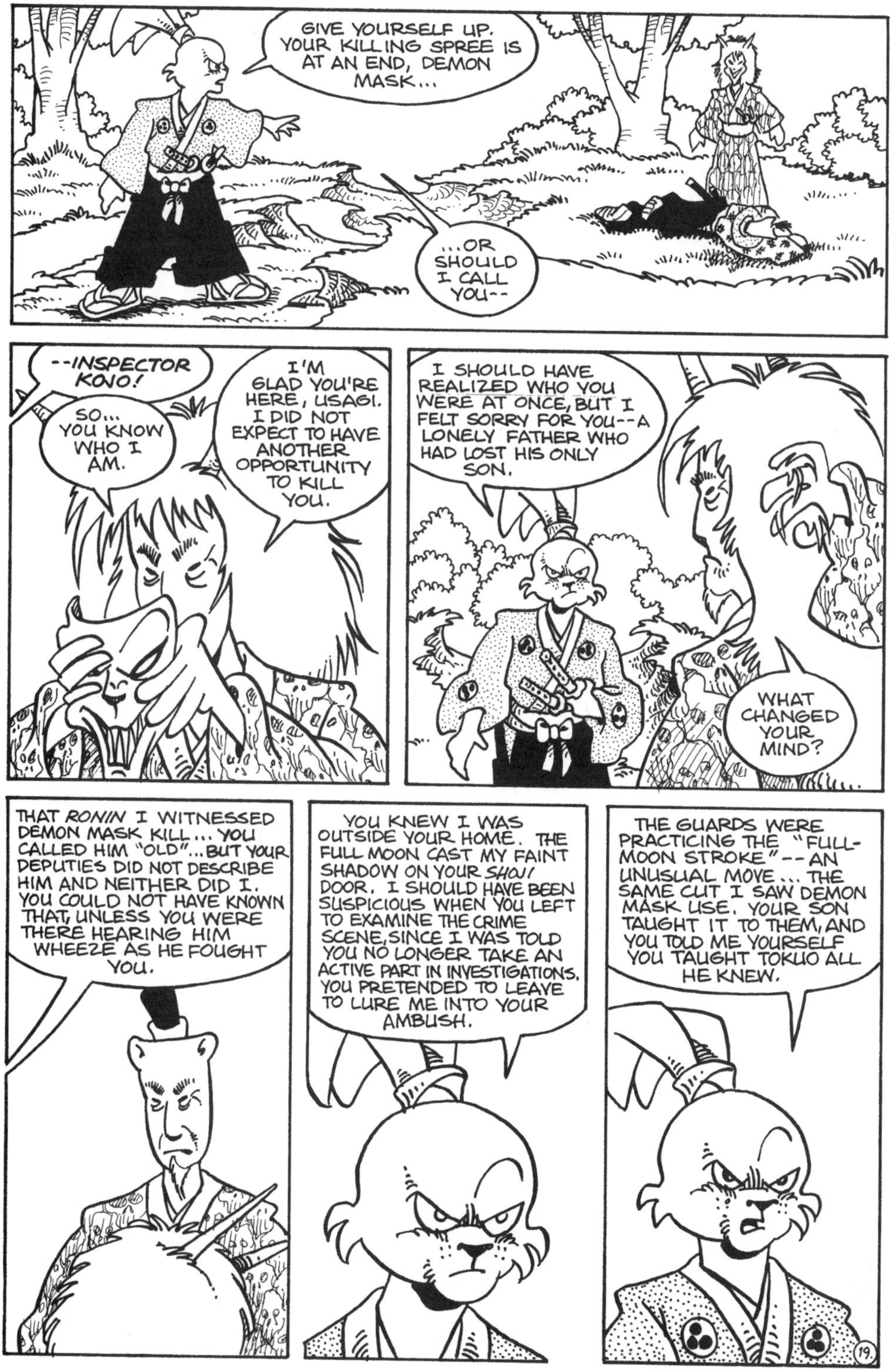
GIVE YOURSELF UP. YOUR KILLING SPREE IS AT AN END, DEMON MASK...
...OR SHOULD I CALL YOU--
--INSPECTOR KOJO!
SO... YOU KNOW WHO I AM.
I'M GLAD YOU'RE HERE, USAGI. I DID NOT EXPECT TO HAVE ANOTHER OPPORTUNITY TO KILL YOU.
I SHOULD HAVE REALIZED WHO YOU WERE AT ONCE, BUT I FELT SORRY FOR YOU--A LONELY FATHER WHO HAD LOST HIS ONLY SON.
WHAT CHANGED YOUR MIND?
THAT *RONIN* I WITNESSED DEMON MASK KILL... YOU CALLED HIM "OLD"... BUT YOUR DEPUTIES DID NOT DESCRIBE HIM AND NEITHER DID I. YOU COULD NOT HAVE KNOWN THAT, UNLESS YOU WERE THERE HEARING HIM WHEEZE AS HE FOUGHT YOU.
YOU KNEW I WAS OUTSIDE YOUR HOME. THE FULL MOON CAST MY FAINT SHADOW ON YOUR *SHOJI* DOOR. I SHOULD HAVE BEEN SUSPICIOUS WHEN YOU LEFT TO EXAMINE THE CRIME SCENE, SINCE I WAS TOLD YOU NO LONGER TAKE AN ACTIVE PART IN INVESTIGATIONS. YOU PRETENDED TO LEAVE TO LURE ME INTO YOUR AMBUSH.
THE GUARDS WERE PRACTICING THE "FULL-MOON STROKE"--AN UNUSUAL MOVE... THE SAME CUT I SAW DEMON MASK USE. YOUR SON TAUGHT IT TO THEM, AND YOU TOLD ME YOURSELF YOU TAUGHT TOKUO ALL HE KNEW.
19.

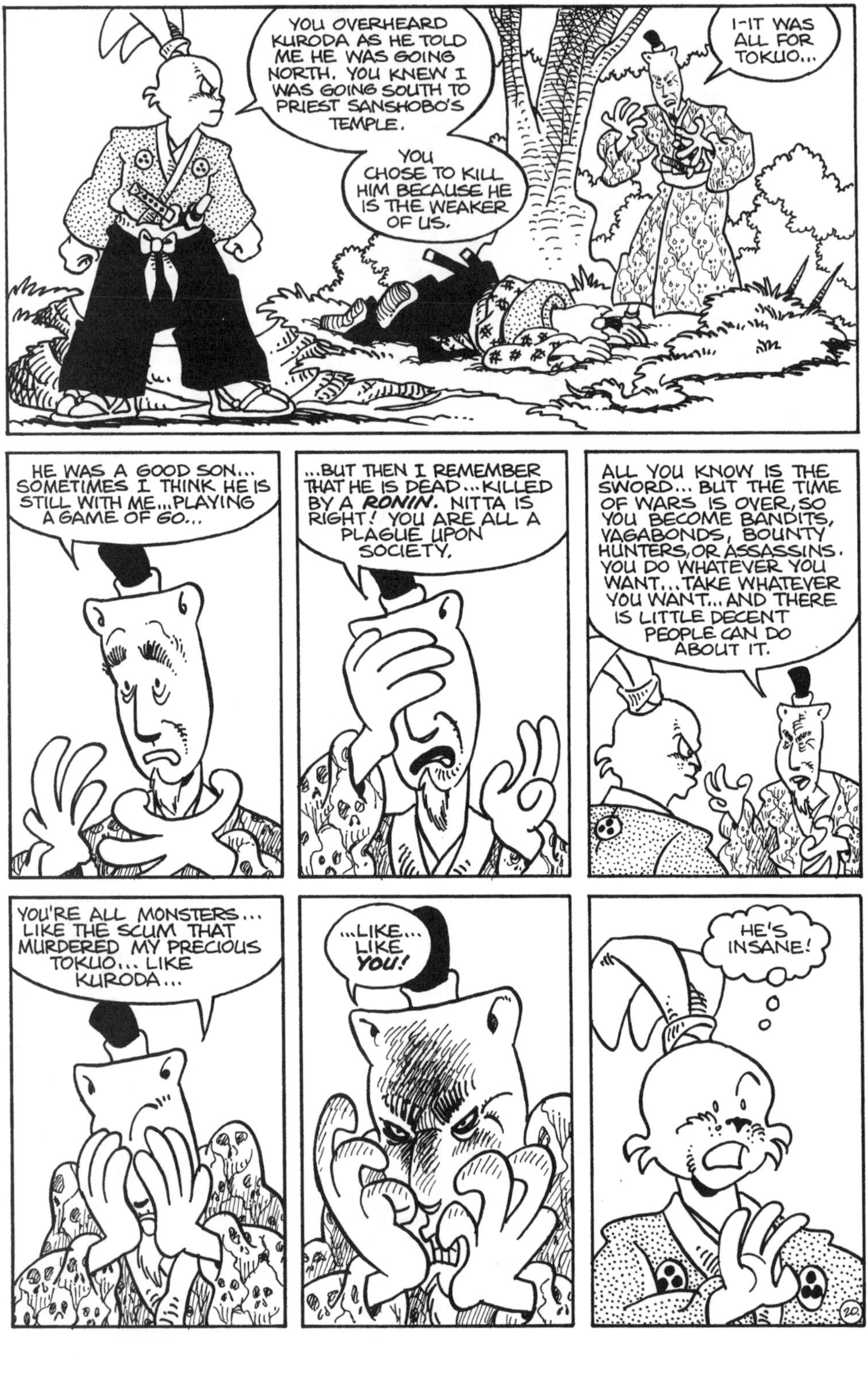
YOU OVERHEARD KURODA AS HE TOLD ME HE WAS GOING NORTH. YOU KNEW I WAS GOING SOUTH TO PRIEST SANSHOBO'S TEMPLE.
YOU CHOSE TO KILL HIM BECAUSE HE IS THE WEAKER OF US.
I-IT WAS ALL FOR TOKUO...
HE WAS A GOOD SON... SOMETIMES I THINK HE IS STILL WITH ME...PLAYING A GAME OF GO...
...BUT THEN I REMEMBER THAT HE IS DEAD...KILLED BY A *RONIN.* NITTA IS RIGHT! YOU ARE ALL A PLAGUE UPON SOCIETY.
ALL YOU KNOW IS THE SWORD... BUT THE TIME OF WARS IS OVER, SO YOU BECOME BANDITS, VAGABONDS, BOUNTY HUNTERS, OR ASSASSINS. YOU DO WHATEVER YOU WANT... TAKE WHATEVER YOU WANT... AND THERE IS LITTLE DECENT PEOPLE CAN DO ABOUT IT.
YOU'RE ALL MONSTERS... LIKE THE SCUM THAT MURDERED MY PRECIOUS TOKUO... LIKE KURODA...
...LIKE... LIKE ***YOU!***
HE'S INSANE!
20.

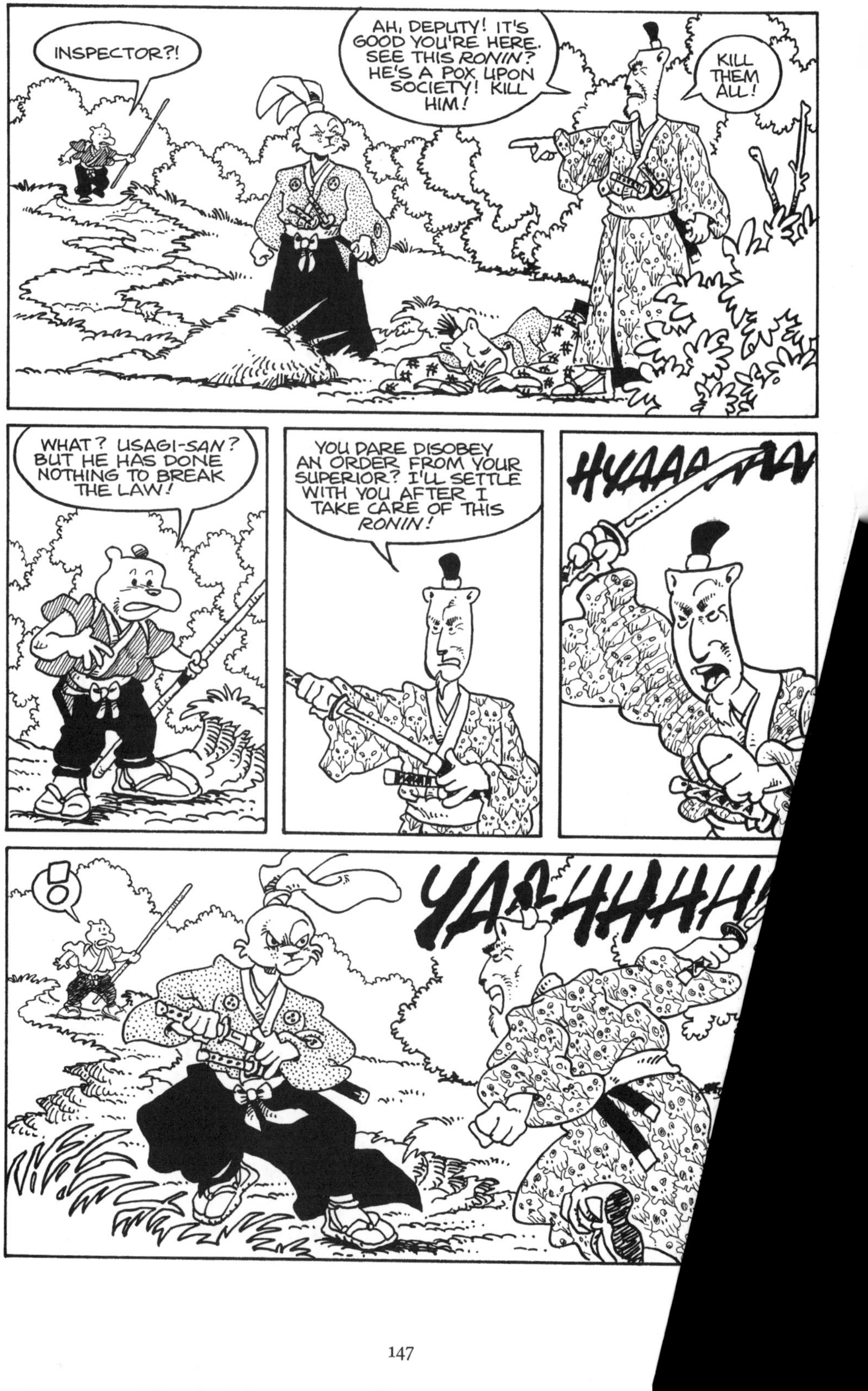
INSPECTOR?!
AH, DEPUTY! IT'S GOOD YOU'RE HERE. SEE THIS *RONIN*? HE'S A POX UPON SOCIETY! KILL HIM!
KILL THEM ALL!
WHAT? USAGI-*SAN*? BUT HE HAS DONE NOTHING TO BREAK THE LAW!
YOU DARE DISOBEY AN ORDER FROM YOUR SUPERIOR? I'LL SETTLE WITH YOU AFTER I TAKE CARE OF THIS *RONIN*!
HYAAAAAA
YAAHHHHH

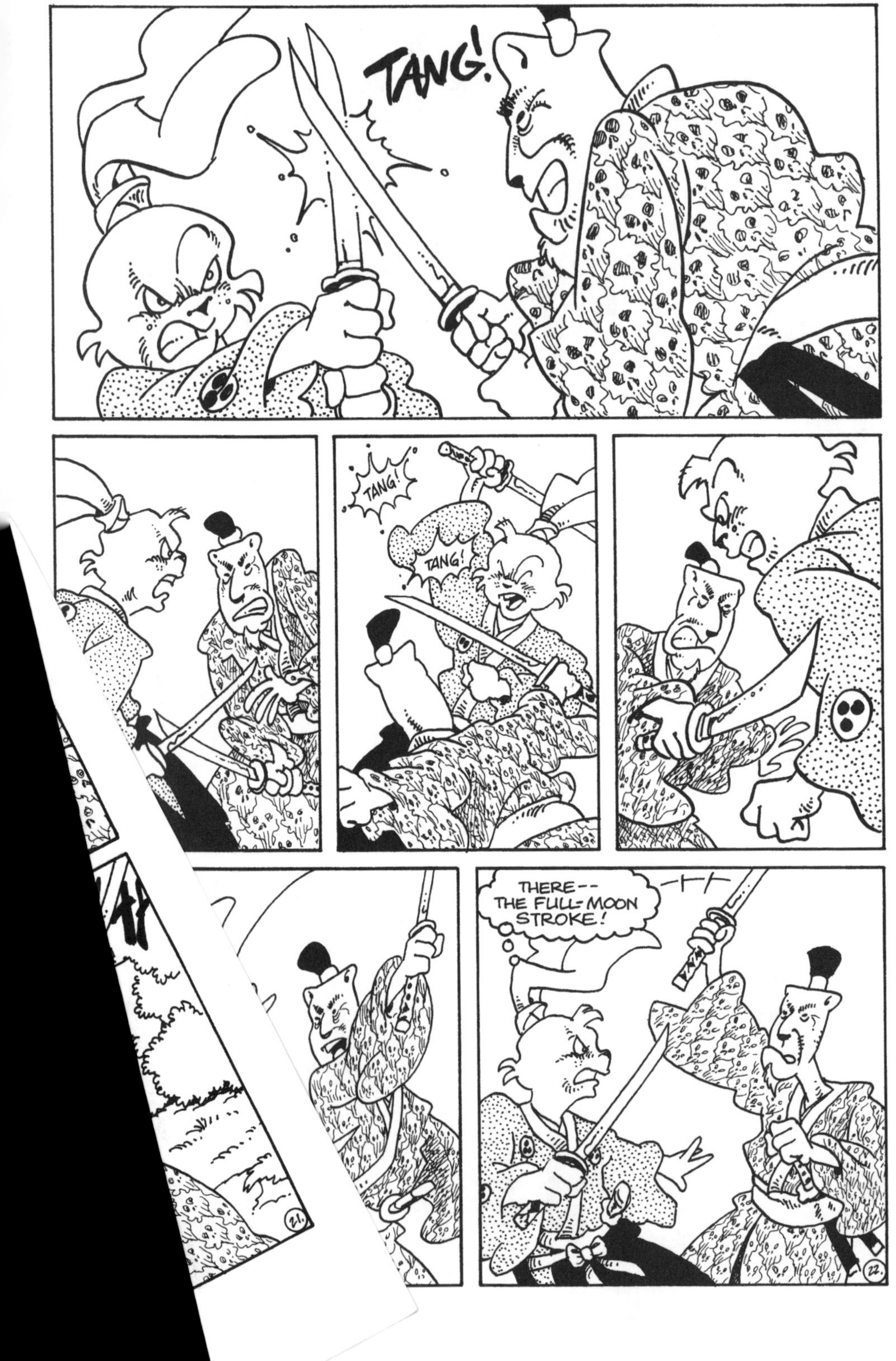
TANG!
TANG!
TANG!
THERE-- THE FULL-MOON STROKE!
21.
22.

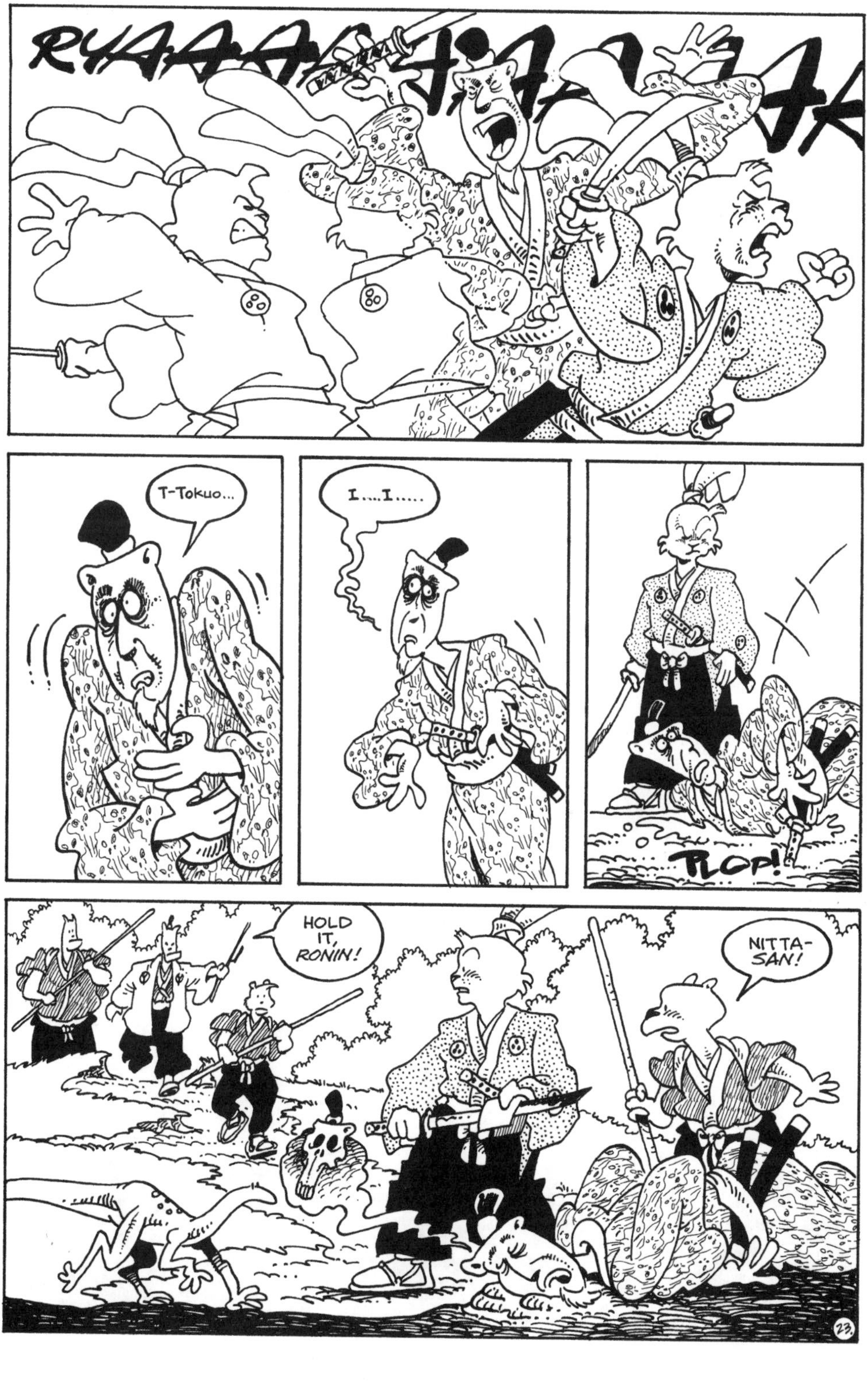
RYAAAAAAAAAAAAAAAAAAAAK
T-Tokuo...
I....I.....
PLOP!
HOLD IT, RONIN!
NITTA-SAN!
23.

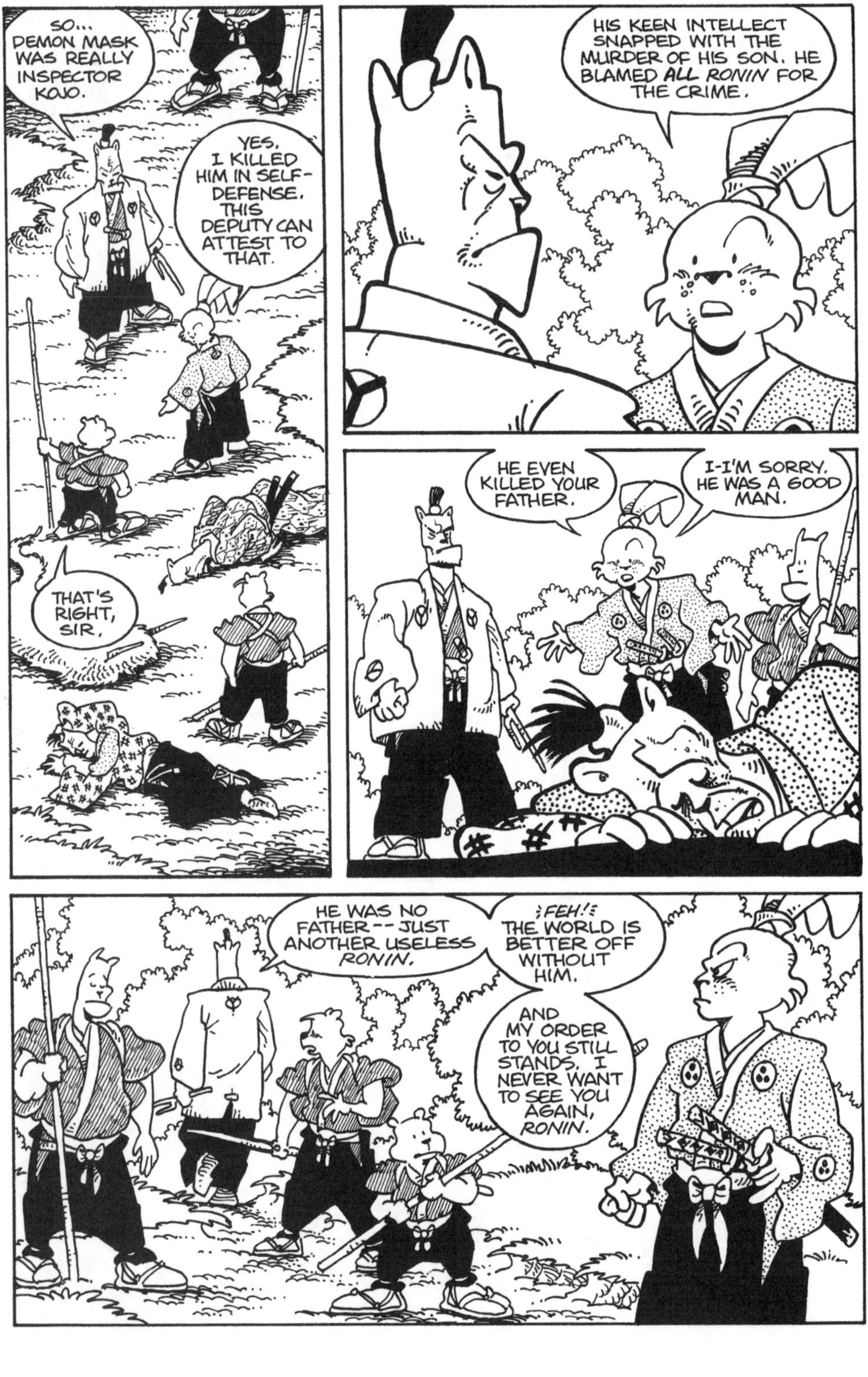
SO... DEMON MASK WAS REALLY INSPECTOR KOJO.
YES. I KILLED HIM IN SELF-DEFENSE. THIS DEPUTY CAN ATTEST TO THAT.
THAT'S RIGHT, SIR.
HIS KEEN INTELLECT SNAPPED WITH THE MURDER OF HIS SON. HE BLAMED **ALL** *RONIN* FOR THE CRIME.
HE EVEN KILLED YOUR FATHER.
I-I'M SORRY. HE WAS A GOOD MAN.
HE WAS NO FATHER--JUST ANOTHER USELESS *RONIN.*
FEH! THE WORLD IS BETTER OFF WITHOUT HIM.
AND MY ORDER TO YOU STILL STANDS. I NEVER WANT TO SEE YOU AGAIN, *RONIN.*

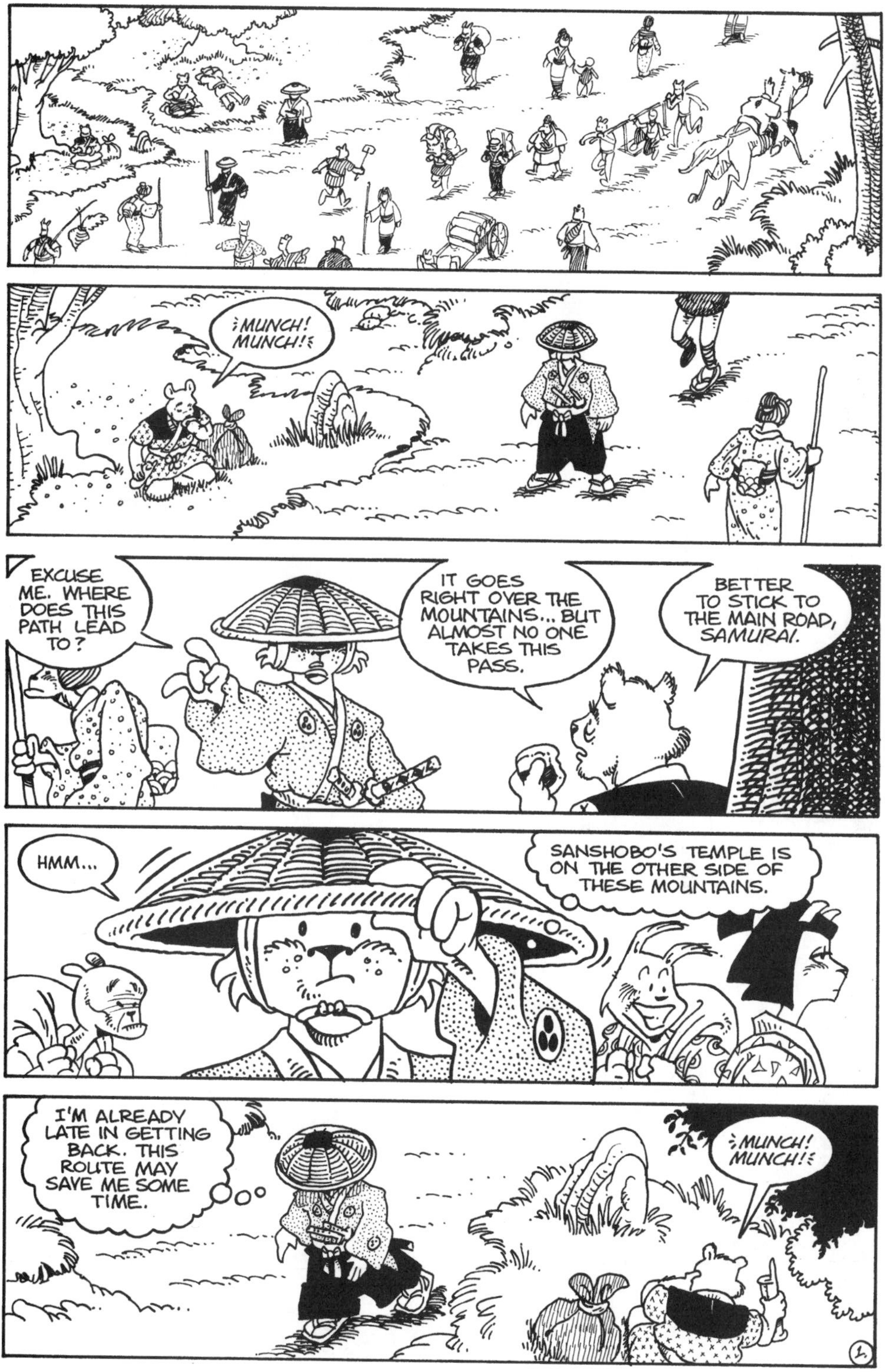
MUNCH! MUNCH!
EXCUSE ME. WHERE DOES THIS PATH LEAD TO?
IT GOES RIGHT OVER THE MOUNTAINS... BUT ALMOST NO ONE TAKES THIS PASS.
BETTER TO STICK TO THE MAIN ROAD, SAMURAI.
HMM...
SANSHOBO'S TEMPLE IS ON THE OTHER SIDE OF THESE MOUNTAINS.
I'M ALREADY LATE IN GETTING BACK. THIS ROUTE MAY SAVE ME SOME TIME.
MUNCH! MUNCH!
2

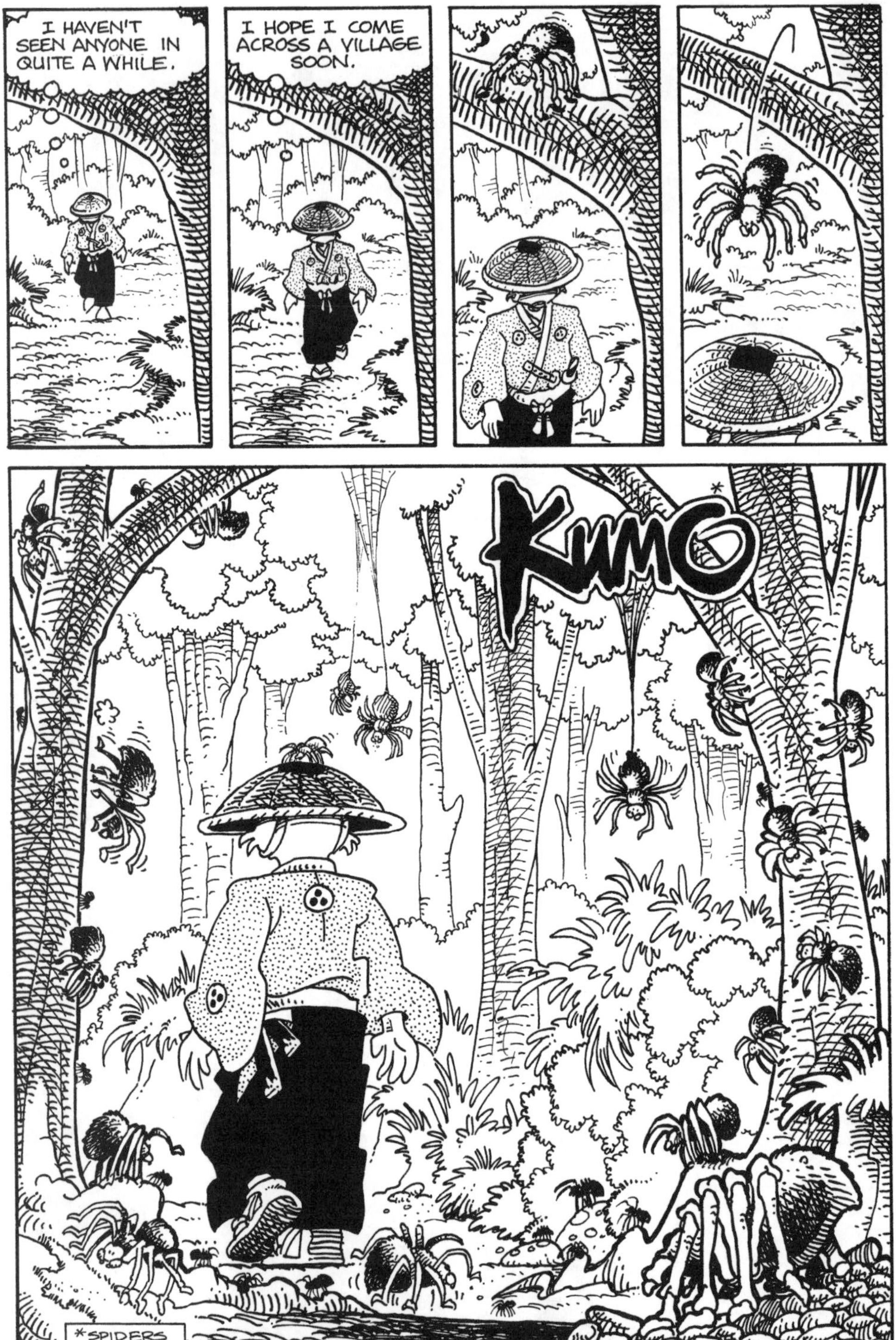
I HAVEN'T SEEN ANYONE IN QUITE A WHILE.
I HOPE I COME ACROSS A VILLAGE SOON.
KUMO*
*SPIDERS
2.

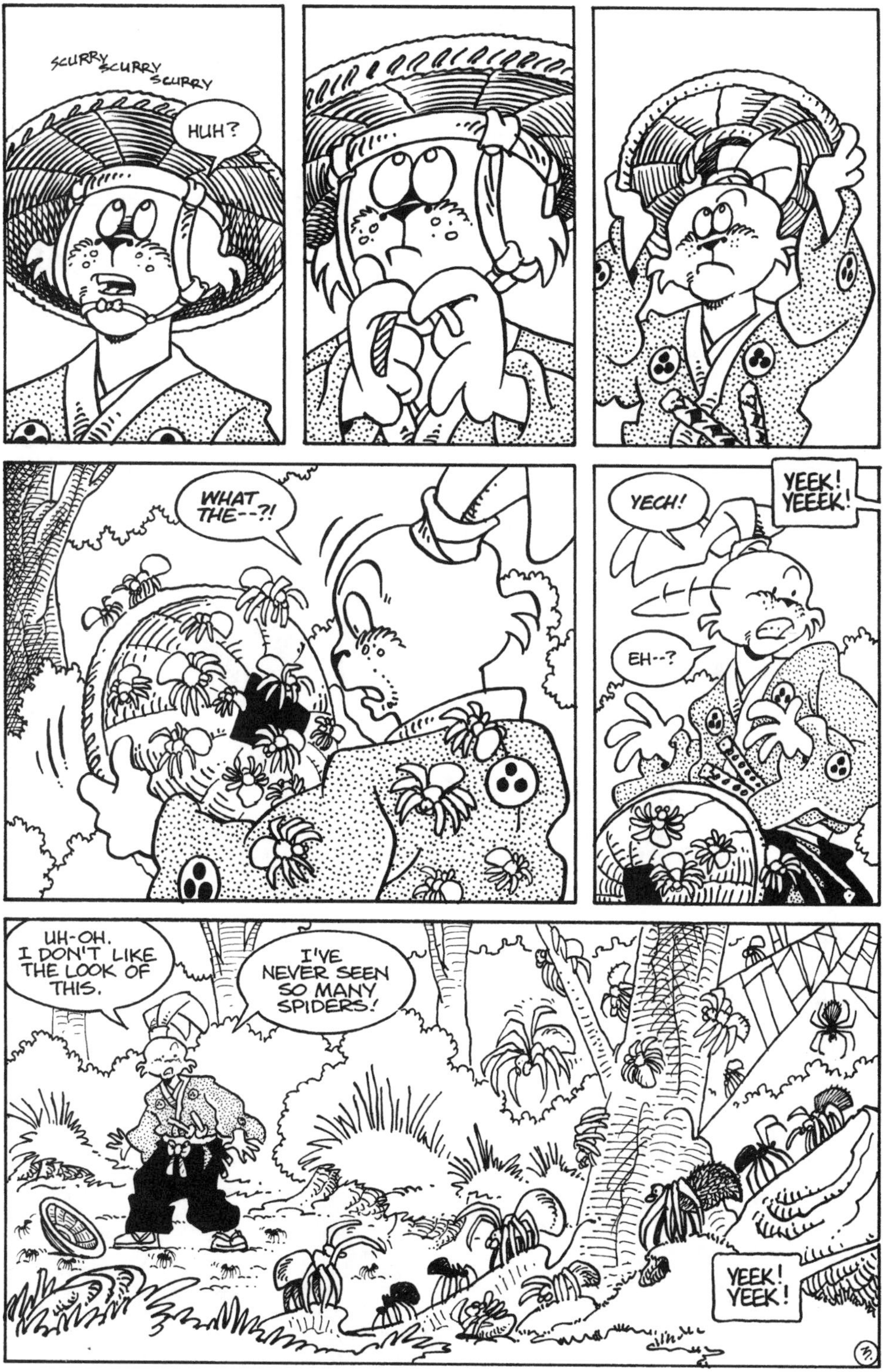
SCURRY SCURRY SCURRY
HUH?
WHAT THE--?!
YECH!
YEEK! YEEEK!
EH--?
UH-OH. I DON'T LIKE THE LOOK OF THIS.
I'VE NEVER SEEN SO MANY SPIDERS!
YEEK! YEEK!
3.

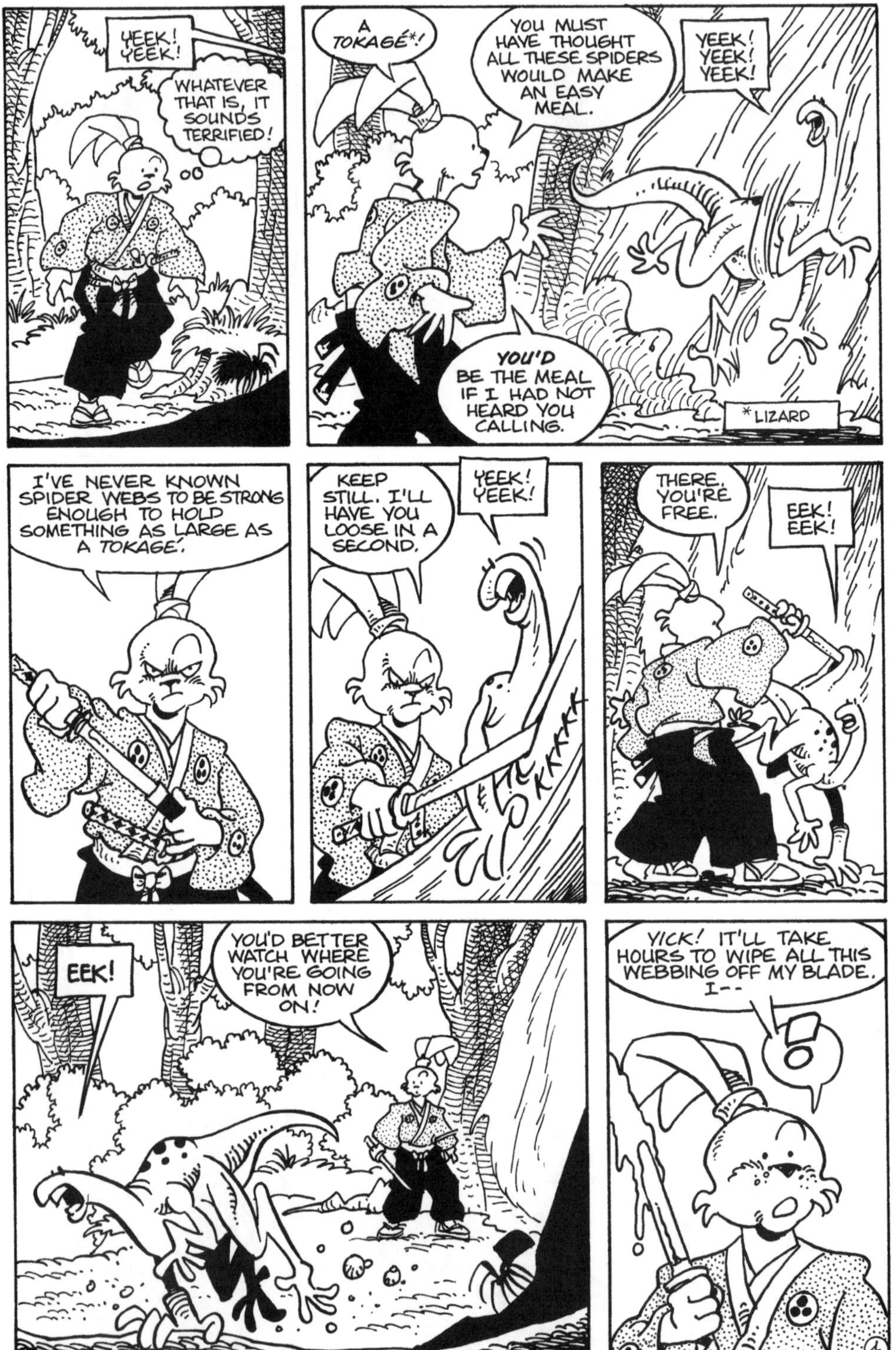
YEEK! YEEK!
WHATEVER THAT IS, IT SOUNDS TERRIFIED!
A TOKAGE*!
YOU MUST HAVE THOUGHT ALL THESE SPIDERS WOULD MAKE AN EASY MEAL.
YEEK! YEEK! YEEK!
YOU'D BE THE MEAL IF I HAD NOT HEARD YOU CALLING.
*LIZARD
I'VE NEVER KNOWN SPIDER WEBS TO BE STRONG ENOUGH TO HOLD SOMETHING AS LARGE AS A TOKAGE.
KEEP STILL. I'LL HAVE YOU LOOSE IN A SECOND.
YEEK! YEEK!
HTCKKKKK
THERE. YOU'RE FREE.
EEK! EEK!
EEK!
YOU'D BETTER WATCH WHERE YOU'RE GOING FROM NOW ON!
YICK! IT'LL TAKE HOURS TO WIPE ALL THIS WEBBING OFF MY BLADE. I--
!
4

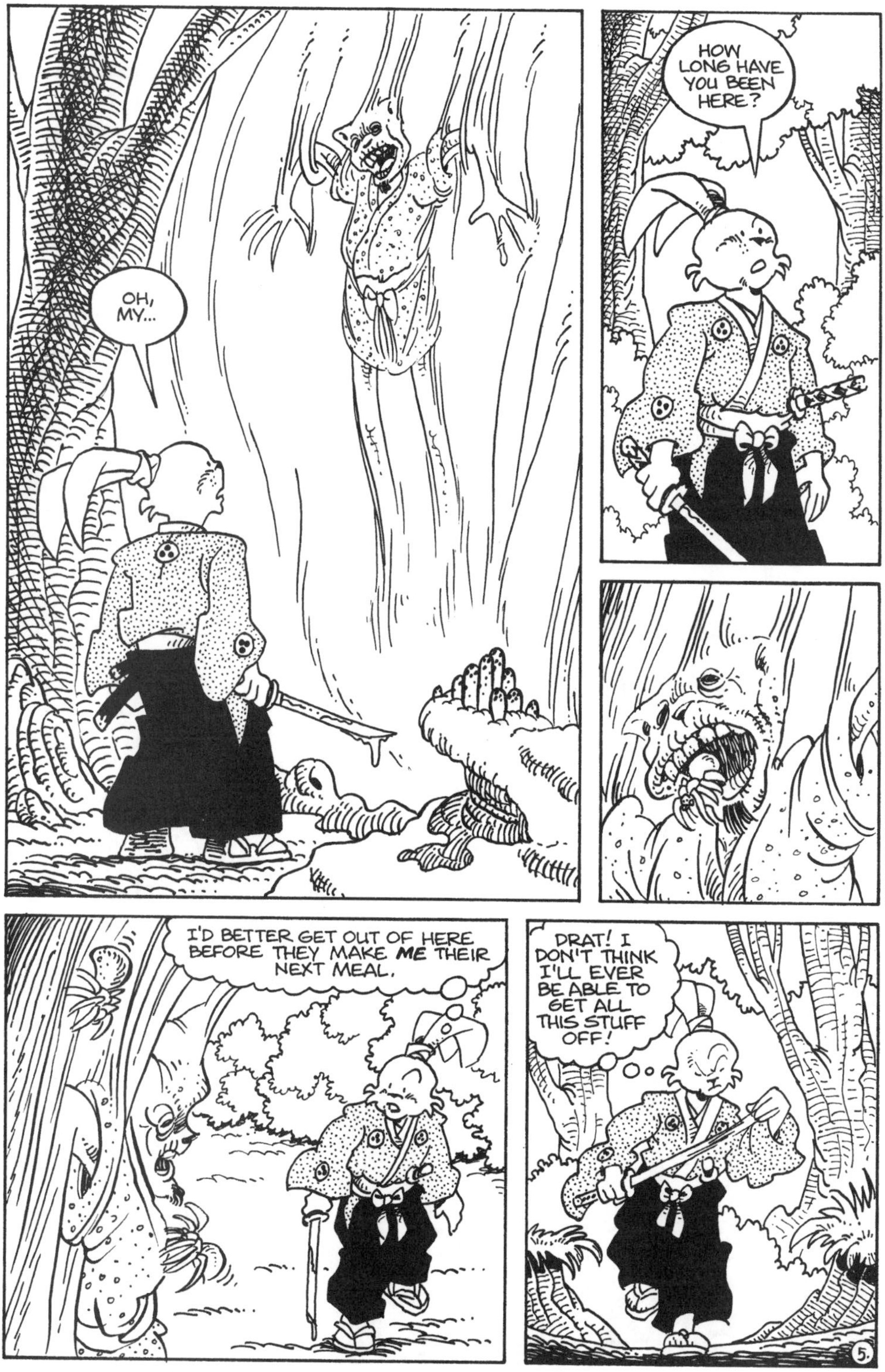
OH, MY...
HOW LONG HAVE YOU BEEN HERE?
I'D BETTER GET OUT OF HERE BEFORE THEY MAKE ME THEIR NEXT MEAL.
DRAT! I DON'T THINK I'LL EVER BE ABLE TO GET ALL THIS STUFF OFF!
5.

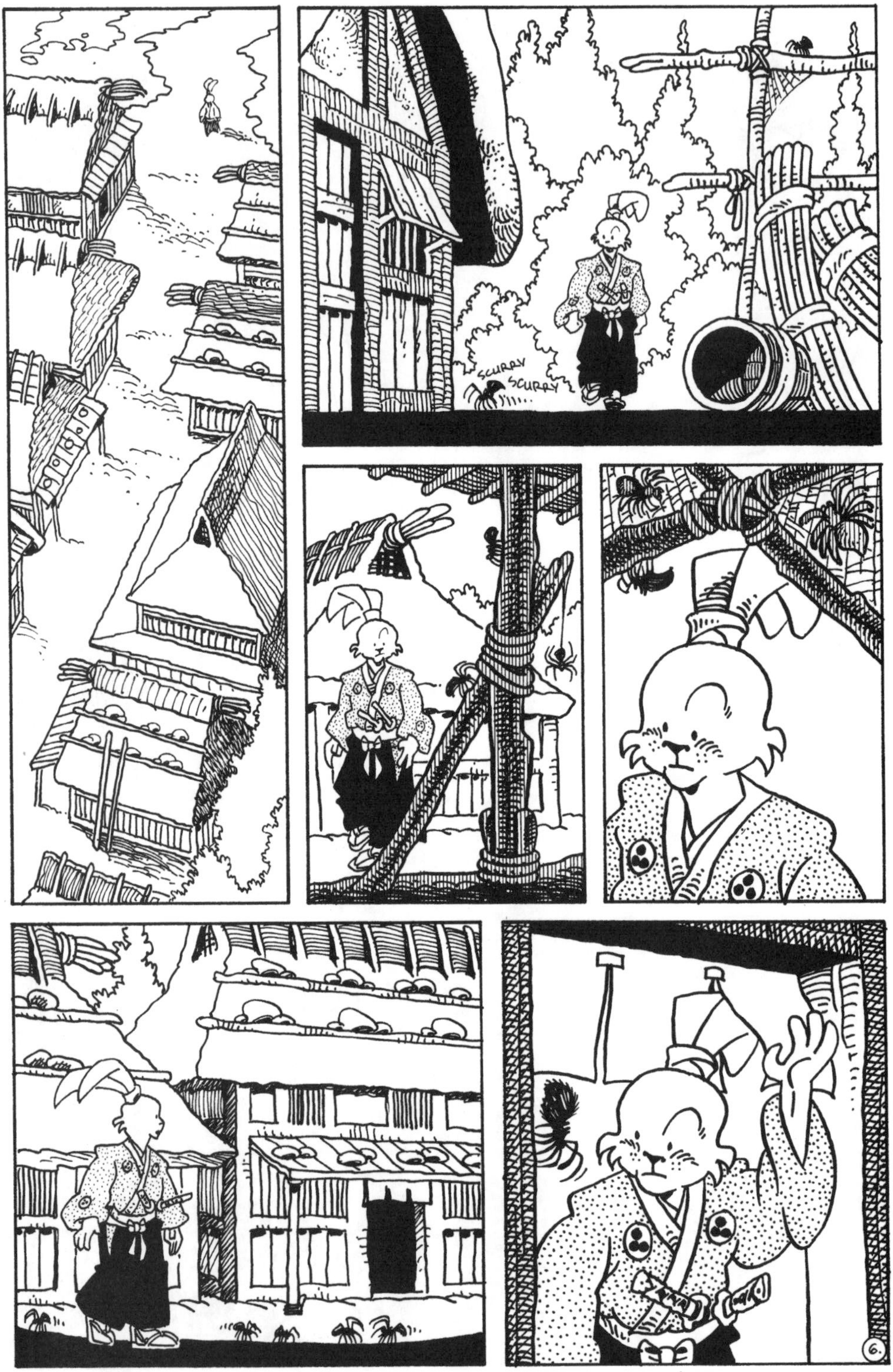
SCURRY
SCURRY
6.

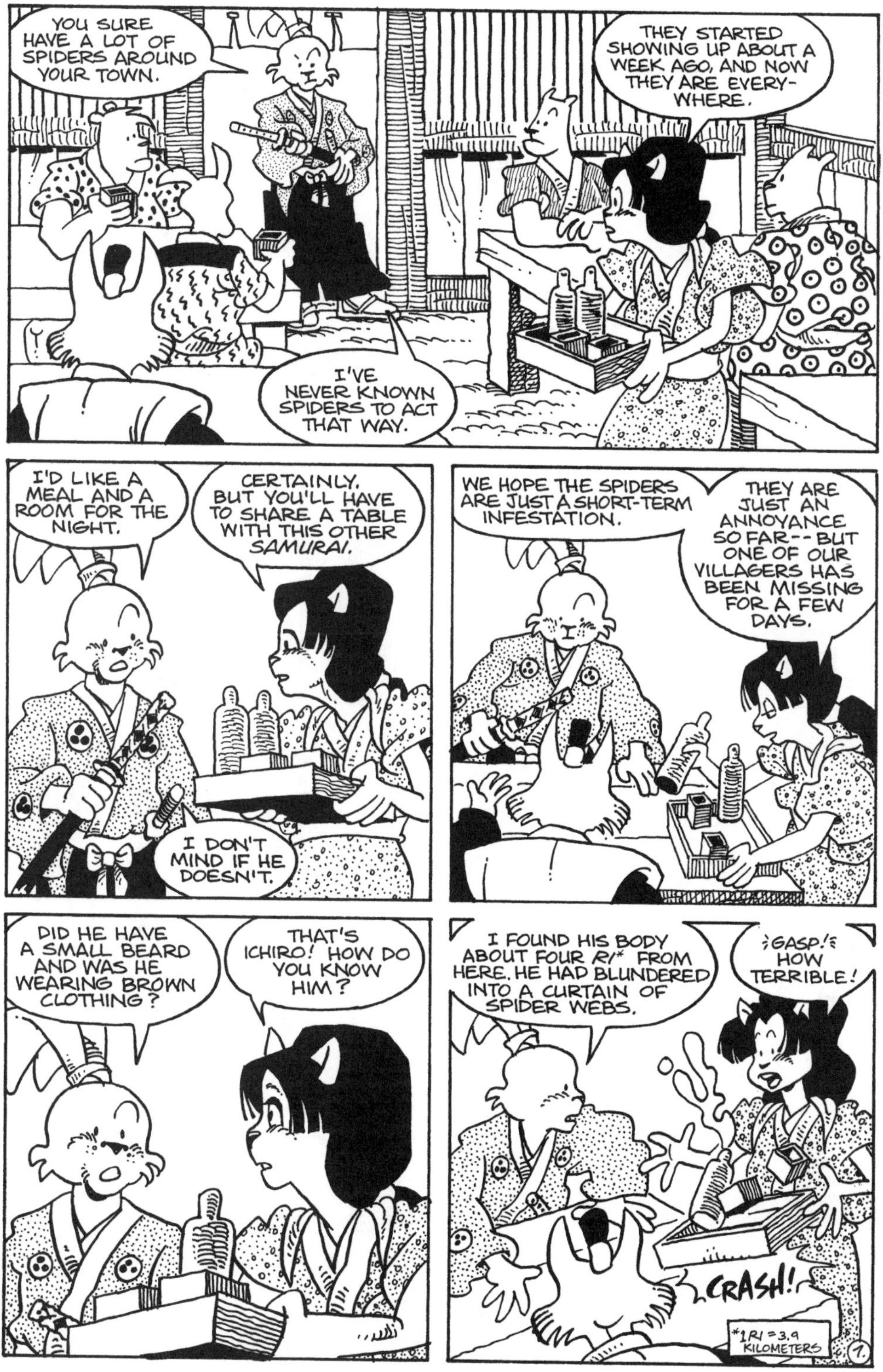
YOU SURE HAVE A LOT OF SPIDERS AROUND YOUR TOWN.
THEY STARTED SHOWING UP ABOUT A WEEK AGO, AND NOW THEY ARE EVERY-WHERE.
I'VE NEVER KNOWN SPIDERS TO ACT THAT WAY.
I'D LIKE A MEAL AND A ROOM FOR THE NIGHT.
CERTAINLY. BUT YOU'LL HAVE TO SHARE A TABLE WITH THIS OTHER *SAMURAI.*
I DON'T MIND IF HE DOESN'T.
WE HOPE THE SPIDERS ARE JUST A SHORT-TERM INFESTATION.
THEY ARE JUST AN ANNOYANCE SO FAR-- BUT ONE OF OUR VILLAGERS HAS BEEN MISSING FOR A FEW DAYS.
DID HE HAVE A SMALL BEARD AND WAS HE WEARING BROWN CLOTHING?
THAT'S ICHIRO! HOW DO YOU KNOW HIM?
I FOUND HIS BODY ABOUT FOUR *RI** FROM HERE. HE HAD BLUNDERED INTO A CURTAIN OF SPIDER WEBS.
GASP! HOW TERRIBLE!
CRASH!
*1 RI = 3.9 KILOMETERS
7.

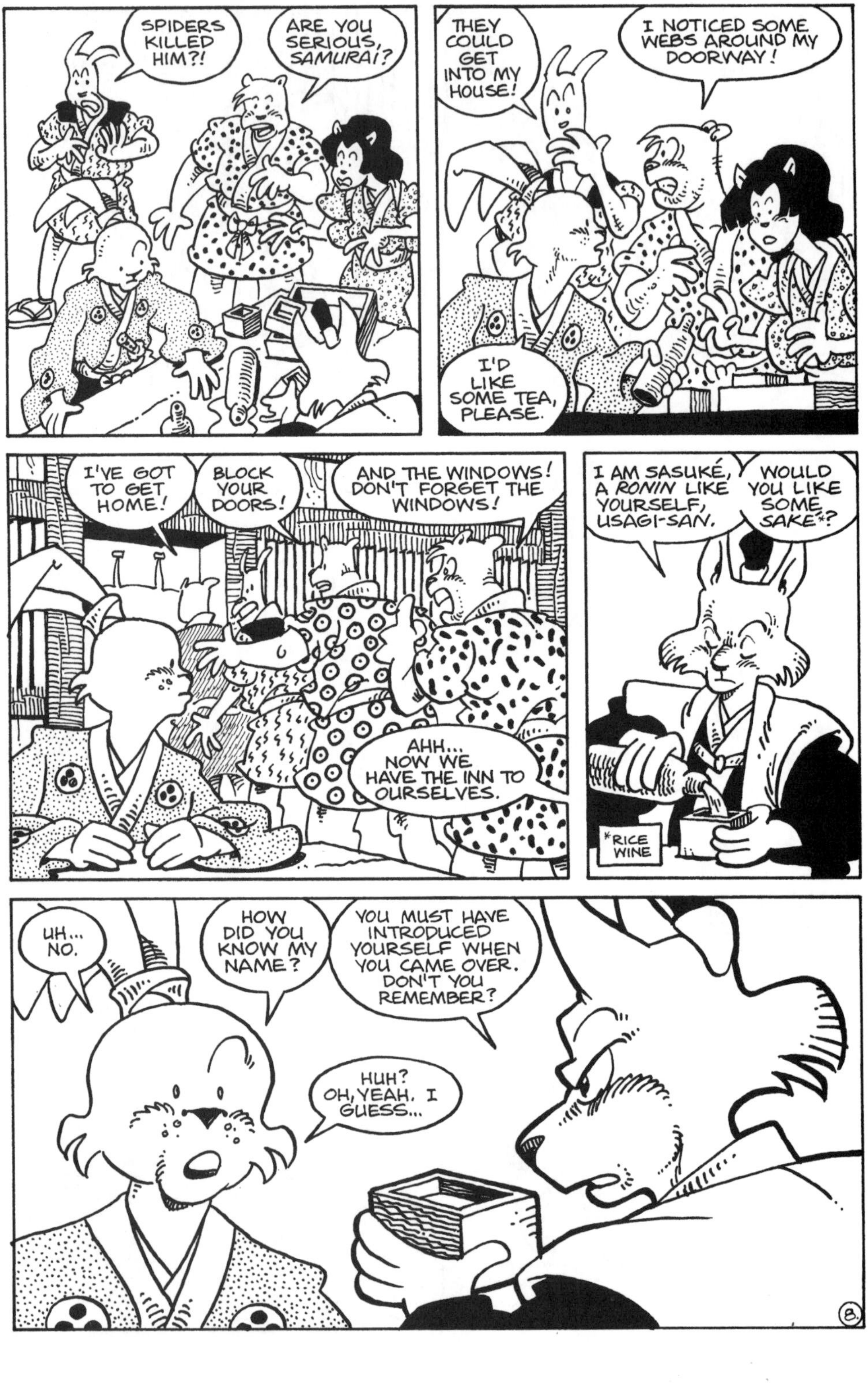
SPIDERS KILLED HIM?!
ARE YOU SERIOUS, *SAMURAI*?
THEY COULD GET INTO MY HOUSE!
I NOTICED SOME WEBS AROUND MY DOORWAY!
I'D LIKE SOME TEA, PLEASE.
I'VE GOT TO GET HOME!
BLOCK YOUR DOORS!
AND THE WINDOWS! DON'T FORGET THE WINDOWS!
AHH... NOW WE HAVE THE INN TO OURSELVES.
I AM SASUKÉ, A *RONIN* LIKE YOURSELF, USAGI-SAN.
WOULD YOU LIKE SOME *SAKE**?
*RICE WINE
UH... NO.
HOW DID YOU KNOW MY NAME?
YOU MUST HAVE INTRODUCED YOURSELF WHEN YOU CAME OVER. DON'T YOU REMEMBER?
HUH? OH, YEAH. I GUESS...
8.

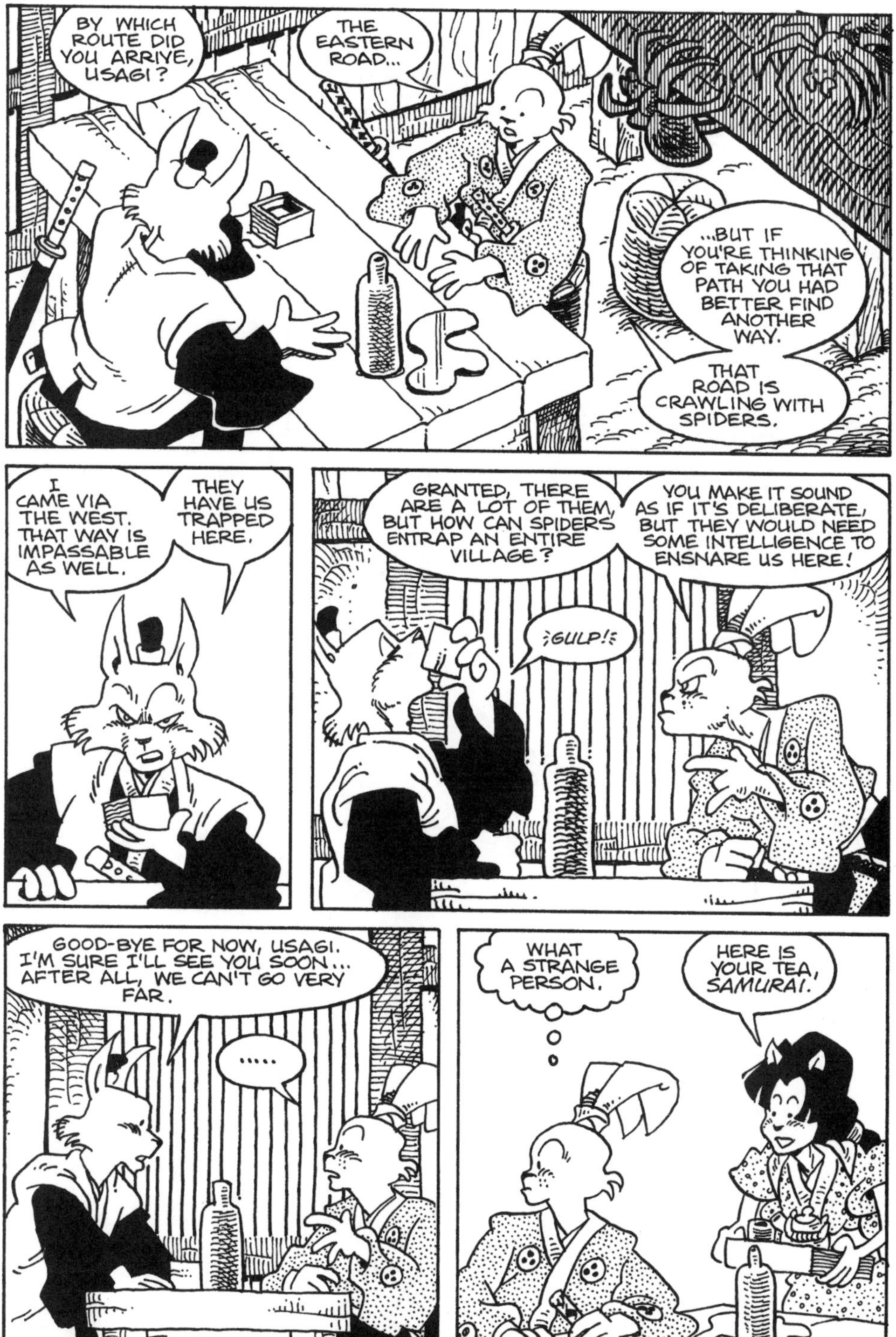
BY WHICH ROUTE DID YOU ARRIVE, USAGI?
THE EASTERN ROAD...
...BUT IF YOU'RE THINKING OF TAKING THAT PATH YOU HAD BETTER FIND ANOTHER WAY.
THAT ROAD IS CRAWLING WITH SPIDERS.
I CAME VIA THE WEST. THAT WAY IS IMPASSABLE AS WELL.
THEY HAVE US TRAPPED HERE.
GRANTED, THERE ARE A LOT OF THEM, BUT HOW CAN SPIDERS ENTRAP AN ENTIRE VILLAGE?
YOU MAKE IT SOUND AS IF IT'S DELIBERATE, BUT THEY WOULD NEED SOME INTELLIGENCE TO ENSNARE US HERE!
;GULP!;
GOOD-BYE FOR NOW, USAGI. I'M SURE I'LL SEE YOU SOON... AFTER ALL, WE CAN'T GO VERY FAR.
.....
WHAT A STRANGE PERSON.
HERE IS YOUR TEA, SAMURAI.
9.

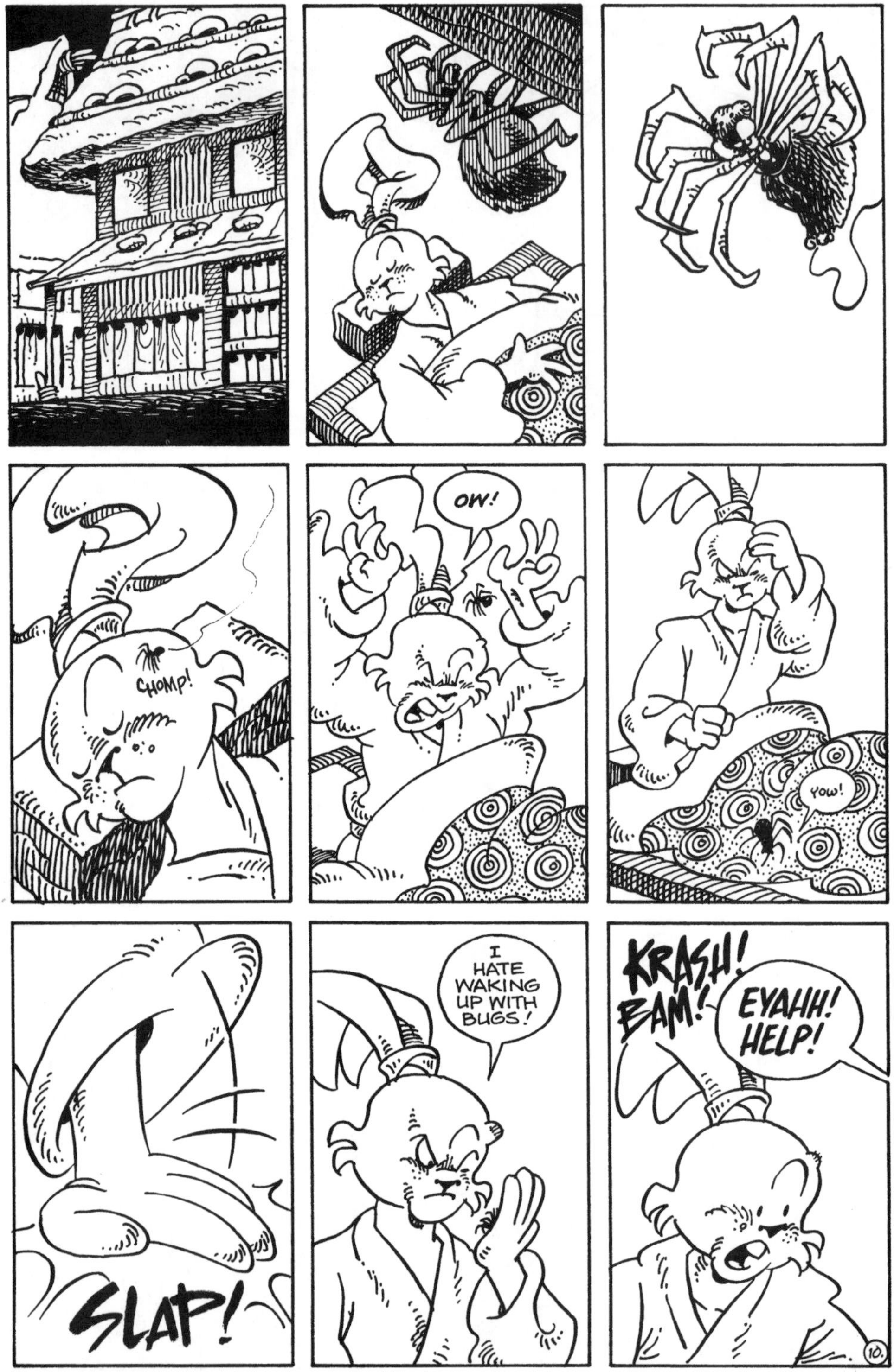
CHOMP!
OW!
YOW!
SLAP!
I HATE WAKING UP WITH BUGS!
KRASH!
BAM!
EYAHH! HELP!
10.

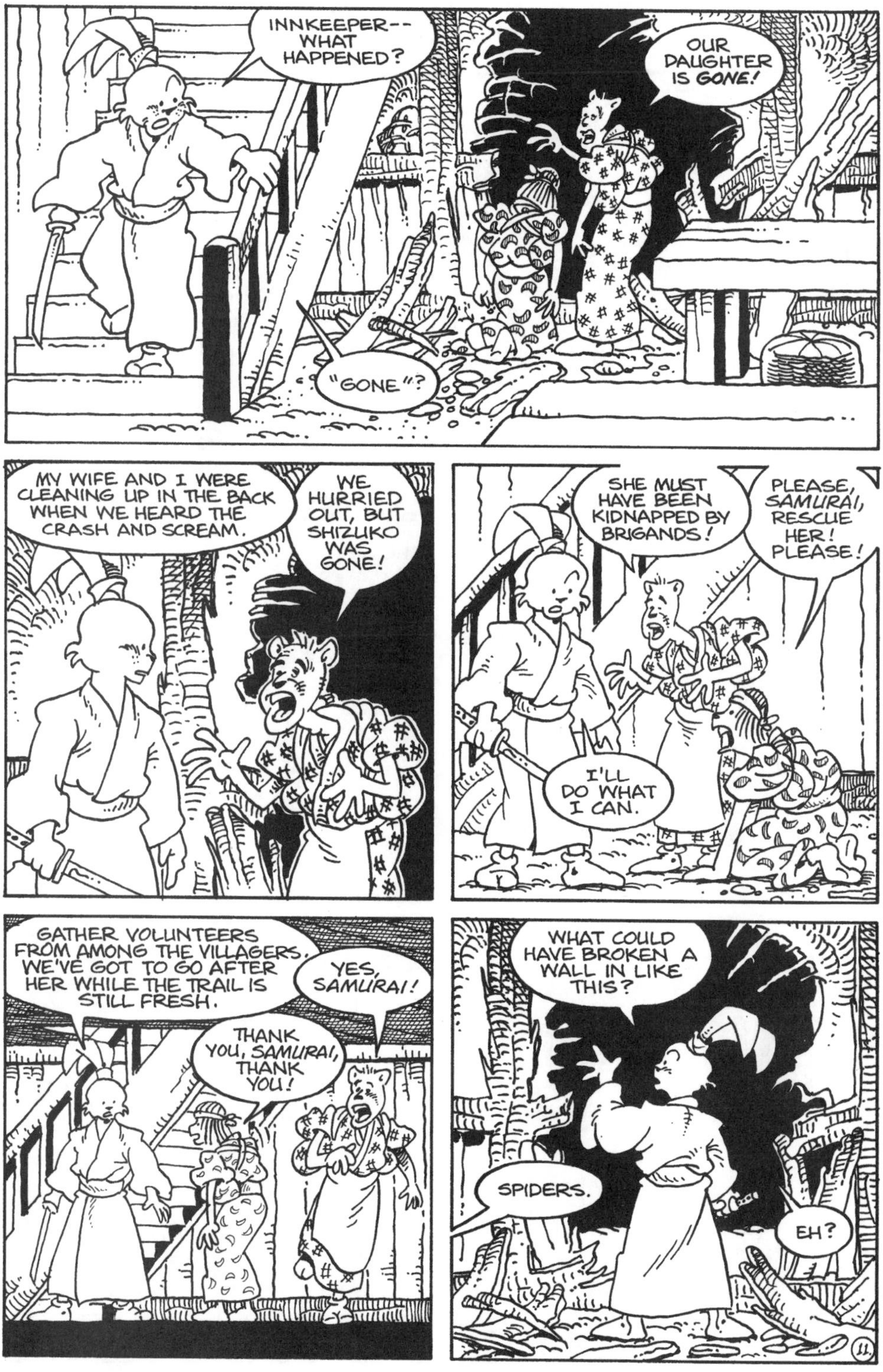
INNKEEPER-- WHAT HAPPENED?
OUR DAUGHTER IS GONE!
"GONE"?
MY WIFE AND I WERE CLEANING UP IN THE BACK WHEN WE HEARD THE CRASH AND SCREAM.
WE HURRIED OUT, BUT SHIZUKO WAS GONE!
SHE MUST HAVE BEEN KIDNAPPED BY BRIGANDS!
PLEASE, SAMURAI, RESCUE HER! PLEASE!
I'LL DO WHAT I CAN.
GATHER VOLUNTEERS FROM AMONG THE VILLAGERS. WE'VE GOT TO GO AFTER HER WHILE THE TRAIL IS STILL FRESH.
YES, SAMURAI!
THANK YOU, SAMURAI, THANK YOU!
WHAT COULD HAVE BROKEN A WALL IN LIKE THIS?
SPIDERS.
EH?
11

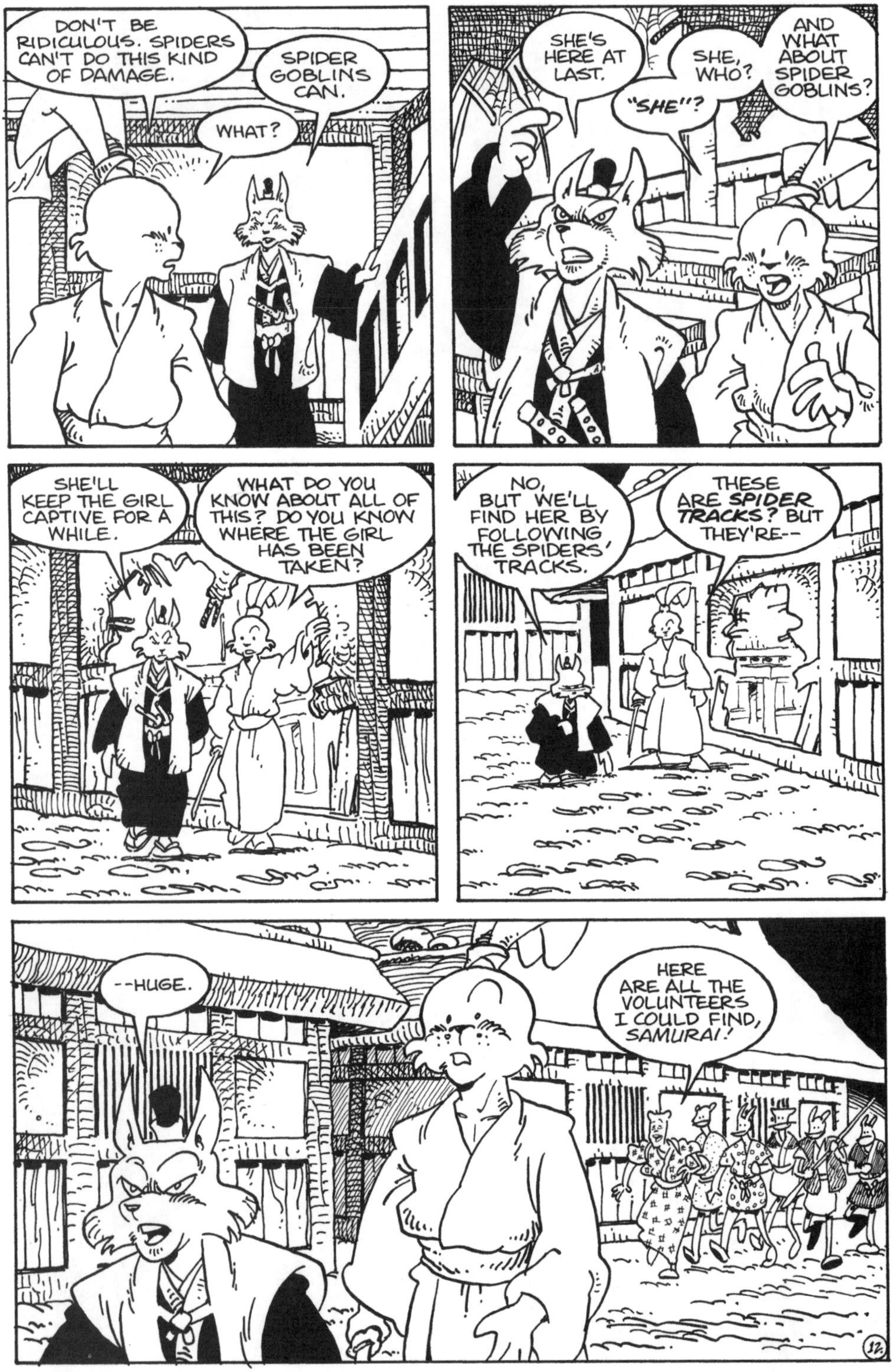
DON'T BE RIDICULOUS. SPIDERS CAN'T DO THIS KIND OF DAMAGE.
SPIDER GOBLINS CAN.
WHAT?
SHE'S HERE AT LAST.
SHE, WHO?
"SHE"?
AND WHAT ABOUT SPIDER GOBLINS?
SHE'LL KEEP THE GIRL CAPTIVE FOR A WHILE.
WHAT DO YOU KNOW ABOUT ALL OF THIS? DO YOU KNOW WHERE THE GIRL HAS BEEN TAKEN?
NO, BUT WE'LL FIND HER BY FOLLOWING THE SPIDERS' TRACKS.
THESE ARE SPIDER TRACKS? BUT THEY'RE--
--HUGE.
HERE ARE ALL THE VOLUNTEERS I COULD FIND, SAMURAI!
12

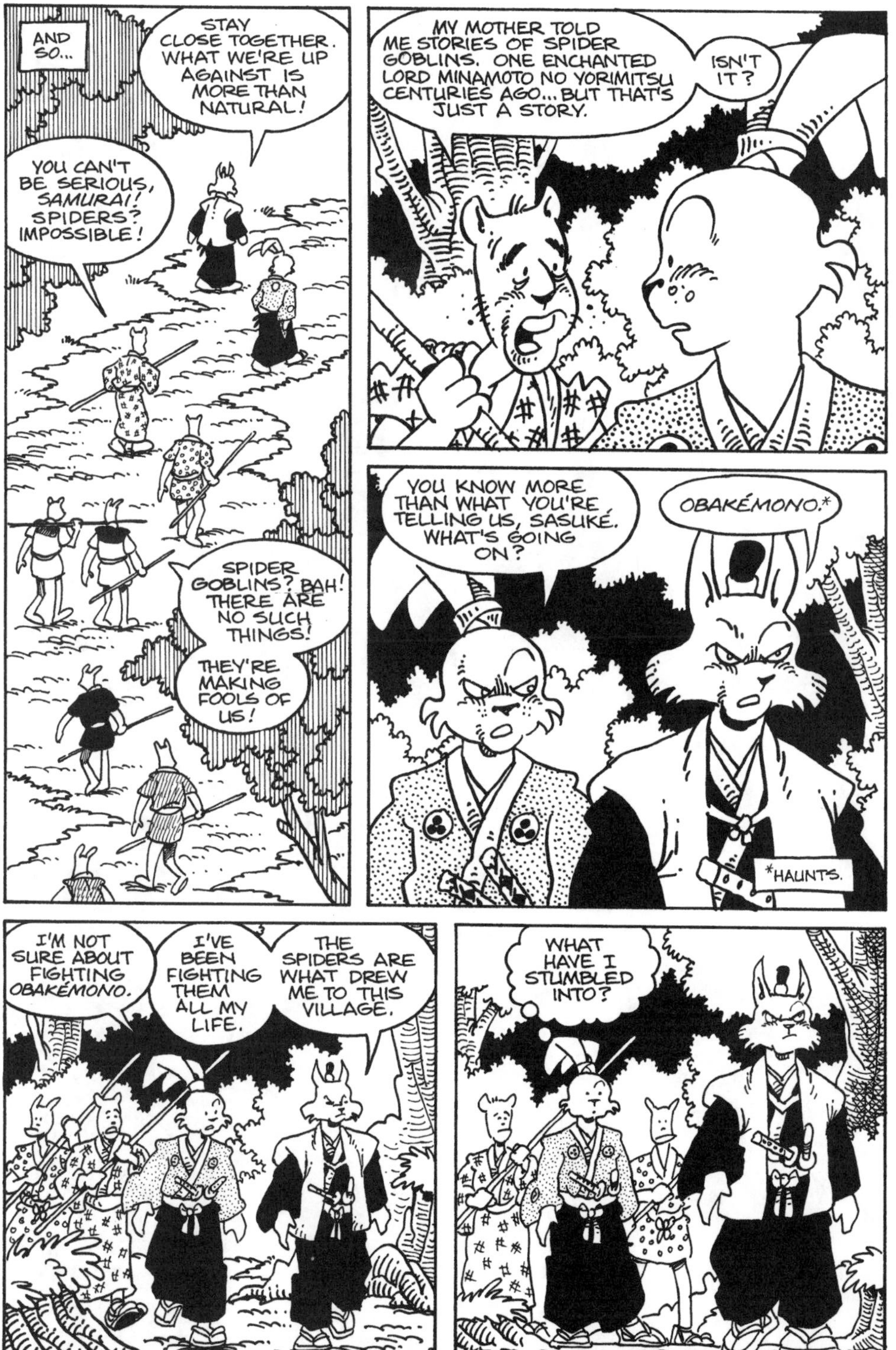

AND SO...
STAY CLOSE TOGETHER. WHAT WE'RE UP AGAINST IS MORE THAN NATURAL!
YOU CAN'T BE SERIOUS, SAMURAI! SPIDERS? IMPOSSIBLE!
SPIDER GOBLINS? BAH! THERE ARE NO SUCH THINGS!
THEY'RE MAKING FOOLS OF US!
MY MOTHER TOLD ME STORIES OF SPIDER GOBLINS. ONE ENCHANTED LORD MINAMOTO NO YORIMITSU CENTURIES AGO... BUT THAT'S JUST A STORY.
ISN'T IT?
YOU KNOW MORE THAN WHAT YOU'RE TELLING US, SASUKÉ. WHAT'S GOING ON?
OBAKÉMONO.*
*HAUNTS.
I'M NOT SURE ABOUT FIGHTING OBAKÉMONO.
I'VE BEEN FIGHTING THEM ALL MY LIFE.
THE SPIDERS ARE WHAT DREW ME TO THIS VILLAGE.
WHAT HAVE I STUMBLED INTO?
13.

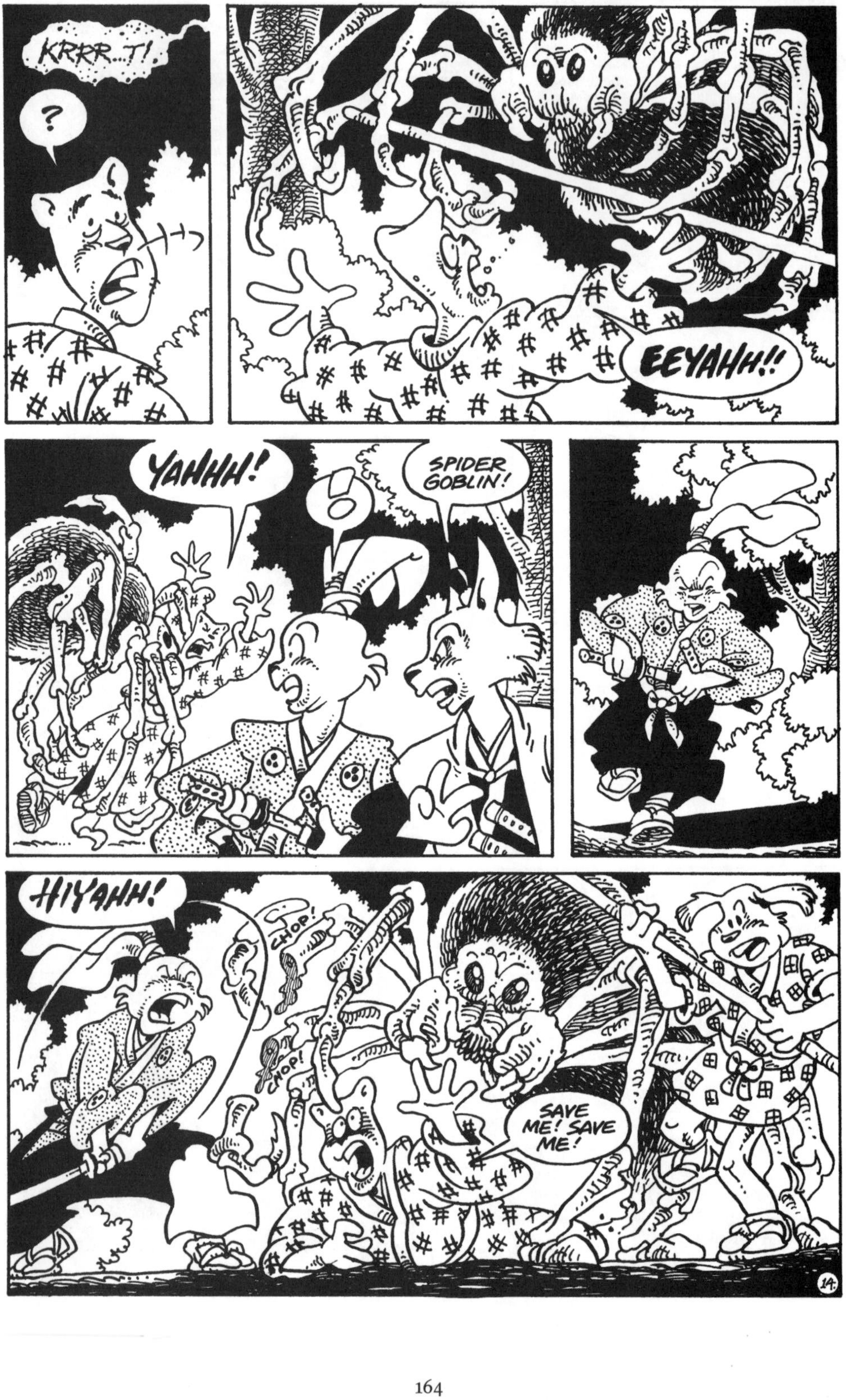
KRRR..T!
?
EEYAHH!!
YAHHH!
!
SPIDER GOBLIN!
HIYAHH!
CHOP!
CHOP!
SAVE ME! SAVE ME!
14.

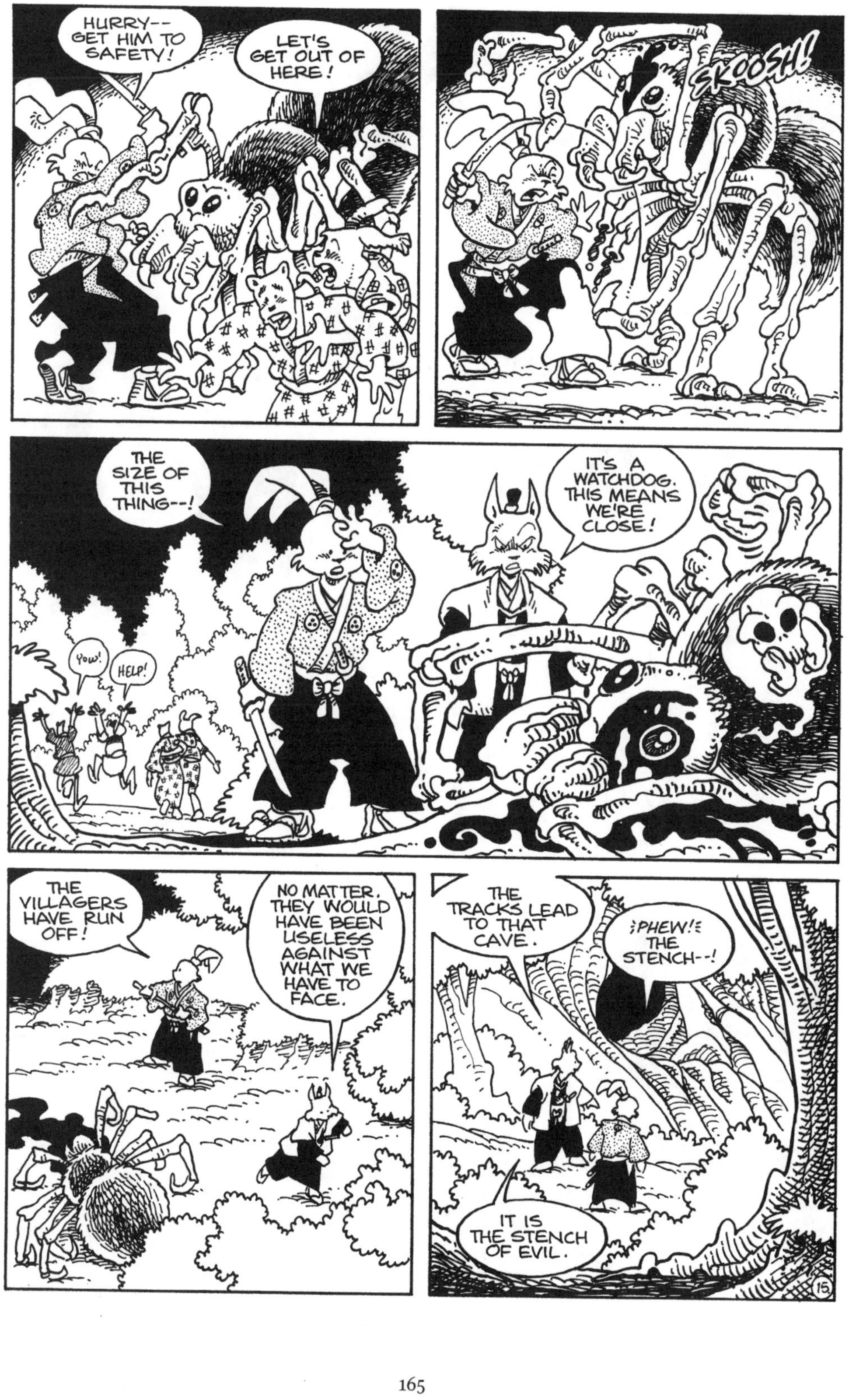
HURRY-- GET HIM TO SAFETY!
LET'S GET OUT OF HERE!
SKOOSH!
THE SIZE OF THIS THING--!
IT'S A WATCHDOG. THIS MEANS WE'RE CLOSE!
YOW!
HELP!
THE VILLAGERS HAVE RUN OFF!
NO MATTER. THEY WOULD HAVE BEEN USELESS AGAINST WHAT WE HAVE TO FACE.
THE TRACKS LEAD TO THAT CAVE.
PHEW! THE STENCH--!
IT IS THE STENCH OF EVIL.
15

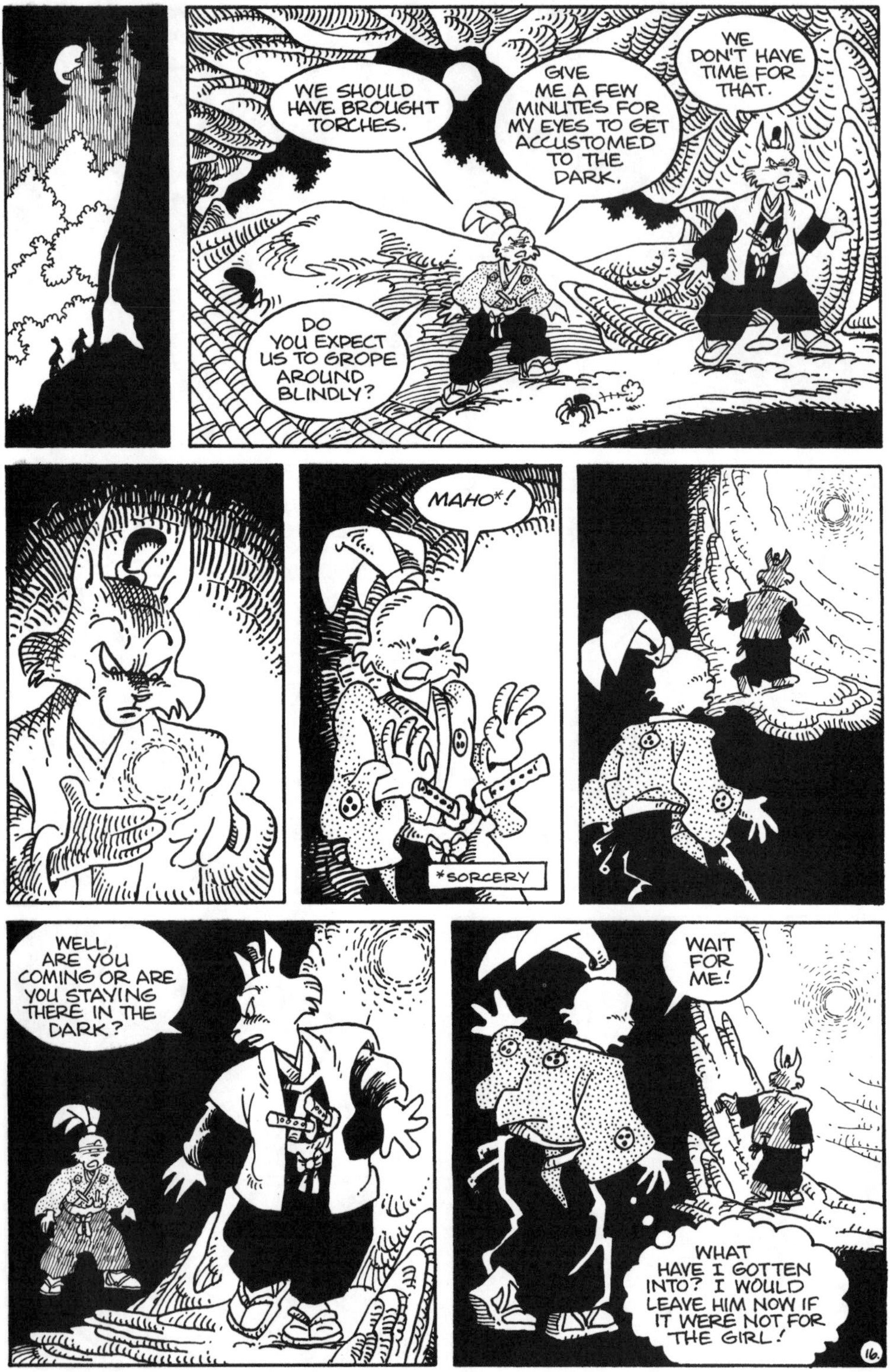
WE SHOULD HAVE BROUGHT TORCHES.
GIVE ME A FEW MINUTES FOR MY EYES TO GET ACCUSTOMED TO THE DARK.
WE DON'T HAVE TIME FOR THAT.
DO YOU EXPECT US TO GROPE AROUND BLINDLY?
MAHO*!
*SORCERY
WELL, ARE YOU COMING OR ARE YOU STAYING THERE IN THE DARK?
WAIT FOR ME!
WHAT HAVE I GOTTEN INTO? I WOULD LEAVE HIM NOW IF IT WERE NOT FOR THE GIRL!
16.

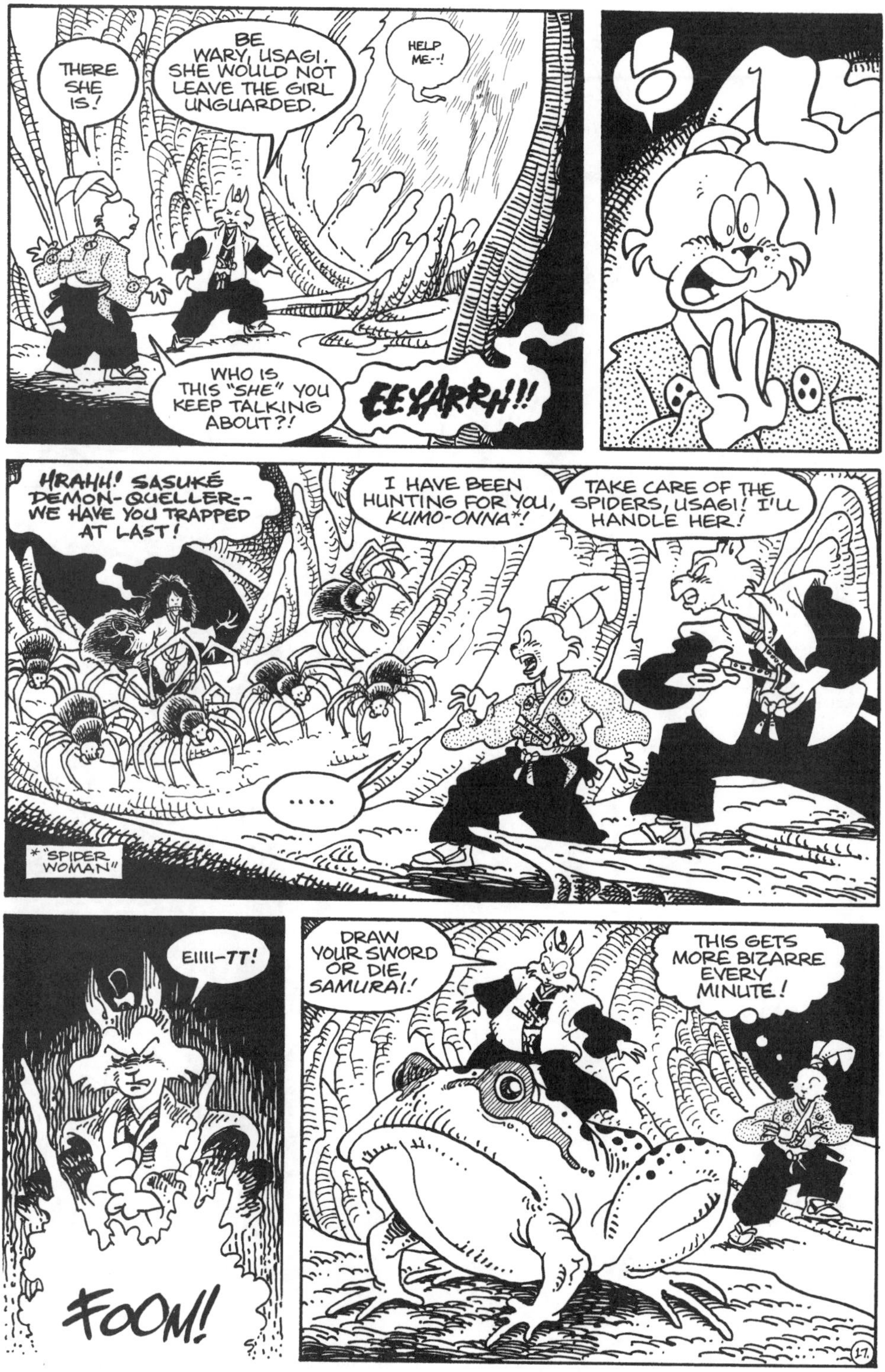
THERE SHE IS!
BE WARY, USAGI. SHE WOULD NOT LEAVE THE GIRL UNGUARDED.
HELP ME--!
WHO IS THIS "SHE" YOU KEEP TALKING ABOUT?!
EEYARRH!!
HRAHH! SASUKÉ DEMON-QUELLER-- WE HAVE YOU TRAPPED AT LAST!
I HAVE BEEN HUNTING FOR YOU, KUMO-ONNA*!
TAKE CARE OF THE SPIDERS, USAGI! I'LL HANDLE HER!
.....
*"SPIDER WOMAN"
EIIII-TT!
FOOM!
DRAW YOUR SWORD OR DIE, SAMURAI!
THIS GETS MORE BIZARRE EVERY MINUTE!
17.

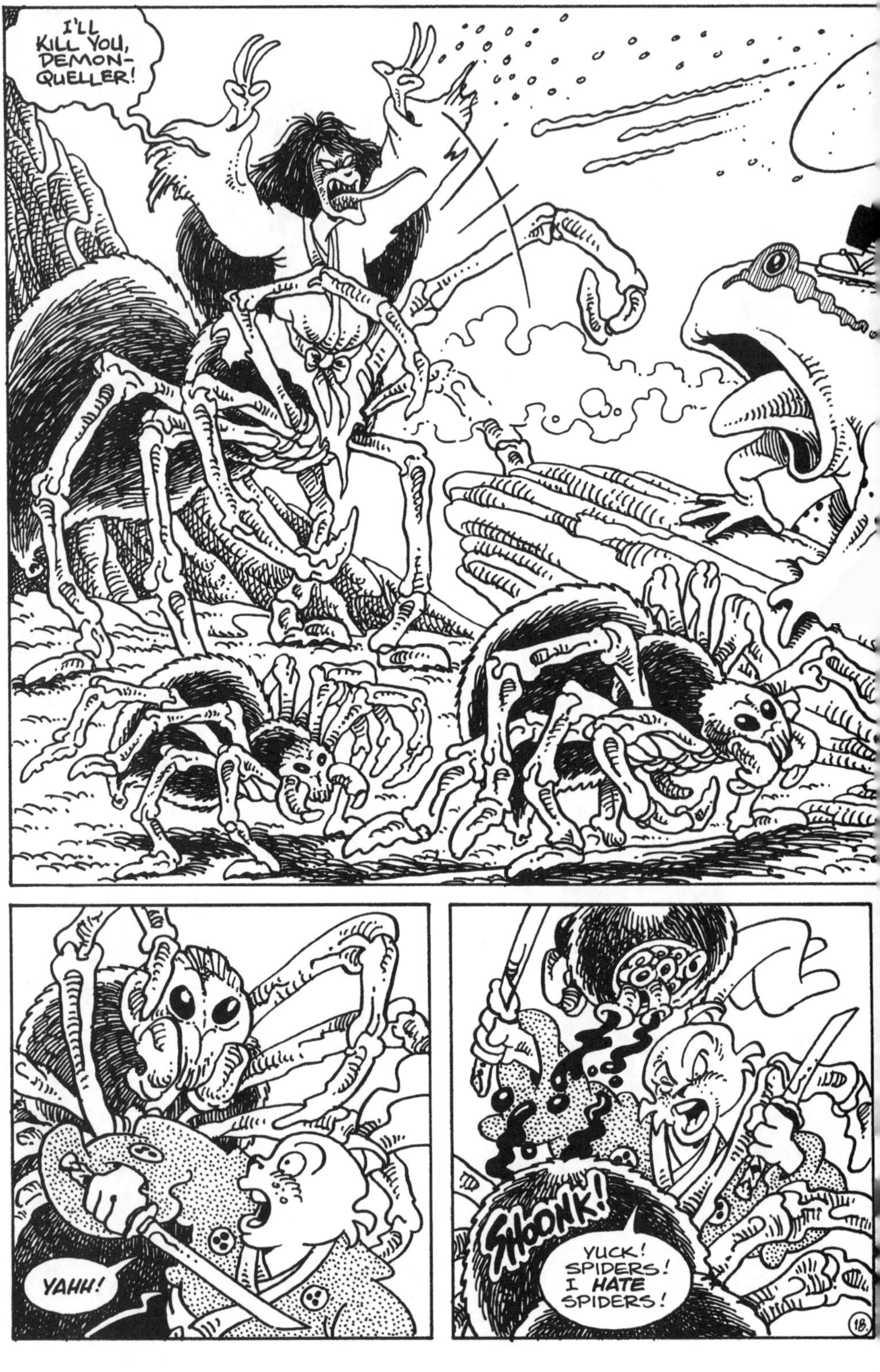
I'LL KILL YOU, DEMON-QUELLER!
YAHH!
SHOONK!
YUCK! SPIDERS! I HATE SPIDERS!
18.

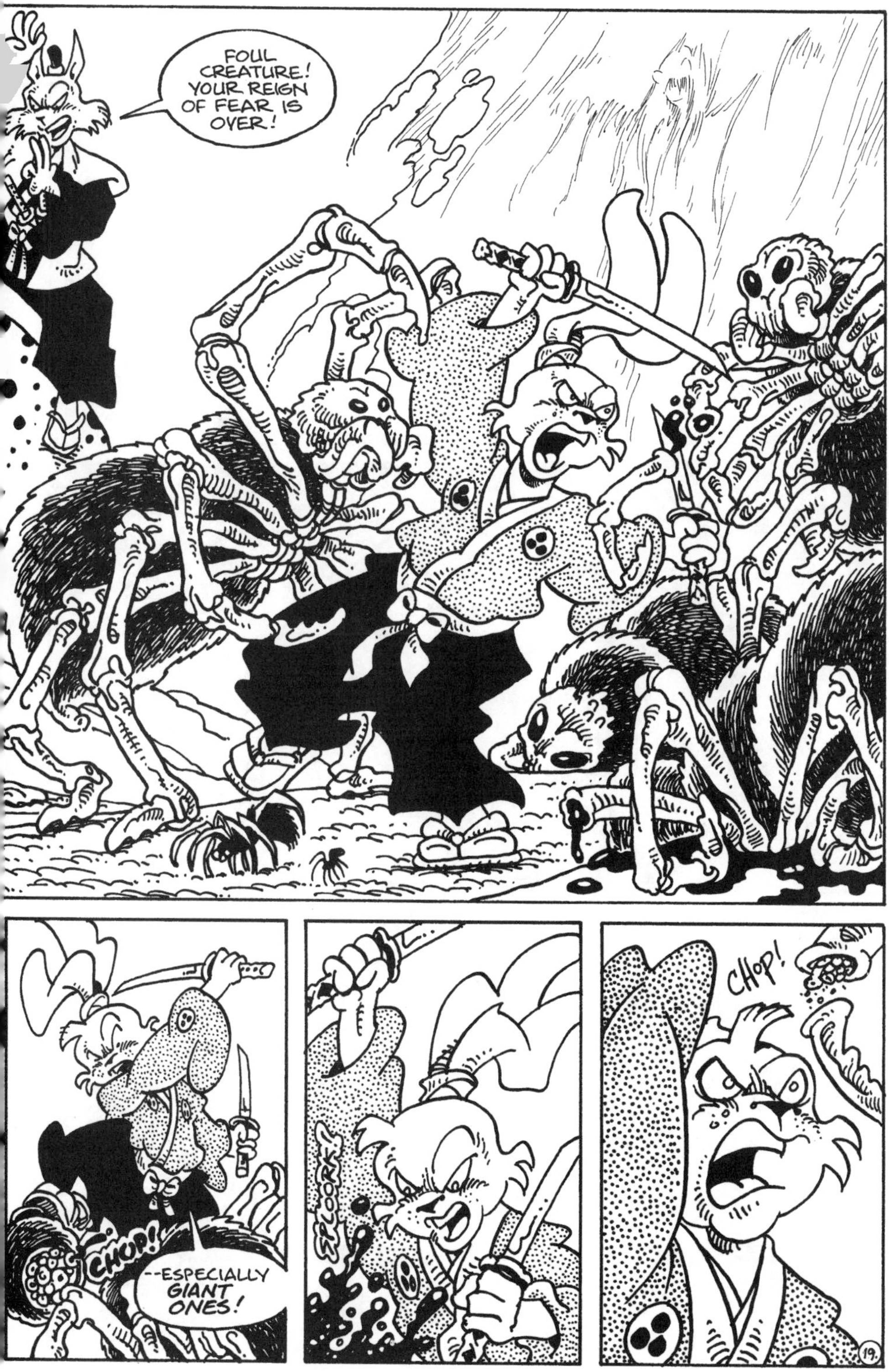
FOUL CREATURE! YOUR REIGN OF FEAR IS OVER!
CHOP!
--ESPECIALLY GIANT ONES!
SPLOORK!
CHOP!
19.

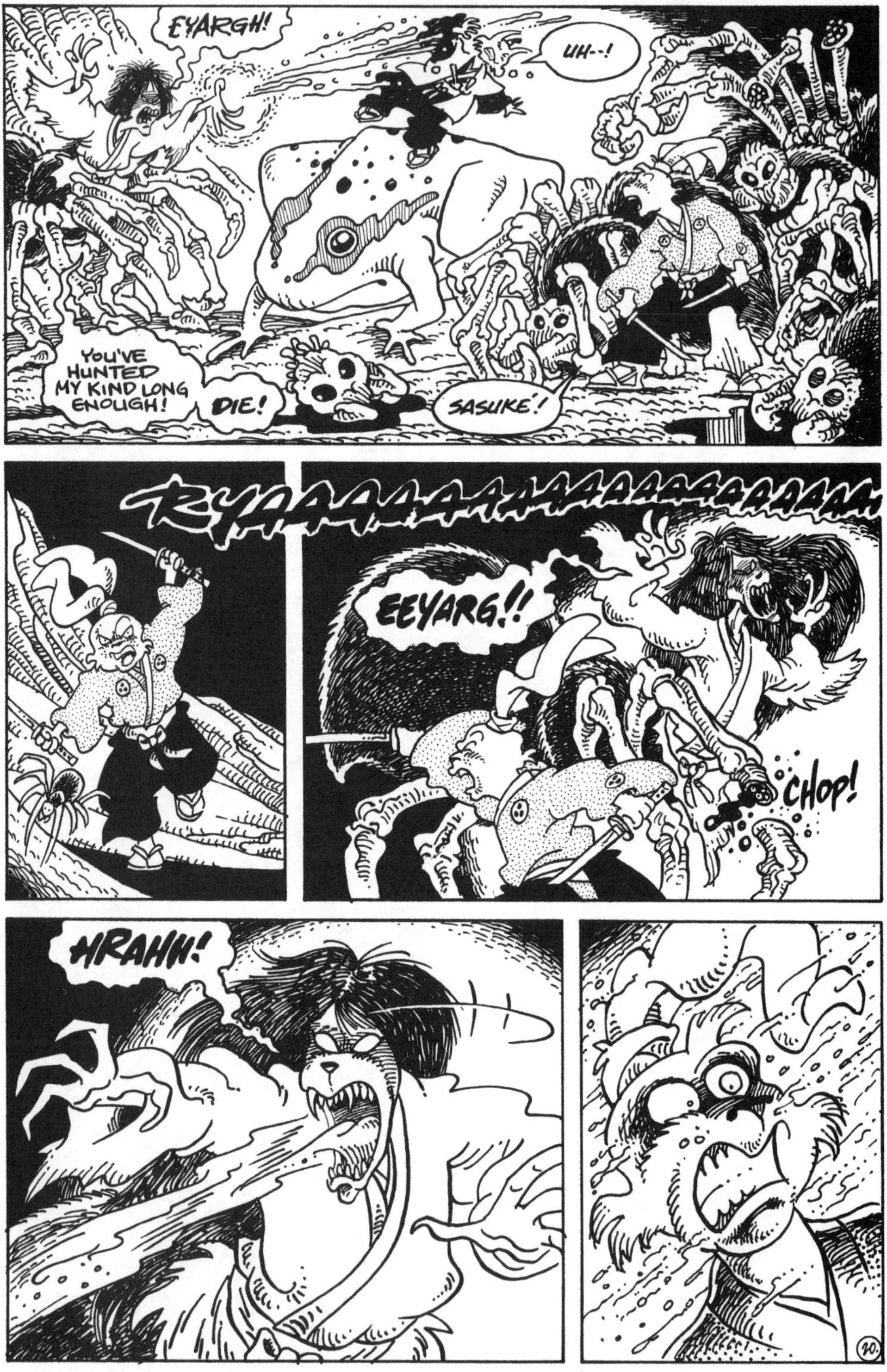
EYARGH!
UH--!
YOU'VE HUNTED MY KIND LONG ENOUGH!
DIE!
SASUKE!
RYAAAAAAAAAAAAAAAAAAAAA
EEYARG!!
CHOP!
HRAHH!
20.

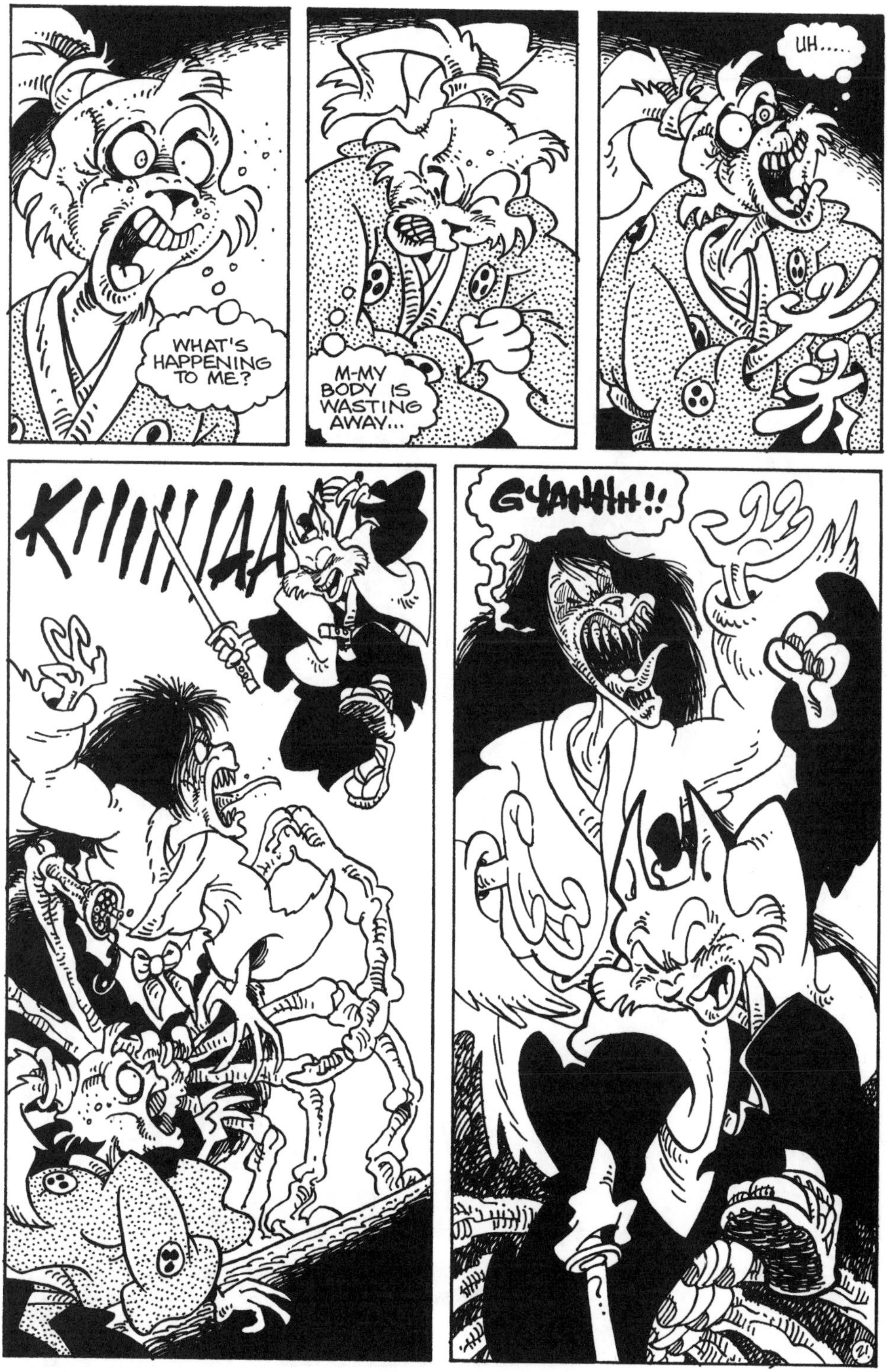
WHAT'S HAPPENING TO ME?
M-MY BODY IS WASTING AWAY...
UH.....
KIIIIIAA
GYAHHH!!
21

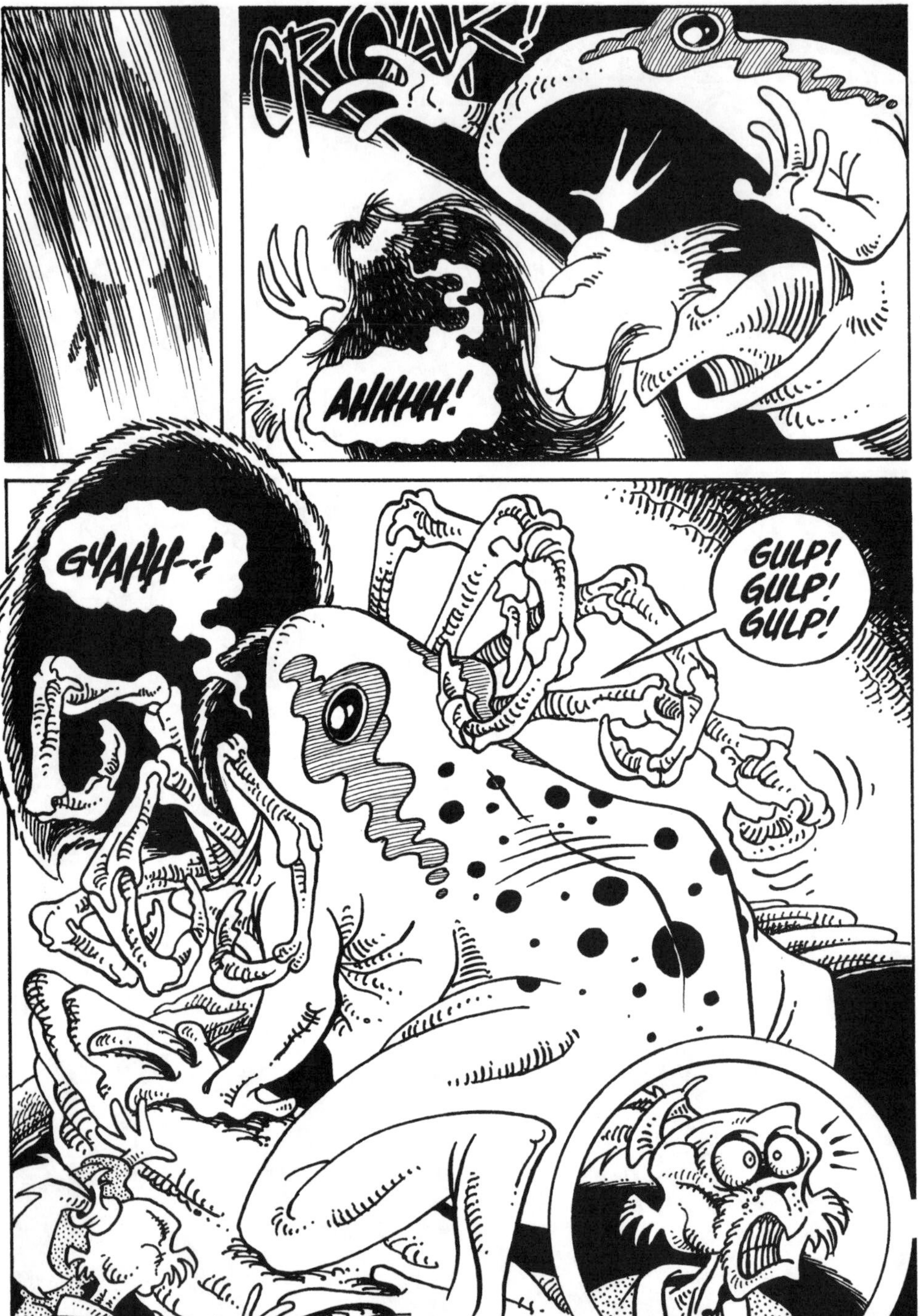
CROAK!
AHHHH!
GYAHH--!
GULP! GULP! GULP!
22

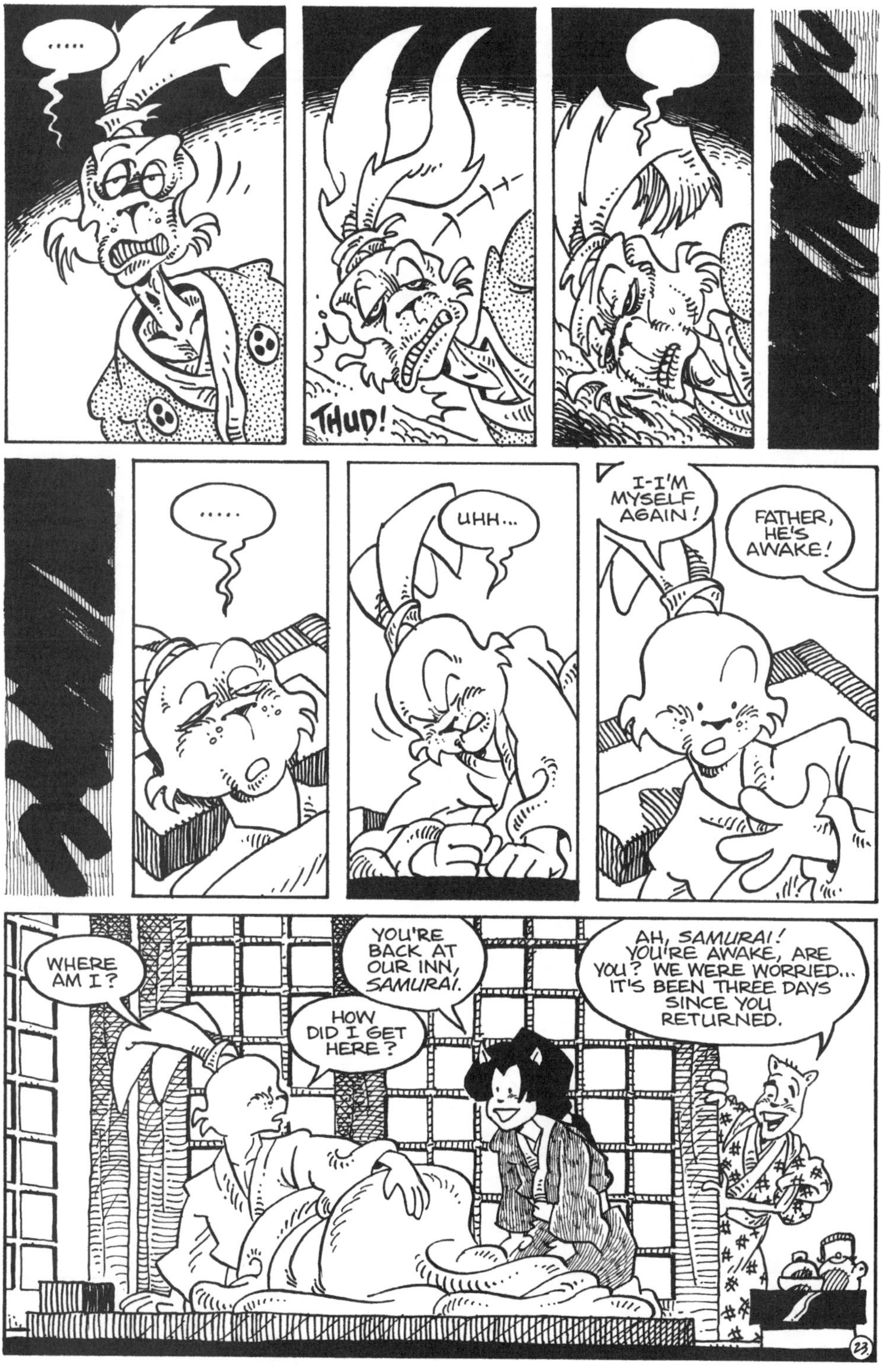
.....
THUD!
.....
UHH...
I-I'M MYSELF AGAIN!
FATHER, HE'S AWAKE!
WHERE AM I?
YOU'RE BACK AT OUR INN, SAMURAI.
HOW DID I GET HERE?
AH, SAMURAI! YOU'RE AWAKE, ARE YOU? WE WERE WORRIED... IT'S BEEN THREE DAYS SINCE YOU RETURNED.
23.

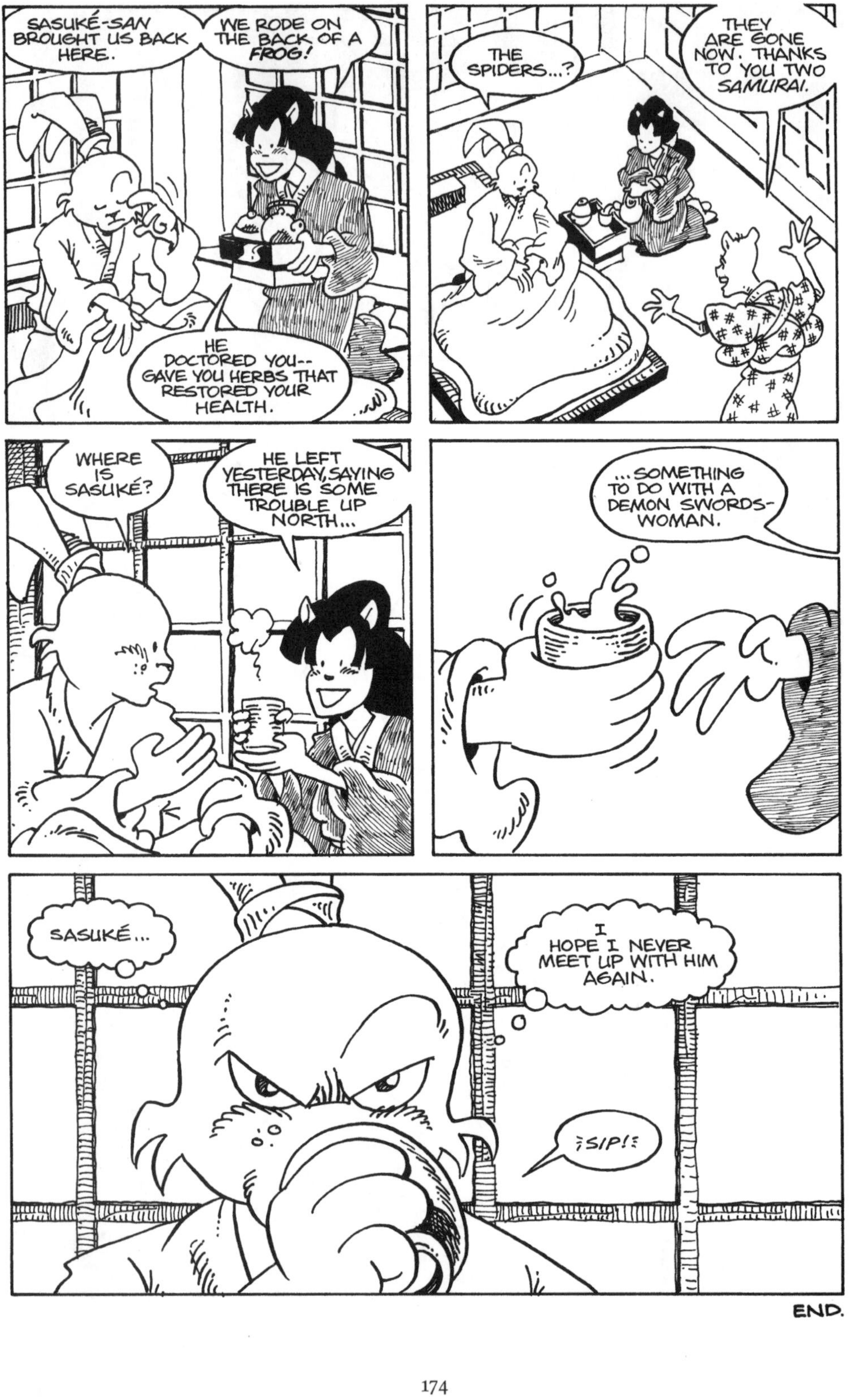
SASUKÉ-SAN BROUGHT US BACK HERE.
WE RODE ON THE BACK OF A FROG!
HE DOCTORED YOU-- GAVE YOU HERBS THAT RESTORED YOUR HEALTH.
THE SPIDERS...?
THEY ARE GONE NOW. THANKS TO YOU TWO SAMURAI.
WHERE IS SASUKÉ?
HE LEFT YESTERDAY, SAYING THERE IS SOME TROUBLE UP NORTH...
...SOMETHING TO DO WITH A DEMON SWORDS-WOMAN.
SASUKÉ...
I HOPE I NEVER MEET UP WITH HIM AGAIN.
¡SIP!
END.

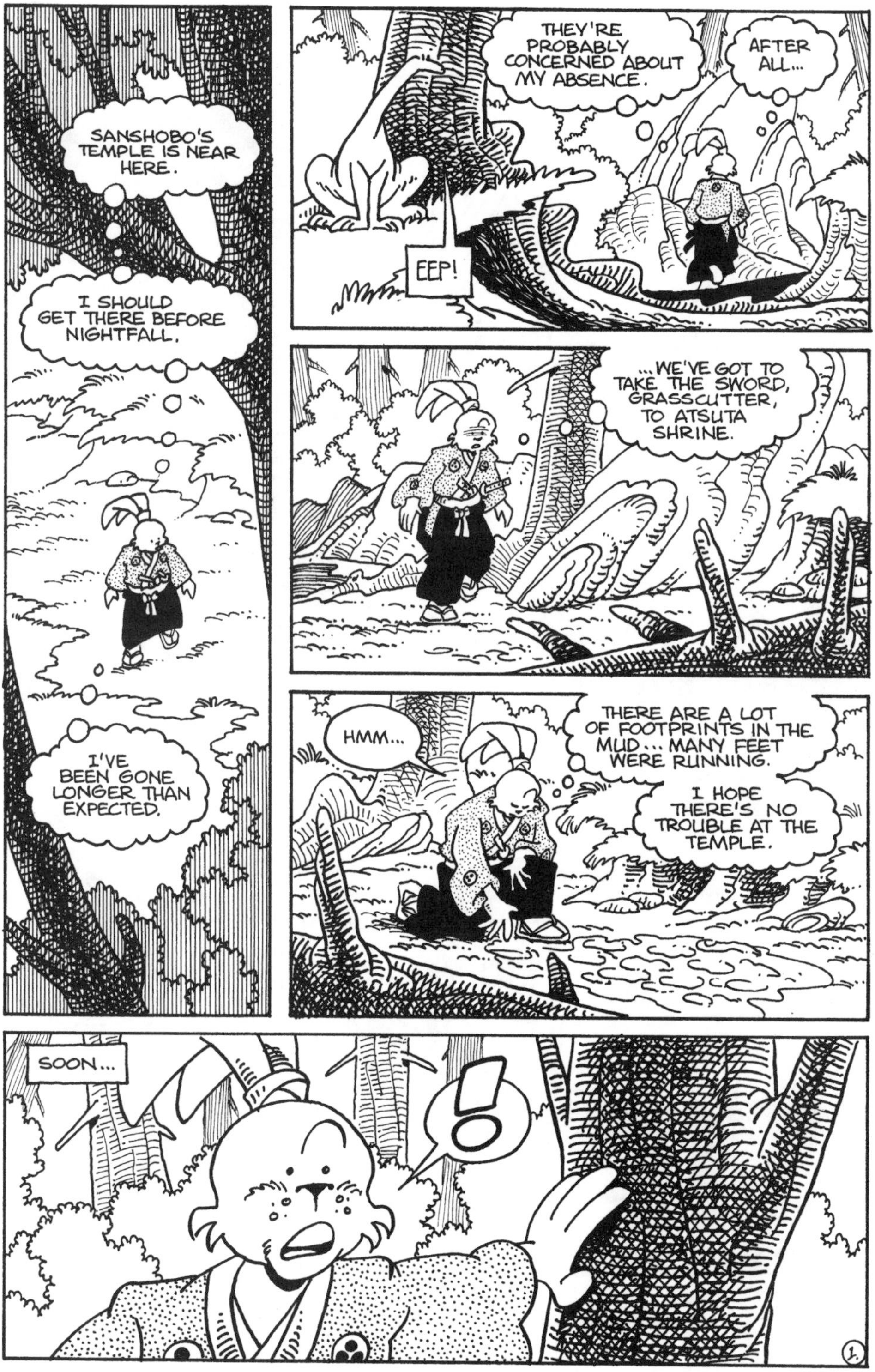
SANSHOBO'S TEMPLE IS NEAR HERE.
I SHOULD GET THERE BEFORE NIGHTFALL.
I'VE BEEN GONE LONGER THAN EXPECTED.
THEY'RE PROBABLY CONCERNED ABOUT MY ABSENCE.
AFTER ALL...
EEP!
...WE'VE GOT TO TAKE THE SWORD, GRASSCUTTER, TO ATSUTA SHRINE.
HMM...
THERE ARE A LOT OF FOOTPRINTS IN THE MUD... MANY FEET WERE RUNNING.
I HOPE THERE'S NO TROUBLE AT THE TEMPLE.
SOON...
!
1.

REUNION

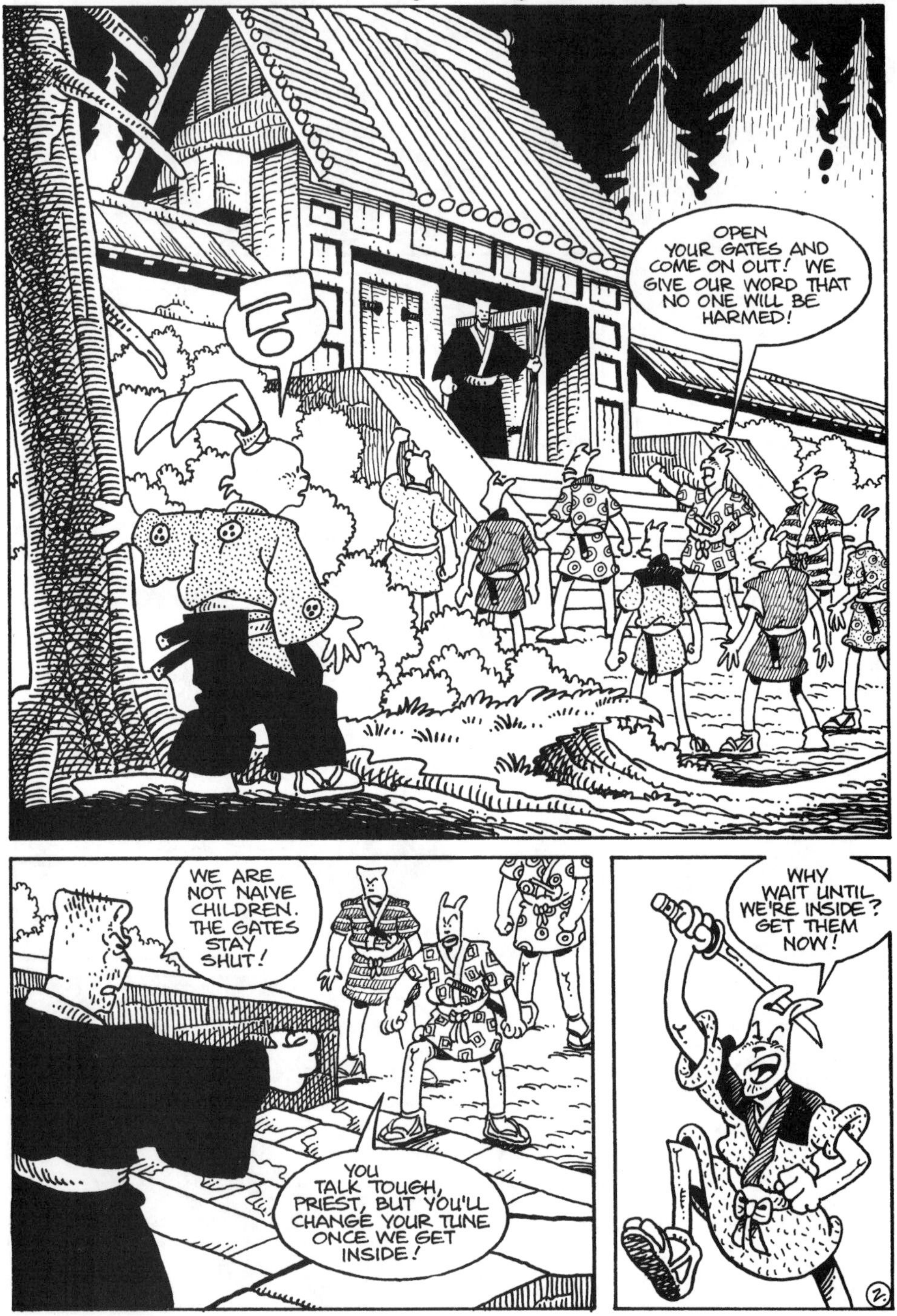
?
OPEN YOUR GATES AND COME ON OUT! WE GIVE OUR WORD THAT NO ONE WILL BE HARMED!
WE ARE NOT NAIVE CHILDREN. THE GATES STAY SHUT!
YOU TALK TOUGH, PRIEST, BUT YOU'LL CHANGE YOUR TUNE ONCE WE GET INSIDE!
WHY WAIT UNTIL WE'RE INSIDE? GET THEM NOW!
2.

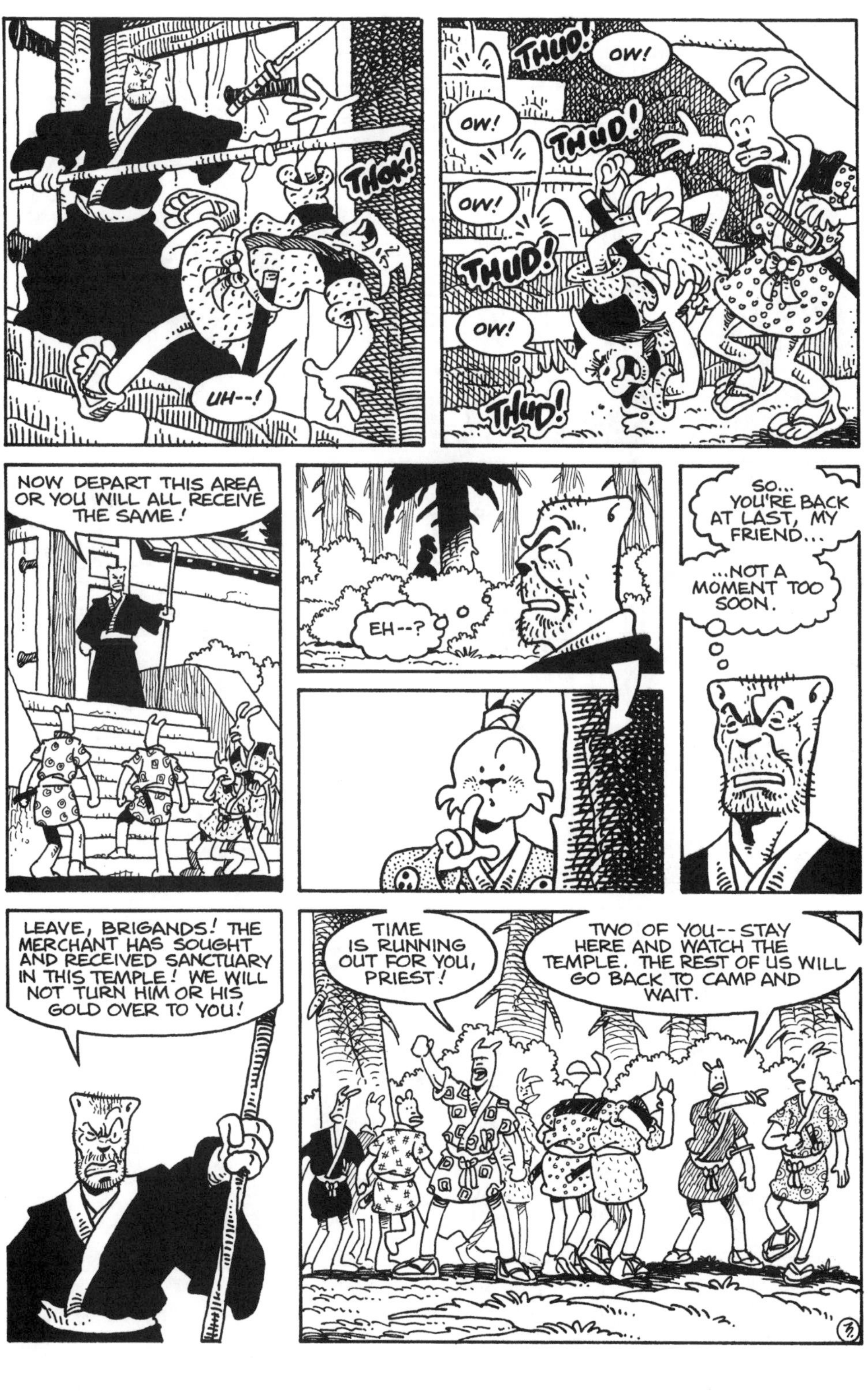
THOK!
UH--!
THUD!
OW!
OW!
THUD!
OW!
THUD!
OW!
THUD!
NOW DEPART THIS AREA OR YOU WILL ALL RECEIVE THE SAME!
EH--?
SO... YOU'RE BACK AT LAST, MY FRIEND...
...NOT A MOMENT TOO SOON.
LEAVE, BRIGANDS! THE MERCHANT HAS SOUGHT AND RECEIVED SANCTUARY IN THIS TEMPLE! WE WILL NOT TURN HIM OR HIS GOLD OVER TO YOU!
TIME IS RUNNING OUT FOR YOU, PRIEST!
TWO OF YOU--STAY HERE AND WATCH THE TEMPLE. THE REST OF US WILL GO BACK TO CAMP AND WAIT.

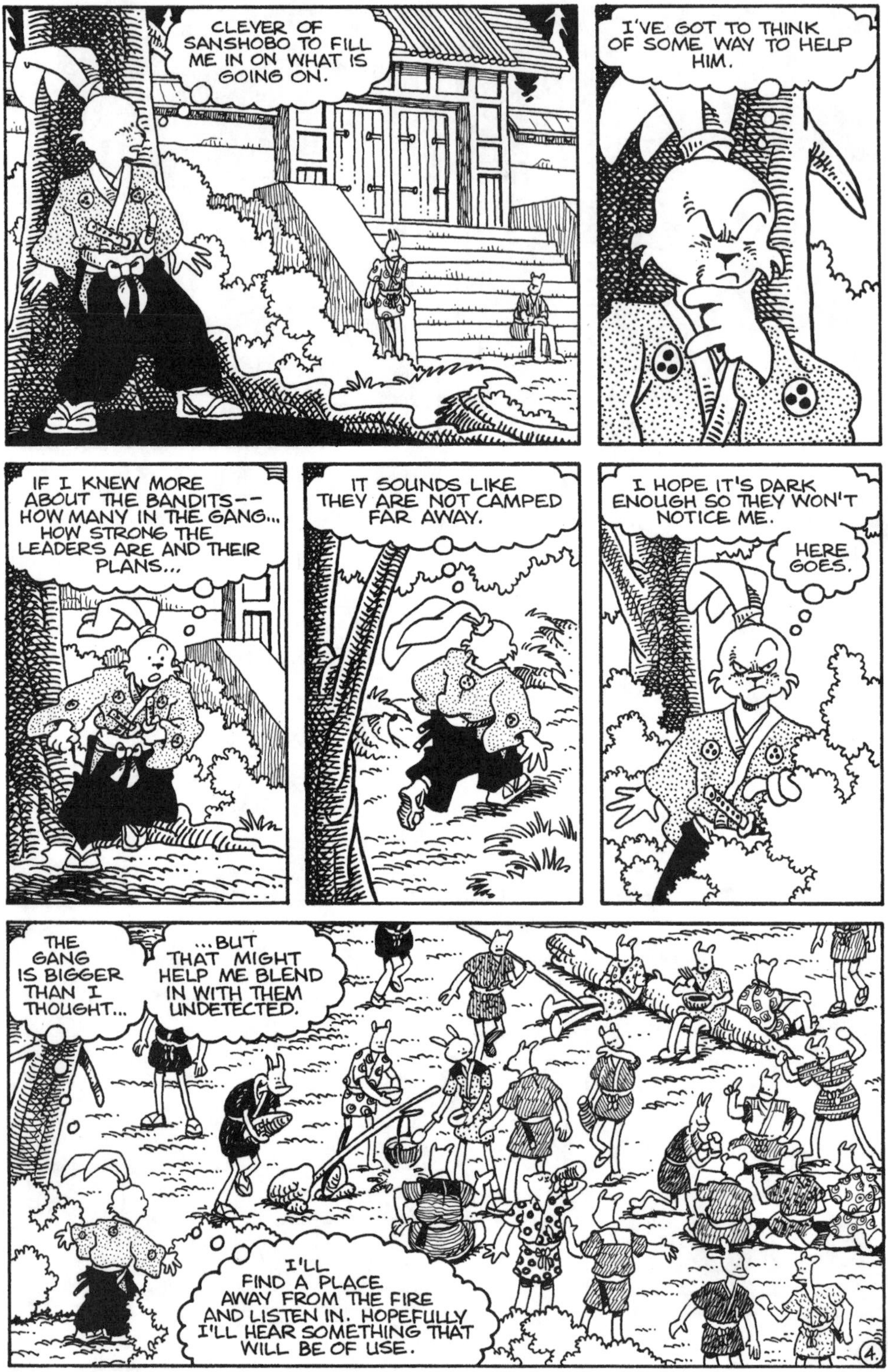
CLEVER OF SANSHOBO TO FILL ME IN ON WHAT IS GOING ON.
I'VE GOT TO THINK OF SOME WAY TO HELP HIM.
IF I KNEW MORE ABOUT THE BANDITS-- HOW MANY IN THE GANG... HOW STRONG THE LEADERS ARE AND THEIR PLANS...
IT SOUNDS LIKE THEY ARE NOT CAMPED FAR AWAY.
I HOPE IT'S DARK ENOUGH SO THEY WON'T NOTICE ME.
HERE GOES.
THE GANG IS BIGGER THAN I THOUGHT...
...BUT THAT MIGHT HELP ME BLEND IN WITH THEM UNDETECTED.
I'LL FIND A PLACE AWAY FROM THE FIRE AND LISTEN IN. HOPEFULLY I'LL HEAR SOMETHING THAT WILL BE OF USE.
4.

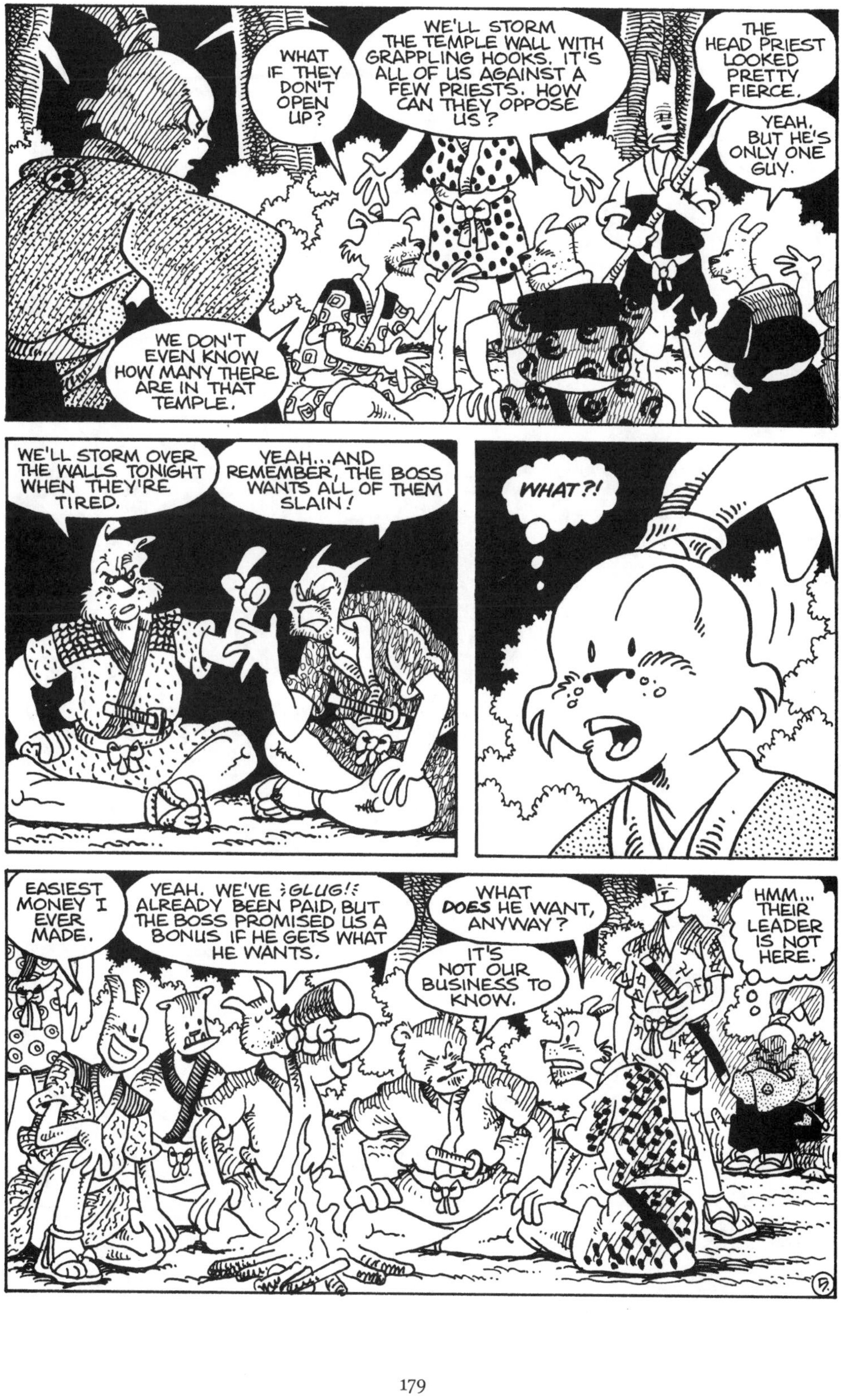
WHAT IF THEY DON'T OPEN UP?
WE'LL STORM THE TEMPLE WALL WITH GRAPPLING HOOKS. IT'S ALL OF US AGAINST A FEW PRIESTS. HOW CAN THEY OPPOSE US?
THE HEAD PRIEST LOOKED PRETTY FIERCE.
YEAH, BUT HE'S ONLY ONE GUY.
WE DON'T EVEN KNOW HOW MANY THERE ARE IN THAT TEMPLE.
WE'LL STORM OVER THE WALLS TONIGHT WHEN THEY'RE TIRED.
YEAH...AND REMEMBER, THE BOSS WANTS ALL OF THEM SLAIN!
WHAT?!
EASIEST MONEY I EVER MADE.
YEAH. WE'VE *GLUG!* ALREADY BEEN PAID, BUT THE BOSS PROMISED US A BONUS IF HE GETS WHAT HE WANTS.
WHAT DOES HE WANT, ANYWAY?
IT'S NOT OUR BUSINESS TO KNOW.
HMM... THEIR LEADER IS NOT HERE.

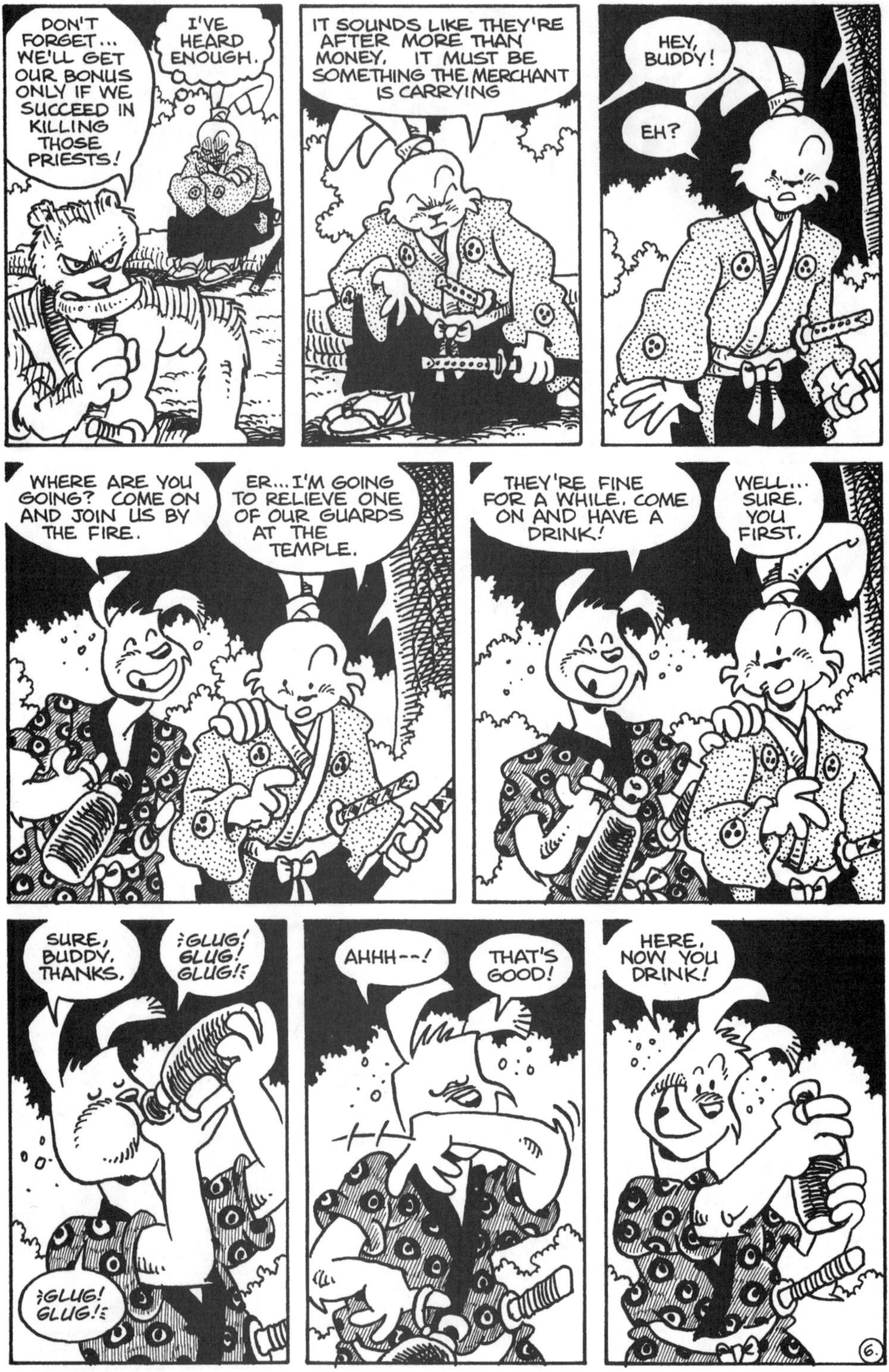
DON'T FORGET... WE'LL GET OUR BONUS ONLY IF WE SUCCEED IN KILLING THOSE PRIESTS!
I'VE HEARD ENOUGH.
IT SOUNDS LIKE THEY'RE AFTER MORE THAN MONEY. IT MUST BE SOMETHING THE MERCHANT IS CARRYING
HEY, BUDDY!
EH?
WHERE ARE YOU GOING? COME ON AND JOIN US BY THE FIRE.
ER... I'M GOING TO RELIEVE ONE OF OUR GUARDS AT THE TEMPLE.
THEY'RE FINE FOR A WHILE. COME ON AND HAVE A DRINK!
WELL... SURE. YOU FIRST.
SURE, BUDDY. THANKS.
GLUG! GLUG! GLUG!
GLUG! GLUG!
AHHH--!
THAT'S GOOD!
HERE, NOW YOU DRINK!
6.

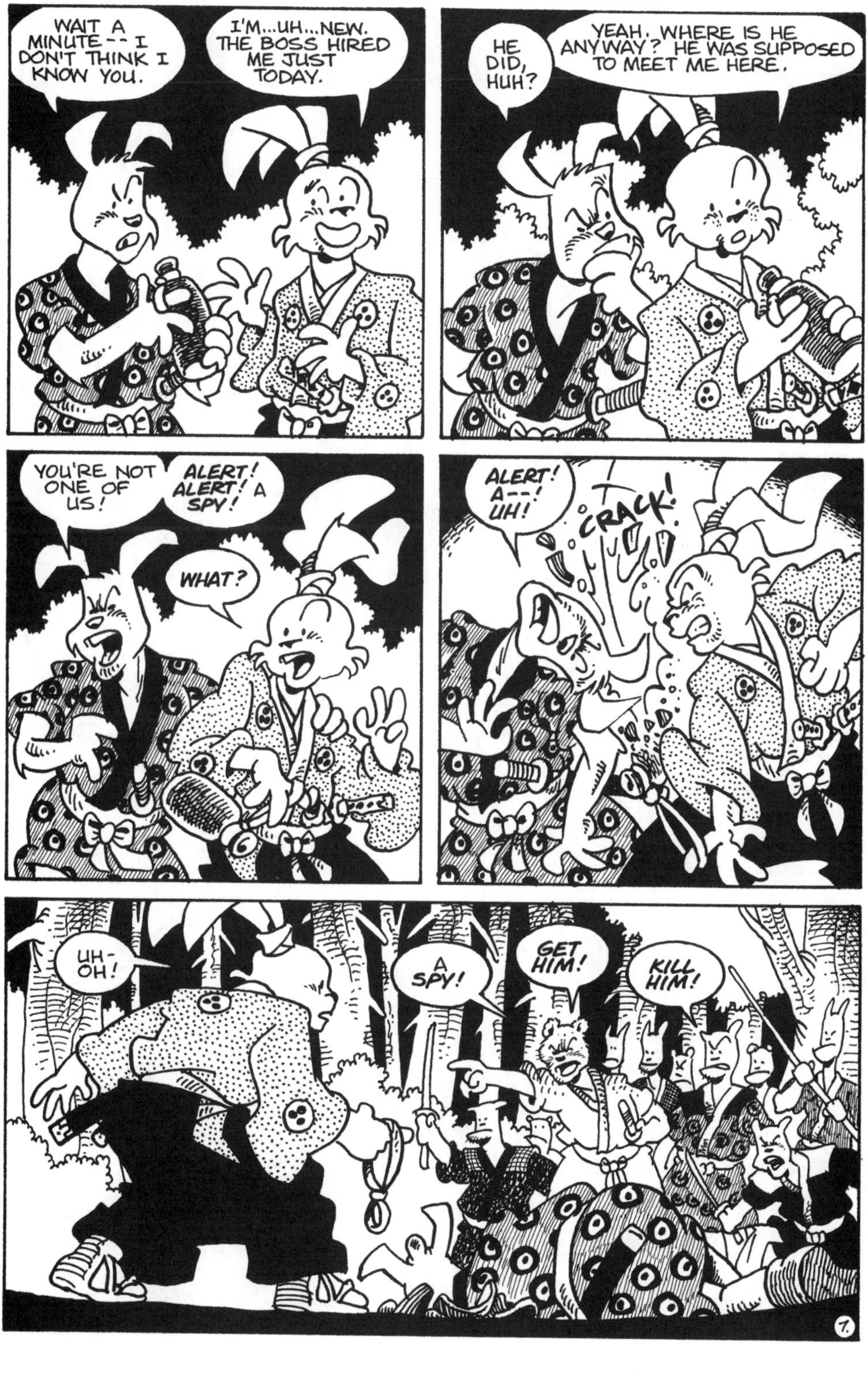
WAIT A MINUTE -- I DON'T THINK I KNOW YOU.
I'M...UH...NEW. THE BOSS HIRED ME JUST TODAY.
HE DID, HUH?
YEAH. WHERE IS HE ANYWAY? HE WAS SUPPOSED TO MEET ME HERE.
YOU'RE NOT ONE OF US!
ALERT! ALERT! A SPY!
WHAT?
ALERT! A--! UH!
CRACK!
UH-OH!
A SPY!
GET HIM!
KILL HIM!
7.

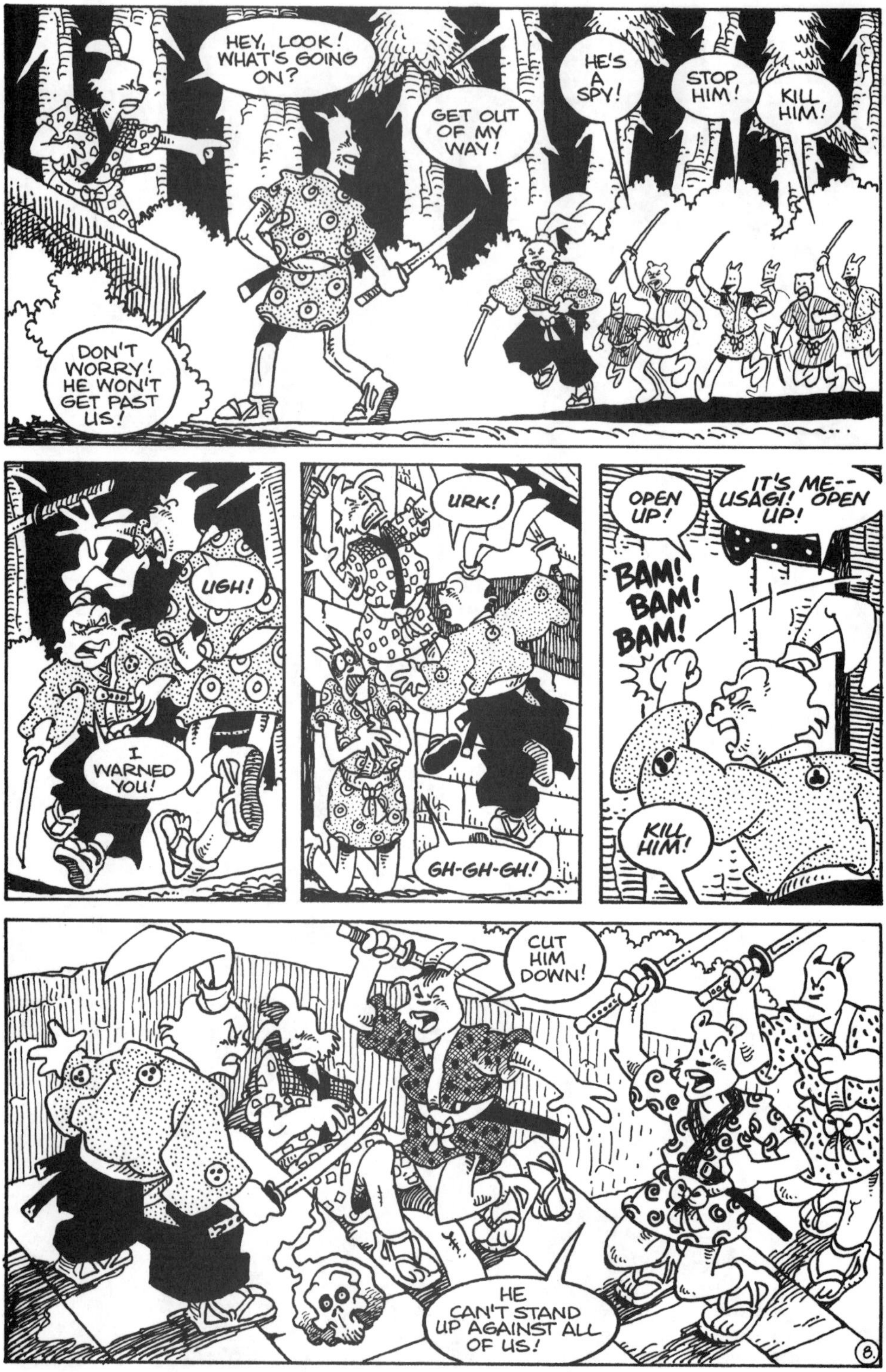
HEY, LOOK! WHAT'S GOING ON?
GET OUT OF MY WAY!
HE'S A SPY!
STOP HIM!
KILL HIM!
DON'T WORRY! HE WON'T GET PAST US!
UGH!
I WARNED YOU!
URK!
GH-GH-GH!
OPEN UP!
IT'S ME-- USAGI! OPEN UP!
BAM! BAM! BAM!
KILL HIM!
CUT HIM DOWN!
HE CAN'T STAND UP AGAINST ALL OF US!
8.

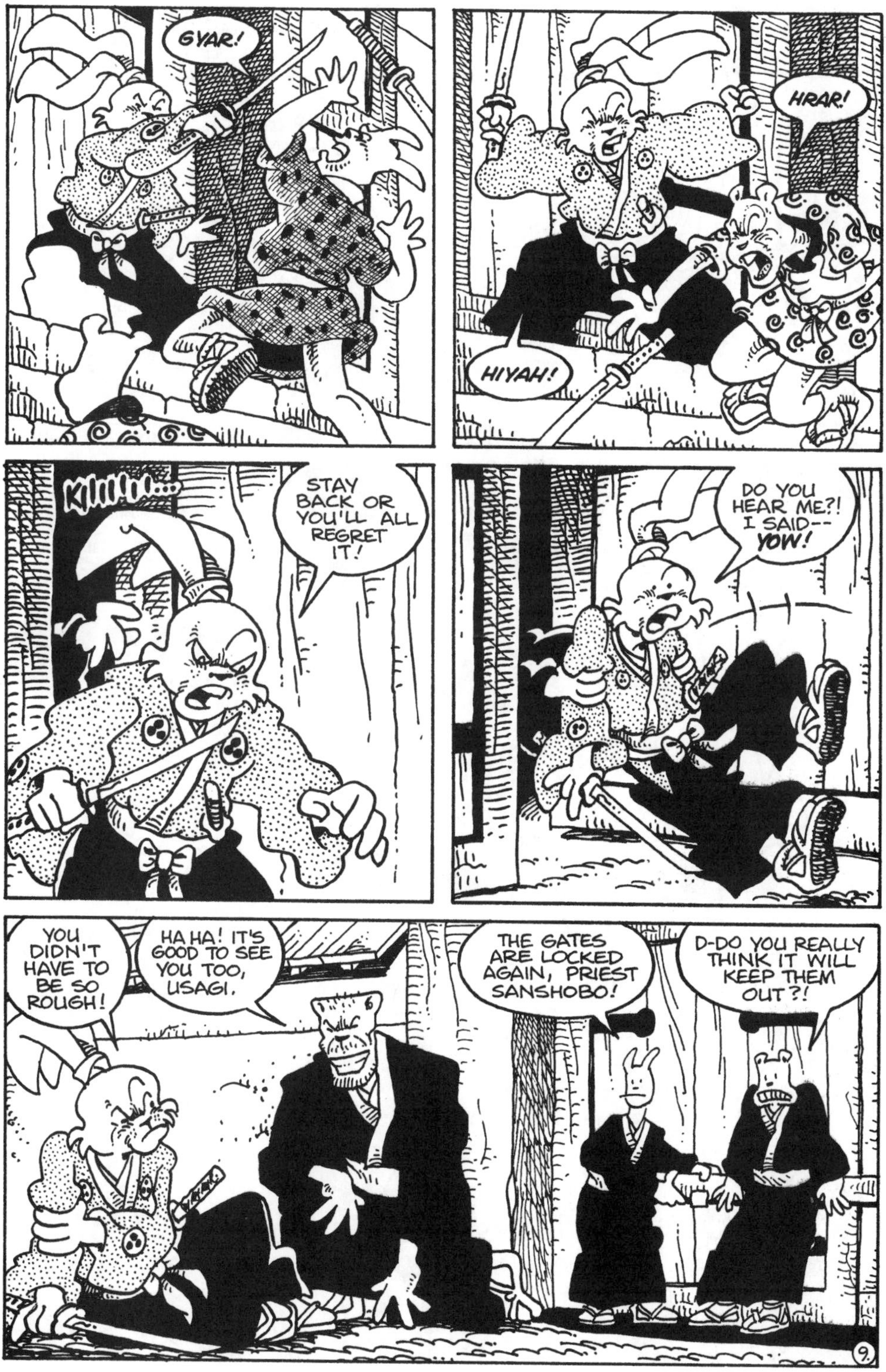
GYAR!
HRAR!
HIYAH!
KIIIIIII...
STAY BACK OR YOU'LL ALL REGRET IT!
DO YOU HEAR ME?! I SAID-- YOW!
YOU DIDN'T HAVE TO BE SO ROUGH!
HA HA! IT'S GOOD TO SEE YOU TOO, USAGI.
THE GATES ARE LOCKED AGAIN, PRIEST SANSHOBO!
D-DO YOU REALLY THINK IT WILL KEEP THEM OUT?!
9.

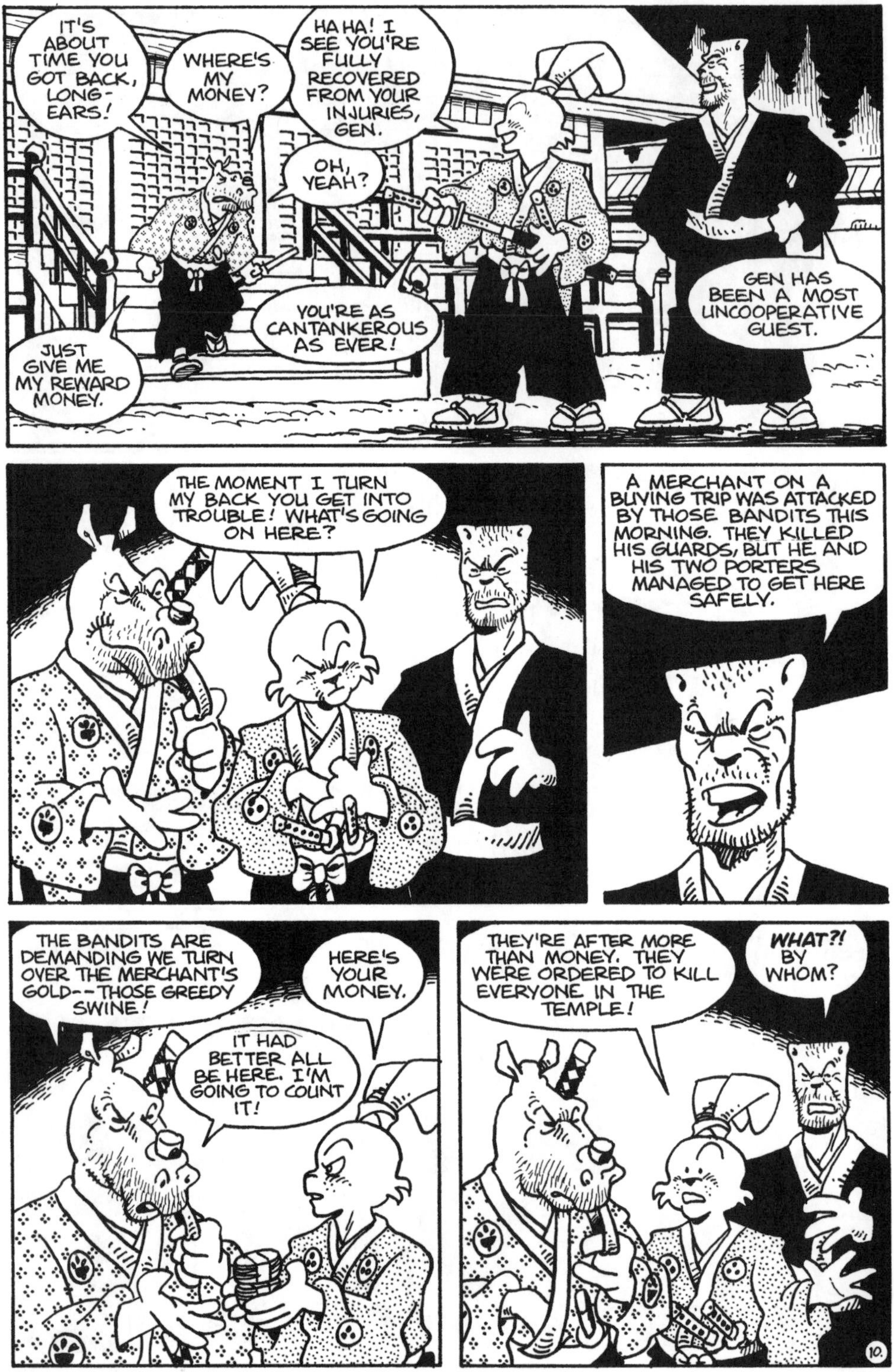
IT'S ABOUT TIME YOU GOT BACK, LONG-EARS!
WHERE'S MY MONEY?
HA HA! I SEE YOU'RE FULLY RECOVERED FROM YOUR INJURIES, GEN.
OH, YEAH?
JUST GIVE ME MY REWARD MONEY.
YOU'RE AS CANTANKEROUS AS EVER!
GEN HAS BEEN A MOST UNCOOPERATIVE GUEST.
THE MOMENT I TURN MY BACK YOU GET INTO TROUBLE! WHAT'S GOING ON HERE?
A MERCHANT ON A BUYING TRIP WAS ATTACKED BY THOSE BANDITS THIS MORNING. THEY KILLED HIS GUARDS, BUT HE AND HIS TWO PORTERS MANAGED TO GET HERE SAFELY.
THE BANDITS ARE DEMANDING WE TURN OVER THE MERCHANT'S GOLD--THOSE GREEDY SWINE!
HERE'S YOUR MONEY.
IT HAD BETTER ALL BE HERE. I'M GOING TO COUNT IT!
THEY'RE AFTER MORE THAN MONEY. THEY WERE ORDERED TO KILL EVERYONE IN THE TEMPLE!
WHAT?! BY WHOM?
10.

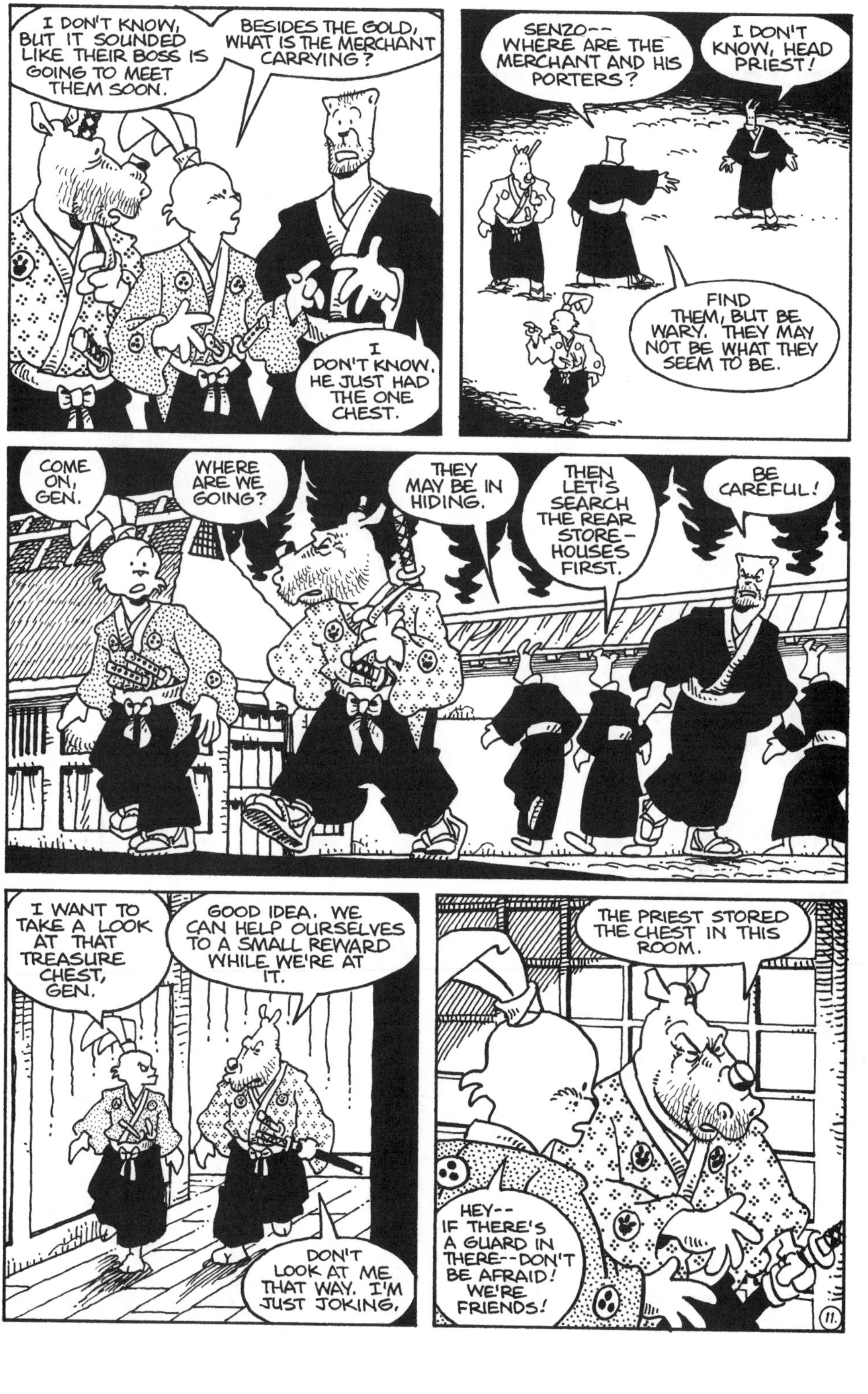
I DON'T KNOW, BUT IT SOUNDED LIKE THEIR BOSS IS GOING TO MEET THEM SOON.
BESIDES THE GOLD, WHAT IS THE MERCHANT CARRYING?
I DON'T KNOW. HE JUST HAD THE ONE CHEST.
SENZO-- WHERE ARE THE MERCHANT AND HIS PORTERS?
I DON'T KNOW, HEAD PRIEST!
FIND THEM, BUT BE WARY. THEY MAY NOT BE WHAT THEY SEEM TO BE.
COME ON, GEN.
WHERE ARE WE GOING?
THEY MAY BE IN HIDING.
THEN LET'S SEARCH THE REAR STORE-HOUSES FIRST.
BE CAREFUL!
I WANT TO TAKE A LOOK AT THAT TREASURE CHEST, GEN.
GOOD IDEA. WE CAN HELP OURSELVES TO A SMALL REWARD WHILE WE'RE AT IT.
DON'T LOOK AT ME THAT WAY. I'M JUST JOKING.
THE PRIEST STORED THE CHEST IN THIS ROOM.
HEY-- IF THERE'S A GUARD IN THERE--DON'T BE AFRAID! WE'RE FRIENDS!
11.

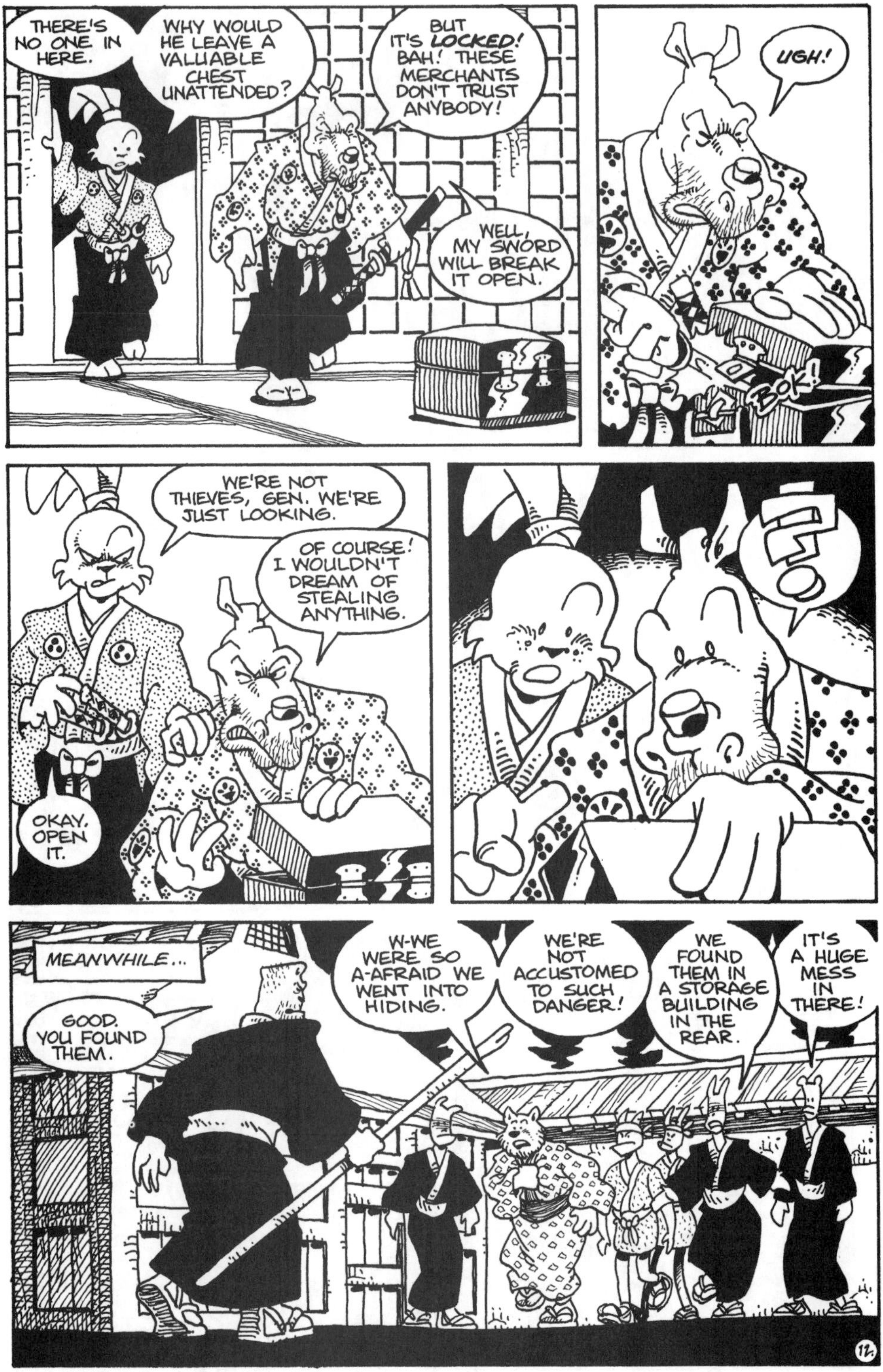
THERE'S NO ONE IN HERE.
WHY WOULD HE LEAVE A VALUABLE CHEST UNATTENDED?
BUT IT'S **LOCKED!** BAH! THESE MERCHANTS DON'T TRUST ANYBODY!
WELL, MY SWORD WILL BREAK IT OPEN.
UGH!
BOK!
WE'RE NOT THIEVES, GEN. WE'RE JUST LOOKING.
OF COURSE! I WOULDN'T DREAM OF STEALING ANYTHING.
OKAY. OPEN IT.
?!
MEANWHILE...
GOOD. YOU FOUND THEM.
W-WE WERE SO A-AFRAID WE WENT INTO HIDING.
WE'RE NOT ACCUSTOMED TO SUCH DANGER!
WE FOUND THEM IN A STORAGE BUILDING IN THE REAR.
IT'S A HUGE MESS IN THERE!
12.

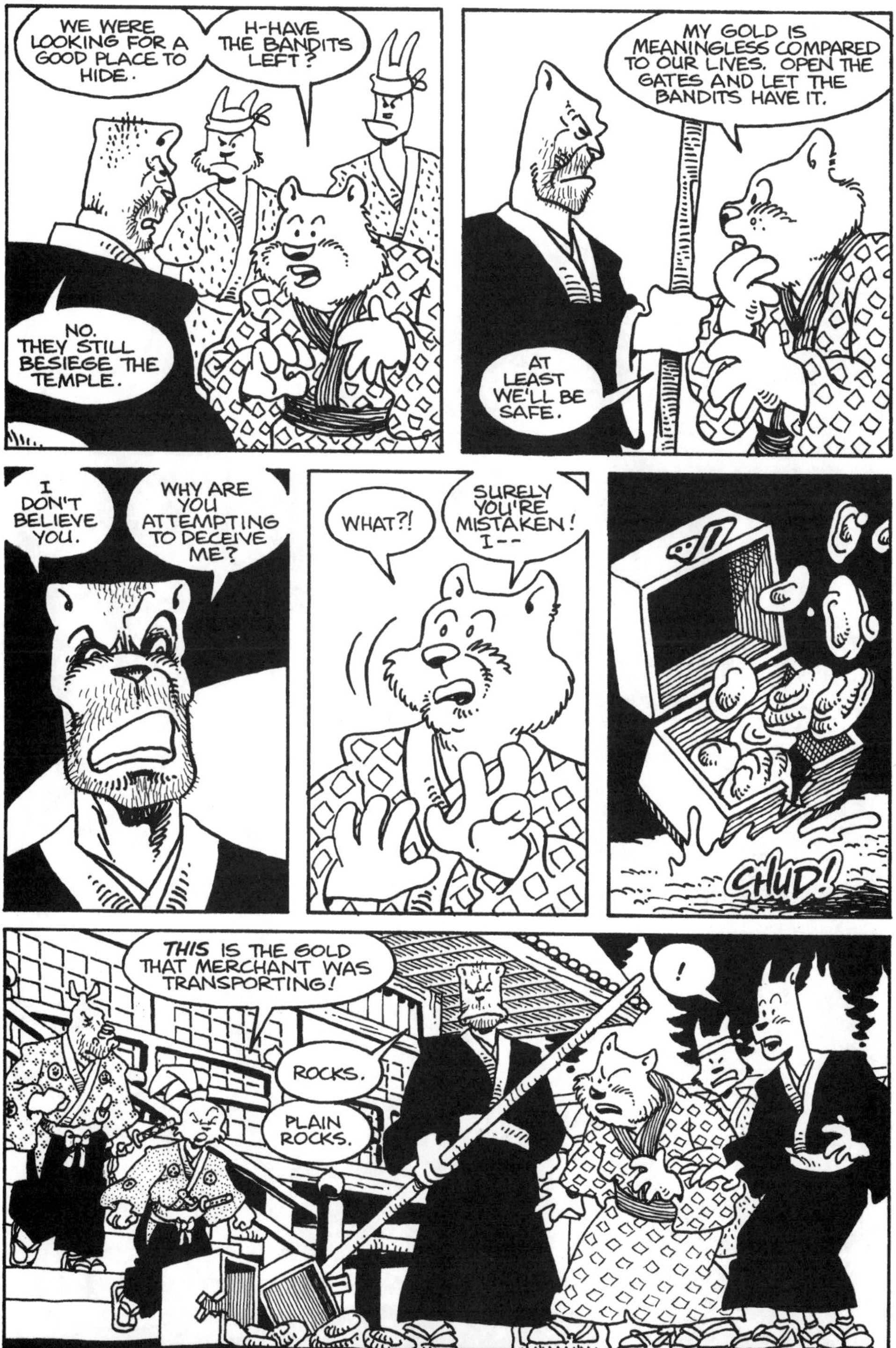
WE WERE LOOKING FOR A GOOD PLACE TO HIDE.
H-HAVE THE BANDITS LEFT?
NO. THEY STILL BESIEGE THE TEMPLE.
MY GOLD IS MEANINGLESS COMPARED TO OUR LIVES. OPEN THE GATES AND LET THE BANDITS HAVE IT.
AT LEAST WE'LL BE SAFE.
I DON'T BELIEVE YOU.
WHY ARE YOU ATTEMPTING TO DECEIVE ME?
WHAT?!
SURELY YOU'RE MISTAKEN! I--
CHUD!
THIS IS THE GOLD THAT MERCHANT WAS TRANSPORTING!
ROCKS.
PLAIN ROCKS.
!
13.

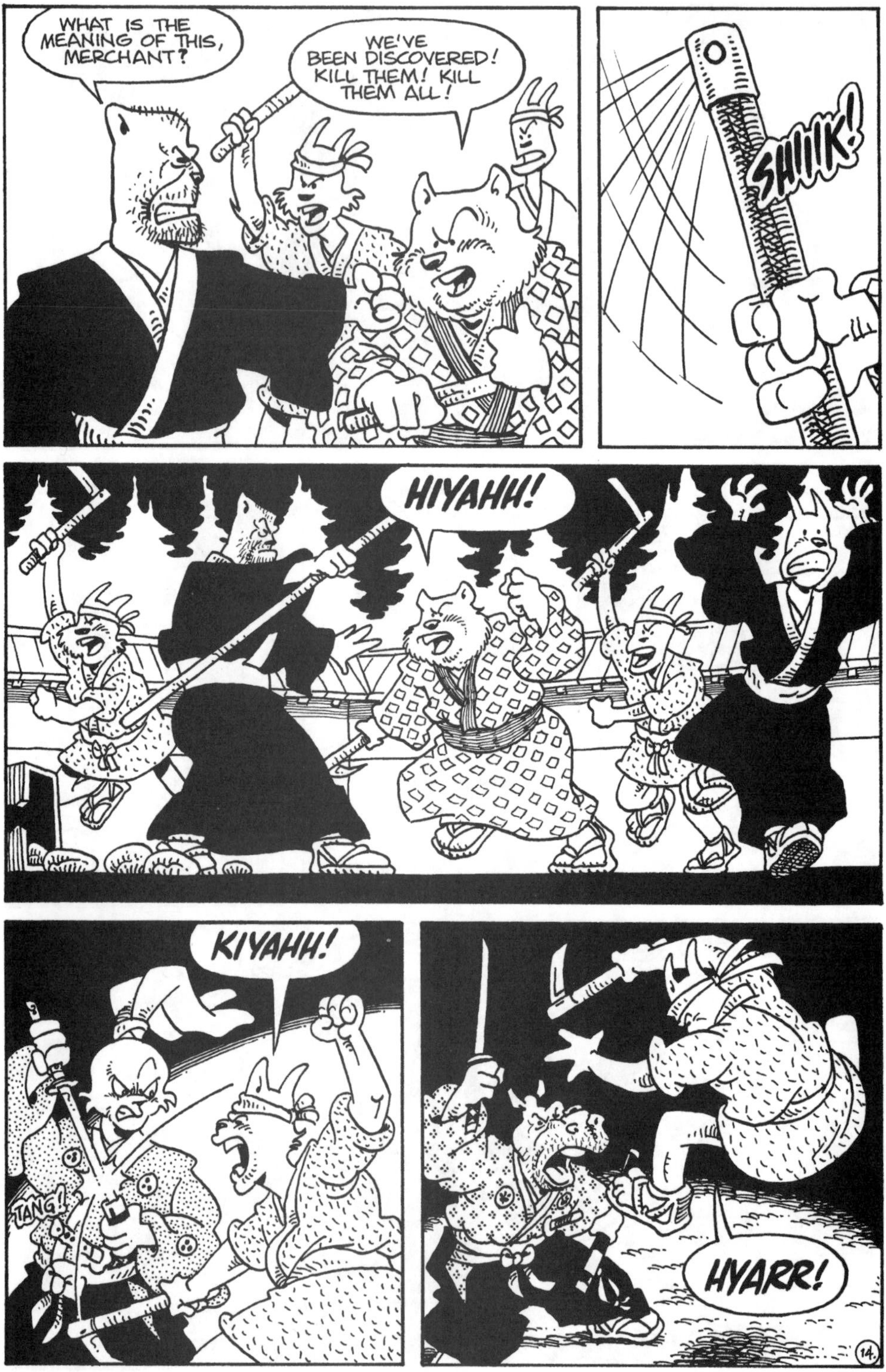
WHAT IS THE MEANING OF THIS, MERCHANT?
WE'VE BEEN DISCOVERED! KILL THEM! KILL THEM ALL!
SHIIIK!
HIYAHH!
KIYAHH!
TANG!
HYARR!
14.

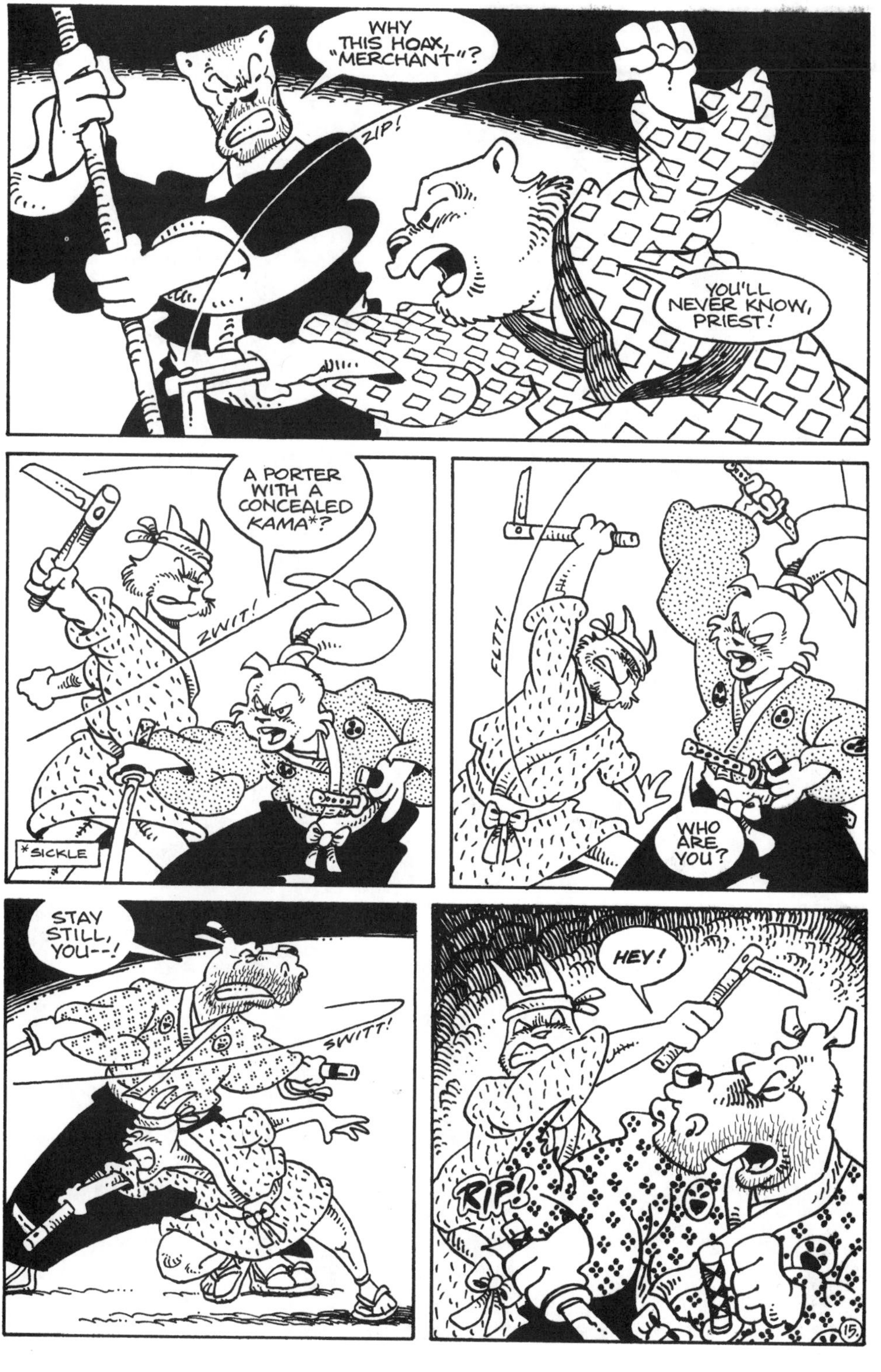
WHY THIS HOAX, "MERCHANT"?
ZIP!
YOU'LL NEVER KNOW, PRIEST!
A PORTER WITH A CONCEALED KAMA*?
ZWIT!
*SICKLE
FLTT!
WHO ARE YOU?
STAY STILL, YOU--!
SWITT!
HEY!
RIP!
15.

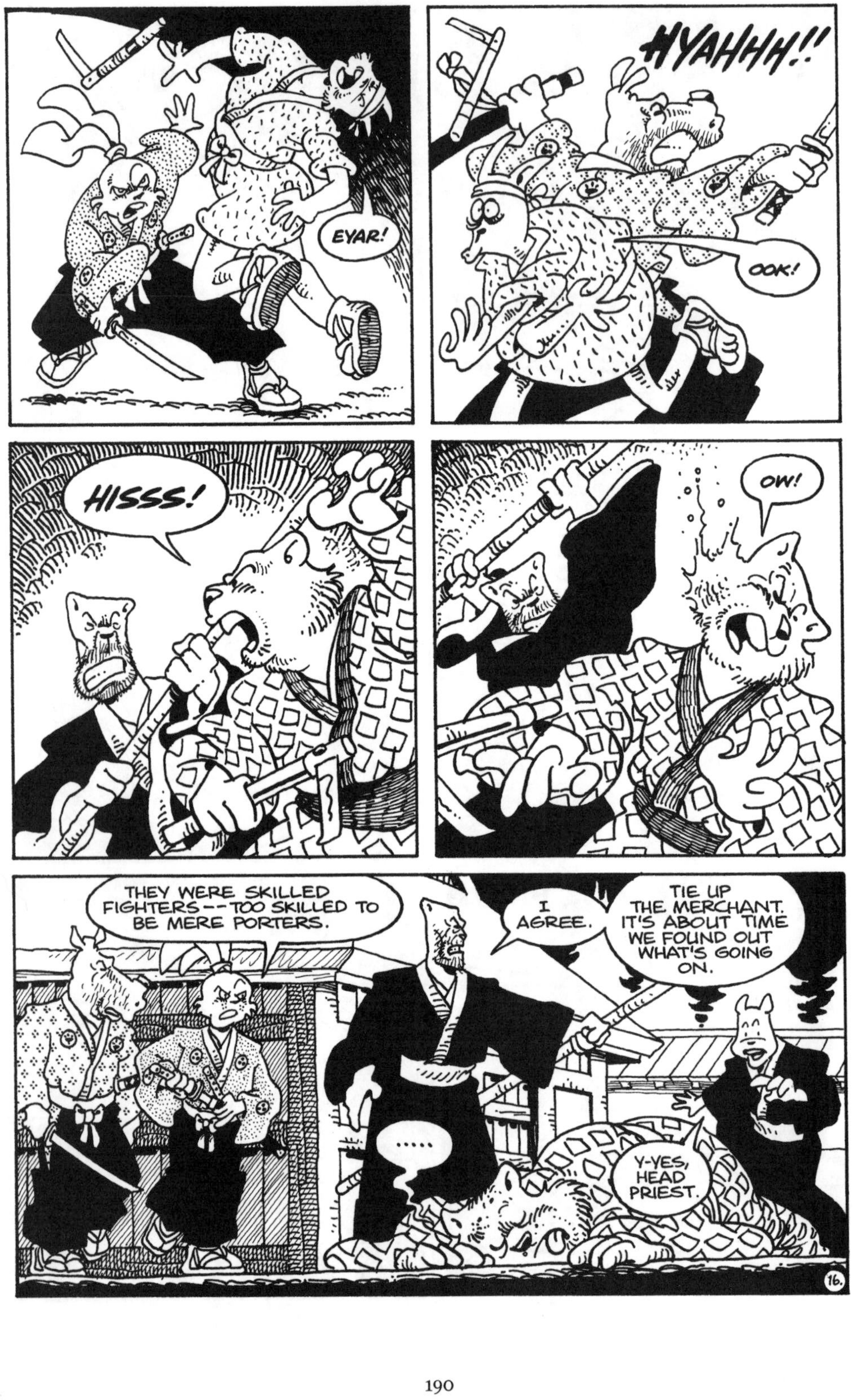
EYAR!
HYAHHH!!
OOK!
HISSS!
OW!
THEY WERE SKILLED FIGHTERS--TOO SKILLED TO BE MERE PORTERS.
I AGREE.
TIE UP THE MERCHANT. IT'S ABOUT TIME WE FOUND OUT WHAT'S GOING ON.
.....
Y-YES, HEAD PRIEST.
16.

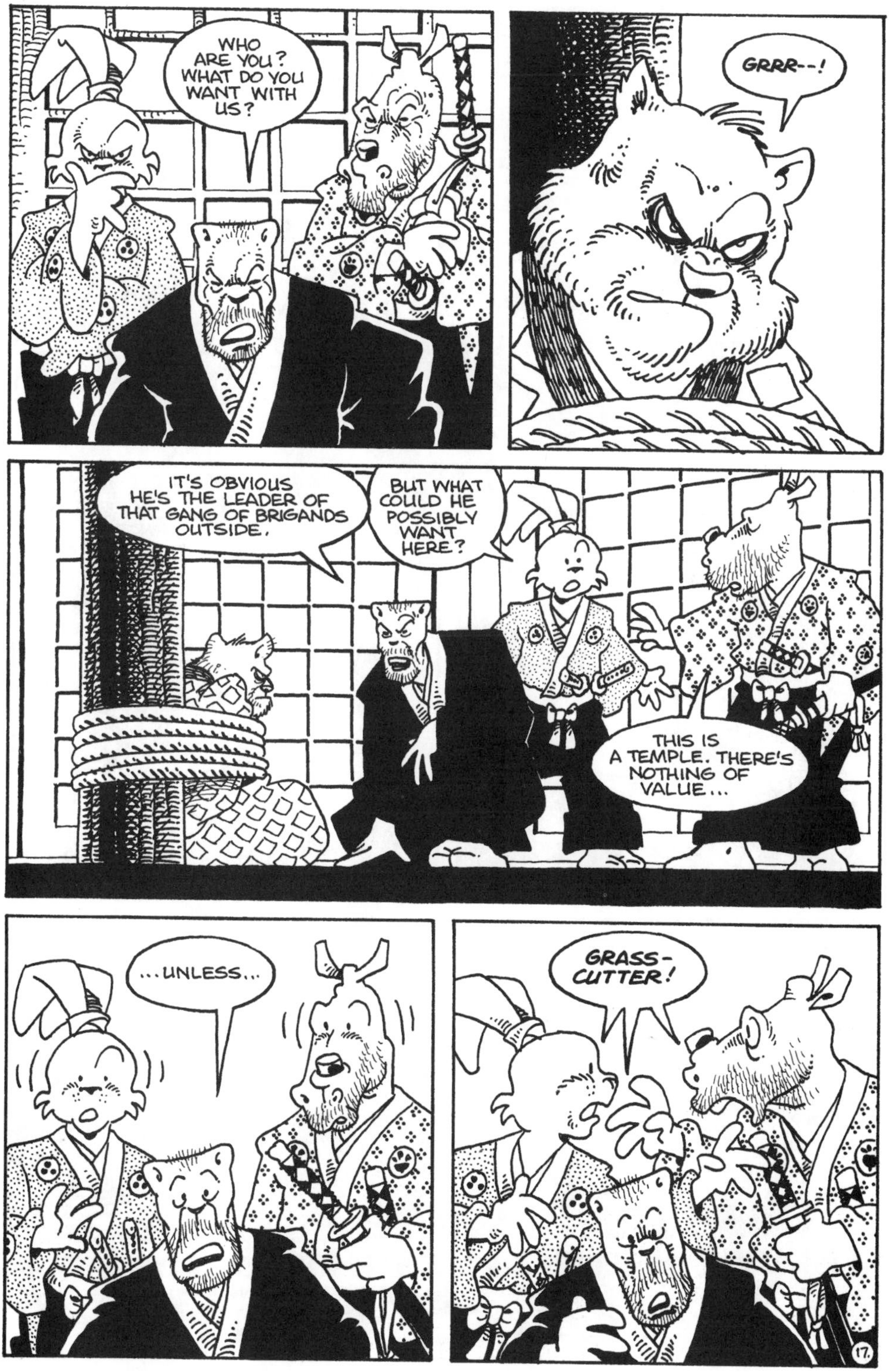
WHO ARE YOU? WHAT DO YOU WANT WITH US?
GRRR--!
IT'S OBVIOUS HE'S THE LEADER OF THAT GANG OF BRIGANDS OUTSIDE.
BUT WHAT COULD HE POSSIBLY WANT HERE?
THIS IS A TEMPLE. THERE'S NOTHING OF VALUE...
...UNLESS...
GRASS-CUTTER!
17.

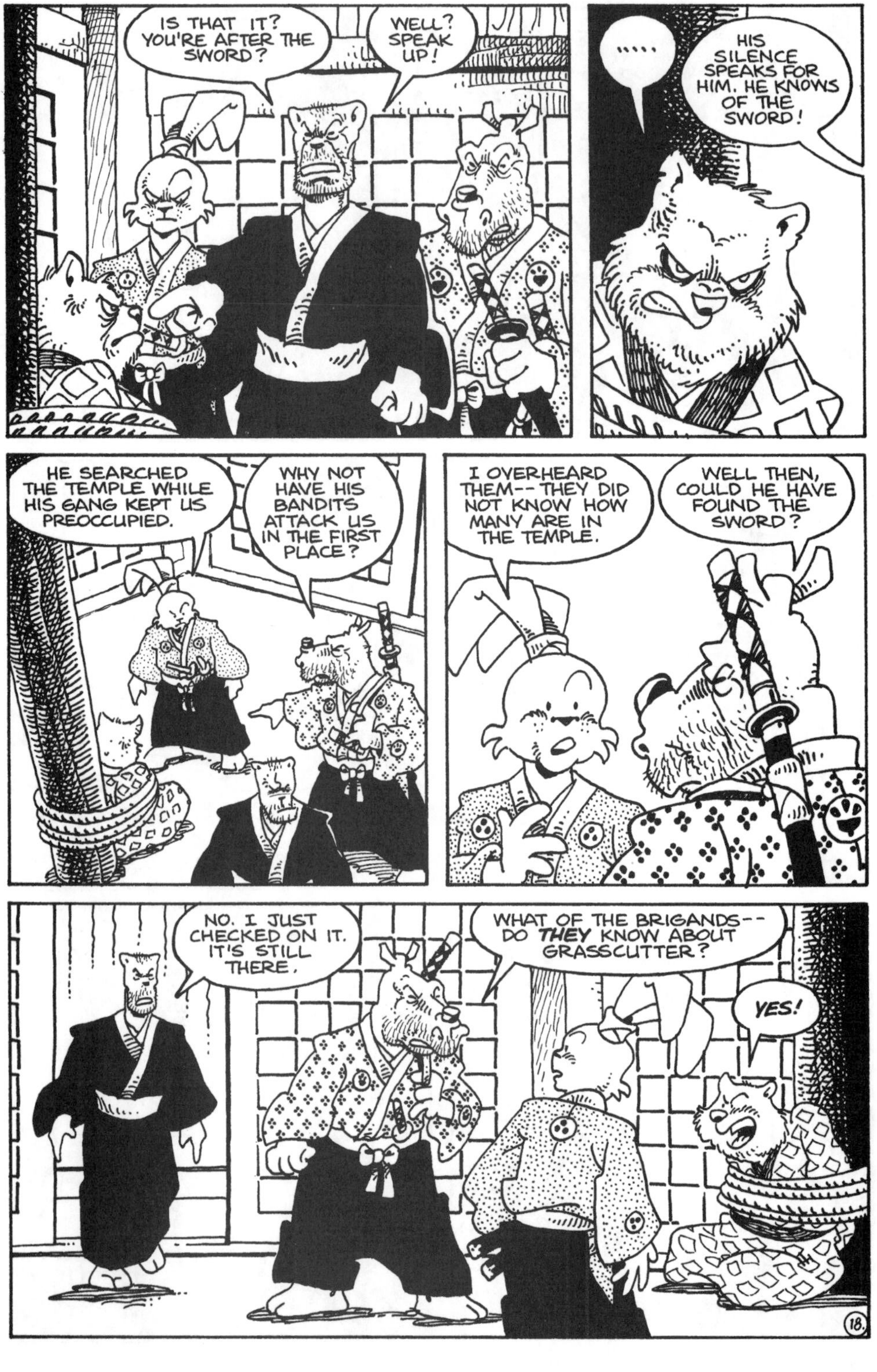
IS THAT IT? YOU'RE AFTER THE SWORD?
WELL? SPEAK UP!
.....
HIS SILENCE SPEAKS FOR HIM. HE KNOWS OF THE SWORD!
HE SEARCHED THE TEMPLE WHILE HIS GANG KEPT US PREOCCUPIED.
WHY NOT HAVE HIS BANDITS ATTACK US IN THE FIRST PLACE?
I OVERHEARD THEM-- THEY DID NOT KNOW HOW MANY ARE IN THE TEMPLE.
WELL THEN, COULD HE HAVE FOUND THE SWORD?
NO. I JUST CHECKED ON IT. IT'S STILL THERE.
WHAT OF THE BRIGANDS-- DO THEY KNOW ABOUT GRASSCUTTER?
YES!
18.

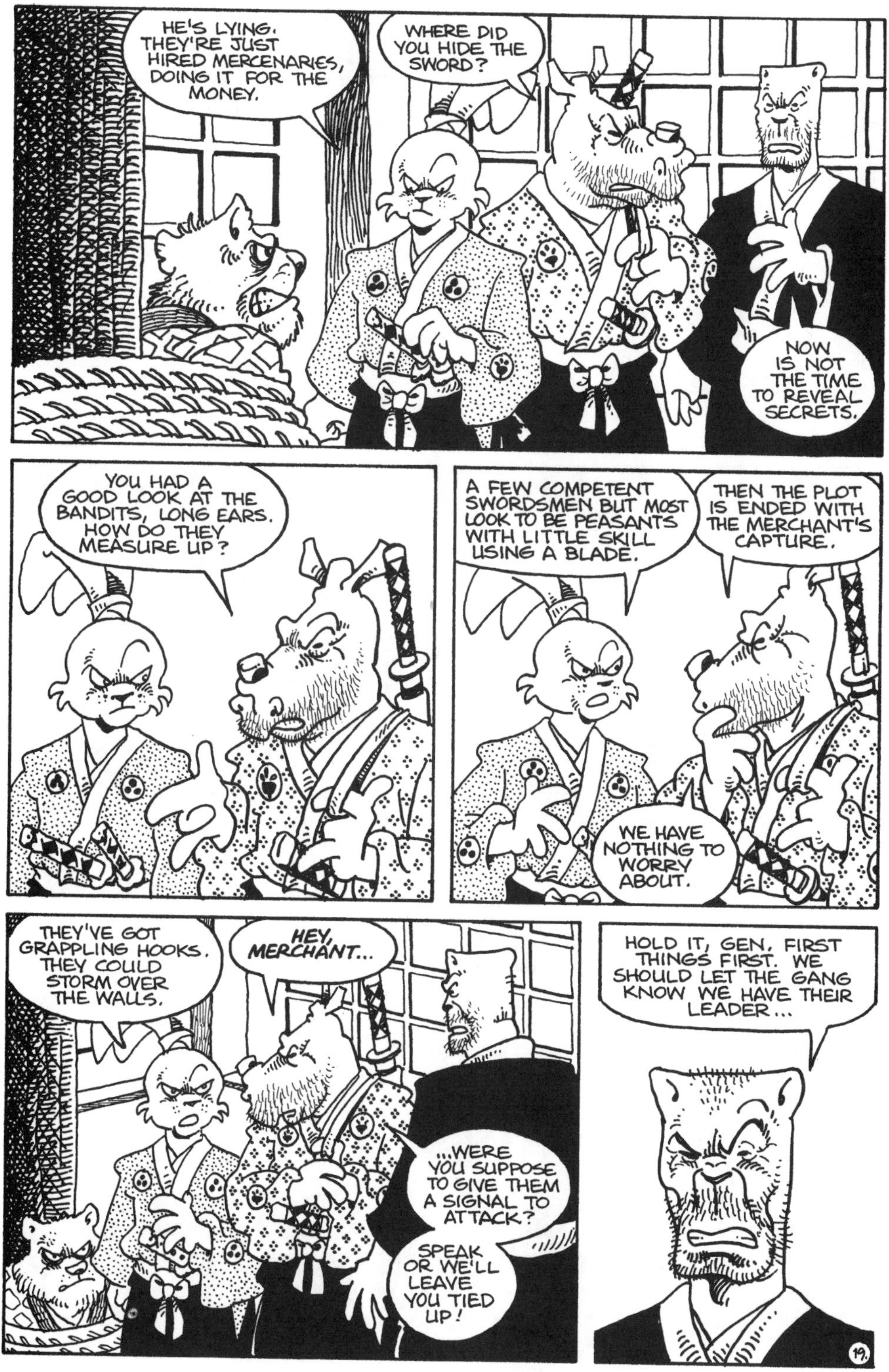
HE'S LYING. THEY'RE JUST HIRED MERCENARIES, DOING IT FOR THE MONEY.
WHERE DID YOU HIDE THE SWORD?
NOW IS NOT THE TIME TO REVEAL SECRETS.
YOU HAD A GOOD LOOK AT THE BANDITS, LONG EARS. HOW DO THEY MEASURE UP?
A FEW COMPETENT SWORDSMEN BUT MOST LOOK TO BE PEASANTS WITH LITTLE SKILL USING A BLADE.
THEN THE PLOT IS ENDED WITH THE MERCHANT'S CAPTURE.
WE HAVE NOTHING TO WORRY ABOUT.
THEY'VE GOT GRAPPLING HOOKS. THEY COULD STORM OVER THE WALLS.
HEY, MERCHANT...
...WERE YOU SUPPOSE TO GIVE THEM A SIGNAL TO ATTACK?
SPEAK OR WE'LL LEAVE YOU TIED UP!
HOLD IT, GEN. FIRST THINGS FIRST. WE SHOULD LET THE GANG KNOW WE HAVE THEIR LEADER...
19.

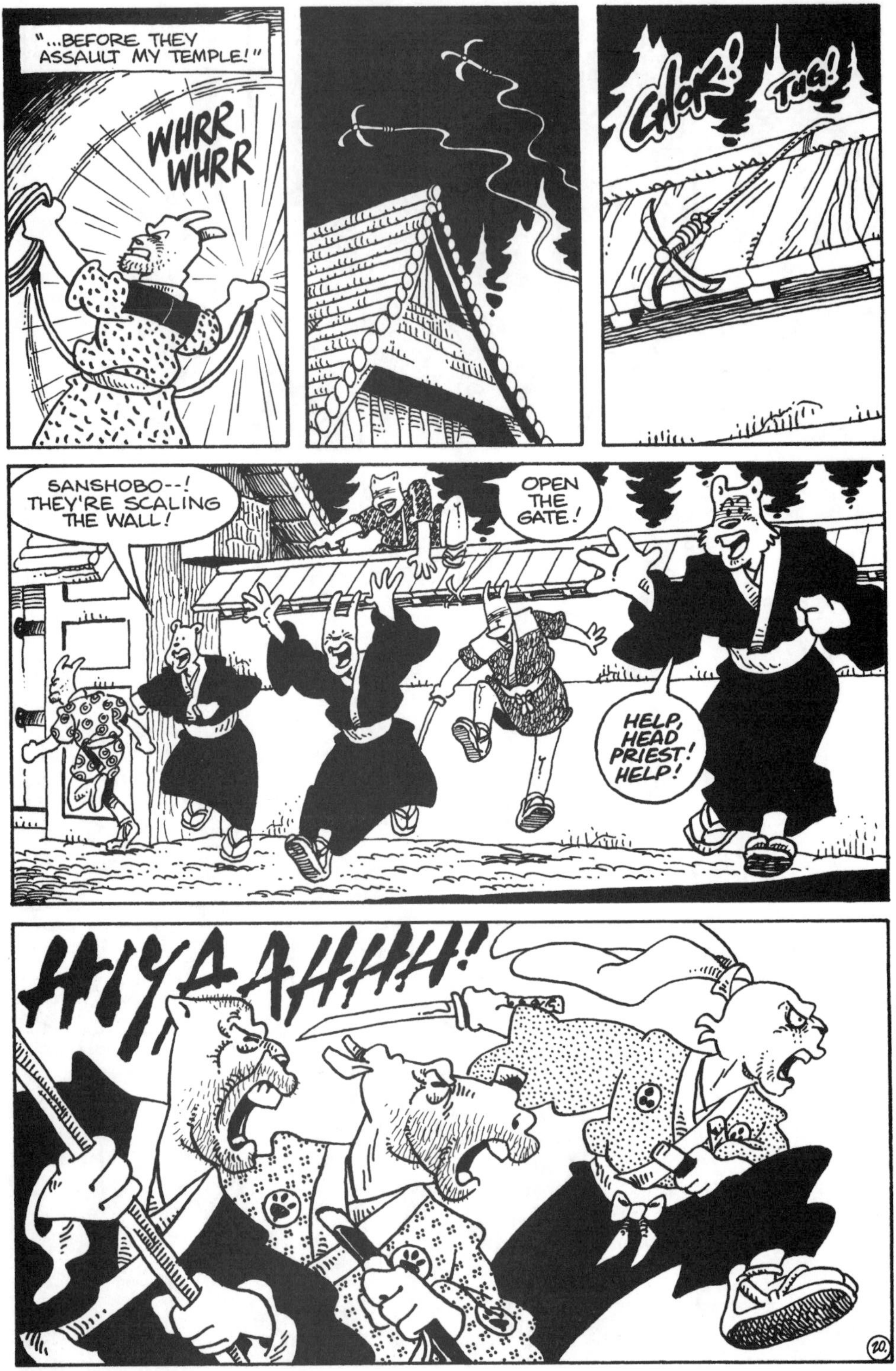
"...BEFORE THEY ASSAULT MY TEMPLE!"
WHRR WHRR
CHOK!
TUG!
SANSHOBO--! THEY'RE SCALING THE WALL!
OPEN THE GATE!
HELP, HEAD PRIEST! HELP!
HIYAAHHH!
20.

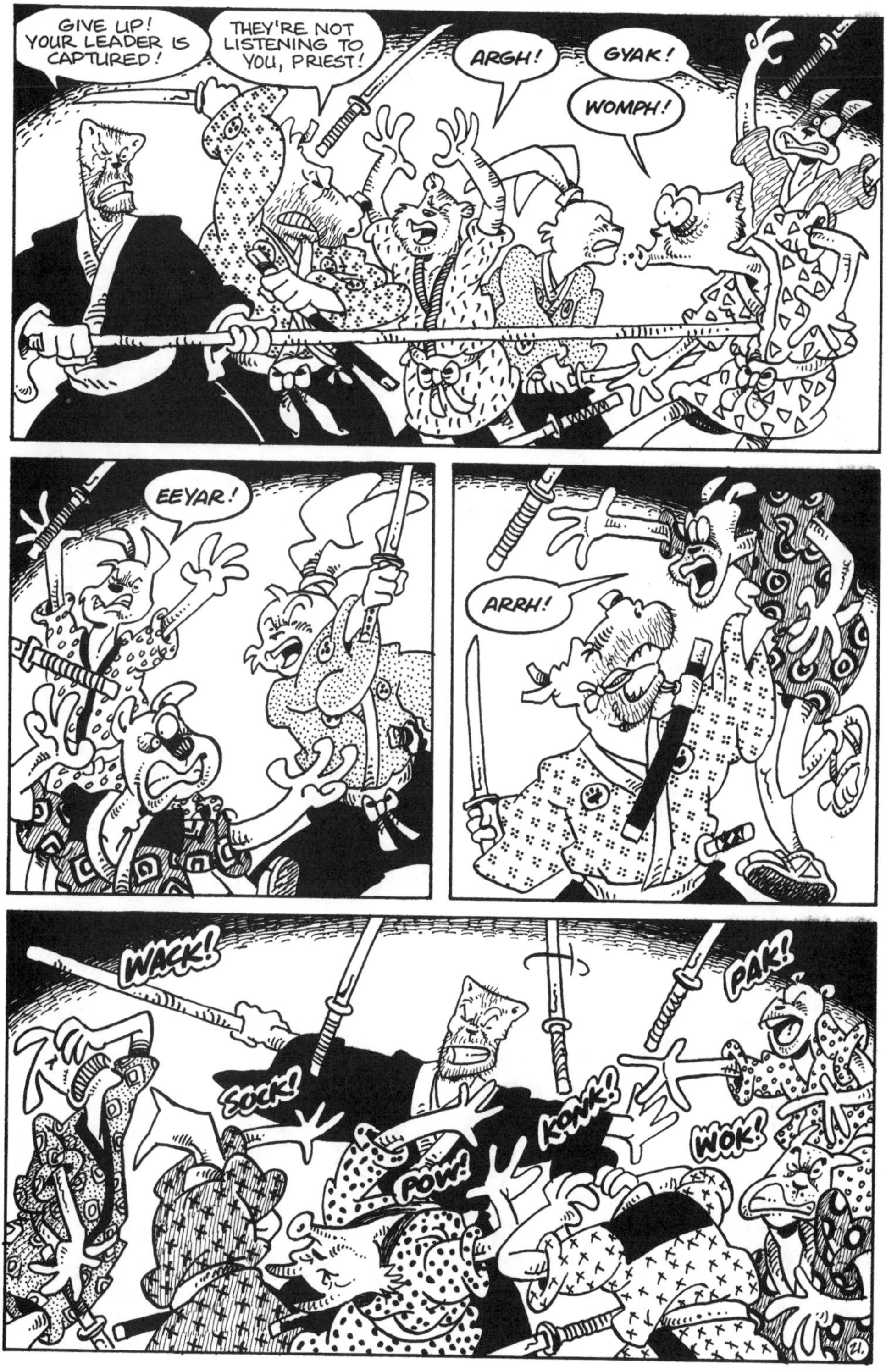
GIVE UP! YOUR LEADER IS CAPTURED!
THEY'RE NOT LISTENING TO YOU, PRIEST!
ARGH!
GYAK!
WOMPH!
EEYAR!
ARRH!
WACK!
PAK!
SOCK!
KONK!
WOK!
POW!
21.

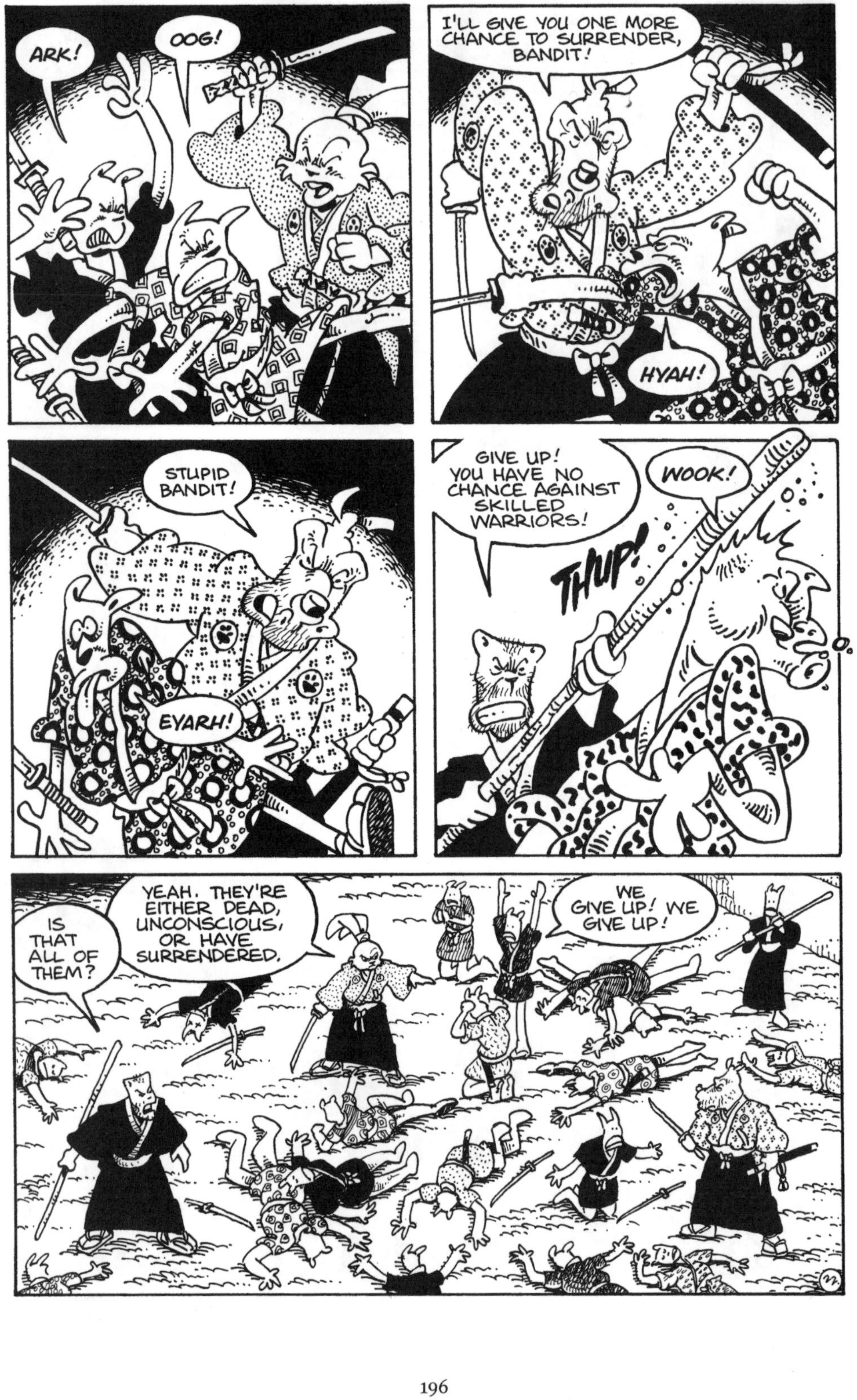
ARK!
OOG!
I'LL GIVE YOU ONE MORE CHANCE TO SURRENDER, BANDIT!
HYAH!
STUPID BANDIT!
EYARH!
GIVE UP! YOU HAVE NO CHANCE AGAINST SKILLED WARRIORS!
WOOK!
THUP!
IS THAT ALL OF THEM?
YEAH. THEY'RE EITHER DEAD, UNCONSCIOUS, OR HAVE SURRENDERED.
WE GIVE UP! WE GIVE UP!

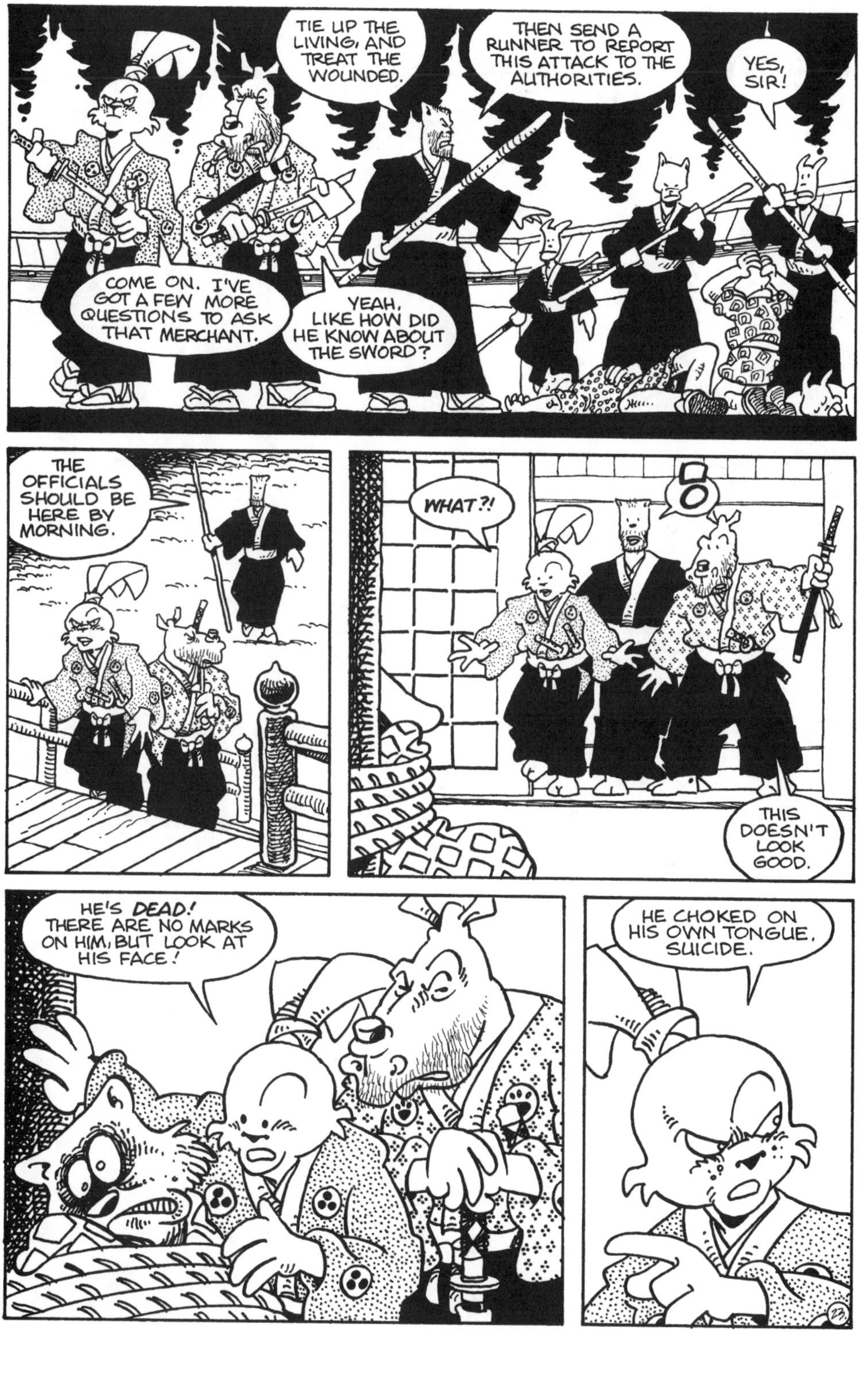
TIE UP THE LIVING, AND TREAT THE WOUNDED.
THEN SEND A RUNNER TO REPORT THIS ATTACK TO THE AUTHORITIES.
YES, SIR!
COME ON. I'VE GOT A FEW MORE QUESTIONS TO ASK THAT MERCHANT.
YEAH. LIKE HOW DID HE KNOW ABOUT THE SWORD?
THE OFFICIALS SHOULD BE HERE BY MORNING.
WHAT?!
THIS DOESN'T LOOK GOOD.
HE'S *DEAD!* THERE ARE NO MARKS ON HIM, BUT LOOK AT HIS FACE!
HE CHOKED ON HIS OWN TONGUE. SUICIDE.
23.

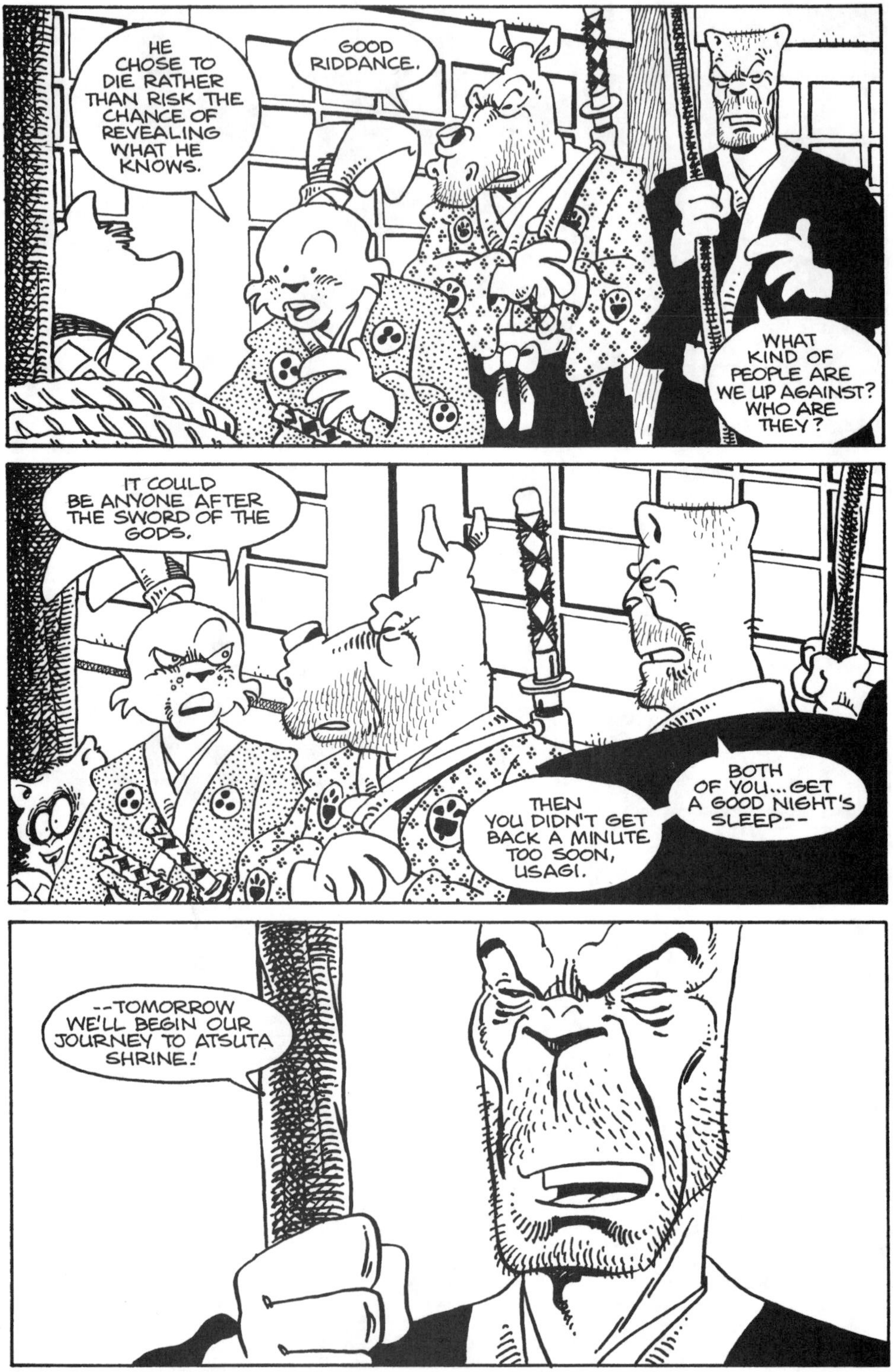
HE CHOSE TO DIE RATHER THAN RISK THE CHANCE OF REVEALING WHAT HE KNOWS.
GOOD RIDDANCE.
WHAT KIND OF PEOPLE ARE WE UP AGAINST? WHO ARE THEY?
IT COULD BE ANYONE AFTER THE SWORD OF THE GODS.
THEN YOU DIDN'T GET BACK A MINUTE TOO SOON, USAGI.
BOTH OF YOU...GET A GOOD NIGHT'S SLEEP--
--TOMORROW WE'LL BEGIN OUR JOURNEY TO ATSUTA SHRINE!

THE END.

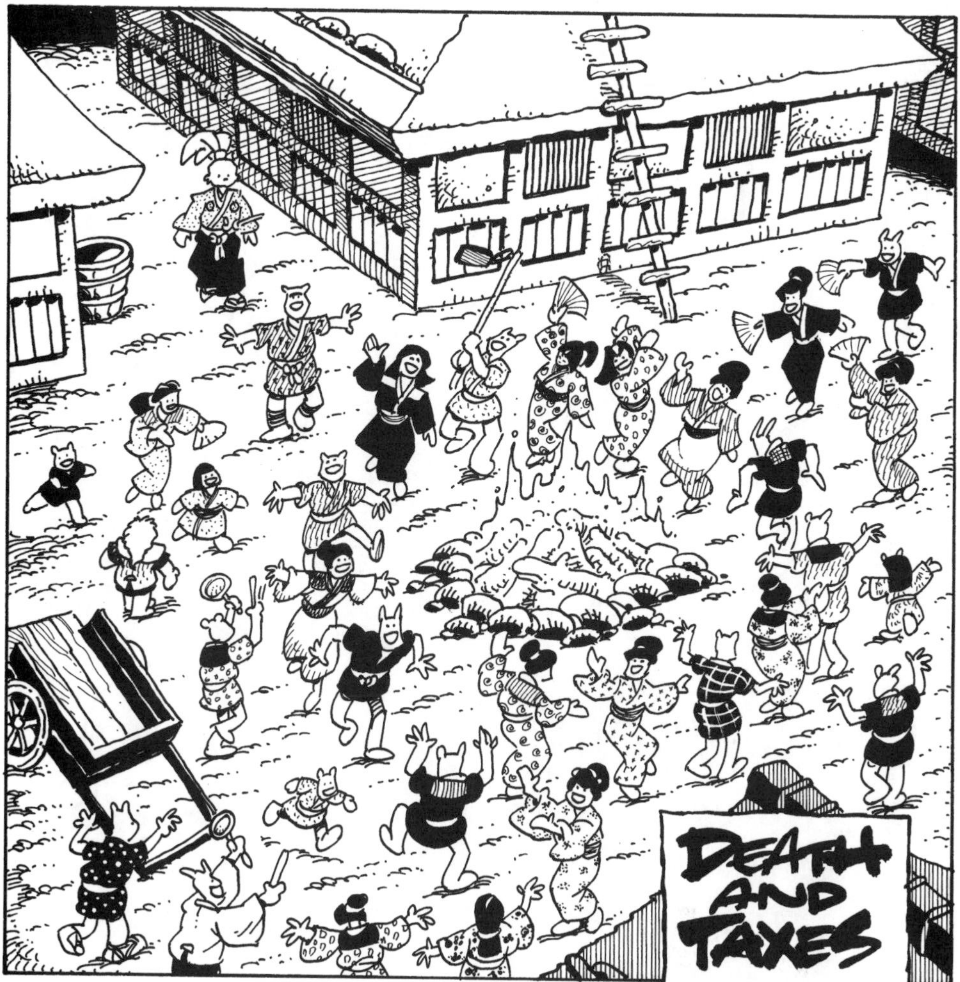
DEATH AND TAXES

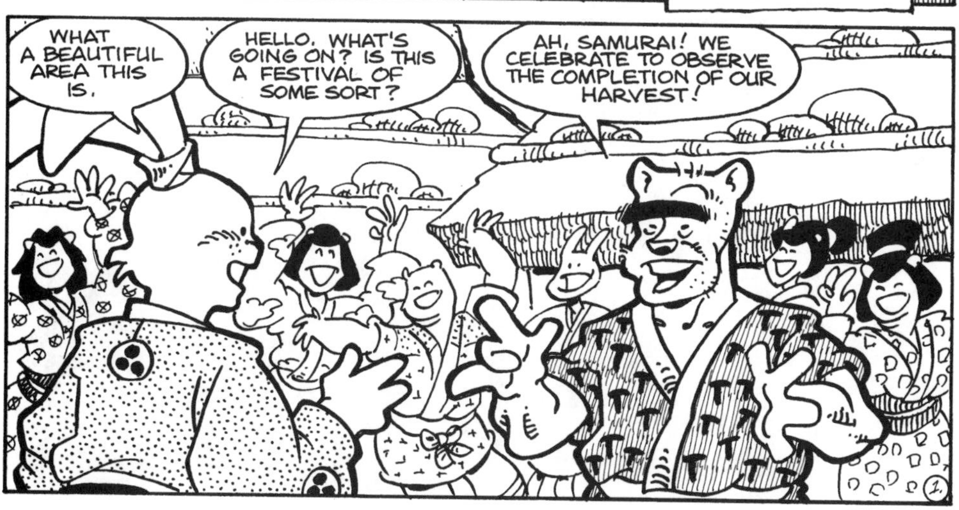
WHAT A BEAUTIFUL AREA THIS IS.
HELLO. WHAT'S GOING ON? IS THIS A FESTIVAL OF SOME SORT?
AH, SAMURAI! WE CELEBRATE TO OBSERVE THE COMPLETION OF OUR HARVEST!
1.

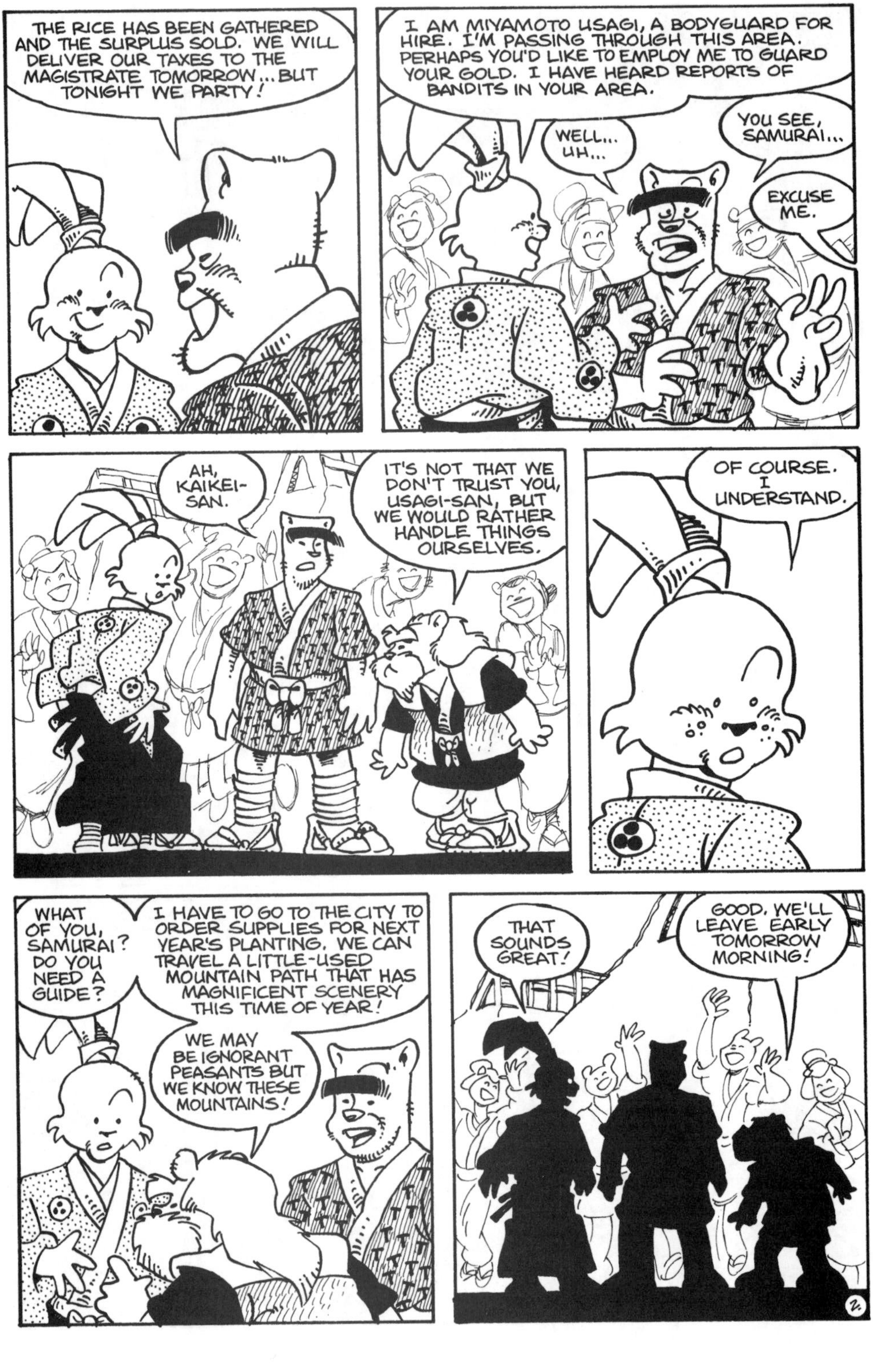
THE RICE HAS BEEN GATHERED AND THE SURPLUS SOLD. WE WILL DELIVER OUR TAXES TO THE MAGISTRATE TOMORROW... BUT TONIGHT WE PARTY!
I AM MIYAMOTO USAGI, A BODYGUARD FOR HIRE. I'M PASSING THROUGH THIS AREA. PERHAPS YOU'D LIKE TO EMPLOY ME TO GUARD YOUR GOLD. I HAVE HEARD REPORTS OF BANDITS IN YOUR AREA.
WELL... UH...
YOU SEE, SAMURAI...
EXCUSE ME.
AH, KAIKEI-SAN.
IT'S NOT THAT WE DON'T TRUST YOU, USAGI-SAN, BUT WE WOULD RATHER HANDLE THINGS OURSELVES.
OF COURSE. I UNDERSTAND.
WHAT OF YOU, SAMURAI? DO YOU NEED A GUIDE?
I HAVE TO GO TO THE CITY TO ORDER SUPPLIES FOR NEXT YEAR'S PLANTING. WE CAN TRAVEL A LITTLE-USED MOUNTAIN PATH THAT HAS MAGNIFICENT SCENERY THIS TIME OF YEAR!
WE MAY BE IGNORANT PEASANTS BUT WE KNOW THESE MOUNTAINS!
THAT SOUNDS GREAT!
GOOD. WE'LL LEAVE EARLY TOMORROW MORNING!
2

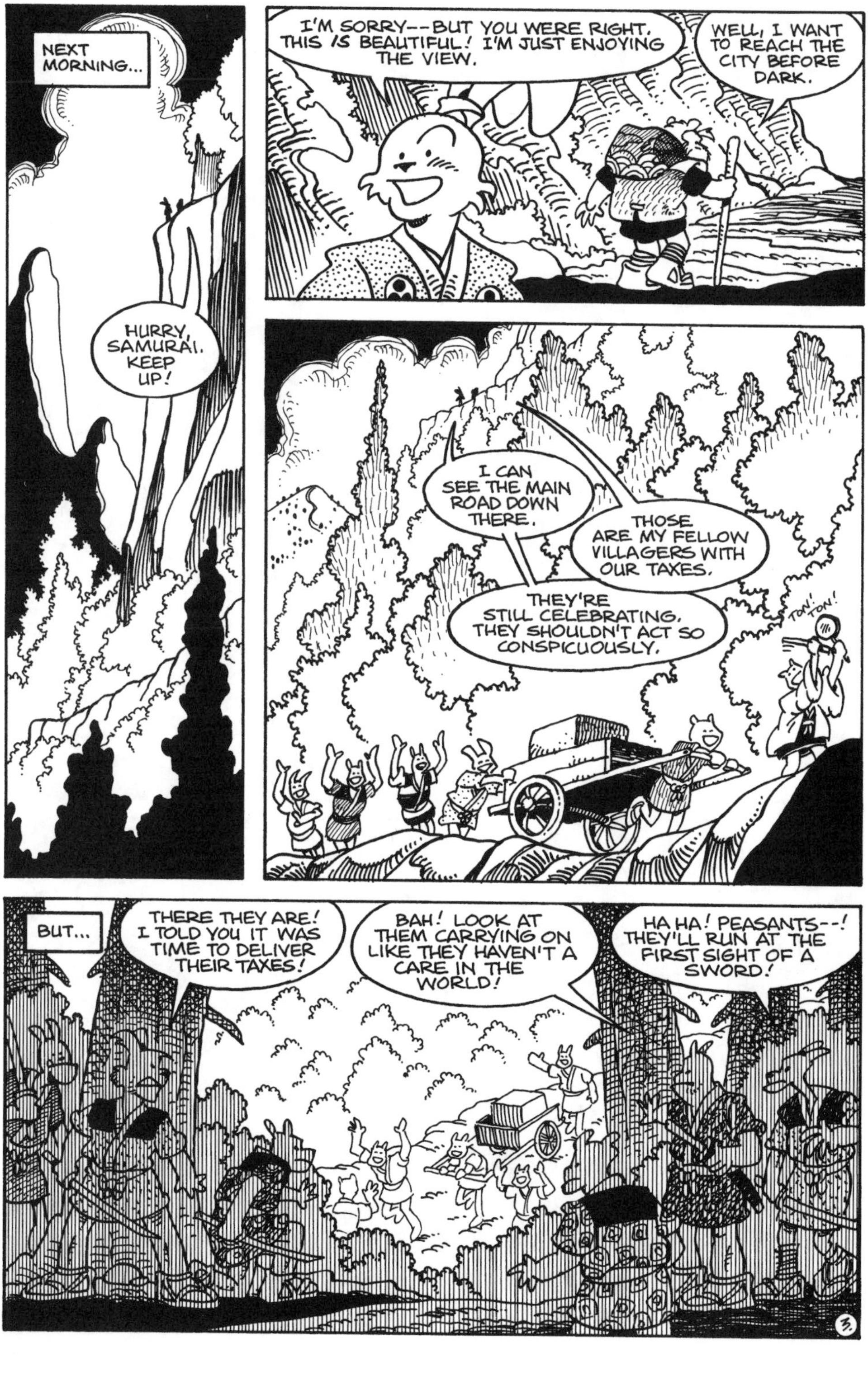
NEXT MORNING...
HURRY, SAMURAI. KEEP UP!
I'M SORRY--BUT YOU WERE RIGHT. THIS IS BEAUTIFUL! I'M JUST ENJOYING THE VIEW.
WELL, I WANT TO REACH THE CITY BEFORE DARK.
I CAN SEE THE MAIN ROAD DOWN THERE.
THOSE ARE MY FELLOW VILLAGERS WITH OUR TAXES.
THEY'RE STILL CELEBRATING. THEY SHOULDN'T ACT SO CONSPICUOUSLY.
TON! TON!
BUT...
THERE THEY ARE! I TOLD YOU IT WAS TIME TO DELIVER THEIR TAXES!
BAH! LOOK AT THEM CARRYING ON LIKE THEY HAVEN'T A CARE IN THE WORLD!
HA HA! PEASANTS--! THEY'LL RUN AT THE FIRST SIGHT OF A SWORD!
3.

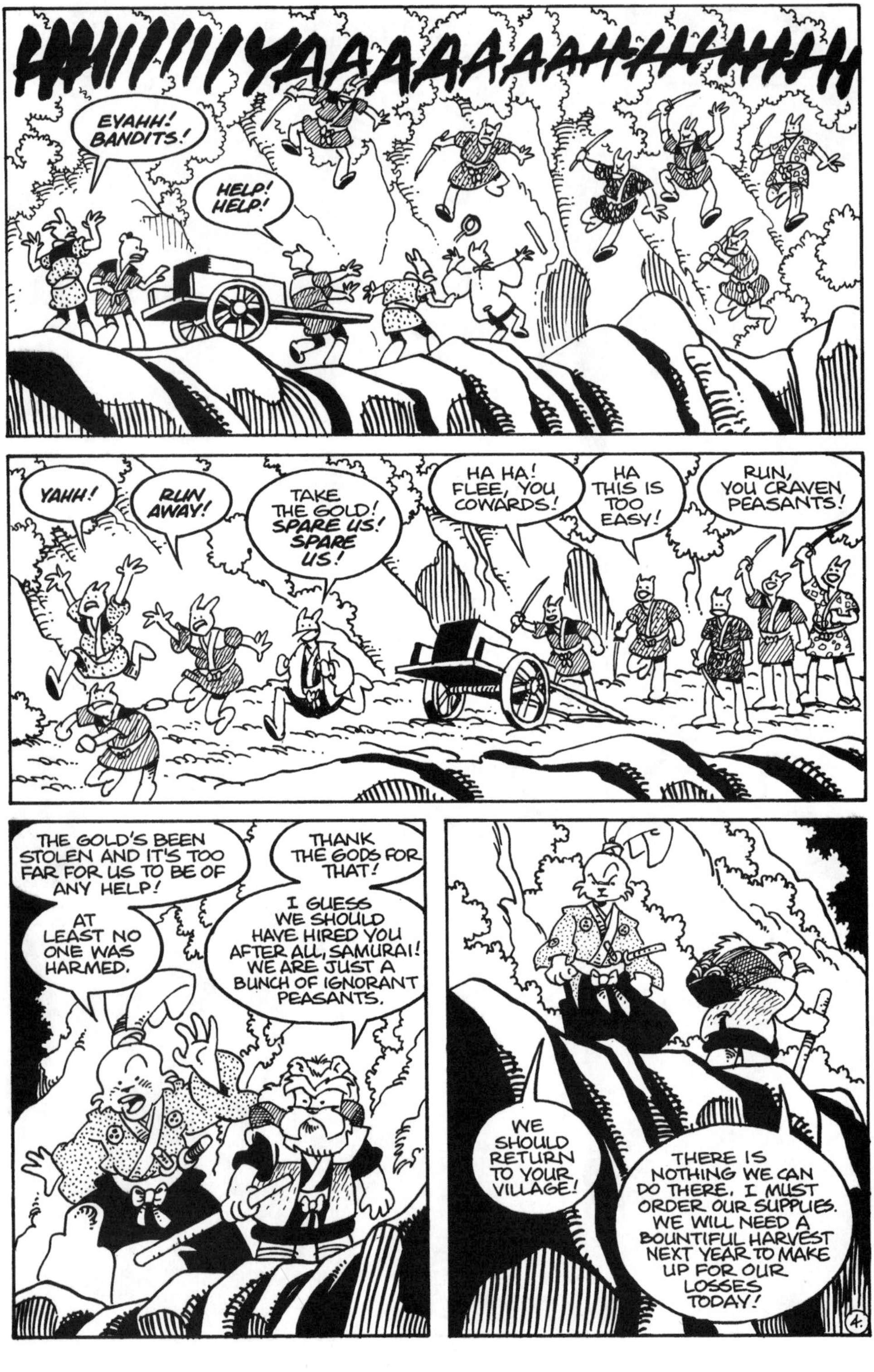
HHHIIIIIYAAAAAAAHHHHHHH
EYAHH! BANDITS!
HELP! HELP!
YAHH!
RUN AWAY!
TAKE THE GOLD! SPARE US! SPARE US!
HA HA! FLEE, YOU COWARDS!
HA THIS IS TOO EASY!
RUN, YOU CRAVEN PEASANTS!
THE GOLD'S BEEN STOLEN AND IT'S TOO FAR FOR US TO BE OF ANY HELP!
AT LEAST NO ONE WAS HARMED.
THANK THE GODS FOR THAT!
I GUESS WE SHOULD HAVE HIRED YOU AFTER ALL, SAMURAI! WE ARE JUST A BUNCH OF IGNORANT PEASANTS.
WE SHOULD RETURN TO YOUR VILLAGE!
THERE IS NOTHING WE CAN DO THERE. I MUST ORDER OUR SUPPLIES. WE WILL NEED A BOUNTIFUL HARVEST NEXT YEAR TO MAKE UP FOR OUR LOSSES TODAY!
4.

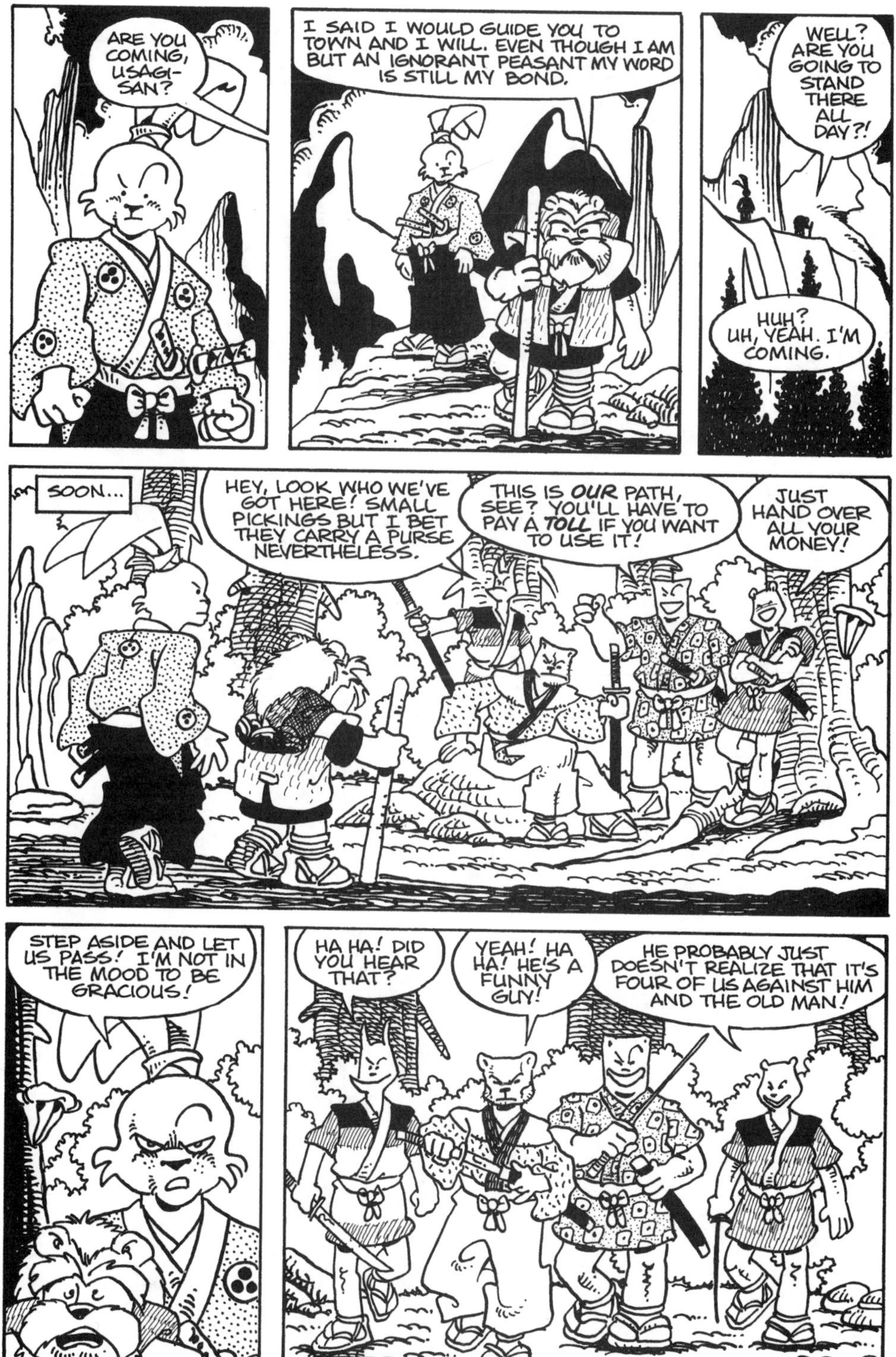
ARE YOU COMING, USAGI-SAN?
I SAID I WOULD GUIDE YOU TO TOWN AND I WILL. EVEN THOUGH I AM BUT AN IGNORANT PEASANT MY WORD IS STILL MY BOND.
WELL? ARE YOU GOING TO STAND THERE ALL DAY?!
HUH? UH, YEAH. I'M COMING.
SOON...
HEY, LOOK WHO WE'VE GOT HERE! SMALL PICKINGS BUT I BET THEY CARRY A PURSE NEVERTHELESS.
THIS IS **OUR** PATH, SEE? YOU'LL HAVE TO PAY A **TOLL** IF YOU WANT TO USE IT!
JUST HAND OVER ALL YOUR MONEY!
STEP ASIDE AND LET US PASS! I'M NOT IN THE MOOD TO BE GRACIOUS!
HA HA! DID YOU HEAR THAT?
YEAH! HA HA! HE'S A FUNNY GUY!
HE PROBABLY JUST DOESN'T REALIZE THAT IT'S FOUR OF US AGAINST HIM AND THE OLD MAN!
5.

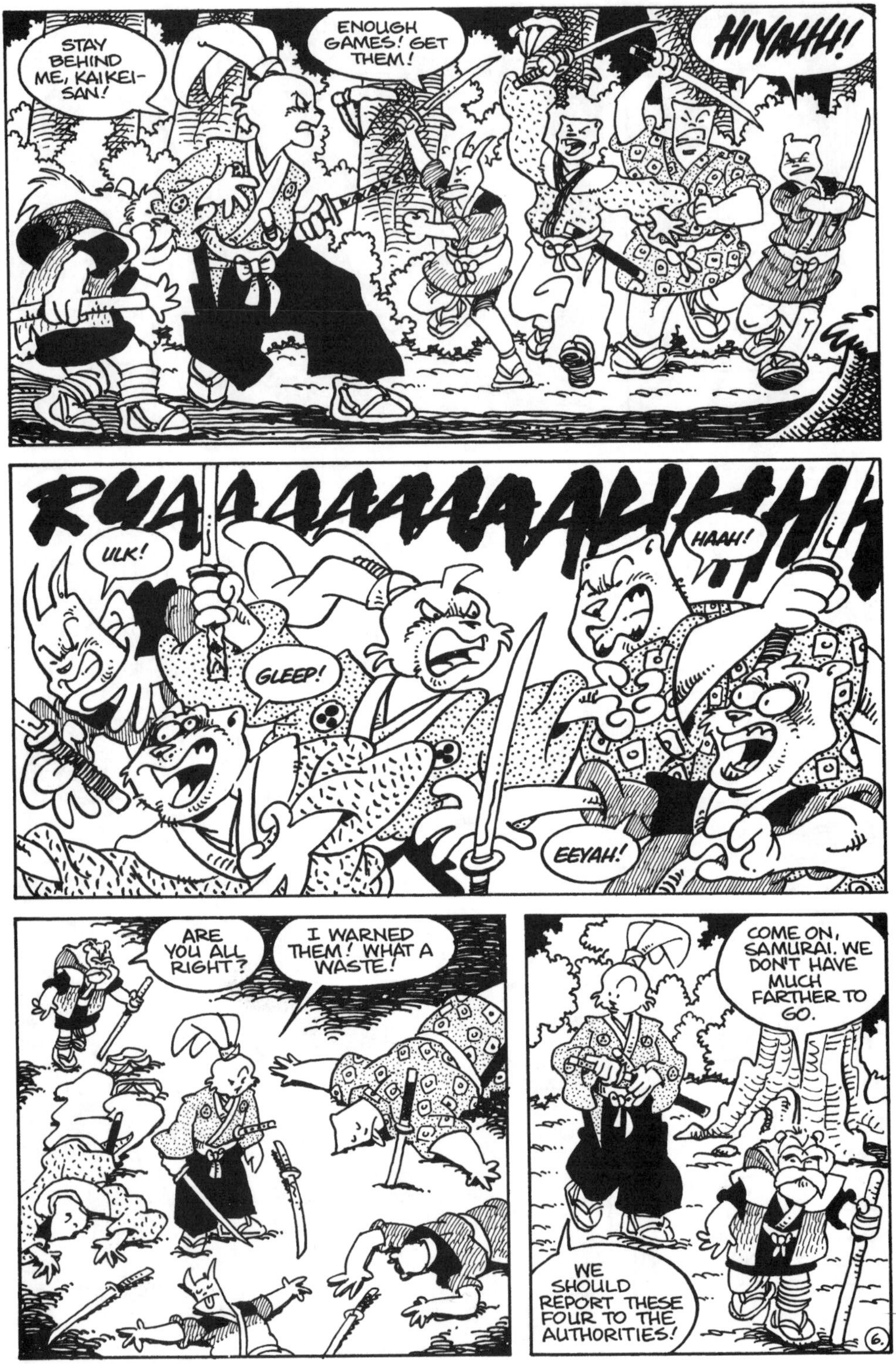
STAY BEHIND ME, KAIKEI-SAN!
ENOUGH GAMES! GET THEM!
HIYAHH!
RYAAAAAAAAAHHHH
ULK!
HAAH!
GLEEP!
EEYAH!
ARE YOU ALL RIGHT?
I WARNED THEM! WHAT A WASTE!
COME ON, SAMURAI. WE DON'T HAVE MUCH FARTHER TO GO.
WE SHOULD REPORT THESE FOUR TO THE AUTHORITIES!
6.

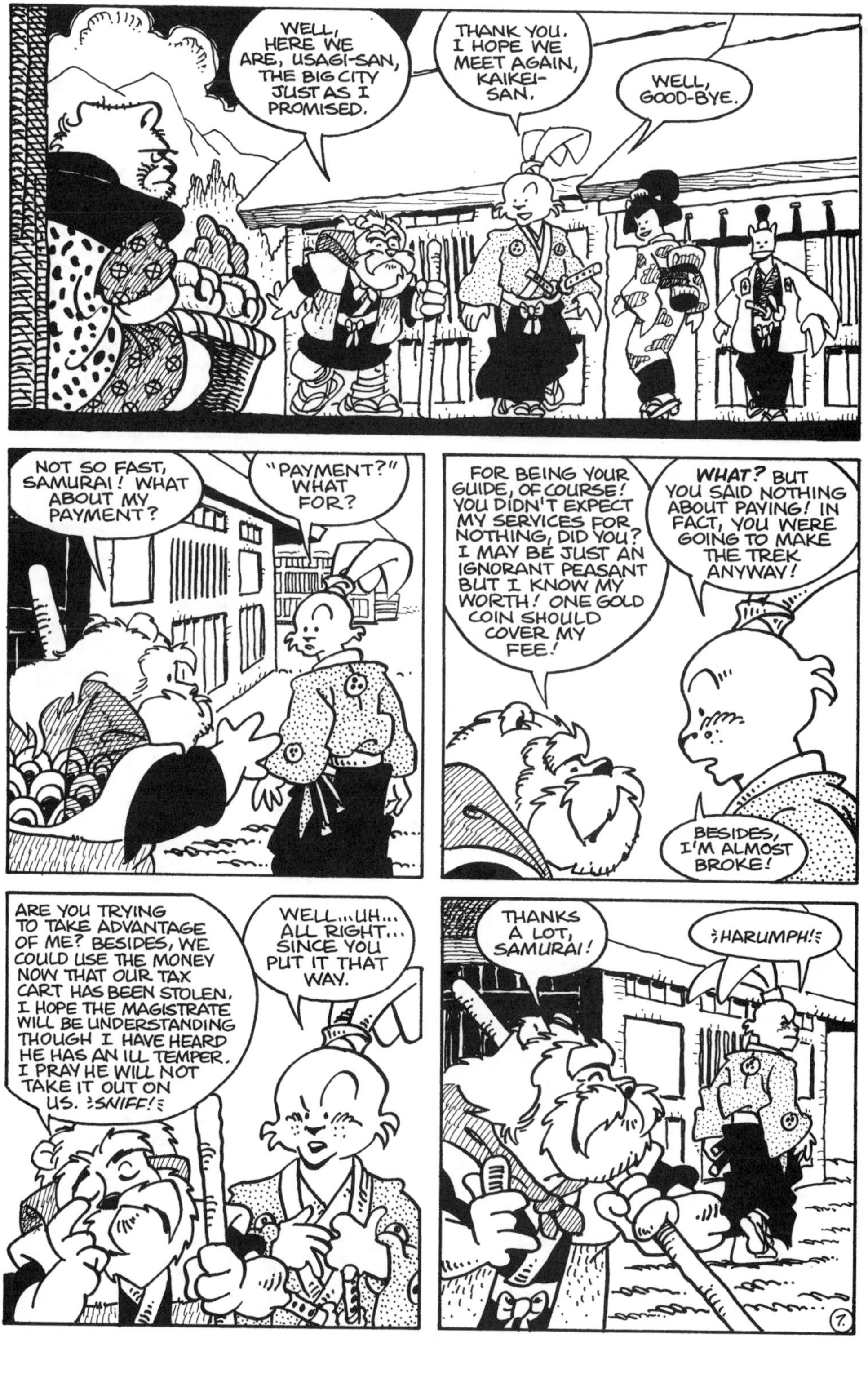
WELL, HERE WE ARE, USAGI-SAN, THE BIG CITY JUST AS I PROMISED.
THANK YOU. I HOPE WE MEET AGAIN, KAIKEI-SAN.
WELL, GOOD-BYE.
NOT SO FAST, SAMURAI! WHAT ABOUT MY PAYMENT?
"PAYMENT?" WHAT FOR?
FOR BEING YOUR GUIDE, OF COURSE! YOU DIDN'T EXPECT MY SERVICES FOR NOTHING, DID YOU? I MAY BE JUST AN IGNORANT PEASANT BUT I KNOW MY WORTH! ONE GOLD COIN SHOULD COVER MY FEE!
WHAT? BUT YOU SAID NOTHING ABOUT PAYING! IN FACT, YOU WERE GOING TO MAKE THE TREK ANYWAY!
BESIDES, I'M ALMOST BROKE!
ARE YOU TRYING TO TAKE ADVANTAGE OF ME? BESIDES, WE COULD USE THE MONEY NOW THAT OUR TAX CART HAS BEEN STOLEN. I HOPE THE MAGISTRATE WILL BE UNDERSTANDING THOUGH I HAVE HEARD HE HAS AN ILL TEMPER. I PRAY HE WILL NOT TAKE IT OUT ON US. SNIFF!
WELL...UH... ALL RIGHT... SINCE YOU PUT IT THAT WAY.
THANKS A LOT, SAMURAI!
HARUMPH!
7.

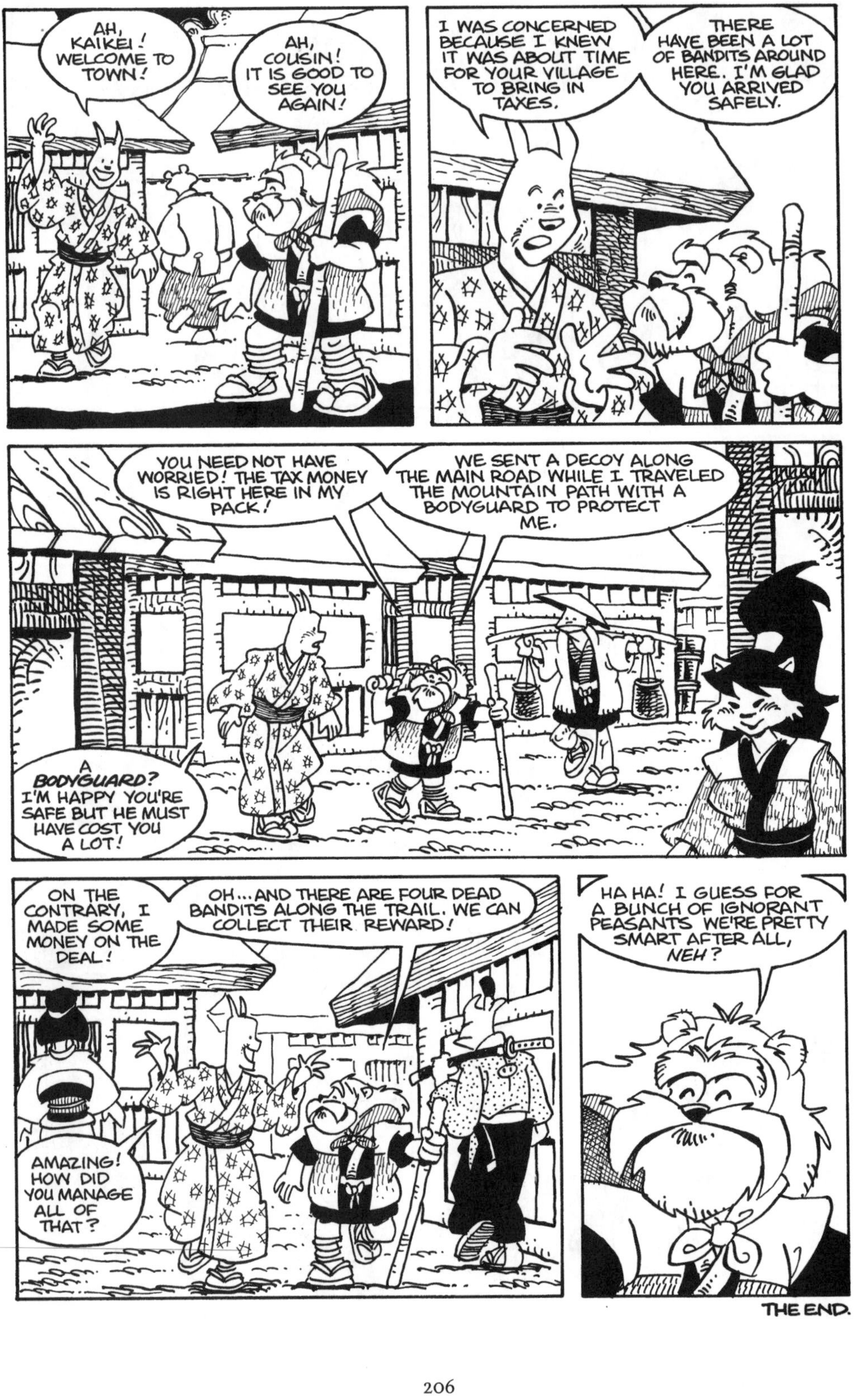
AH, KAIKEI! WELCOME TO TOWN!
AH, COUSIN! IT IS GOOD TO SEE YOU AGAIN!
I WAS CONCERNED BECAUSE I KNEW IT WAS ABOUT TIME FOR YOUR VILLAGE TO BRING IN TAXES.
THERE HAVE BEEN A LOT OF BANDITS AROUND HERE. I'M GLAD YOU ARRIVED SAFELY.
YOU NEED NOT HAVE WORRIED! THE TAX MONEY IS RIGHT HERE IN MY PACK!
WE SENT A DECOY ALONG THE MAIN ROAD WHILE I TRAVELED THE MOUNTAIN PATH WITH A BODYGUARD TO PROTECT ME.
A BODYGUARD? I'M HAPPY YOU'RE SAFE BUT HE MUST HAVE COST YOU A LOT!
ON THE CONTRARY, I MADE SOME MONEY ON THE DEAL!
OH... AND THERE ARE FOUR DEAD BANDITS ALONG THE TRAIL. WE CAN COLLECT THEIR REWARD!
AMAZING! HOW DID YOU MANAGE ALL OF THAT?
HA HA! I GUESS FOR A BUNCH OF IGNORANT PEASANTS WE'RE PRETTY SMART AFTER ALL, NEH?
THE END.

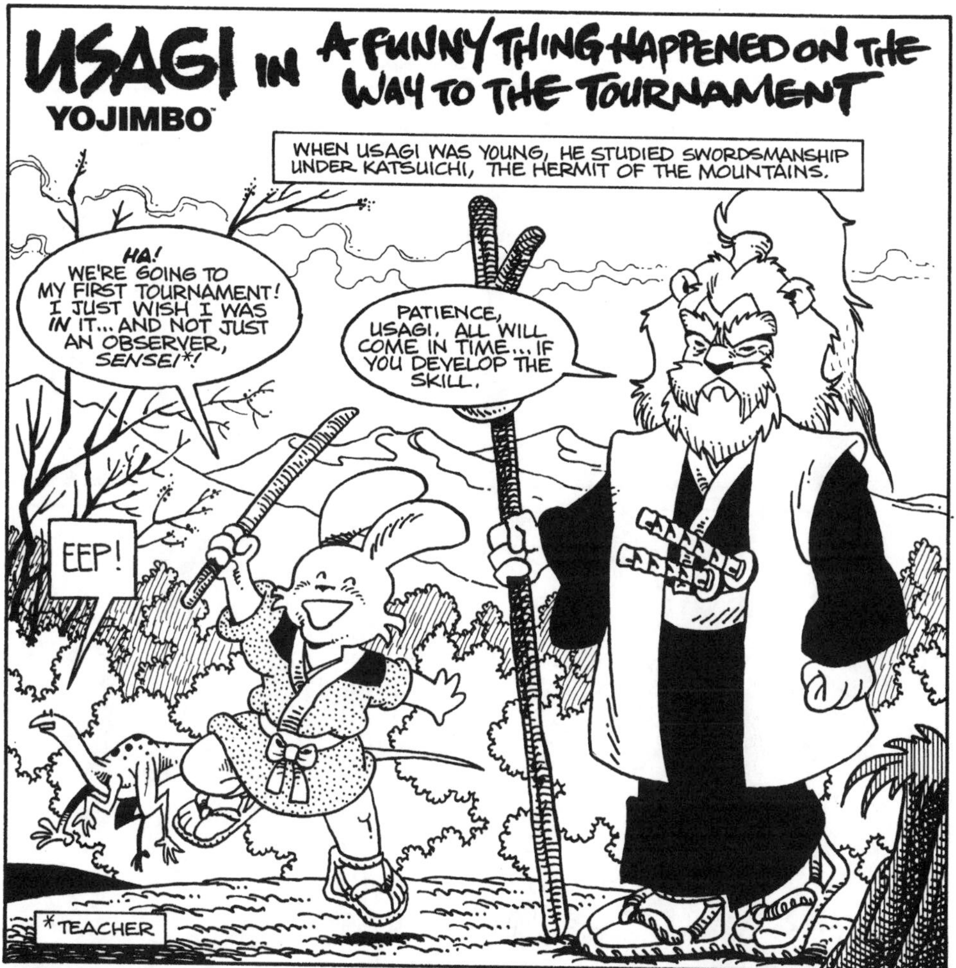
USAGI YOJIMBO IN A FUNNY THING HAPPENED ON THE WAY TO THE TOURNAMENT
WHEN USAGI WAS YOUNG, HE STUDIED SWORDSMANSHIP UNDER KATSUICHI, THE HERMIT OF THE MOUNTAINS.
HA! WE'RE GOING TO MY FIRST TOURNAMENT! I JUST WISH I WAS IN IT... AND NOT JUST AN OBSERVER, SENSEI*!
PATIENCE, USAGI, ALL WILL COME IN TIME... IF YOU DEVELOP THE SKILL.
EEP!
*TEACHER
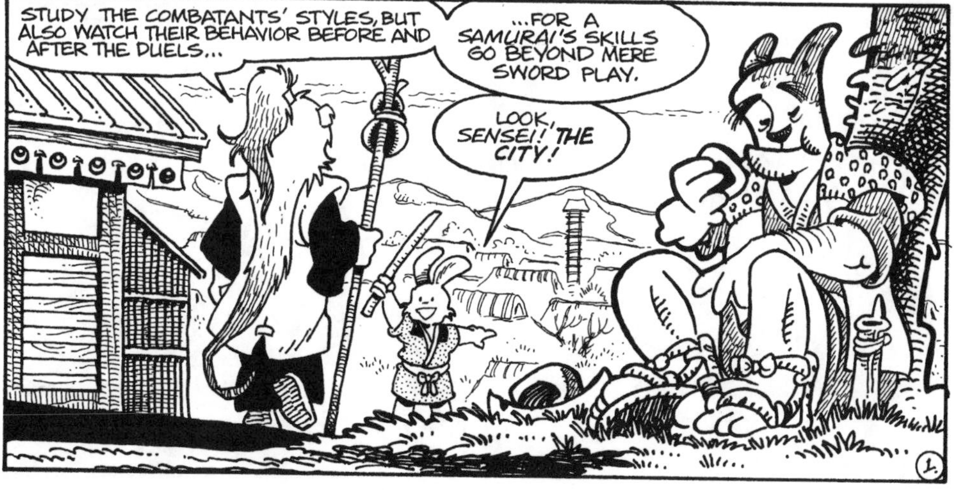
STUDY THE COMBATANTS' STYLES, BUT ALSO WATCH THEIR BEHAVIOR BEFORE AND AFTER THE DUELS...
...FOR A SAMURAI'S SKILLS GO BEYOND MERE SWORD PLAY.
LOOK, SENSEI! THE CITY!
1.

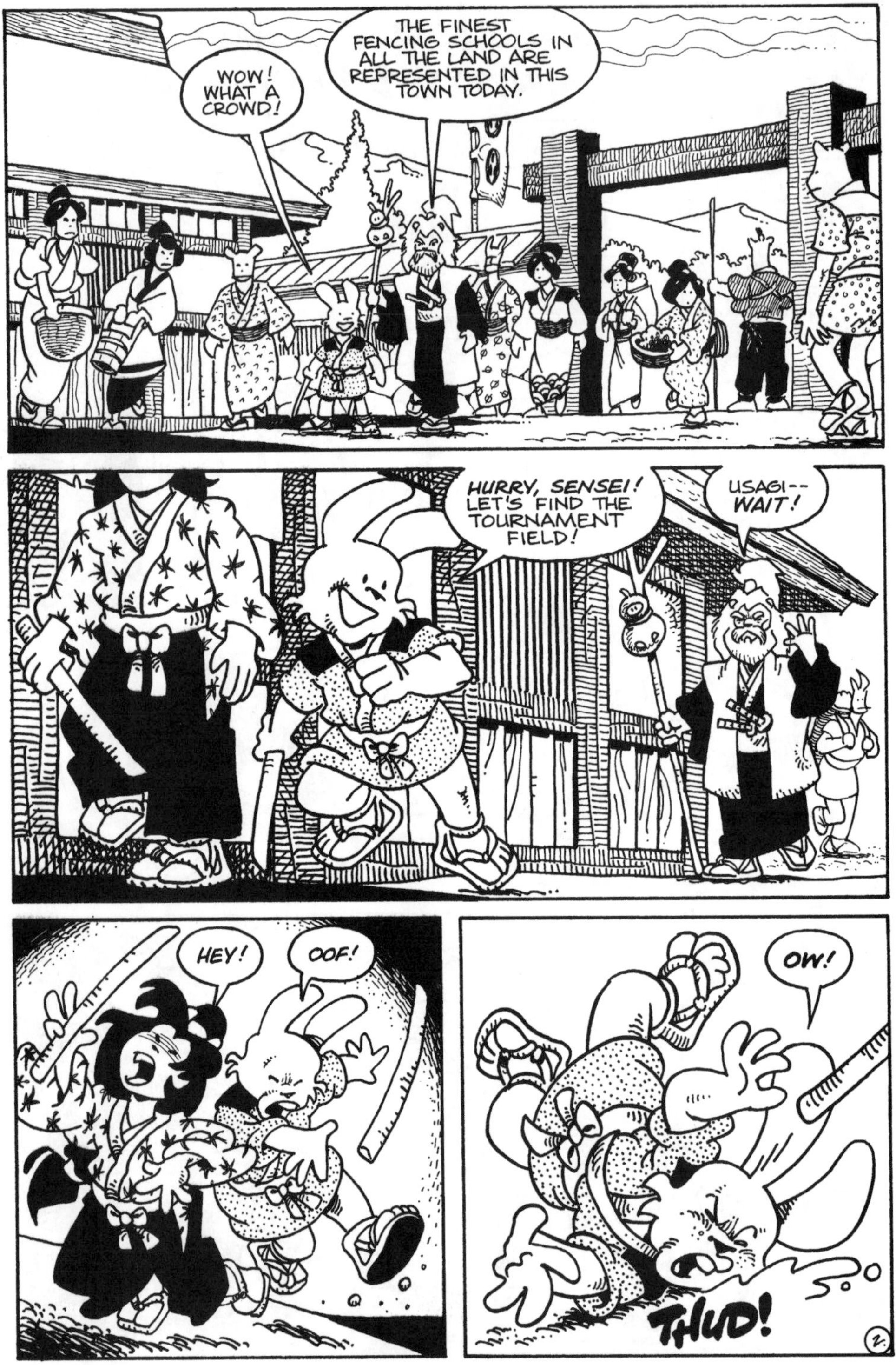
WOW! WHAT A CROWD!
THE FINEST FENCING SCHOOLS IN ALL THE LAND ARE REPRESENTED IN THIS TOWN TODAY.
HURRY, SENSEI! LET'S FIND THE TOURNAMENT FIELD!
USAGI-- WAIT!
HEY!
OOF!
OW!
THUD!
2.

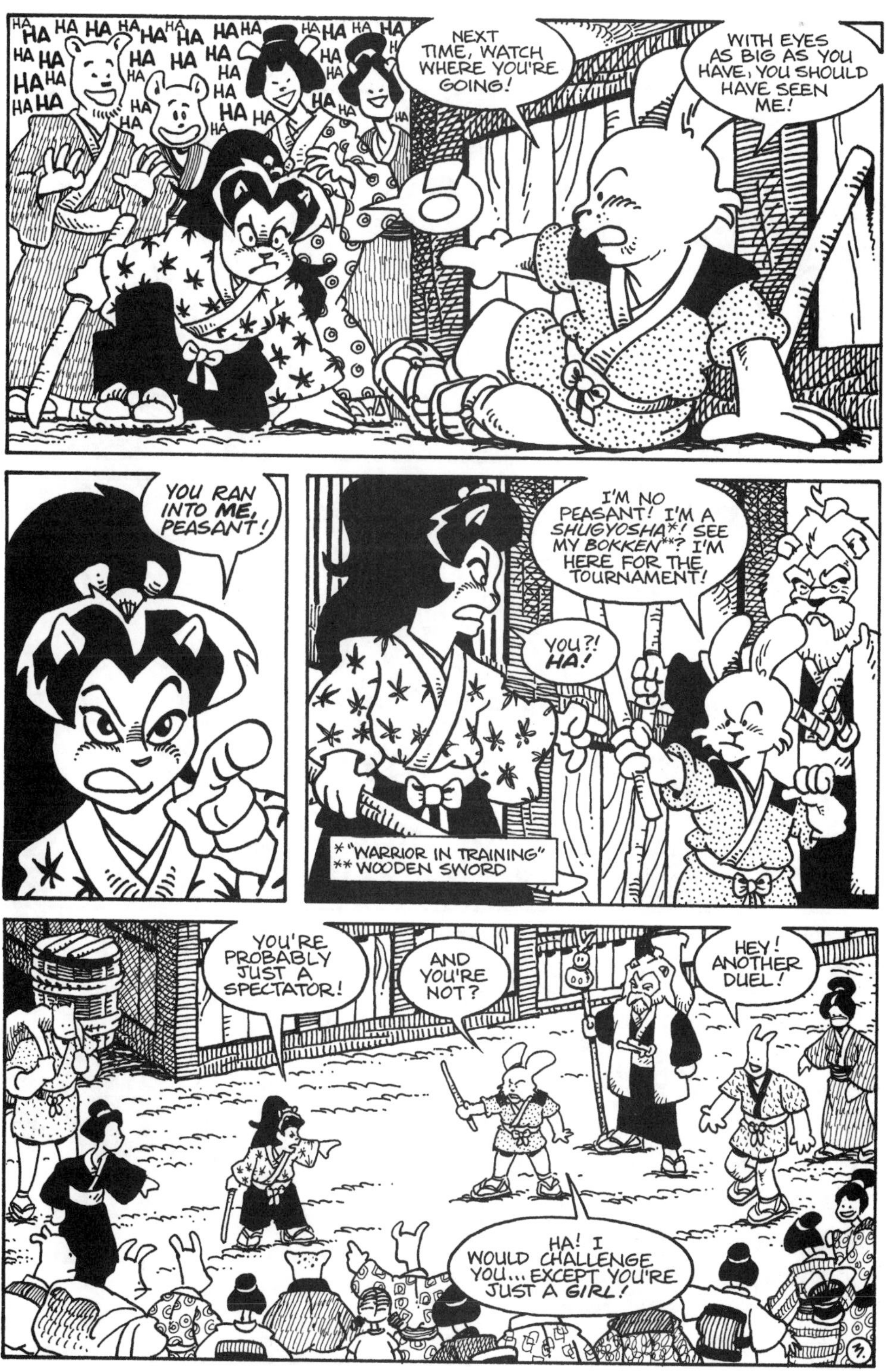
HA HA HA HA HA HA HA HA HA HA HA HA HA HA HA HA HA HA HA HA HA HA HA HA HA HA HA HA HA HA HA HA HA HA HA HA HA HA
NEXT TIME, WATCH WHERE YOU'RE GOING!
WITH EYES AS BIG AS YOU HAVE, YOU SHOULD HAVE SEEN ME!
YOU RAN INTO ME, PEASANT!
I'M NO PEASANT! I'M A SHUGYOSHA*! SEE MY BOKKEN**? I'M HERE FOR THE TOURNAMENT!
YOU?! HA!
*"WARRIOR IN TRAINING"
**WOODEN SWORD
YOU'RE PROBABLY JUST A SPECTATOR!
AND YOU'RE NOT?
HEY! ANOTHER DUEL!
HA! I WOULD CHALLENGE YOU... EXCEPT YOU'RE JUST A GIRL!

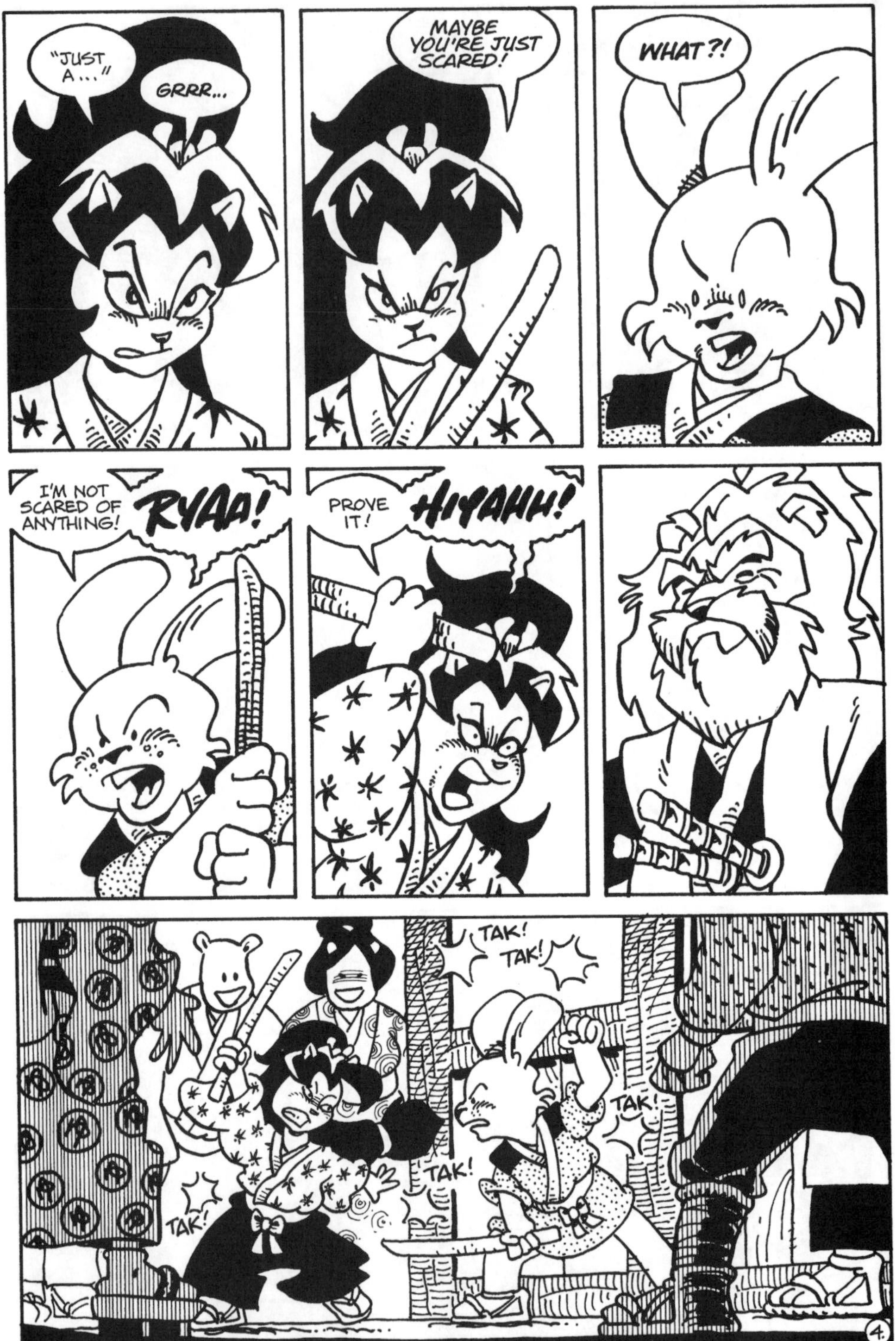
"JUST A..."
GRRR...
MAYBE YOU'RE JUST SCARED!
WHAT?!
I'M NOT SCARED OF ANYTHING!
RYAA!
PROVE IT!
HIYAHH!
TAK!
TAK!
TAK!
TAK!
TAK!
4.

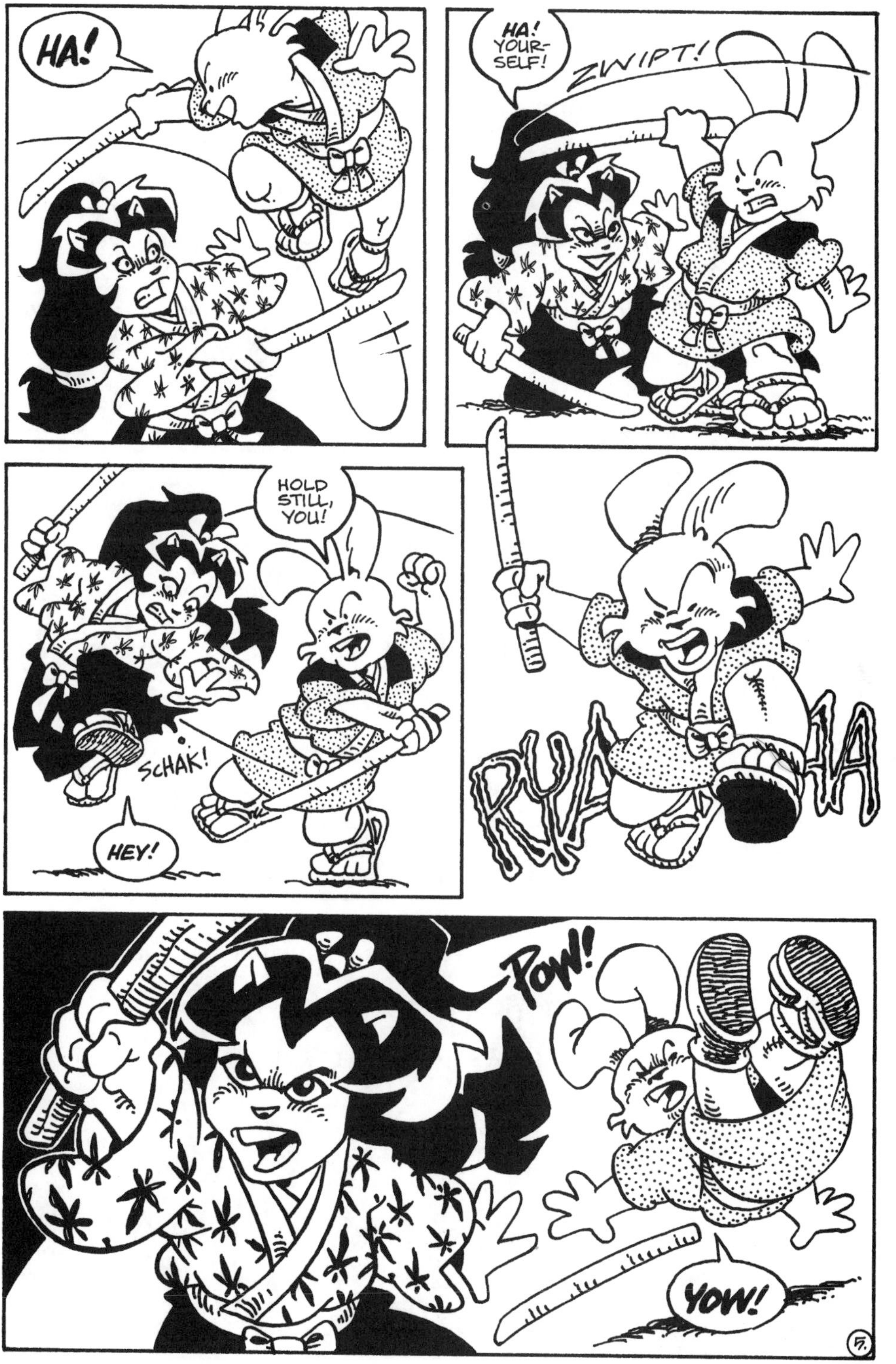
HA!
HA! YOUR-SELF!
ZWIPT!
HOLD STILL, YOU!
SCHAK!
HEY!
RYA
HA
POW!
YOW!
5.

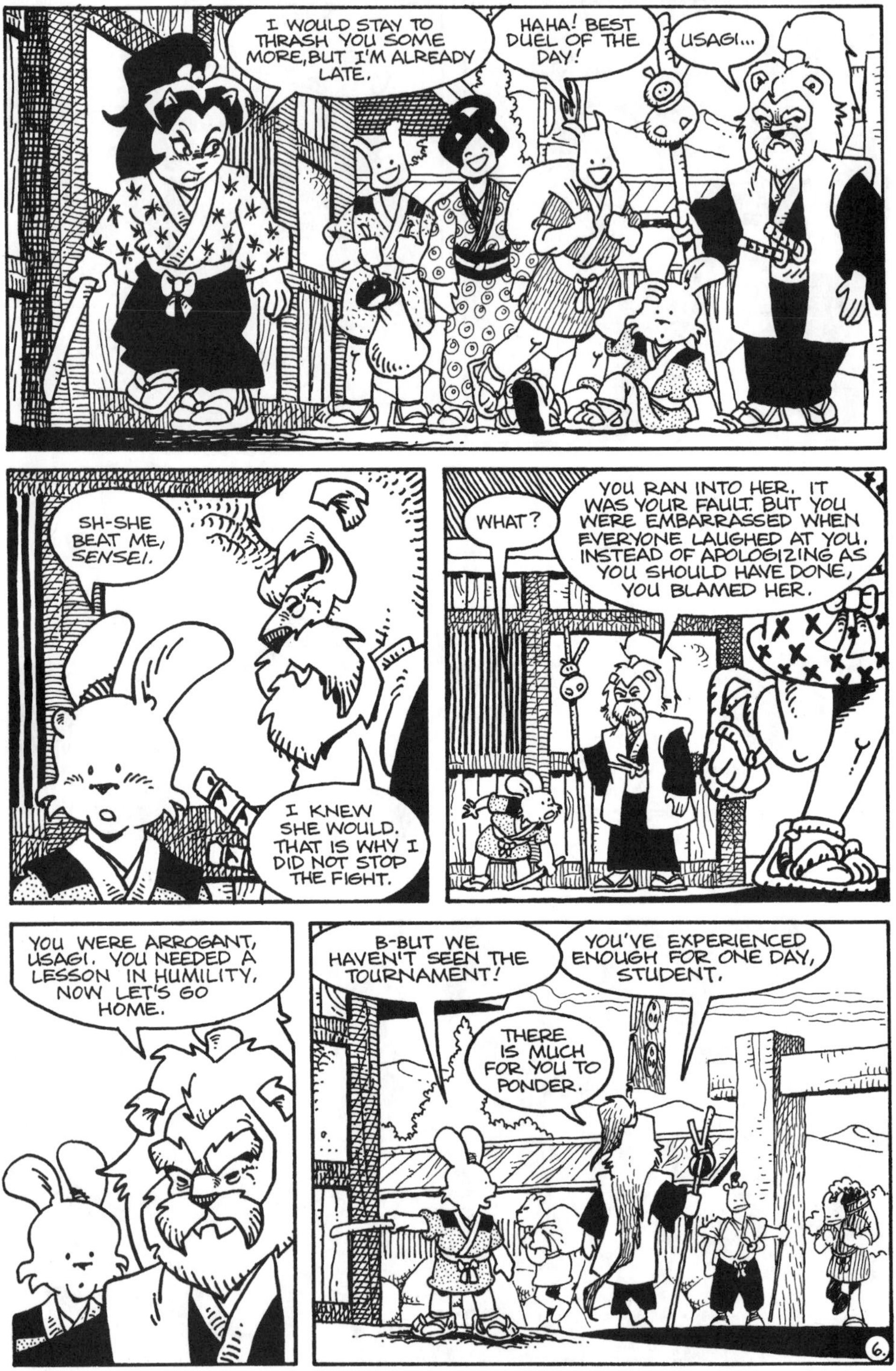
I WOULD STAY TO THRASH YOU SOME MORE, BUT I'M ALREADY LATE.
HAHA! BEST DUEL OF THE DAY!
USAGI...
SH-SHE BEAT ME, SENSEI.
I KNEW SHE WOULD. THAT IS WHY I DID NOT STOP THE FIGHT.
WHAT?
YOU RAN INTO HER. IT WAS YOUR FAULT. BUT YOU WERE EMBARRASSED WHEN EVERYONE LAUGHED AT YOU. INSTEAD OF APOLOGIZING AS YOU SHOULD HAVE DONE, YOU BLAMED HER.
YOU WERE ARROGANT, USAGI. YOU NEEDED A LESSON IN HUMILITY. NOW LET'S GO HOME.
B-BUT WE HAVEN'T SEEN THE TOURNAMENT!
YOU'VE EXPERIENCED ENOUGH FOR ONE DAY, STUDENT.
THERE IS MUCH FOR YOU TO PONDER.
6.

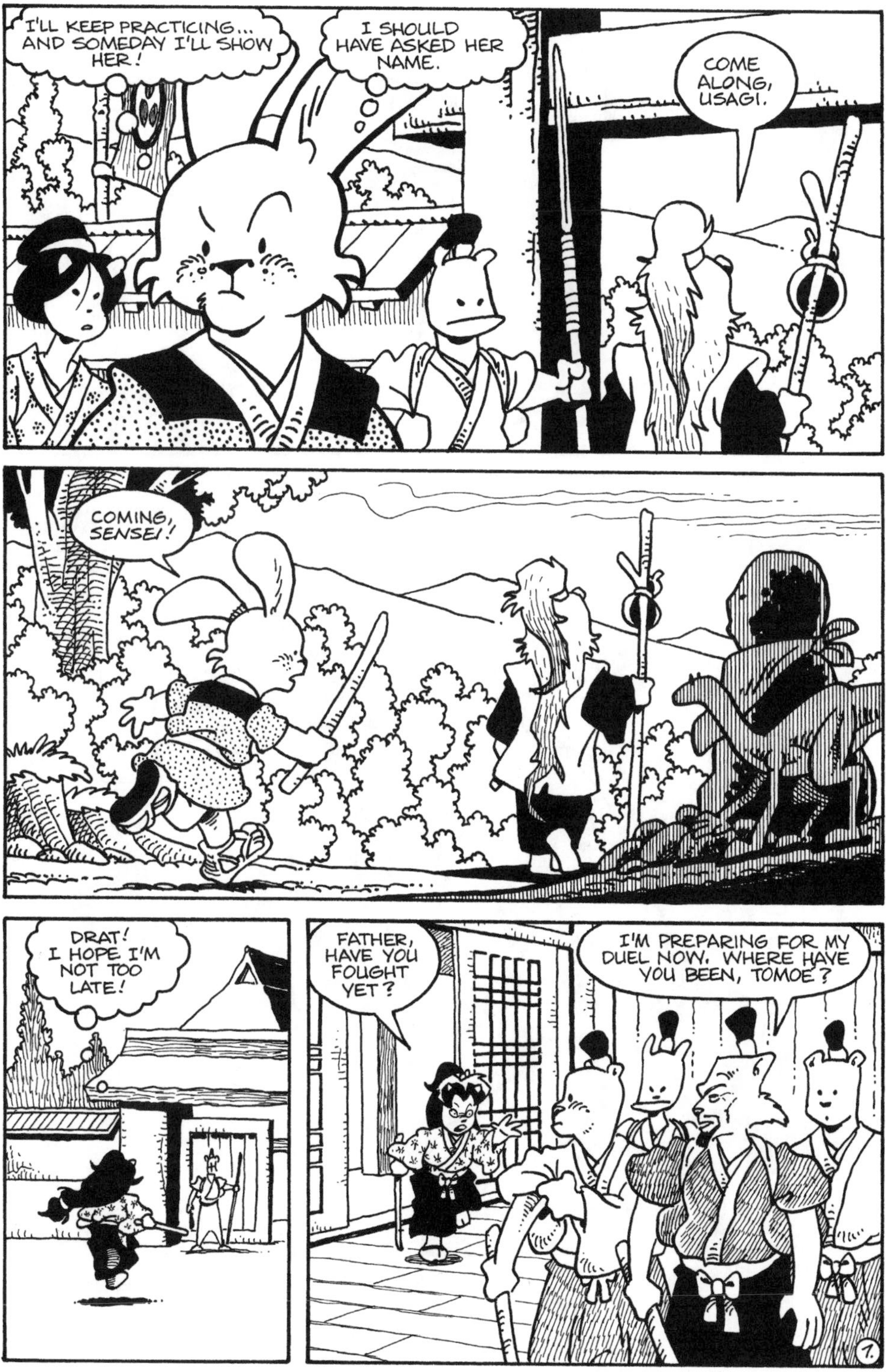

I'LL KEEP PRACTICING... AND SOMEDAY I'LL SHOW HER!
I SHOULD HAVE ASKED HER NAME.
COME ALONG, USAGI.
COMING, SENSEI!
DRAT! I HOPE I'M NOT TOO LATE!
FATHER, HAVE YOU FOUGHT YET?
I'M PREPARING FOR MY DUEL NOW. WHERE HAVE YOU BEEN, TOMOE?
7.

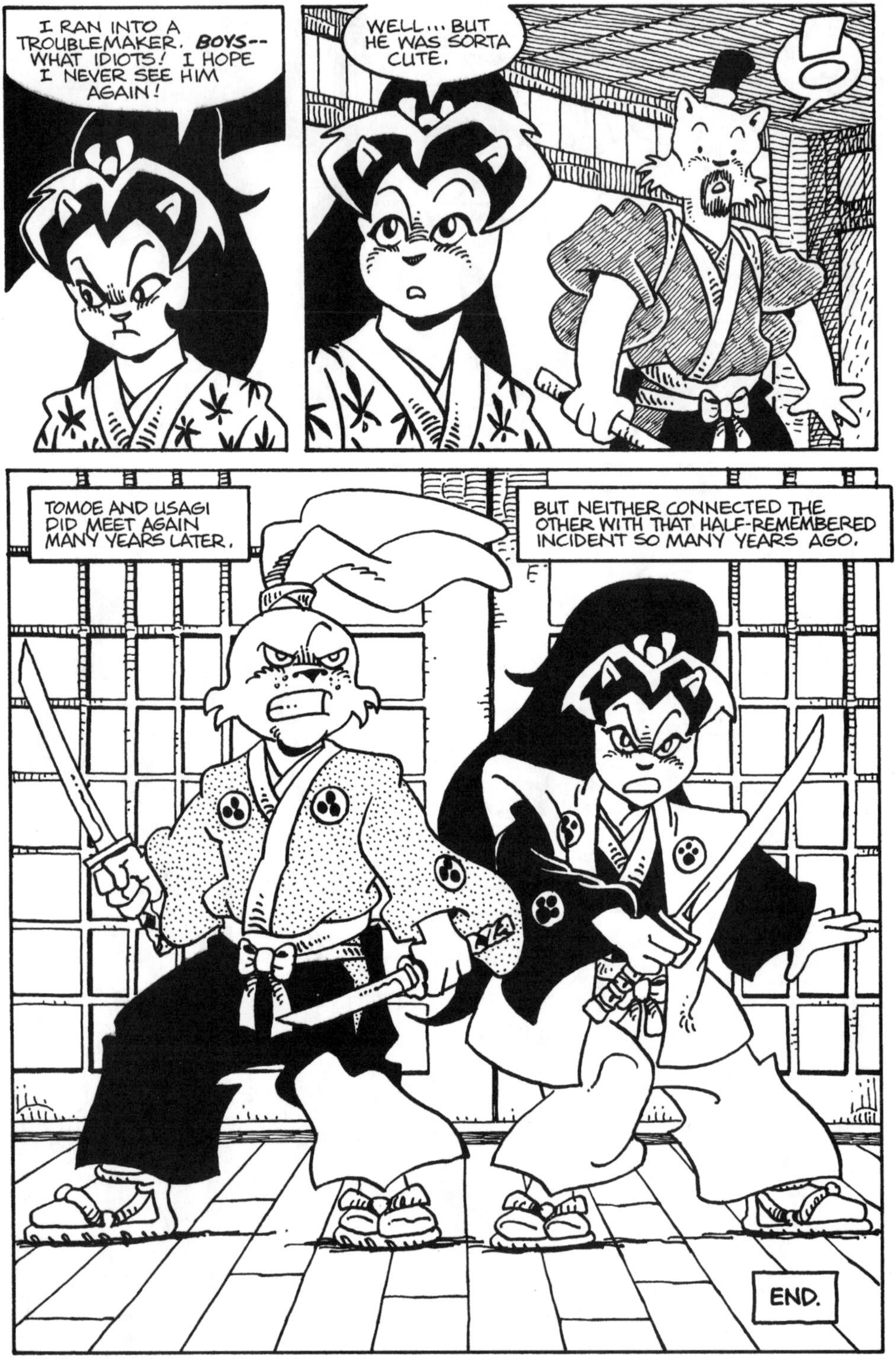
I RAN INTO A TROUBLEMAKER. **BOYS**-- WHAT IDIOTS! I HOPE I NEVER SEE HIM AGAIN!
WELL... BUT HE WAS SORTA CUTE.
!
TOMOE AND USAGI DID MEET AGAIN MANY YEARS LATER.
BUT NEITHER CONNECTED THE OTHER WITH THAT HALF-REMEMBERED INCIDENT SO MANY YEARS AGO.
END.

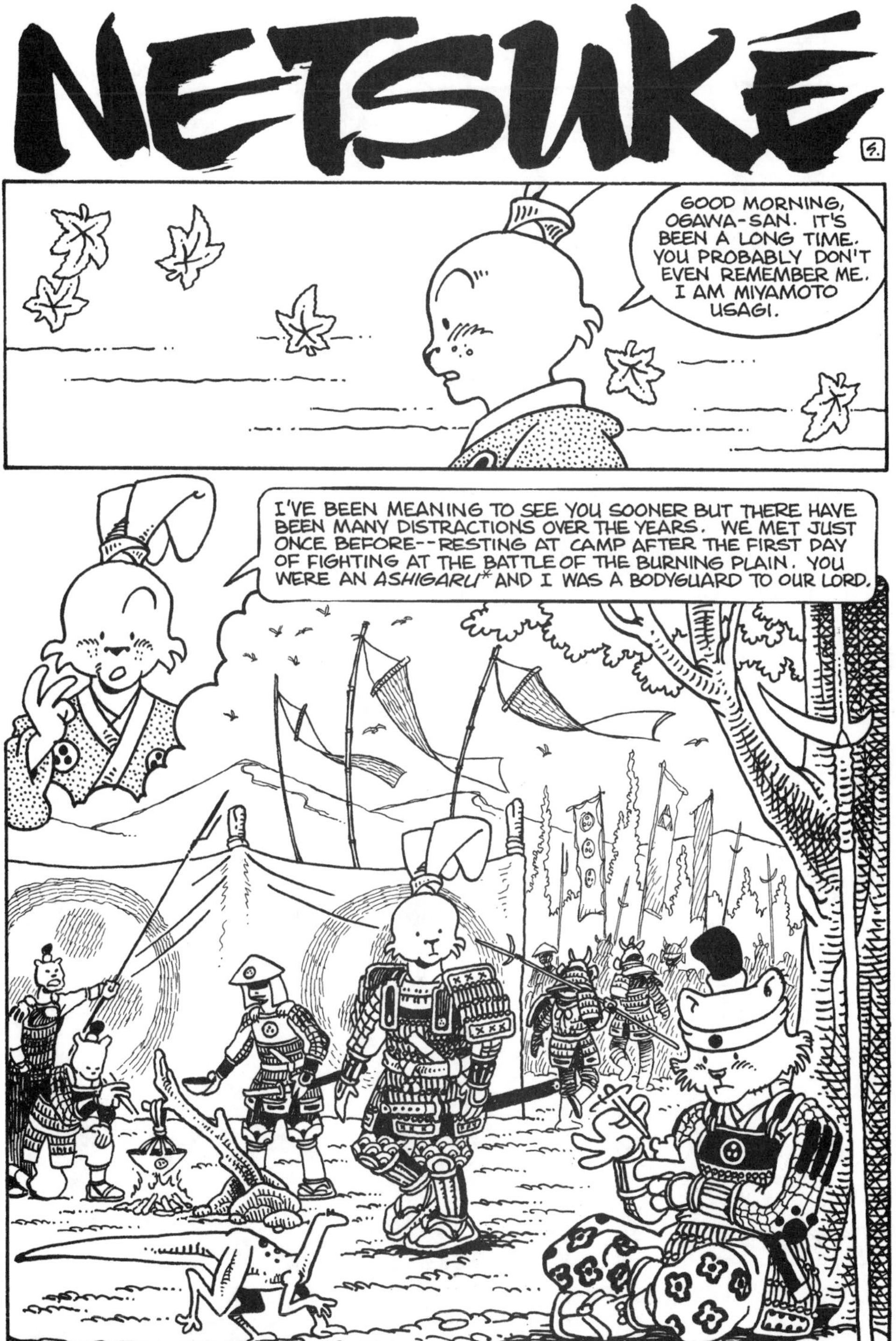
NETSUKÉ
5.
GOOD MORNING, OGAWA-SAN. IT'S BEEN A LONG TIME. YOU PROBABLY DON'T EVEN REMEMBER ME. I AM MIYAMOTO USAGI.
I'VE BEEN MEANING TO SEE YOU SOONER BUT THERE HAVE BEEN MANY DISTRACTIONS OVER THE YEARS. WE MET JUST ONCE BEFORE--RESTING AT CAMP AFTER THE FIRST DAY OF FIGHTING AT THE BATTLE OF THE BURNING PLAIN. YOU WERE AN *ASHIGARU** AND I WAS A BODYGUARD TO OUR LORD.
*FOOTSOLDIER
©1999 SAKAI
1.

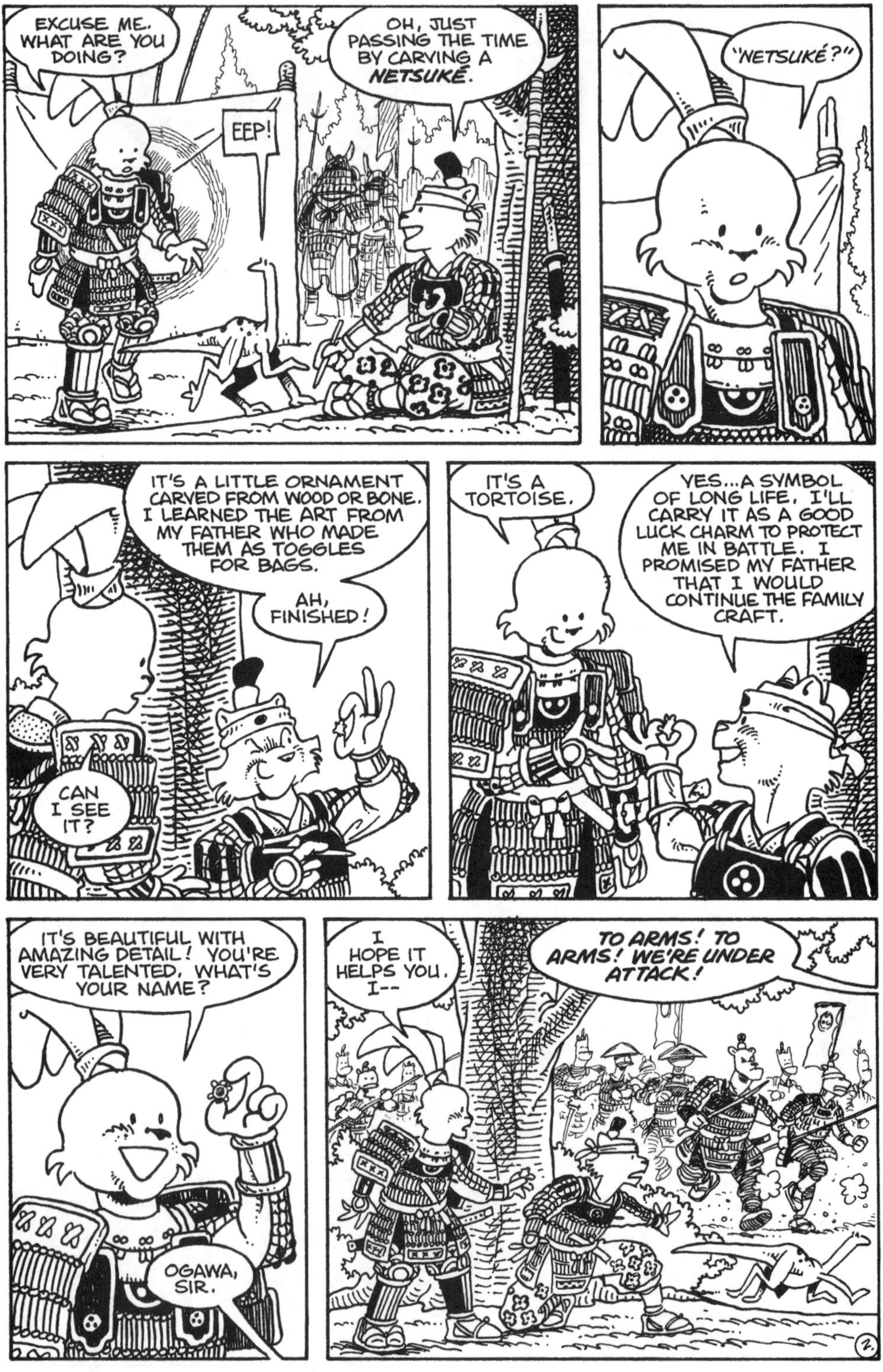
EXCUSE ME. WHAT ARE YOU DOING?
EEP!
OH, JUST PASSING THE TIME BY CARVING A NETSUKÉ.
"NETSUKÉ?"
IT'S A LITTLE ORNAMENT CARVED FROM WOOD OR BONE. I LEARNED THE ART FROM MY FATHER WHO MADE THEM AS TOGGLES FOR BAGS.
AH, FINISHED!
CAN I SEE IT?
IT'S A TORTOISE.
YES...A SYMBOL OF LONG LIFE. I'LL CARRY IT AS A GOOD LUCK CHARM TO PROTECT ME IN BATTLE. I PROMISED MY FATHER THAT I WOULD CONTINUE THE FAMILY CRAFT.
IT'S BEAUTIFUL WITH AMAZING DETAIL! YOU'RE VERY TALENTED. WHAT'S YOUR NAME?
OGAWA, SIR.
I HOPE IT HELPS YOU. I--
TO ARMS! TO ARMS! WE'RE UNDER ATTACK!
2.

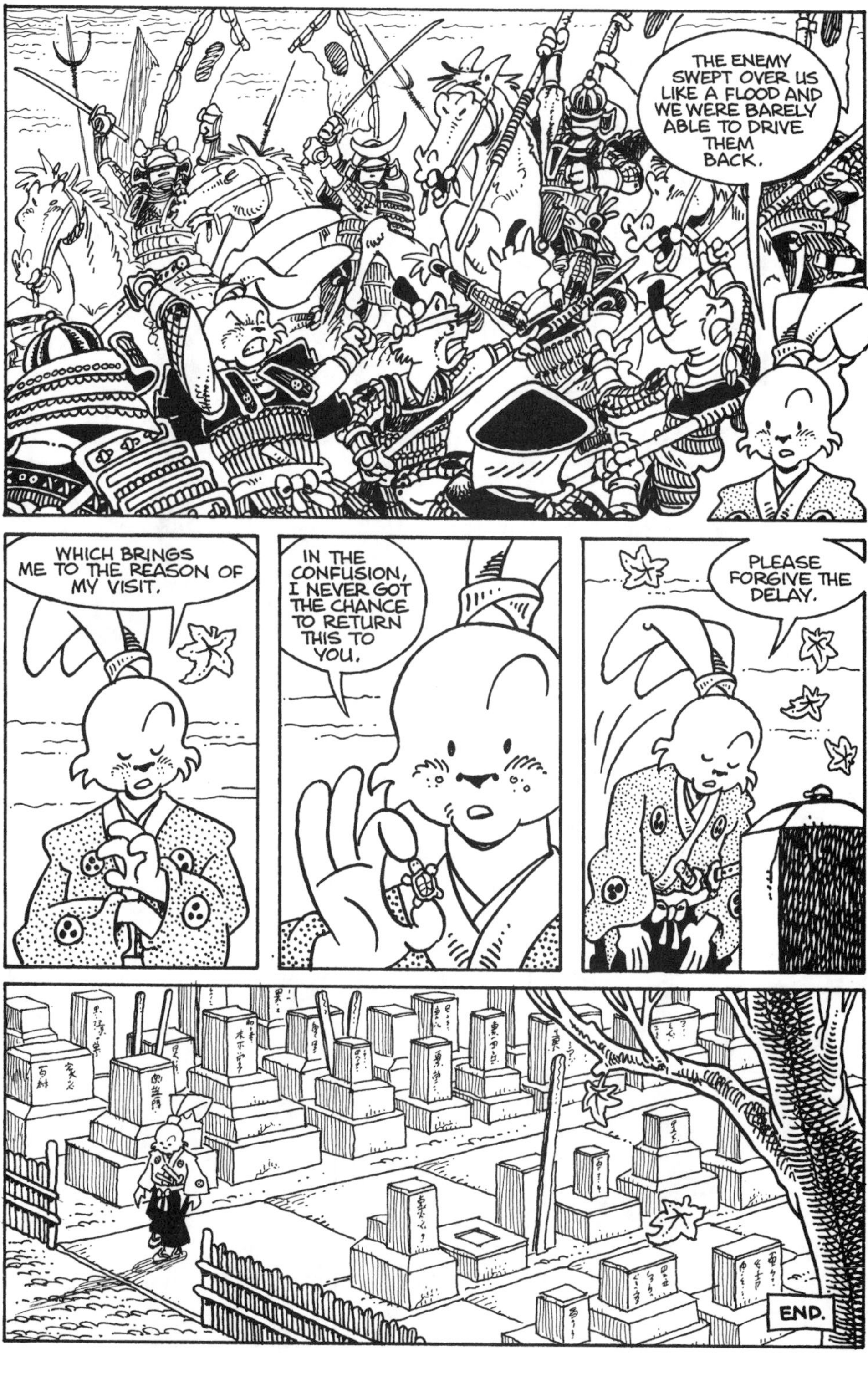
THE ENEMY SWEPT OVER US LIKE A FLOOD AND WE WERE BARELY ABLE TO DRIVE THEM BACK.
WHICH BRINGS ME TO THE REASON OF MY VISIT.
IN THE CONFUSION, I NEVER GOT THE CHANCE TO RETURN THIS TO YOU.
PLEASE FORGIVE THE DELAY.
END.

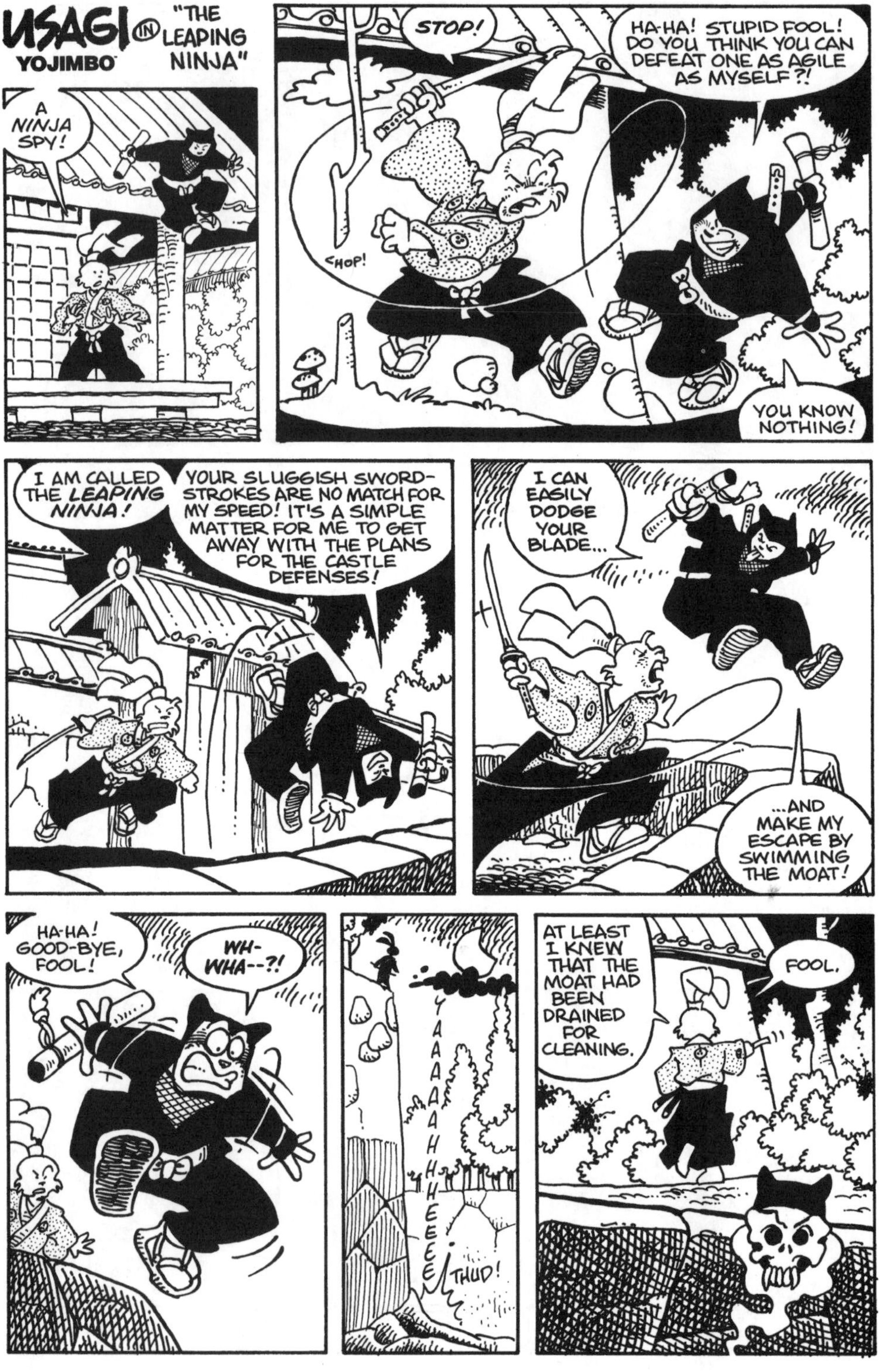
USAGI YOJIMBO IN "THE LEAPING NINJA"
A NINJA SPY!
STOP!
CHOP!
HA-HA! STUPID FOOL! DO YOU THINK YOU CAN DEFEAT ONE AS AGILE AS MYSELF?!
YOU KNOW NOTHING!
I AM CALLED THE LEAPING NINJA!
YOUR SLUGGISH SWORD-STROKES ARE NO MATCH FOR MY SPEED! IT'S A SIMPLE MATTER FOR ME TO GET AWAY WITH THE PLANS FOR THE CASTLE DEFENSES!
I CAN EASILY DODGE YOUR BLADE...
...AND MAKE MY ESCAPE BY SWIMMING THE MOAT!
HA-HA! GOOD-BYE, FOOL!
WH-WHA--?!
YAAAAAAHHHEEEE
THUD!
AT LEAST I KNEW THAT THE MOAT HAD BEEN DRAINED FOR CLEANING.
FOOL.

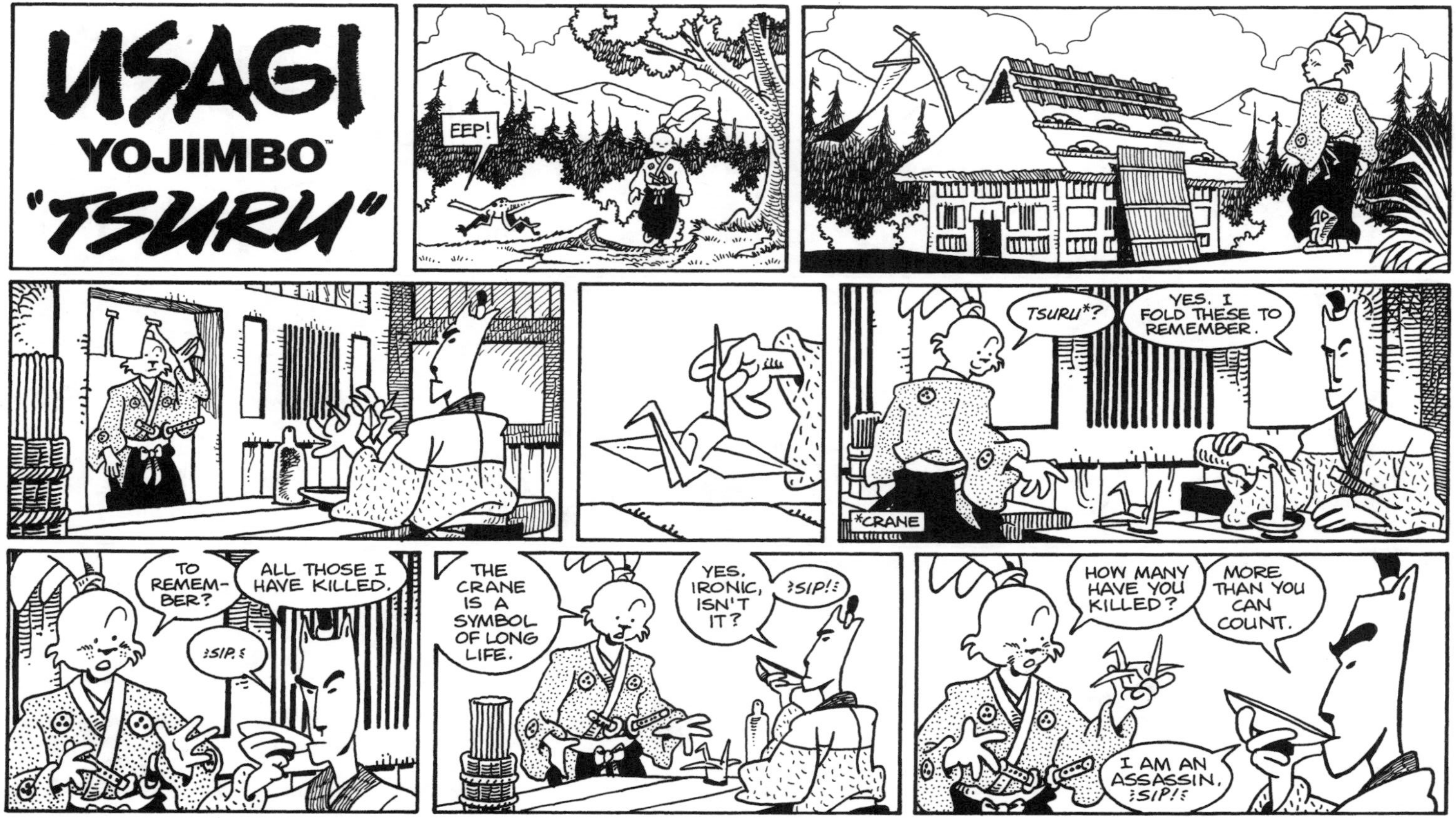
USAGI YOJIMBO™
"TSURU"
EEP!
TSURU*?
YES, I FOLD THESE TO REMEMBER.
*CRANE
TO REMEMBER?
ALL THOSE I HAVE KILLED.
SIP.
THE CRANE IS A SYMBOL OF LONG LIFE.
YES. IRONIC, ISN'T IT?
SIP!
HOW MANY HAVE YOU KILLED?
MORE THAN YOU CAN COUNT.
I AM AN ASSASSIN. SIP!

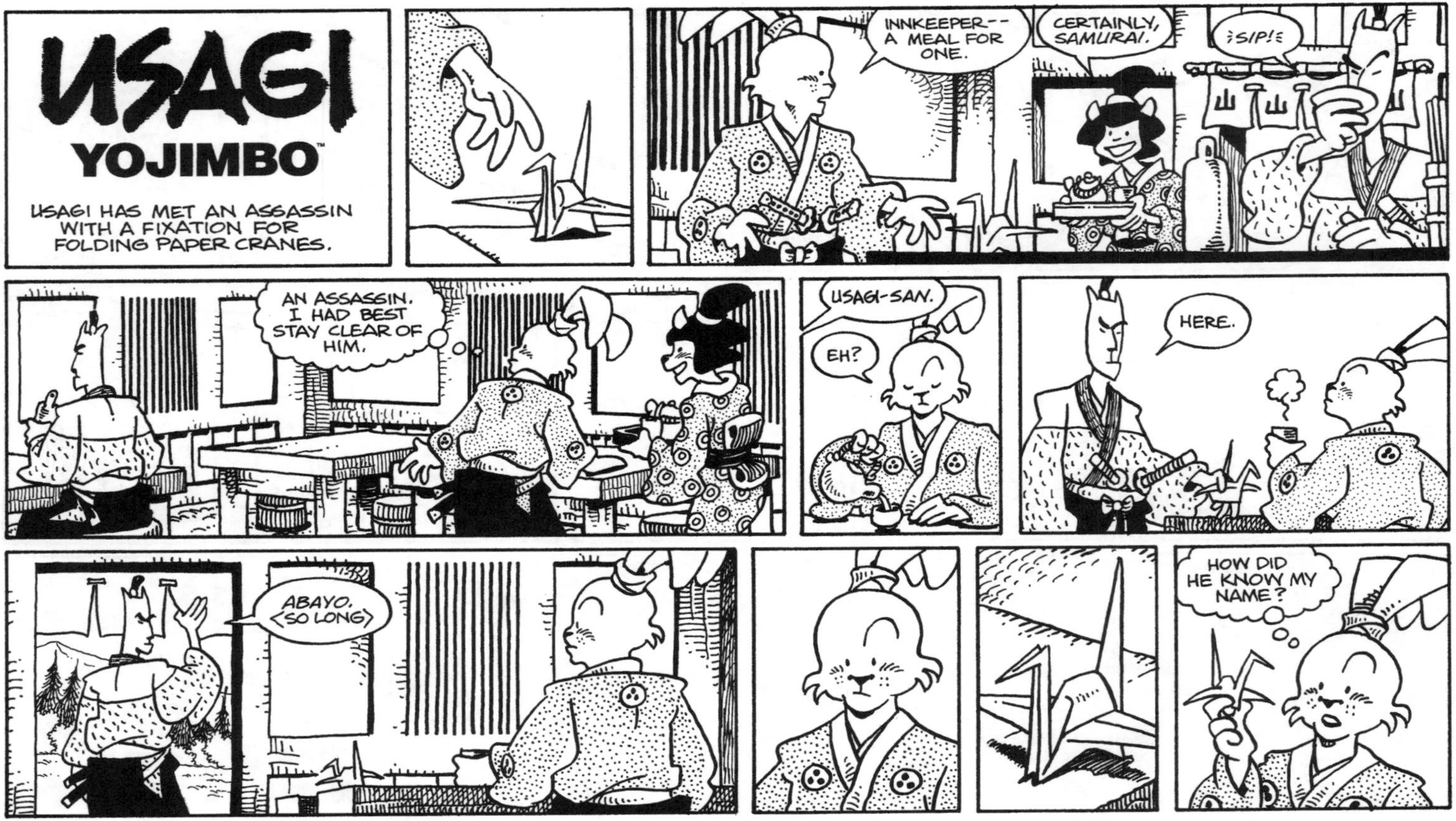
USAGI YOJIMBO™
USAGI HAS MET AN ASSASSIN WITH A FIXATION FOR FOLDING PAPER CRANES.
INNKEEPER-- A MEAL FOR ONE.
CERTAINLY, SAMURAI.
SIP!
AN ASSASSIN. I HAD BEST STAY CLEAR OF HIM.
USAGI-SAN.
EH?
HERE.
ABAYO. <SO LONG>
HOW DID HE KNOW MY NAME?

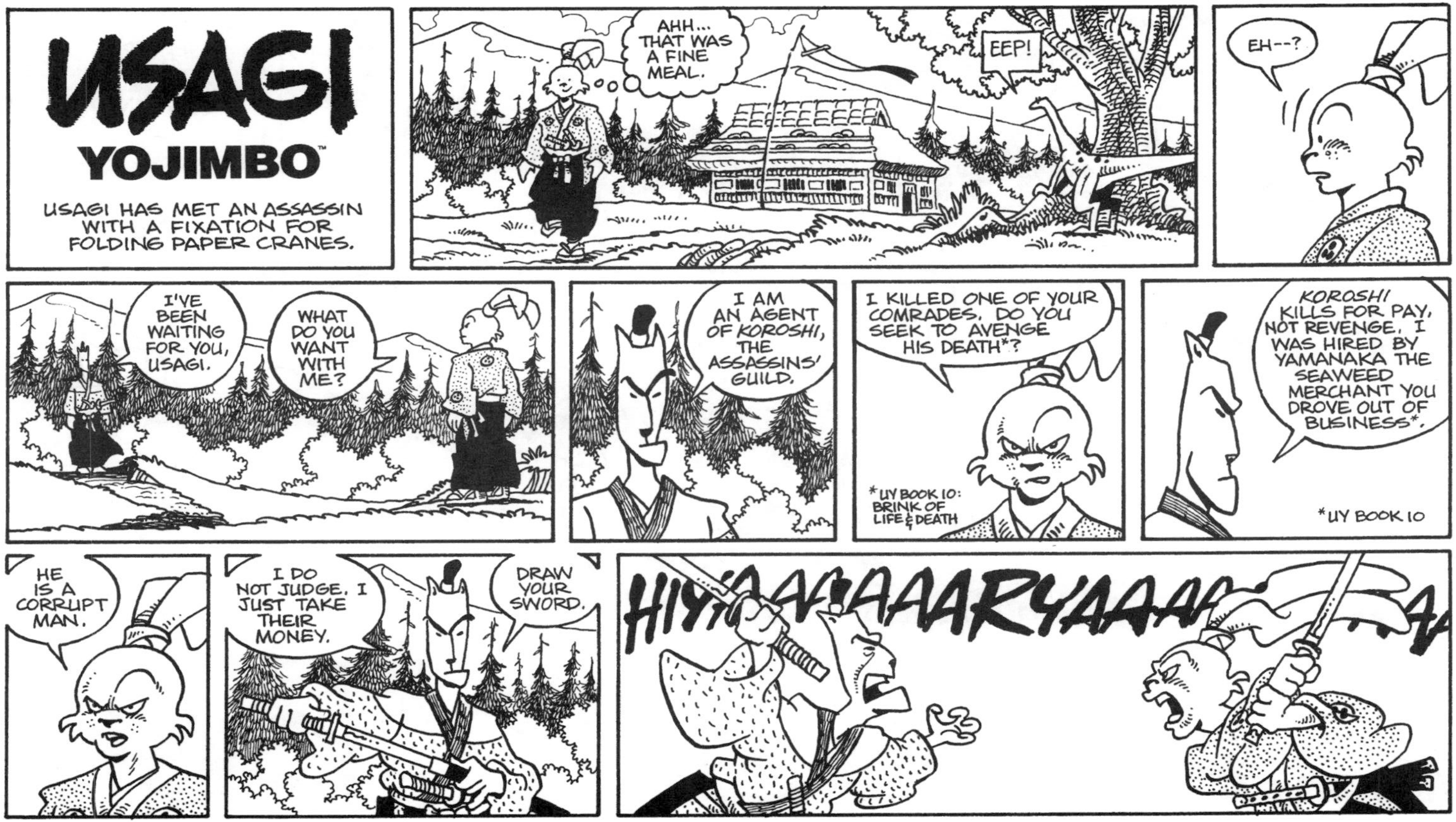
USAGI YOJIMBO™
USAGI HAS MET AN ASSASSIN WITH A FIXATION FOR FOLDING PAPER CRANES.
AHH... THAT WAS A FINE MEAL.
EEP!
EH--?
I'VE BEEN WAITING FOR YOU, USAGI.
WHAT DO YOU WANT WITH ME?
I AM AN AGENT OF KOROSHI, THE ASSASSINS' GUILD.
I KILLED ONE OF YOUR COMRADES. DO YOU SEEK TO AVENGE HIS DEATH*?
*UY BOOK 10: BRINK OF LIFE & DEATH
KOROSHI KILLS FOR PAY, NOT REVENGE. I WAS HIRED BY YAMANAKA THE SEAWEED MERCHANT YOU DROVE OUT OF BUSINESS*.
*UY BOOK 10
HE IS A CORRUPT MAN.
I DO NOT JUDGE. I JUST TAKE THEIR MONEY.
DRAW YOUR SWORD.
HIYAAAAAAARYAAAA

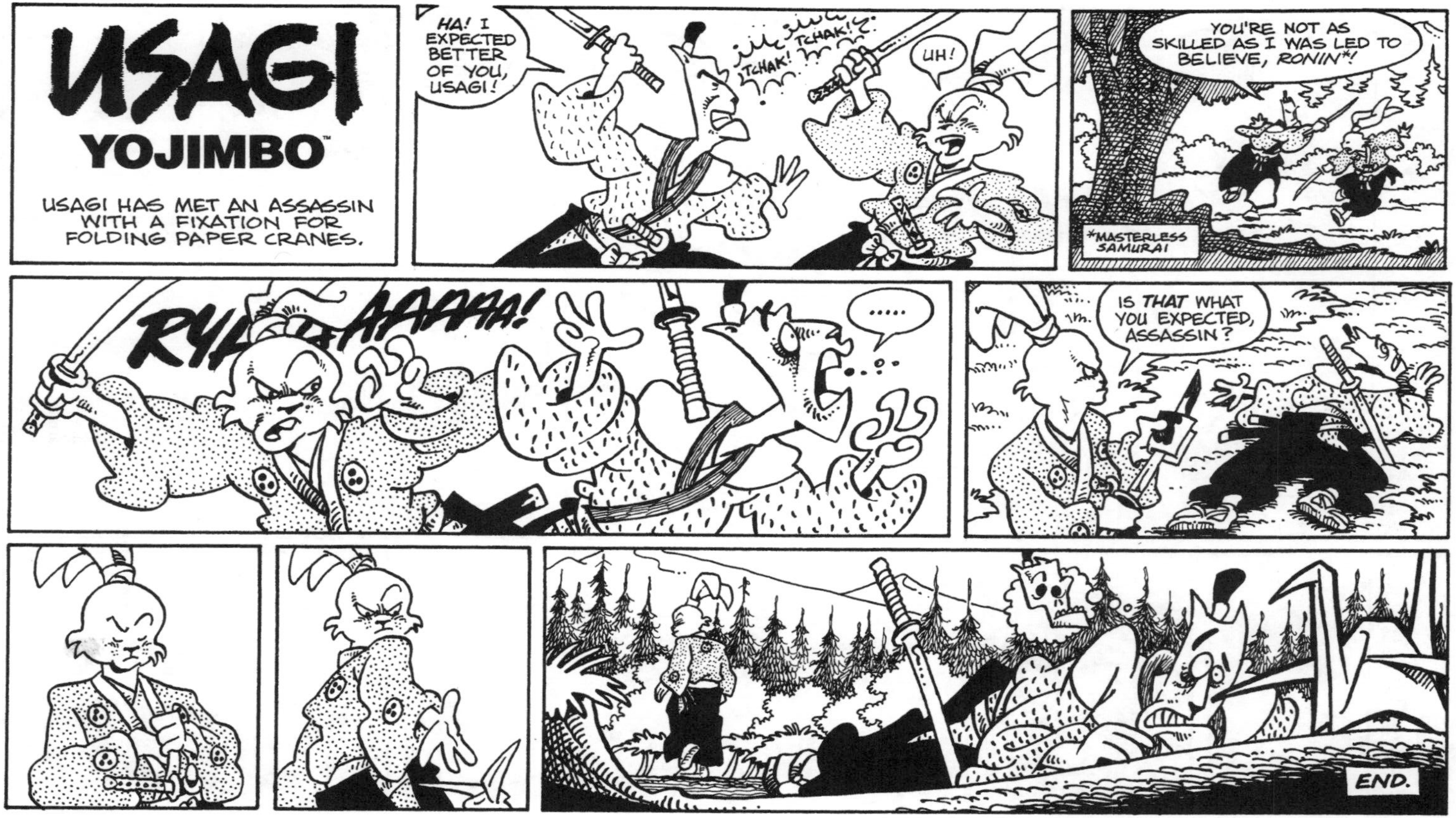
USAGI
YOJIMBO™
USAGI HAS MET AN ASSASSIN WITH A FIXATION FOR FOLDING PAPER CRANES.
HA! I EXPECTED BETTER OF YOU, USAGI!
TCHAK! TCHAK!
UH!
YOU'RE NOT AS SKILLED AS I WAS LED TO BELIEVE, RONIN*!
*MASTERLESS SAMURAI
RYAAAAAA!
.....
IS THAT WHAT YOU EXPECTED, ASSASSIN?
END.

Demon Mask Story Notes

THE INN ON MOON SHADOW HILL

Japan has an incredibly rich tradition of folklore. Usagi has encountered a few of the more maleficent *obake* (haunts), such as the *kappa*, *obakeneko*, the *tengu*, and the *nue*, and will, no doubt, meet up with a few more.

"The Inn on Moon Shadow Hill," however, focuses on some of the weirder of the Japanese monsters of folklore. I grew up hearing of some of these creatures in Hawaii, which has a huge Japanese-American population. A *mujina* (faceless woman) was purported to have haunted the women's restroom at the old Waialae Drive-In Theatre in Honolulu. She really didn't do anything. The story usually unfolds as a woman goes into the restroom and sees a girl combing her long hair. She sees a reflection of her face in the mirror...only there is no face, just a smooth, egg-like shape. The girl may or may not have feet...a trait common to many Japanese ghosts. The drive-in is no longer there, having been torn down to make way for a subdivision.

Many *obakemono* seem to be fairly benign, such as the *rokuroshikubi* (long-neck woman) or the *sasosho* (that hairy foot with the eye)...and what's with that walking umbrella (*bakegasa*)?

For another story of a *mujina* and other strange tales, I suggest *Kwaiden* by Lafeadio Hearn (Dover Publications, NY, 1968).

A POTTER'S TALE

Many believe Japan to have the oldest ceramics tradition in the world. Based on carbon dating, it goes as far back as 10,000 B.C. with the *Jomon* — or "cord marked" pottery.

Unlike in the West, Japanese ceramics is admired as fine art, on a par with painting and sculpture, as well as for its utilitarian purposes. A single teacup crafted by a master potter could command as high a price as 25,000 *koku* by feudal lords. (A *koku* is the amount of rice needed to feed a man for a full year.)

Different areas are known for their unique pottery. Mishiko, a village northeast of Tokyo, is renown for sturdy pieces of glazed stoneware. Shigaraki is famous for large storage jars. The Arita district of Kyushu, Japan's southernmost island, is known for its fine porcelain and is considered the nation's ceramics capital.

Toyotomi, the great unifier of Japan during the later sixteenth century, led an unsuccessful invasion of Korea, and many Korean artisans were taken back to Japan. The Arita porcelain industry was founded by these Korean artisans.

Today, the wares from the Arita kilns are known as Imari ware, after the port from which they are shipped.

The major difference between ceramics and porcelain has to do with the materials used and the firing temperatures. Ceramic pieces consist primarily of clay and are baked at 1000° centigrade. Porcelain is made of finely crushed quartz, feldspar, and kaolin, and is fired above 1300°

References: *The Dawns of Tradition*, 1983, published by Nissan Motor Co., Japan, has a wonderful overview and focuses on two schools, with beautiful photographs of potters at work. In *Japan Day by Day*, by Edward S. Morse, 1990, Cherokee Publishing of Atlanta, GA, the author describes in detail visits to several schools and kilns. Many of the visuals came from two videos: *Ugetsu Monogatari*, 1953, directed by Kenji Mizoguchi, a beautifully photographed ghost story about two peasants who try to seek their fortune; and a National Geographic presentation of the "Living Treasures of Japan," which profiles several artisans working in various traditional arts such as cloth making, sword making, and, of course, pottery.

THE MYSTERY OF THE DEMON MASK

In Japan, the board game *go* is attributed to the Chinese Emperor Shun (2255-2206 B.C.). Legend has it that it was invented to strengthen the weak mind of his son Shang Kiun. It was brought to the Japanese Islands around the year 735 A.D. with the return of the envoy Kibi Daijin. It became a game for the warrior class, and by the thirteenth century it was played by the greatest generals to the meanest foot soldiers. Boards were carried on campaigns, and when the day's fighting was done the soldiers would retire to fight another type of battle. All three of the great generals, Nobunaga, Hideyoshi, and Ieyasu Tokugawa were devotees of *go*. Private and state-endorsed *go* academies were founded, and the highest masters of the land appeared annually to "combat" before the shogun. This ceremony was referred to as *go zen go*, "playing the game before the exalted presence." The custom was maintained until the fall of the Shogunate in 1868.

Go has been likened to western chess. However, whereas chess concerns a single battle, *go* is an entire campaign and so a severe loss on a portion of the board does not mean a loss of the game. The player can take to another part of the field and may even secure a decisive advantage. Battles occur in various parts of the board as positions are besieged and armies are cut off and captured in an effort to acquire the most territory and surround the most vacant spaces possible. A typical game can take an hour or two, but, as in chess, a championship game may be played over a period of days. There is record of such a game lasting nine days. It is said that a player would have to play ten thousand games to reach the lowest professional rank. At a rate of one game a day, that would be about twenty-seven years.

The board, or *ban*, is a solid block of wood, always stained yellow. The feet are cut to resemble the kuchinashi fruit. — *kuchinashi* means "without a mouth" — and are supposed to restrain onlookers from offering comments. The top of the board is painted with thin, black lines, nineteen on each side, dividing it into squares. The intersections of these lines are called *me* or *moku*. Disc-shaped stones are placed on these intersections. Stones are picked from *tsubo* boxes and, with the middle and index fingers, placed on the board so it gives a cheerful little "click."

The game comes to an end when the opposing armies are in absolute contact. The whole board need not be covered.

For people living in wood and paper homes, fire was a big concern. It did not take much to set a house on fire, and any strong wind could quickly spread it out of control.

There were some twenty major fires in Edo from 1600 to 1866. One of the most destructive was in 1657 in which 108,000 people died and half the city was laid to waste.

Many precautions were taken to prevent the spread of fire. Large barrels of water and buckets were kept on streets, and many streets themselves were wide enough to act as fire breaks. Fire towers were erected throughout the city. They were equipped with bells or alarm boards. The location and ferocity of the fires were indicated by the number and strength of the strokes hitting the alarm.

Firefighters were organized by the *daimyo* (lord) to protect his castle and the homes of his retainers and by merchants to protect their own interests. Firefighters were called *tobi-no-mono* or *hikeshi*. The term *tobi-no-mono* (*tobi*=Siberian black kite; *mono*=person) comes from the fact that the hook used had a head shaped like the beak of a kite. *Hikeshi* (*hi*=fire; *keshi*=to extinguish) is a more descriptive term. The *daimyo's* firefighters wore protective leather clothing with hooded helmets, whereas the town's *tobi* wore heavy cotton clothing and were mainly composed of carpenters, roofers, and other construction experts. Large mallets and poles were used to knock down walls, bamboo ladders enabled the firefighters to climb, and hooks tore down burning roofs. Manually operated wooden pumps were introduced in the mid-eighteenth century to shoot streams of water through bamboo pipes. Each company of *tobi* had a standard: a geometric shape mounted on a pole. The standard-bearer took a position as close to the fire as possible, sometimes even on the roof of a burning building. The owner of the saved building would pay a fee to those companies whose standards were represented and who put out the blaze.

References: Reference for the game came from: *The Game of Go, the National Game of Japan* by Arthur Smith, published in 1956 by Charles E. Tuttle Company, Inc. of Rutland, Vermont and Tokyo, Japan; additional information came from the website of the American Go Association. References for the fire-fighting scene were gotten from: *History of Fire*

Fighting in Japan, by Tadayoshi Yamamoto, published in 1981 by Fukuinkan-Shoten, Tokyo, a wonderful picture book depicting the firefighters from the Edo period to the present; *Everyday Life in Traditional Japan*, by Charles J. Dunn, 1969, Charles E. Tuttle Co. of Rutland, VT and Tokyo, described the structure of the fire department; *Kabuki Costume*, by Ruth M. Shaver, with illustrations by Soma Akira and Ota Gako, 1966, Charles E. Tuttle Co., described in detail the *tobi* and his uniform; and *Japan Day by Day*, by Edward S. Morse, 1945, Houghton Mifflin Co. of Boston, gives fascinating accounts of three fires witnessed by the author, one extinguished by traditional means, and one using a foreign-type water pump.

KUMO

Spider Goblins, sometimes called Earth Spiders, are not uncommon in Japanese folklore.

Minamoto no Yorimitsu (944-1021 A.D.) had fallen ill and was brought medicine every midnight by an unfamiliar youth. As his illness worsened, he began to suspect the servant of some evil. One night he attacked the boy, who fled, but not before throwing a sticky spider web at him, entwining him. Yorimitsu's four loyal lieutenants tracked the servant to a cave, where, in his true guise of a spider goblin, he battled them. The monster was killed, and Yorimitsu immediately recovered.

In another story, Kurogumo-oji (Prince Black Spider) was taught magic by the Spider Goblin of Katsurayama to prepare himself for an assassination attempt.

There are two major inspirations for the creation of Sasuke:

Chung K'uei had vowed to the Chinese Emperor Kao-tsu that he would free the world of demons and monsters. The legend was imported to Japan during the Kamakura Period (1185-1392 A.D.) and was integrated into Japanese folklore as *Shoki* (the Japanese reading of Chung K'uei's name). Early woodcut prints depict Shoki as a huge, bearded figure dressed as a Chinese scholar with a double-edged sword, subduing demons.

The other source was Sarutobi Sasuke, a legendary ninja whose exploits are shrouded in mystery and magic. Sasuke, a farmer's son, studied *ninjutsu*, the art of invisibility, under the mountain hermit, Tozawa Hakuunsai. Japanese folklore took the art of invisibility literally and imbued the ninja with magical powers such as transformation, weather manipulation, and, of course, invisibility. Toads and frogs are often associated with these ninja/wizards. They have the ability to hypnotize and to belch deadly gas from their mouths.

References: *Japanese Ghosts and Demons* by Stephen Addiss, 1985, published by George Braziller, Inc. of New York; *Japanese Mythology* by Juliet Piggot, 1969, published by the Hamlyn Publishing Group Ltd. of London, New York, Sydney, Toronto, and England; *Ninja: The True Story of Japan's Secret Warrior Cult* by Stephen Turnbull, 1991, Firebird Books of United Kingdom, gives a comprehensive look at the ninja of history as well as of folklore.